A Modern Guide to Uneven Economic Development

T0313873

ELGAR MODERN GUIDES

Elgar Modern Guides offer a carefully curated review of a selected topic, edited or authored by a leading scholar in the field. They survey the significant trends and issues of contemporary research for both advanced students and academic researchers.

The books provide an invaluable appraisal and stimulating guide to the current research landscape, offering state-of-the-art discussions and selective overviews covering the critical matters of interest alongside recent developments. Combining incisive insight with a rigorous and thoughtful perspective on the essential issues, the books are designed to offer an inspiring introduction and unique guide to the diversity of modern debates.

Elgar Modern Guides will become an essential go-to companion for researchers and graduate students but will also prove stimulating for a wider academic audience interested in the subject matter. They will be invaluable to anyone who wants to understand as well as simply learn.

Titles in the series include:

A Modern Guide to Food Economics
Edited by Jutta Roosen and Jill E. Hobbs

A Modern Guide to Post-Keynesian Institutional Economics
Edited by Charles J. Whalen

A Modern Guide to Creative Economies
Edited by Roberta Comunian, Alessandra Faggian, Jarna Heinonen and Nick Wilson

A Modern Guide to Tourism Economics
Edited by Robertico Croes and Yang Yang

A Modern Guide to Austrian Economics
Edited by Per L. Bylund

A Modern Guide to the Economics of Crime
Edited by Paolo Buonanno, Paolo Vanin and Juan Vargas

A Modern Guide to Knowledge
Francisco Javier Carrillo

A Modern Guide to Uneven Economic Development
Edited by Erik S. Reinert and Ingrid Harvold Kvangraven

A Modern Guide to Uneven Economic Development

Edited by

Erik S. Reinert

Honorary Professor, UCL Institute for Innovation and Public Purpose (IIPP), University College London, UK and Adjunct Professor of Technology Governance and Development Strategies, TalTech, Estonia

Ingrid Harvold Kvangraven

Lecturer, Department of International Development, King's College London, UK

ELGAR MODERN GUIDES

Edward Elgar
PUBLISHING

Cheltenham, UK • Northampton, MA, USA

Published by
Edward Elgar Publishing Limited
The Lypiatts
15 Lansdown Road
Cheltenham
Glos GL50 2JA
UK

Edward Elgar Publishing, Inc.
William Pratt House
9 Dewey Court
Northampton
Massachusetts 01060
USA

Paperback edition 2024

A catalogue record for this book
is available from the British Library

Library of Congress Control Number: 2022948517

This book is available electronically in the **Elgar**online
Economics subject collection
http://dx.doi.org/10.4337/9781788976541

ISBN 978 1 78897 653 4 (cased)
ISBN 978 1 78897 654 1 (eBook)
ISBN 978 1 0353 4444 4 (paperback)

Printed and bound by CPI Group (UK) Ltd, Croydon, CR0 4YY

Contents

PART VI ECOLOGY

Contributors

Bruno Bonizzi is Senior Lecturer in Finance at Hertfordshire Business School, UK. His research focuses on financial integration and financialization, with reference to institutional investors and developing and emerging economies. He is editor of the recently published book titled *Emerging Economies and the Global Financial System: Post-Keynesian Analysis*.

Salah Chafik is a Senior Research Fellow at UCL's Institute for Innovation and Public Purpose, and Visiting Researcher at TalTech in Estonia. His research interests include empirical and theoretical Islamic governance, administration, and economics.

Monica Di Fiore is a researcher at the Institute for Cognitive Sciences and Technologies of the Italian National Research Council. Since 2013 she has been dealing with the crisis of science, responsible research and innovation, science-based regulatory capture, and ethics of quantification.

Sylvi B. Endresen is Associate Professor Emerita at the University of Oslo, Norway (human geography). Her research in economic geography includes theories of technological change; multinational investments; temporary work; and export processing zones. She has undertaken extensive fieldwork in developing countries; and in later years, transition economies in Eastern Europe.

Alf Hornborg is an anthropologist and Professor of Human Ecology at Lund University, Sweden. His books include *The Power of the Machine* (2001), *Global Ecology and Unequal Exchange* (2011), *Global Magic* (2016) and *Nature, Society, and Justice in the Anthropocene* (2019).

Annina Kaltenbrunner is Associate Professor in the Economics of Globalisation and the International Economy at Leeds University Business School, UK. Her research focuses on financial processes and relations in emerging capitalist economies.

Jan Kregel is Professor of Development Finance at Tallinn University of Technology, Estonia. He is an elected member of the Accademia Nazionale dei Lincei, the Società Italiana degli Economisti, and a Life Fellow of the Royal Economic Society (UK).

Marta Kuc-Czarnecka is Assistant Professor at the Gdańsk University of

Technology, Poland, Faculty of Management and Economics, Department of Statistics and Econometrics. Her research interests cover social convergence, quality of life, geographic information systems and composite indicators.

Ingrid Harvold Kvangraven is Lecturer in International Development at King's College, London, UK. Her research is broadly centred on the role of finance in development, structural explanations for global inequalities, the political economy of development, and critically assessing the economics field. She is also founding editor of the blog *Developing Economics*.

Mariana Mazzucato is Professor and Founding Director of the Institute for Innovation and Public Value (IIPP) at the University College London, UK, and Chair of the World Health Organization's Council on the Economics of Health for All. Her most recent book is *Mission Economy: A Moonshot Guide to Changing Capitalism* (2021).

Magdalena Olczyk is Professor of Economics at Gdańsk University of Technology, Poland. Her scientific interests concentrate on Central and Eastern European economies, especially their international competitiveness, structural changes, participation in global value chains, functional specialization and energy transition.

Lyn Ossome is Associate Professor of Political Studies at Wits University, South Africa. Her research interests include gendered labour, agrarian studies, and the state. She is the author of *Gender, Ethnicity and Violence in Kenya's Transitions to Democracy: States of Violence (2018)* and co-editor of *Labour Questions in the Global South* (2021).

Carlota Perez is Honorary Professor at the Institute for Innovation and Public Purpose (IIPP), UCL, at the Science Policy Research Unit (SPRU), University of Sussex, UK, and at the Nurkse Institute at Taltech, Estonia; and also author of the influential *Technological Revolutions and Financial Capital: the Dynamics of Bubbles and Golden Ages.*

Vladimir Popov is Principal Researcher at the Central Economics and Mathematics Institute of the Russian Academy of Sciences. He authored *Mixed Fortunes: An Economic History of China, Russia, and the West* (2014) and edited *When Life Expectancy Is Falling: Mortality Crises in Post-Communist Countries in a Global Context* (2020).

Jeff Powell is a Senior Lecturer in Economics at the University of Greenwich, UK. He is a member of the Institute of Political Economy, Governance, Finance and Accountability (PEGFA) and a founding member of Reteaching Economics.

Jerome R. Ravetz is Research Associate at Oxford University, UK. He is co-creator with Silvio Funtowicz of Post-Normal Science. They also designed the NUSAP system of notations for representing uncertainty and quality in scientific information.

Erik S. Reinert is Professor at Taltech in Estonia, and Honorary Professor at the Institute for Innovation and Public Purpose at UCL in the UK. His book *How Rich Countries got Rich ... and why Poor Countries stay Poor* has been published in 25 languages.

Andrea Saltelli is academic counsellor at the Barcelona Management School, Universitat Pompeo Fabra (UPF-BSM).

Ting Xu is Professor of Law at the University of Essex, UK. Her research interests are situated in the fields of comparative property law; Chinese law; law, governance, and development; property and human rights; law and social theory; and political economy.

Xuan Zhao is Assistant Professor of History of Economic Thought, School of Economics, Shanghai University of Finance and Economics, China. He holds an MA in Technology Governance from Taltech in Estonia, and a PhD in History (history of economic thought) from the University of Manchester, UK.

Introduction: uneven development – addressing causes versus treating symptoms

Erik S. Reinert and Ingrid Harvold Kvangraven

Let us imagine the mythical extraterrestrial being visiting our planet and trying to understand the same question this book is attempting to answer: why some nations and some areas appear to be so much poorer than others. Let us imagine a being with a logic like ours, but not yet having been subject to the terrestrial economics profession.

Our extraterrestrial visitor would find that in some countries people suffered from malnutrition and famine, while in other countries people had health problems because they were eating too much. To understand why, this individual might look for an explanation by observing differences between what people in different countries do for a living. Was there a connection between what people produced, and their welfare? On the individual level there was clearly a connection: across the planet, hospitals paid surgeons better than the people cleaning the floors of the same hospital.

After visiting a few universities on our planet, our visitor will understand that the person often considered a great prophet on understanding wealth and poverty on this planet is a certain Adam Smith (1723–1790), and will seek an explanation for uneven distribution of food in his work. He will consequently be introduced to the role played by the 'invisible hand':

> It is to no purpose, that the proud and unfeeling landlord views his extensive fields, and without a thought for the wants of his brethren, in imagination consumes himself the whole harvest that grows upon them. The homely and vulgar proverb, that the eye is larger than the belly, was never more fully verified than with regard to him. The capacity of his stomach bears no proportion to the immensity of his desires ... The rest he is obliged to distribute ... The rich ... consume only little more than the poor. They are led by an invisible hand to make nearly the same distribution of the necessaries of life, which would have been made, had the earth been divided into equal portions among its inhabitants (*Theory of Moral Sentiments*, first published 1759, in Smith 1812: 317–318)

Having also seen Smith's earliest work, The History of Astronomy (written before 1758; published in Black and Hutton 1795), our visitor understands that an 'invisible hand' may have been a reasonable metaphor for what kept the planets in orbit. But even if it comes from the most revered economist on the planet, the principle that the rich have a limited capacity to consume, and therefore are forced to share with the poor, will not convince him. The invisible hand here appears to be an eerily misplaced metaphor.[1]

Having observed, in the hospital example, what looks like a skill premium – certain skills achieve higher incomes than others – our visitor looks up how Adam Smith explains differences in wages in his 1776 *Wealth of Nations* (Smith 1776 [1976]). In Chapter X of book I, Adam Smith explains what causes differences in wages between professions. In his words: the question as to which circumstances, 'either really, or at least in the imagination of men, make up for a small pecuniary gain in some (employments), and counter-balance a great one in others'.

Smith lists five reasons why some people are paid better than others. The list is remarkable in that in each and every point raised, Adam Smith goes out of his way to explain why human knowledge and human skills do not produce a higher standard of living than ignorance; neither to society nor to the individual. Below we shall see the important role played by these assumptions as the very foundation of David Ricardo's 1817 theory of international trade. Smith explains that if people with more knowledge and more skills have higher incomes – which was of course also observable at the time of Adam Smith – it is never due to the fact that skills and knowledge produce value, but due to one of the following five reasons.

First, wages vary with the agreeableness of the employment. For this reason, 'the most detestable of all employments, that of the public executioner, is, in proportion to the quantity of work done, better paid than any common trade whatever' (Smith 1776 [1976]: 113). Under this point Adam Smith also discusses why human skills and talent are often very well rewarded, attempting to explain what he sees as the 'exorbitant rewards' of artists, 'opera-singers &c.'. The rewards to these talents are to Smith a direct result of 'the discredit which attends the employment of them as the means of subsistence'. To Smith the fact that society rewards extraordinary talent is a direct result of the fact that 'we despise their persons'. 'While we do the one (i.e. despise them), we must of the necessity do the other (i.e. pay exorbitant rewards).' 'Should the public opinion or prejudice ever alter with regard to such occupations, their pecuniary recompense would quickly diminish' (ibid.: 120). Smith argues that if we just would just stop despising our actors, artists and sportsmen, their incomes would fall to the level of an agricultural labourer. His system does not allow for a pecuniary reward which is coupled with admiration: his 'natural' system has to pair 'high reward' with 'despise'.

Second, wages vary with the cost of learning the business. Smith makes it very clear that 'the cost of apprenticeship accounts for the wages of manufacturers being higher than those of country labour' (ibid.: 114). There is therefore no advantage to manufacturing over agriculture, although the earnings in manufacturing 'may be somewhat greater, it seems evidently, however, to be no greater than what is sufficient to compensate the superior expense of their education'. In other words, the mercantilist tradition that nations which export the products from professions of higher skills will be wealthier than nations exporting products with low skills is here strongly refuted. From the point of view of both society and the individual, adding knowledge to labour is, in Smith's system, clearly a zero-sum game.

Third, wages vary with constancy of employment. For this reason, professionals such as masons and bricklayers who 'can neither work in hard frost and foul weather', and who are not secured constant demand for their services, will have a higher wage than people who are permanently employed. 'The high wages of these workmen, therefore, are not so much the recompense of their skill, as the compensation for the inconsistency of their employment' (ibid.: p. 116). Again, any role of skill and knowledge is explained away.

Fourth, wages vary with the trust to be reposed. Some professions – Smith mentions goldsmiths, physicians, lawyers and attorneys – are higher-paid because of the 'great trust which must be reposed in the workmen' (ibid.: 117). We have to have confidence in these people, says Smith, and the reason we pay them more is that we do not have confidence in people who are not well paid. 'Such confidence could not safely be reposed in people of a very mean or low condition. Their reward must be such, therefore, as may give them that rank in society which so important trust requires' (ibid.: 118). To Adam Smith, in other words, we do not pay lawyers and doctors better than people who wash dishes because their skills are more valuable, but because we have to trust these people, and could not dream of having confidence in people from the lower classes of society.

Fifth, wages vary with the probability of success. 'Put your son apprentice to a shoemaker, there is little doubt of his learning to make a pair of shoes: But send him to study law, it is at least twenty to one if ever he makes such proficiency as will enable him to live by his business.' For this reason, Adam Smith looks at the skilled professions as being like a lottery: 'those who draw the prizes ought to gain all that is lost by those who draw the blanks'. Since, according to Smith, only one in 20 lawyers 'make something out of their profession, this one lawyer ought to receive not only the retribution of his own so tedious and expensive education, but that of more than twenty others who are never likely to make anything by it' (Smith 1776 [1976]: 118–119). Again: knowledge is a zero-sum game.

As opposed to today's economists, Adam Smith is consistent in carrying his anti-mercantilist macro theory down to the micro – family – level. Few economists today recommend their children to get a job washing dishes rather than to go to university, using the argument that factor-price equalization is just around the corner anyway.[2] Privately – but not at the national level – today's economists see the value of human capital. Privately, then, they accept United States (US) economist Daniel Raymond's most important point from 1820 (Raymond 1820; Reinert 2015): different professions have different capacities to absorb capital (human or other) profitably; in other words, different professions have different 'windows of opportunity' for creating welfare, and this is a key factor on which national economic strategies must be founded (Skidelsky 2020).

One cannot profitably add as much human capital to the job of washing dishes as to the job of being a lawyer. For this reason economists would often recommend for their children professions which require a university education, although by doing this they express what they – at the macro level of an African nation – would describe as 'a mercantilist preference for one profession to another'. On the macro level the same economists recommend nations to stick to their comparative advantage, whatever it may be. Compared to this modern logical inconsistency in advice between 'my children and the children of Africa', Adam Smith comes across as being much more consistent. He argues that the mechanisms that work on the macro also work at the micro level: all risks considered it is safer to let your son become a shoemaker's apprentice than to become a lawyer (Adam Smith had no children).

Based on the above, Adam Smith – again with a certain logic – reinforces the arguments above, dispensing with skill and knowledge as economic factors based on two assumptions. First, he assumes that labour comes from the same pool of people: 'If, *in the same neighbourhood*, there was any employment either more or less advantageous than the rest, so many people would crowd into it in the one case, and so many would desert it in the other, that its advantages would soon return to the other employments.' So, if the wage differential between the surgeon and the cleaning lady becomes too big, everyone will become surgeons and there will be no one left to wash the floors.

Second, he assumes that skills can be learned extremely fast. Investing in machines and instruments may take a long time, says Smith:

> but when both have been fairly invented and are well understood, to explain to any young man, in the completest manner, how to apply the instruments and how to construct the machines, cannot well require more that the lessons of a few weeks: perhaps those of a few days might be sufficient. In the common mechanical trades, those of a few days might certainly be sufficient.

Adam Smith's discussion on what causes a difference in retribution between professions leads up to a severe criticism of the English statutes of apprenticeship and of his opposition to patents. These statutes dated from Elizabeth I – from the Renaissance cultivation of knowledge per se – and provided apprenticeships of up to seven years. Adam Smith saw apprenticeships as an extreme waste, since he was of the opinion that everything could be learned 'in a few days'. Unlike some later economists, such as Alfred Marshall, Adam Smith was not a practical man: he 'seemed the unlikeliest of guides to the practical world' in the words of Harvard Business School professor Thomas McCraw (1992: 364). Adam Smith's disregard of the role of human knowledge became a necessary foundation for David Ricardo's 1817 theory of international trade. This theory – which most economists meet early in their education – is based on the international barter of labour hours that are completely void of any skills. If Adam Smith's discussion of the irrelevance of knowledge and skills had been a mandatory introduction to Ricardo's theory of international trade and its comparative advantage, it would have been less convincing to the students. But when students meet this same argument as an unstated assumption in a 'scientific' argument such as that of David Ricardo's trade, it is easily accepted as the holiest of truths. Modern economics abounds with theories that are as illogical as this one, but since they are expressed in mathematics rather than in English, they nevertheless come across as being 'scientific'.

We could mention that in a book published one year after Adam Smith's *Wealth of Nations* an alternative way of understanding the world was presented by another Scotsman, William Robertson. In his *History of America*, Robertson (1777) claimed that 'in every inquiry concerning the operations of men when united together in society, the first object of attention should be their mode of subsistence. Accordingly as that varies, their laws and policies must be different'. If Robertson's ideas had ruled in the Washington institutions – the International Monetary Fund (IMF) and the World Bank – instead of Adam Smith's and David Ricardo's, they would have seen a link between Africa's mode of production and the poverty of the continent. Robertson was a much-esteemed principal (rector) of the University of Edinburgh.

In his book *The Rhetoric of Reaction: Perversity, Futility, Jeopardy*, Albert Hirschman (1991) discusses the arguments which since the time of Adam Smith have been used against any form of active and interventionist economic policy. Hirschman divides the arguments against any active strategy on the part of the state into three categories, and finds to his surprise that both the traditional 'right' and the traditional 'left' gradually started to make the same kind of arguments:

1. Perversity. Any attempt at improving the economic or social order will have the opposite effect of that intended. This argument is clearly present already in Adam Smith's late works.
2. Futility. Any attempt at changing the social or economic order is doomed to fail.
3. Jeopardy. Any attempt at changing the social or economic order will carry with it costs that are so high as to jeopardize what has previously been achieved.

As we have seen, Adam Smith's attitude to new knowledge was in strong conflict with influental US economist Daniel Raymond (1786–1849). Smith's view on sustainability sharply contrasts with that of another US economist, Erasmus Peshine Smith (1814–1882) (Hudson 1969). Renaissance economics saw no limits to progress: they truly saw 'a never ending frontier of human knowledge' (Bush 1945). In Adam Smith's system, however, nations reach a stationary state where they can 'advance no further', when that 'full complement of riches which the nature of its soil and climate ... allowed it to require' had been reached (Smith 1776 [1976]: 106). In today's setting, Smith's attitude to new knowledge might have made him into a believer in de-growth.

Erasmus Peshine Smith placed Man's harnessing of Nature's energy as the main moving force of the economy. To Peshine Smith, Nature's resources – especially her energy resources – have infinite potential. Whereas the theories of Adam Smith developed into pessimistic Malthusianism, Peshine Smith's theories kept alive the spirit of the Renaissance and of Man's undeveloped potentials (Smith 1853).

Peshine Smith (1853) sought to develop economics into a quantitative engineering science: 'to construct a skeleton of political economy upon the basis of purely physical laws'. He believed all economic laws to have their counterparts in those of the natural sciences, and proceeded to characterize the reproduction of wealth as a vast energy-transfer system within Nature's overall equilibrium, the basic question being the extent to which Man would proceed to exploit Nature's latent wealth. He wrote to Henry Carey, a fellow economist: 'The entire universe then is motion, and the only point is how much of the universal and ceaseless motion we shall utilise, and how much we shall permit to be working against us.' His holistic view of the planet is described in the 'Law of Endless Circulation in Matter and Force'. Equally Renaissance economics sees no limits to progress – they truly see 'a never ending frontier of human knowledge'.[3] As noted above this is the complete opposite position to that of Adam Smith's system, where a stationary state will be reached.

The increased wealth produced by increased productivity was to Peshine Smith a product of the forces of nature – harnessed by Man – substituting for manual labour. 'Twenty years ago,' he says, 'a paper box of matches sold for a shilling. Now as many matches, of superior quality, are sold for a halfpenny' – i.e. the price had been reduced to 1/24. '[I]n the meantime, by improved chemical and mechanical combinations, twenty-five boxes had come to be made by the same expenditure of human labor as one match required in its day.' In a box with 25 matches, says Peshine Smith, 24 may be regarded as the contribution from Man's harnessing of Nature – a Nature who gives her aid, and asks no recompense – and one as the result of muscular action. His 'circulation in Matter and Forces' is decidedly both 'modern' and 'ecological'. This principle is of course what is behind the shift to green energy.

As opposed to Peshine Smith, classical and neoclassical economics do not have a relevant theory of production, and of the role of human knowledge in this process. Thorstein Veblen in his 'Preconceptions of Economic Science' says it this way: 'To sum up: classical economics, having primarily to do with the pecuniary side of life, is a theory of the process of valuation' (Veblen 1919a: 144). Production is left out. In the words of Werner Sombart: 'There is like a tacit agreement [in the profession] that one has reached the conviction that the science of economic life, in so far as this is studied by the economics profession, is a science of the circulation and distribution of goods' (Sombart 1928: 917). To say it in German (which is not our native language) mainstream economics too often operates with qualitätslose Grössen: quantities that are devoid of any qualitative understanding or content.

In the understanding of wealth and poverty, the Cold War gave us a strange set of mutually exclusive countermovements: on the one hand, the Marshall Plan (1947) that emphasized the importance of manufacturing industry; but on the other hand, Paul Samuelson's revival in 1948–1949 of David Ricardo's 1817 trade theory (Samuelson 1948, 1949) that 'proved' the exact opposite: whatever a country produced there would be a tendency for the prices of the factors of production – capital and labour – to 'equalize'. The latter became the centrepiece of post-war international trade policy.

However, recent n-gram technology has made it possible to illustrate how David Ricardo and his theory of comparative advantage were virtually neglected until Paul Samuelson brought them into the core of economics at the start of the Cold War in 1948–1949. Communism advanced under the utopian slogan 'From each according to his ability, to each according to his needs'. With his new interpretation of David Ricardo, Paul Samuelson produced a counter-utopia: under the standard assumptions of neoclassical economics free trade would produce a tendency towards factor price equalization: the prices of labour and capital would tend to equalize across the planet.

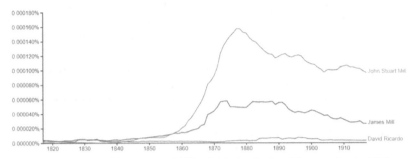

Note: Frequency of use of the term 'David Ricardo' during the first 100 years after the 1817 publication of his main work, *Principles of Economics*, compared to that of two, then much more famous, English economists.

Figure I.1   The frequency of use of the term 'David Ricardo'

This far-fetched theory brought David Ricardo out of the shadows as a marginal economist. Compared to two other English economists and economic philosophers, father and son James and John Stuart Mill, David Ricardo had indeed been a 'nobody' during the first 100 years after his 1817 theory. As seen in Figure I.1, the by far most influential 19th century economist had been John Stuart Mill, who importantly did understand the importance of infant industry protection for poor countries. Figure I.2 shows the frequency of use of the term 'comparative advantage' since 1817.

The Cold War brought into focus a theory – although old – that until then had never been very popular. Until then, economics had the skills of going back and forth between the theoretical models and the real world, between

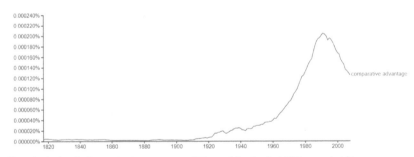

Note: As is clearly shown the term was very little used for the first 100 years, but its use exploded with the start of the Cold War in the late 1940s.

Figure I.2   Frequency of use of the term 'comparative advantage' from 1817 until today

theory and experience. The loss of this skill, and a general lack of historical knowledge, contributes to what Thorstein Veblen calls 'the contamination of instincts': today's standard educational economics too often fails to communicate with what to practical people is common sense. In this vein, a distinguished committee of the American Economic Association pointed in 1991 to the danger that 'graduate programs (in economics) may be turning out a generation of too many *idiots savants*, skilled in technique but innocent in real economic issues' (Krueger 1991: 1044–1045). An unfortunate result of this is that common sense is often applied to things in your own country, but in places far away from home the *idiots savants* are in charge of global policies.

The really confusing thing about Adam Smith – in the same 1759 book from which our first quotation comes – is that he seems to contradict the statements we have quoted from him earlier in this chapter. Here, Adam Smith makes a clear and forceful argument:

> The same principle, the same love of system, the same regard to the beauty of order ... frequently serves to recommend those institutions which tend to promote the public welfare ... When the legislature establishes premiums and other encourage-ments to advance the linen or woollen manufactures, its conduct seldom proceeds from pure sympathy with the wearer of cheap or fine cloth, and much less from that with the manufacturer or merchant. The perfection of police (i.e. policy), the exten-sion of trade and manufactures, are noble and magnificent objects. The contempla-tion of them pleases us, and we are interested in whatever can tend to advance them. They make part of the great system of government, and the wheels of the political machine seem to move with more harmony and ease by means of them. We take pleasure in beholding the perfection of so beautiful and grand a system, and we are uneasy till we remove any obstruction that can in the least disturb or encumber the regularity of its motions. (Smith 1812: 320)

The chapters in this book appear to be much more in line with this particular version of Adam Smith. Had the following claim not been made by an English economist, Lord Lionel Robbins, we would not have dared to make it, but we agree with him that 'Smith and the classical economists were cosmopolitan only as far as international free trade favored Britain – they were Englishmen first and economists second' (Robbins 1952: 10–11). This observation is in no way unique. As US economists and public policy now turn against free trade, we can make a similar observation.[4] To follow the logic of Thorstein Veblen (1919a), vested interests unfortunately become part of science. This is used with strategies of increasing sophistication; contesting the evidence with their own proprietary science, contesting the legitimacy of regulators, all the way to acting so as to colonize the space of public intermediation between science and society (Veblen 1919b).

Neoclassical and neoliberal economics of the Cold War did not produce the harmony that theory had predicted (Veblen 1919a). For the problems close to home, the policies coming out of the political process in Washington – be they from Sanders or Trump or Biden – protect US manufacturing. A few blocks away in the same Washington, DC, the Washington institutions – the World Bank and the IMF – still tend to be stuck in the logic of what the American Economic Association called *idiots savants* which prevents such protection in the poor world, where it is more needed.[5]

The economics field has only narrowed further since then, theoretically and methodologically. As noted by Reinert et al. (2018), there was a drastic increase in publications using the term 'poverty alleviation' between 1950 and 2000, and a reduction in publications referring to 'development economics' (Reinert et al. 2018). This trend is in line with an observed turn in development economics towards more micro-oriented problems associated with poverty alleviation, and a move away from studies of underlying causes of global uneven development, related to the historical evolution of institutions, the political economy of trade agreements, structural transformations of agriculture and industry, and the various drivers and manifestations of imperialism. As Reinert and Reinert put it, this trend can be likened to putting on the play 'Hamlet *without* the Prince of Denmark', given that the traditional problems of development centred around production have been marginalized from contemporary development discourses (Reinert and Reinert 2006).

The 2019 Nobel Prize in Economics[6] illustrates this development very clearly. It was awarded to Abhijit Banerjee, Esther Duflo and Michael Kremer for having 'introduced a new approach to obtaining reliable answers about the best ways to fight global poverty' (Royal Swedish Academy of Sciences 2019). What is notable in the justification for this prize is the attention to methods rather than theoretical advances. The method that Banerjee, Duflo and Kremer pioneered is the use of randomized control trials (RCTs) to test the effects of targeted development interventions. The so-called randomistas argue that experimental methods are able to deliver unbiased estimates, meaning that with repeated trials we would get estimates that tend to get closer on average to the true value of parameters (Ravallion 2020). Notably, Banerjee and Duflo have repeatedly claimed that such experiments allow development economists to be less impacted upon by big ideological debates, and to focus more on empirical questions where the findings can speak for themselves (e.g., Banerjee 2005; Banerjee and Duflo 2011). However, there are two fundamental flaws with this argument about pure empiricism. The first is that evidence always requires interpretation, and there is thus no such thing as findings speaking for themselves, as such (Kabeer 2020; Bédécarrats et al. 2020). Indeed, the randomistas' interpretation of experimental results through a neoclassical lens limits their understanding of social phenomena because it fails to understand how structures constrain individual behaviour (see Kvangraven 2020 for a review and discussion). The second flaw in the empiricist reasoning is that a focus on issues that can be randomized limits the kinds of questions that can be asked. Given that the randomistas draw clear boundaries around what is considered legitimate knowledge, it limits our ability to conceptualize and solve problems (Reddy 2012), and it especially limits the field's capacity to study the major drivers and manifestations of uneven development that this book is concerned with.

Despite increased attention to poverty and claims of an empirical turn in the field, the policies pushed by powerful agencies of economic development remain remarkably similar to the highly contested structural adjustment programmes of the 1980s, which were associated with increased poverty across the developing world. The ways that the COVID-19 pandemic has been handled is an apt illustration of this. Despite urgent needs for increased health spending, the IMF has been conditioning its loans on austerity policies that force developing countries to cut back on spending in the face of serious health and economic crises (Tamale 2021). As the field of economic development grapples with a severely limited toolbox for understanding the increasingly complex challenges associated with understanding and confronting the persistent uneven development we see in the world, this book is an attempt to broaden the theoretical and methodological lens through which we can view these issues.

In this book we attempt to bring back the real-world material issues that today's mainsteam economics tend to assume away, and to demonstrate explicitly how the vantage point that you theorize from makes a difference for the insights that can be derived about the causes and implications of uneven development.

Part I of the book considers sources of uneven development, with a focus on insights from different geographical regions. In Chapter 1, Erik Reinert identifies ten blind spots in mainstream economics which have prevented us from understanding why economic development – by its very nature – is a very uneven process. These assumptions are not to be looked at one by one and then put back into the theoretical structure, in order to create a theory based on human experience rather than unrealistic assumptions, these assumptions all need to be discarded simultaneously.

In Chapter 2, Erik Reinert, Salah Chafik and Xuan Zhao explore non-ethnocentric approaches to geography and uneven development. While they argue that there is an important link between the mode of production and the social structures of a society, which can be posited as a critique of the model of geographic diffusionism, they also argue that both in Europe and in the Americas the proximity of radically different geographical niches seems to have been key to understanding economic progress.

In Chapter 3, Mariana Mazzucato and Carlota Perez explore the role of innovation policy for growth, with a particular focus on Europe. They show that knowledge of how innovation occurs, and its relationship to finance, is central for an active economic policy to support growth in Europe. The chapter takes issue with prevailing beliefs which favour a limited role of the state in supporting investment and innovation, and shows how historically the state has been central in driving innovation, which in turn has driven growth under capitalism.

Part II of the book is centred on different kinds of theoretical approaches to uneven development. Together, the chapters demonstrate how making alternative assumptions and abstractions from the mainstream of the economics field leads to fundamentally different insights about the drivers of uneven development.

In Chapter 4, Erik Reinert, Monica Di Fiore, Andrea Saltelli and Jerome Ravetz unpack how neoliberal ideology continues to be prevalent in economics, and how this ideology is connected to the simplified vision of what cotemporary economics is about. They specifically explore the role of markets in this vision, and investigate the role of Cartesian and Ricardian dreams in present-day science and economics.

In Chapter 5, Lyn Ossome unpacks the relationship between gender and uneven development along three major themes that relate to the development of capitalism in the Global South, namely the colonial political economy and the regime of gendered labour that had been the primary basis for the stabilization of colonial capitalist accumulation and dispossession of the colonized; imperialism and the gendered nature of ongoing primitive accumulation in the Global South, and the gendered component of national sovereignty, which Ossome argues must be understood concretely in relation to the question of the surplus population, land poverty and the crisis of social reproduction.

In Chapter 6, Ingrid Kvangraven considers the role of dependency theory in our understanding of uneven economic development. She outlines how dependency theory, as a Global South-centric intellectual tradition, brings radically different insights regarding the drivers of uneven development to the table. In addition to elaborating on the main insights to be learned from the tradition, and reflecting on how and why it was marginalized during the Cold War, she also addresses some potential weaknesses and spaces for further development of the tradition.

In Chapter 7, Ingrid Kvangraven shows what it means to centre imperialism in the study of uneven development, in the context of the plethora of theories of and approaches to imperialism that exist. The chapter does not rehash the many rich debates about specific theories of imperialism, as that has been done elsewhere, but draws in some key contributions from the past two centuries. To make the theoretical discussion more concrete, the chapter also demonstrates how centring imperialism is helpful for understanding the evolution of the financial systems of Ghana and Senegal in particular.

Following from this, in Chapter 8, Xuan Zhao discusses the unequal treaties of modern China and Japan throughout the past century, through the lens of imperialism. In addition to discussing the diversity of such treaties, he also unpacks how they provided the legal foundation for the other hundreds of contemporary treaties and agreements between Chinese central and local governments and foreign countries. Furthermore, he argues that the history of unfair treaties laid the foundation for modern Chinese political ideology, which is strongly centred on sovereignty.

Moving on from theoretical debates, Part III delves into concrete mechanisms that have historically created and prevented inequality. In Chapter 9, Andrea Saltelli and Erik Reinert unpack the problems with the French Enlightenment, which they argue started the tradition which made it possible to base economic theory on far-fetched assumptions tailored to serve vested interest of specific groups. They argue that the Italian Enlightenment, on the other hand, had approaches, values and contexts that were entirely different, leading them to pose the question: did economics emulate the wrong Enlightenment?

In Chapter 10, Sylvi Endresen demonstrates how her Schumpeterian interpretation of modernization in reverse, building on her recent book, can explain cases of technological retrogression, drawing on examples of fisheries in Sri Lanka and Malaysia. In those cases, she observed a substantial reversal of modernization caused by increased prices of input in the one case, and over-exploitation of resources in the other. The chapter shows how technological retrogression served as an engine of increased inequality and the persistence of poverty.

Moving on, in Part IV the book considers how systems and nations decline and collapse. In Chapter 11, Erik Reinert discusses the relevance of Jacob Bielfeld's 'On the Decline of States' from 1760. Bielfield's insights stand in sharp contrast to today's equilibrium economics, as his work starts from the basic assumption that everything in the world is characterized by instability. In the chapter, the various ways in which Bielfeld organized his thinking are unpacked, including his taxonomic approach to economic order, which is today often associated with biology.

In Chapter 12, Marta Kuc-Czarnecka, Andrea Saltelli, Magdalena Olczyk and Erik Reinert assess the implications of opening up Central and Eastern European (CEE) countries to free trade. The chapter revisits contrasting narratives about the benefit of both free trade and the European Union enlargement for CEE countries, and empirically explores the effects of reforms undertaken. The chapter demonstrates how free trade policies led to significant losses for the CEE countries, leading to de-industrialization and migration.

The book then goes on to consider recent escapes from poverty in Part V. In Chapter 13, Ting Xu discusses how China escaped the poverty trap. The chapter builds on the work by Yuen Yuen Ang (2016), *How China Escaped the Poverty Trap*, but extends it to expand Ang's analytical framework by combining it with insights from evolutionary economics, and putting it in the context of property regime transformation in China. What is more, beyond providing extensive analysis of the role of diversity in property in giving rise to 'innovative property transformation' in China, the chapter also shows how China's escape from the 'poverty trap' has itself been highly uneven, with many parts of China's central and western regions remaining economically underdeveloped.

Furthermore, in Chapter 14, Vladimir Popov discusses the recent experiences of successful economic policies in Uzbekistan. The chapter demonstrates that while the rapid market-oriented reforms in the Union of Soviet Socialist Republics (USSR) successor states did not pay off, the gradual reformers performed better. Popov shows how even among top performers in the post-Soviet space, the Uzbekistan case is unique because it overcame the transformational recession in the first half of the 1990s and since then has been an extremely successful economy. This chapter argues that the crucial factor in the successful economic performance of Uzbekistan was not liberalization per se, but the ability to preserve the institutional capacity of the state.

Part VI of the book delves into the role of finance and its relationship to the rest of the economy. In Chapter 15, Bruno Bonizzi, Annina Kaltenbrunner and Jeff Powell argue that what is often studied under the heading of financialization should be located within a global system of financialized capitalism, in which developing economies adopt a specific subordinate role, in both production and finance. The chapter shows how lived experiences of financialized capitalism differ based on where one sits in an uneven hierarchy of classes and nation-states, and elaborates a specific theory of (subordinate) financialized capitalism.

In Chapter 16, Jan Kregel revisits Keynes's paradox of savings to understand the constraints imposed on Italy through the single currency system in the eurozone. The chapter connects challenges associated with the elimination of policy space for national exchange rate adjustments with divergences in national debt and deficits in the eurozone, showing how a key remaining domestic policy instrument in the periphery of the European Union has been domestic wage and price adjustments relative to eurozone and non-eurozone trading partners. Finally, it concludes with thoughts on where the solutions to these inequalities lie.

The final theme of the book is about the pressing issue of climate change and environmental collapse. Given the serious inequalities embedded in the system that has produced climate breakdown and the unequal impacts of climate change, the focus in Part VII is on this unevenness. Chapter 17 by Alf Hornborg is thus concerned with identifying ecologically unequal exchange in the world-system, and laying out the implications of this inequality. The chapter discusses different ways of measuring ecologically unequal exchange, and argues that the asymmetric transfers of embodied resources must be represented and understood in other than monetary terms, which implicates biophysical realities beyond the horizons of economics. The chapter explains how the relevance of biophysical asymmetries in international trade lies not in underpayment per se, but in their contributions to the uneven growth of material infrastructures for profit-generating production, their indications of skewed patterns of consumption, and their implications for the unequal distribution of resource exhaustion and environmental degradation.

Finally, the book closes with a concluding chapter by the editors, which assesses the challenges and possibilities for reversing uneven development.

NOTES

1. For a discussion of this metaphor, see Samuels (2011).
2. When Paul Samuelson reintroduced David Ricardo's (1817) trade theory in the immediate post-World War II period he predicted that with free international trade the prices of the factors of production (capital and labour) would tend to equalize across the planet (Samuelson 1948, 1949).
3. For two recent books on the subject, see Galluzzi (2020) and Markey (2020).
4. For a discussion see Hirsh (2019).
5. Exceptions here are two former World Bank Chief Economists, Paul Romer and Justin Yifu Lin.
6. The fact that economics positions itself as a hard science by emulating a Nobel Prize for its field says a lot about how it consideres itself more prestigious and scientific than other social sciences. Though it is often referred to as a Nobel Prize, its official name is the Sveriges Riksbank Prize in Economic Sciences in Memory of Alfred Nobel.

REFERENCES

Ang, Yuen Yuen. 2016. *How China Escaped the Poverty Trap*. Ithaca, NY: Cornell University Press.
Banerjee, Abhijit V. 2005. 'New Development Economics and the Challenge to Theory', *Economic and Political Weekly* 40 (40): 4340–4344.
Banerjee, Abhijit V. and Esther Duflo. 2011. *Poor Economics: A Radical Rethinking of the Way to Fight Global Poverty*. New York: PublicAffairs.
Bédécarrats, Florent, Isabelle Guérin and François Roubaud. 2020. 'Microcredit RCTs in Development: Miracle or Mirage?', in *Randomized Control Trials in Development: A Critical Perspective*, edited by F. Bédécarrats, I. Guérin, and F. Roubaud, pp. 186–226. Oxford: Oxford University Press.
Bielfeld, Jacob. 1760. 'On the Decline of States', Chapter XV in *Institutions Politiques*, Vol. 2. The Hague: Pierre Gosse.

Black, Joseph and Hutton, James, eds. 1795. *Essays on Philosophical Subject by the Late Adam Smith, LLD.* London and Edinburgh: T. Cadell Jun. and W. Davies (Successors to Mr. Cadell) in the Strand, and W. Creech, Edinburgh.

Bush, Vannevar. 1945. *Science, the Endless Frontier. A Report to the President by Vannevar Bush, Director of the Office of Scientific Research and Development, July 1945.* Washington DC: United States Government Printing Office.

Galluzzi, Paulo. 2020. *The Italian Renaissance of Machines.* Cambridge, MA: Harvard University Press.

Hirschman, Albert O. 1991. *The Rhetoric of Reaction. Perversity, Futility, Jeopardy.* Cambridge, MA: Harvard University Press.

Hirsh, Michael. 2019. 'Economists on the Run', *Foreign Policy*, 22 October. https://foreignpolicy.com/2019/10/22/economists-globalization-trade-paul-krugman-china/ (accessed 24 April 2022).

Hudson, Michael. 1969. 'E. Peshine Smith: A study in Protectionist Growth Theory and American Sectionalism', PhD Thesis, New York University.

Kabeer, Naila. 2020. 'Women's Empowerment and Economic Development: A Feminist Critique of Storytelling Practices in "Randomista" Economics', *Feminist Economics* 26 (2): 1–26.

Krueger, Anne. 1991. 'Report of the Commission on Graduate Education in Economics', *Journal of Economic Literature* 29 (3): 1035–1053.

Kvangraven, Ingrid Harvold. 2020. 'Nobel Rebels in Disguise – Assessing the Rise and Rule of the Randomistas', *Review of Political Economy* 32 (3): 305–341.

Markey, Lia (ed.). 2020. *Renaissance Invention. Stradanus's Nova Reperta.* Evanston, IL: Northwestern University Press.

McCraw, Thomas. 1992. 'The Trouble with Adam Smith', *American Scholar* 61 (3): 364.

Ravallion, Martin. 2020. 'Highly Prized Experiments', *World Development* 127: 1–2.

Raymond, Daniel. 1820. *Principles of Political Economy.* Baltimore, MD: Fielding Lucas.

Reddy, Sanjay. 2012. 'Randomise This! On Poor Economics', *Review of Agrarian Studies* 2 (2): 60–73.

Reinert, Erik S. 2015. 'Daniel Raymond (1820): A US Economist who Inspired Friedrich List, with Notes on Other Forerunners of List from the English-speaking Periphery', *Festschrift to Jürgen Backhaus*, edited by Helge Peukert, pp. 517–536. Marburg: Metropolis.

Reinert, Erik S., Jayati Ghosh and Rainer Kattel, eds. 2018. *Handbook of Alternative Theories of Economic Development.* Cheltenham, UK and Northampton, MA: Edward Elgar Publishing.

Reinert, Hugo and Erik S. Reinert. 2006. 'Creative Destruction in Economics: Nietzsche, Sombart, Schumpeter', in *Friedrich Nietzsche (1844–1900)*, edited by Jürgen G. Backhaus and Wolfgang Drechsler, pp. 55–85. Boston, MA: Springer.

Ricardo, David. 1817. *The Principles of Political Economy and Taxation.* London: John Murray.

Robbins, Lionel. 1952. *The Theory of Economic Policy in English Classical Political Economy.* London: Macmillan.

Robertson, William. 1777. *History of America.* London: Printed for W. Strahan, T. Cadell, in the Strand, and J. Balfour, at Edinburgh.

Royal Swedish Academy of Sciences. 2019. Sveriges Riksbank Prize in Economic Sciences in Memory of Alfred Nobel, 'Press Release: The Prize in Economic

Sciences 2019'. 28 October. https://www.nobelprize.org/prizes/economic-sciences/2019/press-release (accessed 24 April 2022).

Samuels, Warren J. 2011. *Erasing the Invisible Hand: Essays on an Elusive and Misused Concept in Economics*. Cambridge: Cambridge University Press.

Samuelson, Paul A. 1948. 'International Trade and the Equalisation of Factor Prices', *Economic Journal*, 58: 163–184.

Samuelson, Paul A. 1949. 'International Factor Price Equalisation Once Again', *Economic Journal*, 59: 181–197.

Skidelsky, Robert. 2020. *What's Wrong with Economics? A Primer for the Perplexed*. New Haven, CT: Yale University Press.

Smith, Adam. 1776 [1976]. *Wealth of Nations*. Chicago, IL: University of Chicago Press.

Smith, Adam. 1812. *The Theory of Moral Sentiments*, in *The Collected Works of Adam Smith*, Vol. 1. London: Cadell & Davies.

Smith, Erasmus Peshine. 1853. *A Manual of Political Economy*. New York: Putnam.

Sombart, Werner. 1928. *Der moderne Kapitalismus*, Vol. 2: *Das europäische Wirtschaftsleben im Zeitalter des Frühkapitalismus*. Munich and Leipzig: Duncker & Humblot.

Tamale, Nona. 2021. 'Adding Fuel to Fire – How IMF Demands for Austerity Will Drive Up Inequality Worldwide', Oxfam Briefing Paper, August.

Veblen, Thorstein Bunde. 1919a. 'The Preconceptions of Economic Science', in *The Place of Science in Modern Civilisation and other Essays*, pp. 56–81. New York: Huebsch.

Veblen, Thorstein Bunde. 1919b. *The Vested Interests and the State of the Industrial Arts*. New York: Huebsch.

PART I

Nature-made versus policy-made sources of
uneven development

1.   Uneven economic development: identifying the blind spots of mainstream economics

Erik S. Reinert

Two main events came to form today's mainstream economics: the choice of metaphor and the choice of language. First, with the founding father of neo-classical economics – Alfred Marshall and his 1890 *Principle of Economics* – the very foundation of the economics profession came to be a metaphor from physics: equilibrium. Second, after United States (US) economist Paul Samuelson in his 1941 PhD thesis argued that 'mathematics is a language', this language relatively fast came to replace other languages – such as German or French – as mandatory language requirements for US PhD students in economics (Collier 2016).

These two events combined came, to a large extent, to define what kind of problems economists look for. As the old saying, sometimes attributed to Mark Twain, goes: 'If you define your tool as a hammer, you are going to spend the rest of your life searching for things that look like nails'. The two events carried economics to a very high level of abstraction and created important blind spots. US economist Paul Krugman is one of the few who have recognised the importance of these blind spots in economics: 'I think there's a pretty good case to be made that the stuff that I stressed in the models is a less important story than the things that I left out because I couldn't model them' (MacFarquhar 2010).

In this chapter I identify ten blind spots that, if they were included again in economics, would not only give us a much better qualitative understanding of uneven economic development, but also help us to rediscover policy tools that became unfashionable with Cold War economics and the Washington Consensus.

The insights I hope to contribute in this chapter are based on other traditions in economics. These traditions include evolutionary economics (based on metaphors from biology); the historical method, as it was once used everywhere, usually defined as a method based on connecting previously unconnected facts; economic anthropology; and institutional economics from the Renaissance kind with Leonardo Bruni (1369–1444) to the traditional kind with Thorstein Veblen (1857–1929). These sum up what I have defined as the Other Canon approach in economics, comprising all the traditions of economics except those based on equilibrium and expressed in mathematics.

The equilibrium model and its main language, mathematics, carry with them the blind spots of neoclassical economics. Taken as a whole, the ten factors below prevent the built-in harmony-creating mechanisms of neoclassical economics, such as the factor price equalisation in trade theory, from coming even close to being realised. In other words, this chapter outlines the factors that neoclassical economics left out of the analysis; essentially because they were incompatible with the basic assumptions on which the theory built, and/or were outside the reach of their chosen language: mathematics.[1] The language problem is discussed in a separate section towards the end of the chapter. My contention is that the cumulative effects of the blind spots listed below, in distorting the reality as it is seen by mainstream economics, are formidable, as are their effects on the inability to cure poverty.

TEN BLIND SPOTS

1.   Synergies

The basic insight that synergies, based on the diversity of economic activities in an area, are an important wealth-creating mechanism creating a common good – a *ben comune* – dates back to the Florentine philosopher and statesman Brunetto Latini (1220–1294) and to Niccolò Machiavelli (1469–1513)[2] (Latini [1254] 1993). The growth of towns and cities brought these synergies into evidence. Towns permitted communication that unleashed individual freedom, creativity, diversification and synergies that together created unprecedented wealth. This was the fundamental observation of one of the earliest best-selling books in economics, *Delle Cause della Grandezza delle Città* written by Giovanni Botero (1543–1617) (see Botero 1589). The English translation, published in London in 1606, is entitled *The Cause of the Greatnesse of Cities*. The subject was kept alive over centuries, and came back strongly with Schumpeter's student August Lösch (1954), his French translator François Perroux (1955), with Jane Jacobs (1984), and Harvard Business School's Michael Porter (1990, 1998) and his clusters. But in spite of all this accumulated knowledge the World Bank and the International Monetary Fund (IMF) fail to see the dangers when they fail to warn poor countries against monoculture and lack of economic diversity more than 500 years later.

It may be said that Adam Smith's division of labour illustrates this phenomenon, but this insight has left no traces in neoclassical economics. Says US economist George Stigler: 'Almost no one used or now uses the theory of division of labour, for the excellent reason that there is scarcely such a theory ... There is no standard, operable theory to describe what Smith argued to be the mainspring of economic progress' (Stigler, quoted in McCraw 1992: 362). In fact, Smith's example of the pin factory had already been used to explain the division of labour by German economist Ernst Ludwig Carl (1722–1723). Recently the role of diversity and complexity has been added in a project by Ricardo Hausman and Cesar Hidalgo (2014), but these are ideas that hardly ever make it to the policy level where they are sorely needed.

Historically the most important of all synergies was specified already in 1767 by David Hume, Adam Smith's best friend, when he discussed the reign of Henry VII (starting in 1485): 'Promoting husbandry ... is never more effectually encouraged than by the increase of manufactures' (Hume 1767: 65). The introduction of manufactures creates employment, increases wages, and diminishes population pressure, and is at the core of the cumulative causations which we call development. As US Secretary of State George Marshall expressed in his Harvard speech in June 1947, announcing what came to be called the Marshall Plan: 'the farmer has always produced the foodstuffs to exchange with the city dweller for the other necessities of life ... This division of labor is the basis of modern civilization' (OECD 1947).

2. Institutions

'It is not sufficient to inquire whether an institution of the state is attested to have been founded by our ancestors. Rather it is necessary that we understand and explain *why* it was instituted. For it is by knowing the *cause* that we gain knowledge of a thing'. This statement on methodology is found in an analysis of the Florentine Constitution written in 1413 (Baron 1966) at the request of Emperor Sigismund of the Holy Roman Empire. The author, Leonardo Bruni (1369–1444), represents what has become known as the school of civic humanism: the ideology of the successful Italian city-states of the Renaissance.

Bruni's description of Florence and its institutions represents something of a watershed in the social sciences. While earlier literature tended to focus on mere descriptions of facts, Bruni created an analysis of economic institutions combining both the dynamics of causality and deliberate design. Institutions, he argued, tend to be created with a clear purpose in mind, as part of a conscious strategy aimed at achieving defined dynamic political and/or economic goals. These were institutions aimed at breaking the static equilibrium of the Middle Ages; they were change-inducing and change-enabling institutions that I suggest calling Schumpeterian institutions. The ability to create such Schumpeterian institutions which enable the structural change that we call economic development, and to change these institutions when new conditions so require, comes across as a key feature of the organisational capability of any society.

Adam Smith, however, largely removed human institutions from economic theory. Says Harvard Business School historian Thomas McCraw:

> [Adam Smith] exhibits a powerful aesthetic aversion to any type of collective action, a visceral distaste bordering on revulsion. For him 'human institutions' so invariably produce 'absurd' results that they have no presumptive legitimacy. His atomistic view removed all systemic effects and constructs a theory of individuals void of any uniqueness, all governed by their 'human nature' which is the same in all human beings. (McCraw 1992)

Some institutional innovations are crucial to create economic growth. Primogeniture – the right of the first-born legitimate son (or child) to inherit his parents' entire estate – has created stability in European kingdoms compared, for example, to the Arab world. In agriculture, primogeniture prevented farm sizes from diminishing into or beyond self-sufficiency. Werner Sombart, the great historian of capitalism, sees the birth of two institutions – double-entry book-keeping and bankruptcy – as the key innovations making the system possible. Historically these institutions bring us back to Venice in the 12th and 13th centuries (Mueller and Lane 1997).

It is generally most useful to see institutions as born out of problems in the production system. Risk-sharing in the long-distance trading system in Venice was once solved by distributing the ownership of a boat and its cargo in, say, 40 shares, each owner having 2.5 per cent. Insurance as an institutional innovation externalised this problem by sharing risks among a large number of boats. The problem came before the solution: it is not that the Venetians invented insurance so that they could have long-distance trading, it is the other way around. In contrast, in their 2012 book *Why Nations Fail: The Origins of Power, Prosperity, and Poverty*, Daron Acemoglu and James Robinson in practice come to the defence and salvation of neoclassical theory by blaming former European colonies for not 'getting the institutions right' (Acemoglu and Robinson 2012). They seem to disregard the key point that the 'extractive institutions' they blame for the lack of development represent the very essence of Western colonialism. When explaining that 'North America became more prosperous [than Peru and Mexico] precisely because it enthusiastically adopted the technologies and the advances of the Industrial Revolution' (ibid.: 53), Acemoglu and Robinson leave out that Peru and Mexico for a long time were colonies, and that a key element in colonial policies was precisely to prohibit manufacturing there. When Peru and Mexico later gained formal independence, they were still de facto colonies, as power just shifted from Spaniards in Spain to Spaniards residing locally, locked into the same system of exporting raw materials. In this way, Acemoglu and Robinson appear to be blaming the victims of colonialism for their own poverty.

3.   Knowledge/Technology Adding Value

Giovanni Botero's (1589) bestselling *On the Greatnesse of Cities* explains the wealth of cities mainly by the value added to raw materials, emphasising the difference between 'a heap of logs and stones and a house', and 'a marble block and what Michelangelo does to it'. What Nietzsche called *Geist und Willenskapital* – Mankind's wit and will (Nietzsche 1995: 239) – is there in Schumpeterian evolutionary economics, but not in mainstream neoclassical economics. At one point this idea reappeared in classical development economics. As a young man in the 1970s this author, employed as a research assistant at the Latin American Institute at the University of St Gallen in Switzerland, was sent to a number of Latin American countries in order to recruit students to a course in Switzerland and find a product in each country where adding value could increase gross domestic product (GDP) (for example, banana paste for baby food from Ecuador, instead of bananas). The course was financed by the Swiss Foreign Office and the United Nations Conference on Trade and Development (UNCTAD) in Geneva.

In a 1994 article, I produced a Quality Index of Economic Activities, ranking the ability of economic activities to produce wealth for a nation (see Figure 1.1). The more advanced Renaissance economists focused on what I have called 'The labour-hour-terms-of trade' (Reinert 1980). This was the important variable to watch if one was interested in the welfare of the common man. In 1994 the world's most efficient producers of baseballs (which are hand-sown) worked in Haiti earning US$0.30 an hour; whereas the world's most efficient producers of golf balls (a mechanised production), in the United States, made at least $9 an hour. In the mercantilist/Renaissance view, by exporting baseballs and importing golf balls Haiti exchanged 30 hours of labour (in baseball production) for one hour of labour (in golf ball production). At the time, Haiti had a very large share of the world market in baseballs. The key thing to keep in mind here is that both baseball producers and golf ball producers are in this example producing with state-of-the-art technology: whereas golf ball production is mechanised, all the capital of the United States has yet to mechanise the production of baseballs. This uneven advance of technical change makes it possible for a nation to be locked into a comparative advantage of being poor and ignorant. This possibility is ignored in today's economic theory, but was clearly perceived by the more sophisticated Renaissance mercantilists, who held the variables of skill and knowledge up front.

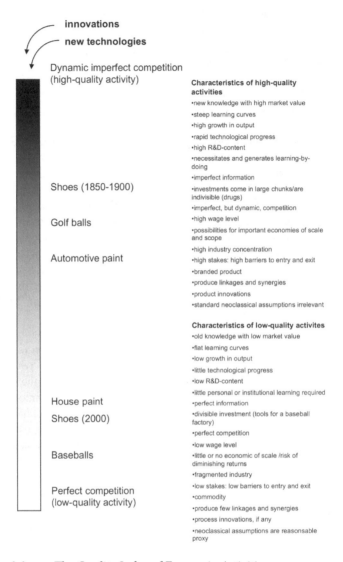

Figure 1.1   The Quality Index of Economic Activities

4.   Time-Specific Technological Contexts Produce Different Windows of Opportunity for Growth

Here also, Giovanni Botero's 1589 book is an early mover. He finds that there are more opportunities for innovation in city activities than in countryside activities. Also, when we talk about historical periods as the Stone Age and Bronze Age we implicitly understand that at a certain point the opportunities for innovation are greater in Bronze Age activities than in Stone Age activities. We find this as a basis of the work of Carlota Perez (2003) and her techno-economic paradigms. Recently Lord Sainsbury, former United Kingdom Minister of Science and Innovation, recognised this in his book *Windows of Opportunity* (Sainsbury 2020).

5.   Diminishing and Increasing Returns

Former World Bank Chief Economist Justin Yifu Lin very succinctly writes: 'Except for a few oil-exporting countries, no countries have ever gotten rich without industrialization first' (Lin 2012: 350). At the core of an explanation for this lies the dichotomy between diminishing returns (in raw material) and increasing returns (in industry). Explaining wealth and poverty by contrasting increasing and diminishing returns entered economics in 1613, in a book written in a prison cell in Naples by a certain Antonio Serra (see also Patalano and Reinert 2016).

Diminishing returns – what happens if production increases when one factor of production is not available at the same quality as before – has been observed since Ancient Greece. In modern production: (1) diminishing returns in the production of raw materials combines with (2) perfect competition (commodity competition), and (3) price volatility to form a 'triple curse' of factors that mutually reinforce each other in maintaining vicious circles of poverty and unsustainable growth. If we ask ourselves why the most efficient farmers in the world, in the European Union (EU) and US, to such a large degree depend on protection and subsidies, the reasons are the same: diminishing returns, perfect competition (no market power), and price volatility due to variabilities in climates and harvests (demand normally being stable, it happens that the total value of a yearly harvest is lower when the harvest is huge than when it is small).

In his 1890 textbook mentioned above, Alfred Marshall uses a biblical quote to describe the effects of diminishing returns: 'And the land was not able to bear them, that they may dwell together' (Genesis XIII, 6). He also points out that diminishing returns is 'the cause of most migrations of which history tells' (Marshall 1890: 201). This also certainly applies to today's international migration: from raw material-producing countries to industrialised countries, and from countries being de-industrialised (such as Ukraine) to countries keeping their industries.

Alfred Marshall recommended taxing diminishing returns industries (agriculture, fisheries and mining) in order to give bounties to activities produced under increasing returns (industrial goods) (Marshall 1890: 452). The first part has proved difficult, due to the low income in the agricultural sector, but the second part – giving bounties (and protection) to manufacturing industry – has been necessary in all countries that have travelled the road pointed to by Justin Yifu Lin at the beginning of this subsection.

My 1980 PhD thesis tested out Serra's theory in contemporary Latin America (Reinert 1980). This showed, as Serra predicted, that with increasing production productivity fell, often considerably: in banana production in Ecuador, in cotton production in Peru and in tin mining in Bolivia. Recently the Organisation for Economic Co-operation and Development (OECD) found that in spite of Chile having the largest copper reserves in the world, every extra tonne of copper mined comes at a higher cost than the previous one did.

There are very important connections between diminishing returns and both sustainability and population pressures. If a country exclusively specialised in fisheries, the nation could fish the oceans empty (Endresen 2021; Chapter 10 in this volume). If it specialised in mining, the nation would have to mine deposits with decreasing quality of ore. As a result, the resource-based nation is locked into an economic activity which yields less and less as its specialisation in the resource-base activity deepens.

Alfred Marshall faced the problem that the diminishing/increasing returns dichotomy was not compatible with the equilibrium metaphor he had chosen as the theoretical foundation of economics. This is reflected in the way this issue is treated through the eight editions of his 1890 book. The importance of this dichotomy is gradually reduced. In the 1930s, Harvard economist Jacob Viner eliminated increasing returns from international trade theory on the account that it was not compatible with equilibrium (Viner 1937). The obvious choice – from a pragmatic point of view – would have been to eliminate the equilibrium metaphor because it was not compatible with the key mechanisms that make rich countries rich and keep poor countries poor.

In 1981 – at the age of 28 – later Nobel economist Paul Krugman briefly reintroduced Antonio Serra's increasing/diminishing returns dichotomy in international trade (Krugman 1981). His source was US economist Frank Graham's in my view very convincing 1923 article on the subject (Graham 1923). Reintroducing this dichotomy, Krugman found what others had been finding for centuries: in a world with increasing and diminishing returns to scale, some countries may find themselves specialising in diminishing returns industries and consequently being poor.

Amusingly, the young Krugman not only refers to what the classical development economists had been saying about this, but also to Lenin's theory of imperialism. In 1981 it was not a good idea for an aspiring American economist to come out in defence of Lenin's theories.

Some years ago, I had a student go through Krugman's later writings, and he never found the increasing/diminishing returns dichotomy used again.

Schumpeter had invented the 'Ricardian vice': the tendency for economists to make and test theories that are not troubled by the complexities of reality, resulting in theories that are mathematically beautiful but largely useless for practical applications. As a result of this article, I added the 'Krugmanian vice': having produced a much more relevant theory than Ricardo, but refusing to apply it in practical economic policy.

So, in practical policy this literature had no influence whatsoever on the policy recommendations of the Washington Consensus. Krugman had rediscovered the medicine that worked against poverty, but refused to use it, apparently for ideological and/or career reasons. With the evidence shown by history in general, and by Justin Yifu Lin specifically, I find it deeply unethical that economists as a community – starting with the mature Alfred Marshall – have so systematically shown so much more loyalty to their models than to the fate of the poor. In my imagination this resembles a medical doctor having an effective medicine on the shelf, but refusing to use it for ideological reasons.

6.   How the Benefits from Innovations Spread

The fruits of new knowledge and new technology may spread in the economy in two different ways, reflecting two different regimes of appropriation: in the classical mode, through reduction in prices to the consumer; in the collusive mode, through higher profits to the capitalist, higher wages to the producer, and a larger economic base for government to tax. Here, rents from new innovations are shared between capital, labour and government.

In the classical mode, technological change and new knowledge will spread in the economy in terms of reduced prices. This is how the young David Ricardo assumes this to happen, and no doubt – particularly with dramatic technical change – this is an important mechanism. In commodity competition, this is the main way that the benefits from technological change spread.

The word 'collusion' here does not imply any conspiracy. The whole idea of Schumpeterian growth indicates a large degree of the collusive spread of technical change. The entrepreneur will constantly see their profits eroded by imitators and must continuously innovate to keep their profits up. In industries that might be labelled 'high-quality activities', this profit-enhancing innovation can involve increasing the skill levels of workers. Note that this will increase workers' value in the labour market; this is precisely the US 19th century 'high-wage strategy' argument. Under Schumpeterian competition, a high degree of collusive spread is normal; the individual rent-seeking of the Schumpeterian entrepreneur is converted into collective rent-seeking on behalf of society. Under these conditions, what's good for General Motors generally is what's good for the country.

In avoiding ruinous price-competition, the dynamic process of Schumpeterian rent-seeking produces an ever-increasing diversity of products; competition is based on product differentiation and different quality levels. Development and the impact of innovation will – over time – fan out to encompass more and more of the economy.

In any system with differing degrees of increasing and diminishing returns, and with a mixture of collusive and classical means of distributing gains from technical progress, some nations will be better off under autarchy than under free trade; at least until they have secured a competitive base in increasing-returns/collusive spread activities. This is the basic reason why Werner Sombart and most other German historical economists were critical of free trade between nations at different levels of technological development.

In a world where the benefits from innovation spread in these two different ways, it is virtually impossible for an agricultural nation to innovate itself out of poverty. The only way to do this is by being part of an industrial society, and converting agricultural products into niche products, restricting the area in which the products are produced, such as Parmesan cheese and Parma ham. This strategy was first invented in 1716 with the Gallo (rooster) brand for Chianti wine by Grand Duke Cosimo III of Florence. Table 1.1 summarises the characteristics of the two modes of diffusion of productivity improvements.

In 2004, Rainer Kattel and myself created a taxonomy of different forms of economic integration, of which colonialism was one of several (Reinert and Kattel 2004). Since the end of the Cold War the economic strategy of Europe had, in the spirit of Friedrich List, been based on a symmetrical form of integration among nations at approximately the same level of industrialisation and technical sophistication. The underlying assumption, which was left from the spirit of the Marshall Plan, was that manufacturing matters.

The integration of Spain into the EU had taken place in the 1980s by gradually reducing Spain's import duties – which had been very high – in order to make sure that advanced industries, such as the car industry, survived. We later found the opposite mechanism – a shock therapy type of integration – and documented how this form of integration of former Comecon (Council for Mutual Economic Assistance) countries very frequently led to a de-industrialisation of these countries. As a consequence, the social structures of these countries became more like those found in Latin America. With reference to Table 1.1, the wage-raising activities in the left column were diminished or frequently lost. In a joint 2007 paper, Kattel and I even went so far as suggesting 'an economic suicide' of the previous European model of integration (Reinert and Kattel 2007). In this process we noticed what we called the Vanek–Reinert effect:[3] with rapid trade liberalisation the most efficient industries in the least developed of the trading partner countries are the first to become extinct. Branco Milanovic (2016) has commented on this phenomenon as 'the greatest

Table 1.1   *Characteristics of the two modes of diffusion of productivity improvements*

	The collusive mode	The classical mode
Characteristics of mode		
Divisibility of investments	Indivisible, comes in 'chunks'	Divisible
Degree of perfect information	Imperfect (e.g., patents, internal research and development)	Perfect (competitive market for technology itself)
Source of technology from user company point of view	Internal, or external in big chunks = high degree of economies of scale	External
Type of innovation	Product innovation	Process innovation
Barriers to entry	Increase	No change
Industry structure	Increases concentration	Neutral
Economies of scale	Increase	No change
Market shares	Very important	Unimportant
How benefits spread		
Gross national product as measured	Highly visible	Tends not to appear (Solow paradoxes)
Profits level	Increases stakes: possibilities for larger profits or losses	No change
Monetary wages	Increase	No change
Real wages (nationally)	Increase	Increase
Price level	No change	Decreases
Terms of trade	No change	Turns against industries experiencing technological progress
Examples of innovations in the two groups	New pharmaceuticals, mainframe computers, automotive paint production	Electricity, telephones, sewing machines, use of personal computers, dispersion paint production, containers
Where found	Mainly in industry, in recent products and processes	In primary and tertiary sectors, use of new generic technologies, mature industry

reshuffle of individual incomes since the Industrial Revolution' (see also Autor and Dorn 2013).

7.   The Two Roles of Human Beings: Consumers and Producers

During the 19th century US debate on protectionism, the Americans granted the English free traders the point that locally produced goods in the US initially would become more expensive, punishing the US consumers. But, the Americans countered, in the long run this would be more than compensated by the much higher wages the same consumers would receive as producers in an industrialised economy, rather if they had stayed employed as farm hands. In a dynamic setting, high wages would also be driving technological development, forcing employers to make productivity-enhancing investments. This was made clear in German economics in the 1930s (Bauer 1932: 56).

Counterintuitively I found how an apparently irresponsible wage policy in Italy in the 1970s and 1980s – a period when I ran my own manufacturing firm there – in fact led to massive investments in new machinery and a GDP growth rate at times higher than that of Germany in the same period (Reinert 2014). The failure of neoclassical economics to see the advantages of high wages, combined with a lack of understanding of any positive role of unions (after all, trade unions increase demand), has clearly prevented technological development and caused unnecessary poverty in the US. Former Secretary of Labor Robert Reich has been fighting a lonely battle here, arguing against 'corporate welfare' and instead upgrading the technological skill of workers. One hundred years ago, the high wages in the US were seen as an important explanation of the country's success. Werner Sombart (1906) showed that at the time US workers earned two to three times as much as comparable workers in Germany, and tied that to positive feedback mechanisms between high wages and advanced technology. One of Sombart's key arguments was that the availability of free land westwards had kept wages on the East Coast high. As with Robert Reich, Werner Sombart's argument directly contradicts the neoclassical arguments against minimum wages.

8.   Innovations and the Role of Less Religion

If one takes a stroll through the famous Uffizi Gallery in Florence, one can observe the start of the Renaissance when the motives for the paintings were no longer purely religious. Suddenly bucolic scenes and scenes involving pagan motives based on pre-Christian deities, such as Venus, appear. The fall of Constantinople (1453) brought new influences to Italy, and the prestige that cities had won from stealing bodies of saints – such as Venice stealing the body of St Mark from Alexandia in AD 828 – now came from stealing the bodies of important philosophers. In 1465, Sigismondo Malatesta, the Ruler of Rimini, returned home from the war in Peloponnesus (Hutton 1926). As one text says 'induced by the mighty love with which he burned for men of learning', Malatesta brought the bones of Georgios Gemistos Plethon (1355?–1450) to his home town. Plethon was the man who, with the ideas of Plato, was key in bringing the Renaissance attitude to learning to Italy and Europe. His coffin can still be seen in the unfinished cathedral of Rimini, the Tempio Malatestiano.

How the creativity of the Italian Renaissance came to an end is best symbolised by a 'populist' monk in Florence, Girolamo Savonarola (1452–1498), who attacked the symbols of Renaissance culture, such as the precious arts. He and his followers literally set fire to the symbols of the Renaissance, in the so-called bonfire of the vanities. The mental openness that started the Renaissance was closed by the religious fanatism of Savonarola.

Leopold von Ranke (1795–1886) is often considered the father of history as a science. Ranke's juxtaposition of Savonarola and Luther gives us an explanation for the ending of the Renaissance, and why the frontier of knowledge and economic development moved northwards in Europe (Ranke [1919] 2011). While Martin Luther opened up the minds of Protestants by allowing them to communicate directly with God, Savonarola 'closed' the formerly open minds of the Catholic Renaissance. Says Ranke: 'One of Luther's largest accomplishments for the later development of the world lies in the distinction between civic and religious life. Savonarola wanted to make the connection between the two even closer than they already were'. It is significant that the most famous artist of the moment, Sandro Botticelli, himself brought his paintings to be burned at Savonarola's bonfire of the vanities (Sebregondi and Parks 2011). Savonarola's rule in Florence lasted only four years, and the same kind of mob who made him popular then had him hanged and burned. His demagoguery had been extremely divisive and destructive. He has recently been compared to Donald Trump (Goldin and Kutarna 2017).

In Northern Europe we also see a new attitude towards creating new knowledge. Here novelties and innovations used to be bad words: Roger Bacon (1214–1292) was jailed for 'certain suspicious novelties'. Almost 400 years later, in his essay 'Of Innovations' (Bacon 1625), his namesake Francis Bacon (1561–1626) – heavily influenced by Giovanni Botero – placed innovations as the centrepiece of progress. Francis Bacon also made an interesting distinction between two kinds of people – those who collect knowledge and those who collect money – and suggested that they cooperate (Trace 2018). Bacon wrote that 'money is like muck, not good except it be spread', and that 'money is a good servant, but a bad master'. Most importantly, Francis Bacon reflected the change in religious attitude towards new knowledge: 'God has, in fact, written two books, not just one. Of course, we are all familiar with the first book he wrote, namely Scripture. But he has written a second book called Creation.'[4]

The Renaissance and modern capitalism both had their sources of ethical rules of behaviour. As part of Renaissance development came a set of bourgeoisie values first codified by the Florentine scholar Leon Battista Alberti (1404–1472)[5] and later made famous in the writings of Benjamin Franklin (1706–1790),[6] whose *Way to Wealth*, reaching more than 1100 editions before 1850, no doubt is the top economic bestseller in history.[7]

During the Dark Ages of Europe, Muslims provided the more knowledge-friendly religion. The Golden Age of Islam lasted from the 8th to the 12th century, and came to an end with the invasion of the Mongols. Most of the texts of the Ancient Greek philosophers reached the West via Arabic, translated from Greek in 'translation factories' in Baghdad during this period. In the contemporary world, my dealing with the Muslim Council of Singapore in the publication of one of my articles showed me the different attitudes compared to the Muslim Council of Kabul.

9.   Separating Productive Capital from Mammon

A key element in Western culture has been the prevention of hoarding. In other words, making sure that money was circulating, not idle. The biblical term for idle money is *mammon*. We find a clear expression of this principle in the Bible (Matthew 25: 14–30), where servants/slaves are given money (*talents*), and later, the servant who has simply buried the money – instead of putting it into circulation – is severely punished. The 14th century monetary theorist Nicolas Oresme testifies to the importance of keeping money in circulation in order for the real economy – and the very process of life – to keep going (Oresme [1356] 1956). We also find this issue raised by Martin Luther (1483–1546), whose measure of good and bad was 'does it serve life?'. Luther lived in a time when a lot of money was buried in the ground instead of being in circulation. In the US tradition we find this focus on 'the process of life' in John Dewey, and in economics with Thorstein Veblen and Clarence Ayres.

Continental European economics has always continued this in a sense Biblical separation of the financial economy from the real economy. We find this from Marx (1966; in Volume 3 of *Das Kapital*) on the left of the political axis, to the conservative Schumpeter on the right. Figure 1.2 renders Schumpeter's idea of separating the money (*Rechenpfennige*, accounting units) from what you can buy for money in the real economy (*Güterwelt*, the world of goods and services).

In good times the financial economy serves as scaffolding for the real economy; as a bridge in time, as Keynes put it. If allowed to grow in ways that do not positively impact upon the real economy – by making money on money without going through production in the real economy – the financial sector will become like a parasite which grows at the expense of the real economy. Since the times of Hammurabi, 1500 BC, societies which survived have managed to cancel unpayable debt. Bankruptcy, like bookkeeping, was a necessary invention in the early centuries of capitalism. At the moment the combination of printing new money, which is an asset in the financial sector but a liability in the real economy, coupled with austerity in the real economy,

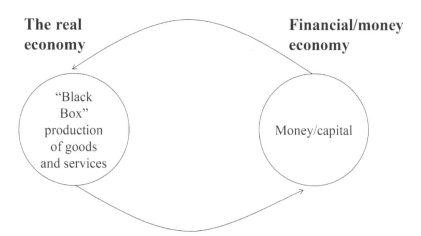

The real economy

Financial/money economy

"Black Box" production of goods and services

Money/capital

Note: Separating the real economy in a Schumpeterian fashion, *Güterwelt* = the world of goods (and services), *Rechenpfennige* = accounting units. The EU solution to the financial crisis has been to create more accounting units, inflating the size of the financial sector, but – through austerity – to a large extent preventing these newly created accounting units from reaching the real economy in the form of increased demand for goods and services. In this way the financial economy goes from working in symbiosis with the real economy, into being a parasite decreasing the size of the real economy.

Figure 1.2   The circular flow of economics

may be producing the situation Lenin looked forward to: the last stage of capitalism will be when financial capital takes the reins.

With a single-minded focus on preventing inflation at all costs, Mario Draghi was elected head of the European Central Bank for an eight-year period, from 2011 to 2019. In practice, Draghi's quantitative easing ends up being the opposite of Keynesianism: creating money instead of creating jobs. It is surprising that this ideological turnaround has not created more political discussions than it has.

An early writer on monetary issues, Nichols Oresme (1325–1382), already quoted, judged the ethical dilemma surrounding unused money (gold and silver) and the needs of human beings:

> And therefore so much of them [gold and silver] ought not to be allowed to be applied to other uses that there should not be enough left for money. It was this consideration that led Theodoric, king of Italy [493–526], to order the gold and silver deposited according to pagan custom in the tombs, to be removed and used for coining for the public profit, saying: 'It was a crime to leave hidden among the dead and useless, what would keep the living alive'. (Oresme [1356] 1956: 6)

10.   Unlearning the Balance of Countervailing Powers

The most successful and powerful states of the Renaissance – Venice and Florence – both had systems which consciously created a political balance of countervailing powers preventing both the concentration of powers and corruption. In Venice the head of government, the Doge, was elected in a process so full of checks and procedures that to modern eyes it seems exaggerated. With the privilege and honour of being Doge came the duty to give up all his business interests, and he was in a sense a prisoner in his own city. Government – the Council of the 10, Consiglio dei Dieci – was elected for one year only. Once (in 1355) 'the 10' even pronounced a death sentence for a Doge, who was executed for attempting a *coup d'état* from the inside, what in Latin America is called an *autogolpe*, or self-coup. This term has been used in connection with the activities of former US President Donald Trump.

In Florence the Prince ruler was not elected, but his government of eight or ten persons – *la Signoría* – all represented different branches of trade and industry. So this government only had a minority of one single person representing both bankers and dealers in gold and silver. This prevented the problems listed under point 7 above.

The importance of institutions creating a balance of countervailing powers was again brought into focus by Charles Montesquieu (1689–1755), and is reflected in Western constitutions. The freedom from arbitrary power is an important goal of these institutions. It was this freedom that eventually – in some areas well into the 20th century – killed feudalism in Europe.

In his 1952 book *American Capitalism: The Concept of Countervailing Power*, US economist John Kenneth Galbraith (1908–2006) explained to us how capitalism functioned at its best when subject to three countervailing powers: big business, big government and big labour. Neoliberalism removed big government and big labour, and left big business, inside which finance gradually took on more and more power.

From the perspective of this chapter, Thomas Piketty's volumes on inequality[8] – in spite of their very deserved success – suffer from being too heavily based on neoclassical economic analysis, excluding many of the factors listed above. James Galbraith's review of his first book elaborates these weaknesses well (Galbraith 2014). Two important books in the 1930s carried the title *Types of Economic Theories* (Spann 1930; Mitchell 1931), but the profession that developed during the Cold War essentially narrowed into one single type.

Finding this quote from Friedrich Nietzsche many years ago put into words my scepticism about mainstream economics:

> The only seeing which exists is a seeing in perspective, a seeing with perception; and the more feelings we allow to get involved about an issue, the more eyes –

different eyes – that we mobilise to observe one thing, the more complete will our concept of this thing, our objectivity, be. (Nietzsche 1988: 365, my translation)

An absence of multiple perspectives often appears to come into conflict with what German philosophers used to call 'common sense' (*der gesunde Menschenverstand*). Whatever the modern versions of David Ricardo's trade theory might tell us, a factor price equalisation resulting from trade between Amazonian tribes and Silicon Valley comes across as supporting some Veblenian type of vested interests in mathematical wrappings (Veblen 1924). This logic used to be a defence of British colonialism. This chapter indirectly argues very strongly for the reintroduction of different types of economic theory; what is now called 'scientific pluralism' in economics (Ludwig and Ruphy 2021; see also Rodrik 2015).

LANGUAGE

The cumulative combination of the ten factors mentioned above has made today's standard textbook economics into what Lionel Robbins termed a *Harmonielehre*, a system where the resulting economic harmony is built into the very assumptions of the theoretical structure (Robbins 1952: 22–29). Related to this, the profession clearly has a language problem.

The choice of language matters. We all understand that if we want to write a thesis on snow, we will find that the Sami language spoken by Arctic reindeer herders, who have more than 300 words for snow (Eira 2012), is a more appropriate language than Swahili. If we ask ourselves why so few legal theses and court cases are written in mathematics, the answer may point to a similar weakness of that specific language. If we go back to the study of economics before World War II, we find that in Europe economics was often studied with law. Joseph Schumpeter was also a lawyer and practiced as one. Law requires an ability to see things from more than one angle. This may point us to one of the weaknesses of modern mainstream economics.

As mentioned initially, Paul Samuelson – who was to become the most influential economist of the post-World War II era – made an important statement on the opening page of his 1940 doctoral dissertation at Harvard University: 'Mathematics is a Language'. The fashion of seeing economics in this way spread rapidly, as the best universities in the USA changed their foreign language requirements to allow the substitution of mathematics for one of the two foreign language requirements for PhD candidates in economics.

An underlying focus in this chapter is the level of abstraction at which economic analysis is carried out. It is indispensable to keep in mind that economics has existed based on different metaphors – equilibrium if the profession is based on physics, or evolution if biology is the underlying metaphor – and also, as is history, on narratives. The strength and weaknesses of the language chosen – for example, English, German, or mathematics – will also influence the scientific conclusions. Mathematics-based neoclassical economics tends to disregard context, and to be free from a system of categories that was so important when the natural sciences classified the world. We fail to see that a form of understanding based on mathematical symbols is fundamentally different from a qualitative form of understanding, as when we understand another person (Drechsler 2004).

Its limited vocabulary and limited classification system automatically carry modern mainstream economics to a high level of abstraction. When economists advise their children as to their choice of profession, they leave theory aside and return to common sense: they do not say to them 'My son, my daughter, I have observed that you have a comparative advantage in washing dishes and cleaning up the kitchen. I would advise you to make a career in restaurant kitchens.' Parents tend to understand that real economic life consists of a hierarchy of professions, while the same persons, as economists, would – based on the theories of David Ricardo – deliver proof that communities following whatever comparative advantage – be it washing dishes or designing computers – would optimise world income. To some extent economics has become a science that proves as 'correct' what intuitively is 'wrong'.

In my years in manufacturing industry – my company employing about 120 people in three European countries – I was in the business of reproducing colours. One interesting theoretical aspect of this job was how many different colours a normal human eye could distinguish. The estimate at the time was around 7 million, a number which falls within today's estimates. Following this logic into economics, I found it mind-boggling that while the human mind is able to distinguish about 7 million colours, in the foundational work of mainstream trade economic theory there is only one single kind of economic activity: every labour hour in David Ricardo's theory is assumed qualitatively equal. Or, alternatively, all are assumed to be equally void of any skills. An economic theory predicting economic harmony seemed to me simply to be a necessary by-product of a very unscientific inability to see differences and create categories. Adding just two categories – increasing and diminishing returns as in point 5 above – adds tremendous predictive powers to the models.

It seems fairly obvious that the more categories you have to describe a situation, the better you will be able to describe and handle a given situation. The example of the Sàmi language versus Swahili mentioned above is but one example. Having substituted enormous and nuanced vocabularies in English and other languages with mathematics, many details and nuances disappeared from the economics profession. For Joseph Schumpeter there was a trade-off between accuracy and relevance in economics; and limiting the language to mathematics from my point of view profoundly sacrificed relevance. It was like deliberately attempting to write a thesis on snow in Swahili, instead of in Sami: the task was simpler, but at the cost of relevance. Not having the 300 words for snow of the Sami, a thesis on snow in Swahili would be a banality. As is, in my view, some of the economics written in mathematics.

Some people see things earlier than others. When discussing his 2020 book *Windows of Opportunity*, Lord Sainsbury and I found that we had one earlier indirect connecting point. My first job after a 1980 PhD in economics had been a project for the Irish Prime Minister's office, with US consulting firm Telesis. In 1982, Lord Sainsbury had read a book called *Minding America's Business* by two young Americans called Ira Magaziner and Robert Reich (1982). They explained that the poor growth rate of the USA was due to a loss of competitive advantage in the high value-added sectors of its economy. Certainly, a very early warning. The same Ira Magaziner headed Telesis when I worked for the company in Ireland in 1980, and the same Robert Reich has been courageously defending the link between low wages and the loss of competitive advantage of American industry in high value-added sectors.

When we look at how irrelevant economic theory became during the Cold War – starting with Paul Samuelson's articles in the late 1940s that free trade would produce factor price equalisation – one important explanation is on the demand side. In a fierce ideological battle with communism there was strong demand for theories that 'proved' the superiority of capitalism. Here the tool of mathematics offered a welcome solution, and the Cowles Commission was key in the promotion of this agenda (Christ 1994). Mathematics delivered the necessary level of abstraction – and the necessary lack of any categories – that made economic theory the harmony-making machinery it became. Had there been categories – such as those mentioned above – we could have employed more common sense and understood that in competition between different categories of nations, outcomes would be as predictable as they are in boxing and wrestling: the outcome between a match heavyweight and a featherweight boxer is as predictable as guessing the GDP of a high-tech nation and a nation stuck in a diminishing returns industry. The use of high levels of abstraction seems effectively to block this kind of intuition that used to be commonplace in other types of economic theory.

When Germany and the United States were forging ahead of the United Kingdom around 1900, and free trade was no longer in their interest, British ideology changed (Dangerfield 1935). At the time one of the cabinet ministers even used the German word for the successful customs union, *Zollverein*, when suggesting a solution for the British Empire: 'The Imperial Zollverein'. We now see a similar development, as free trade is no longer in the interest of the United States. Neoclassical trade theory is being abandoned in the United States, but is still forced upon poor countries in the world through the Washington institutions, the IMF and the World Bank. It remains a mystery to this author that this abhorrent moral inconsistence seems not to become a political issue.

CONCLUSION: CONTRASTS

Where I studied in Norway, economics was a high school (*Gymnasium*) subject. To me the subject only became interesting when, at the age of 18, I visited Peru. Most people I observed in Lima – people handling luggage at the airport, bus drivers, waiters, barbers – were equally as efficient as their Norwegian counterparts. Why, then, did the Oslo bus driver have a salary 15 times that of his equally efficient Lima counterpart? I came from a background in industrial production and was used to wages differing with the skill level. The same skill ought to produce the same wage; why this contrast? When I got back to Norway, I looked for explanations and did not find them. With the years, I came to find the explanations in the factors listed above.

When I came to Harvard Business School I observed another contrast: between what is taught on the two banks of the River Charles, the river separating Harvard Business School from the rest of the Harvard campus. At the business school I was taught why some companies make more money and can pay higher salaries than other companies. In the Economics Department on the other side of the river, international economics is taught as if these factors – those determining wealth and poverty in markets by creating barriers to entry and imperfect competition – do not exist. Harvard Business School teaches its students to separate the few crucial items on a balance sheet and focus on them. Economics departments tend to concentrate on facts that are compatible with the assumptions needed for their models to work. At the Business School I recognised the methodology of the German Historical School, the remnants of which I had met when studying for my BA in St Gallen in Switzerland. There is a connection here: Edwin Gay (1867–1946), the founder of Harvard Business School and Dean during the first 11 years, had studied economic history at German-speaking universities for 12 years.

I found a third contrast in the huge difference between economic writings before World War II and afterwards, during the Cold War. I found that had I been born 100 years earlier – the same year as Cambridge economist Herbert Foxwell – I would have been a fairly mainstream economist. Foxwell – who was also President of the Royal Economic Society – shared my desperation with the practical irrelevance of David Ricardo's economic theories. Herbert Foxwell also built the book collection that, below, is referred to as the Kress Library at Harvard Business School. Slowly I developed the idea that the economics profession, as other things in life, had cyclical aspects. Similar contexts – such as the Hungry Forties of the 1840s – might produce similar theoretical responses. These cyclical aspects were emphasised in a paper written for the United Nations in 2009 (Reinert 2009).

After many years of exile in the 'real world' of business following my Cornell PhD in Economics, I came back to academia in the early 1990s. As during my studies in Switzerland, I was fortunate to communicate with economists who also had their education from before the Cold War, in this case Stanford's Moses Abramowitz and Sussex's Christopher Freeman. To my pleasant surprise both were very supportive of my idea of a Quality Index of Economic Activities, dynamically ranking them as to their potential – at any time – to contribute to economic growth (see point 3 above). The very idea of such a ranking is so foreign to neoclassical economics that, if it had not been for the strong support of pre-neoclassical economists, what so far has been a 30-year research project would probably have been stillborn.

My wife Fernanda Reinert has contributed much, both directly and indirectly, to this chapter. Her job as a librarian among old books in what was then the Kress Library at Harvard Business School, specialising in pre-1850 economics, was one of the several coincidences that made me into a 'necrophile' economist. Our joint work on the historically bestselling economics books is an important foundation for this chapter.[9]

This chapter ends with a comparative table (Table 1.2) contrasting the different starting points of neoclassical economics (standard textbook economics) in the left-hand column, and of the Other Canon – that is, the alternative experience-based tradition mentioned initially – in the right-hand column. These few pages were the outcome of a two-day meeting held at what was then The Inn at Harvard in July 1999. I would like to thank the other participants, in alphabetical order, Leonardo Burlamaqui, Ha-Joon Chang, Michael Chu, Peter Evans, Geoff Hodgson and Jan Kregel. We often see in academia that the restrictive assumptions in the left-hand columns are taken out one by one and studied, but only to then be put back into the structure again. In this way the irrelevant main structure is kept. If we could simultaneously free our minds from all the assumptions that keep economics in the unrealistic left-hand column – and if the IMF and the World Bank shifted their conditionalities to poor countries accordingly – we could get rid of world poverty.

Table 1.2   Two different ways of understanding the economic world and the wealth and poverty of nations

Starting point for the standard canon	Starting point for the 'Other Canon'
Equilibrium under perfect information and perfect foresight	Learning and decision-making under uncertainty (Schumpeter, Keynes, Shackle)
High level of abstraction	Level of abstraction chosen according to problem to be resolved
Man's wit and will absent	Moving force: *Geist- und Willenskapital*: Man's wit and will, entrepreneurship
Not able to handle novelty as an endogenous phenomenon	Novelty as a central moving force
Moving force: capital per se propels the capitalist engine	Moving force: new knowledge which creates a demand for capital to be provided from the financial sector
Metaphors from the realm of physics	Metaphors (carefully) from the realm of biology
Mode of understanding: Mechanistic (*begreifen*)	Mode of understanding: Qualitative (*verstehen*), a type of understanding irreducible only to numbers and symbols
Matter	*Geist* precedes matter
Focused on Man the Consumer A. Smith: 'Men are animals which have learned to barter'	Focused on Man the Innovator and Producer.A. Lincoln: 'Men are animals which not only work, but innovate'
Focused on static/comparative statics	Focused on change
Not cumulative/history absent	Cumulative causations/ 'history matters'/ backwash effects (Myrdal, Kaldor, Schumpeter, German Historical School)
Increasing returns to scale and its absence a non-essential feature	Increasing returns and its absence essential to explaining differences in income between firms, regions and nations (Kaldor)
Very precise (would rather be accurately wrong than approximately correct)	Aiming at relevance over precision, recognises the trade-off between relevance and precision as a core issue in the profession
'Perfect competition' (commodity competition/ price competition) as an ideal situation = a goal for society	Innovation- and knowledge-driven Schumpeterian competition as both engine of progress and ideal situation; with perfect competition, with equilibrium and no innovation, capital becomes worthless (Schumpeter, Hayek)
The market as a mechanism for setting prices	The market also as an arena for rivalry and as a mechanism selecting between different products and different solutions. (Schumpeter, Nelson and Winter)

Starting point for the standard canon	Starting point for the 'Other Canon'
Equality Assumption I: No diversity	Diversity as a key factor (Schumpeter, Shackle)
Equality Assumption II: All economic activities are alike and of equal quality as carriers of economic growth and welfare	Growth and welfare are activity-specific: different economic activities present widely different potentials for absorbing new knowledge
Both theory and policy recommendations tend to be independent of context ('one medicine cures all')	Both theory and policy recommendations highly context-dependent
The economy largely independent from society	The economy as firmly embedded in society
Technology as a free good, as 'manna from heaven'	Knowledge and technology are produced, have cost and are protected; this production is based on incentives of the system, including law, institutions and policies
Equilibrating forces at the core of the system and of the theory	Cumulative forces are more important than equilibrating ones, and should therefore be at the core of the system
Economics as *Harmonielehre*: The economy as a self-regulating system seeking equilibrium and harmony	Economics as an inherently unstable and conflict-rich discipline; achieving stability is based on Man's policy measures (Carey, Polanyi, Weber, Keynes)
Postulates the representative firm	No 'representative firm'; all firms are unique (Penrose)
Static optimum; perfect rationality	Dynamic optimisation under uncertainty; bounded rationality
No distinction made between real economy and financial economy	Conflicts between real economy and financial economy are normal and must be regulated (Minsky, Keynes)
Saving caused by refraining from consumption and a cause of growth	Saving largely results from profits (Schumpeter) and saving per se is not useful or desirable for growth (Keynes)

NOTES

1. I am here largely leaving out the clear precedents for these ideas in Greek and Arab literature (for example, Ibn Khaldoun, 1332–1406). The advice of General and Governor Thahir Ibn al Husein (775–822) on the issue of equity is equally relevant in Western politics today, 1200 years later: 'Distribute [taxes] ... among all taxpayers in a fair, just and equitable manner and make them general, not exempting anyone because of his noble rank or great riches.. and do not levy on anyone a tax which is beyond his capacity to pay'. The quotation comes from the *Prolegomena* of Ibn-Khaldun (1332–1406), cited in Neumark (1975: 274).
2. 'Il ben comune a quello che fa grandi le città' says Machiavelli ([1531] 1971).
3. Named after my Cornell professor Jaroslav Vanek (1930–2017), who mentioned this mechanism in class but never wrote about it.

4. For excellent discussions on religion and economics, see Tawney (1926) and Samuelsson (1957).
5. The first modern publication of his work on this is Alberti (1734). On Alberti, see Grafton (2000).
6. For the classical discussion on the values of capitalism, see Sombart (1913). Sombart discusses both Alberti and Franklin.
7. See http://waytowealth.org (accessed 6 November 2021). For a discussion on Franklin's work, see Sophus Reinert (2015).
8. The first of which was Piketty (2014).
9. This project originated in the Kress Library at Harvard Business School, when Fernanda Reinert's boss Kenneth Carpenter in 1975 had identified 40 economics books published in ten editions or more before 1850. When Mr Carpenter retired, he left the project for us to continue. Reinert et al. (2017) and Reinert and Reinert (2018) are two publications that came out of this project. The project continues, and we have now identified 102 economics books published in ten editions or more before 1850. The surprising element in this project is to find how many old bestsellers in economics are now completely forgotten.

REFERENCES

Acemoglu, Daron and James Robinson, *Why Nations Fail: The Origins of Power, Prosperity, and Poverty*, New York: Crown, 2012.
Alberti, Leon Battista, *Trattato del Governo della Famiglia*, Florence: Tartini e Franchi, 1734.
Autor, David and David Dorn, 'The Growth of Low-Skill Service Jobs and the Polarization of the US Labor Market', *American Economic Review* 103 (5), 2013: 1553–1597.
Bacon, Francis, 'Of Innovations', in *The Essayes or Councels, Civill and Morall, of Francis Lo. Verulam, Viscount St Alban*, London: Haviland, 1625, pp. 139–141.
Baron, Hans, *The Crisis of the Early Italian Renaissance*, Princeton, NJ: Princeton University Press, 1966.
Bauer, Wilhelm, *Die wirtschaftliche Bedeutung hoher Löhne*, Heidelberg: Verlag der Weiss'schen Universitätsbuchhandlung, Published by Heidelberger Studien aus dem Institut für Sozial-und Staatswissenschaften, in Verbindung mit Alfred Weber, Emil Lederer und Carl Brinkmann. Herausgegeben von Arthur Salz, Band II, Heft 4, 1932.
Botero, Giovanni, *Della Ragion di Stato: Libri dieci, con Tre Libri delle Cause della Grandezza, e Magnificenza delle Città*, Venice: Gioliti, 1589.
Carl, Ernst Ludwig, *Traité de la richesse des princes, et de leurs etats: et des moyens simples et naturels pour y parvenir*, 3 vols, Paris: Chez T. Legras, 1722–1723.
Christ, Carl F. 'The Cowles Commission Contributions to Econometrics at Chicago: 1939–1955', *Journal of Economic Literature* 32 (1), 1994: 30–59.
Collier, Irwin. 'Columbia. Mathematics Satisfies Second Foreign Language Reqt for Economics PhDs, 1950', *Economics in the Rear-View Mirror*, 15 July 2016. http://www.irwincollier.com/columbia-mathematics-satisfies-second-foreign-language-economics-phds-1950/ (accessed 4 November 2021).
Dangerfield, George, *The Strange Death of Liberal England*, New York: Smith & Haas, 1935.

Drechsler, Wolfgang, 'Natural versus Social Sciences: On Understanding in Economics', in Erik S. Reinert (ed.), *Globalization, Economic Development and Inequality: An Alternative Perspective*, Cheltenham, UK and Northampton, MA, USA: Edward Elgar Publishing, 2004, pp. 71–87.

Eira, Inger Marie Gaup, *Muohttaga jávohis giella. Sámi árbevirolaš máhttu muohttaga birra dálkkádatrievdanáiggis / The Silent Language of Snow. Sámi Traditional Knowledge of Snow in Times of Climate Change*, Tromsø: University of Tromsø, 2012.

Endresen, Sylvi (2021). *Technological Retrogression: A Schumpeterian Interpretation of Modernization in Reverse*, London: Anthem, 2021.

Galbraith, John Kenneth, *American Capitalism: The Concept of Countervailing Power*, Boston, MA: Houghton Mifflin, 1952.

Galbraith, James K. 'Kapital for the Twenty-First Century?', *Dissent Magazine* Spring 2014. https://www.dissentmagazine.org/article/kapital-for-the-twenty-first-century (accessed 5 November 2021).

Goldin, Ian and Chris Kutarna, 'Why Donald Trump is a second Savonarola', *Irish Times* 6 November 2017. https://www.irishtimes.com/culture/books/why-donald -trump-is-a-second-savonarola-1.3281556 (accessed 2 November 2021).

Grafton, Anthony, *Leon Battista Alberti. Master Builder of the Italian Renaissance*, New York: Hill & Wang, 2000.

Graham, Frank, 'Some Aspects of Protection Further Considered', *Quarterly Journal of Economics* 37, 1923: 199–227.

Hausmann, Ricardo and Cesar Hidalgo, *The Atlas of Economic Complexity. Mapping Paths to Prosperity*, Cambridge, MA: MIT Press, 2014.

Hume, David, *History of England*, Vol. III, London: Millar / Cadell, 1767.

Hutton, Edward, *The Mastiff of Rimini: Chronicles of the House of Malatesta*, London: Methuen, 1926.

Jacobs, Jane, *Cities and the Wealth of Nations: Principles of Economic Life*, New York: Random House, 1984.

Krugman, Paul, 'Trade, Accumulation and Uneven Development', *Journal of Development Economics* 8 (2), 1981: 149–161.

Latini, Brunetto [1254]. *The Book of the Treasure = Li livres dou tresor*. New York: Garland Publishing, 1993.

Lin, Justin Yifu, *New Structural Economics: A Framework for Rethinking Development and Policy*, Washington DC: World Bank Publications, 2012.

Lösch, August, *Economics of Location: A Pioneer Book in the Relations between Economic Goods and Geography*, New Haven CT: Princeton University Press, 1954.

Ludwig, David and Stéphanie Ruphy, 'Scientific Pluralism', in Edward N. Zalta (ed.), *The Stanford Encyclopedia of Philosophy*, Winter 2021 edition. https://plato.stanford .edu/archives/win2021/entries/scientific-pluralism (accessed 24 April 2022).

MacFarquhar, Larissa, 'The Deflationist', *New Yorker* 1 March 2010. https://www .newyorker.com/magazine/2010/03/01/the-deflationist (accessed 24 April 2022).

Machiavelli, Niccolò [1531], *Discorsi sopra la prima Deca di Tito Livio*, Libro secondo, Capitolo 2. Sansoni Editore, Firenze, 1971.

Magaziner, Ira C. and Robert Reich, *Minding America's Business: The Decline and Rise of the American Economy*, New York: Harcourt Brace Jovanovich, 1982.

Marshall, Alfred, *Principles of Economics*, London: Macmillan, 1890.

Marx, Karl, *Das Kapital*, 3 vols, Berlin: Dietz, 1966.

McCraw, Thomas, 'The Trouble with Adam Smith', *American Scholar* 61 (Summer) 1992.

Milanovic, Branco, *Global Inquality: A New Approach for the Age of Globalisation*, Cambridge MA: Harvard University Press, 2016.

Mitchell, Wesley Clair, 'Lectures on Types of Economic Theory', delivered at Columbia University, New York, 1931.

Mueller, Reinhold and Frederic Lane, *The Venetian Money Market: Banks, Panics, and the Public Debt: 1200–1500*, Baltimore, MD: Johns Hopkins University Press, 1997.

Neumark, Fritz, 'Zyklen in der Geschichte ökonomischer Ideen', *Kyklos* 28 (2), 1975.

Nietzsche, Friedrich, *Human, all too Human*, Stanford, CA: Stanford University Press, 1995.

Nietzsche, Friedrich, 'Zur Genealogie der Moral', in *Sämtliche Werke*, Vol. 5, dtv/de Gruyter, Munich, 1988.

OECD, 1947. 'The "Marshall Plan" speech at Harvard University', 5 June 1947. https://www.oecd.org/general/themarshallplanspeechatharvarduniversity5june1947.htm (accessed 2 November 2021).

Oresme, Nicolas [1356], *De Moneta. Translated from the Latin ... by Charles Johnson*, London: T. Nelson & Sons, 1956.

Patalano, Rosario and Sophus A. Reinert (eds), *Antonio Serra and the Economics of Good Government*, London: Palgrave, 2016.

Perez, Carlota, *Technological Revolutions and Financial Capital: The Dynamics of Bubbles and Golden Ages*, Cheltenham, UK and Northampton, MA, USA: Edward Elgar Publishing, 2003.

Perroux, François, 'Note sur la notion de pôle de croissance', *Economie Appliquée*, 8, 1955: 307–320.

Piketty, Thomas, *Capital in the Twenty-First Century*, Cambridge, MA: Belknap Press, 2014.

Porter, Michael E., *The Competitive Advantage of Nations*, New York: Free Press, 1990.

Porter, Michael E. 'Clusters and the New Economics of Competition', *Harvard Business Review* 76 (6), 1998.

Ranke, Leopold von, *Savonarola und die florentinische Republik gegen Ende des fünfzehnten Jahrhunderts*, Munich: Hirth, 1919; and *Savonarola*, Bremen: Dearbooks, 2011.

Reinert, Erik, *International Trade and the Economic Mechanisms of Underdevelopment*, Ann Arbor, MI: University Microfilm, 1980.

Reinert, Erik S., 'The Terrible Simplifiers: Common Origins of Financial Crises and Persistent Poverty in Economic Theory and the new "1848 Moment"', UN DESA Working Paper No. 88, December 2009.

Reinert, Erik S., 'Financial Crises and Countermovements: Comparing the times and attitudes of Marriner Eccles (1930s) and Mario Draghi (2010s)', in Dimitri Papadimitriou (ed.), *Contributions of Economic Theory, Policy, Development and Finance: Essays in Honor of Jan A. Kregel*, London: Routledge, 2014, pp. 319–344.

Reinert, Erik S., Kenneth Carpenter, Fernanda Reinert and Sophus A. Reinert, '80 Economic Bestsellers before 1850: A Fresh Look at the History of Economic Thought', The Other Canon Foundation and Tallinn University of Technology Working Papers in Technology Governance and Economic Dynamics, No. 74, 2017.

Reinert, Erik S. and Rainer Kattel, 'The Qualitative Shift in European Integration: Towards Permanent Wage Pressures and a "Latin-Americanization" of Europe?', Praxis Working Papers No. 17, Praxis Foundation, Estonia, 2004. https://ideas.repec.org/p/pra/mprapa/47909.html (accessed 13 November 2021).

Reinert, Erik S. and Rainer Kattel, 'European Eastern Enlargement as Europe's Attempted Economic Suicide?', The Other Canon Foundation and Tallinn University of Technology Working Papers in Technology Governance and Economic Dynamics No. 14, 2007. http://technologygovernance.eu/eng/the_core_faculty/working _papers/ (accessed 24 April 2022).

Reinert, Erik S. and Fernanda Reinert, '33 Economic Bestsellers published before 1750', *European Journal of the History of Economic Thought*, 25 (6), 2018: 1206–1263.

Reinert, Sophus A. 'The Way to Wealth Around the World: Benjamin Franklin and the Globalization of American Capitalism', *American Historical Review*, 120 (1), 2015: 61–97.

Robbins, Lionel, *The Theory of Economic Policy in English Classical Economics*, London: Macmillan, 1952.

Rodrik, Dani, *Economics Rules: Why Economics Works, When it Fails, and How to Tell the Difference*, Oxford: Oxford University Press, 2015.

Sainsbury, Lord David, *Windows of Opportunity, How Nations Create Wealth*, London: Profile Books, 2020.

Samuelsson, Kurt, *Religion and Economic Action, a Critique of Max Weber*, New York: Harper & Row, 1957.

Sebregondi, Ludovica and Tim Parks, *Money and Beauty. Bankers, Botticelli, and the Bonfire of the Vanities*, Florence: Giunti, 2011.

Serra, Antonio, *Breve trattato delle cause che possono far abbondare li regni d'oro e argento dove non sono miniere*, Naples: Lazzaro Scoriggio, 1613. English translation: *A Short Treatise on the Wealth and Poverty of Nations (1613)*, edited by Sophus A. Reinert, London: Anthem, 2011.

Sombart, Werner, *Warum gibt es in den Vereinigten Staaten keinen Sozialismus?*, Tübingen: J.C.B. Mohr (P. Siebeck), 1906.

Sombart, Werner, *Der Bourgeois: Zur Geistesgeschichte des Modernen Wirtschaftsmenschen*, Munich: Duncker & Humblot, 1913. Published in English as *The Quintessence of Capitalism: a Study of the History and Psychology of the Modern Business Man*, New York: E.P. Dutton, 1915.

Spann, Othmar, *Types of Economic Theory*, London: Allen & Unwin, 1930.

Tawney, Richard, *Religion and the Rise of Capitalism: A Historical Study*, London: J. Murray, 1926.

Trace, Jamie, 'Giovanni Botero and English Political Thought', PhD dissertation, University of Cambridge, 2018.

Veblen, Thorstein, *The Vested Interests and the Common Man*, London: Allen & Unwin, 1924.

Viner, Jacob, *Studies in the Theory of International Trade*, New York: Harper, 1937.

2. Geography, uneven development and population density: attempting a non-ethnocentric approach to development

Erik S. Reinert, Salah Chafik and Xuan Zhao

> In every inquiry concerning the operations of men when united together in society, the first object of attention should be their mode of subsistence. Accordingly as that varies, their laws and policies must be different. (William Robertson 1721–1793, *The History of America*, 1777)

At the very start of his bestselling book *The Wealth and Poverty of Nations* (Landes 1998), Harvard economic historian David Landes laments the loss of geography as an academic discipline: 'When Harvard simply abolished the geography department after World War II, hardly a voice protested ... Subsequently a string of leading universities – Michigan, Northwestern, Chicago, Columbia – followed suit, again without serious objection. These repudiations have no parallel in the history of American higher education'.

One general explanation for this would be that 'the hardening of the paradigm' of development economics (Jomo and Reinert 2005: xxii) increasingly left out qualitative issues, much as happened to history – the so-called historical schools virtually died out – giving way to mathematics. However, as regards geography, Landes has a more specific explanation, one that hits much harder today than it did when the book was written in the 1990s: 'Geography had been tainted with a racist brush and no one wanted to be contaminated' (Landes 1998: 4).

Landes emphasizes the role of Yale University professor Ellsworth Huntington (1876–1947), who 'in spite of much useful and revealing research' (Landes 1998: 3), went too far in connecting the physical environment and human activity (Huntington 1925). It became a defence of Eurocentrism and, in the end, racism. This was, in the words of James M. Blaut, *The Colonizer's Model of the World* (Blaut 1993; see also Blaut 2000; Krugman 1991).

We certainly agree with Blaut that the model of geographic diffusionism is essentially based not on the facts of history and geography, but on the ideology of colonialism. As indicated in the initial quotation in this chapter, we believe that the arrow of causality tends to go from mode of production to social structures. Still – as we shall try to show here – distance and other geographical features play important roles.

German economist Franz Oppenheimer (1864–1943) uses the concept *Transportwiderstand* – transport resistance – as a mechanism that prevents goods, activities and welfare from spreading evenly (Oppenheimer 1923). Traditional service activities – such as haircuts – have an absolute transport resistance: production and consumption must take place simultaneously. The effects of transport resistance on industrialization work in two different ways. The high cost of transporting electricity – the energy lost for every kilometre – gave Norway for about 100 years a considerable comparative advantage in energy-intensive industrialization (for example, artificial fertilizers, aluminum production). On the other hand, the extremely long distance and high transportation costs from England to its colonial outposts in Australia and New Zealand, for a long time made local industrialization easier for the settlers there.

If all economic activities had been like haircutting, geography would hardly have mattered. When we look at early advanced economic development later in this chapter, we shall see that both in Europe and in the Americas the proximity of radically different geographical niches seems to have been a key to understand economic progress. We find the footprint of Oppenheimer's transport resistance in the earliest processes of development.

Friedrich List (1789–1846), the great promotor of industrialization, insisted on combining policies of industrialization with heavy investments in railways.[1] High transportation costs combined with important economies of scale in manufacturing made the reduction of transportation costs within Germany a key priority for List; in other words, he wanted to reduce the *Transportwiderstand*. Industries in latecomer countries needed economies of scale – large volumes of production – to achieve the low costs of production that England had achieved. Also in Russia the idea of industrialization was intimately tied to the idea of railway building by one single person, Sergei Witte (1849–1916), who was both Finance Minister under two Tsars and Russia's first Prime Minister. In 1889, Witte wrote a book promoting the ideas of Friedrich List, and he later organized the construction of the Trans-Siberian Railway (von Laue 1963).

Attempting to avoid the unintended by-products of studying economic geography, Alfred Chandler's framework of *Scale and Scope* (Chandler 1990) allows us to understand the geographical elements contributing to uneven development. Economies of scale – or increasing returns to scale – is key to lower unit costs in industrial production, but also a key factor producing human agglomerations, as Henry Ford's factories once represented for Detroit.

In industrial terms, Henry Ford's assembly plant created huge economies of scale that lowered unit costs, gave market power and increased the barriers to entry into this economic activity; thus leading to increased profits, higher wages and high population density. Economies of scope create similar effects, but independent of geographical proximity. The almost 39 000, geographically very spread, McDonald's restaurants gain similar advantages by the economies of scope of their operations, but scope does not affect wages and population density to the same effect as scale. While Ford's innovations and economies of scale acted as a 'wage setter' – as when he doubled his workers' wages to $5 a day in January 1914 – McDonald's employees are 'wage takers'. They tend to be paid the minimum wage wherever they happen to be located. The point here is that economies of scale, and the accompanying barriers to entry into an activity, have geographical dimensions that contribute to economic development being uneven, to the patterns of human settlements, and thus the variations in population density. One could even mention that there is a connection between the economies of scale in industry and the possibility of caring for the environment: the productivity and wage explosion at Henry Ford's factories created an economy that could afford for President Woodrow Wilson to found the United States (US) National Park Services two years later, in 1916.

GEOGRAPHY, CLIMATE AND DEVELOPMENT

The 'climate thesis' posits that tropical climates are, *ceteris paribus*, poor candidates for development. One of the factors mentioned has been that the tropics have maiming diseases (for example, malaria) that leave people unable to work, while colder climate have diseases which kill outright (heart attacks). The most cited work in this area seems to be Gallup et al. (1998). Historically, however, a country such as Switzerland also had malaria (Italian: *mal aria* = foul air), but it was eradicated by draining the wetlands to create agricultural land and hydropower (Bircher 1992). Also, the indisputable success of Singapore – located slightly more than 1 degree from the Equator – is a counterexample suggesting that industrialization and technology beat climate as a main explanation for generalized wealth.

One of the theories resurrected in Landes's work is the 'hydraulic thesis' expressed in Karl A. Wittfogel's (1957) *Oriental Despotism: A Comparative Study of Total Power*. The many books written by Terje Tvedt[2] show the same points: how rivers tie cultures together by essentially facilitating transport and communication. This will reduce transport resistance and lead to possibilities for larger-scale production, but it does not necessarily lead to despotism. We shall see that geographical proximity of different ecological niches may also have the same centralizing and synergetic effects.

Geography, firstly, affects the degree of transport resistance and thereby the efficient scale and size of an operation; and secondly, variations in geography affect the scope of economic operations. When the European explorers gradually came to understand the Americas, they found it somewhat contradictory that what to them looked like huge fertile prairies in North America had a relatively small population, while the seemingly inhospitable Andes probably had the largest population density on the whole continent. Estimates of 1492 populations are as low as 3.8 million for the contiguous US 48 states plus Canada, while the population of the apparently inhabitable Andes was as high as 15.7 million (Denevan 1992). Clearly the population density is also related to the technologies used: North American natives were hunters and gatherers, while the cultures in the Andes had reached the agricultural stage. One could argue that the concept of sustainability as it relates to populations only becomes meaningful after the technology variable is introduced.

A good explanation for this high population density is found in the landscape ecology of extreme climates as explained by German geographer Carl Troll (1899–1975). Troll envisioned a world consisting of a huge number of ecological niches, which with differences in altitudes would form what he called landscape belts (*Landschaftsgürtel*). On the North American prairies, one could travel for weeks inside the same climatic niche, while in mountainous areas such as the Andes (see Figure 2.1) very different ecological niches – such as those fit for growing cotton and those fit for growing potatoes – are found geographically relatively near to each other (Troll 1966).

Carl Troll's work was continued by anthropologist John Murra (1916–2006).[3] Studying a huge number of Peruvian court documents from colonial times and present annual migration patterns, Murra found that Peruvian labour had been highly mobile between the different ecological niches, sequentially following the seasons where harvests and other work was found. Murra developed the concept of a 'vertical archipelago' of ecological niches that – due to the great variations in climate from sea level to more than 4000 metres above sea level – are relatively close to each other in terms of kilometres and travelling time (Murra 1975, 2002). If we look at the cradle of European agricultural civilization, in places such as Armenia and Georgia, we can observe the same short geographical distances between climate zones: for example, between a climate suitable for cotton and a climate suitable for potatoes (seen in today's crops).

Moving between different ecological niches is the key to traditional nomadism, such as in the Andes and for the reindeer herders in Northern Eurasia. Moving according to where nature produces food is the very key to survival.[4] The more extreme the climate, the greater the number of ecological niches needed to survive. In other words, the more extreme the climate, the longer the annual nomadic migrations will tend to be.

Geography is of course closely linked to temperature. In Carl Troll's geography of extreme climates, one particular range of temperature – the days of the year when the temperature is both above and below zero during the same 24 hours – is crucial. Whether it is 20 or 30 below zero is normally not impor-

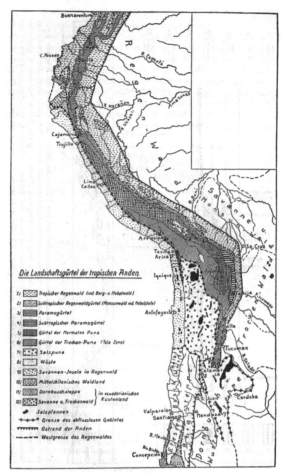

Note: The proximity of qualitatively different niches – from sea level to 4000 metres above sea level – allowed for a very high population density in the pre-Columbian cultures here. Different products would dominate niches at different altitudes: fish and cotton near sea level, fruits higher up, then maize, and further up potatoes; and at the top level around 4000 metres, *quinua*, a key crop related to millet (millet was an important crop in Europe before the arrival of potatoes and maize from the Americas), and the herding of different types of animals: llamas, alpacas, vicuñas. In the Arctic such ecological niches are even closer together. The efficient management of herding across this 'archipelago' of different ecological niches is the very core of reindeer herding.
Source: Illustration by Troll (1931), reproduced in Troll (1966: 111).

Figure 2.1   The geographical proximity of widely different ecological niches (or landscape belts) in the Andes

tant; however, what German geographers refer to as *Frostwechselhäufigkeit* – how often you find freezing and thawing in the same 24 hours – is extremely important.

In the Andes, a high *Frostwechselhäufigkeit* would allow the production of a staple food such as freeze-dried potatoes (*chuño*): freezing the potatoes every night and subsequently drying them in the sun during the daytime. It has been argued that the nutritional importance of *chuño* explains why the three main pre-Columbian cities in present Ecuador, Peru and Bolivia are all located above 3000 metres: Quito, Cuzco, and the area around Lake Titicaca. At this altitude the frequency of *Frostwechselhäufigkeit* is sufficient to make the production of *chuño* possible (Troll 1931, 1966; Murra 1975;[5] Gade 1996, 2016).

Karl Polanyi (1944) is the one who most efficiently contrasted capitalism to pre-capitalist societies. The pre-capitalist societal organization of herders is extended family groups, in the Andes called *ayllu* and in Sami called *siida*. Work inside a *siida* is divided and shared as a kind of joint venture inside a family group. It is important to note that the ownership of reindeer is individual, but the management of the herd is done by the *siida* 'joint venture'. If the tasks so require, the *siida* can also be split according to seasons.

Karl Polanyi has pointed to what he calls the three 'fictitious commodities' of capitalism, that are all missing in pre-capitalist societies: money, labour as a commodity, and private ownership of land. This still today essentially applies inside the Sami production system, while their relationship with the outside world of course is organized according to the market system. Instead of land ownership, pre-capitalist societies – including the Sami herders – have well-organized sequential usufruct of land. The different groups have the right to use and benefit from the land at different times of the year.

This difference in population density between the prairie and the Andes allows us to bring in another important factor, that of diversity. From Giovanni Botero (1592) onwards, manufacturing has been seen as the key to wealth. However, the argument is generally not one of manufacturing per se, but again and again the diversity of the manufacturing sector is emphasized. Rephrasing the understanding of development in the age of Botero we could say that if you would like to know the wealth of a city, go into the city and count the number of professions: the larger the number of professions (the larger the division of labour), the richer the city. The first description we have of virtuous circles of development (Serra 2011 [1613]) has at its core the diversity of manufacturing activities (the number of different professions) plus the increasing returns to scale in these industries.

The surprisingly high population density in pre-Columbian times has similarly been convincingly explained as the result of diversity. The apparently inhospitable Andes are home to a variety of climatic niches in close geographical proximity to each other (Troll 1931; Murra 1975). At a time when large distances impose high costs – what Oppenheimer (1923) calls high *Transportwiderstand* – the extreme climate of the Andes reduced this cost of time and transportation by bringing widely divergent climatic niches close in time and distance. The importance of diversity as a key to having a high population density and prosperity recently returned to the economic debate with Hausmann and Hidalgo's (2014) *Atlas of Economic Complexity: Mapping Paths to Prosperity*. By showing the importance of economic diversity, Hausmann and Hidalgo vindicate a key and very influential argument in early economic theory.

WE AND 'THE OTHERS': FROM MONSTERS IN ANTIQUITY TO ADMIRATION DURING THE RENAISSANCE, AND ON TO THE INTOLERANCE OF THE ENLIGHTENMENT

The types and degrees of European ethnocentrism have varied over time. We can essentially distinguish between three stages: the non-Europeans as 'monsters' (from the Romans until the Age of Discovery), the non-Europeans as admirable cultures (the Renaissance), the age of Eurocentrism (the Enlightenment, starting around 1750). It is indeed notable that the so-called Enlightenment was not enlightened when it came to racial issues. Voltaire, probably the most famous philosopher of the Enlightenment, was openly anti-Semitic.

Roman natural historian Pliny the Elder – who died during the eruption of Vesuvius in the year 79 – influenced Western ideas for centuries. Pliny described the monster-like beings that supposedly lived where no European had ever set foot. This appealed to people's curiosity and their sense for the grotesque. We find these in books as late as in the 1600s.

These myths slowly died out with the Great Explorations, starting around 1450, when information about geography and ethnology from the rest of the world reached Europe.[6] Italian Jesuit Govanni Botero (1544–1617) was the first to collect a work on global geography and ethnology, *Relazioni Universali*, in 1592.

Botero, a Jesuit, worked in the Vatican, in a group producing the index of books that were prohibited in the Catholic Church (*index librorum prohibitorum*). He therefore had almost exclusive access to many books that were not generally available. A fundamental feature of Botero's 1592 work – which had enormous influence all over Europe for the next more than a century[7] – was not just a mere acknowledgement of, but rather a fundamental celebration of the diversity in the Creation as it could be observed across the globe. Botero unabashedly proclaimed and appreciated the sophistication of the economic and socio-political structures, traditions, and innovations of his known world.

Note: The category of 'monsters' still existed in the works of Linnaeus until the 1740s.
Source: https://retrospectjournal.com/2020/12/07/blemmyae-a-history-of-the-headless-men/.

Figure 2.2   *Examples of human 'monsters' which Pliny the Elder (23–79
                   BC) thought inhabited the world that had not yet been
                   'discovered'*

Looking for a copy of Botero's *Relazioni Universali* in a Florence bookstore
in the 1980s provided a surprise. The book dealer immediately asked the
customer (Reinert): 'With or without monsters?' After Botero passed away in
1617, at least one edition was illustrated with the monsters that had lived in
human fantasy since Pliny the Elder had created them about 1500 years earlier
(Figure 2.2). The customer ended up buying one with monsters, and one with
more ethnographically correct illustrations.

   One of the many sources who Botero had access to was another Jesuit,
Matteo Ricci (1552–1610), the missionary to China. Ricci represented the
two-way communication Jesuits were keen on between Europe and the rest of
the world. In China, Ricci only translated the Bible into Chinese, but he also
translated the Chinese philosopher Confucius into Latin. Much later, Swedish
clergyman Lars Levi Læstadius (1800–1861) played a similar role in cultural
bridge-building in Northern Fennoscandia. He preached to the local Sámi in
their own language, but also translated part of their mythology into Swedish
(Læstadius 1997).

From our point of view today, the Renaissance thirst for knowledge and relative lack of prejudices seems remarkable. There was an attitude of positive curiosity. Cultures that later would be called 'primitive races' were seen as sophisticated users of extremely diverse and often challenging geographic surroundings. Sciences were of course less sophisticated than they are now, but they had what in our view is a very healthy focus on the context in which events took place: a deep and qualitative understanding of the connection between nature and culture. The contrast to the Eurocentric way in which Europeans and North Americans later would treat China and Japan is frightening (see Chapter 7 in this volume).

With one of the authors (Reinert) having worked as an adjunct professor in the economics of reindeer herding at Sámi University College in Kautokeino in Northern Norway, it is interesting to compare the present official Norwegian interpretation of this activity being 'backward' (Reinert 2006) with that of Botero. In the *Relazioni Universali*[8] Botero packs a lot of information on the Sami into just over one page on what he calls the Sami nation (Botero 1622 [1592]: 96–97), which he calls *Lappia* and *Lapponia*, which 'borders to Norway' (*confina con la Norvegia*). He describes their great abilities in archery, and admires their ability to build boats without nails. 'They have had a long war against the Norwegians', Botero writes about the nation Lapponia,[9] and informs us that they have gradually had to yield their independence, and that they pay taxes to Norway in the form of animal hides (Botero 1622 [1592]: 97). As always, Botero describes the relationship between nature and culture when he describes the Sami: 'Instead of horses, Nature has given the Saami the reindeer'.[10] He attempts to describe the reindeer: the size of a mule, hide like a donkey, and horns like a deer but with fewer branches. Botero admiringly describes the enormous distance, 50 *miglia*, that the Sami reindeer snow-sleighs are able to cover in 24 hours.

Renaissance man saw himself as created in the image of God, herefore had a duty pursue creative excellence and beauty, just as the Lord had done when he created the Earth and all its creatures (see Reinert and Daastøl 1997 [1998]). With this followed the duty to respect the enormous variety that could be observed in Nature. All human beings were equal in the eyes of the Creator. The difficult balance between duty-bound human beings as part of a *Ganzheit* (an indivisible whole), and the later Enlightenment focus on individuals driven by their own self-interest, is clearly still with us today. With the Enlightenment, particularly from 1770 and onwards, we see a sharp contrast in the attitude towards aboriginal cultures.

As we see in the above quotation from Botero, 'Nature' is the generous spirit that provides resources, not a specific deity. Non-European cultures were often pictured as utopias that showed Europeans alternative ways of organizing society: the existing diversity widened the realm of the thinkable. Admiration for things Chinese started with Marco Polo (1250–1324) and continued for centuries. In Germany the admiration for China was strong and probably lasted longer than in English-speaking countries.

In his 1750 work, Christian Wolff – an important German philosopher – expressed his admiration for China and its institutions,[11] but Justi (1762) also admired the Inca Empire in the Andes. The Inca Empire was particularly difficult to classify for Europeans.

Wolff (1679–1754) came to personally experience the conflict between the previous tolerant Renaissance view on other cultures and the new Eurocentrism. In 1721 he held a lecture on 'The Practical Philosophy of the Chinese' at the University of Halle, in Prussia, where he held a professorship. Here he used the texts of Confucius as proof that ethics and civilization could be created independently of Christendom. As a result, he was banned from Prussia, with the threat of the death penalty if he did not leave the country within 48 hours. Here the fragmentation of Germany into small states came to his rescue. Wolff could get on his horse and ride to Marburg in the neighbouring state of Hesse, where he was received as a hero at the university. At a time of more or less enlightened regimes, the multiplicity of small states provided diversity among which a 'best practice' often slowly developed by trial and error. Arthur Schopenhauer (1788–1860), Nietzsche's 'educator', was also influenced by Asian philosophy.

In Sweden – which for a long time had been an important political and intellectual power in Europe – probably the most famous intellectual at the time, Carl von Linné (1707–1778), still held the Renaissance view of the Sami as 'noble'. In a country where economics at the time – as in Germany – was called Cameralism, Linnaeus describes the Sami as 'the ideal cameralists'; and one of his best-known portraits shows him dressed as a Sami (Aslaksen 2007).

The Renaissance admiration for the diversity of the Creation changed relatively abruptly over a few decades during the latter part of the 1750s. Aboriginal cultures should no longer be understood within the logic of divine Creation: rather, they were subjugated to the interest of other cultures. From the 1500s the Jesuits had functioned as cultural bridge-builders. Matteo Ricci's double translation – the Bible into Chinese and Confucius into Latin – has already been mentioned. In Latin America, the Jesuits gathered the natives into villages – *reducciones* – which sometimes were run by the native *caciques*, or chiefs, rather than by Europeans. This project recalls the idea of Jesuit Giovanni Botero that wealth was best created in urban-like surroundings.

But the tolerance of the Jesuits stood in the way of a Europe in search of colonies and labour. They were thrown out of Portugal around 1760, out of the Spanish colonies in 1767, and in 1773 the Jesuit Order was prohibited by the Pope, a prohibition that lasted until 1814. The present Pope Francis is the first Pope ever from the Jesuit order, which was founded in 1534.

So, during the 1770s the Jesuits, who had been the defenders of the original inhabitants in Asia and America, were thrown out of these continents. The Jesuits believed in education for all and also taught the natives to paint and to play music. The *reducciones* – their settlements for the natives – can still be seen as impressive ruins in Argentina and Paraguay.

We can observe the same change of attitude towards the native inhabitants elsewhere. In the 1775 draft of the US Constitution they are referred to as 'indian nations', but when the Constitution was approved the next year, they had been reduced to 'indian tribes'.

The same pattern was observed in Northern Fennoscandia. Also here, the conscious destruction of aboriginal language and cultures starts in the 1770s. In Norway the Seminarium lapponicum, which had been established to teach Sami to the priests, was closed in 1774. It was ordered that the language spoken by the Sami should be scrapped, 'the Norwegian language introduced, and children will learn their Christendom in Norwegian' (Friis 1933 [1881]: 73). This policy continued in Norway until very recently.

So we can observe that the changing mentality towards non-European inhabitants of the world changed fairly rapidly and simultaneously around the world. An important economic consequence, which was identical on both sides of the Atlantic, was that legal ownership was only given to settled farmers. The sequential usufruct of land which dominated outside Europe was not classified as legal ownership. This turnaround in policy away from the ideals of Giovanni Botero provided the Europeans with: (1) land that could be taken from the natives for free; and (2) cheap labour, once the protection of the Jesuits became outlawed.

The paradox of the Enlightenment was that it was apparently dominated by reason and tolerance, but that – compared to the Renaissance – it also represented worsening conditions for minorities and a massive growth of slavery, which came to an end in France only in 1840 and in the US in 1865. Voltaire, probably the most respected philosopher of the Enlightenment, in 1763 wrote *A Treatise on Toleration*, while at the same time being an antisemite.[12] In the same vein, Enlightenment philosopher Jacques Rousseau, who excelled in abstract arguments for human rights in his work on the social contract (Rousseau 1762), nevertheless pictures women almost as inferior beings. The Enlightenment gives us the modern mainstreaming of the ethnocentrism of the West and the demeaning stereotype of 'the others', as Edward Said (1978) expressed in *Orientalism*.

One important point here is that the Enlightenment coincided with the collapse of the old empires – that by definition consisted of many ethnic groups – and the consolidation of new nation-states. Inside the old empires, minorities were often allowed to have their own institutions and their own language. Be they Armenian, Basque, Jews or Sami, they suddenly represented a threat against the consolidation and unity of the new nation-states. Two of the largest genocides in history, against Jews and Armenians, as well as the most recent genocide in Europe, against Bosnians, came about where ethnic minorities 'stood in the way of' new or potential nation-states.

If we create a categorization of the relationship between us (the West) and 'the others' there are three very different periods: (1) from Pliny the Elder (AD 23/24–79) and his 'monsters' to the Middle ('Dark') Ages; then (2) an ambivalent period of rapid European colonial expansion on the one hand, and on the other the Great Discoveries (and the consolidation of the knowledge collected by the discoveries) alongside extraordinary interest, tolerance and respect for non-European cultures (for example, Giovanni Botero in the late 1500s until around 1750); which is then followed by (3) an unequivocal period of exploitation and racism which we still live with today.

EUROPEAN ETHNOCENTRISM SEEN FROM THE ISLAMIC WORLD

The period between classical Greco-Roman civilization and the Great Discoveries, commonly referred to as the 'Dark Ages' of Europe's history, is what Joseph Schumpeter ([1954] 1987), in his *History of Economic Analysis*, referred to as the 'Great Gap' in terms of philosophical and scientific contributions, especially with regard to economics. Although Schumpeter gives high praise to the practical aspects of governance and policy in this period, namely Charlemagne and the Eastern Empire (Byzantines), his view is that intellectual questions were simply not addressed, and if they were, the writings did not survive; therefore declaring: 'we may safely leap over 500 years to the epoch of St. Thomas Aquinas (1225–74)' (Schumpeter [1954] 1987: 70). If we do indeed take this leap to Aquinas, it follows that the European Renaissance was achieved as an independent European development.

Such a leap, however, requires overlooking the tremendous and far-ranging accomplishments resulting from the Golden Era of the Islamic world (discussed below) and, by extension, the direct pathways of transmission of science and thought of the former to Europe (Saliba 2007).

To start with, the scientific method itself was developed and systematized by Muslim scholars during the Great Gap period, with Ibn Al-Haytham (965–1040) being the earliest and most prominent example of utilizing systematized empirical experimentation for his revolutionary work on optics. Through a series of experiments, Ibn Al-Haytham put forth the first known description of physical light reflecting from an object and its subsequent reception by the eye (not vice versa), and the first theory of how light received through the eye is transmitted to the brain through an optic nerve (that is, the mechanics of human vision) (Smith 1992).

In governance, the rapid expansion of Islam since its early days led to an overstretch as regards governability and administrative capacity. This could only partly be countered by decentralization and the inclusion of local elites (which resulted in the existence of diverse cultural/ethnic groups); already well described by the historian Abu Al-Hasan Al-Baladhuri (820–892) in his 9th century work *Futūh al-Buldān*. The Golden Era period featured similarly important developments in terms of statecraft and administration (Samier 2017). Take, for instance, the vizier and scholar Nizam Al-Mulk (1018–1092) and his *Siyāsatnāma*, which despite being over 900 years old presents a detailed, workable and weirdly current concept of state administration, such as the need for superiors to avoid interference in routine administration (or in today's parlance, not to micro-manage), and the non-delegatability of responsibility for those over whom one rules (Drechsler 2015; Al-Mulk 1960).

Within mathematics, although numerous Muslims put forth major contributions to the field, the example of the Persian polymath Muhammad ibn Musa Al-Khwarizmi (780–850) alone suffices as a rebuttal to the Great Gap narrative: his treatise *Hisab al-Jabr wa al-Muqabala* took (often complex) scenarios from Islamic inheritance laws to outline the first systematic solution to linear and quadratic equations, introducing the mathematical concept of *sifr* (zero) along the way, and making him the founder of algebra; that is, the second word of the title of his treatise, *al-Jabr* (Afridi 2013). The Latin translation of Al Khwarizmi's *Hisab* was used as the foundational text in European universities until the 16th century, and another Latin translation of his work on arithmetic introduced the decimal numeric system to Europe, today known as Arabic numerals.

In Islam, there are various Quranic and Prophetic injunctions to seek and develop knowledge regardless of its origin; what is imperative is that the knowledge benefits Creation without violating or encroaching upon divine edicts. The House of Wisdom, founded in the late 8th century by Caliph Harun Al-Rashid, was a paragon of this imperative and embodied the translation movement of texts from Greek, Roman and Hindi into Arabic, which introduced ancient thought and science to Islamic civilization (Lyons 2011). This was a proactive and intentional effort to appropriate the knowledge of earlier traditions, in particular that of Ancient Greece; not as 'a re-enactment of the glories of ancient Greece' via translation, but rather as a basis for furthering intellectual thought and scientific innovation (Saliba 2007: 2). Similarly, the 9th century pious aristocrat Fatima Al Fihri used the fortune she inherited to build what became the oldest continually operating university and the first degree-awarding educational institution in the world: al Qarawiyyin in Fes, Morocco.

In the realm of medicine, the United States National Library of Medicine recognizes the *bimaristan* (early Islamic healthcare institutions) as the first hospitals, with the oldest being built in 805, also under the reign of Caliph Harun Al-Rashid (National Library of Medicine 1994). The work of Muslim physicians from the Great Gap period not only laid the foundations for Western medicine, but at times proved to be remarkably precocious. The encyclopaedic *Cannon of Medicine*, written in 1025 by Ibn Sina (Avicenna), was the main text used to teach medicine at European universities until as late as the 18th century (McGinnis 2010). Today the area of mind and body wellness (that is, the integration of physical and behavioural health) has increasingly, especially since the start of the COVID-19 pandemic, captured the attention of contemporary medical scholars and practitioners. Over 11 centuries ago, Abu Zayd al-Balkhi (850–934) asserted that prophylactic and treatment approaches must focus on both the body and the mind, because they are together the foundation of well-being (Awaad et al. 2019).

An important precursor to the Eurocentric Great Gap narrative was the systemic borrowing of ideas by European scholastics from Muslim scholars without acknowledgement. There are three key reasons for this lack of credit: (1) the denigrating view of Islam and Muslims that scholastics held, and by extension, the impossibility of acknowledging anything of value or merit originating from them; (2) the opportunity for scholastics to take self-credit; some even viewed this as a way to 'emancipate knowledge from the clutches of Arabs' (Sezgin 1984: 127); and (3) that borrowing without acknowledgement was a widespread and accepted practice (Islahi 2014). Despite this, the reality of pathways of transmission is clear, as illustrated by the Escuela de Traductores de Toledo (Toldeo School of Translators) founded in the 12th century to translate texts (most prominently those of Ibn Rushd/Averroes who was known in the West simply as 'The Exegete' for his commentary on Greek classics) from Arabic into Latin, and later into what became an early standardized version of Spanish.

Indeed, thousands of Arabic words have made their way into Western languages. In Venice, the residence-warehouses of foreign embassies were, and still are, called *fondaco* (Arabic for warehouse). The names of professions in Spanish (*alfarero*, potter; *alfaiate*, tailor; and many more) show that the division of labour took place when the country was under Arab rule. This also to some degree applies to Portugal: a key institution was and is *alfandega*, customs office. The Spanish word for the same thing, *aduana*, comes via Persian and Arabic. The word 'algorithm' comes from the Latinized version of the aforementioned Al-Khwarizmi's name, and the Arabic word he used for zero, *sifr*, is also the origin of the words 'cipher' and 'decipher'.

As for economics, to turn back to Schumpeter's mention of Saint Thomas Aquinas, we agree that he was one of the most influential Western thinkers and perhaps the single most important scholar in the transition from the European Dark Ages. What is often overlooked is that Aquinas was deeply influenced by, and borrowed generously from, Muslim thinkers before him; in particular Ibn Sina and Abu Hamid Al-Ghazali (Smith 1944). The latter is considered one of the greatest scholars of Islam, from any time period.

Among various other topics, Al-Ghazali (1058–1111) theorized on key aspects of economic development such as the stages of production and specialization of labour (he uses needles as an illustration of his argument, which is uncannily similar to the pin factory example of Adam Smith seven centuries later), market regulations (for example, via an oversight institution known as *al-hasbah*), currency debasement (notably predating early Renaissance scholar Nicholas Oresme's 1956 [1356] *Treatise on Money*), and flexibility in public borrowing and public expenditures for the purpose of ensuring broad societal goals, for example, socio-economic justice, security, and developing a prosperous society (Ghazanfar and Islahi 1990).

Nearly three centuries later, Ibn Khaldun (1332–1406) – who is recognized as a founding father of social science writ large, and specifically of sociology, historiography and economics – expanded on Al-Ghazali's economic thought. In his *Al-Muqaddima* (Arabic for *The Introduction*), he discusses how specialization of labour is a result of no one human being able to do everything, and more importantly, the greater specialization of labour, the more industries and crafts flourish, and in turn the more wealth is generated (Ibn Khaldun 2004); which foreshadows Botero's heuristic of counting the number of professions in an area to know how wealthy it is. Continuing Ibn Khaldun's argument: greater wealth in a society results in governments having more revenues to spend on people's well-being and creating economic opportunities, which results in both a natural rise in the population and the arrival of immigrants of varying backgrounds, which subsequently diversifies and boosts human and intellectual capital, increases demand for goods and services, builds up industries, raises incomes, augments the sciences and education, and ultimately spurs further development (Chapra 2008). We believe that although a brilliant economist in his own right, Schumpeter's suggestion to safely leap over such contributions is an incorrect one.

EUROPEAN ETHNOCENTRISM SEEN FROM CHINA

It seems that when the Roman world was under the rule of the 'Five Good Emperors', China for the first time heard about this civilization at the other end of Eurasia from the Arsacid Persia (Yü 1986: 461; He 2017: 173). Compared with the European image of 'the others' as monsters, China highly praised the wealth and civilization of Roman Europe, and named it Ta Ch'in (or Da Qin, 大秦; literally, 'the Grand China'). This name implied that the Chinese thought so highly of this civilization that it was deemed worthy of being treated as an equal of China, as 'Ch'in' meant and was the origin of the word

'China' (ibid.). However, there was hardly any direct contact between China and Rome, because the Pathian intentionally blocked them in order to keep its position as the monopolist of the Silk Road trade (Yü 1986: 461). In the following centuries, China's contact with the European civilization was limited to the occasional communication with Ta Ch'in, namely, Rome and its eastern successor, the Byzantine Empire. Only after Genghis Khan's offspring merged the crowns of the Mongolian Khan and the Chinese Emperor, did the Catholic Church start to reach out to Chinese emperors, seeking to convert this vast empire to Catholicism (He 2017: 507–513). The Mongolian khans/emperors showed great interest in this religion, and asked the Church to dispatch a cardinal to China (ibid.: 513). This plan was never fulfilled, due to the overturn of Mongolia's regime in China.

Starting with the Great Discoveries, Europe found direct access to China. Chinese emperors started to receive European diplomatic representatives with different objectives (Wills 1998; Wills and Cranmer-Bying 2016; He 2017: 836–878). Among them, they welcomed the Jesuits the most. Unlike Mongolian emperors, Chinese emperors' interest in European missionaries now did not lie in religious curiosity, but in the useful knowledge mastered by the Jesuits: astronomy, mathematics, medicine, mechanics, map-making, fine arts, and especially firearm-making (He 2017: 634–636; Wills 1998: 363–366; Witek 2016). However, after 1722, the Jesuits were expelled from the imperial court due to their alliance with what ended up being the wrong side of the princes' competition for the throne (Witek 2016: 361).

Jesuits' activities 'led to some fascinating interactions in religion, scholarship, science, literature, and art' (Wills 1998: 363). This list also included economic thought. To the Renaissance Continental economic thinkers, Chinese economy and economic thought provided a strong supporting case proving that their ideas could actually work. Giovanni Botero was a high-profile Sinophile. He regarded China as the most developed economy from which principles of economic development could be learned. Above all, Botero noticed that China had 'countless multitudes of artisans and merchants' (Botero 1956 [1589]: 143). Clearly, Botero took China as the living example of his principle of making a country rich: the more diversified a country's manufacturing activities are, the richer the country will be. He also made this observation regarding European cities (Botero 2012 [1588]).

Christian Wolff was also an enthusiastic Sinophile. Wolff's natural law theory provided the philosophical foundation of the Continental enlightened despotism and the German cameralism (Haakonssen 2006; Tribe 1988: 30–34). His economic doctrines were typically mercantilist (cameralist), which was common at the time (Wolff 1736: 212–590). Yet the most striking characteristic of Wolff's economic thought was that he followed in the footsteps of Leibniz in spreading Scientific Revolution and the spirit of innovation in the German world (Reinert and Daastøl 1997 [1998]). Wolff advocated that it was a natural obligation of humans to acquire as much knowledge as possible and to invent as much as possible (Wolff 1743: 165–168, 191–202). Wolff wrote: 'those who are able to invent useful human arts or improve inventions are obliged to do so' (Wolff 1756: 170). Therefore, in addition to his mercantilist/cameralist policy program, Wolff proposed that the state should create academies of sciences, aiming at generating and spreading inventions useful to industries (Wolff 1743: 241–249). In Wolff's thought, it was the state that should play the key role in generating industrial innovations.

Just like Botero, Wolff referred to China for the evidence supporting his ideas. Wolff believed that China was a living example of the rational and prosperous civilization which was built on the principles agreeing with his philosophy (Wolff 1985 [1721]; Kanamori 1997). Especially, Wolff found that China provided the evidence supporting his proposal of the state as the innovation generator. Wolff regarded the ancient Chinese as people enjoying happiness under the rule of philosopher kings (Wolff 1750). Wolff believed that these ancient Chinese emperors 'settled that model of government, where in it now excels all other models in the world', and this model of government continued flourishing until Wolff's time (ibid.: 15). The characteristic of this model of government was that the ruler engaged in making inventions useful to the economy and society, and acted as the 'master of the time and opportunity requisite for the business of invention, and of philosophical reasonings, without neglecting the affairs of a vast empire' (ibid.). Wolff's observation was largely accurate, for it was a common function of the Chinese state in history to act as the key promoter of crafts and inventions. In the *Rites of Zhou* (周礼), a Confucian classical text about the ideal organization of a monarchy, there is listed a ministry named 司空 (Si Kong) which was in charge of manufacturing and artisanry and their skills (百工), and the task of this ministry was 'to make the country rich' (以富邦国). In medieval China, namely the Tang and Song Dynasties (618–1279), one of the imperial government agencies was 少府监 (Shao Fu Jian), which managed all state manufactories, 'concentrated all crafts under the heavens' (聚天下之伎), and was specifically in charge of 'policies regarding crafts' (掌百工伎巧之政令).

From these cases, we could say that two key elements behind the European economic development in the early modern period – the pursuit of maximizing the diversity of the manufacturing sector, and the state policy promoting innovations and the progress of skills – were both discovered by European economists (Botero and Wolff) with reference to the Chinese case. This explains that after the decline of imperial China as well as its pursuit of manufacturing and innovation, when the last group of Chinese Confucian literati thought about catching up with the West, they actually found the reason for European development was that they practiced what their ancestors believed, but this was abandoned later (e.g., Xue 1994: 164–165; Zheng 1994 [1894]: 241, 246). To a certain degree, we could say that from a Chinese perspective, compared with the late imperial China, European economies were more developed, which is a key pillar supporting the eurocentrism, because in some key respects they were more 'Chinese'.

THE ELEPHANT IN THE ROOM: UNDERSTANDING POPULATION DENSITY

Human history has for a long time been related to stages of economic development, typically a stage of hunting and gathering, a stage of herding and nomadism, a stage of agriculture, and a stage of industrialism (Bücher 1893; Ely 1903; Hildebrand 1864, 1876; Kalveram 1933; Rostow 1960; Reinert 2000; Schefold 1988, 1994/1995; Sombart 1928; Sommer 1948). As already suggested by Botero, an important aspect of economic stage theories is that they are a tool that helps us understand the nexus between productive structure of a nation, social organization and wealth.

Furthermore, different economic stages correspond to a carrying capacity – a level of sustainability – in terms of population. Clearly very fertile and well-irrigated areas such as China would have a very much higher carrying capacity than most others in an agricultural society; but if we refer to countries in general, the suggested relationship between technological stage of development and population density will hold. Among hunters and gatherers in the Amazon, 1–2 persons per square kilometre is a lot; in an advanced industrial and service economy such as that of Holland, 400 persons per square kilometre does not mean 'overpopulation'.

In the spring of 2015, Reinert found himself as an advisor to the government of Eritrea. Somewhat unusually, he was invited to a government cabinet meeting. Eritrea had found itself in an exceptionally industry-friendly colonial period under Italy, until 1941[13] when it came under British military administration. Migration was an important issue and came up in the cabinet meeting. Seemingly, when the national population density approached 40 persons per square kilometre, migration from Eritrea increased, and migration went for example to Holland, which has over 400 persons per square kilometre (Table 2.1). The economic structure of Holland, an advanced industrial sector combined with an advanced service sector and an agricultural sector with high barriers to entry (for example, flower bulbs), made this possible.

In the meeting it was suggested that Eritrea should try to industrialize in order to slow migration; there were still some manufacturing plants left. The elderly guard in the cabinet meeting, largely veterans from the war, were fairly enthusiastic about the proposal. What killed the idea completely was a cabinet minister who had been working with the World Bank and who – with this con-

Table 2.1   Economic stages and typical maximum population density

Economic stage	Population density
Hunting and gathering societies	1–2 persons / km2
Agricultural societies	40 persons / km2
Industrial societies, e.g. Holland	400 persons / km2

vincing authority – single-handedly killed the idea. Reinert was subsequently invited to talk at a meeting in a park outside Stockholm where over 10 000 Eritreans resident in Europe gathered for a meeting; a truly amazing event.

At the beginning of the Cold War the Morgenthau Plan and its successor, the Marshall Plan, give us a very important insight into the relationship between economic structure and population density. When it was clear that the Allies would win World War II, the question of what to do with Germany, which in three decades had precipitated two world wars, came onto the agenda. Henry Morgenthau Jr, US Finance Minister from 1934 to 1945, formulated a plan to keep Germany from ever again threatening world peace (Morgenthau 1943). Germany, he argued, was to be entirely deindustrialized and turned into an agricultural nation. All industrial equipment was to be removed or destroyed; the mines were to be flooded with water or concrete. This programme, the Morgenthau Plan, was approved by the Allies during a meeting in Canada in late 1943, and was immediately implemented when Germany capitulated in May 1945.

During 1946 and 1947, however, it became clear that the Morgenthau Plan was causing serious economic problems in Germany: deindustrialization caused agricultural productivity to plummet. This was indeed an interesting experiment. The mechanisms of synergy between industry and agriculture, so key to Enlightenment economists, also worked in reverse: killing industry reduced the productivity of the agricultural sector. More people on the same land created diminishing returns. Former President Herbert Hoover – who at the time played the role of the old and wise statesman – was sent to Germany with orders to report to Washington what the problem was. His investigation took place in early 1947, and Hoover wrote three reports. In the last, dated 18 March 1947, he concluded: 'There is the illusion that the New Germany left after the annexations can be reduced to a "pastoral state". It cannot be done unless we exterminate or move 25 000 000 out of it'.

Observing the dark consequences of deindustrialization, Herbert Hoover had reinvented the old mercantilist theory of population: an industrial state could feed and maintain a far larger population than an agricultural state occupying the same territory. The practical result of this was seen when Germans moved from the British, French, and American sectors of Germany – all subject to the Morgenthau Plan – into the Soviet sector where manufacturing industry was still permitted. Less than three months after Hoover's warning, on 5 June 1947, then US Secretary of State George Marshall delivered a speech at Harvard announcing what came to be called the Marshall Plan, completely reversing the Morgenthau Plan. West Germany was to reindustrialize; and in the period that followed this industrialization plan created 'a sanitary belt' of wealthy countries from Western and Southern Europe all the way to Taiwan, South Korea and Japan. This industrialization clearly contributed to stopping communism.

The fact that famines tend to occur only in countries specialized in agriculture underlines the power of industry, of the division of labour, and of the importance of the intersectorial synergies that create and maintain welfare. But today's neoclassical trade theory does not allow a theory simultaneously employing increasing and diminishing returns – such as Herbert Hoover implicitly did – that would not be compatible with the core notion of equilibrium. If the West is interested in stopping migration, industrializing the Third World would be the simplest measure (Reinert 2003). It would require the kind of industrial policy that Donald Trump reinvented for the United States, but refused to African countries. One problem in the West in general seems to be that the same people who are most vigorously against immigration are also the people who are most fervently in favour of free trade. This is truly a contradiction, that could be solved by a better knowledge of the underlying mechanisms of economics. We seem to be stuck with the analysis of Acemoglu and Robinson (2012), that poor counties simply lack the right institutions, without seeing that these right institutions were once lacking in the rich world as well; until they were created as an outcome of industrial development.

NOTES

1. Christopher Freeman (1921–2010), the inspirator of modern evolutionary economics, argues that Friedrich List is the originator of the idea of national innovation systems (Freeman 1995).
2. See Tvedt and Østgaard (2006).
3. One of the authors, Reinert, studied under Murra at Cornell University.
4. Francis Bacon (1620) in his *Novum Organum* states in translation: 'Nature, to be commanded, must be obeyed'.
5. Particularly Chapter 3, 'El control vertical de un máximo de pisos ecológicos en la economía de las sociedades andinas', pp. 59–117.
6. There were of course also earlier contacts, such as Marco Polo's stay in China from 1271 to 1295.
7. Interestingly, early translations in Germany from the original Italian text were both into Latin (1596, 1599, 1620, 1664 and 1670) and into German (1596, 1599, 1604, and 1611).

8.	Botero, Giovanni, *Le Relationi Universali, Diviso in sette parti*, Venice: Alessandro Vecchi, 1622. This is the 5th edition. The first edition was published in 1592.
9.	'Hanno guerreggiato lungamente co i Noruegi' he says in his old-fashioned Italian.
10.	'In vece di cavalli, la natura gli ha dato il rangifero.'
11.	The English title of Wolff (1750) is interesting; see the References.
12.	Volume 3 of the history of antisemitism carries the title 'from Voltaire to Wagner' (Poliakov 1975).
13.	Apparently fairly different from other Italian colonies.

REFERENCES

Acemoglu, Daron and James Robinson (2012), *Why Nations Fail: The Origins of Power, Prosperity, and Poverty*, New York: Crown.
Afridi, Muhammad A. (2013), 'Contribution of Muslim scientists to the world: an overview of some selected fields', *Revelation and Science*, 3(1), 40–49.
Al-Mulk, Nizam (1960), *The Book of Government or Rules for Kings: Syiāsát-nāma or Siyar al-Mulk*, London: Routledge & Kegan Paul.
Aslaksen, Iulie (2007), 'Carl von Linné – botaniker med økonomiske visjoner', *Økonomisk Forum*, 61(9), 38–43.
Awaad, Rania, Alaa Mohammad, Khalid Elzamzamy, Soraya Fereydooni and Maryam Gamar (2019), 'Mental health in the Islamic Golden Era: The historical roots of modern psychiatry', in H. Moffic, J. Peteet, A. Hankir and R. Awaad (eds), *Islamophobia and Psychiatry*, New York: Springer, pp. 3–17.
Bacon, Francis (1620), *Novum Organum*, London: Apud Joannem Billium.
Bircher, S. (1992), 'Die Malaria im St. Galler Rheintal', in *Internationale Rheinregulierung – Der Alpenrhein und seine Regulierung 1892–1992*, Buchs: Buchs Druck und Verlag, pp. 120–126.
Blaut, J.M. (1993), *The Colonizer's Model of the World*, New York: Guildford Press.
Blaut, J.M. (2000), *Eight Ethnocentric Historians*, New York: Guilford Press.
Botero, Giovanni (1592), *Relazioni Universali*, Ferrara: Appresso Benedetto Mammarelli.
Botero, Giovanni (1622 [1592]), *Le relationi Universali, Diviso in sette parti*, Venice: Alessandri Vecchi.
Botero, Giovanni (1956 [1589]), *The Reason of State*, trans. by P.J. Waley, London: Routledge & Kegan Paul.
Botero, Giovanni (2012 [1588]), *Delle Cause Grandezze della Grandezza delle Città*, Rome: Martinelli. English translation *On the Causes of the Greatness and Magnificence of Cities*, Toronto: University of Toronto Press.
Bücher, Karl (1893), *Die Entstehung der Volkswirtschaft*, Tubingen: Laupp (1st edition in one volume) last edition (in two volumes) 1927. English translation, as Carl Bücher (1902), *Industrial Evolution*, London: George Bell & Sons / New York: Henry Holt (translated from the 3rd German edition). Translations also into Czech, French and Russian.
Chandler, Alfred (1990), *Scale and Scope. The Dynamics of Industrial Capitalism*, Cambridge, MA: Harvard University Press.

Chapra, M. Umer (2008), 'Ibn Khaldun's theory of development: does it help explain the low performance of the present-day Muslim world?', *Journal of Socio-Economics*, 37(2), pp. 836–863.

Denevan, William M. (ed.) (1992), *The Native Population of the Americas in 1492*, Madison, WI: University of Wisconsin Press.

Drechsler, Wolfgang (2015), 'Paradigms of non-Western PA and governance', in Andrew Massey and Karen Johnston (eds), *The International Handbook of Public Administration and Governance*, Cheltenham, UK and Northampton, MA, USA: Edward Elgar Publishing, pp. 104–132.

Ely, Richard (1903), *Studies in the Evolution of Industrial Society*, New York: Chautauqua Press.

Freeman, Chris (1995), 'The "National System of Innovation" in historical perspective', *Cambridge Journal of Economics*, 19(1), 5–24.

Friis, J.A. (1933 [1881]), *Lajla*, Oslo: Gyldendal.

Gade, Daniel W. (1996), 'Carl Troll on nature and culture in the Andes', *Erdkunde*, 50(4), 301–316.

Gade, Daniel (2016). 'Urubamba verticality: reflections on crops and diseases', in Daniel Gade (ed.), *Spell of the Urubamba: Anthropogeographical Essays on an Andean Valley in Space and Time*, Cham: Springer, pp. 83–129.

Gallup, John Luke, Jeffrey Sachs and Andrew Mellinger (1998), 'Geography and economic development', National Bureau of Economic Research, Working Paper 6849.

Ghazanfar, Shaikh M. and A. Azim Islahi (1990), 'Economic thought of an Arab scholastic: Abu Hamid al-Ghazali (AH 450–505/AD 1058–1111)', *History of Political Economy*, 22(2), 381–403.

Haakonssen, Knud (2006), *The Cambridge Companion to Adam Smith*, New York: Cambridge University Press.

Hausmann, Ricardo and Cesar Hidalgo (2014), *The Atlas of Economic Complexity: Mapping Paths to Prosperity*, Cambridge, MA: MIT Press.

He, Xinhua [何新华] (2017), *A Diplomatic History of China: from Xia to Qing* [中国外交史：从夏至清], Beijing: China Economic Publishing House.

Hildebrand, Bruno (1864), 'Natural-, Geld- und Kreditwirtschaft', in *Jahrbücher für Nationalökonomie und Statistik*, Vol. II, pp. 1–24, reprinted in Hans Gehrig (ed.) (1922), *Die Nationalökonomie der Gegenwart und Zukunft und andere gesammelte Schriften von Bruno Hildebrand*, Jena: Gustav Fischer.

Hildebrand, Bruno (1876), 'Die Entwicklungsstufen der Geldwirtschaft', in *Jahrbücher für Nationalökonomie und Statistik*, Vol. XXVI, pp. 15–26; reprinted in Hans Gehrig (ed.) (1922), *Die Nationalökonomie der Gegenwart und Zukunft und andere gesammelte Schriften von Bruno Hildebrand*, Jena: Gustav Fischer.

Huntington, Ellsworth (1925), *Civilization and Climate*, New Haven, CT: Yale University Press.

Ibn Khaldun, Abd Al-Rahman (2004), *Al-Muqaddima* [The Introduction, المقدمة], Beirut: Dar Yorab.

Islahi, A. Azim (2014), *History of Islamic Economic Thought: Contributions of Muslim Scholars to Economic Thought and Analysis*, Cheltenham, UK and Northampton, MA, USA: Edward Elgar Publishing.

Jomo, K.S. and Erik S. Reinert (2005), 'Introduction', *The Origins of Development Economics, How Schools of Economic Thought Have Addressed Development*, London: Zed Publications / New Delhi: Tulika Books, pp. vii–xxii.

Justi, J.H.G. von (1762), *Vergleichungen der Europäischen mit den Asiatischen und andern vermeintlich Barbarischen Regierungen*, Berlin: Rüdiger.

Kalveram, Gertrud (1933), *Die Theorien von den Wirtschaftsstufen*, Leipzig: Hans Buske.

Kanamori, Shigenari (1997), 'Christian Wolff' Speech on Confucianism: Confucius Compared with Wolff', *European Journal of Law and Economics*, 4, 299–304.

Krugman, Paul (1991), *Geography and Trade*, Louvain: Louvain University Press / Cambridge, MA: MIT Press.

Læstadius, L.L. ([1840–45] 1997), *Fragmenter i lappska mythologien*, Åbo [Turku]: Nordic Institute of Folklore Publications.

Landes, David (1998), *The Wealth and Poverty of Nations*, New York: Norton.

Lyons, Jonathan (2011), *The House of Wisdom: How the Arabs Transformed Western Civilization*, London: Bloomsbury Publishing.

McGinnis, Jon (2010), *Avicenna*, Oxford: Oxford University Press.

Morgenthau, Henry, Jr (1943), *Germany Is Our Problem*, New York and London: Harper & Brothers.

Murra, J. (1975), 'El "control vertical" de un máximo de pisos ecológicos en las sociedades andinas', *Formaciones económicas y políticas del mundo andino*, Lima: Instituto de Estudios Peruanos.

Murra, J. (2002), *El Mundo Andino. Población, medio ambiente y economía*, Lima: Instituto de Estudios Peruanos / Universidad Católica.

National Library of Medicine (1994), *Islamic Culture and the Medical Arts: Hospitals*. https://www.nlm.nih.gov/exhibition/islamic_medical/islamic_12.html.

Oppenheimer, Franz (1923), *System der Soziologie*, Vol. 3, Tome 1, 5th edn, Jena: Gustav Fischer.

Oresme, Nicolas (1956 [1356]), *De Moneta*, translated from the Latin by Charles Johnson, London: Nelson & Sons.

Polanyi, Karl (1944), *The Great Transformation*, Boston, MA: Beacon.

Poliakov, Léon (1975), *The History of Anti-Semitism. Volume III. From Voltaire to Wagner*, London: Routledge & Kegan Paul.

Reinert, Erik S. (2000), 'Karl Bücher and the geographical dimensions of techno-economic change', in Jürgen Backhaus (ed.), *Karl Bücher: Theory – History – Anthropology – Non-Market Economies*, Marburg: Metropolis Verlag, pp. 177–222.

Reinert, Erik S. (2003), 'Increasing poverty in a globalised world: Marshall Plans and Morgenthau Plans as mechanisms of polarisation of world incomes', in Ha-Joon Chang (ed.), *Rethinking Economic Development*, London: Anthem, pp. 453–478.

Reinert, Erik S. (2006), 'The economics of reindeer herding: Saami entrepreneurship between cyclical sustainability and the powers of state and oligopolies', *British Food Journal*, 108(7), 522–540.

Reinert, Erik S. and Arno Daastøl ([1997] 1998), 'Exploring the genesis of economic innovations: the religious gestalt-switch and the duty to invent as preconditions for economic growth', *European Journal of Law and Economics*, 4(2/3), 233–283; republished in *Christian Wolff. Gesammelte Werke, Materialien und Dokumente*, Hildesheim: Georg Olms Verlag, 1998.

Robertson, William (1777), *The History of America*, London and Edinburgh: Strahan, Cadell, & Balfour.

Rostow, Walt Whitman (1960), *The Stages of Economic Growth: A Non-Communist Manifesto*, Cambridge: Cambridge University Press.

Rousseau, Jean-Jacques (1762), *Du Contrat Social; ou, principes du droit politique*. Amsterdam: Marc Michel Rey.

Said, Edward (1978), *Orientalism*, New York, Pantheon Books.

Saliba, George (2007), *Islamic Science and the Making of the European Renaissance*, Cambridge, MA: MIT Press.

Samier, Eugenie A. (2017), 'Islamic public administration tradition: historical, theoretical and practical dimensions', *Administrative Culture*, 18(1), 53–71.

Schefold, Bertram (1988), 'Karl Bucher und der Historismus der Deutschen Nationalökonomie', in Notker Hammerstein (ed.), *Deutsche Geschichtswissenschaft um 1900*, Stuttgart: Steiner.

Schefold, Bertram (1994/1995), *Wirtschaftsstile*, 2 volumes (Vol. 1: *Studien zum Verhältnis von Ökonomie und Kultur*; Vol. 2: *Studien zur ökonomischen Theorie und zur Zukunft der Technik*), Frankfurt: Fischer Taschenbuch Verlag.

Schumpeter, Joseph Alois ([1954] 1987), *History of Economic Analysis*, London: Routledge.

Serra, Antonio (2011 [1613]), *Breve trattato delle cause che possono far abbondare li regni d'oro e argento dove non sono miniere*, Naples: Lazzaro Scoriggio. English translation, *A Short Treatise on the Wealth and Poverty of Nations*, edited by Sophus A. Reinert, London: Anthem.

Sezgin, Fuat (1984), *Muhādarāt fī Tarīkh al-Ulūm al-Arabīyah wa'l- Islāmiyah* [Lectures on Arabic and Islamic Sciences, محاضرات في خيرات العلوم العربية و الإسلامية], Frankfurt: Institut für Geschichte der Arabisch-Islamischen Wissenschaften.

Smith, John D. (1992), 'The remarkable Ibn al-Haytham', *Mathematical Gazette*, 76(475), 189–198.

Smith, Margaret (1944), *Al-Ghazali, The Mystic*, London: Luzac.

Sombart, Werner (1928), *Der moderne Kapitalismus*, 6 volumes, Munich and Leipzig: Duncker & Humblot.

Sommer, Artur (1948), 'Über Inhalt, Rahmen und Sinn älterer Stufentheorien (List und Hildebrand)', in Edgar Salin (ed.), *Synopsis. Festgabe für Alfred Weber*, Heidelberg: Lambert Schneider, pp. 535–565.

Tribe, Keith (1988), *Governing Economy: The Reformation of German Economic Discourse 1750–1840*, Cambridge: Cambridge University Press.

Troll, Carl (1931), 'Die geographische Grundlage der Andinen Kulturen und des Inkareiches'. *Ibero-Amerikanisches Archiv*, 5, 1–37.

Troll, Carl (1966), *Ökologische Landschaftsforschung und vergleichende Hochgebirgsforschung*, Wiesbaden: Steiner.

Tvedt, Terje and Terje Østgaard (2006), *A History of Water*, 3 volumes, New York and London: I.B. Tauris.

Von Laue, Theodore (1963), *Sergei Witte and the Industrialization of Russia*, New York: Columbia University Press.

Wills, John E. (1998), 'Relations with maritime Europeans, 1514–1662', in Denis Twitchett and Frederick W. Mote (eds), *The Cambridge History of China*, Vol. 8, Cambridge: Cambridge University Press, pp. 333–375.

Wills, John E. and John L. Cranmer-Bying (2016), 'Ch'ing relations with maritime Europeans', in Willard J. Peterson (ed.), *The Cambridge History of China*, Vol. 9, Pt 2, Cambridge: Cambridge University Press, pp. 264–328.

Witek, John W. (2016), 'Catholic missionaries, 1644–1800', in Willard J. Peterson (ed.), *The Cambridge History of China*, Vol. 9, Pt 2, Cambridge: Cambridge University Press, pp. 329–371.

Wittfogel, Karl A. (1957), *Oriental Despotism: A Comparative Study of Total Power*, New Haven, CT: Yale University Press.

Wolff, Christian (1736), *Vernünfftige Gedancken von dem Gesellschafftlichen Leben der Menschen*, Frankfurt and Leipzig: Renger.

Wolff, Christian (1743), *Vernünfftige Gedancken von der Menschen Thun und Lassen*, Frankfurt and Leipzig: Renger.

Wolff, Christian (1750), *The Real Happiness of a People under A Philosophical King Demonstrated; Not only from the Nature of Things, but from the undoubted Experience of the Chinese under their first Founder Fohi, and his Illustrious Successors, Hoam Ti, and Xin Num*. London: M. Cooper, at the Globe.

Wolff, Christian (1756), *Jus Naturae Methodo Scientifica Pertractatum*, Frankfurt and Leipzig: Renger.

Wolff, Christian (1985 [1721]), *Rede über die praktische Philosophie der Chinesen*, translated from Latin by Michael Albrecht, Hamburg: Felix Meiner Verlag.

Xue, Fucheng [薛福成] (1994), *Chou Yang Chu Yi* [Xue Fucheng's collection on foreign affairs, 筹洋刍议], Shenyang: Liaoning People's Publishing House.

Yü, Ying-Shih (1986), 'Han foreign relations', in Denis Twitchett and John K. Fairbank (eds), *The Cambridge History of China: Vol. 1*, Cambridge: Cambridge University Press, pp. 377–462.

Zheng, Guanying [郑观应] (1994 [1894]). *Sheng Shi Wei Yan* [Words of warning in a flourishing age, 盛世危言], Shenyang: Liaoning People's Publishing House.

3. Redirecting growth: inclusive, sustainable and innovation-led

Mariana Mazzucato and Carlota Perez

INTRODUCTION

The advanced world is facing a crucial moment of transition. After the response to the 2008 bubble collapses was pouring masses of money into the financial sector with no conditionality in terms of supporting the real economy, low investment, low productivity and increasing inequality were the results. The COVID-19 pandemic then revealed the polarisation of incomes, the precarious quality of employment, low growth and a global financial casino that is steering further and further away from funding the real economy, that builds mountains of debt to finance financial gambles, invests in real estate and other rent-providing assets, harming the prospects of economic revival and social progress (Mazzucato 2017). Indeed, the current policy emphasis on 'fixing finance', while leaving the real economy sick, sets the stage for successive bubbles and a boom-and-bust economy. The war in Ukraine – and the energy crisis it has unleashed – makes it even more urgent to undertake a bold policy course that can seriously tackle the environmental threat as a direction for investment, innovation, growth and new forms of social well-being.

In this chapter, we argue that the theories underlying current policies are misguided, and that expecting the market to solve the problems it has created is a fundamental misunderstanding. Current problems have become structural after four decades of unfettered markets and financialisation. In particular, we take issue with the prevailing beliefs about private and public investment and about the role of the state in such investment. We also provide a different narrative of the state, in which what is needed is not just countercyclical spending, but an investment-driven, 'mission-oriented' (Foray et al. 2012; Mazzucato 2021) and courageous state that can not only guide Europe out of the crises, but also steer and direct growth when it is achieved (Mazzucato 2013a, 2021). As increasing numbers of policy-makers are recognising, dogged subscription to neoliberal orthodoxy is a dead end: markets alone cannot return us to prosperity. Our work has shown that investment is driven by innovation;

specifically, by the perception of where new technological opportunities lie (Pavitt 1984; Perez 2016; Mazzucato et al. 2020b; Mazzucato 2021). Private investment only kicks in when those opportunities are clear; public investment must be directed towards creating those opportunities across all policy spaces and affecting the entire economy. Furthermore, the state's role as an investor of first resort involves taking risks: win some, lose some. Such risks must be rewarded, so that taxpayers not only socialise the risks, but also share in the rewards (Lazonick and Mazzucato 2013; Mazzucato 2021).

We hold that success in the current digital and green transition requires bringing innovation to the centre of government thinking and action. Innovation policy must become growth policy, and vice versa. In doing so, innovation–growth policy will affect all other policies: financial market reform, labour market policy, and especially taxation. A clear understanding of the innovation potential inherent in the current historical moment will inform the direction that such policies take. Naturally, different pathways can be chosen while moving in this direction, but recognising the role of policy in choosing it enables a better understanding of the 'boundaries' within which civil society and other forces can successfully operate (Stirling 2009). Ambitious and clear missions are a productive way to implement directionality, form collaborations between multiple actors and catalyse investment (Mazzucato 2021).

This chapter focuses on applying our knowledge of the ways in which innovation occurs (clustered and wave-like; collective; uncertain; and cumulative[1]) in order to understand what must be done to generate long-run growth which is both 'smart' and 'inclusive'. It fundamentally seeks to understand both what has gone wrong and how to repair those failings. We first look at the role that innovation has played as the driver of economic growth since the start of the Industrial Revolution, using the long-term lens of technological regimes and paradigms (Dosi et al. 1988; Perez 2002, 2010) to characterise the current transition period in its historical context. These insights enable us to understand that the challenge today is not to 'fix' finance while leaving the economy sick, but rather to change the way that the real economy works. This change must include de-financialising the economy and redirecting investments towards productive mission-oriented areas (Mazzucato 2017, 2021).

We argue that the way to get the real economy to operate in the current context is to employ a policy direction that is smart, inclusive and green. 'Green growth' can become the next big technological and market opportunity, stimulating and leading private and public investment. This brings us to a discussion on the role that the government plays in ensuring that such opportunities exist, and particularly the importance of being able to invest – welcoming the underlying risk and uncertainty – along the entire innovation chain, not only in areas characterised by positive externalities (such as research and development (R&D)). We then offer some criteria for specific fiscal/tax policies in order to achieve such a reorientation (making it more profitable for productive investments, and less profitable for speculative or polluting ones), and for creating the 'smart' governance necessary to implement such policies. Without smart government at the organisational level, smart (innovation-led) growth is impossible. We look at the effect that such policies have on steering missions and promoting more inclusive growth, where the state socialises not only risks but also rewards. We argue that such policies are themselves innovation policies, and conclude by summarising nine key criteria that we believe can help growth policy be guided by long-run value creation.

HISTORY MATTERS

It is not enough to agree, as many economists do, that innovation is a key driver of economic growth. In order for this assertion to have real meaning and to produce coherent recommendations across policy arenas, the underlying assumptions of the models and frameworks that guide the policies must be connected with a deep understanding of how innovation actually comes about. Here, a major strength of the Schumpeterian evolutionary theoretical framework is the significant attention that it has placed in recent decades on understanding the 'process' of innovation (Freeman 1994).

Contrary to other investment decisions (such as those relating to stocks, bonds or business expansion), which entail a calculable economic risk, innovation is a non-probabilistic process with odds of success or failure that cannot be calculated in advance (Knight 1921). Furthermore, innovation is not a 'random' variable (that is, independently and identically distributed), but is instead subject to clustering in systems (Freeman and Perez 1988; Schumpeter 1934 [1912]). Indeed, it tends to be cumulative and path-dependent, with innovation today building on yesterday's innovation (David 2004; Dosi 2005; Lazonick 2011). This is very different from the view in new growth theory (Romer 1994), where innovation is seen as risky (as opposed to uncertain) and R&D can be modelled as a lottery and be random in its outcomes (with little possibility of fat tails and clustering).

In this context, it is crucial to understand the deep sense in which Schumpeter saw innovation as the driver of growth in capitalism. While he claimed that bankers are at the heart of capitalism, and that credit creation is what brings expansion (Schumpeter 1934 [1912]), he was clear that this was as a response to innovation opportunities. In Schumpeter's view, it is not the availability of money that leads to innovation, investment and growth; it is the availability of potential innovations, as investment opportunities, that brings forth the money (Schumpeter 1982 [1939]). Without such opportunities, no amount of tax breaks, quantitative easing or toxic debt will expand the real economy.

Indeed, Pavitt's (1984) taxonomy of innovation places technological opportunities (along with conditions of appropriability and knowledge base) as a key driver of investment. This is related to a key finding in industry dynamics, that entry rates in new sectors are uncorrelated with current rates of profits; it is the perception of future profits and growth rates that drives entry (Dosi and Lovallo 2007). Indeed, this is what Keynes meant by 'animal spirits' (Keynes 1936). As opposed to short-term casino-type speculation, production investment is driven by a gut instinct about future technological and market opportunities, not the current bottom line. Therefore, the question for policy-makers should not be how to make it easier for businesses to invest, but how to stimulate their courage and desire to do so. As discussed in Mazzucato (2013a), we are not faced with a lion in a cage that needs to be released by taking away the impediments (tax and regulation); rather, we must first turn the pussycat into a lion. Indeed, Keynes's assertion that businessmen were not lions, tigers or wolves, but domesticated animals (Keynes 1992 [1938][2]), poses a very different policy agenda, even for Keynesians. While countercyclical spending is an important part of the solution, it also involves moving the boom in the right direction, with businesses willing and able to spend in the uncertain technological areas that could be the key drivers of growth in the future.

Great Surges, Technological Paradigms and Bubbles

To understand how to drive public and private investment around mission-led innovations (Mazzucato 2021), it is first necessary to understand similar challenges in previous crisis periods. The current emphasis on 'financialisation' – that is, too much speculative investment and not enough productive investment – makes speculation and short-termism appear unprecedented (Haldane 2011). However, this view is theoretically short-sighted, because it discards the possibility of learning from history and understanding why, for example, we are now in a period that is more similar to the 1930s than to the 1980s. Applying insights from Perez's (2002) work on technological paradigm shifts, bubbles and great surges of development enables us to grasp the specificities of each historical period of development, and how the patterns observed in each of those periods are replicated today. The crash of 1929 ended the prosperity bubble of the roaring twenties in the United States (US), just as the NASDAQ crash in 2000 and the collapse of 2007–2008 ended the bubble booms of the 1990s and 2000s, respectively. The 1920s had seen the emergence of the automobile, universal electricity, petrochemicals, radio and the mass production paradigm (Freeman and Perez 1988). The 1990s and 2000s witnessed the explosion of information and communications technologies (ICT), the spread of flexible production systems (Womack et al. 1990), and the installation of the global Internet and its consequences on globalised finance, trade and production (Boyer 2000). Both of those real investment booms turned into 'casino capitalism' (Perez 2002). In each case, there was a significant shift in the rankings of industries and countries; in each, the bust led to a freezing of 'animal spirits', revealed the decoupling of the financial world from the real economy (Krippner 2005; Dore 2008), and also caused growing income polarisation. On both occasions, a huge innovation potential was installed and ready to flourish, but then as now, 'financialisation' and resistance to government action stood in the way.

It is this understanding that points to a parallel between today's crises and opportunities and those of the 1930s rather than to those of the 1980s. The call for unfettered free markets in the 1980s assumed that the cause of the recession was government regulation (Derthick and Quirk 1985). However, when viewed with an understanding of the pattern of technological revolutions, the stagflation of the 1980s was not caused by excess government, but by a lack of innovation potential. It was the exhaustion of the mass production trajectories that had driven the post-war boom, while the ICT revolution was only just emerging; albeit with great speed and great promise, but without enough weight to drive the whole economy out of stagflation and decline (Perez 2002). The pro-market policies enabled the survival of companies with mature technologies. With less regulation, these companies were able to close down facilities, move offshore, reduce personnel, pay lower wages and taxes, and regain profitability through cost-cutting (Lazonick and O'Sullivan 2000). Higher productivity did not occur then due to increasing returns to scale, as would have been expected by the Verdoorn effect (Verdoorn 2002 [1949]; Kaldor 1966), but rather due to the radical elimination of less-productive facilities and many jobs, applying what Freeman and Soete (1994) called the 'Verdun effect'.[3]

By contrast, the government strategy around microelectronics, and the computer revolution itself, was very active (Block and Keller 2011) and created increasing opportunities for new entrants. Funding for small businesses through the Small Business Innovation Research (SBIR) programme in the US (benefiting Compaq, Intel, Hewlett Packard, and others), public procurement for high-tech companies, and R&D funding for universities and government labs all provided the groundwork for the key technologies that would lead to the personal computer (PC) boom, and later, when the government handed over the Internet to the private sector, to the dot.com boom and further revolutionary technology systems.

Thus, the bubble boom of the 1990s was not the result of less government, but instead the explosion of the ICT revolution riding on government-funded technologies ranging from integrated circuits to the Internet (Block and Keller 2011; Lazonick and Tulum 2011; Mazzucato 2013a). Equally, the global boom of the 2000s was enabled by governments (national and foreign) providing

masses of funds and easy credit. Where governments did fail to provide adequate regulation was in the financial sector, with the unfettered proliferation
of toxic financial instruments having catastrophic consequences (Perez 2009).
Today, as in the 1930s, both economists and politicians are increasingly concerned with the reluctance of finance to fund the real economy. As Keynes
(1972 [1930/1931]) wrote in 'The Grand Slump of 1930': 'there cannot be
a real recovery, in my judgment, until the idea of lenders and the idea of productive borrowers are brought together again … Seldom in modern history has
the gap between the two been so wide and so difficult to bridge.' We now turn
to the relationship between finance and innovation.

INNOVATION AND FINANCE

Today, as in the West in the 1930s, governments across the world are trying
to 'rebalance' the economy away from speculative finance and towards
productive finance that can nurture growth in the real economy. Figure 3.1
shows the problem, especially in countries such as the United Kingdom (UK)
and the US, where finance outgrew the real economy for years, leading to
the crisis (Krippner 2005; Dore 2008). Financialisation has been caused by
two factors. The first is the financial sector mainly lending to itself rather
than to the real (production) economy,[4] with the risks being far higher but
severely underpriced (Mazzucato 2017). The second factor is the corporate
sector's concentration on short-term boost to profitability – through mergers
and acquisitions (M&A) activity and divestiture from long-run areas such as

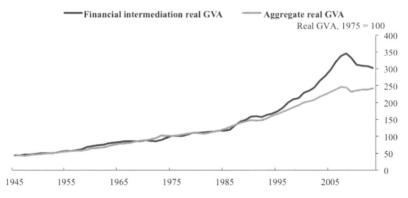

Source: Alessandri and Haldane (2009); 2009–2013 data extended by authors with data from the
Bank of England.

*Figure 3.1   Financial intermediation as a percentage of gross value
              added (GVA), UK, 1945–2013*

R&D – and boosting stock prices and stock options (hence executive pay) through the increased trend of share buybacks; in the last decade, these have exploded to $3 trillion for the Fortune 500 companies alone (Lazonick and Mazzucato 2013). Because price is understood to represent value, such activities are predominantly considered productive, as adding value to the economy. However, these forms of rent-seeking, generating income without producing anything new, extract value from the economy, promoting inequality and preventing further investment in the real economy. The failure to differentiate between value creation and value extraction, as well as unearned income and profits, has meant that the disproportionate capture of rents in the private sector has gone largely unnoticed (Mazzucato 2017; The WHO Council on the Economics of Health for All 2022).

The financial sector's continued reinvestment in itself resulted in bank assets ballooning, but these assets were increasingly fictitious. In 2008, when asset prices fell and bank equity was wiped out, banks were so highly leveraged that it required only a 3 per cent fall for the major bust to occur. Before that happened, however, bank assets and profits expanded relative to the rest of the economy, increasing their value-added contributions, as this is measured indirectly by their interest margin (see Figure 3.1 for the UK). This has caused company profits to be reinvested in speculative areas, and also led to record levels of hoarding, reducing the endogenous creation of new opportunities for future growth: human capital and R&D.

In this context, finance is not playing the role of the 'ephor' of capitalism (Schumpeter 1934 [1912]: 74), and business is not displaying the investment behaviour that Keynes wished for. Instead, the traditional banks and even the venture capitalists have become increasingly risk-averse. Venture capital is focused on the exit, within three years, usually via an initial public offering (IPO) (Lazonick and Tulum 2011). However, major innovations can take 15–20 years to fully develop, which means that this particular financing model only works for gadgets that ride on existing technology, rather than the big waves of the future. Thus, secular stagnation is a result of this financialisation, not an excuse for it. Indeed, while a common excuse for buybacks is that they are used when there are no opportunities for investment,[5] Figure 3.1 shows that they are actually causing the dismantling of future opportunities, not reacting to a lack of them. Technological and market opportunities have always been a function of the private and public sectors interacting in dynamic ways. Indeed, a recent MIT report shows that the real problem is the lack of an engaged private sector, with the current absence of large R&D laboratories at private companies, such as Xerox Parc and Bell Labs that co-invested alongside the state in the 1960s (MIT 2013).

Given the short-termist financial sector and the financialised real economy, policies based on the false assumption of the existence of a shortage of finance are doomed to failure (Mazzucato 2021). In order to understand why it is not the quantity of finance but the quality that is important, it is necessary to first look more closely at the relationship between finance and innovation.

Uncertain Cumulative Innovation Requires Patient, Long-term, Committed Capital

Innovation and finance affect each other. Different kinds of companies and industries, depending on their stage of evolution, require different types of finance, but the finance they actually receive affects their investment patterns and company characteristics (Mazzucato 2013b; O'Sullivan 2005). Those companies that want to invest in truly radical new technologies or in sectors in which innovation has a long lead time (such as pharmaceuticals) require finance that is patient and long-term in nature. Also, because innovation is cumulative, finance must always be 'committed'. Across the globe, this long-term funding has often come about through public institutions, whether they are public agencies such as the Defense Advanced Research Project Agency (DARPA) in the USA, or through state investment banks such as the German KfW or the Chinese Development Bank (Block and Keller 2012; Mazzucato 2013a; Mazzucato and Penna 2014). Indeed, 'mission-oriented' public sector investments have been fundamental in creating the new opportunities that later drive the private sector to enter new sectors and invest in new technologies (Mowery 2010; Mazzucato 2021).

Understanding the feedback relationship between innovation and the type of finance also helps us to understand the relationship between technology and bubbles (Perez 2002, 2009; O'Sullivan 2005). Periods during which low-cost finance is widely available but there are few profitable opportunities in the real economy will result in unproductive paper bubbles. Bubbles may still result when finance is chasing real technological opportunities, but the infrastructural remnants (new railways, new electrical networks, new Internet technology) will continue to fuel growth for decades. What the government provided in the 1990s boom was not easy money, but new opportunities in the form of new technology (the Internet) that was a powerful platform for innovation; indeed, a 'general purpose technology' (Lipsey et al. 2005). The high real interest rates prevalent at that time in the US (approximately 7 per cent) were the same as they were during the stagflation of the 1980s, yet this did not deter investors, who recognised the above-mentioned opportunities (Figure 3.2A).

During the dot-com bubble, however illusory the promised gains turned out to be, they looked like real opportunities. Therefore, the high cost of credit was no deterrent; at the peak of the bubble, 60 percent of the IPOs in the US stock markets were in ICT stocks (Figure 3.2B). The fact that real technological opportunities underlay the overinvestment meant that even though a (dot-com)

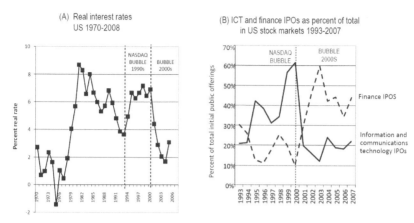

Source: Perez (2009) with data from World Development Indicators (A), and Perez (2009) with data from Thompson (B).

Figure 3.2   Without technological opportunities, easy money leads to casino finance

bubble collapse followed, it still left behind a worldwide telecommunications network that facilitated globalisation and a social learning process around the web that enabled the innovations that emerged in social networks and mobile telephony. By contrast, the much lower interest rates (between 2 and 5 per cent) that prevailed in the 2000s (Figure 3.2A) led to the development of new financial instruments for reaping capital gains without having to invest in new (now 'risky') technologies. During that period, easy credit inflated the housing bubbles, while the (much reduced) flow of investment to the stock market involved twice as many finance IPOs as ICT ones. Finally, the post-pandemic boom, enabled by cheap credit, led to rapid and easy profits in cryptocurrencies, synthetic instruments, derivatives and any other financial (not real-economy) investment. The war in Ukraine induced collapses in the stock and currency markets in the 2020s and the accompanying inflation is having a devastating effect on business and the population, confronting the threat of stagflation.

There was no reason to expect that zero interest rates would bring a good outcome. Indeed, the recent floods of money into the banks, euphemistically referred to as 'quantitative easing', led to meagre innovation, investment, and growth results, and mainly led to stock market inflation (which increases inequality) and to much leaked speculation in the emerging markets. This again shows that the revival of real investment does not depend mainly on the amount of finance available or on its low cost, but on the way it is introduced into the economy. Only by directing the creation of money – for example, by co-financing European Central Bank (ECB) bonds with European Investment Bank (EIB) bonds and guiding the former towards productive investments all over Europe, as the European Union (EU) is in theory trying to do with the Next Gen EU recovery programme – will the stimulus finally lead to long-run growth rather than short-run blips.

Supply of Finance versus Demand for Finance

The assumption that there is a finance shortage on both the public and the private sides is not only untrue, but also leads to incorrect policies. Today, capital is not scarce (Christensen and van Bever 2014): in 2010, almost $1.2 trillion was being hoarded in the private sector in the US and close to $0.7 trillion in Europe (Zenghelis 2011). What this ignores is that finance is not neutral: its form and structure matter.

A related false assumption, among both mainstream and some heterodox economists, is that there is a 'financing gap'; that is, a credit crunch that requires policy to induce the banks to lend. In reality, with regard to important innovation, there is as much of a demand-for-finance problem as there is a supply-of-finance problem. By insufficient demand, we mean that there are not enough courageous firms that see clear profit opportunities and are willing to make long-run commitments to high growth areas that require major innovations (NESTA 2009; Storey 1994). It is that sort of demand which can drive the revival of growth and employment. This cannot be achieved by pushing the banks to lend or by making life easier for businesses through various types of tax reductions and tax credits.

An illustration of the abundance of money and the perception of lack of good investment options is the flood of money pouring into cryptocurrencies. The price of a bitcoin reached an all-time high in November 2021 with its value exceeding $65 000 after breaking $1 ten years prior.[6] By the end of 2021, trading in all crypto was over 100 billion per day.[7] The search for easy gains kept potential investment money occupied. And some of that idle money looking for quick gains may have come from the 'quantitative easing' policy that provided unconditional liquidity to the banks buying doubtful assets at premium prices for an amount reaching 10 per cent of US GDP, and similar levels in the UK (Kinateder and Choudhury 2022).

The question, then, is not how to provide easy money, but how to bring forth the opportunities, how to mobilise the supply of innovation, how to activate entrepreneurship both public and private. The opportunities will bring forth the money toward better purposes. Here, conditionalities can be an important tool to align public–private partnerships with purposeful missions and to ensure that the rewards of investment are shared equitably (Mazzucato

2021). The CHIPS Act in the United States, for example, aims to incentivise companies to build new factories within the US through including conditions on economic and national security interests. Additionally, to prevent rent-seeking and value-extracting behaviour in the private sector, the Act also includes conditions on limiting stock buybacks and dividends (White House 2022). The emphasis on commercialisation assumes that all that is needed is intermediary institutions, and that the quality and quantity of the science base is not a problem. In reality, there has been a massive underinvestment in many countries, particularly across Europe in key science areas, leading to knowledge transfer policies 'pushing on a string' (Dosi et al. 2006).

It is not sufficient to simply recognise the importance of innovation; it is these accompanying assumptions that matter. The differences in how we understand innovation (path-dependent and cumulative versus a random variable), uncertainty, and the characteristics of investment (driven by the perception of future technological opportunities versus driven by easy and cheap money) will determine the details of innovation policies and, most importantly, our growth policies.

Returning to the 1930s, we see that both Keynes and Roosevelt, coming from completely different angles, not only tried to make investors pull their money out of the banks and bring it into production, but also saw the state as the only entity capable of mobilising the economy. They argued that this should be done not by giving money to the banks, but by 'pulling' investment and innovation, either through government investment and procurement and/ or by putting money into the hands of those with a high propensity to consume. Following Keynes and Roosevelt, such dynamic sources of reliable demand would create the necessary inducement for idle money to invest in production and revive the economy. Innovation was not in their vocabulary, nor in their explicit thoughts; yet the nature of the innovation potential that had been installed during the 1910s and 1920s was inherent to their plans. What made growth actually happen, however, was having a direction for its deployment.

THE GREEN DIRECTION

It is important to emphasise the distinction between a technological revolution, the potential inherent in that revolution, and the direction of investment and innovation in which that potential is deployed (Perez 2013a, 2013b, 2016, 2019). Technological revolutions, such as those that brought the railway age in the 19th century, the age of mass production in the early 20th century and the information age now, are based on an interrelated set of new technologies, industries and infrastructural networks that develop in intense feedback, providing markets and suppliers for each other (in the way that computers generated markets for micro-chips and the Internet generated markets for computers, and so on). In the process, these revolutions also provide a new potential to transform and enable innovations in all other industries. We now have smart grids, cars and soon houses, with the 'Internet of things'; nanotech and biotech are completely ICT-enabled and, in turn, can help to innovate in other industries; artificial intelligence (AI) is opening a world of possibilities, as is robotics. Even the globalisation of production and trade has been made possible by the Internet, which is revolutionising logistics handling across the economy. However, these possibilities are disparate and often unconnected; ICT can be used and shaped in different ways, and profitability depends on relative costs and, especially, dynamic demand. Moreover, the missions required for a green transition are as much as social and economic as technological in nature. Greening the economy requires nothing less than a moonshot-worthy mission. To tackle the climate crisis, we need cross-sectoral change across the entire economy (Mazzucato 2021). Only a common direction can contribute such synergies. Thus, in contrast with the specific revolutionary industries, the direction chosen for using the whole of the new potential across the economy becomes a socio-political choice.[8] The direction provides convergent trajectories for the multiple and disparate industries to innovate, while generating common synergies (suppliers, skills, equipment, service and distribution networks, demand patterns, and so on) that provide advantages for all participants (Perez 2013b). Suburbanisation and the Cold War played that role in the post-war boom in the West; today, 'green growth' can serve as a powerful global direction for deploying the potential of the information revolution. If it is widely understood, such a socio-political choice can reorient innovation across the entire economy, providing a variety of energy sources, a major increase in the productivity of natural resources, and new sustainable lifestyles and patterns of production (Perez and Murray-Leach 2018). It would also enable full global development, given that the continuation of the American way of life for the billions of new consumers entering the market in the emerging and developing worlds would soon reach planetary limits (Rockström et al. 2009) if it were not reshaped for sustainability.

Innovation Potential, Direction and Deployment

The effect of a green direction would be the equivalent of the effect that suburbanisation and the energy-intensive and materials-intensive lifestyles had on the potential of the mass production revolution after World War II. Such successful deployment periods result from purposeful strategic policies. When Keynes said it was fine to simply 'dig ditches and fill them up again', he was desperately trying to put income in the hands of consumers: enabling mass consumption to entice mass production. The specific conditions of his time allowed him to ignore the great importance of the 'direction' of stimulus spending. Yet, World War II inadvertently provided this direction by creating massive demand for military innovation and for deploying the mass production of equipment. Having learned that lesson, reluctant businesses (and many equally unwilling politicians) finally accepted state involvement in the economy. Bretton Woods and the welfare state stabilised international trade and established a reliable expectation of increased disposable income across the national population for the spread of the successive innovations of the American way of life.

To understand the importance of giving a direction to the potential, we must delve again into the neo-Schumpeterian understanding of innovation. Products are not developed in isolation, but in technology systems (Freeman 2008) where each innovation creates problems that call forth solutions from suppliers (Rosenberg 1983), which spur investments and can lead to entire new industries. Universal low-cost electricity brought mass use of refrigerators and freezers, which spawned innovations in frozen foods, which created the need for innovations in packaging methods and materials. This clustering of inter-dependent users and producers, and of self-reinforcing capabilities, results in synergies and support networks that make further innovations easier and prof-itable (that is, they involve less uncertainty) (Lundvall et al. 2002). At the same time, the aims of 'disposability' and 'reducing work in the home' converged to become common guidelines for innovation trajectories across many industries during the post-war boom. Multiple plastic materials were developed so that dishes and bottles did not have to be washed or returned; synthetic fibres were designed to allow no-iron garments; and plastic disposable packaging was made available for processed, refrigerated and frozen foods. This encouraged the production of special equipment and the training of personnel for shaping, casting, extruding and otherwise making it easy to innovate using plastics, which increased the markets and reduced the cost through economies of scale. This made it even easier to replace natural materials with synthetic ones when making electrical appliances for kitchen and entertainment. However, without the welfare state and official labour unions, which made home ownership and instalment buying a reality for the great majority, the mass demand would not have been there to generate the scale and the synergies that made it all possible (Perez and Murray-Leach 2018).

Indeed, suburbanisation – based on cheap houses built on cheap land, full of electrical appliances and with a car at the door – was not only stimulated with roads and other means, but often publicly guaranteed, as was the early case of the Federal National Mortgage Association (Fannie Mae) in the US in 1938. The installed technological potential then benefited from cheap energy and from standardised consumption patterns, enabling economies of scale to be exploited. This lifestyle shift was aided by labour unions keeping salaries apace with productivity increases, shorter working hours, unemployment insurance and pensions. This social security framework, strengthened by the personal credit system, facilitated a steady increase in per-household consumption that brought forth successive series of interrelated innovations spreading across individual domestic markets and overflowing into the rest of the world. In Europe, which had a stronger social democratic tradition, even bolder innovations were spurred by government funding and procurement in national health systems, education and other public services. Depending on the specific context of each advanced country, there was a varying degree of expenditure in the two aspects of the Cold War – the arms race, and the provision of social welfare and good living for the majority of people – both of which contributed to innovation and market expansion.

In essence, the huge innovation potential of the mass production revolution, which had been installed by the 1930s, was only expressed in growth and prosperity when the government provided a direction for its deployment, together with the institutions that sustained it. This is why it is so important to move away from a view of the state simply providing a fix to a market failure, to one that makes and stimulates investments and mission-oriented innovations (Mowery 2010). When one asks what missions could drive investment today, and what direction can be given to the full deployment of the ICT industries and to their capacity to transform all other activities, the answers are very different answers from those arising from doomsday scenarios that see a lack of technological potential, and therefore no substantial opportunities for growth (Gordon 2012), or the overoptimistic scenarios that rely on technology and markets to do the job (Brynjolfsson and McAfee 2011) with a few educational nudges from the state and in the current – financialised – conditions.

What Is Green Growth?

Green growth is more than just low-carbon and renewable energies. From a technological point of view, renewables alone do not constitute a synergistic technology system. There is not enough technological convergence in knowledge, suppliers, engineering or skills between solar, wind, wave, geothermal or hydroelectric energy equipment. In order to benefit from all the potential synergies, the environmental challenge must be seen with a wider lens. Apart from the technologies that enable flexibility and interaction in the space of renewable energy, such as batteries, smart grids and the like, the green direction would have to encompass what can be termed green growth. This would include conservation; pollution control; reduction of material content per product; designing for durability; replacing products, possession and waste with services, rental and maintenance, and recycling, respectively; promoting the flourishing of the creative economy; making cities more liveable and less polluting; revamping transport systems and the built environment; promoting collaborative and sharing economies; focusing on health (including preventive and personalised medicine); and promoting all forms of education, in and out of schools. This type of growth implies a redefinition of the optimal production practices and a different view of the 'good life', shaping the desires and aspirations of the majority. In other words, green growth involves a gradual transformation of the entire economy, reversing the mass production and consumption patterns of the previous revolution, and making it cost-effective and profitable to introduce a wide range of innovative changes in production and lifestyles that would increase sustainability and reduce carbon, while improving the quality of life for all.

A Political Choice for Growth, Convergence and Synergies

> The good news is we are sitting on a complete revolution of technology that allows us to move in a sustainable direction. That's a matter of choice though. Markets alone won't take us there. We have to decide on planetary scale, we're going for a sustainable, green, inclusive economy. (Sachs 2014)

Why cannot markets find the green direction on their own? The reason is that there is no ready-made route which will make the multiple possible directions and disparate innovations profitable. The main characteristic of innovation is uncertainty, and it is only in the context of a revolution or when a direction has been clearly chosen and made reality through policy action that the risks will diminish, and innovations proliferate in that space and start to create synergies for each other. There are already innumerable experiments in the private sector, not only in alternative energy, batteries, electric cars and the like, but also in radically new environmentally friendly production methods, such as the circular economy (Ellen McArthur Foundation 2012/2013) or 'cradle to cradle' (McDonough and Braungart 2002), which aim to eliminate effluents and waste; or industrial symbiosis (Chertow 2000; Lombardi and Laybourn 2012), in which industries use each other's waste as inputs. There have also been significant efforts to stimulate policies in the public sector. Early examples include the German, Danish and Swedish policies on renewable energies; the EU directives on recycling; and tax and other policies in various countries that aimed to increase consumer purchases of zero-emission cars or installation of solar panels. And indeed, Tesla cars sold very well in Norway early on (the country at one point was responsible for 80 percent of purchases) because the Norwegian government made it a convenient and profitable purchase: no tax is paid on purchase, no city parking permit is needed, and drivers can use taxi lanes.

However, all of these separate attempts were far from sufficient and evolved too slowly to yield the required growth results. Most of them were too uncertain to attract finance, and too dispersed to guarantee demand and generate strong synergies. Only an intense collective push will lead to a real take-off, and Europe is a large enough market to be able to make a difference if its member countries act in unison. The problem is that there is still a somewhat fundamentalist understanding of the nature of the free market as neutral and unregulated, when in fact markets would be much more dynamic and profitable if the playing field were clearly and intelligently tilted. As mentioned above, businesses were fiercely resistant to the New Deal and government intervention until they experienced the advantages of receiving state support and a clear direction during World War II. In the heyday of free markets in the 19th century, the British Empire, with its procurement practices, served as the pace-setter for business expansion and innovation.

The complex feedback loops between government policy, business strategies and consumer preferences are unpredictable, but without clear and stable policies they may take even longer or not happen at all. What the green direction can do today, through a clear, coherent and stable set of government policies, is to tilt the playing field strongly towards sustainability. This involves governments taking on the high-risk R&D investments to unleash the truly new systems, and setting up policies so that demand, taxes, regulation, prices, procurement and all other contextual elements favour attaining profitability by increasing the productivity of resources. Industries and services that saw such opportunities would readily shift their strategies and innovation trajectories to apply criteria of conservation, durability, easy recycling, low-carbon and environmental preservation.

Such convergence in the direction of innovation would create more and more synergies, making it easier and easier to find suppliers and markets, and to grow and to restore employment levels. For the advanced countries, this may imply respecialising in two types of activities: those for high-quality or high-complexity demand sectors (in equipment and consumer goods or in services) that cannot be based on low-cost labour, and those for domestic quality of life that cannot be offshored. The former can aim to serve the high ends of the consumer markets and the infrastructure, equipment and engineering needs of the growing developing world. Among the latter, one can count on the greening of the built environment, the sharing and the rental economies, the preventive and personalised health care services, other activities related to quality of life, and so on.

After the 1929 crash, it took 12 years and a major war before governments finally set in place the institutional innovations that led to the wave of investment innovation and expansion, and fully unleashed the potential that had been installed from the 1910s through the 1930s. The same force must be applied in today's context, giving a direction for the full deployment of ICT; this is a challenge that requires a re-examination of the prevailing consensus on the minimal role of the state.

STATE AS LEAD MARKET-CREATING 'INVESTORS', NOT MARKET-FIXING 'SPENDERS'

The current fashion for keeping government out and for trusting markets to bring prosperity is a misreading of recent experience that does not stem from a deep understanding of the drivers of growth and of the central role played by technical change. Worse still, it ignores the role of the state as the driver of the real growth miracles of the past few decades: Japan, South Korea, Singapore, China and others in Asia (Wade 1990; Amsden 1989); and Germany and Denmark in Europe. Most of all, it misrepresents the entrepreneurial role of the public sector in driving the ICT revolution in the USA (Mazzucato 2013a). The global boom of the 2000s was fuelled by the offshoring and outsourcing movement, but not by innovation in new sectors. In most advanced countries, innovation was centred on the synthetic financial instruments that led to the housing bubbles and to the Lehman Brothers crash (Perez 2009). Those bubbles were primarily enabled by governments providing easy credit after 9/11, and by the flows of Japanese and Chinese surplus to the West in order to fuel demand for their own export boom. Financial markets were able to exploit this new potential by lifting barriers and removing old regulations. However, no amount of market freedom could have made the private sector risk the huge investments that the US government made in the development and setting up of the Internet in the 1970s and 1980s, or nanotechnology in the 1990s (Block and Keller 2011).

Mazzucato (2013a, 2021) argued that areas of the world which have indeed experienced innovation-led growth, such as Silicon Valley in the past or China today, are characterised by mission-oriented investments, with direct public spending in a wide host of different areas. For example, all of the technologies behind the iPhone were directly funded by government-led investments. Indeed, Apple has one of the lowest R&D expenditures in the PC industry (Mazzucato 2013a), precisely because it (ingeniously) uses mostly existing, government-funded technologies; Apple's secret has been to add the crucial element of design. The emergence of phone microchips is due to the US military and space programmes, which comprised almost the entire early market for the breakthrough technology (ibid.: Ch. 5), driving the price of the initially costly chips down 50 times in only a few years, enabling numerous new applications. Cellular communication itself has its foundations in radiotelephony capabilities advanced throughout the 20th century with support from the US military. The technologies underpinning the Internet, which put the 'smart' into smart phones, were developed and funded by the United States

Defense Department's Advanced Research Projects Agency in the 1960s and 1970s. The Global Positioning System (GPS) was created and deployed in the 1980s–1990s by the US military's NAVSTAR satellite programme, while the revolutionary multi-touch interface was first developed by University of Delaware researchers with support from National Science Foundation (NSF) and Central Intelligence Agency (CIA) grants (Breakthrough Institute 2010). Even the latest SIRI, iPhone 5's personal assistant, was initially developed with DARPA funding. The same applies in such areas as biotechnology, where private venture capital followed massive public investments that amounted to $31 billion in 2012 alone (Mazzucato 2013a).

Growth occurs when a significant technological opportunity is located in a favourable context, and when high-risk, capital-intensive investments are made to kick-start the innovation 'machine'. No amount of price signals would have created the Internet, just as today a carbon tax or an emissions market would be crucial but not sufficient to get clean tech going. This is not only about the simple fact that Silicon Valley could not have appeared, grown and prospered in the old Soviet Union or in Sicily, for example. It is also about the conscious provision of a set of investments, incentives and conditions that will significantly reduce the risks and increase the potential profitability of what is now technologically feasible, but highly uncertain, encouraging convergence in order to create further and further synergies. Policy cannot be limited to temporary countercyclical spending, applying a shallow understanding of Keynesian advice. In *The End of Laissez-Faire*, Keynes (1926) defined the role of government intervention in very direct terms: 'The important thing for Government is not to do things which individuals are doing already, and to do them a little better or a little worse; but to do those things which at present are not done at all.' Many companies, both large and small, are currently experimenting in the green direction, but they are far from doing it with sufficient scale and boldly and quickly enough to make a significant difference in growth and jobs. In order for this to be done intensively, kicks and pushes are required, not just gentle nudges, and governments must themselves take courageous risks. Because the delivery of core services and functions has often been outsourced to third parties, such as consulting companies and think tanks, the state's capacity to ambitiously direct growth has often been undermined (Collington and Mazzucato 2022; Mazzucato and Collington forthcoming). Accordingly, moving beyond outsourcing and investing in dynamic in-house capabilities is essential for the state's ability to respond flexibly to the ever-evolving demands many of the current crises have prompted today (Kattel and Mazzucato 2018; Mazzucato et al. 2022). Moreover, generating consensus in identifying and strengthening context-specific paths in that direction (and the narrower specialisations within them) is necessary in order to revive each country's economy in the current global context.

INCLUSIVE GROWTH

Rising inequality, together with unemployment and low-grade jobs, are key elements of the current disintegration of many economies and can be seen as both a cause and an effect of the 2008 financial crisis in both developed and developing countries. This was evidenced during the COVID-19 pandemic and in the catastrophic effects of inflation during the Russian war in Ukraine. However, national and transnational ambitions to generate growth that is both smart and inclusive (Mazzucato 2018) are not working. This is due not only to vested interests, but also to the lack of a theoretical framework in economics which will allow that connection to be posited strongly. While it used to be that economists who studied innovation also studied the distributional impacts (consider the studies of the Classical economists on the effect of mechanisation on profits and wages, as in Ricardo 1817), there has been a sharp divide over the last century, with economists interested in innovation focusing on technology, learning, and the dynamics of capabilities. This has left issues of distribution and inequality to be studied by labour economists, mostly within a traditional neoclassical approach and without including innovation. In turn, governments have also divided innovation policy, labour policy and economic policy into three distinct worlds with different thinking (and no communication among them).

Fortunately, there has been a return to thinking about the relationship between innovation and inequality, through new growth theory, which focuses on 'skill-biased technical change' (SBTC) (Acemoglu 2002; Acemoglu and Restrepo 2018). Apart from methodological concerns with this method (such as the underlying assumption about how labour markets work), a key issue is SBTC's inability to explain the most dramatic increase in inequality between the top 1 per cent or top 0.1 per cent and the bottom income groups. In the USA, real incomes for the bottom 90 per cent of earners rose only about 4 per cent from 2000 to 2007, compared around 94 per cent for the top 0.1 percent (Piketty and Saez 2010; Piketty 2014). Although it is more complex to measure comparable data across the European Union, the indices that have attempted to do this reveal that, similarly, the 'top deciles capture an increasing part of the income generated in the economy, while the poorest 10% are losing ground' (Fredriksen 2012; cf. European Commission 2011). And the *World Inequality Report* (2018) made a global effort with equivalent results across the planet. Is it realistic to explain these extremes in terms of skills? We argue that it is not, and that there is a much deeper relationship between the character of innovation and its consequences on the workforce and on income distribution.

Unemployment and the Need for Respecialisation

One of the causes of major job loss or displacement is the fact that technical change occurs in clusters corresponding to successive technological revolutions. As the main industries approach maturity and exhaust their ability to increase innovation, productivity or markets, they must shed labour, close down facilities, migrate in search of lower costs and new markets, or disappear (Freeman and Perez 1988). The modernisation option, using the emerging technologies and infrastructures of the next technological revolution, will imply radical skill changes, but only appears years later. That was the case with the application of mass production techniques in the early 20th century, and more recently with flexible production and the globalisation of value chains brought about by the ICT revolution (Van Ark 2001). These processes are at the root of the changing production landscape, with some regions declining as others flourish, and some skills being devalued (or jobs disappearing) as others gain in value, and as new activities find entrepreneurial use for the displaced workers (Brynjolfsson and McAfee 2011). Understanding the fundamental nature of these changes is essential for designing policies with a chance of success, especially in Europe and the US which have seen the most dramatic upheaval of their previously successful production fabric.

The most extensive job losses in USA manufacturing did not occur after the 2007–2008 collapse, but during the easy credit bubble. Those were the years of the massive shift of production to Asia. Manufacturing employment in the US fluctuated at around 18 million from the mid-1960s to 2000, then dropped by over one-third, from 17 million to 13 million, in the seven years of the easy credit boom. Those jobs are not recoverable except through high-tech redesign of a segment of the products involved, and/or with the creation of non-offshorable segments in the economy. A rental economy in the durable goods sector could create hundreds of thousands of jobs in maintenance, distribution and recycling; supporting investment in the Global South could create highly skilled jobs in the capital goods and engineering industries; but a return to high growth and high-quality lives will only come by inducing bold innovation and new technology systems.

Although the phenomenon may be less acute in some European countries than in the US, it is of the same nature. In the UK, for instance, there was a greater intensity of job losses in manufacturing during the NASDAQ boom of the 2000s (1 million, or 25 per cent) than during the current recession (nearly half a million). Thus, it is essential to recognise that technological or globalisation job losses cannot be recovered with economic 'revival'. Only large-scale innovation can replace these jobs with new ones. And thanks to the MIT project Production in the Innovation Economy (MIT 2013), it can now be said – with abundant empirical evidence – that without domestic manufacturing activities and capabilities, innovation cannot be turned into production and jobs. It is time to seriously rethink active respecialisation.

New jobs will not be brought about by maintaining austerity policies or by providing stimulus via the banks. It is only through a major innovation effort, which increases both public and private sector commitments to long-run investments in human capital, R&D and infrastructure, that we can begin to engage in a dialogue in which innovation and employment are not seen as trade-offs. There is nothing 'natural' about 'secular stagnation' (Summers 2013). Not by chance, the term was coined by Alvin Hansen (1939) in the 1930s Depression. It is not an exogenous fate, but an endogenous outcome of the lack of investments being made and the lack of an innovation direction being chosen.

Apart from the employment shifts brought by technological revolutions, there is also a strong polarisation of income. This is directly linked to the intense financialisation of the economy that has historically accompanied the initial decades of diffusion and the resultant major technology bubbles (Perez 2002, 2009, 2013a, 2013b). Long-term data gathered by Piketty and Saez (2010) on US income distribution among taxpayers shows how similar the polarisation in the recent bubbles is to that of the 'roaring twenties' (see Figure 3.3). Both periods of extreme income inequality are in stark contrast with the resulting reversal in the post-war boom, when suburbanisation, the Cold War

% of income earned by top 1% of taxpayers (including capital gains) - USA 1913-2018

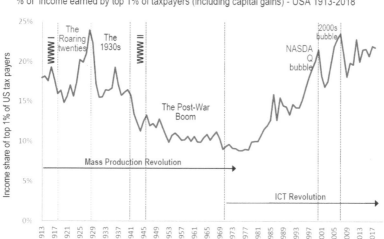

Source: Piketty and Saez (2018), period indications by CP.

Figure 3.3   *How financialisation polarises income during bubbles*

and mass production innovation brought jobs and growth, while labour unions, the tax structure and the welfare state ensured that the incomes of the majority of citizens increased with productivity.

Lazonick and Mazzucato (2013) argued that inequality of such an extreme form has to do with the ability of some agents in the economy – specifically the financial ones – to 'extract' value from the innovation process. Hence, the problem of inequality (regardless of whether Piketty's 2014 wealth tax proposal is applied) needs to be faced directly by innovation/industrial policy. It is no use arguing that skill changes are the source of the current inequality. Skills are endogenous to the investment process (that is, skills are actively created and are not manna from heaven). Therefore, it is necessary to make sure that all investment, and especially public–private partnerships, increase rather than decrease the incentives of private companies to invest in human capital formation, and other long-term areas such as research and development.[9]

It is clear that unless industrial policy also asks what kind of innovation ecosystems we want, we risk creating ones that are not symbiotic but parasitic, in which a disproportionate share of the rewards from innovation go to a narrow group of actors, who call themselves the great value creators but are in reality the great value extractors; again, this is a problem tied to the financialisation of the economy.

In addition, socio-political choices in terms of who reaps the rewards of productivity can make a huge difference. When commentators complain about the high-income assembly jobs being taken to China, they do not point to the fact that they became low-income jobs as soon as they got there. Wage levels are not in the nature of the jobs or the technologies; they result from political decisions related to the direction given to the economy and to the importance given to social fairness and progress.

Sharing Both Risks and Rewards

In ignoring the entrepreneurial role of the state as lead investor and risk-taker, and focusing only on the role of the public sector as setting the background (horizontal) conditions, orthodox economic theory has also ignored the way in which the socialisation of risks should be accompanied by the socialisation of rewards. Indeed, the more downstream the public investments, in particular technologies and firms, the higher the risk that one of those technologies or firms will fail. But this is indeed normal, as any venture capitalist would admit: for every success, there are many failures. The most successful capitalist economies have had active states that made risky investments, some of them contributing to technological revolutions.

But this raises the fundamental question of how to make sure that, like private venture capital funds, the state can reap some return from the successes (the 'upside'), to cover the inevitable losses (the 'downside') and finance the next round of investments. This is especially important given the path-dependent and cumulative nature of innovation. Returns arise slowly. Indeed, companies in areas such as information and communications technology, biotechnology and nanotechnology, had to accept many years of zero profits before any returns were in sight. If the collective process of innovation is not properly recognised, the result will be a narrow group of private corporations and investors reaping the full returns of projects that the state helped to initiate and finance (Laplane and Mazzucato 2020).

So who gets the reward for innovation? Some economists argue that returns accrue to the public sector through the knowledge spillovers that are created (new knowledge that can benefit various areas of the economy) and via the taxation system. But the evolution of the patenting system has made it easier to take out patents on upstream research, meaning that knowledge dissemination can effectively be blocked, and spillovers cannot be assumed. At the same time, the global movement of capital means that the particular country or region funding initial investments in innovation is by no means guaranteed to reap all the wider economic benefits, such as those relating to taxation. Indeed, corporate taxation has been falling globally, and corporate tax avoidance and evasion have been rising. Perhaps most importantly, while the spillovers that occur from upstream 'basic' investments should not be thought of as needing to earn a direct return for the state, downstream investments targeted at specific companies and technologies are qualitatively different. Precisely because some investments in firms and technologies will fail, the state should treat these investments as a portfolio and enable some of the upside success to cover the downside risk.

Picking a Direction for the Willing

In this context, it is important to note that a mission-oriented approach is not about government 'picking winners' in vertical industrial sectors, but about choosing directions for change – such as a green transition – that require horizontal investment and innovation in many sectors. The full power of policy instruments should be used to create projects that elicit solutions from many different willing actors. De-risking assumes a conservative strategy that minimises the risks of picking losing projects but does not necessarily maximise the probability of picking winners, which requires the adoption of a portfolio approach for public investments (Rodrik 2013). In such an approach, the success of a few projects can cover the losses from many projects, and the public organisation in question also learns from its loss-making investments (Mazzucato 2013a). Research on the developmental state (Block and Keller 2011) suggests that these goals are best achieved not through heavy top-down policies, but through a decentralised structure in which the organisation(s) involved remain nimble, innovative and dynamic from within (Breznitz and Ornston 2013). This strand of thinking can benefit from looking at the ways in which public–private partnerships were created when seeking the joint creation of new products and services, including vaccines (Chataway et al. 2007).

In particular, there is a strong case for arguing that, where technological breakthroughs have occurred as a result of targeted state interventions benefiting specific companies, the state should reap some of the financial rewards over time by retaining ownership of a small proportion of the intellectual property it had a hand in creating. This is not to say that the state should ever have exclusive licence or hold a large enough proportion of the value of an innovation to deter its diffusion (and this is almost never the case). But by owning some of the value it has created, which over time has the potential for significant growth, funds can be generated for reinvestment into new potential innovations.

Large digital companies, such as Facebook, Google and Apple, have received a large share of income produced by a collective value creation process. For instance, Google's revenue in 2021 was $185 527 billion but it employed only 139 995 staff, while Apple's revenue was $274 515 billion with only 147 000; each corporation relying largely on the collective value created by the billions of users of its platform and products worldwide.[10] If that value is shared more equally, there is no doubt that the share going to these large companies will be lower. Thus, not only must they be paying their fair share of tax, often avoided through tax gimmicks (Mazzucato et al. 2020a), but also they should be capturing a lower share in the first place. There could be, in the future, a clause in the grant which says that if the grant does not lead to any commercial success, the company owes nothing back. But if the profits made on the back of the public grant or loan leads to X billion in profits for the company, a share of that profit goes to a public wealth fund that can help to replenish the public pot to create more Googles.

Another way to socialise rewards in a non-monetary way is to make sure that the companies receiving public subsidies, guarantees and direct investments operate in a way that serves the public. For example, the extraction of value from the real economy that has been a result of the increasing use of share buybacks (Lazonick 2014) can be reversed through conditionalities which assure that profits being earned from a process of collective wealth creation are reinvested back into the economy. The direction of that investment can also be a condition; for example, making sure that energy companies which receive subsidies transition more to renewables.

There are good examples emerging from the ongoing COVID-19 crisis. When negotiating bailouts for industries suffering, such as airlines not flying, some states are seeking concrete societal benefits. To accelerate greening of industrial sectors, Austria has made its airline industry bailouts conditional on the adoption of climate targets, while France has also introduced five-year targets to lower domestic carbon dioxide emissions. Conditionalities are indeed a way for risks and rewards to be shared, so the 'deal' for the government is investment towards beneficial areas; truly 'building back better'.

Similarly, governing innovation for the public good has been highlighted during the COVID-19 pandemic. To maximise the impact on public health, the innovation ecosystem must be steered to use collective intelligence to accelerate advances. Science and medical innovation thrive and progress when researchers exchange and share knowledge openly, enabling them to build upon one another's successes and failures in real time. The COVID-19 technology access pool (C-TAP), which is a voluntary pool for health technology-related knowledge, intellectual property and data proposed by Costa Rica and adopted and launched by the World Health Organization on 29 May 2020, has offered a pragmatic solution with game-changing significance (World Health Organization 2020). However, it remains unused to this day.

CONCLUSION: GREEN GROWTH REQUIRES INNOVATIVE, SMART, GREEN GOVERNMENT

Understanding the problem and the nature of the solutions is only a first, albeit indispensable step. Implementing the necessary directionality also requires effective public actors, and this requires sector- and technology-specific expertise to be located in government so that public interventions are not just making it easier (via subsidies) but also raising the stakes and commitment by all and 'making things happen that otherwise would not' (Keynes 1936). Government must not only fund innovation, but also innovate 'within' (Kattel et al. 2022). One of the most important innovations introduced by government during the Victorian boom in the 1850s was the introduction of exams for entering the civil service (Cohen 1941). It was the knowledgeable and meritocratic structure of the British government that allowed such a small country to effectively govern an empire which covered a third of the planet. Before that, posts in the civil service had been bought or granted. Today, many public servants are as competent and highly educated as top managers in private companies (as are many politicians), but as long as governments are presented as boring bureaucracies that get in the way of the creative people, they will not bring forth existing talent or be able to attract new talent, which is precisely what is needed in the areas that drive growth (Kattel et al. 2022).

Another necessary change refers to the ways of measuring and judging performance. Governments, like innovative companies, must welcome rather than fear the failures that are inevitable when undertaking uncertain innovations. Those countries that are currently growing through innovation, such as China, Finland, South Korea and Singapore, have expertise in innovation within top levels of government, not just in the ministries for innovation and industry. They have also set up dynamic agencies that are willing to explore in a trial-and-error process. President Obama's active post-crisis stimulus programme (until 2010) was heavily influenced by a Nobel Prize laureate scientist, Steve Chu, in the Department of Energy, who was responsible for setting up the Advanced Research Projects Agency – Energy (ARPA-E) (Grunwald 2012). BNDES, Brazil's active and successful state investment bank before the Bolsonaro government dismantled it, which doubled its lending since the crisis, directed investments not only in infrastructure but also in key sectors such as pharma, biotech and clean-tech; and it was run by two non-neoclassical innovation economists. By contrast, when the state is filled with a fear of 'picking winners' and industrial policy is sidelined by the treasury, there is almost a self-fulfilling prophecy that leads to failure, with agencies responsible for industrial policy becoming marginal to the economic strategy, and ending up with a patchy innovation policy that is at odds with macro growth policy.

New Context, New Direction, New Policy Criteria

The world is at a turning point similar to the 1930s, with major institutional innovations needed to overcome a distorted financialised economy and a society with profoundly polarised incomes. As on that occasion, huge innovation potential must be turned into profitable opportunities, while creating the conditions for a fairer social sharing of the benefits.

We have also argued that in order for innovation-led growth to occur, an understanding of how innovation comes about must lead financial reform as well as growth and development policies. Smart and inclusive growth must be government-led and innovation-driven, as it has been in past 'golden ages'. It must also go hand-in-hand with changes in corporate governance, which provide better incentives for companies to reinvest their profits in long-run value creation areas such as human capital and R&D, rather than share buy-backs. Furthermore, government policy must be understood as not only fixing markets but also actively shaping and creating them. This requires providing a clear direction for innovation, investing in it, and providing a coherent set of policies (direct and indirect) to tilt the playing field so that it rewards those firms which are willing and able to invest in the opportunities of the future, and makes it less profitable to continue along the old harmful paths. There is a world of technological possibilities to bring to fruition across the global economy. Secular stagnation is in no way inevitable; it is a result of (endogenous) choices that are the opposite of the ones we outline below.

Our policy criteria can be summarised as follows:

1. Public investments as mission/challenge-oriented. It is important for innovation policy to be guided more by the need to actively shape and create markets than just to fix market failures or to compensate for imperfect information. Mission orientation puts the grand challenges of our time at the heart of policy-making, business models and value chains. This means the ability to catalyse many sectors under big 'challenges' (such as tackling climate change, or the limits to natural resources, or the ageing crisis), forming purposeful collaborations between governments, businesses and citizens. It also means having an overview of the support needed along the entire innovation chain, not just the clear public good areas.

2. Direct and indirect. It is unrealistic to think that tax incentives (indirect public spending) alone will work, because business investment is driven by perceptions of opportunities, not just cost. Such opportunities are often created through direct public investments in high-risk areas, which the private sector is still too risk-averse to enter into. Procurement contracts, grants and loans are important government tools that can award risk-taking investors, aiming to solve public goals. As was the case with the ICT revolution, innovation must be directed along the entire chain, from basic research, to applied research and early-stage financing of companies. This also requires creating the conditions for massive investment across the world, from the strongest to the weakest countries, in order to apply those advances widely and to create dynamic demand for digital and green consumer and equipment goods.

3. Use the national development banks and the multilateral ones to kick-start innovation-led growth and provide patient capital towards achieving the green transition. A combination of government policies tilting the playing field, and clearly directioned investment funding, can unleash a process of growth as well as of decreasing inequality within and between nations. Conditionalities are critical in aligning public–private partnership with ambitious policy goals, making sure that the rewards of bold investments are distributed equally. They can promote investments in the real economy, rewarding value creation over value extraction.

4. Green as key challenge and redirection. The 'green transformation' will only occur if such directed challenge/mission-oriented investments can be geared towards green (as defined above). If sustainable growth is the ambition and the need is urgent, it is important to understand that this direction will be chosen by policy, not by markets with the required intensity. This is not about picking specific technologies or firms, but considering the portfolio of different investments, direct and indirect, that must be made to actively influence production and consumption patterns

to reverse the energy- and materials-intensive model inherited from mass production; in other words, effecting a complete redirection of the entire world economy. The mass production revolution received such direction-ality from suburbanisation and the Cold War. Global green growth is an option in which ICT in connection with other new technologies can be used to enable convergent innovations across the entire economy today. However, a such a green transition requires a firm push from both supply and demand. Supply in the sense of direct mission-oriented investment in research, development and tax subsidies that make it clearly profit-able to invest in renewable energies, special materials, conservation, recyclability, productivity of resources, and so on. Demand in terms of fostering changes in consumer behaviour and stimulating the development of the lagging countries, whose markets for appropriate technology for infrastructure and capital goods can become a positive-sum game with the advanced world. Given that advanced countries cannot compete in cheap-labour, low-value products or services, it is essential to define – or create – high-quality, high-value demand areas.

5. Finance: quality not quantity. While it is often assumed that innovation requires finance, the nature of this financing is often overlooked. With its increasingly short-termist goals, the venture capital (VC) model can only play a limited role. Growth-driving innovation requires long-term com-mitted capital. Public development banks are financing up to 34 per cent of worldwide renewable energy projects, compared to only 19 per cent for corporate actors (Mazzucato and Penna 2014). It is important for finance policy to consider the different forms of patient long-term committed capital that are required, and also to accept the high failure rates that this might entail. Equally, when public funds take the form of public venture capital, it should be possible to benefit from the upside, so that losses can be covered, and the next round supported via a 'revolving fund'. This would also render investment more 'social', as called for by Keynes: 'Socialization of investments helps to replan the environment of our daily life … Not only shall we come to possess these excellent [technological] things, but … we can hope to keep employment good for many years to come' (Keynes 1972 [1930/1931]).

6. Definancialisation. Achieving this goal requires a dual emphasis. The total value added of the non-financial sector must be increased by induc-ing finance to lend not to itself, but to value-creating projects in the real economy, and to definancialise the real economy by incentivising firms to reinvest profits in areas such as human capital, equipment, software and R&D, rather than speculative areas that only aim to boost share prices (such as share buybacks), or find a way to limit those practices.

7. Regulation for shifting profitability. As emphasised by Polanyi (2001 [1944]), markets are always regulated, deeply embedded in political processes. The question is how they are regulated and for what purpose. Intelligent regulation (including taxation) can shift profitability towards innovation-led growth that serves the public good, which in turn can stimulate further innovation. For example, a rule that requires returning a product on disposal (as the EU directive on electrical and electronic goods does; European Union 2012) stimulates redesign for disassembly and recycling, rewarding the most successful designs and reducing the cost to the community. Planning rules in cities and environmental regulation of the construction industry for minimising energy consumption and maintenance will enhance the value of the properties and reduce running costs. Restricting industrial effluents can lead to 'industrial symbiosis' (Chertow 2000), where one industry profits from using the by-products of another. Once there is a stable and consistent direction – such as 'green growth' can be – both regulation and innovation will tend to converge along a known trajectory and the policy-maker's criteria can coincide with those of the business strategist.

8. Taxation. Crucial in the design of an innovation and growth strategy will be a radical and bold restructuring of the tax system. Tax structures must reward long-run investments – in labour and areas such as R&D – rather than quick trades that are geared at value extraction and lead to asset inflation. If well designed, a modernised tax system would discourage casino-type financial activities, drastically reduce the advantage of high-frequency trading, radically decrease global tax avoidance, penalise resource use while reducing the tax on labour, and favour patient capital as well as investment in the real economy. Such an innovation-prone tax system is likely to include a global 'financial transactions' tax aimed at funding green investment in the Global South; an increased capital gains tax (with a decreasing scale in time); a shift of taxes from value-added (which is levied on salaries and profits) to energy, transport and materials use; and policies that focus on stimulating R&D and human capital formation.

9. Upgrading the public sector. The tasks that confront governments at all levels to successfully overcome the threat of disastrous climate change, to reverse social inequality and achieve global growth with increased productivity of both labour and resources, will require what amounts to an institutional revolution. New and appropriate institutions with highly trained personnel to handle the new policies using ICT, not as a heavy computerisation of stiff rules, but as highly efficient and simplified tools to provide an easy-to-use effective public service. Government should

become so efficient and creative as to attract the best minds and the most dedicated persons (Kattel et al. 2022).

The 'unfettered markets', 'minimum government' and 'too big to fail' ideas behind the policies formulated since the financial collapse of 2007–2008 have not contributed greatly to reviving economies, restoring decent employment levels, reducing climate risk or reversing income polarisation. Saving the banks – rather than the economy, society and the planet – by pouring masses of liquidity (quantitative easing, QE) into the already decoupled and global financial system without any conditionality has actually worsened the problem. Low growth, low investment, low productivity, together with high inequality and carbon footprint, have been the result. The time has come for a serious rethinking of both the policies and the premises behind them. Understanding innovation as a driver of growth, employment and well-being, and recognising the essential role of the state in innovating, creating new markets, stimulating and giving direction to innovation, is the foundation for a strategic redesign. In order for there to be a real chance of success, growth and development policies must be innovation policies.

ACKNOWLEDGEMENTS

The authors would like to thank Professor Rainer Kattel and Carla Rainer for their useful comments and editorial assistance on this chapter.

NOTES

1. This brief definition draws on histories of innovation studies that have empha-sised these characteristics, such as Dosi and Nelson (1994), Freeman (1994) and Lazonick (2009).
2. In a private letter to Franklin D. Roosevelt, 1 February 1938, John M. Keynes wrote:

    Businessmen have a different set of delusions from politicians, and need, therefore, different handling. They are, however, much milder than politicians, at the same time allured and terrified by the glare of publicity, easily persuaded to be 'patriots', perplexed, bemused, indeed terrified, yet only too anxious to take a cheerful view, vain perhaps but very unsure of themselves, pathetically responsive to a kind word. You could do anything you liked with them, if you would treat them (even the big ones), not as wolves or tigers, but as domestic animals by nature, even though they have been badly brought up and not trained as you would wish ... (Keynes 1992 [1938])

3. A pun, referring to the destruction of the French positions in Verdun by heavy German artillery, during the First World War.
4. By 'real economy', we mean growth of production in both manufacturing and services that leads to job creation. It is common to distinguish the growth of 'real' value added from value added in finance and agriculture.

5.	Of course, what they mean by 'no opportunities' is no easy three-year, high-return opportunities that can yield as much as financial gains. It is this distorted market situation that needs to be put right by policy action.
6.	Figures taken from https://www.statista.com/statistics/326707/bitcoin-price -index/.
7.	See https://www.statista.com/statistics/1272903/cryptocurrency-trade-volume/.
8.	Hitler, Stalin and the Western democracies made profoundly different choices for innovation with the potential of mass production across the economies involved.
9.	The risk is that the 'open innovation' model has increased the number of alliances, but not enhanced the degree of commitment needed by each of the partners involved. In the US in pharmaceuticals, for example, as the state has stepped up its role in the research element of R&D, the private sector has decreased its support, dedicating more of its retained earnings to development, marketing, takeovers and stock buybacks
10.	See https://growthrocks.com/blog/big-five-tech-companies-acquisitions/.

REFERENCES

Acemoglu, D. (2002). Technical Change, Inequality and the Labor Market. *Journal of Economic Literature* 40(1), 7–72.
Acemoglu, D. and Restrepo, P. (2018). Artificial Intelligence, Automation and Work. Working Paper No. 24196. National Bureau of Economic Research, Cambridge. https://www.nber.org/system/files/working_papers/w24196/w24196.pdf, https://doi.org/10.3386/w24196.
Alessandri, P. and Haldane, A. (2009). Banking on the State. Bank of England, November.
Amsden, A.H. (1989). *Asia's Next Giant: South Korea and Late Industrialization*. New York: Oxford University Press.
Block, F.L. and Keller, M.R. (eds) (2011). *State of Innovation: The U.S. Government's Role in Technology Development*. Boulder, CO: Paradigm Publishers.
Block, F.L. and Keller, M.R. (2012). Explaining the Transformation in the US Innovation System: The Impact of a Small Government Program. *Socio-Economic Review* (30 September), 1–28. doi:10.1093/ser/mws021. Available at: http://ser .oxfordjournals.org/content/early/2012/09/30/ser.mws021.full.pdf+html (accessed 13 February 2013).
Boyer, R. (2000). Is a Finance-Led Growth Regime a Viable Alternative to Fordism? A Preliminary Analysis. *Economy and Society*, 29(1), 111–145.
Breakthrough Institute (2010). Where Good Technologies Come From: Case Studies in American Innovation. Oakland, CA: Breakthrough Institute, December. Available at: http://thebreakthrough.org/blog/Case%20Studies%20in%20American %20Innovation%20report.pdf (accessed 24 January 2013).
Breznitz, D. and Ornston, D. (2013). The Revolutionary Power of Peripheral Agencies: Explaining Radical Policy Innovation in Finland and Israel. *Comparative Political Studies*, 46, 1219–1245.
Brynjolfsson, E. and McAfee, A. (2011). *Race Against The Machine: How the Digital Revolution is Accelerating Innovation, Driving Productivity, and Irreversibly Transforming Employment and the Economy*. Lexington, MA: Digital Frontier Press.

Chataway, J., Brusoni, S., Cacciatori, E., Hanlin, R. and Orsenigo, L. (2007). The International AIDS Vaccine Initiative (IAVI) in a Changing Landscape of Vaccine Development: A Public/Private Partnership as Knowledge Broker and Integrator. *European Journal of Development Research*, 19, 100–117.

Chertow, M.R. (2000). Industrial Symbiosis: Literature and Taxonomy. *Annual Review of Energy and the Environment*, 25(1), 313–337.

Christensen, C.M. and van Bever, D. (2014). The Capitalist's Dilemma. *Harvard Business Review*, 92(6), 60–68.

Cohen, E.W. (1941). *The Growth of the British Civil Service, 1780–1939*. London: Allen & Unwin.

Collington, R. and Mazzucato, M. (2022). Beyond Outsourcing: Re-embedding the State in Public Value Production. UCL Institute for Innovation and Public Purpose, Working Paper Series (IIPP WP 2022-14). Available at: https://www.ucl.ac.uk/bartlett/public-purpose/wp2022-14.

David, P.A. (2004). Understanding the Emergence of Open Science Institutions: Functionalist Economics in Historical Context. *Industrial and Corporate Change*, 13(4), 571–589.

Derthick, M. and Quirk, P.J. (1985). *The Politics of Deregulation*. Washington, DC: Brookings Institution Press.

Dore, R. (2008). Financialization of the Global Economy. *Industrial and Corporate Change*, 17(6), 1097–1112.

Dosi, G. (2005). Statistical Regularities in the Evolution of Industries: A Guide through some Evidence and Challenges for the Theory. LEM Working Paper Series, No. 2005/17. Scuola Superiore Sant'Anna, Laboratory of Economics and Management (LEM), Pisa.

Dosi, G., Freeman, C., Nelson, R.R., Silverberg, G. and Soete, L. (eds) (1988). *Technical Change and Economic Theory*. London: Pinter.

Dosi, G, Llerena, P. and Labini, M.S. (2006). The Relationships between Science, Technologies and Their Industrial Exploitation: An Illustration through the Myths and Realities of the So-Called 'European Paradox'. *Research Policy*, 35(10), 1450–1464.

Dosi, G. and Lovallo, D. (2007). Rational Entrepreneurs or Optimistic Martyrs? Some Considerations on Technological Regimes, Corporate Entries, and the Evolutionary Role of Decision Biases. In R. Garud, P.R. Rattan and Z. Shapira (eds), *Technological Innovation: Oversights and Foresights*. Cambridge: Cambridge University Press, pp. 41–68.

Dosi, G. and Nelson, R. (1994). An Introduction to Evolutionary Theories in Economics. *Journal of Evolutionary Economics*, 4(3), 153–172.

Ellen MacArthur Foundation (2012/2013). *Towards the Circular Economy. Economic and Business Rationale for an Accelerated Transition*. Circular Economy Report Vols 1 & 2.

European Commission (2011). Social Situation Monitor, EU-SILC 2005-2011. Available at: http://ec.europa.eu/social/main.jsp?catId=1050&intPageId=1871&langId=en (accessed 11 April 2014).

European Union (2012). Directive 2012/19/EU of the European Parliament and of the Council of 4 July 2012 on Waste Electrical and Electronic Equipment (WEEE). *Official Journal of the European Union*, L 197, 24 July 2012, Available at: http://eur-lex.europa.eu/legal-content/EN/TXT/?uri=OJ:L:2012:197:TOC. (accessed 11 April 2014).

Foray, D., Mowery, D.C. and Nelson, R.R. (2012). Public R&D and Social Challenges: What lessons from mission R&D programs? *Research Policy*, 41(10), 1697–1702.

Fredriksen, K. (2012). Income Inequality in the European Union. OECD Economics Department Working Papers, No. 952. OECD Publishing.

Freeman C. (1994). Innovation and Growth. In M. Dodgson and R. Rothwell (eds), *Handbook of Industrial Innovation*. Aldershot, UK and Brookfield, VT, USA: Edward Elgar Publishing, pp. 78–93.

Freeman, C. (2008). *Systems of Innovation: Selected Essays in Evolutionary Economics*. Cheltenham, UK and Northampton, MA, USA: Edward Elgar Publishing.

Freeman, C. and Perez, C. (1988). Structural Crises of Adjustment: Business Cycles and Investment Behaviour, in Dosi et al. (eds.). *Technical Change and Economic Theory*. London: Pinter. pp. 38–66.

Freeman C. and Soete, L. (1994). *Work for All or Mass Unemployment: Computerised Technical Change into the 21st Century*. London: Pinter.

Gordon, R. (2012). Is US Economic Growth Over? Faltering Innovation Confronts the Six Headwinds. Working Paper 18315, National Bureau of Economic Research, August. http://www.nber.org/papers/wI8315.

Grunwald, M. (2012). *The New New Deal: The Hidden Story of Change in the Obama Era*. New York: Simon & Schuster.

Haldane, A.G. (2011). The Short Long. Speech at the 29th Société Universitaire Européene de Recherches Financières Colloquium: New Paradigms in Money and Finance? Brussels; Bank of England.

Hansen, A.H. (1939). Economic Progress and Declining Population Growth. *American Economic Review*, 29(1), 1–15.

Kaldor, N. (1966). *Causes of the Slow Growth in the United Kingdom*. Cambridge: Cambridge University Press.

Kattel, R., Drechsler, W. and Karo, E. (2022). *How to Make an Entrepreneurial State.* New Haven, CT, USA and London, UK: Yale University Press.

Kattel, R. and Mazzucato, M. (2018). Mission-Oriented Innovation Policy and Dynamic Capabilities in the Public Sector. UCL Institute for Innovation and Public Purpose, Working Paper Series (IIPP WP 2018-5). Available at: http://www.ucl.ac.uk/bartlett/public-purpose/wp2018-05.

Keynes, J.M. (1926). *The End of Laissez-Faire*. London: L. & V. Woolf.

Keynes, J.M. (1972 [1930/1931]). The Grand Slump of 1930. In *Essays in Persuasion. The Collected Writings of John Maynard Keynes, Vol. XI*. London: Macmillan for the Royal Economic Society, pp. 126–149.

Keynes, J.M. (1936). *The General Theory of Employment, Interest and Money*. New York: Harcourt, Brace & Company.

Keynes, J.M. (1992 [1938]). Private letter to Franklin Delano Roosevelt, 1 February 1938. In D.E. Moggridge, *Maynard Keynes: An Economist's Biography*. London, UK and New York, USA: Routledge, pp. 543–627.

Kinateder, H. and Choudhury, T. (2022). Guest Editorial: Cryptocurrencies: Current Trends and Future Perspectives. *Studies in Economics and Finance*, 39(3), 345–346.

Knight, F. (1921). *Risk, Uncertainty and Profit*. New York: Augustus M Kelley.

Krippner, G.R. (2005). The Financialization of the American Economy. *Socio-Economic Review*, 3(2), 173–208.

Laplane, A. and Mazzucato, M. (2020). Socializing the Risks and Rewards of Public Investments: Economic, Policy, and Legal Issues. *Research Policy*, 49. https://doi.org/10.1016/j.repolx.2020.100008.

Lazonick, W. (2009). *Sustainable Prosperity in the New Economy? Business Organization and High-Tech Employment in the United States*. Kalamazoo, MI: WE Upjohn Institute.

Lazonick, W. (2011). The Innovative Enterprise and the Developmental State: Toward an Economics of 'Organizational Success', The Academic-Industry Research Network. Available at: https://www.ineteconomics.org/uploads/papers/BWpaper_LAZONICK_040811.pdf

Lazonick, W. (2014), Profits without Prosperity. *Harvard Business Review*. Available at: https://hbr.org/2014/09/profits-without-prosperity.

Lazonick, W. and Mazzucato, M. (2013). Risks and Rewards in the Innovation–Inequality Relationship. In special issue of *Industrial and Corporate Change*, M. Mazzucato (ed.), 22(4): 1093–1128.

Lazonick, W. and O'Sullivan, M. (2000). Maximizing Shareholder Value: A New Ideology for Corporate Governance. *Economy and Society*, 29(1), 13–35.

Lazonick, W. and Tulum, O. (2011). US Biopharmaceutical Finance and the Sustainability of the Biotech Business Model. *Research Policy*, 40(9), 1170–1187.

Lipsey, R., Carlaw, K.I. and Bekhar, C.T. (2005). *Economic Transformations: General Purpose Technologies and Long-Term Economic Growth*. Oxford: Oxford University Press.

Lombardi, D.R. and Laybourn, P. (2012). Redefining Industrial Symbiosis. *Journal of Industrial Ecology*, 16:1, 28–37.

Lundvall, B.-Å., Björn, J., Andersen, E.S. and Dalum, B. (2002). *Research Policy*, 31(2), 213–231.

Mazzucato, M. (2013a). *The Entrepreneurial State: Debunking Private vs. Public Sector Myths*. London: Anthem Press.

Mazzucato, M. (2013b). Finance, Innovation and Growth: Finance for Creative Destruction vs. Destructive Creation. In special issue of *Industrial and Corporate Change*, M. Mazzucato (ed.), 22(4): 869–901.

Mazzucato, M. (2017). *The Value of Everything: Making and Taking in the Global Economy*. London: Allen Lane.

Mazzucato, M. (2018). The challenges and opportunities of framing the EC 2020 'challenges' as 'mission-oriented' policies. ISI Growth Policy Brief.

Mazzucato, M. (2021). *Mission Economy: A Moonshot Guide to Changing Capitalism*. London: Allen Lane.

Mazzucato, M. and Collington, R. (forthcoming). *The Big Con: How the Consulting Industry Weakens Our Businesses, Infantilizes Our Governments, and Warps Our Economies*. Allen Lane.

Mazzucato, M., Entsminger, J., and Kattel, R. (2020a), Public Value and Platform Governance. UCL Institute for Innovation and Public Purpose, Working Paper Series (IIPP WP 2020-11). Available at: https://www.ucl.ac.uk/bartlett/public-purpose/wp2020-11.

Mazzucato, M., Kattel, R. and Ryan-Collins, J. (2020b). Challenge-driven Innovation Policy: Towards a New Policy Toolkit. *Journal of Industry, Trade and Competition*, 20, 421–437.

Mazzucato, M. and Penna, C. (2014). Beyond Market Failures: The Role of State Investment Banks in the Economy. Unpublished working paper.

McDonough, W. and Braungart, M. (2002). *Cradle to Cradle: Remaking the Way We Make Things*. New York: North Point Press.

MIT (Massachusetts Institute of Technology) (2013). A Preview of the MIT Production in the 'Innovation Economy Report', edited by Richard M. Locke and Rachel

Wellhausen, mit.edu, 22 February. Available at: http://web.mit. edu/press/images/documents/pie-report.pdf (accessed 25 February 2013).

Mowery, D.C. (2010). Military R&D and innovation. In B.H. Hall and N. Rosenberg (eds), *Handbook of the Economics of Innovation*. Amsterdam: North-Holland, pp. 1219–1256.

NESTA (National Endowment for Science Technology and the Arts) (2009). The Vital 6 per cent: How High-Growth Innovative Businesses Generate Prosperity and Jobs. Research Summary. London: NESTA.

O'Sullivan, M. (2005). Finance and Innovation. In J. Fagerberg, D. Mowery and R.R. Nelson (eds), *The Oxford Handbook of Innovation*. Oxford: Oxford University Press, pp. 240–265.

Pavitt, K. (1984). Sectoral Patterns of Technical Change: Towards a Taxonomy and a Theory. *Research Policy*, 13(6), 343–373.

Perez, C. (2002). *Technological Revolutions and Financial Capital: The Dynamics of Bubbles and Golden Ages*. Cheltenham, UK and Northampton, MA, USA: Edward Elgar Publishing.

Perez, C. (2009). The Double Bubble at the Turn of the Century: Technological Roots and Structural Implications. *Cambridge Journal of Economics*, 33(4), 779–805.

Perez, C. (2010). Technological Revolutions and Techno-economic Paradigms. *Cambridge Journal of Economics*, 34(1), 185–202.

Perez, C. (2013a). Financial Bubbles, Crises and the Role of Government in Unleashing Golden Ages. In A. Pyka and H.P. Burghof (eds), *Innovation and Finance*. London: Routledge, pp. 11–15.

Perez, C. (2013b). Unleashing a Golden Age after the Financial Collapse: Drawing Lessons from History. *Environmental Innovation and Societal Transitions*, 6, 9–23.

Perez, C. (2016). Capitalism, Technology and a Green Global Golden Age: The Role of History in Helping to Shape the Future. In M. Mazzucato and M. Jacobs (eds), *Rethinking Capitalism*. London: Wiley Blackwell, pp. 191–217.

Perez, C. (2019). Transitioning to Smart Green Growth: Lessons from History. In Roger Fouquet (ed.), *Handbook on Green Growth*. Cheltenham, UK and Northampton, MA, USA: Edward Elgar Publishing, pp. 447–463.

Perez, C. and Murray-Leach, T. (2018). Smart & Green: A New 'European Way of Life' as the Path for Growth, Jobs and Wellbeing. In Austrian Council for Research and Technology Development (eds), *Re:Thinking Europe. Positions on Shaping an Idea*. Vienna: Verlag Holzhausen. pp. 208–223.

Piketty, T. (2014). *Capital in the 21st Century*. Cambridge, MA: Harvard University Press.

Piketty, T. and Saez, E. (2010 [2003]). Income Inequality in the United States, 1913–1998. *Quarterly Journal of Economics* 115(1), 1–39.

Piketty, T. and Saez, E. (2018 [2004]). Income Inequality in the United States. Available at https://eml.berkeley.edu/~saez/piketty-saezOUP04US.pdf (data series updated to 2018).

Polanyi, K. (2001 [1944]). *The Great Transformation: The Political and Economic Origins of Our Time*. Boston, MA: Beacon Press.

Ricardo, D. (1817). *On the Principles of Political Economy and Taxation*. London: John Murray.

Rockström, J., Steffen, W., Noone, K., Persson, Å., Chapin, F.S. III, Lambin, E., et al. (2009). Planetary Boundaries: Exploring the Safe Operating Space for Humanity. *Ecology and Society*, 14(2), 32. Available at: http://www.ecologyandsociety.org/vol14/iss2/art32/.

Rodrik, D. (2013). Green Industrial Policy. Princeton University Working Paper.

Romer, P.M. (1994). The Origins of Endogenous Growth. *Journal of Economic Perspectives*, 8(1), 3–22.

Rosenberg, N. (1983) *Inside the Black Box: Technology and Economics.* Cambridge: Cambridge University Press.

Sachs, J. (2014). We Need a Sixth Wave of Sustainable and Green Technologies. Green Week Conference 2014, European Commission, Brussels, 3 June. Available at: http://cordis.europa.eu/news/rcn/36601_en.html (accessed 22 April 2014).

Schumpeter, J.A. (1934 [1912]). *The Theory of Economic Development: An Inquiry into Profits, Capital, Credit, Interest, and the Business Cycle.* Cambridge, MA: Harvard University Press.

Schumpeter, J.A. (1982 [1939]). *Business Cycles.* Philadelphia, PA: Porcupine Press.

Stirling, A. (2009). Direction, Distribution and Diversity: Pluralising Progress in Innovation, Sustainability and Development. STEPS Working Paper 32. Brighton: STEPS Centre.

Storey, D.J. (1994). New Firm Growth and Bank Financing. *Small Business Economics*, 6, 139–150.

Summers, L. (2013). Why Stagnation Might Prove to be the New Normal, *Financial Times*, 15 December. Available at: http://www.ft.com/cms/s/2/87cb15ea-5d1a-11e3-a55800144feabdc0.html#axzz35Bf2xOBb (accessed 22 April 2014).

Van Ark, B. (2001). *The Renewal of the Old Economy: An International Comparative Perspective.* Paris: OECD.

Verdoorn, J.P. (2002 [1949]). Factors that Determine the Growth of Labor Productivity. In J. McCombie, M. Pugno, and B. Soro (eds) *Productivity Growth and Economic Performance.* London: Palgrave Macmillan, pp. 28–36.

Wade, R. (1990). *Governing the Market: Economic Theory and the Role of Government in East Asian Industrialization.* Princeton, NJ: Princeton University Press

White House (2022). Fact Sheet: CHIPS and Science Act Will Lower Costs, Create Jobs, Strengthen Supply Chains, and Counter China. Available at: https://www.whitehouse.gov/briefing-room/statements-releases/2022/08/09/fact-sheet-chips-and-science-act-will-lower-costs-create-jobs-strengthen-supply-chains-and-counter-china/.

The WHO Council on the Economics of Health for All (2022). Strengthening Public Sector Capacity, Budgets and Dynamic Capabilities towards Health for All. Available at: https://cdn.who.int/media/docs/default-source/council-on-the-economics-of-health-for-all/who_councileh4a_councilbrief4.pdf?sfvrsn=275a7451_5&download=true.

Womack, J.P., Jones, D.T. and Roos, D. (1990). *The Machine That Changed the World.* New York: Rawson Associates.

World Health Organization (2020). COVID-19 Technology Access Pool. Available at: https://www.who.int/initiatives/covid-19-technology-access-pool.

World Inequality Report (2018). Co-edited by F. Alvaredo, L. Chancel, T. Piketty, E. Saez and G. Zucman. Harvard University Press. Available at: wir2018-full-report-english(1).pdf (wid.world).

Zenghelis, D. (2011). *A Macroeconomic Plan for a Green Recovery.* Centre for Climate Change Economics and Policy, Grantham Research Institute on Climate Change and the Environment Policy Paper, January. Available at: http://www2.lse.ac.uk/GranthamInstitute/publications/Policy/docs/PP_macroeconomic-green-recovery_Jan11.pdf (accessed 1 May 2014).

PART II

Assumptions, abstractions and approaches to uneven development

4. Altered states: Cartesian and Ricardian dreams

Erik S. Reinert, Monica Di Fiore, Andrea Saltelli and Jerome R. Ravetz

INTRODUCTION

'Everyone seems to agree that the economics profession had a near death experience in 2008' (Wilsdon 2016). As examples, the 'death of [economic] theory' was hypothesised by Noah Smith (2013); conferences were held entitled 'What's Wrong with Economics?'; Queen Elizabeth II questioned the predictive capacity of British economists (Pierce 2008); a similar moment occurred among United States (US) economists in a Senate hearing (Mirowski 2013: 275–286); Paul Romer denounced the use of ideologically laden mathematical models (Romer 2015); 33 theses were nailed to the door of the London School of Economics (Macfarlane 2017; Reinert and Saltelli 2018); and new curricula were developed to 'fix' the teaching of the craft (Cassidy 2017). The list could go on, making the case that economics lives in a moment of crisis, where some of the prevalent core assumptions of the discipline are being disputed. Has this ever happened before?

There was a time in the recent past where Ricardian economics was declared dead. This occurred after the economic crises of 1848, with the critique reaching maturity early in the 20th century. Herbert Foxwell (1899), a Cambridge economist, warned his contemporaries of the 'extreme dangers' of Ricardian economics, arising 'from the unscientific use of hypothesis and social speculations, from the failure to appreciate the limited application to actual affairs of highly artificial and arbitrary analysis'. In the US the same critique took to the extreme of sarcasm in the famous line from Thorstein Veblen when he criticised English 19th century economic and political philosophy: 'A gang of Aleutian Islanders slashing about in the wrack and surf with rakes and magical incantations for the capture of shell-fish are held, in point of taxonomic reality, to be engaged in a feat of hedonistic equilibration in rent, wages, and interest' (Veblen 1919a: 193).

Today, as then, a subject of criticism was the level of abstraction of economic theorising; what we would today associate with mathematical modelling in the famous assertion by Milton Friedman that 'Truly important and significant hypotheses will be found to have "assumptions" that are wildly inaccurate descriptive representations of reality, and, in general, the more significant the theory, the more unrealistic the assumptions (in this sense)' (Friedman 1953: 14). Against this vision, Wolfgang Drechsler was quoted in Hudson (2010) as saying that mathematics has helped to enthrone 'irrelevance as methodology'.

The background to Friedman's assertion enables an even stronger assessment. Among other issues, the 'marginalist controversy' included a debate between Richard Lester, a labour economist at Princeton, and the eminent Fritz Machlup, on the marginalist theory of the firm. Lester conducted an empirical survey of cotton-spinning firms, to see whether, as the theory predicted (and as every student of economics was taught) they stopped increasing production when increasing marginal costs equalled the decreasing marginal returns. He found that they had no idea at all about marginal entities, and in any case their internal accounting systems could not trace them. He concluded that the marginalist theory of the firm had no basis in the real world of practice. Machlup defended the theory, with his arguments eventually becoming similar to the classic formulation of Friedman (Ravetz 1994).

History tells us that economics became quantitative in the first place – in the second half of the 18th century – only to fall periodically back into scholasticism (Reinert 2000). Thus, economics emerged from the sterile pursuits of medieval scholasticism. Francis Bacon (1561–1626), who attempted to create experience-based science, describes how scholasticism makes science degenerate:

> Surely, like as many substances in nature which are solid, do putrefy and corrupt into worms; so it is the propriety of good and solid knowledge to putrefy and dissolve into a number of subtle, idle, unwholesome and, as I may term them, vermiculite questions, which have indeed a kind of quickness, and life of spirit, but no soundness of matter, or goodness of quality. This kind of degenerate learning did chiefly reign amongst the schoolmen [i.e., the scholastics], who, having sharp and strong wits, and abundance of leisure, and small variety of reading, but their wits being shut up in the cells of a few authors ... as their persons were shut up in the cells of monasteries and colleges, and knowing little history, either of nature or time, did, out of no great quantity of matter, and infinite agitation of wit, spin out unto us those laborious webs of learning which are extant in their books. (Bacon 1605, quoted in E.S. Reinert 2007)

Mathematics was an important ingredient of the quantitative programme, but a fanatical commitment to formal models ended up pushing economics back into scholasticism – into 'working upon itself' – thus closing the circle. When mathematics was first introduced in economics in the 18th century, accusations of scholasticism reappeared (S.A. Reinert 2007).

The ideological elements of the economic theory are very much at the core of the present moment of economic angst, although different readings have been put forward. For Rajan and Zingales (2004), 'Capitalism's biggest political enemies are … the executives in pin-striped suits extolling the virtues of competitive markets with every breath while attempting to extinguish them with every action'. History shows that developed countries, having achieved their level of wealth by protecting their industrial sectors at birth, needed to maintain now the postulation of perfect competition and efficient markets as an expedient to prevent developing countries from creating an industrial sector of their own (E.S. Reinert 2007).

In reality, an economic theory modelling international trade as the barter of qualitatively identical labour hours, whether in Silicon Valley or in a tribe of hunter-gatherers in the Amazon, will fail to realise that 'free trade' may benefit some types of economic activities more than others. This analysis of *cui prodest* (who benefits?) follows a long intellectual tradition and can be found in England with Josiah Tucker (1713–1799). Tucker (1782) was in the habit of directly or indirectly asking '*cui bono*', in relation to economic theorising. In the United States this tradition was followed up by Thorstein Veblen (1857–1929). Veblen analysed the power of 'vested interests', which he defined as 'a legitimate right to get something for nothing, usually a pre-scriptive right to an income which is secured by controlling the traffic at one point or another' (Veblen 1919b: 161–162).

It might be pointed out that we present a caricature of economics here; after all, there is a lot of literature on imperfect competition. However, it is important to note that key policy decisions on the global level, whether they are from the World Trade Organization (WTO), the World Bank or the International Monetary Fund, tend to revert back to Ricardianism in its crude forms. We saw this, for example, in 1997 when WTO Director-General Renato Ruggiero declared that we should unleash 'the borderless economy's potential to equalise relations among countries and regions' (Ruggiero 1997). This illusion – that trade under all circumstances would tend to even out eco-nomic differences among nations – is the main mechanism that has created the increasing inequality crisis between nations (E.S. Reinert 2007). The World Bank's *Doing Business Report* gives us an example of the indirect damage of using a frictionless Ricardian framework as an implicit ideal: cutting welfare to the poor would boost a country's score on this index. Implicitly admitting to the problem, in August 2020 the World Bank announced that the publication of this report was to be suspended 'until it conducts a review and audit'. An ongoing controversy inside the World Bank, related to Paul Romer leaving his post as Chief Economist, focused on India's rating under the autocratic regime of Prime Minister Narendra Modi rising by 67 slots in this survey, while the rating of more social democratic Chile fell.

In this chapter we discuss the present status of health of economics, moving from a somewhat different perspective: starting from the considerations that economics presents itself as a science, all the more so when the ambition of economics is to parallel physics in its reliance on equilibrium-based mathematics as a key to the reading of the world. As part and parcel of the house of science, economics participates in the vicissitudes of science. Thus, we first discuss how science *qua* science is currently undergoing a serious moment of crisis, mostly impacting its governance and quality assurance system; then we investigate the extent to which the crisis of economics is different from the crisis in science.

Our thesis is that the two crises have more in common than is acknowledged at present, and that a useful reading of the present crises can be provided by the crafts of history and philosophy of science and of economics. Only once this is done will the peculiarities and idiosyncrasies of economics need to be called to the fore.

A CRISIS IN THE HOUSE OF SCIENCE

The year 2016 saw the first example of artificial intelligence (AI) beating the best Go player, and the confirmation of the existence of gravitation waves. The previous year was the year of *Homo naledi* and the pentaquark. In 2014, a probe was positioned on the surface of a comet. In 2013, a fast and precise new method for editing snippets of the genetic code, the so-called CRISPR technology, was developed. In 2012, the Higgs boson was experimentally detected. In 2011 another AI program beat humans in *Jeopardy*, a quiz show.

Talking about a crisis in science in this situation might seem unwarranted, and some readers of the crisis add that the 'crisis of science' narrative is irresponsible (Fanelli 2018; Jamieson 2018). The situation is complicated by instrumental use of the 'irreproducible science' narrative to advance anti-regulation agendas (Wood and Randall 2018), especially in the United States (Oreskes 2018; Saltelli 2018).

Indeed, the crisis is a poorly kept secret. Much is played out in public spaces and the media, even beyond academic fora. As early as 2013, *The Economist* (2013a, 2013b) devoted its cover to 'Bad Science' ('How Science Goes Wrong'; 'Trouble at the Lab'), reporting an unprecedented crisis of reproducibility in several disciplines, from psychology to cancer research.

Journals such as *Nature* (2015) and *The Lancet* (Horton 2015) have run concerned editorials, and six international conferences were held between 2007 and 2019 on Research Integrity.[1] The issue is debated in academia and think tanks (Horton 2015). In social science an important experiment was led by Brian Nosek, a psychologist at the University of Virginia, co-founder of the Center for Open Science and leader of the Reproducibility Project: Psychology. The experiment zoomed in on 100 major studies, and could only replicate 35 per cent of the total. Further, the size of the effects was systematically smaller in the replica than in the original (Open Science Collaboration 2015). Several scholars, including John P.A. Ioannidis, have investigated the extent to which different disciplines are diseased, from medicine (Ioannidis 2016) to economics (Ioannidis et al. 2017), nutrition (Magni et al. 2017) and social sciences in general (Hardwicke et al. 2019), while Fanelli compared the seriousness of the problem with Auguste Compte's hierarchy of science (Fanelli 2010), with, for example, psychology faring worse than space science, and social sciences being more vulnerable than natural ones.

The crisis should also be seen in the context of our symbiotic relation with technology and innovation (Arthur 2009). Recent years have seen unprecedented progresses of automation in what is now called the second machine age (Brynjolfsson and McAfee 2016), while concepts such as 'crowd' and 'platform' continue to acquire new meanings (McAfee and Brynjolfsson 2017). Concerned eyes (Lanier 2006, 2018; Zuboff 2019) have looked at the impact of platform (or surveillance) capitalism on society and democratic representation. While most analyses have set the reproducibility crisis aside from the crisis in our relation to technology, we consider them here as related, following Benessia et al. (2016), Ravetz (2016), Ravetz and Saltelli (2015) and Saltelli and Funtowicz (2017).

In this reading, the crisis has ethical, epistemological, methodological and even metaphysical dimensions. Its root causes were diagnosed long ago by philosopher Jerome R. Ravetz (1971), whose predictions have found abundant verification in present-day historical critique of commodified science (Mirowski 2011, 2018). The crisis of science *qua* science impacts upon science as used for policy. Identified points of friction are the paradigm of evidence-based policy (Saltelli and Giampietro 2017), the use of science to produce implausibly precise numbers and reassuring techno-scientific imaginaries (Benessia and Funtowicz 2015; Porter 2012; Scoones and Stirling 2020), and the pretended use of science to 'compel' decision by the sheer strength of 'facts' (Muller 2018).

Writing on the crisis of science is complicated by the rapid unfolding of events, with the discipline of statistics at the forefront of the storm. The saga of the p-value – revolving around the use or abuse of this particular statistic for the identification of effects in various types of experiments – is still ongoing, with the issuing of recommendations on its use by the American Statistical Association (Wasserstein and Lazar 2016) and lively discussion among practitioners (Gigerenzer and Marewski 2015; Leek et al. 2017; Leek and Peng 2015; Saltelli and Stark 2018). The latest convulsion of the crisis of statistics involves a petition to abolish the concept of significance altogether (Amrhein et al. 2019). Like other disciplines, economics has also been a victim of the reproducibility crisis (Ioannidis et al. 2017).

In summary, the different readings of the crisis in science (Benessia et al. 2016) include:

- Poor training, poor statistical design, hubris of data mining, perverse incentives, use of counterproductive metrics to appraise science and scientists.
- Science a victim of its own success; senility by exponential growth and hyper-specialisation. A prediction in this direction was made by Derek de Solla Price (de Solla Price 1963: 1–32), the father of scientometrics. This reading is today brought to an extreme conclusion by Millgram (2015: 21–53), for whom science has contributed to the undoing of the Enlightenment, creating a world of serial hyper-specialisers, where man's capacity to make sense of reality is compromised.
- Science as another victim of the neoliberal ideology. This is the thesis upheld by Philip Mirowski (2011, 2018). According to Mirowski, since the 1980s neoliberal ideologies have established that the market is the best answer to the question of how best to fund research. At present, much research is performed by contract research organisations (CROs) that operate under significant budget and time pressures; that this may impact on reproducibility is unsurprising.
- Science is a social enterprise. Its quality control apparatus suffers under the mutated conditions of technoscience. This reading is mostly due to Ravetz (1971, 2011), who predicted in 1971 that, in the passage from small science to big science, the form of commitment necessary for the performance of good-quality scientific work would come under increasing strain. Recent analytic work (Smaldino and McElreath 2016) accurately confirmed that prediction, going so far as to identify a Darwinian superior fitness in bad science.

THE HOUSE OF ECONOMICS

A recent study of the 80 most important economics books – measured as the number of editions – before 1850 showed an important discrepancy compared with what is presently taught in most courses in the history of economic thought (Reinert et al. 2017). The origin of modern economics is normally seen as the 18th century French physiocrats who – based on the logic that ultimately food was the key commodity of man – decided that agriculture was the only 'productive' branch of the economy. The historical records of economic best-sellers show that the physiocrats were outnumbered by works against physiocracy by a factor of about four to one.[2] The theories that dominated economic policy were based on empirical studies, not the highly abstract theories of the physiocrats. Recent works have re-evaluated the importance of physiocracy by analysing its limited influence on economic policy at the time, comparing this to its overwhelming presence in today's history of economic thought (Klotz et al. 2017; Kaplan 2015).

In their book *The Invisible Hand: Economic Equilibrium in the History of Science*, Ingrao and Israel (1990) traced the use and misuse of equilibrium in the history of economics. In economics, vested interests shine through more clearly than in the hard sciences. It was obvious that the physiocrats' emphasis on agriculture represented political support to the feudal landowning class. However, a direct result of this policy was that more money was to be made not by bringing grain into Paris, but rather by storing it and waiting for prices to rise. In fact, this early belief in 'the magic of the market' was responsible for the shortage of bread that was the main cause of the French Revolution (Kaplan 2015). The Storming of the Bastille happened when news reached Paris that the ardent anti-physiocrat Jacques Necker had lost his job as Minister of Finance. Necker, who is virtually unknown as an economist, is the only author with four different works in the bestseller list mentioned above.

Thus, economics has been a tool of political vested interests from its very conception. At a time when England was the only industrialised country, and clearly had an interest in continuing to hold that position, David Ricardo (1817) constructed his theory of international trade, visualising the world economy as a system of bartering labour hours, all of identical quality. Here is a context-free world, with no capital, no skills and no knowledge. David Ricardo 'proved' that the world would be richer if every country stuck to its 'comparative advantage', whether it was in the Stone Age or the Machine Age. By the end of the 19th century, Ricardo was completely out of fashion. In his 1897 inaugural address as Rektor of the University of Berlin, Gustav Schmoller criticised the two political extremes – communism and the Manchester School (today's neoliberalism) – as 'twins of an ahistorical rationalism'. In a sense, Ricardo was father of both 'twins': of communism with his labour theory of value, and of Manchester liberalism with his theory of international trade:

> The simplistic optimism of 'laissez-faire' and the childish and frivolous appeal to revolution, the naive hope that the tyranny of the proletariat would lead to world happiness, increasingly showed their real nature, they were twins of an ahistorical rationalism ... The old doctrines of individualistic natural law were transformed from the humanistic idealism of an Adam Smith to the hard mammonism of the Manchester School [and were useless for the present situation] ... The period 1870–1890 led to the theoretical and practical bankruptcy of both the old schools. (Schmoller 1897)

Unfortunately, what Schmoller referred to as the two bankrupt schools came to be at the centre of what we can call Cold War economics. Early in the Cold War, US economist Paul Samuelson (1948, 1949, 1983), using the usual assumptions, employed Ricardo's trade theory to 'prove' that, under the standard assumptions, international trade would tend to equalise the prices for the factors of production: capital and labour. At approximately the same time, also in the US, the Cowles Commission started sponsoring influential economic research based on market equilibrium models, producing more than ten Nobel laureates in economics. With the benefit of hindsight it is reasonably clear that the extremely high level of abstraction employed in both Ricardian trade theory and equilibrium models ideologically underpinned the perfection of the capitalist model during the Cold War. The utopian free trade model appears to be collapsing only now as it hits the United States like a boomerang. No longer the world economic hegemon – as England was when David Ricardo wrote – free trade is no longer in the interest of the United States.

Relevant to the issue of the Cartesian dream treated here, the great physiocrat Quesnay wrote a few pages on economics, and hundreds of pages on bloodletting (*salasso/sangria*) as a cure-all (his 1770 work on the subject has 734 pages). It is believed that bloodletting contributed to the death of Descartes at the Stockholm castle (Clarke 2006). Quesnay was perhaps as wrong on bloodletting as he was on economics.

IS THE CRISIS JUST ONE?

The word 'crisis' originates from a Greek verb (*krínein*) for 'to decide, separate, judge'. We should clarify what we mean by crisis by separating its different elements, and by judging their seriousness and relevance. Already, some voices have wondered whether there is not perhaps a 'crisis of the crisis?' (Ortmann 2016), and different claims have been put forward regarding the status of health of the various disciplines.

Cartesian Dream and Science Hubris

For some scholars, the last four centuries have been those of scientific hubris, of rationality becoming a substitute for reason; to use the words of Stephen Toulmin (2001), of a 'Cartesian dream' (Pereira and Funtowicz 2015). A vivid illustration of the dream is Francis Bacon's *Magnalia Naturae*, in the New Atlantis (Bacon 1627), *Wonders of Nature, in Particular with Respect to Human Use*. This ancient work contains one full-page listing – four centuries ago – of all future conquests of science, from the retardation of age to the mitigation of pain, to the creation of new materials, and so on. Thanks to science, with the exception of the long-distance transfer of smells (which he once mentions), no item in Bacon's list has been left unachieved.

The same dream was shared by Descartes and was later enriched by Condorcet (2010 [1796]), although in his prediction of the future progress of humanity Condorcet made the assumption that scientific and moral progress would go hand in hand.

The scientific revolution, with Galileo and Descartes, opened the path to dominant faith that the truth would only be achieved through science; with the Cartesian dream, the mission of science 'to knowledge highly useful in life' coincides with 'knowing the force and action of fire, water, air, the stars, the heavens, and all the other bodies that surround us' (Descartes 1637); that is, objective facts, not on understanding of personal ignorance (Ravetz 1993). The vision of science as 'the art of the soluble' (Medawar 1968) entails the removal of what is not soluble because it is not scientific; therefore, it does not exist. Descartes's positive dream of a certain truth and absolute power has resulted in the systematic suppression of any understanding of the Platonic and Socratic ignorance (Ravetz 1993), what we would today call a refutation of Knightian ignorance (Knight 1921). Science is about certainty. Uncertainty is to be evicted. It exists only in the form of 'soluble' scientific inquiry, at the edge of scientific knowledge, and ignorance must be pushed beyond the research problems boundaries (Ravetz 1994).

Since then, human reason and the use of mathematics, as opposed to the use of wisdom and self-knowledge (that is, humanistic learning), are the positive elements of the European of understanding of science (Ravetz 1993). Mathematics can vanquish uncertainty, 'studying the world in simplified, isolated bits, with only moderate uncertainty' (Ravetz 2015). This 'reductionism' set a partial view of the world against its complexity, dismissing the importance of complementary perspectives (Ravetz 2019).

Condorcet's insight, in his essay *Outlines of an Historical View of the Progress of the Human Mind* (Condorcet 2010 [1796]), was to add to the Baconian list of achievements that science would have tamed social problems as well, thanks to the power of mathematics. Condorcet was one of the fathers of modern decision theory. It is curious to note that the unique possibly non-realised item in Bacon's list of wonder is something he called 'Natural Divinations', possibly the capacity to predict the future. However, here we might find modellers advocating that this has been mastered as well. The promise of control and prediction rooted in the Cartesian dream of rigorous technical models and precise scientific metrics in handling the uncertainties did not survive the test of a radically uncertain world (Scoones and Stirling 2020).

It was the extraordinary success of science – continuing to the present day – that ensured the persistence and vitality of the dream. If science makes airplanes fly, skyscrapers stand, metro and cars run without human intervention, surely science can tame human problems, inform policies and resolve disputes by the sheer accumulation of facts. Indeed, artificial intelligence does beat human intelligence in a growing set of contexts.

Without much success, philosophers, scholars and ecologists have taken issue with this dream. This critique has often addressed innovation as a source of never-ending growth, for bringing about as many new problems as those which are solved. The same conversation today pits techno optimists (Nijhuis 2015; Rifkin 2015) against the more prudent reading of Brynjolfsson and McAfee (2016), and of Pope Francis's own *Laudato Si* (Pope Francis 2015); for example, on the effect of automatisation on the labour market. An underlying problem here is that economics – from Ancient Greece to the more recent historical and institutional schools – has traditionally had ethics as a built-in element. Only with its methodological individualism and physics envy has modern neoclassical economics externalised this part of the analysis.

Ricardian and Cartesian Dreams and Their Vices

Economics might be considered part of the implementation of the Cartesian dream. The earlier successes of that programme were always mixed with failures. After all, it was Descartes' disciple Huygens who summed up a lifetime of attempts to prove the system with the phrase 'un beau roman de physique'.

Such a Ricardian dream within a Cartesian dream appears to have pushed aside more ancient sources of economic thought originating centuries ago in Italy, and kept alive by generations of economists, especially in Germany, until almost all of the 19th century (E.S. Reinert 2007). In brief:

> The mainstream canon is a product of the Enlightenment, in opposition to Renaissance values and outlook. Rationality and individuality during the Renaissance were based on an image of man as a spiritual being: creative and productive. The Enlightenment had a more materialistic understanding of human rationality and individuality: mechanical and consuming. (Reinert and Daastøl 2004)

This quotation recalls the theses of Toulmin's works *Cosmopolis* (Toulmin 1992) and *Return to Reason* (Toulmin 2001), as well as Harold Innis's theories of cycles, to which we shall return later.

In the Ricardian system (especially as it developed), 'the market' becomes the 'pineal gland' that explains everything and nothing. Criticism of an overly formalistic economics would converge on three key aspects of the Ricardian economy which, if applied to policy, would turn out to be distortive. Reinert (2013) identified these as 'Ricardo's three vices':

1. 'Ricardo's assumption-based rather than empirically based theory'. Joseph Schumpeter originally described it as the original Ricardian vice. He referred to the use of unrealistic assumptions, producing elegant but often practically useless theories.
2. 'Ricardo's built-in defence of colonialism'. Removing any qualitative features from the theory of international trade on the barter of labour hours, the Ricardian economic theory considered all economic activities to be equally generative of economic welfare, making colonialism legitimate.
3. 'Ricardo's failure to distinguish the financial sector from the real economy'. In other words, 'between the monetary (financial) sphere of the economy and the real economy of goods and services' (Reinert 2013).

A curious aspect of David Ricardo is that his labour theory of value is, simultaneously, the foundation both for communism (Marx made this concept the core of his economic theory, as it gave primacy to the industrial working class) and for the neoliberal theory of international trade with its 'comparative advantage'.

As for the role of economics, Ravetz (1994) advances the provocative hypothesis that it has remained an elite folk science, one where the production of stable 'facts' is less important than its ideological functions of providing justification and guidance for policies. Most economists would likely disagree, but if natural and social scientists can be said to be the heirs of the Cartesian dream, it should be acceptable to say that mainstream economists are today the heirs of the Ricardian dream.

While Ricardian vices may be so to an economist's sensibility, Cartesian vices may appear more evident to an ecologist, or to a sociologist:

1. 'Man as master and possessor of nature' is, by design, entitled to exploit the same nature as much as needed or wished. The most conspicuous examples of the rape of the Earth come to mind, from the poison cups left by mining, to shale gas and tar sands extractions of fossil fuels, and from collapsing fisheries to the burning of Amazonian forests.
2. In the Cartesian world, environmental and social affairs can be predicted and controlled, ignorance can be tamed, and even climate can eventually be regulated with the right amount of 'negative emissions' (Curvelo 2015). The ecosystem becomes an occasion for 'services' whose functioning can be evaluated and optimally allocated.
3. Finally, to a sociologist's sensitivity, there is in the predominant status assigned to geometry and mathematics as an element of education and regimentation (Ernest 2018). Descartes' denunciation of humanities and

philosophy as castles built on sand starts a long historical process that leads eventually to the modern emphasis on science, technology, engineering and mathematics (STEM), and the disciplined learning of mathematics as a contribution to the making of modern citizens, apt subjects of a knowledge economy. Unsurprisingly, this is reflected in current measures of education (Araujo et al. 2017).

Economics and the Scholasticism Wave

As mentioned in the introduction, the crisis of economics can be framed in the context of recurring cycles of economic thought (Reinert 2000), with economics first out, then back again into scholasticism. When did economics become scholastic and lose touch with reality?

A rich strand of literature, which has Philip Mirowski as its champion, argues that economics is a recurring victim of its physics envy (Mirowski 1991; Morus 2013). In late Victorian times, a surge of popularity and prestige for physics might have been the birth of physics envy.

There was a general background in the late 19th century when, at an accelerating pace, disciplines were being formed and 'scholasticised'. This could be seen in connection with history, psychology and anthropology: practitioners taught their craft and reflected on its foundations; they wanted to make it a science, also by using quantification as 'guarantee of truth'. Mathematisation 'becomes more than a tool, it becomes a safety-foundation of an almost mythical nature' (Drechsler 2004). the University of Cambridge was crucial here, given the high prestige of its physics, Alfred Marshall establishing economics, and the added local feature of the Tripos examination in mathematics, which had all the features of a scholastic enterprise (Warwick 2003). All that could have been the context for the creation of a mathematical-scholastic science of economics, whose content was arcane puzzles where the variables had real-sounding names.

Economist Paul Romer (2015) coined the term 'mathiness' to denote an improper use of mathematics to veil or obfuscate normative or ideological stances. The roots of the problem of 'mathiness' were born within Alfred Marshall's 1890 *Principles of Economics*. In Marshall's text, the law of increasing returns and the law of diminishing returns led Marshall to recommend, in line with Mill, subsidising manufacturing, which obeyed the law of increasing returns. However, this is not included in the models in the appendices, nor in the further development of formal economics: the increasing/diminishing returns dichotomy, which is the main determinant of the wealth and poverty of nations, was thrown out of the models because it was not compatible with equilibrium. Instead, they should have thrown out equilibrium because it was not compatible with reality. This problem was analysed extensively by Ingrao and Israel (1990).

In a sense, the rot started with a theory that provided the extremely simplifying assumptions that made the mathiness possible. Herbert Foxwell, a Cambridge economist, clearly saw the problems with Ricardo: in an introduction to an 1899 book by Anton Menger, Foxwell pointed to the key problems with Ricardo:

> Ricardo, and still more those who popularised him, may stand as an example at all time of the extreme danger which may arise from the unscientific use of hypothesis in social speculations, from the failure to appreciate the limited applications to actual affairs of a highly artificial and arbitrary analysis. His ingenious, though perhaps over-elaborated reasonings became positively mischievous and misleading when they were unhesitatingly applied to determine grave practical issues without the smallest sense of the thoroughly abstract and unreal character of the assumptions on which they were founded. (Foxwell 1899)

Mathiness: The Cartesian and Ricardian Legacy

As just mentioned, economist Paul Romer (2015), with his use of the term 'mathiness', has led a courageous debate against 'freshwater economists' (an allusion to Chicago and the Great Lakes region, distinct from the 'saltwater' economics of institutions on the East and West coasts) or 'sympathisers' for their use of mathematics as Latin, in the sense that mathematics would be used to scare off debate and veil ideological stances.

In a later blog entry, Paul Romer based his plea to fellow economists for the importance of intellectual honesty on a famous speech by Richard Feynman, perhaps the most beloved US physicist ever. Feynman's speech, entitled 'Cargo Cult Science' (Feynman et al. 1985), famously argued for a distinctive feature of science – that of being falsifiable – and for the moral commitment of scientists to go out of their way to try to falsify their own work. Hence, in the moment in which economics performs its ethical self-examination, it is to physics (again) that Romer turns.

The moment of truth for economics has coincided with the inability of mathematical modelling – in the form of dynamic stochastic general equilibrium (DSGE) models – to forewarn of the oncoming global financial crisis, with the ensuing inquiries involving the US Senate as well as the British Crown (Mirowski 2013: 275–286). The use of mathematics to obfuscate rather than illuminate would correspond to the use of 'Latin' of a decaying science, according to Harold Innis (1951), for whom periodical crises of the 'core' speaking in Latin[3] are resolved by injections from the periphery speaking vernacular. Innis's description of links among economic fashion, quantification and power relations can be summarised as follows:

> Canadian economist Harold Innis (1894–1952) suggests that scientific fashions of what Veblen called esoteric and exoteric knowledge follow a pattern, and in his scheme it becomes clear that scientific fashions may be driven by what Veblen dubbed 'vested interests.' I shall argue that sectors of the economies may actually be collecting rents from irrelevant economic theories. Without reference to Veblen, Innis sees that abstract science, communicated in Latin, gets more and more abstract, monopolises knowledge and enters into alliances with the political elites (with Veblen's vested interests). [Innis 1951] Today's Latin would be mathematics, and today a de facto alliance exists between mainstream (neo-classical) economics and the financial sector. (Reinert 2012a)

Economics is presently a master discipline as far as policy advice is concerned. Almost by definition, cost–benefit analyses, promoted by engineers and economists (Porter 1995), are the method of choice to adjudicate the feasibility of policy options.

In the academic world, economists command the highest salaries (Fourcade et al. 2014) and make decisions about the desirability of austerity policies. In the case of Harvard professors Kenneth Rogoff and Carmen Reinhart, this decision was based on flawed spreadsheet computation (Cassidy 2013). Rogoff and Reinhart calculated that a public debt to gross domestic product ratio above 90 per cent would be bad for countries. This calculation was used worldwide to justify austerity policies in the middle of the present recession, but a later reanalysis by researchers from the University of Massachusetts at Amherst disproved their finding, tracing it to a coding error in the authors' original software (coded in MS Excel). It is significant that the policies based on that error remained in force after its exposure.

The Rogoff and Reinhart model made an even more fundamental mistake: they analysed only the liability side of the balance sheets of nations. England's sovereign debt after winning very long wars with France during the late 1700s was huge, and so was the debt of the United States in the years following its independence in 1776. We can trace bookkeeping – separating assets and liabilities to find net worth – back to 13th century Venice and the very origins of capitalism, but today's macroeconomists fail to see the world from this angle. From Hammurabi as the ruler of Mesopotamia (around 1750 BC), through the Bible, to the economics of Marx and Schumpeter, we find the separation of the financial economy (money) and the real economy (the production of goods and services) (Reinert 2012b). From this also follows the separation between unproductive hoarding and savings productively invested. The gradual loss of these distinctions has led us to an economy where the financial sector is growing at the expense of the real economy.

Economists have recently attempted to extend their reach to adjudicate disputes such as climate change. In particular, Nicholas Stern called for more and better modelling (using the contested DSGE) to show how serious the consequences of climate change will be (Stern 2015).

Scholars of the study of science and technology (Collingridge and Reeve 1986; Funtowicz and Ravetz 1994), as well as fathers of the ecologist movement (Ernest Friedrich Schumacher, Lewis Mumford, Langdon Winner), have long argued that the enrolment of quantification in support of environmental policy, in the form of risk or cost–benefit analysis, should be resisted, lest one remains trapped in 'tar' (Winner 1989: 151). For Ernest Freidrich Schumacher:

> quality is much more difficult to 'handle' than quantity, just as the exercise of judgment is a higher function than the ability to count and calculate. Quantitative differences can be more easily grasped and certainly more easily defined than qualitative differences: their concreteness is beguiling and gives them the appearance of scientific precision, even when this precision has been purchased by the suppression of vital differences of quality. (Schumacher 1973)

The movement known as post-normal science (PNS) (Funtowicz and Ravetz 1993) can be seen as a reaction to the hyper-precision of cost–benefit and risk analysis as applied to solve ecological problems. 'How much is a songbird worth?' is the incipit of a paper in the same style (Funtowicz and Ravetz 1994). It is interesting to note that, even then, in order to show the vacuity of a certain style of quantification, Funtowicz and Ravetz (1994) selected the economics of climate change as their target; again, a cost–benefit analysis.

One could argue that the issue is not with statistics, or cost–benefit analysis, but more in general with an improper use of quantification, so that books apparently treating different endeavours such as algorithms (O'Neil 2016), metrics (Muller 2018) and mathematical models (Pilkey and Pilkey-Jarvis 2009), and many others, are in fact wrestling with very similar pathologies, including the neglect of the non-neutrality of the technique (Saltelli et al. 2020b; Scoones and Stirling 2020).

There is currently resurgent interest in issues of the ethics of quantification, first proposed by Espeland and Stevens (2008), both in relation to mathematical modelling (Saltelli et al. 2020a) and to other forms of quantification (Bruno et al. 2014a, 2014b; Didier 2020; Saltelli 2020; Saltelli and Di Fiore 2020).

THE CARTESIAN AND RICARDIAN DREAMS: COMMON THREAD, SAME ETHOS?

Thus, it would seem that the Cartesian and Ricardian dreams share more than one thread. Both can be seen in a historical perspective as the following cycles: that between the Renaissance's reasonableness and qualitative understanding versus the Enlightenment's rationality and increasing quantification; that between the power of the centre and its periphery; and that between Latin and the vernacular. In both dreams, mathematics appears to contribute cyclically to relevance and irrelevance, when its adoption as the language needed to read the book of nature (and of man) is taken too far.

Asking if science suffers more under the stupor of the Cartesian dream or the Ricardian one recalls the dialogue of Italian poet Giacomo Leopardi about whether Death or Fashion kills the most, where the poet adjudicates in favour of Fashion. One can say that while the Cartesian dream served science well in many of the excellent things science did and does for us – with the key idea that many problems can indeed be subdivided into simple ones and solved one at a time until the entire edifice is built – the same cannot be said for the Ricardian dream. In this sense, in an ideal context between Ricardo and Descartes about who did the most damage, Leopardi would probably adjudicate in favour of Ricardo – as the damage done by this thinker was not balanced by useful services made to society. Reawakened today, Leopardi would probably note that present-day economics has reversed its relation with science: science is now part of the economy, more than economy is a part of science.

Another common thread linking the Cartesian and Ricardian dreams is a common origin that both, through the use of implicit and explicit assumptions, bring theory up to a level of abstraction where the conclusions suffer from a *reductio ad absurdum*, while an increasing number of observers, both inside and outside of the economics profession, argue that the use of mathematics in economics in some areas has reached a point of diminishing or even negative returns (Muller 2018; Porter 2012; Stirling 2019).

Following Ravetz (1971), we would like primarily to note that both economics and science are social activities, and their ethos (and its changes) determines their function, quality and outcome. The perceived collapse of quality assurance, most visible in statistics, is an indication of the decline of that dream (Amrhein et al. 2019; Gelman 2019). Nevertheless, a legitimate question is whether science at large and economics share the same ethos.

According to a lively strand of literature, economics exhibits some distinctive features when it comes to the prevailing norms of the craft. Clearly the moral progress of Enlightenment economics was a result of a century-long effort to sort out the ethics of the market; a process that started with Bernard Mandeville's *Fable of the Bees* (Mandeville 1723). Mandeville recognised that 'private vices' are at the core of the growth into a liberal economic system, replacing the role of virtue of Renaissance civic humanism. Later, Count Pietro Verri of Milan discovered the limits of Mandeville's theory and counterbalanced its main revolutionary claim: that any private interest is good greed. Instead, Verri's Rule stated that the coincidence of private with public interest is the boundary between good greed and bad (or predatory) greed (Reinert 2013).

For Ruske (2015), politicians with a past as economists are more likely to be corrupted. That claim was extended by Frank and Schulze (2000) from politicians to the entire citizenry. Those who have watched Charles Ferguson's movie *Inside Job* will recall an interview with Frederic Mishkin, a banking professor at Columbia University, praising Iceland's 'strong' banking regulation system two years before it went bust. Mishkin had been paid US$124 000 by the Icelandic Chamber of Commerce to write the paper. The episode suggests:

> a troubling possibility: that prominent academic financial economists, such as those portrayed in the movie, had lucrative connections with private financial firms that they did not disclose to the public even when they were proffering public policy advice on financial matters that could affect the financial fortunes of those financial firms (Carrick-Hagenbarth and Epstein 2012)

The investigation by Carrick-Hagenbarth and Epstein (2012) focused on the financial affiliations of 19 prominent academic financial economists active in proposing reforms in the wake of the 2008 global financial crisis, and found that 'private affiliations were common but that these academic economists disclosed these affiliations infrequently and inconsistently'. In 2015, Campaign for Accountability, an advocacy group, revealed how a payday lending industry trade association paid for and edited a controversial academic paper claiming that payday loans do not leave consumers trapped in cycles of debt.

All of the above are anecdotes. Contrasting 'virtuous' natural scientists against 'sinful' economists is possibly a caricature. Here the former would follow Mertonian norms of scientific ethos[4] and the latter a more profit-seeking (or utility-maximising) attitude, like that of Frederic Mishkin in real life or the fictional Gordon Gekko, immortalised by Michael Douglas in Oliver Stone's movie *Wall Street*. As anticipated by Ravetz (1971), and discussed by Benessia et al. (2016), Mertonian principles were more plausible in describing pre-war 'little science' than modern techno-science, and more for amateur gentlemen scientists than for young researchers on the verge of a precarious profession.

What one can observe is that today's economics is much closer to the exercise of power than any other discipline at possibly any point in the history of mankind; only churches have historically enjoyed as much leverage. Notwithstanding the existence of a healthy level of disagreement within the craft of economics, mainstream economics plays an important role in the maintenance of existing economic order, inclusive of its distortion of the balance between the real and the financial economy, which we now all take as a fact of life but which would have terrified 'Old Canon' economists.

Perhaps the most telling difference between today's economics and science's other disciplines is in the mismatch between status (and ambition) of economics and the quality of its achievements. The inability of economists to predict or explain the credit crunch testifies to the limited predictive capacities of the discipline. In a three-page letter to Queen Elizabeth II, ten economists explained the failure to forecast the extent and harshness of the credit crunch, writing that: 'in recent years economics has turned virtually into a branch of applied mathematics, and has been become detached from real world institutions and events' (Hodgson 2009). The spirit of the letter goes in the direction of escaping from the Cartesian and Ricardian legacy, and enabling economics to embrace a diversity of approaches.

CONCLUDING REMARKS

A recent book on science's crisis (Benessia et al. 2016) advanced a number of hypotheses about what could, or would, need to be done to achieve progress:

1. Ongoing initiatives from inside the house of science – to overhaul the peer review system, to ease retractions, to increase reproducibility and transparency, to revise the use of perverse metrics, and overall to change the existing system of perverse incentives – are useful, but at the same time insufficient. As noted in a blog at the London School of Economics, it is difficult to detach oneself from old habits (Moriarty 2015). For example, one cannot ask young researchers, caught in the struggle to secure an insecure job – and requested to publish to achieve their PhD – to do this while fighting existing metrics and bad practices. Along the same lines, we have already mentioned the Darwinian 'fitness' of bad science (Smaldino and McElreath 2016). Things are likely to become worse before they get better (Saltelli 2017; Gillis 2019).

2. In a paper exposing the abuse and misuse of statistical tools, Gigerenzer and Marewski (2015) noted that, in 'Bacon's view, it is better to have no beliefs than to embrace falsehoods, because false idols block the way toward enlightenment'. Benessia et al. (2016) called this the need to 'unlearn' before progress can be achieved, and the list of unlearning extends from blind reliance on quantitative tools to the aspects of the Cartesian dream already discussed.

3. Ravetz (2018) called for a resistance movement against bad and corrupt practices and against the proletarianisation of research. Statistics, one step ahead as usual, already has a movement of statistical resistance, named French Statactivisme (Bruno et al. 2014a, 2014b), and one of its missions is the fight against 'funny numbers' (Porter 2012).

4.   The history and philosophy of science, science and technology studies, and similar sociological tools to understand the crisis are important and should be heard. In the experience of the authors, if there is one thing that both conservatives and progressive scientists agree upon, it is their disdain of philosophers. Scientists might have difficulty living through their structural contradictions; for example, between science's public image and its role (Ravetz 2011). Scientists' responsibilities have been defined as 'the elephant in the room we can't ignore' (Macilwain 2016). Criticism should not become a pretext for yet another round of science wars between the two cultures.

What conclusions can one draw by revisiting the above list with economics in mind? Economics shares science predicaments as to the hyper-reliance of perverse metrics and incentives, and must therefore give serious consideration to the ongoing activities to fight perverse incentives. Economics could also consider strengthening its quality control mechanisms and tools. This would involve reintroducing craft skills in handling numbers. Education would play an important role in this, as well as better strategies for the screening of mathematical evidence, such as the use of pedigrees for quantitative information (Funtowicz and Ravetz 1990) or testing the quality of the narrative supported by numbers (Saltelli et al. 2013; Saltelli and Giampietro 2017). Finally, the work of historians of economic thought – such as Philip Mirowski and others quoted in this chapter – shows that, even in economics, a useful critique can emerge from the history of the discipline. This should be more visible in present economics curricula.

Paul Romer's discussion of mathiness, cited previously, shows that the level of debate in economics on what should be unlearned is advanced. However, Romer's very brief tenure as Chief Economist of the World Bank (October 2016 to January 2018) and the conditions under which he left point to a structure that was unwilling to tolerate his view of the problems with economics. Even in economics, one should abandon the belief that nothing can go wrong when there are quantitative data and mathematical techniques. As we have discussed in this chapter, the Ricardian dream would need to be revisited, as per the Cartesian one.

ACKNOWLEDGEMENT

This chapter was pre-published as UCL-IIPP working paper 2021/07 with the same title and authors, https://www.ucl.ac.uk/bartlett/public-purpose/publications/2021/mar/altered-states-ricardian-and-cartesian-dreams.

NOTES

1. http://www.wcri2019.org/.
2. It should be added that the physiocrats mainly published in journals, not in books. However, the books came in very few editions.
3. Models as Latin are also discussed in Saltelli et al. (2013).
4. 'In his essay "The normative structure of science", Thomas Merton attributed to modern science a unique ability to provide "certified" knowledge, thanks to the institutionalization of distinctive social norms in the scientific community, in the form of a specific ethos that drove progress … The ethical and epistemic value of science ensured by the Mertonian norms of communalism, universalism, disinterestedness and organized scepticism helped to delimit a "republic of science" – an autonomous community of peers, self-governed through shared knowledge and under no form of authority other than knowledge itself' (Benessia et al. 2016: 76).

REFERENCES

Amrhein, V., Greenland, S., and McShane, B. (2019). Scientists Rise up against Statistical Significance. *Nature* 567(7748): 305–307. http://www.nature.com/articles/d41586-019-00857-9 (accessed: 31 March 2019).

Araujo, L., Saltelli, A., and Schnepf, S.V. (2017). Do PISA Data Justify PISA-Based Education Policy? *International Journal of Comparative Education and Development* 19(1): 20–34. http://www.emeraldinsight.com/doi/10.1108/IJCED-12-2016-0023.

Arthur, B.W. (2009). *The Nature of Technology: What It Is and How It Evolves.* New York: Free Press.

Bacon, F. (1627). *Magnalia Naturae, Praecipue Quoad Usus Humanos.* https://archive.org/details/worksfrancisbaco05bacoiala.

Benessia, A., Funtowicz, S., Giampietro, M., Saltelli, A., Pereira, Â.G., et al. (2016). *Science on the Verge.* Arizona State University. https://books.google.es/books?id=bjGVjwEACAAJ.

Benessia, A., and Funtowicz, S. (2015). Sustainability and Techno-Science: What Do We Want to Sustain and for Whom? *International Journal of Sustainable Development* 18(4): 329. http://www.inderscience.com/link.php?id=72666 (accessed: 10 May 2010).

Bruno, I., Didier, E., and Prévieux, J. (2014a). *Statactivisme. Comment Lutter Avec Des Nombres.* Paris: Zones, La Decouverte.

Bruno, I., Didier, E., and Vitale, T. (2014b). Editorial: Statactivism: Forms of Action between Disclosure and Affirmation. *Open Journal of Sociopolitical Studies* 2(7): 198–220.

Brynjolfsson, E., and McAfee, A. (2016). *The Second Machine Age: Work, Progress, and Prosperity in a Time of Brilliant Technologies.* New York: W.W. Norton & Company.

Campaign for Accountability (2015). Academic Deception. https://www.scribd.com/document/288230891/Academic-Deception (accessed: 11 May 2018).

Carrick-Hagenbarth, J., and Epstein, G.A (2012). Dangerous Interconnectedness: Economists' Conflicts of Interest, Ideology and Financial Crisis. *Cambridge Journal of Economics* 36(1): 43–63. https://academic.oup.com/cje/article-lookup/doi/10.1093/cje/ber036 (accessed: 11 May 2018).

Cassidy, J. (2013). The Reinhart and Rogoff Controversy: A Summing Up. *The New Yorker*, 26 April. http://www.newyorker.com/news/john-cassidy/the-reinhart-and -rogoff-controversy-a-summing-up (accessed: 27 August 2017).

Cassidy, J. (2017). A New Way to Learn Economics. *The New Yorker*. https://www .newyorker.com/news/john-cassidy/a-new-way-to-learn-economics.

Clarke, D.M. (2006). *Descartes: A Biography*. Cambridge University Press. https:// books.google.es/books?id=G 2JBCIn5UCkC&printsec=frontcover&dq= inauthor: %22Desmond+M.+Clarke%2 2&hl=en&sa=X&ved=0ahUKEwio2vGlsfvaAhV- J7BOKHU6kATOO6AEIJzAA#v=onepage&q&f=false (accessed: 10 May 2018).

Collingridge, D., and Reeve, C. (1986). *Science Speaks to Power: The Role of Experts in Policy Making*. New York: St Martin's Press.

Condorcet, N. de (2010 [1796]). *Outlines of an Historical View of the Progress of the Human Mind*. Baltimore: Printed by G. Fryer, for J. Frank, 1802.

Curvelo, P. (2015). Geoengineering Dreams. In Pereira, A.G. and Funtowicz, S. (eds), *Science, Philosophy and Sustainability: The End of the Cartesian Dream*. London and New York: Routledge, pp. 114–131.

Descartes, R. (1637). *Discours de La Méthode Pour Bien Conduire Sa Raison, & Chercher La Verité Dans Les Sciences*. Leiden: Jan Maire.

Didier, E. (2020). *America by the Numbers: Quantification, Democracy, and the Birth of National Statistics*. Cambridge, MA: MIT Press.

Drechsler, W. (2004). Natural vs. Social Sciences: On Understanding in Economics. In Reinert, E.S. (ed.), *Globalization, Economic Development and Inequality: An Alternative Perspective*. Cheltenham, UK and Northampton, MA, USA: Edward Elgar Publishing, pp. 71–87.

The Economist (2013a). How Science Goes Wrong. https://www.economist.com/ leaders/2013/10/21/how-science-goes-wrong (accessed: 11 August 2017).

The Economist (2013b). Trouble at the Lab. https://www.economist.com/briefing/ 2013/10/18/trouble-at-the-lab (accessed: 11 August 2017).

Ernest, P. (2018). The Ethics of Mathematics: Is Mathematics Harmful? In Paul Ernest (ed.), *The Philosophy of Mathematics Education Today*. Cham: Springer, pp. 187–216.

Espeland, W., and Stevens, M.L. (2008). A Sociology of Quantification. *European Journal of Sociology* 49(3): 401–436.

Fanelli, D. (2010). 'Positive' Results Increase Down the Hierarchy of the Sciences. Ed. Enrico Scalas. *PLoS ONE* 5(4): e10068. http://dx.plos.org/10.1371/journal.pone .0010068 (accessed: 25 August 2017).

Fanelli, D. (2018). Opinion: Is Science Really Facing a Reproducibility Crisis, and Do We Need It To? *Proceedings of the National Academy of Sciences of the United States of America* 115(11): 2628–31. http://www.ncbi.nlm.nih.gov/pubmed/ 29531051 (accessed: 26 March 2018).

Feynman, R.P., Leighton, R. and Hutchings, E. (1985). *Surely You're Joking, Mr. Feynman!* New York: W.W. Norton & Company.

Fourcade, M., Ollion, E., and Algan, Y. (2014). *The Superiority of Economists*. http:// www.maxpo.eu/pub/maxpo_dp/maxpodp14-3.pdf (accessed: 10 May 2018).

Foxwell, H.S. (1899). Introduction. In Anton Menger, *The Right to the Whole Produce of Labour*. London: Macmillan & Co., pp. v–cx.

Frank, Bjorn and Schulze, Günther (2000). 'Does Economics Make Citizens Corrupt?' *Journal of Economic Behavior and Organization* 43(1): 101–113.

Friedman, M. (1953). *Essays in Positive Economics*. Chicago, IL: University of Chicago Press.

Funtowicz, S., and Ravetz, J.R. (1990). *Uncertainty and Quality in Science for Policy*. Dordrecht: Kluwer.

Funtowicz, S., and Ravetz, J.R. (1993). Science for the Post-Normal Age. *Futures* 25(7): 739–755. https://www.sciencedirect.com/science/article/abs/pii/001632879390022L?via%3Dihub (accessed: 11 August 2017).

Funtowicz, S., and Ravetz, J.R. (1994). The Worth of a Songbird: Ecological Economics as a Post-Normal Science. *Ecological Economics* 10(3): 197–207. http://linkinghub.elsevier.com/retrieve/pii/0921800994901082 (accessed: 11 August 2017).

Gelman, A. (2019). Retire Statistical Significance: The Discussion. *Blog: Statistical Modelling, Causal Inference and Social Sciences*. https://statmodeling.stat.columbia.edu/2019/03/20/retire-statistical-significance-thediscussion/.

Gigerenzer, G., and Marewski, J.N. (2015). Surrogate Science. *Journal of Management* 41(2): 421–440.

Gillis, A (2019). The Rise of Junk Science. *The Walrus*. https://thewalrus.ca/the-rise-of-junk-science/.

Hardwicke, T.E., Wallach, J.D., Mallory, C.K., and Ioannidis, J.P.A. (2019). *An Empirical Assessment of Transparency and Reproducibility-Related Research Practices in the Social Sciences (2014–2017)*. MetaArXiv Preprints, 29 April. https://osf.io/preprints/metaarxiv/6uhg5/ (accessed: 6 May 2019).

Hodgson, G.M. (2009). Letter to the Queen. https://www.geoffreymhodgson.uk/letter-to-the-queen (accessed: 11 September 2020).

Horton, R. (2015). Offline: What Is Medicine's 5 Sigma? *The Lancet* 385: 1380. http://www.thelancet.com/pdfs/journals/lancet/PIISO140-6736%2815%2960696-1.pdf (accessed: 14 August 2017).

Hudson, M. (2010). The Use and Abuse of Mathematical Economics. *Real-World Economics Review* (54): 2–22.

Ingrao, B., and Israel, G. (1990). *The Invisible Hand: Economic Equilibrium in the History of Science*. Cambridge, MA: MIT Press.

Innis, H.A. (1951). *The Bias of Communication*. Toronto: University of Toronto Press.

Ioannidis, J.P.A. (2016). Evidence-Based Medicine Has Been Hijacked: A Report to David Sackett. *Journal of Clinical Epidemiology* 73: 82–86. http://linkinghub.elsevier.com/retrieve/pii/S0895435616001475 (accessed: 24 March 2018).

Ioannidis, J.P.A., Stanley, T.D., and Doucouliagos, H. (2017). The Power of Bias in Economics Research. *Economic Journal* 127: F236–F265.

Jamieson, K.H. (2018). Crisis or Self-Correction: Rethinking Media Narratives about the Well-Being of Science. *Proceedings of the National Academy of Sciences of the United States of America* 115(11): 2620–2627. http://www.ncbi.nlm.nih.gov/pubmed/29531076 (accessed: 26 March 2018).

Kaplan, S.L. (2015). *Bread, Politics and Political Economy in the Reign of Louis XV*, 2nd edition. London: Anthem Press.

Klotz, G., Minard, P., and Orain, A. (2017). *Les Voies de La Richesse? La Physiocratie en Question (1760–1859)*. Rennes: Presses Universitaires de Rennes.

Knight, F.H. (1921). *Risk, Uncertainty and Profit*. Boston, MA: Houghton Mifflin Company, University Press Cambridge.

Lanier, J. (2006). *Who Owns the Future?* London: Penguin Books.

Lanier, J. (2018). *Ten Arguments for Deleting Your Social Media Accounts Right Now*. New York: Henry Holt & Co.

Leek, J., Colquhoun, D., McShae, B.B., Gelman, A., Nuijten, M.B., and Goodman, S.N. (2017). Five Ways to Fix Statistics. *Nature* 551: 557–559.

Leek, J., and Peng, R.D. (2015). P Values Are Just the Tip of the Iceberg. *Nature* 520: 612.

Macfarlane, L. (2017). *33 Theses for an Economics Reformation – New Thinking for the British Economy*. https://neweconomics.opendemocracy.net/33-theses-economics -reformation/ (accessed: 23 October 2022).

Macilwain, C. (2016). The Elephant in the Room We Can't Ignore. *Nature* 531(7594): 277. http://www.nature.com/doifinder/10.1038/531277a (accessed: 11 August 2017).

Magni, P., Bier, Dennis M., Pecorelli, Sergio, Agostoni, Carlo, Astrup, Arne, et al. (2017). Perspective: Improving Nutritional Guidelines for Sustainable Health Policies: Current Status and Perspectives. *Advances in Nutrition* 8(4): 532–545. http://www.ncbi.nlm.nih.gov/pubmed/28710141 (accessed: 4 May 2018).

Mandeville, B. (1723). *The Fable of the Bees, or, Private Vices, Public Benefits*. http:// oll.libertyfund.org/titles/mandeville-the-fable-of-the-bees-or-private-vices-publick -benefits-vol-1#chapter_66840 (accessed: 11 May 2018).

Marshall, Alfred (1890). *Principles of Economics*. London: Macmillan.

McAfee, A., and Brynjolfsson, E. (2017). *Machine, Platform, Crowd: Harnessing Our Digital Future*. New York: W.W. Norton and Company. http://books.wwnorton .com/books/Machine-Platform-Crowd/ (accessed: 10 May 2018).

Medawar, P.B. (1968). *The Art of the Soluble*. London: Methuen.

Millgram, E. (2015). *The Great Endarkenment: Philosophy for an Age of Hyperspecialization*. New York: Oxford University Press.

Mirowski, P. (1991). *More Heat than Light: Economics as Social Physics, Physics as Nature's Economics*. Cambridge: Cambridge University Press.

Mirowski, P. (2011). *Science-Mart, Privatizing American Science*. Cambridge, MA: Harvard University Press.

Mirowski, P. (2013). *Never Let a Serious Crisis Go to Waste: How Neoliberalism Survived the Financial Meltdown*. London: Verso. https://books.google.es/books?id =5mdelx-86jwC.

Mirowski, P. (2018). The Future(s) of Open Science. *Social Studies of Science* 48(2): 171–203. http://journals.sagepub.com/doi/10.1177/0306312718772086 (accessed: 10 May 2018).

Moriarty, P. (2015). Addicted to the Brand: The Hypocrisy of a Publishing Academic. *London School of Economics Impact Blog*. http://blogs.lse.ac.uk/impactofsocia lsciences/2016/03/14/addicted-to-the-brand-the-hypocrisy-of-a-publishing -academic/ (accessed: 11 May 2018).

Morus, I.R. (2013). *When Physics Became King*. Chicago, IL: University of Chicago Press.

Muller, J.Z. (2018). *The Tyranny of Metrics*. Princeton, NJ: Princeton University Press.

Nature (2015). Misplaced Faith. *Nature* 522(7554): 6. http://www.nature.com/ doifinder/10.1038/522006a (accessed: 11 August 2017).

Nijhuis, M. (2015). Is the Ecomodernist Manifesto the Future of Environmentalism? *The New Yorker*. https://www.newyorker.com/tech/elements/is-the-ecomodernist -manifesto-the-future-of-environmentalism.

O'Neil, C. (2016). *Weapons of Math Destruction: How Big Data Increases Inequality and Threatens Democracy*. London: Random House Publishing Group.

Open Science Collaboration (OSC) (2015). Estimating the Reproducibility of Psychological Science. *Science* 349(6251): aac4716. https://science.sciencemag .org/content/349/6251/aac4716.

Oreskes, N. (2018). Beware: Transparency Rule Is a Trojan Horse. *Nature* 557(7706): 469–469. http://www.nature.com/articles/d41586-018-05207-9 (accessed: 26 May 2018).

Ortmann, A. (2016). So, Is There a Crisis? Or Is There a Crisis of the Crisis, or What? On Replicability, Reproducibility, and Other Current Challenges in the Social Sciences. *Core Economics*, 18 March.

Pereira, A.G., and Funtowicz, S. (2015). *Science, Philosophy and Sustainability: The End of the Cartesian Dream.* London: Routledge.

Pierce, A. (2008). The Queen Asks Why No One Saw the Credit Crunch Coming. *The Telegraph*, 5 November.

Pilkey, O.H., and Pilkey-Jarvis, L. (2009). *Useless Arithmetic: Why Environmental Scientists Can't Predict the Future.* New York: Columbia University Press.

Pope Francis (2015). *Laudato Si'.* http://w2.vatican.va/content/francesco/en/encyclicals/documents/papa-francesco_20150524_enciclica-laudato-si.html (accessed: 11 May 2018).

Porter, T.M. (1995). *Trust in Numbers: The Pursuit of Objectivity in Science and Public Life.* Princeton, NJ: Princeton University Press. https://books.google.es/books?id=oK0OpgVflN0C.

Porter, T.M. (2012). Funny Numbers. *Culture Unbound* 4: 585–598.

Quesnay, F. (1770). *Traité Des Effets et de l'usage de La Saignée.* Paris: La Veuve d'Houry.

Rajan, R., and Zingales, L. (2004). *Saving Capitalism from the Capitalists: Unleashing the Power of Financial Markets to Create Wealth and Spread Opportunity.* Princeton, NJ: Princeton University Press. https://press.princeton.edu/titles/7822 .html (accessed: 10 May 2018).

Ravetz, J.R. (1971). *Scientific Knowledge and Its Social Problems.* Oxford: Clarendon Press.

Ravetz, J.R. (1993). The Sin of Science. *Knowledge* 15(2): 157–165.

Ravetz, J.R. (1994). Economics as an Elite Folk Science: The Suppression of Uncertainty. *Journal of Post Keynesian Economics* 17: 165–184. https://www.jstor .org/stable/4538434 (accessed: 11 May 2018).

Ravetz, J.R. (2011). Postnormal Science and the Maturing of the Structural Contradictions of Modern European Science. *Futures* 43(2): 142–148.

Ravetz, J.R. (2015). Preface: Descartes and the Rediscovery of Ignorance. In Pereira A.G. and Funtowicz S. (eds), *Science, Philosophy and Sustainability, the End of the Cartesian Dream.* London: Routledge, xv–xviii.

Ravetz, J.R. (2016). How Should We Treat Science's Growing Pains? *The Guardian.* https://www.theguardian.com/science/political-science/2016/jun/08/how-should-we -treat-sciences-growing-pains (accessed: 25 August 2017).

Ravetz, J.R. (2018). Reflections on Informed Critical Resistance, Reform and the Making of Futures. Post-Normal Science Symposium, University of Oxford, Institute for Science, Innovation and Society. https://www.insis.ox.ac.uk/article/post -normal-science-symposium-address-jerome-ravetz.

Ravetz, J.R. (2019). Ignorance, Uncertainty and 'What-If?', in Ziauddin Sardar (ed.), *The Postnormal Times Reader.* Herndon, VA: International Institute of Islamic Thought, pp. 159–167.

Ravetz, J.R., and Saltelli, A. (2015). The Future of Public Trust in Science. *Nature* 524(7564): 161. http://www.nature.com/articles/524161d (accessed: 10 May 2018).

Reinert, E.S. (2000). Full Circle: Economics from Scholasticism through Innovation and Back into Mathematical Scholasticism. *Journal of Economic Studies* 27(4/5):

364–376.   http://www.emeraldinsight.com/doi/10.1108/01443580010341862 (accessed: 11 August 2017).

Reinert, E.S. (2007). *How Rich Countries Got Rich and Why Poor Countries Stay Poor*. London: Constable.

Reinert, E.S. (2012a). Economics and the Public Sphere: The Rise of Esoteric Knowledge, *Refeudalization, Crisis and Renewal*. http://publicsphere.ssrc.org/reinert-economics-and-the-public-sphere/ (accessed: 10 May 2018).

Reinert, E.S. (2012b). Mechanisms of Financial Crises in Growth and Collapse: Hammurabi, Schumpeter, Perez and Minsky. Tallinn University of Technology Working Papers in Technology Governance and Economic Dynamics, No. 39, TUT Ragnar Nurkse Department of Innovation and Governance.

Reinert, E.S. (2013). Civilizing Capitalism: 'Good' and 'Bad' Greed from the Enlightenment to Thorstein Veblen (1857–1929). MPRA Paper 47931, University Library of Munich, Germany.

Reinert, E.S., Carpenter, K., Reinert, F., and Reinert, S. (2017). 80 Economic Bestsellers before 1850: A Fresh Look at the History of Economic Thought. Working papers in Technology Governance and Economic Dynamics No. 74. https://developingeconomics.files.wordpress.com/2017/06/reinert-et-al-80-economic-bestsellers-before-1850-3.pdf (accessed: 10 May 2018).

Reinert, E.S., and Daastøl, A.M. (2004). The Other Canon: The History of Renaissance Economic. In Reinert, Erik (ed.), *Globalization, Economic Development and Inequality*. Cheltenham, UK and Northampton, MA, USA: Edward Elgar Publishing, pp. 21–70.

Reinert, E.S., and Saltelli, A. (2018). Debate: What Is Missing in the 33 Theses for an Economics Reformation. *The Conversation*, 29 March.

Reinert, Sophus A. (2007). One Will Make of Political Economy What the Scholastics Did with Philosophy: Henry Lloyd and the Mathematization of Economics. *History of Political Economy* 34(4): 643–677.

Ricardo, David (1817). *The Principles of Political Economy and Taxation*. London: John Murray.

Rifkin, J. (2015). *The Zero Marginal Cost Society: The Internet of Things, the Collaborative Commons, and the Eclipse of Capitalism*. New York: Palgrave Macmillan.

Romer, P. (2015). Mathiness in the Theory of Economic Growth. *American Economic Review* 105(5): 89–93. Available at http://pubs.aeaweb.org/doi/10.1257/aer.p20151066 (accessed: 11 August 2017).

Ruggiero, R. (1997). Services in Borderless Economy. Speech in Berlin, 23 October. https://www.wto.org/english/news_e/sprr_e/berlin_e.htm.

Ruske, R. (2015). Does Economics Make Politicians Corrupt? Empirical Evidence from the United States Congress. *Kyklos* 68(2): 240–254. https://onlinelibrary.wiley.com/doi/abs/10.1111/kykl.12082 (accessed: 11 May 2018).

Saltelli, A. (2017). Science's Credibility Crisis: Why it Will Get Worse before it Can Get Better. *The Conversation*, 9 November.

Saltelli, A (2018). Why Science's Crisis Should Not Become a Political Battling Ground. *Futures* 104: 85–90.

Saltelli, A. (2020). Ethics of Quantification or Quantification of Ethics? *Futures* 116(102509). doi: doi.org/10.1016/j.futures.2019.102509.

Saltelli, A., Bammer, G., Bruno, I., Charters, E., Di Fiore, M., et al. (2020a). Five Ways to Ensure That Models Serve Society: A Manifesto. *Nature* 582: 482–484. https://www.nature.com/articles/d41586-020-01812-9.

Saltelli, A., Benini, L., Funtowicz, S., Giampietro, M., Kaiser, M., et al. (2020b). The Technique Is Never Neutral: How Methodological Choices Condition the Generation of Narratives for Sustainability. *Environmental Science and Policy* 106: 87–98.

Saltelli, A., and Di Fiore, M. (2020). From Sociology of Quantification to Ethics of Quantification. *Humanities and Social Sciences Communications* 7(69). https://doi.org/10.1057/s41599-020-00557-0.

Saltelli, A., and Funtowicz, S. (2017). What Is Science's Crisis Really about? *Futures* 91: 5–11.

Saltelli, A., and Giampietro, M. (2017). What Is Wrong with Evidence Based Policy, and How can it be Improved? *Futures* 91: 62–71. http://www.sciencedirect.com/science/article/pii/SOO 16328717300472 (accessed: 19 June 2017).

Saltelli, A., Guimaraes Pereira, A., Van der Sluijs, J.P., and Funtowicz, S. (2013). What Do I Make of Your Latinorum? Sensitivity Auditing of Mathematical Modelling. *International Journal of Foresight and Innovation Policy* 9 (2/3/4): 213–234. http://www.inderscience.com/link.php?id=58610 (accessed: 11 August 2017).

Saltelli, A., and Stark P.B. (2018). Fixing Statistics is More than a Technical Issue. *Nature* 553(7688): 281. http://www.nature.com/doifinder/10.1038/d41586-018-0064 7-9 (accessed: 25 March 2018).

Samuelson, Paul (1948), International Trade and the Equalisation of Factor Prices. *Economic Journal* 58(June): 163–184.

Samuelson, Paul (1949). International Factor-Price Equalisation Once Again. *Economic Journal* 59(June): 181–197.

Samuelson, P.A. (1983). *Foundations of Economic Analysis (1946)*. Cambridge, MA: Harvard University Press.

Schmoller, G. (1897). *Wechselnde Theorien Und Feststehende Wahrheiten Im Gebiete Der Staats- Und Socialwissenschaften Und Die Heutige Deutsche Volkswirtschaftslehre, Rede Bei Antritt Des Rectorats*. Berlin: W. Buxenstein.

Schumacher, E.F. (1973). *Small ls Beautiful: Economics as if People Mattered*. New York: Harper Perennial.

Scoones, I., and Stirling, A. (eds) (2020). *The Politics of Uncertainty*. Pathways to Sustainability series. Abingdon, UK and New York, USA: Routledge. https://www.taylorfrancis.com/books/9781000163445 (accessed: 3 August 2020).

Smaldino, P.E., and McElreath, R. (2016). The Natural Selection of Bad Science. *Royal Society Open Science* 3: article 160384.

Smith, N. (2013). Noahpinion: The Death of Theory? *Noahpinionblog*. http://noahpinionblog.blogspot.com.es/2013/08/the-death-of-theory.html?m=1 (accessed: 10 May 2018).

de Solla Price, D. (1963). *Little Science, Big Science*. New York: Columbia University Press. https://books.google.es/books?id=MWOPAOAAMAAJ.

Stern, N.H. (2015). *Why Are We Waiting? The Logic, Urgency, and Promise of Tackling Climate Change*. Cambridge, MA: MIT Press.

Stirling, A. (2019). How Politics Closes down Uncertainty. STEPS Centre, 20 February. https://steps-centre.org/blog/how-politics-closes-down-uncertainty/ (accessed: 31 March 2019).

Toulmin, S. (1992). *Cosmopolis: The Hidden Agenda of Modernity*. Chicago, IL: University of Chicago Press.

Toulmin, S. (2001). *Return to Reason*. Cambridge, MA: Harvard University Press.

Tucker, J. (1782). *Cui Bono? Or, An Inquiry, What Benefits Can Arise Either to the English or the Americans, the French, Spaniards, or Dutch, from the Greatest*

Victories, or Successes, in the Present War, Being a Series of Letters, Addressed to Monsieur Necker, Late Control. London: T. Cadell.

Veblen, T. (1919a). *The Place of Science in Modern Civilization*. New York: Huebsch.

Veblen, T. (1919b). *The Vested Interests and the State of the Industrial Arts*. New York: Huebsch.

Warwick, A (2003). *Masters of Theory: Cambridge and the Rise of Mathematical Physics Masters of Theory*. Chicago, IL: University of Chicago Press.

Wasserstein, R.L., and Lazar, N.A. (2016). The ASA's Statement on p-Values: Context, Process, and Purpose. *American Statistician* 70(2): 129–133.

Wilsdon, J. (2016). *The Metric Tide: The Independent Review of the Role of Metrics in Research Assessment and Management*. Los Angeles, CA: SAGE Publications. https://uk.sagepub.com/en-gb/eur/the-metric-tide/book251812 (accessed: 24 March 2018).

Winner, L. (1989). *The Whale and the Reactor: A Search for Limits in an Age of High Technology*. Chicago, IL: University of Chicago Press.

Wood, P., and Randall, D. (2018). How Bad Is the Government's Science? *Wall Street Journal*, 17 April.

Zuboff, S. (2019). *The Age of Surveillance Capitalism: The Fight for a Human Future at the New Frontier of Power*. New York: Public Affairs, Hachette Book Group.

5. Gender and uneven development

Lyn Ossome

INTRODUCTION

The law of uneven development suggests that differences in natural conditions and historical connection affect the rate of growth of productive forces, and produce structural disparities that result in varying rates and extents of growth for different groups, classes, social institutions, cultural fields and branches of economy. The primary preoccupation of theorists of uneven development is thus with an understanding of the nature and effect of asymmetries that occur between countries (and internal to them) as a result of historically determined social and productive forces. The disproportionate development of these factors give rise to contradictory tendencies in the overall trajectories of countries, which may either advance very rapidly or become stifled by factors outside of their control.

Structural barriers historically imposed on periphery countries have led to their uneven integration into the global capitalist political economy. This historical process has been elaborated in the literature in varying ways. Marxists, for instance, understand capitalist development as a temporally and spatially uneven combination of progress and regress (McIntyre 2009). Samir Amin (1976) dealt with this preponderance through an assessment of the problems of peripheral capitalism, which he elaborated through a number of key theses, four of which I highlight for the purpose of my enquiry in this chapter.

First, that the external imposition of the capitalist mode of production upon pre-capitalist formations caused certain crucial retrogressions that stunted local industrial production and precipitated the agrarian crisis in the Third World today (ibid.: 200–202).

Second, Amin exposes the problem of extraversion, through which the level of wages in the periphery became lower, and the development of industries is limited through a system that compelled the periphery to the role of complementary supplier of products of production (mainly agricultural produce and minerals) for which it had a natural advantage (ibid.). Third, he cautioned against mapping the trajectory of peripheries against the centre: underdevelopment of the periphery needed to be understood as an outcome of economic domination by the centre, expressed in the forms of international specialization (that is, the structure of world trade where the centre shapes the periphery in accordance with its own needs) and in the dependence of the structures whereby growth in the periphery is financed (ibid.).

Fourth are the political relations that organize the dominance of central capital over the world system, which in the peripheries enable the rise of a petty bourgeois strata and tendency towards state capitalism. On this latter point, I am interested in the ways in which gender ideology is deployed as a response to underdevelopment, and the backlash that this precipitates in the form of sustained structural violence against minorities.

Relatedly, ecosocialist theorizations frame the question of underdevelopment around the conditions produced by ecologically (environmentally) unequal exchange and appropriation of carbon sinks. The theory of environmentally unequal exchange, writes Ajl (2021: 14), 'emphasizes that it is not only goods and labor that are enmeshed in unequal exchange ... it is not merely the natural wealth, the free gifts provided by nature, which are consumed unevenly along North/South lines. It is also the environment itself'. A central problem is the loss by poor people of control over their lives, labour, environments and land (ibid.: 118), enforced by a capitalist colonial structure which relies on labour in the periphery, cheapened through the maintenance of vast labour reserves and unequal rural agrarian structures, widespread malnourishment, and punishment against countries that defy this structure. Agrarian reform within this colonial agrarian structure is thus foreclosed, as a result also foreclosing any shifts in equitable land ownership so central to changing food and agriculture systems (ibid.: 122). These arguments are necessarily framed around an anti-imperialist politics (Ajl 2021; Hickel 2020). The ways in which this ecological assault deepens capitalism's reproductive crisis, and accompanying demands of agrarian reforms that acknowledge this rift, are central to the questions raised being raised in the feminist agrarian scholarship emerging from the Global South.

The South agrarian scholarship is divided on the impacts of inequality which colonialism had on the distribution of resources. A key debate in this regard has been between Mafeje (1991) and Moyo (2018). For instance, although recognizing that indirect colonial rule had altered various organizational aspects of rural society in non-settler Africa,[1] Mafeje (1991) insisted that land concentration and agrarian class formation based on capitalist property relations and labour exploitation had been limited before and during colonization, and that lineage-based household landholding systems remained dominant and secured relatively adequate land for small cultivators. Against this argument, Moyo argues that Mafeje 'underestimated the processes of land alienation, concentration and commodification that were being consolidated after independence, particularly when neoliberalism was taking root in Africa from the 1980s' (Moyo 2018: 218).

The gendered manifestations of this colonial structure and postcolonial inheritance has been elaborated by Moyo and Yeros (2005) as a 'functional dualism' that emerged in the late-colonial policy of confining women to communal areas by institutionalized means, under despotic chieftaincies as the means of securing male labour for mines and farms (ibid.: 34). This dualism, they argue, is generalizable in the periphery. They furthermore note the instrumentalization of gender hierarchy that has continued under structural adjustment policies (SAPs), with the curtailing of social services and reliance on female reproductive labour (ibid.; see also Naidu and Ossome 2016).

Ideologically, however, despite the increasing recognition by agrarian movements of patriarchy as a problem, and adoption in some instances of a conscious gender policy (Moyo and Yeros 2005: 49–50), my co-author and I have shown elsewhere the insufficiency of empirical evidence that merely highlights shifts in gendered patters of (land) ownership and access without dealing concretely with gendered contradictions that are rendered apparent only through an analysis of the structural dimensions of gender in the midst of agrarian transitions (Ossome and Naidu 2021: 346), and which suggests an 'agrarian question of gendered labour' that is core to understanding the historical trajectory of gendered relations in the uneven course of capitalist development (ibid.). I address this question in some detail below.

Lastly, these various positions address the fundamentally political question of the state – the fulcrum around which the organization/reorganization of periphery economies has proceeded – from the extraversion instituted by the colonial state and inherited by the postcolonial state, to the undue influence of international financial institutions (IFIs) over states under neoliberalization. Even under globalization, these forces, rather than diminish the role of the state, reassert the centrality of the state. This is primarily because the national question regains relevance as the basis for the resolution of contemporary questions of uneven development, not least of which are new agrarian questions emerging in the Third World, but expressed globally through imperialism's stranglehold. Indeed, as Moyo and Yeros (2005) observe, under the pretext of a 'crisis of development':

> a standard surgical operation has ensued: the deregulation of national currencies and prices; the commercialization and privatization of previously state-controlled industries and public services; the cutting of social services; the unilateral withdrawal of support for agriculture; the titling and commodification of peasant agricultural land; and the flexibilization of labour relations. The results have been the intensification of socioeconomic degradation, the reinforcement of the peripheral tendency of crisis, and an unprecedented degree of dependence since the end of formal imperialism. (Moyo and Yeros 2005: 12–13)

It is hardly surprising then, that one of the greatest casualties of extraverted development under monopoly financialized capitalism has been the social capacity of the state. The social depletion that is characteristic of a 'crisis of care' is an:

> acute expression of the social reproductive contradictions of financialized capitalism … [suggesting that] the present strains on care are not accidental but have deep systemic roots in the structure of our social order … [and indicative of] something rotten not only in capitalism's current, financialized form but in capitalist society per se. (Fraser 2016: 99–100)

The wholesale displacement of the social reproductive burden onto the private sector – which remains in an impossible competition with working-class households, between which two the preponderant demand is for women's unpaid, underpaid and devalued labour – means that 'development' continues to rely on a substratum of unequal gender relations that are historical but marginalized in considerations of the 'economy proper', and therefore of state policy. The persistence of unequal integration and hierarchy, Getachew (2019) argues, 'highlights processes of integration and interaction that produce unevenly distributed rights, obligations and burdens. These processes of unequal integration are structural and embedded in the institutional arrangements of the international order [and] create the international conditions of ongoing imperial domination' (Getachew 2019: 32–33). Unequal integration, in other words, is fundamentally a problem of empire.

GENDERED DEVELOPMENT IN HISTORY

The primary question which feminist theorizations pose to the issue of development relates to the social and historical structures and conditions which both require the production of gendered inequalities in order to sustain development, and therefore reproduce these inequalities as the basis of development. A key debate that highlights this problem is the historical question of primitive accumulation, and in particular its basis in (gendered) labour. First-generation theorists of social reproduction such as Silvia Federici (2004) partly responded to this question by placing it within the context of capitalist expansion, by documenting changes in women's social status and their social degradation as a result of witch hunts, whose backdrop was the transition from feudalism to capitalism. Federici shows how the witch hunts of 16th and 17th century Europe served to create and enforce a newly established role in society for women there, who had been consigned to unpaid reproductive labour to satisfy the needs of a rising capitalist order. These processes ensured the separation of production from reproduction, and utilized extreme violence in the creation and enforcement of the resulting sexual division of labour.

One of the most devastating insights in that work is the recognition of everything that women lost in terms of social power in the transition to capitalism. Witches embodied everything that capitalism had to destroy: 'the heretic, the healer, the disobedient wife, the woman who dared live alone, the woman who poisoned the master's food and inspired the slaves to revolt' (Heenan 2017). The process of capitalist expansion was in no way a progressive moment in changing social relations, and at every stage, new rounds of primitive accumulation involving violence and expropriation of land can be observed.

Earlier, Rosa Luxemburg (1951) addressed the colonial question of primitive accumulation, with the insight that non-capitalist forms of production were essential for capitalism. The incursion of capital and consumer goods into rural areas and the dispossession that accompanies commodification force rural populations to purchase from the market what they used to produce for themselves. The accompanying shrinking of the non-capitalist strata means that some rural households cannot keep up with the socially determined level of consumption, thus lowering the living standards of all workers. Luxemburg argued, however, that capitalism does not benefit from the complete destruction of non-capitalist economies, as this would lead to a 'standstill of accumulation' (Luxemburg 1951).

Other theorists highlight the cost and conditions of labour in ways that illustrate the dependent and divisive nature of colonial capitalist accumulation. For instance, Walter Rodney's (1981) insights from his analysis of what would determine Guyana's ability to keep the plantation system alive, even as this system collapsed in much of the Caribbean, was that much more than capital, 'having a labor supply of a particular type' had been essential (ibid.: 646). In a fine-grained analysis, he considered the crucial contestation as not between an issue of labor supply versus no labor supply, but rather that 'the labor must be cheap and plentiful, and, even more important, the labor must be easily controlled'; he showed that a functioning plantation system would have been impossible 'unless labor [could] be provided under conditions that maximize the industrial control' (ibid.).

For Rodney, the capital–labour nexus was thus central to an understanding of the capacity for emancipation, the political form which could not be abstracted from economic emancipation:

> the real question was whether the ex-slaves, the freed slaves, could create a new way of life in which labor enters a relationship with capital under conditions that are at least partially determined by labor, whether labor could free itself from some of the absolute controls characteristic of slavery. It is that issue that was resolved to

the advantage of the planters and to the detriment of the ex-slaves in the years after emancipation. (ibid.)

Patnaik (2020) has elaborated on this duality, and the fact that while free wage labour is an indisputable fact in the core countries, so is lack of freedom imposed on peripheral populations:

> The Marxist analysis of the relation between the growth of free wage labour at one pole of capitalist accumulation and of chattel slavery at the other pole … must take into account the dialectical interaction of these two antithetical forms of exploitation. The freedom of workers in the core countries was historically conditional on the imposition of unfreedom on non-European peoples. The capitalist ruling classes imposed servitude on many non-European peoples, forcibly removed them from their communities, enslaved and transported millions of persons to the other side of the globe to work plantations for their own benefit, treating slave rent as profit. After the formal abolition of slavery, another form of unfreedom continued under the indentured labour system. (Patnaik 2020: 273)

Rodney's own argument is of a primary contradiction between the plantation system in which African labour is the backbone, and the shift in the consciousness and form of labour without an accompanying shift in the mode of production. Emancipation brings qualitative changes in labour which takes gendered form in a new kind of bondage. Drawing a definite distinction between male adult labour on the one hand, and the labour of women and children on the other, Rodney argues that the slave system and the plantation system, in order to function effectively, operated on the basis of exploiting family labour, where every member of the family was considered an asset to the plantation. He argues, however, that what is important in the post-slavery era is that:

> given the historical conditions of the time, women were discriminated against in terms of the rate of wages, and, of course, children were paid still less. Thus, the ability to command family labor was at the same time the ability to incorporate cheap labor, because women and children were paid less (Rodney 1981: 650)

The transition to a modern capitalist mode of production did not modify or affect the unequal (gendered) incorporation of labour that had been characteristic of the plantation economy. This might suggest two contradictory positions: either that the exploitation of gendered labour was a primary condition for the expansion of production and transition to capitalism (as the social reproduction literature suggests); or, conversely, that its articulation was to a political superstructure that was required for the reproduction of the social conditions that were necessary for the continuation of production. This is a question of the material culture underlying forced labour: a concern with how labour responded to the social conditions which the plantation imposed on it, and the mechanisms through which the disciplining and regimentation of labour could be assured. It requires theorization of the plantation as not just an economic model, but rather as a 'total system' in which social, cultural and political relations were reproduced towards the stabilization of the integrated whole. The gendering of labour, in other words, was a non-economic basis for the devaluation and degradation of African labour as a whole, and therefore, structurally integrated as such into subsequent trajectories of colonial development.

I have made a similar argument elsewhere in relation to the historical subjugation of women and the stabilization of colonial domination in Africa. The appropriation and exploitation of women's productive and reproductive labour towards the reproduction of the settler colonial political economy had functioned to ensure that women constituted a crucial condition of indirect rule and colonial accumulation. The bifurcation of the state constituted the political and social mechanisms of colonial rule (Mamdani 1996), but the structural dynamics which facilitated the stabilization of these bifurcated domains of rule was thoroughly gendered. The stabilization of the tribalized domains of native authority was highly articulated to the productive and reproductive roles to which labouring women in the colonies had been confined as the migrant cash crop economy expanded (Ossome 2018: xvi). This uneven structure of gendered, tribalized and racialized integration of women and men was a core feature of the colonial political economy; to overcome it, the postcolonial developmental state had necessarily to do away with the structures which had institutionalized these social inequalities. But democratization as the panacea has failed miserably, in its liberal form, to account for subjectivities that are 'non-economic': gender and ethnicity are thus treated as aberrations, rather than as modern edifices of the colonial and postcolonial state and capitalist structure that ought to be central to the social and economic stabilization of any state.

Lastly, and in relation to the present, the devastation caused by contemporary crises reflect again the dual nature of economies organized around historically gendered labour patterns, with imperialism retaining two distinct labour reserves in centres and peripheries (Yeros 2021). This, for instance, is evident with the social and economic crisis precipitated by the COVID-19 pandemic. An estimated 2.7 billion workers, or roughly 81 per cent of the world's workforce (ILO 2020) work and earn less due to the COVID-19 recession, with those in lower-middle-income developing countries losing most. In the imperialist centres, prior to the pandemic, the proletariat consisted of approximately 86 per cent of the working-age population, followed by 78 per cent in Central and South Eastern Europe, 65 per cent in Latin America and the Caribbean, 50 per cent in North Africa and East Asia, and as low as 21 per cent in South Asia and sub-Saharan Africa, according to data provided by the

International Labour Organization (ILO). Conversely, the unwaged working population (the self-employed, or unpaid family labour) was lowest in the imperialist centres, around 10 per cent, followed by 20 per cent in Central and South Eastern Europe, 32 per cent in Latin America and the Caribbean, 26–31 per cent in North Africa and East Asia, and as high as 78 per cent in South Asia and sub-Saharan Africa where, in fact, population growth is highest. The size of the two labour reserves differs dramatically; those in the imperialist centres also have closer interaction with the world's active army of labour – the proletariat proper – which is concentrated in the centres. Very different conditions, of massive and permanent marginality, prevail in peripheral social formations (Yeros 2021: 30).

This impoverished population is sustained primarily, although not exclusively, by a regime of exploited and/or unpaid gendered labour. Yet most macroeconomic considerations have tended to conceal the structurally gendered dimensions of this crisis: that is, the political economy of survival that historically sustained the populace of neoliberalizing countries, and which has again taken shape in response to the COVID-19 induced economic shock (Ossome 2020b: 69). The social substratum that meets the daily and generational needs of poor working-class households in the absence of adequate provisioning by the state and market, and the social and political significance of this realm of gendered labour in relation to neoliberal state responses to COVID-19 in Africa (ibid.) is thoroughly historical, as the foregoing discussion suggests. It ought to be understood as the social cost of the postcolonial failure to dismantle an inherited unequal structure of production that assumes the availability of gendered labour without any material concern with its reproduction or survival.

LAND AND THE SOCIAL REPRODUCTIVE CRISIS OF UNEVEN DEVELOPMENT

Ding and Yin (2015), reference Sam Moyo's observation that neoliberalism continues to make the Global South's agriculture subservient to the interests of the developed world, with two core strategies: removal of price support mechanisms that have helped peasants to sell their goods in the face of cheaper commodities from other countries; and a sustained attack on peasant-owned or -occupied land in the name of 'development'. The reaction of the 2007–2008 food crisis was a new scramble for land in Africa to feed a price bubble in food and biofuels. Neoliberalism and the food crisis also created a speculative bubble in land prices, further impoverishing and driving more peasants from the land. The alternative depended on the ability of the state to subsidize sections of the economy and offer agrarian reforms as a countervailing strategy (Ding and Yin 2015: 589).

Solidarity with the peasant path among Global South agrarian scholars is much more than an intervention into old Marxian debates regarding the role of the peasantry in the process of agrarian transitions. Rather, at its core and in the contemporary phase of capitalist dispossession, the peasantry and their demand for land take on renewed significance as a primary basis of social reproduction and, furthermore, a recognition that the weakening of state and national sovereignty renders impossible the process of autocentric development. Moyo et al. (2013) elaborated the social and political implications of setting aside the national question and its land and peasant components, and laid out the basis for re-engagement with earlier debates that had been 'more organic to the peasant struggles of the Third World, for whom backwardness was seen as *a dynamic process intrinsic to imperialism* and industrialization as *an aspect of a larger strategic objective: national liberation*' (ibid.: 96). The point here is that rather than flatten the trajectories of development to reflect growth paths in the centre, the necessity lies in examining the social forces that have emerged organically in the periphery, precisely because of the uneven trajectories of development that entail not only the primitive accumulation of resources, but also political peripheralization that also constitutes the locus of struggles for sovereignty.

Through a thoroughgoing critique of the industrialization thesis that was central to the classical agrarian question, Moyo et al. (2013) highlight the emergence of contemporary agrarian questions – including gender equity, ecological sustainability and regional integration – which reflect the trajectories of development in Third World countries and which continue to shape relations of inequality in the periphery. But these problems cannot be addressed in any meaningful way within the same systemic structure that reproduces them through circuits of bonded labour, global agribusiness value chains, financialization, debt and militarism; as they more succinctly put it: '[n]either gender equity, nor ecological sustainability, nor autonomous regional integration can be expected to progress under the tutelage of monopoly capitalism' (ibid.: 103–104).

How, then, guided by this framing, should theorists of development approach capitalism's entrenched reproductive crisis? And how do we approach this question from a Third World vantage point? Elsewhere I have argued that critiques of capitalism must grapple concretely with the question of accumulation, highlighting earlier work by (mainly Western) left feminist theorists who readily accepted the capitalist division of labour between private housework (reproductive work) and public productive (wage) work (Ossome 2020a). In the ensuing debates, feminists attempted to show that the housewife and her labour are not outside the process of surplus value production, but constitute the very foundation upon which this process can begin (e.g. Dalla Costa and James 1972). They argued that as capital is able to command the unpaid labour of the wife as well as well as the paid labour of the wage labourer, it is impossible to understand the exploitation of wage labour without understanding the exploitation of non-wage labour. But these claims of an exploitative relationship between the household and capital did not sufficiently demonstrate the relationship between the social reproduction of labour power, the exploitation and alienation of women, and surplus value extraction for the capitalist (Ossome 2020a: 75). Therefore, the question regarding what it is that lends reproductive labour to the structural workings of capitalism remains the subject of intense debate among feminist economists.

These debates are significant, given that they place the question of gendered labour within the analytical purview of structural inequality. However, beyond the problem itself of the reproductive crisis is the question of its manifestation in contexts bearing historical legacies of underdevelopment. There, the state (public sector) as the basis of social provisioning has long been under strain or altogether collapsed, the private sector is beyond the reach of the majority, and recourse to nature – including land and the commons – takes on particular significance for semi-proletarianized households, which in turn are reliant on gendered labour to extract use values from the land and the commons. Yet even this latter option is now under severe attack. Utsa Patnaik (2012) elaborates with clarity a structural framing of the problem, pointing to the 'reproductive limits' which capitalist development imposes.

Patnaik also critiques the 'absolute immiserization' that has accompanied the renewed dominance of finance capital and its attempt to control land, minerals and other primary resources in the Global South through the promotion of an economic 'discipline' of domestic fiscal contraction, free trade and free capital flows (ibid.: 250–251). This new process of primitive accumulation and accompanying immiserization, she argues, does not simply signify greater inequality: unlike the European colonizing migrant of yesteryear, today's displaced peasants and displaced workers of the South simply have nowhere to go. In the competition they face with capital over land and resources, they pose the question of sovereignty of food and natural resources (ibid.). In impoverished nations and agrarian societies, the relevance of land and landed resources thus cannot be reduced to a developmentalist agenda, and ought to be understood also as a primary basis of the survival of those immiserated by capitalism.

Under neoliberal capitalism, serious consideration must also be given to the growing surplus population – those daily expended and pauperized by industry – who place the greatest pressure on the deepening reproductive crisis. The invisibilized human labours that daily go into preserving and presenting a 'reassuring world view' to capital must form the locus of our analysis of the gendered legacies which uneven development has bequeathed upon most of the world. These legacies are manifest through the demand for, and appropriation of, differing resources, labours and time at different historical conjunctures; but these differences do not diminish the need for an internationalist and anti-imperialist politics that ought to frame struggles against these problems that time will only worsen, for countries of both the North and the South.

NOTE

1. Mafeje adopted Samir Amin's (1972) three-way categorization of the incorporation of African countries into the world capitalist system to explain the continent's different paths of agrarian transformation. This highlighted the fact that in the former settler colonies where large-scale land alienation had occurred, capitalist farming based on the exploitation of cheap labour had generated increased agrarian productivity and accumulation, albeit at a tremendous social cost (Mafeje 2003). This was in contrast to the limited concession of land towards mining and plantation enclaves in parts of Central Africa, where natural resources plunder prevailed. Elsewhere, in non-settler East and West Africa, the land and agrarian question was shaped by the promotion of commodity export economies based on household labour and production activities, directed by foreign merchants with state support (ibid., cited in Moyo 2018: 215).

REFERENCES

Ajl, Max (2021), *A People's Green New Deal*, London: Pluto Press.

Amin, Samir (1972), 'Underdevelopment and Dependence in Black Africa: Origins and Contemporary Forms', *Journal of Modern African Studies*, 10(4): 503–524.

Amin, Samir (1976), *Unequal Development: An Essay on the Social Formations of Peripheral Capitalism* [trans. Brian Pearce], London: Harvester Press.

Dalla Costa, Mariarosa and Selma James (1972), *The Power of Women and the Subversion of the Community*, Bristol: Falling Wall Press.

Ding, Xiaoqin and Xing Yin (2015), 'The Uneven and Crisis-Prone Development of Capitalism: A Review of the Tenth Forum of World Association for Political Economy', *World Review of Political Economy*, 6(4): 583–601.

Federici, Silvia (2004), *Caliban and the Witch: Women, the Body and Primitive Accumulation*, Brooklyn, NY: Autonomedia.

Fraser, Nancy (2016), 'Contradictions of Capital and Care', *New Left Review*, 100: 99–117.

Getachew, Adom (2019), *Worldmaking after Empire: The Rise and Fall of Self-Determination*, Princeton, NJ: Princeton University Press.

Heenan, Natasha (2017), 'Silvia Federici, Caliban and the Witch', *Progress in Political Economy*, https://www.ppesydney.net/silvia-federici-caliban-witch/ (accessed on 25 August 2021).

Hickel, Jason (2020), *Less is More: How Degrowth Will Save the World*, London: Windmill Books.

ILO (2020), 'Covid-19: Stimulating the Economy and Employment', https://www.ilo.org/global/about-the-ilo/newsroom/news/WCMS_743036/lang–en/index.htm (accessed 18 July 2020).

Luxemburg, Rosa (1951), *The Accumulation of Capital*, London: Routledge.

Mafeje, Archie (1991), *The Theory and Ethnography of African Social Formations: the Case of the Interlacustrine Kingdoms*, Dakar: CODESRIA Book Series.

Mafeje, Archie (2003), 'The Agrarian Question, Access to Land, and Peasant Responses in Sub Saharan Africa', Geneva: UNSRID Civil Society and Social Movements Programme Paper No. 6.

Mamdani, Mahmood (1996), *Citizen and Subject: Contemporary Africa and the Legacy of Late Colonialism*, Princeton, NJ: Princeton University Press.

Moyo, Sam (2018), 'Debating the African Land Question with Archie Mafeje', *Agrarian South: Journal of Political Economy*, 7(2): 211–233.

Moyo, S., P. Jha and P. Yeros (2013), 'The Classical Agrarian Question: Myth, Reality and Relevance Today', *Agrarian South: Journal of Political Economy*, 2(1): 93–119.

Moyo, Sam and Paris Yeros (eds) (2005), *Reclaiming the Land: The Resurgence of Rural Movements in Africa, Asia and Latin America*, London: Zed Books.

McIntyre, Richard (2009), 'Theories of Uneven Development and Social Change', *Rethinking Marxism: A Journal of Economics, Culture and Society*, 5(3): 75–105.

Naidu, Sirisha and Lyn Ossome (2016), 'Social Reproduction and the Agrarian Question of Women's Labour in India', *Agrarian South: Journal of Political Economy*, 5(1): 50–76.

Ossome, Lyn (2018), *Gender, Ethnicity and Violence in Kenya's Transitions to Democracy: States of Violence* (Korean trans. Jiwon Na), New York and London: Lexington Books.

Ossome, Lyn (2020a), 'The Agrarian Question of Gendered Labour in Sam Moyo's Scholarship', in Paris Yeros and Praveen Jha (eds), *Rethinking the Social Sciences with Sam Moyo*, New Delhi: Tulika Books.

Ossome, Lyn (2020b), 'The Care Economy and the State in Africa's Covid-19 Responses', *Canadian Journal of Development Studies/Revue canadienne d'études du développement*, 42(1–2): 68–78.

Ossome, Lyn and Sirisha Naidu (2021), 'Does Land Still Matter? Gender and Land Reforms in Zimbabwe', *Agrarian South: Journal of Political Economy*, 10(2): 344–370.

Patnaik, Utsa (2012), 'Some Aspects of the Contemporary Agrarian Question', *Agrarian South: Journal of Political Economy*, 1(3): 233–254.

Patnaik, Utsa (2020), 'Looking Back at Karl Marx's Analysis of Capitalism in the Context of Colonialism', in Paris Yeros and Praveen Jha (eds), *Rethinking the Social Sciences with Sam Moyo*, New Delhi: Tulika Books.

Rodney, Walter (1981), 'Plantation Society in Guyana', *Review (Fernand Braudel Center)*, 4(4): 643–666.

Yeros, Paris (2021), 'Elements of a New Bandung: Towards an International Solidarity Front', *Agrarian South Network Research Bulletin*, 10: 26–40.

6. Dependency theory: strengths, weaknesses, and its relevance today

Ingrid Harvold Kvangraven

Once a vibrant field of research across the globe, dependency theory almost disappeared from the academic curricula during the 1970s and 1980s (Kufakurinani et al. 2017). However, in recent decades there has once again been a revival in academic literature on dependency theory.[1] To get a flavour of the nature and intensity of the revival, consider that in 2021 alone there were edited volumes on dependency theory published (e.g. Madriaga and Palestini 2021); articles redefining dependency theory (e.g. Kvangraven 2021); a series of articles evaluating the relevance of dependency theory, and Samir Amin in particular in the *Review of African Political Economy*;[2] and a series of articles assessing dependency theory, its relation to Marxism and its relevance today in *Latin American Perspectives*.[3]

With the aim to clarify the relevance of dependency theory for understanding uneven development today, this chapter deals with the following three sets of questions.

Firstly, what are some of the theoretical and methodological debates within dependency theory? Anyone just familiarizing themselves with dependency theory must be forgiven for being confused about the main concepts as well as the main debates and tensions between the different strands. Questions that may arise are: Is it possible to categorize different kinds of dependency theories under the same theoretical and ideological umbrella? Are the different approaches complementary to each other, or in opposition? What are the intellectual origins of dependency theories, and on what grounds have they been delegitimized?

Secondly, given the radical changes in the global economy since the heyday of dependency theory in the 1950s and 1960s, one can be forgiven for assuming that the theories are simply outdated. Perhaps they cannot account for the far-flung global value chains and spread of manufacturing activities to the Global South? Perhaps globalization and global financialization renders dependency theory irrelevant?

Third, what are some key weaknesses of dependency theory, and how can they be addressed? In particular, separating clearly between symptoms and causes of 'dependence' is a key challenge in parts of the dependency literature, and much of the literature neglects other important inequalities such as race and gender. How can we address such critiques if we want to take research on dependency theory forward?

DEPENDENCY THEORY: THE INTERNAL AND EXTERNAL DEBATES

While there are many different approaches to dependency theory, the core idea which they all have in common is that advanced countries (the centre) benefit from the current global system at the expense of developing countries (the periphery). As formulated by dos Santos (1970: 231), dependency 'is a situation in which the economy of certain countries is conditioned by the development and expansion of another'. All dependency approaches are also in one way or other critiques of linear historiography and they involve a distinction between centre and periphery, which is one Prebisch first made in a lecture in 1944 (Love 1980).[4] While Prebisch and Singer were not originally dependency theorists, dependency theorists build on and extend many of their core concepts, such as attention to centre–periphery dynamics.

There is no unified dependency theory. Depending on their analytical categories, dependency scholars have different interpretations and understandings of the nature of dependency. The articulation of different theories of dependency was a result of complex discussions with internal controversies, although others have often consumed it as a 'corpus of testable propositions' (Cardoso 1977: 15). This is actually in contrast to dependency research's emphasis on global, dynamic and interactive analysis, which goes against the idea of isolating specific variables for hypothesis testing (Cardoso and Faletto 1979; Kay 1989; Vasconi 1971). Given that dependency research is the study of structural relations which are intimately related, and how they evolve over time, those relations cannot be 'tested' by doing cross-country regressions (Valenzuela and Valenzuela 1978: 556). Instead, dependency research is replete with empirical in-depth and comparative case studies.

There have been many recent attempts to define dependency theory (Heller et al. 2009; Mahoney and Rodríguez-Franco 2018; Stallings 2020). I have argued elsewhere that dependency theory is best thought of as a framework (Kvangraven 2018) or a research programme (Kvangraven 2021), rather than a singular theory, given that there is so much disagreement among dependency theorists (Madriaga and Palestini 2021 develop this definition further). In Kvangraven (2021) I argue that at the core of a dependency research programme is an attempt to explain why global economic development has a tendency to be polarizing rather than equalizing. While this is the central question of the research programme, I also identify four core tenets of the programme, namely: (1) a global historical approach; (2) theorizing of the polarizing tendencies of global capitalism; (3) a focus on structures of production; and (4) a focus on the specific constraints faced by peripheral economies. Dependency scholarship contains all four of these pillars, and it is this combination that makes the research programme unique. Nonetheless, the research programme remains broad enough to encompass rich theoretical and methodological debates.

The emphasis on how uneven development is produced and reproduced differs depending on the strand of dependency theory. For example, the neo-Marxists tend to focus on the historical development of capitalism and its extension to the developing world as the key factor, while the structuralists tend to focus on the structures of production and consumption in developing countries and the internal and external constraints they face. The analysis of class formations and relations varies between the approaches, as does the way political and historical aspects of dependency are treated. The plethora of sub-theories within dependency theory led Cardoso (1977: 17) to argue that it is its own field: 'dependency studies'.

Although the term 'dependency theory' originated in Latin America and was for a long time 'held to be a distinctively Latin American analysis of Latin American development' (Sanchez 2003: 31), separate strands of dependency theory developed in other parts of the world long before. Ideas associated with dependency theory can be found in literature across the world and spanning centuries, such as colonial drain theory, French scholarship on the need to protect French industry from Italy in the 16th century, Japanese scholarship on the power relations between centre and periphery, radical African scholarship, Soviet development theory, Canadian 'staple theory',[5] and the Caribbean dependency school (Kvangraven 2021). What is more, the neo-Marxist strand, popularized by Frank (1967) who drew heavily on Sweezy (1942) and Baran (1957), was developed in the United States, but also had proponents in Latin America (for example, dos Santos) and Africa (for example, Samir Amin).

There are many ways to separate the strands. Palma (1978a), for example, distinguishes between three approaches to dependency, namely the American Marxists, the Latin American structuralists who wanted to extend the United Nations Economic Commission for Latin America and the Caribbean's (ECLAC/CEPAL) analysis (for example, Furtado and Sunkel), and those that did not (for example, Cardoso). Both Cardoso (1973) and Lall (1975) make similar categorizations, but for slightly different reasons. For example, Cardoso splits dependency studies into analysis that critiques obstacles to national development and discusses how they can be overcome (the 'diffusion model'), analysis that incorporates analysis of international capitalism in its monopolistic phase (e.g. Baran and Sweezy), and Cardoso's own approach to dependency as a historical-structural process. Whereas Lall's categorization is fairly similar, his categorization is based on the degree to which development of the periphery is considered to be possible within the framework. It is also common in the literature to make a distinction between neo-Marxists and structuralists (e.g. Kay 1989).

Insights From and Debates Within the Latin American Structuralist Tradition

Structuralist dependency theory in Latin America builds on the work of Raúl Prebisch (1950), Celso Furtado (1956) and Anibal Pinto (1969) at CEPAL. A central point for the Latin American structuralists was that the countries of the periphery were structurally and institutionally different from the industrialized countries of the centre, thus rendering orthodox economic theory inapplicable. The theoretical approach is founded on the idea that imperialism has perpetuated the uneven development of metropolitan and peripheral countries.[6]

Prebisch's assertion that there was something fundamentally different about developing countries and how they were inserted into the international economy was novel in the 1940s (Love 1980). While Prebisch is best-known for pointing out that countries in the periphery face unfavourable terms of trade for their primary commodity exports, he argued from the beginning that the 'fundamental economic problem of Latin America lies in increasing its real per capita income by virtue of an increase in productivity' (Prebisch 1950: 8). Therefore, Ocampo and Parra (2003) maintain that too much attention has been given to the terms of trade debate, displacing attention from other relevant factors that Prebisch and Singer had noted. For example, Singer (1950: 476) advocates for industrialization because it generates strong technological externalities and other indirect benefits such as 'its general effect on education, skill, way of life, inventiveness, habits, store of technology, creation of new demand, etc.'

Prebisch (1950) and Singer (1950) also argued that the changing terms of trade between developed and developing countries reflected differences in the market structure between the periphery and the core, with the industrial markets of the core countries being more oligopolistic, and the primary goods markets of the periphery countries being more competitive. Prebisch therefore found that while workers in advanced countries can absorb real economic gains in the booms, their wages do not fall proportionally during the downturn. Meanwhile, as workers are not well organized in the periphery, they are the ones that tend to absorb most of the system's income contraction. Thereby, trade would become a vehicle for uneven development and the 'changing terms of trade a reflection of the distribution of market and pricing power' (UNCTAD 2016: 129). This point on rigidity of the centre's wages made by Prebisch was later to be picked by Samir Amin (1974: Vol. 1, 83–84).

It is worth noting that the terms of trade debate is in no way settled, and the long-term direction of the terms of trade between the core and periphery is still under investigation (e.g. Reinert 1980; Ocampo and Parra-Lancourt 2004; Caraballo and Jiang 2016). There is a growing body of evidence that supports this insight that declining terms of trade may be associated not so much with what a country is exporting, as with the institutional and economic structure of the less-developed countries (UNCTAD 2016). For example, the United Nations Conference on Trade and Development (UNCTAD) finds that the commodity terms of trade have worsened to a greater extent for man-ufacturing-exporting developing economies compared with developing econ-omies as a group, between 1980 and 2014 (partly because of some developing economies benefiting from the commodity boom in the 2000s). UNCTAD (2016: 130) therefore argues that manufacturing in developing economies has 'taken on the features of primary commodities in the global trade regime as a source of structural disadvantage'.

A 'new dependency' emerged in the 1960s that builds on Prebisch and Singer, but that is more focused on technological-industrial dependence characterized by big capital in hegemonic centres and the significance of the rise of multinational corporations (see e.g. dos Santos 1970), as well as financial dependency and cultural dependency (Chilcote 1974).[7] Within the financial dependence view, the recurrent external debt crises of the periphery are a central characteristic of centre–periphery interactions. In this view, it is the lack of finance, in particular foreign finance and the limits imposed by balance-of-payments constraints, that leads to low levels of growth (Vernengo 2006). Because technological development is believed to result from the ability to expand demand, it is a result and not a cause of the development process. In a world with quite open capital accounts, peripheral countries would be forced to keep interest rates high to attract capital and avoid capital flight. Therefore, peripheral countries are not able to pursue countercyclical policies in the same way that central countries can.

Furtado (1959) was arguably the most influential structuralist thinker on issues of colonialism and culture.[8] Furtado defined demand as cultural colo-nization, by which he meant that the elite and upper middle class avidly buy goods that are consumed by the affluent in the advanced countries (Furtado 1973). Other structuralist work on cultural dependency includes that of Juan Corradi (1971) on the culture and ideology adopted by local elites; and Corradi (1971), Quijano (1971) and Lalive d'Epinay's (1971) studies of ways that dependency relates to ideologies such as developmental nationalism and developmentalism. Meanwhile, Silva Michelena and Sonntag (1970) and Sunkel (1969) consider how the university system contributes to maintaining dependency (a debate which was recently been revisited through the debates on decolonizing the university).

Cardoso (1973) criticizes the *dependistas* before him to assume a lack of dynamism in dependent economies, and for assuming that imperialism unifies the interests of dominated nations. In Cardoso and Faletto's (1979) seminal book *Dependency and Development*, they argue that 'associated dependent development' is possible within capitalism. This approach has later been labelled a 'historical-structural approach' (Evans 2009) because of its emphasis on a dialectical relationship between external factors and a range of internal factors, such as the economic organization of production and class relationships of the specific countries being studied.

Insights From and Debates Within Neo-Marxist Dependency Theories

André Gunder Frank (1967) popularized the neo-Marxist approach to dependency theory, largely building on Baran and Sweezy.[9] Baran's (1957) *The Political Economy of Growth* is usually considered to be the origin of the Marxist dependency tradition (for example, by Palma 1978b), although there were several Latin American Marxists who made similar arguments in the 1940s, such as Bagú (1949). This tradition further laid the foundations for the work by Samir Amin, Arghiri Emmanuel, Patnaik and Patnaik, and others.

There is vast debate both within the neo-Marxist framework and between the classical Marxist and neo-Marxist approaches to dependency, as evidenced by a whole special issue of Latin American Perspectives dedicated to 'Issues of Theory in Dependency and Marxism' in 1981 (Chilcote 1981).[10] Baran (1957) challenged the stageist view of some of his Marxist contemporaries who believed that the developed nation showed the underdeveloped 'the image of its own future' (Marx 1967: 8–9). Foster (2013) traces the work of Baran back to the efforts of the early Communist International (Comintern) under the leadership of Lenin to formulate a theory of imperialism that captured the full dimension of the imperialist exploitation of developing countries. As Baran was born and educated in Russia, he was well aware of these debates, which influenced his own theoretical work. Indeed, Lenin (1967) inspired many dependency theorists to incorporate imperialism into their analysis, often through the lens of monopoly capitalism (e.g. Baran and Sweezy 1966; Amin 1974; Foster 2013).

Baran (1957) argues that since foreign capital tends to control domestic markets, the periphery enters straight into the monopolistic phase of capitalist development. The surplus extracted by monopoly capital, therefore, might be reinvested in productive activities, but not in the host country. A central distinction between competitive capitalism and monopoly capitalism, according to the neo-Marxists, is that while in competitive capitalism profits arise from the production process, in monopoly capitalism profits can also arise due to the possession of monopoly power, and therefore they can arise from the exchange process as well (Sawyer 1988).[11]

Frank (1967) extends the ideas of Baran to explain the historical (under) development of Latin America since the 16th century, drawing on the concrete historical development experiences of Chile and Brazil. The persistence of what Frank calls the 'underdevelopment-generating contradiction of capitalism' (ibid.: xi) is evident in all the case studies. As with Baran and Frank, the only political solution that he saw which could break the circle of dependency was a revolution; this is no more explicit than in Frank's (1969) *Latin America: Underdevelopment or Revolution*.

Frank and Baran agree that it was the extension of capitalism to the periphery that led to the core–periphery relationship, which makes capitalist development impossible for the periphery; but they depart somewhat in their historical analysis of capitalist dynamics. Baran (1957) argues that it was the way in which developing countries were incorporated into the world economy that was the problem. As many economies in the periphery still relied on large semi-feudal estates in plantation systems, he argued that when such economies entered the orbit of global capitalism they would find themselves in 'the twilight of feudalism and capitalism, enduring the worst of both worlds' (Baran 1957: 44). He argues that while capitalism helped to raise productivity dramatically in advanced countries, it was prevented from spreading to developing areas by Western political and economic domination. For Frank (1967), however, the capitalist 'development of underdevelopment' in the regions colonized by Europeans in the 16th century and onwards was the result of the incorporation of these regions into the world market and their 'subordination' to the system of capital accumulation on a world scale (Frank 1969: 27–29). In his review of Chilean history, he argues that it was capitalism with its internal contradictions that generated the underdevelopment of Chile, and not the supposed partial survival of a feudal structure, which he claims never existed there in whole or in part.

Frank's (1967) thesis is that in a chain-like fashion the contradictions of metropolis/satellite polarization penetrate the underdeveloped countries by creating an internal structure of underdevelopment. Thus, contrary to common criticism of Frank, he does not consider the only problem to be external underdevelopment,[12] but rather the imposition of capitalism itself. Frank argues that for 'the generation of structural underdevelopment, more important still than the drain of economic surplus ... is the impregnation of the satellite's domestic economy with the same capitalistic structure and its fundamental contradictions' (ibid.: 10).

This historical depiction of the historical extension of capitalism to the periphery to extract surplus has been criticized by classical Marxists and others.[13] Brenner (1977) and Laclau (1971) both argue that the (neo-Marxist) dependency school wrongly defines capitalism as a system of global exchange, thereby downplaying the relations of production. Frank (1972: 23) explicitly refers to class structures as something that 'developed in response to the predatory needs of the overseas and the Latin American metropolis', thereby locating the source of development and underdevelopment in an abstract process of capitalist expansion. By doing so, he fails to specify the particular historically developed class structures through which these processes actually work themselves out, and through which their fundamental character was determined (Brenner 1977: 91). In Brenner's view, Frank's theory then leads to the conclusion that incorporation into the world market automatically breeds underdevelopment, so the policy recommendation would then be 'autarky, rather than socialism' (ibid.: 91).[14] A more generous reading of Frank would lead to the conclusion that a viable policy option in light of his analysis may be some form of partial 'delinking' as advocated by Samir Amin.[15]

Unequal exchange is another key concept associated with the neo-Marxist dependency theorists. It was Arghiri Emmanuel and Sami Amin who popularized this concept, with modifications from Prebisch's original idea (Love 1980). Broadly, unequal exchange theories attempt to explain factor price non-equalization in the world economy, where factor price refers to the remuneration to labour or other primary non-produced factors. In the unequal exchange literature, the centre and periphery are the units of analysis of international exchange. Throughout the analysis, there is emphasis on relations of exchange rather than of production.

Versions of unequal exchange originating within the dependency tradition are often based on some concern with monopoly and centre–periphery trade relations, and this is closely connected to the idea of surplus extraction. One interpretation of unequal exchange is that it is the consequence of unequal wage rates in different areas, which produce the same commodity with the same technique and at equal rates of profit. Sutcliffe (1972: 188) points out that a key element of unequal exchange is that 'exporters in the industrialized countries possess more monopoly power than exporters of underdeveloped countries'. If the capitalists of the rich country face strong unions, but no institutional pressure to increase wages in the poor country, then at a constant rate of profit the gains from technical change in the poor country can be used to increase wages in the rich country (Evans 1975). An implication of this model is that any short-run gains in productivity may be 'bargained away' by the richer countries.

In Emmanuel's (1972) model productivity of labour is generally lower in the periphery, but the wage rate is even lower. He argues that while the productivity of the average worker in underdeveloped areas is 50–60 per cent of that of the average worker in the core, the average wage in the core is about 30 times the average wage in the periphery. The cheap labour attracts foreign investment. This phenomenon has been called 'superexploitation', which is the situation where the workers in the South are exploited by local capitalist classes and exposed to unequal exchange relations (Amin 1974; Marini 1978; Bambirra 1978). The 'superexploitation' argument is not logically in line with Marx, because this means that one could in theory say that a labourer could be exploited an infinite number of times, depending on how many times the good produced is exchanged on the market for a lower value.[16] However, in classical Marxist analysis, the exploitation happens when another class appropriates the socially produced goods at the time of production itself, and at no later stage. For Marx, class relations meant precisely the exchange of 'unequal' (different) surplus value. By focusing on the unequal exchange, the nature of market relations is prioritized over the exploitation of labour.

Shaikh takes issue with unequal exchange literature of Emmanuel (1972) and Amin (1974). In his critique of Emmanuel, Shaikh (1980) argues that two major types of transfers are to be considered. Industries with high organic compositions[17] have prices of production above direct prices,[18] while those with low organic compositions have prices of production below direct prices. This means that surplus value is transferred from industries with low organic compositions to those with high, as prices of production will deviate from direct prices (prices will not correspond to social value). On average, commodities sell at prices of production, not direct prices (see also Bettelheim 1972). Based on this reasoning, Shaikh argues that the net value transfers involved result from two types of transfers, namely intra-industry and inter-industry transfers. For any individual set of capitals, defined for example by their location, nationality or degree of development, the net transfer of surplus value will be the sum of the two effects. The interregional wage differentials therefore need not affect the net transfers of value between industries or between capitals within an industry. This means that there will not necessarily be a net transfer of surplus value between regions.

Amin (1974), on the other hand, argues that periphery exports are characterized by the dual structure that Shaikh also observes, with high organic composition producers in modern sectors co-existing with low organic composition producers in other sectors. While Amin assumes an equalization of profits both across industries and within industries, Shaikh (1980) argues that in reality competition forces all producers to sell at the same price, meaning that producers having different efficiencies will have different unit costs but the same selling price, and therefore different rates of profit. So, within an industry, individual profit rates will generally differ, while competition of capitals equalizes average profit rates across industries. Amin (1974: 57) overlooking this detail leads him to claim that his treatment of the subject constitutes a strong argument in support of Emmanuel's view of unequal exchange. However, Shaikh argues that had Amin not made this mistake, he would have been led to the opposite conclusion: namely, that there is no necessary tendency for a net transfer of value from the periphery to the core.

It does not follow from Shaikh's reasoning that wage differences are of no consequence for individual capitals. For capital located in the periphery, the lower wage will mean more surplus value extracted from a given number of workers, and thereby higher profits. And for high organic composition capitals in the periphery, their already higher profitability arising from their higher efficiency is further enhanced by lower regional wages. For the low organic composition capitals in the periphery, low wages offset their low productivity and can therefore perpetuate backward methods of production. Furthermore, in the foregoing analysis, Shaikh (1980) does not argue that transfers of surplus value do not in fact exist. Rather, he demonstrates that these transfers, if and when they do exist, are in themselves phenomena of international uneven development, not its major causes. Their significance – indeed, their net direction – must be assessed in the light of this understanding. There is an international division of labour, but that division is not the cause of underdevelopment. Rather, it is an effect of real competition on an international scale (see also Shaikh 2016). The transfers of value emerge as secondary phenomena, not the primary cause of underdevelopment.

In relation this this discussion, Brenner (1977) famously refers to Frank and Wallerstein's approach as 'neo-Smithian', by which he means a reliance on a definition of capitalism that implicitly derives from the doctrines of Smith (rather than Marx). The aspect of Smith that neo-Marxists built on is the idea that the essence of capitalism was the development of the division of labour and extension of exchanges among producers involved in ever more specialized work. This understanding of capitalism is based on its development of market relations rather than production relations. Furthermore, Brenner (1977: 67) argues that development is something much more than simply a transfer of surplus from the periphery to the core, leading to underdevelopment in the former and development in the latter. Marx himself showed that concentration and centralization were immanent tendencies of capitalist development, fostered by the competition of capitals. Shaikh (1980) therefore argues that the notion of monopoly actually 'stems from orthodox theory, whose analysis is located in the sphere of circulation and refers to the ability of individual capitalists to control and influence the conditions of purchase and sale'. Grossman (1979) makes a similar observation, noting that transfers of the surplus value produced in the less-developed country take place within the sphere of circulation in the world market; but went on to study how these transfers took place in a very precise manner between Cuba and North America (Grossman 1979). However, classical Marxian analysis is located primarily in production and reproduction. Here, it is not the will of individual capitalists, but the limits imposed upon them by sets of relations of production, that define the capitalist mode of production. As classical Marxists tended to see the difference in organic composition of capital as the principal cause of unequal exchange, they critiqued scholars such as Emmanuel and Amin for focusing merely on the symptoms of a deeper problem (Bettelheim 1972; Grossman 1979). While disagreements were rampant, as Dussel (2001: 208) sees it, 'what was gained in that debate is that it is necessary to look at the difference in average national wages as well as the difference between the organic composition of national capitals, which is extremely important'. Notably, the debate which one could have expected to play out among dependency theorists in the wake of Brenner's (1977) devastating critique did not follow.

Marx himself did not argue that social relations of production or unequal trade relations should be seen as mutually exclusive categories, as both are important to understand uneven development. For example, competition between capitalist nations is not in opposition to the exploitation of one class by another, but can rather be 'perfectly well articulated alongside it' (Dussel 2001: 213). Indeed, in his discussion of competition and its impact of extraction of surplus value in dependency theory, Dussel (2001: 219) constructively puts the theoretical problem as follows:

> we can say that there is 'theoretical space' in Marx's strict discourse for this question which is so central to Latin American social sciences. Not only is there space – it was explicitly traversed by Marx himself. However, it requires our continuing it theoretically. (It is erroneous to think that Marx completed the theoretical discourse and it is only up to us to apply it.)

In other words, there is still further theoretical development and exploration to be done. This may indeed be why the discussion of Marx's role in dependency theory is still central in the contemporary revival of dependency theory (e.g. Felix 2021; Martins 2021; Osorio 2021; Prado 2021; Rubbo 2021).

External Critiques of Dependency

Beyond the intense internal discussions within dependency theory, there were serious external critiques of the tradition too.[19] While the debt crisis of the 1980s is often thought to discredit structuralist dependency theory, the rise of East Asia is often considered to be in contradiction with neo-Marxist analysis, as it illustrated that late development is, in fact, possible in global capitalism. Other common critiques are that neo-Marxist dependency theory is not rooted in rigorous application of Marxist economic theory, and that it is not rooted in rigorous deductive theory (Booth 1985). It has also been criticized for being 'mechanico-formal' and therefore static and ahistorical (Palma 2016).

The debates between Marxists have included many attacks on Baran and Sweezy's concept on monopoly capitalism (e.g. Semmler 1981). For example, while Baran argues that advanced countries are experiencing monopoly capitalism, which is thought to raise prices (in relation to costs) and restrict output, he recognizes that the share of profits did not rise over the five to seven decades associated with monopoly capitalism that he is studying, and that the wage share remained constant in this period (Baran 1957: 56). However, as Kaldor (1958) points out, this contradiction is left completely unexplained.[20]

Frank's work has been acknowledged as perhaps not being the strongest version of neo-Marxist dependency theory, even by Frank (1974) himself, and has received a lot of critique. Critics have found Frank's description of class structure as being overly schematic (e.g. Henfrey 1981; Chilcote 1974), and his analysis has been criticized for being static, as he does not demonstrate or discuss in depth how forms of dependency have changed over time. His description of the concept of dependency has been criticized for not being operational, and for lacking a clear definition (e.g. Lall 1975). Although Frank argues that he addresses several of these problems in later work (e.g. Frank 1972, 1974), the issues of class dynamics are arguably still not comprehensively addressed (Henfrey 1981).

Although Weeks (1981) argues that Marxist theory and dependency theory are separate theories with different intellectual origins, and that they are largely incompatible, the exposition of the theories in this chapter suggests otherwise. The degree of compatibility will depend on which dependency theory and which Marxist theory. Both traditions are rich, and full of overlapping theoretical debates.

DEPENDENCY THEORY'S RELEVANCE FOR UNDERSTANDING UNEVEN DEVELOPMENT TODAY

Despite arguments about the dependency tradition being outdated, this chapter argues that the research programme is of particular relevance for understanding the recent changes that we see in the global economy, such as globalization of production and global financialization (building on Kvangraven 2021). Considering how the COVID-19 pandemic is exacerbating inequalities in the world also points to the usefulness of a dependency research programme that takes such inequalities as a starting point.

In terms of production, we have seen developing countries integrate deeply into global value chains (GVCs). However, how industry is structured globally still reproduces relations of dependence, which left workers in developing countries especially exposed during the pandemic. Rather than increased efficiency (Grossman and Rossi-Hansberg 2008) and flattening of the world (Friedman 2005), the spread of GVCs is associated with rigid power imbalances (Durand and Milberg 2019) and deep vulnerabilities (Suwandi 2019) for those at the bottom of the hierarchy. While many developing countries have moved into manufacturing, it has mostly been into just-in-time manufacturing, which is characterized by relatively low-skilled and low-tech work, and a heavy reliance on companies concentrated in the centre.

China, in contrast to many peripheral countries exploring unsophisticated, standard products with little potential for upgrading, has made significant advances in terms of upgrading within GVCs. However, even though China has massively expanded its manufacturing exports based on its integration into GVCs, the expansion has involved a strong dependence on foreign direct investment (FDI), denationalization of the export-oriented manufacturing sector, and relatively low levels of domestic innovation in exports (Ferrarini and Scaramozzino 2015). Therefore, Fischer (2015) makes the argument that even the development of China and its integration into GVCs can be fruitfully understood through a lens of peripherality. Meanwhile, Macheda and Nadalini (2020) argue that a dependency theory framework such as that of Samir Amin can be a fruitful starting point to understand how the Chinese economy subordinated the domestic market to the logic of internal development. When studying global production through a dependency research programme, it is necessary to pay attention to the institutional context of the chains, the role of the state, the extent of delinking, analysis of ownership and how power is exerted in the chain, and a concern for world-historical processes that shape opportunities for inclusion and exclusion in global development (Neilson 2014).

In terms of finance, again, COVID-19 laid bare the periphery's vulnerability to financial cycles generated by the centre, which was a key insight highlighted by dependency theorists (Lampa 2021). The reversals of capital flows at the height of the financial turmoil at the beginning of the pandemic led to the largest reversal of capital flows ever recorded. This prompted UNCTAD – a UN organization established by one of the forefathers of dependency theory, Raúl Prebisch – to propose the establishment of an international body to oversee developing-country debt relief programmes in the wake of COVID-19. What is more, the emerging work on subordinate financialization is important for understanding how financialization affects the periphery in ways that change, but do not challenge, its relationship to the centre (see Bonizzi et al., Chapter 15 in this book). Musthaq (2021) demonstrates how dependency theory can be extended to account for global financialization, and how Samir Amin's conceptualization of imperialist rent can be particularly helpful to account for the hierarchical nature of global monetary and financial relations. While emerging markets have certainly financialized in a variety of ways that lead to new dependencies, there are important ways in which many peripheral economies experience more continuity than novelty in terms of the ways in which they are integrated into global finance (Koddenbrock et al.

2020). This is an area with much potential for further theoretical and empirical exploration within a dependency research programme (Alami et al. 2021 try to elaborate how such a research programme on international financial subordination might be approached).

GOING FORWARD: AVENUES FOR FURTHER THEORETICAL DEVELOPMENT

As I have argued in this chapter and elsewhere, the key tenets of dependency theory – a global historical approach, theorizing of the polarizing tendencies of global capitalism, a focus on structures of production, and a focus on the specific constraints faced by peripheral economies – remain important for understanding inequalities in global production and finance. This means learning from the dependency theorists of the past, but not applying their concepts dogmatically. It also means that there will be, as there always has been, debate within the research programme, given that different scholars inevitably theorize differently about the polarizing tendencies of capitalism. Within the research programme, there is space for theorizing from a series of theoretical vantage points, including Marxist, structuralist, Keynesian and institutionalist.

In the spirit of non-dogmatism, and with a view to pushing the research programme forward, it is important to recognize the limits and weaknesses of dependency theory and to explore how to address them. For example, one key theoretical weakness in Frank and others is the focus on the symptoms of dependency without rigorously theorizing the mechanisms. As Dussel (2001: 203) puts it:

> I would say that many economists, historians, and sociologists share the error of examining dependency not as an international social relation and a transfer of surplus value between total national capitals of different organic composition, in the framework of competition in the world order, but through its particular forms or merely by means of aspects that are secondary phenomena. They thus confuse the essence with the appearance.

Thus, with such an analytical frame in mind, it is not sufficient to refer to dependency as a condition (e.g. dos Santos 1970) or a situation (Cardoso and Faletto 1979). Indeed, descriptive approaches that aim primarily at uncovering the symptoms of dependence technically fall outside the dependency research programme as defined by Kvangraven (2021), as they do not explicitly theorize about the polarizing nature of the global economy that gave rise to uneven development in the first place.

Even Frank (1981) himself noted that an explicit theory of dependence was necessary and that it had yet to be formulated. As Dussel (2001) points out, Frank's work does not build on fundamental theoretical categories (for example, value, price of production, transfer of surplus value), but this is arguably the case for other dependency theorists too. Because of this theoretical confusion in parts of the dependency literature, the dependency tradition has generally been critiqued for being circular and tautological (e.g. Lall 1975).

Another key weakness to be addressed is the mechanic nature of some dependency theory (in particular neo-Marxist strands), which arguably leaves relatively little room for agency. While uneven development cannot be explained solely by studying the local level and individual actors, Johnson (1981: 112) points out that theory can also move to the other extreme version, resulting in 'structuralist superdeterminism', which fails to account for complex interrelations of international and national forces throughout history. As Cardoso (1977: 21) once wrote, some dependency theorists are under the 'blissful illusion that their findings can remove from history all its ambiguities, conjectures, and surprises'. Indeed, a key strength of the dependency research programme is that it historicizes and contextualizes unequal and exploitative relations between classes in the centre and periphery, which is essential for understanding uneven development.[21]

Furthermore, another key theoretical and methodological question underlying these discussions about dependency is the national question. As many dependency theorists analyse how the nation-state is subordinate in a global hierarchy (and implications for balance-of-payment constraints, the trade imbalance, lack of competitiveness, technological capabilities, and so on), the tradition has been critiqued for focusing too much on the nation-state as a unit of analysis (Blaney 1996; Evans 2009; Palma 2016). Although many dependency theorists have preferred to highlight domestic units of analysis (Cardoso and Faletto 1979), or even global units such as the global working class (Marini 1973), to what extent the national level is a helpful unit of analysis to grapple with in anti-colonial scholarship is an old and legitimate question that dependency scholarship must deal with. Indeed, it dates to Marx's 'List critique' of 1845, where Marx dismisses List's proposal to protect German industry from free trade as bourgeoise ideology (Szporluk 1988; Pradella 2014). Szporluk (1988) argues, however, that Marx was strongly influenced by List, given that his position evolved to open for the possibility that perhaps a case could be made for the existence of a 'relatively progressive national bourgeoisie' in a 'developing country' struggling against 'imperialism' (Marx's speech on free trade, cited in Szporluk 1988: 41). This latter insight, which accepts some of the premises of List's analysis, although perhaps as a temporary solution, resonated with many anti-colonial politicians and scholars during the colonial and post-colonial era. Whether economic development can be conceived of as a national project, whether socialist or not, has remained an important political and methodological question for dependency theorists, given their theorizing from the vantage point of subordinate nations in a hierarchical global economy.

Other theoretical or conceptual weaknesses that have been identified with regard to dependency theory have to do with the lack of intersectional analysis, given the strong emphasis on class. Although some parts of the dependency literature do explore racial inequalities (Casanova 1965; Cotler 1967; Stavenhagen 1965; see also de Oliveira 2021b on the intersectional potential of Bambirra and Marini), gender is rarely discussed (Scott 1995, 2021). The dependency research programme would benefit from building further on this work to consider how racism and sexism shape the structures of production, and how this affects constraints to development in the periphery.

As Edwards (2020: 160) points out, the Black radical tradition originally emphasized that 'global capitalism is dependent upon worldwide exploitation of racialized masses through colonial relations'. In that sense, this tradition can be considered a precursor to dependency theory, but with a focus on race, class and colonial domination as organizing structures for exploitation. As the 'mainstream' of the dependency tradition does not consider race relations, and the Black radical tradition has tended to pay less attention to capitalism as an international system of the subjugation of racialized workers over time, there is much scope and potential for a renewal of dependency analysis coupled with insights from the original insights of Du Bois (1935/1992), Rodney (1982), and others. Edwards (2020) outlines the fruitful insights that can be gained from such a coupling, including how attending to race can improve our understanding of the character and orientation of the domestic capitalist class, the race–class structures that follow from settler colonialism, how race is often constitutive to the production of a cheap labour force, how racial structures shape agrarian classes, how race is key for understanding and assessing middle-class interests and alliances, and how analysis of racialized ideologies and racial solidarities and conflicts can enable us to better understand the relationship between the state and the domestic capitalist class.

More generally, it is pertinent for any analysis of uneven development within a dependency framework to be wary of establishing 'laws' of dependency or of exploitation. By establishing laws, we lose sight of the historical, political and institutional specificities of uneven development. By establishing laws, we remove room for local, national or regional agency by social groups. Dependency theory may be part of a vast and at times confusing field of contradictory views. If we are to bring dependency theory back into economic analysis, we must unpack the precise meaning of the different concepts that make up the different strands of dependency. However, with clarity on these elements, the research programme on dependency can open up fruitful ways of understanding contemporary manifestations of uneven development, such as globalized production, international financial subordination and global intersectional inequalities.

NOTES

1. According to Scopus data, there was a dip in publications mentioning dependency theory between 1985 and 2000, before a boom in publications took place from 2000 to 2021. Felipe Antunes de Oliveira presented this data in a tweet on 10 November 2021. Available here: https://twitter.com/Faobr/status/1458391811370754052 (accessed 9 December 2021).
2. Ajl (2020), Ghosh (2021), Musthaq (2021), Ndlovu-Gatsheni (2021), Kvangraven et al. (2021), Pérez (2021), Scott (2021) and Sylla (2021).
3. Bichir (2021), Castro (2021), Felix (2021), de Oliveira (2021a), Katz (2021), Kaysel and Mussi (2021), Martins (2021), Osorio (2021), Paulani (2021), Prado (2021), Raposo et al. (2021), Rubbo (2021) and Wasserman (2021).
4. Love (1980) traces the origin of the terms 'centre' and 'periphery' back to Werner Sombart (1928: xiv–xv), who wrote about the need to 'distinguish ... the central capitalist nations from a mass of peripheral countries viewed from that center; the former are active and directing, the latter, passive and serving'. However, Sombart did not develop this theory further, and Prebisch was the first to construct a theoretical framework explicitly based on centre–periphery analysis.
5. The debate about Canadian staple theory is interesting, given that it is going on within the Global North as it investigates how Canada is dependent on the United States in particular. See Easterbook and Watkins (1984) for an overview.
6. For more in-depth discussion of structuralist theory, see Palma (1987) or Bielschowsky (2009).
7. The neo-Marxist work of Frank has also been called 'new' dependency, so this term has different meanings in different contexts.
8. Rather than using Prebisch's term 'periphery', Furtado used 'colonial structure' to describe Latin American nations and to specifically emphasize the legacy of the colonial period.
9. The work of Baran, Sweezy and Frank also had important ramifications in the works of Theotônio Dos Santos, Marini, Anibal Quijano and Bambirra, thus illustrating that the dichotomy American/Latin American is somewhat misleading (Vernengo 2006).
10. There is also, for example, the 'modes of production' approach to Marxist dependency theory, which argues that the capitalist mode of production has different tendencies and functions depending on its stage of development, and that the nature of capitalism which dominates the international system can influence the kind of capitalism that comes to dominate in specific societies in any given historical period (e.g. Chinchilla and Dietz 1981).
11. The distinction between competitive capitalism and monopoly capitalism may not be as sharp as is often suggested. For example, in the classical Marxian view the equalization of the profit rate is only a tendency; while the monopoly capital view does allow entry to occur, for example by mistakes of the established firms. The consequence is that 'in one case it is recognized that profit rates may change only slowly while in the other case the profit rates may change somewhat over time' (Sawyer 1988: 69).
12. This criticism is explicit in Kay (1975).

13. For example, Kaldor (1958: 164) argues that Baran (1957) raises important questions, but also makes 'far-reaching generalizations on insufficient and selected evidence'.

14. Perhaps with this dilemma in mind, Baran (1957: 403) saw 'monopoly capitalism and imperialism in the advanced countries and economic and social backwardness in the underdeveloped countries [as being] intimately related, represent[ing] merely different aspects of what is in reality a global problem'. He considered the necessary solution to be a socialist transformation of the advanced countries, as this would not only lead to progress in the West, but also enable 'the peoples of underdeveloped countries to overcome rapidly their present condition of poverty and stagnation'.

15. By delinking, Amin does not mean autarky. What delinking means to him is an attempt to compel the system to adjust to your needs, rather than simply going along with having to unilaterally adjust to the needs of the core (see Amin 1987, or the interview with him in Kvangraven 2017).

16. In the first volume of *Capital*, Marx discusses the futility of comparisons between different degrees of exploitation in different nations, and the methodological problems such a debate entails (see also Johnson 1981; Leys 1977).

17. The Marxian term 'composition of capital' is defined as the ratio of constant capital (capital invested in plant, equipment and materials) to variable capital (capital invested in the labour costs involved in hiring employees).

18. If a commodity sells at its direct price, the value of the price of the commodity is identical to the value of the commodity itself. In other words, the direct price of a commodity is the price at which the amount of abstract labour embodied in the gold bullion represented by that price is exactly equal to the amount of abstract labour embodied in that commodity.

19. See, for example, Leys (1977), Taylor (1979) and Weeks (1981), in addition to Shaikh and Brenner. Frank (1974) also discusses various critics, ranging from the critics on the right, to critics on the Marxist left and critics on the new left.

20. Baran tries to get out of the dilemma in a few different ways, such as referring to the role of unions (Baran 1957: 58), but while he in one sentence suggests that trade union policies offset the pressures of monopoly capital, in another sentence he denies that trade unions have any power to affect wages (Kaldor 1958: 166).

21. While Cardoso's 'associated dependent development' approach seemingly escapes some of the critiques of structuralist dependency theory as being deterministic, it is also worth considering whether he has gone too far in the opposite direction in his analysis of national conditions. As his analysis is inductive, through concrete situations, rather than through a fixed theory, he runs the danger of exchanging the determinism and generalizations of Frank and others for merely empirical descriptions. While the descriptions may be factually more accurate, they may not be clearly guided by theory and clear analytical concepts (see also Henfrey 1981).

REFERENCES

Ajl, Max. 2020. 'The hidden legacy of Samir Amin: delinking's ecological foundation', *Review of African Political Economy* 48(167): 82–101.

Alami, Ilias, Carolina Alves, Bruno Bonizzi, Annina Kaltenbrunner, Kai Kodddenbrock, et al. 2021. 'International financial subordination: a critical research agenda', Greenwich Papers in Political Economy No. 33233.

Amin, Samir. 1974. *Accumulation on a World Scale: A Critique of the Theory of Underdevelopment* (2 vols). New York: Monthly Review Press.

Amin, Samir. 1987. 'A note on the concept of delinking', *Review* (Fernand Braudel Center) 10(3): 435–444.

Bagú, Sergio. 1949. *Economía de la sociedad colonial*. Buenos Aires: El Ateneo.

Bambirra, Vania. 1978. *Teoria de la dependencia: una anticritica*. Mexico City: Ediciones Era.

Baran, Paul. 1957. *The Political Economy of Growth*. New York: Monthly Review Press.

Baran, Paul. and Paul Sweezy. 1966. *Monopoly Capital – An Essay on the American Economic and Social Order*. New York: Monthly Review Press.

Bettelheim, Charles. 1972. 'Theoretical comments', in Arghiri Emmanuel, *Unequal Exchange: A Study of the Imperialism of Trade*. New York: Monthly Review Press, pp. 271–322.

Bichir, Maíra Machado. 2021. 'Fascism and dependency in Latin America in the thinking of Theotônio dos Santos', *Latin American Perspectives*. https://doi.org/10.1177/0094582X211059153.

Bielschowsky, Ricardo. 2009. 'Sixty years of ECLAC: structuralism and neo-structuralism', *Cepal Review* 97: 171–190.

Blaney, David. 1996. 'Reconceptualizing autonomy: the difference dependency theory makes', *Review of International Political Economy* 3(3): 459–497.

Booth, David. 1985. 'Marxism and development sociology: interpreting the impasse', *World Development* 13(7): 761–787.

Brenner, Robert. 1977. 'The origins of capitalist development: a critique of neo-Smithian Marxism', *New Left Review* 1(104): 25–92.

Caraballo, José G. and Xiao Jiang (2016) 'Value-added erosion in global value chains: an empirical assessment', *Journal of Economic Issues* 50(1): 288–296.

Cardoso, Fernando Henrique. 1973. *Notas sobre estado e dependencia*. Sao Paulo: Centro Brasileiro de Análise e Planejamento (Caderno 11).

Cardoso, Fernando Henrique. 1977. 'The consumption of dependency theory in the United States', *Latin American Research Review* 12(3), 7–24.

Cardoso, Fernando Henrique and Enzo Faletto. 1979. *Dependency and Development in Latin America*. Los Angeles, CA: University of California Press.

Casanova, Pablo Gonzalez. 1965. 'Internal Colonialism and National Development', *Studies in Comparative International Development* 1(4): 27–37.

Castro, Lucas Crivelenti e. 2021. 'Brazilian Dependent Capitalism Under the Hegemony of Financialized Capital', *Latin American Perspectives*. https://doi.org/10.1177/0094582X211053011.

Chilcote, Ronald H.1974. 'Dependency: a critical synthesis of the literature', *Latin American Perspectives* 1(1): 4–29.

Chilcote, Ronald. H. 1981. 'Issues of theory in dependency and Marxism', *Latin American Perspectives* 8(3): 3–16.

Chinchilla, Norma Stoltz and James Lowell Dietz. 1981. 'Toward a new understanding of development and underdevelopment', *Latin American Perspectives* 8(3–4): 138–147.

Corradi, Juan. 1971. 'Cultural dependence and the sociology of knowledge: the Latin American case', *International Journal of Contemporary Sociology* 8(January): 36–55.

Cotler, Julio. 1967. 'The mechanisms of internal domination and social change in Peru', *Studies in Comparative International Development* 3(12): 229–246.

dos Santos, Theotonio. 1970. 'The structure of dependence', *American Economic Review* 60(2), 231–236.

Du Bois, W.E.B. 1935/1992. *Black Reconstruction in America*. New York: Athenaeum.

Durand, Cédric and William Milberg. 2019. 'Intellectual monopoly in global value chains', *Review of International Political Economy* 27(2): 404–429.

Dussel, Enrique. 2001. *Towards an Unknown Marx – A Commentary on the Manuscripts of 1861–63*. London and New York: Routledge.

Easterbook, Tom W. and Mel H. Watkins (eds). 1984. *Approaches to Canadian Economic History*. Montreal: McGill-Queen's University Press.

Edwards, Zophia. 2020. 'Applying the black radical tradition: class, race and a new foundation for studies of development', in Barry Eidlin and Michael McCarthy (eds), *Rethinking Class and Social Difference*. Bingley: Emerald Publishing.

Emmanuel, Arghiri. 1972. *Unequal Exchange: A Study of the Imperialism of Trade*. New York and London: Monthly Review Press.

Evans, David. 1975. 'Unequal exchange and economic policies: some implications of the neo-Ricardian critique of the theory of comparative advantage', *Institute of Development Studies Bulletin* 6(4): 28–52.

Evans, Peter. 2009. 'From situations of dependency to globalized social democracy', *Studies of Comparative International Development* 44(4): 318–336.

Felix, Gil. 2021. 'On the concept of the reserve army of labor in Ruy Mauro Marini', *Latin American Perspectives*. https://doi.org/10.1177/0094582X211045402.

Ferrarini, Benno and Pasquale Scaramozzino. 2015. 'The product space revisited: China's trade profile', *World Economy* 38(9): 1368–1386.

Fischer, Andrew. 2015. 'The end of peripheries? On the enduring relevance of structuralism for understanding contemporary global development', *Development and Change* 46(4): 700–732.

Foster, John Bellamy. 2013. 'Introduction to the second edition of The Theory of Monopoly Capitalism', *Monthly Review* 65(3): 107–134.

Frank, André Gunder. 1967. *Capitalism and Underdevelopment in Latin America*. New York: Monthly Review Press.

Frank, André Gunder. 1969. *Latin America: Underdevelopment or Revolution*. New York: Monthly Review Press.

Frank, André Gunder. 1972. *Lumpenbourgeoisie: lumpendevelopment*. New York: Monthly Review Press.

Frank, André Gunder. 1974. 'Dependence is dead, long live dependence and the class struggle: an answer to critics', *Latin American Perspectives* 1(1): 87–106.

Frank, André Gunder. 1981. *Crisis in the Third World*. New York: Holmes & Meier.

Friedman, Thomas L. 2005. *The World Is Flat: A Brief History of the Twenty-first Century*. New York: Straus & Giroux.

Furtado, Celso. 1956. *Uma Economia Dependente*. Rio de Janeiro: Ministerio da Educacao e Cultura.

Furtado, Celso. 1959. *Formação econômica do Brasil*. Rio de Janeiro: Fundo de Cultura.

Furtado, Celso. 1973. 'The concept of external dependence in the study of underde-velopment', in Charles K. Wilber (ed.), *The Political Economy of Development and Underdevelopment*. New York: Random House.

Ghosh, Jayati. 2021. 'Interpreting contemporary imperialism: lessons from Samir Amin', *Review of African Political Economy* 48(167): 8–14.

Grossman, Gene M., and Esteban Rossi-Hansberg. 2008. 'Trading tasks: a simple theory of offshoring', *American Economic Review* 98(5): 1978–1997.

Grossmann, Herschel. 1979. *La leyde la acumulación yel derrumbe del sistema capitalista*, México: Siglo XXI. (Translation from *Das Akkumulations- und Zusammenbruchsgesetz des kapitalistischen Systems*, New York: B. Franklin, 1970.)

Heller, Patrick, Dietrich Rueschemeyer and Richard Snyder. 2009. 'Dependency and development in a globalized world: looking back and forward', *Studies in Comparative International Development* 44(4): 287–295.

Henfrey, Colin. 1981. 'Dependency, modes of production, and the class analysis of Latin America', *Latin American Perspectives* 8(3–4): 17–54.

Johnson, Dale L. 1981. 'Economism and Determinism in Dependency Theory', *Latin American Perspectives* 8(3/4): 108–117.

Kaldor, Nicholas. 1958. 'The Political Economy of Growth by Paul A. Baran', *American Economic Review* 48(1): 164–170.

Katz, Claudio. 2021. 'The cycle of dependency 50 years later', *Latin American Perspectives*. https://doi.org/10.1177/0094582X211018475.

Kay, Geoffrey. 1975. *Development and Underdevelopment: A Marxist Analysis*. New York: Macmillan.

Kay, Geoffrey. 1989. *Latin American Theories of Development and Underdevelopment*. London: Routledge.

Kaysel, André and Daniela Mussi. 2021. 'Francisco Weffort and the dependency theory: populism, class, and nation', *Latin American Perspectives*. https://doi.org/10 .1177/0094582X211052016.

Koddenbrock, Kai, Ingrid Harvold Kvangraven and Ndongo Samba Sylla. 2020. 'Beyond financialisation: the need for a longue durée understanding of finance in imperialism', *OSF Preprints*. DOI: 10.31219/osf.io/pjt7x.

Kufakurinani, Ushehwedu, Ingrid Harvold Kvangraven, Frutoso Santanta and Maria Dyveke Styve (eds). 2017. *Dialogues on Development – Dependency Theory*. New York: Institute for New Economic Thinking.

Kvangraven, Ingrid Harvold. 2017. 'Samir Amin', in U. Kufakurinani, I.H. Kvangraven, F. Santanta and M.D. Styve (eds). *Dialogues in Development – Dependency Theory*. New York: Institute for New Economic Thinkings.

Kvangraven, Ingrid Harvold. 2018. 'Unpacking and repackaging dependency theory', *Essays on Global Development, Trade and Finance*. Ann Arbor, MI: ProQuest LLC.

Kvangraven, Ingrid Harvold. 2021.'Beyond the stereotype: restating the relevance of the dependency research programme', *Development and Change* 52(1): 76–112.

Kvangraven, Ingrid Harvold, Maria Dyveke Styve and Ushehwedu Kufakurinani. 2021. 'Samir Amin and beyond: the enduring relevance of Amin's approach to political economy', *Review of African Political Economy* 48(167): 1–7.

Laclau, Ernesto. 1971. 'Feudalism and capitalism in Latin America', *New Left Review* 1(67): 19–38.

Lalive d'Epinay, Christian. 1971. 'Cultura y dependencia en América', *Cuadernos de la Realidad Nacional* 7(March): 33–50.

Lall, Sanjaya. 1975. 'Is dependence a useful concept in analysing underdevelopment?', *World Development* 3(11/12): 799–810.

Lampa, Roberto. 2021. 'Capital flows to Latin America (2003–17): a critical survey from Prebisch's business cycle theory', *Review of Political Economy* 33(1): 103–125.

Lenin, Vladimir. I. 1967. *Selected Works in Three Volumes*. Moscow: Progress Publishers.

Leys, Colin. 1977. 'Underdevelopment and dependency: critical notes', *Journal of Contemporary Asia* 7(1): 92–107.

Love, Joseph L. 1980. 'Raul Prebisch and the origins of the doctrine of unequal exchange', *Latin American Research Review* 15(3): 45–72.

Macheda, Francesco and Roberto Nadalini. 2020. 'Samir Amin in Beijing: delving into China's delinking policy', *Review of African Political Economy* 6 November: 119–141.

Madariaga, Aldo and Stefano Palestini. 2021. *Dependent Capitalisms in Contemporary Latin America and Europe*. Cham: Palgrave Macmillan.

Mahoney, J. and D. Rodríguez-Franco. 2018. 'What is dependency theory?', in C. Lancaster and N. van de Walle (eds), *The Oxford Handbook of the Politics of Development*. Oxford: Oxford University Press.

Marini, Ruy Mauro. 1973. *La dialectica de la dependencia*. Mexico City: Ediciones Era.

Marini, Ruy Mauro. 1978. 'Las razones del neodesarollismo (respuesta a F.H. Cardoso y J. Serra)', *Revista Mexicana de Sociologia* 40(E): 57–106.

Martins, Carlos Eduardo. 2021. 'The longue durée of the Marxist theory of dependency and the twenty-first century', *Latin American Perspectives*. https://doi.org/10.1177/0094582X211052029.

Marx, Karl. 1967. *Capital, Vol. I*. New York: International Publishers.

Musthaq, Fathimath. 2021. 'Dependency in a financialised global economy', *Review of African Political Economy* 48(167): 15–31.

Ndlovu-Gatsheni, Sabelo J. 2021. 'Revisiting Marxism and decolonisation through the legacy of Samir Amin', *Review of African Political Economy* 48(167): 50–65.

Neilson, Jeffrey. 2014. 'Value chains, neoliberalism and development practice: the Indonesian experience', *Review of International Political Economy* 21(1): 38–69.

Ocampo, Jose and María Ángela Parra. 2003. 'Terms of trade for commodities in the twentieth century', *Revista de la CEPAL* 79: 7–35.

Ocampo, Jose Antonio and Mariangela Parra-Lancourt. 2004. 'The terms of trade for commodities in the twentieth century', *CEPAL Review* 79: 7–35.

de Oliveira, Felipe de Antunes. 2021a. 'Lost and found: bourgeois dependency theory and the forgotten roots of neodevelopmentalism', *Latin American Perspectives*. https://doi.org/10.1177/0094582X211037341.

de Oliveira, Felipe Antunes. 2021b. 'Who are the super-exploited? Gender, race, and the intersectional potentialities of dependency theory', in Aldo Madariaga and Stefano Palestini (eds), *Dependent Capitalisms in Contemporary Latin America and Europe*. Cham: Palgrave Macmillan.

Osorio, Jaime. 2021. 'Assessing a proposal for updating the Marxist theory of dependency', *Latin American Perspectives*. https://doi.org/10.1177/0094582X211047906.

Palma, Gabriel. 1978a. 'Dependency: a formal theory of underdevelopment or a methodology for the analysis of concrete situations of underdevelopment?', *World Development* (6): 881–924.

Palma, Gabriel. 1978b. 'Underdevelopments and Marxism: from Marx to the theories of imperialism and dependency', Thames Papers in Political Economy no. 78(2). London: North East London Polytechnic.

Palma, Gabriel. 1987. 'Structuralism', in *The New Palgrave: A Dictionary of Economics*, New York: Palgrave Macmillan.

Palma, Gabriel. 2016. 'The "dependency school" and its aftermath: why Latin America's critical thinking switched from one type of absolute certainties to another', in E. Reinert, J. Ghosh and R. Kattel (eds), *Handbook of Alternative Theories of Economic Development*. Cheltenham, UK and Northampton, MA, USA: Edward Elgar Publishing.

Paulani, Leda Maria. 2021. 'Dependency 4.0: theoretical considerations and the Brazilian case', *Latin American Perspectives*. https://doi.org/10.1177/0094582X211060844.

Pradella, Lucia. 2014. 'New developmentalism and the origins of methodological nationalism', *Competition and Change* 18(2): 180–193.

Prado, Fernando Correa. 2021. 'The ideology of development, the Marxist theory of dependency, and the critique of the popular-democratic strategy', *Latin American Perspectives*. https://doi.org/10.1177/0094582X211043182.

Pérez, Francisco. 2021. 'East Asia has delinked – can Ethiopia delink too?', *Review of African Political Economy* 48(167): 102–118.

Pinto, Aníbal. 1969. *Concentration of Technical Progress and its Fruits in Latin American Development*. Santiago, Chile: Editorial Universitaria

Prebisch, Raúl. 1950. *The Economic Development of Latin America and Its Principal Problems*. New York: United Nations.

Quijano, Aníbal. 1971. 'Cultura y dominación', *Revista Latinamericana de Ciencias Sociales* 12(June–December): 39–56.

Raposo, Bruna Ferraz, Niemeyer Almeida Filho and Marisa Silva Amaral. 2021. 'the pattern of capital reproduction in dependent and financialized capitalism', *Latin American Perspectives*. https://doi.org/10.1177/0094582X211061878.

Reinert, Erik S. 1980. *International Trade and the Economic Mechanisms of Underdevelopment*. Cornell University.

Rubbo, Deni Alfaro. 2021. 'The diffusion and circulation of Marxism in the periphery: Mariátegui and dependency theory', *Latin American Perspectives*. https://doi.org/10.1177/0094582X211037328.

Rodney, W. 1982. *How Europe Underdeveloped Africa*. Washington, DC: Howard University Press.

Sanchez, Omar. 2003. 'The rise and fall of the dependency movement: does it inform underdevelopment today?', *Estudios Interdisciplinarios de América Latina* 14(2): 31–50.

Sawyer, Malcolm C. 1988. 'Theories of monopoly capitalism', *Journal of Economic Surveys* 2(1): 47–76.

Scott, Catherine. 1995. *Gender and Development: Rethinking Modernization and Dependency Theory*. Boulder, CO: Lynne Rienner Publishers.

Scott, Catherine. 2021. 'The gender of dependency theory: women as workers, from neocolonialism in West Africa to the implosion of contemporary capitalism', *Review of African Political Economy* 48(167): 66–81.

Semmler, Willi. 1981. 'Competition, monopoly and differentials of the profit rates: theoretical considerations and empirical evidence', *Review of Radical Political Economy* 13: 39–52.

Shaikh, Anwar. 1980. 'Foreign trade and the law of value', *Science and Society* 44(1), 27–57.

Shaikh, Anwar. 2016. *Capitalism: Competition, Conflict, Crises*. London and New York: Oxford University Press.

Silva Michelena, H. and Heinz Rudolf Sonntag. 1970. *Universidad, dependencia y revolución*. Mexico City: Siglo Veintiuno Editores.

Singer, Hans. 1950. 'The distribution of gains between investing and borrowing countries', *American Economic Review* 40(2): 473–485.

Sombart. Werner. 1928. *Der moderne Kapitalismus, III: Das Wirtschaftsleben im Zeitalter des Hochkapitalismus, erster Halbband*. Munchen: Deutscher Taschenbuch Verlag.

Stallings, Barbara. 2020. *Dependency in the 21st Century? The Political Economy of China–Latin America Relations*. Cambridge: Cambridge University Press.

Stavenhagen, Rodolfo. 1965. 'Classes, colonialism, and acculturation: essay on a system of inter-ethnic relations in Mesoamerica', *Studies in Comparative International Development* 1(6): 53–77.

Sunkel, Osvaldo. 1969. 'National development policy and external dependence in Latin America', *Journal of Development Studies* 6(October): 23–48.

Sutcliffe, Robert B. 1972. 'Imperialism and industrialisation in the Third World', in Roger Owen and Robert B. Sutcliffe (eds), *Studies in the Theory of Imperialism*. London: Longman.

Suwandi, Intan. 2019. *Value Chains – The New Economic Imperialism*. New York: Monthly Review.

Sweezy, Paul. 1942. *The Theory of Capitalist Development*. New York: Monthly Review Press.

Sylla, Ndongo Samba. 2021. 'Fighting monetary colonialism in francophone Africa: Samir Amin's contribution', *Review of African Political Economy* 48(167): 32–49.

Szporluk, Roman. 1988. *Communism and Nationalism: Karl Marx Versus Friedrich List*. New York and Oxford: Oxford University Press.

Taylor, John. 1979. *From Modernization to Modes of Production: A Critique of Sociologies of Development and Underdevelopment*. London: Macmillan.

UNCTAD. 2016. *Trade and Development Report 2016 – Structural Transformation for Inclusive and Sustained Growth*. Geneva: United Nations Conference on Trade and Development.

Valenzuela, J. Samuel and Arturo Valenzuela. 1978. 'Modernization and dependency: alternative perspectives in the study of Latin American underdevelopment', *Comparative Politics* 10(4): 535–557.

Vasconi, Tomás Amadeo. 1971. 'Dependencia y superestructura' ['Dependency and superstructure'], in T.A. Vasconi and I. Reca (eds) *Modernizacion y Crisis en la Universidad Latinoamericana* [*Modernization and Crisis in the Latin American University*]. Santiago: Centro de Esudios Socio-Economicos (CESO), Universidad de Chile.

Vernengo, Matias. 2006. 'Technology, finance, and dependency: Latin American radical political economy in retrospect', *Review of Radical Political Economics* 38(4): 551–568.

Wasserman, Claudia. 2021. 'Dependency theory in the academic self-reports of the Brasília Group', *Latin American Perspectives*. https://doi.org/10.1177/0094582X211036767.

Weeks, John. 1981. 'The differences between materialist theory and dependency theory and why they matter', *Latin American Perspectives* 8(3–4): 118–123.

7. The need to centre imperialism in studies of uneven development

Ingrid Harvold Kvangraven

The key argument of this chapter is that to grasp the global and uneven character of capitalist development, it is crucial to place imperialism at the core of our analysis. This is of particular importance at a time when the study of development has been increasingly characterized by both methodological individualism and methodological nationalism (van der Linden 2008; Pradella 2014; Kvangraven et al. 2021b). Centring imperialism, in contrast, allows us to see capitalism as a global system of exploitation, which is essential to shed light on the drivers and manifestations of contemporary global phenomena such as financialization.

To what extent imperialism plays a role in shaping uneven development today is a subject of much disagreement. There has been a wave of scholars arguing that imperialism is no longer relevant (Hardt and Negri 2000; Robinson 2005; Roy 2018), or at least not relevant for all developing countries (Chowdhury 2018). Even among radical scholars, this is a highly controversial topic, given the plethora of theories of and approaches to imperialism that exist. This chapter discusses what it means to centre imperialism, drawing on some key scholarly contributions. It does not rehash the many rich debates about specific theories of imperialism, as that has been done elsewhere, but draws in some key contributions from the past two centuries. The chapter then goes on to discuss what centring imperialism does for analyses of finance in uneven development, before demonstrating how centring imperialism is helpful for understanding the evolution of the financial systems of Ghana and Senegal in particular. Finally, the chapter concludes.

WHAT IT MEANS TO CENTRE IMPERIALISM

Imperialism has taken many forms through history. Given that the empires mutate over time and are historically and geographically contingent, there is no one theory of imperialism. Ellen Wood (2003) traces imperialism from the English domination of Ireland to its extension overseas in America, and from the 'second' British Empire in India to contemporary, United States-dominated globalization. Imperialism today, often called 'new imperialism', is clearly different from the imperialism that involved direct coercive control in the colonial period. While under colonialism the exploitation could be more directly enforced by the colonial 'masters', in a postcolonial capitalist world the compulsions are likely to be imposed by markets, but always with the assistance of extra-economic forces such as the state and international organizations. Centring imperialism in an analysis of uneven development, then, means to unpack these forms of global exploitation and trace what kind of economic and extra-economic forces that together shape economies. To do so, an analysis of capitalism as a global system of exploitation is necessary.

Marx wrote about capitalism as emerging as a world system, and refers to a process that creates a division of the world suited to centres of industries in *Capital* Vol. I. In *Grundrisse* he wrote about his intention to deal with the 'international relation of production. International division of labor ... The world market and crises' (Marx 1993: 108).[1] In unpublished work, Marx also recognizes the 'world-polarising and ever-expanding' characteristics of capitalism, reflecting the tendency of the capital of the dominant states (Pradella 2015: 117). Furthermore, he argued that capital would also make recourse to methods of 'primitive accumulation' to expand and increase the exploitation of workers across the globe. In Marx's activism within the First International, 'he affirmed the fundamental importance of building a real solidarity between class struggles in imperialist countries and anti-colonial resistance in colonised and dependent countries' (Pradella 2015: 117). Even though they were not aware of all the ideas Marx had about imperialism, the Marxist theorists of imperialism in the 20th century developed and expanded on some of these aspects that were already present in Marx's work, and reaffirmed the centrality of the critique of imperialism at the economic and political levels in their own work (Pradella 2014, 2015).

These Marxist theorists, including Luxemburg (1913/1951), Hilferding (1910/1980) and Lenin (2000), became preoccupied with the interactions between capitalism and the non-capitalist world. The reasons given to explain imperialism – the expansion of foreign capital – were diverse and varied from one author to another (finding new outlets, decline in the rate of profit, increased competition between national capitals, and so on). Despite the rich debates and disagreements between them, many of them shared one premise: 'that imperialism had to do with the location of capitalism in a world that was not – and probably never would be – fully, or even predominantly, capitalist' (Wood 2003: 126). In other words, a non-capitalist environment was assumed, which made sense given the historical period they were writing in. Moreover, their analysis also centred on global hegemony in the context of colonial domination and war, while new imperialism studies how hegemony emerges as empire (Arrighi 1994; Wood 2003).

In the postcolonial period, the predominance of economic forms of domination makes imperialism distinct from other forms of coercion (Wood 2003). Nonetheless, the predominance of the economic imperatives in this period does not mean that capitalist imperialism can dispense with extra-economic force. In capitalism, there are two distinct, yet related, moments of class exploitation, namely the appropriation of surplus labour and the coercive power that enforces it (ibid.: 16). To understand the latter, we need to also understand the public power of the state. The state is needed in capitalism for a variety of purposes, for example to ensure that those without property are available as labour for capital, maintaining a reserve army of labour. During colonialism, this coercion involved the limiting of industrialisation in the colonies, in combination with extraction that supported industrialisation in the colonisers, thus laying the foundation for the uneven economic system that we see today, where the centre and the periphery produce qualitatively different kinds of goods (Rodney 1972; Reinert 2007). While some newly independent states were able to counter this structure through protectionist industrial policies and a favourable geopolitical environment, most postcolonial countries did not have the capacity or opportunity to do this (Reinert 2007; Kvangraven 2021).

The most basic condition of capitalist expansion beyond the limits of political and military domination, and a key foundation of new imperialism, is the imposition of economic imperatives, introducing compulsions of the market where they do not exist and sustaining them where they do (Wood 2003). Indeed, developing economies across the world have since formal independence largely been forced to open up and structure their economies to the dictates of the capitalist market, through for example structural adjustment programmes, free trade agreements and bilateral pressure. Given the weak economic and political structures of these economies due to colonial legacies, this often leaves those economies vulnerable to exploitation by imperial capital. This opening up to imperial capital entails social transformations such as, for example, the transformation of peasants into market-dependent farmers. As Wood (2003: 21) notes, 'bringing about such social transformations ... has been a major function of capitalist imperialism since its inception'.

There have been a variety of theoretical arguments made through centring imperialism. For example, some see imperialism as intrinsic to the system's need to realize unconsumed surplus at the core (Luxemburg 1913/1951); as a mode of reproducing unequal exchange (Amin 1974); as related to the need to maintain the value of money in the centre, thus imposing income deflation in the periphery (Patnaik and Patnaik 2017); as a 'new, imperialist stage of capitalist development' where the driving force is the high degree of exploitation present in export-oriented industries of developing economies (Smith 2018: 39); or as the political superstructure of monopoly capital and expanding finance (Lenin 2000).[2]

The debates within the imperialism literature are vast. While going deep into the debates is beyond the scope of this chapter,[3] there are a few fault lines that are worth highlighting. Firstly, there is the question of whether imperialism is intrinsic to capitalism or a stage of it. For example, Rosa Luxemburg (1913/1951) takes off from Marx's reproduction scheme, arguing that the capitalist system is demand-constrained given that workers are paid less than the value of their labour and capitalists consume proportionately less than workers of the surplus they receive (see also Hobson's 1902 underconsumption view of imperialism). She argues that conceiving capitalism as a closed system is unrealistic, given the system's need for the periphery to realize the unconsumed surplus at the core. Luxemburg's view of imperialism as intrinsic to capitalism stands in contrast to others who see imperialism as a stage (e.g. Foster 2010).

Another line of disagreement runs between non-Marxist theories of imperialism (e.g. Pachter 1970) that tend to associate imperialism with military expansion, therefore obscuring mechanisms through which imperialism has been internalized (Chilcote 1974). Those theories also tend to focus more on political and military explanations, rather than economic explanations. However, to complicate things further, there are also important fault lines within the Marxist theories. For example, there are those who focus primarily on economic imperatives inherent to imperialism (e.g. Patnaik and Patnaik 2016), and those who argue that more aspects beyond the economic must be considered (e.g. Fraser 2019; Wood 2003). For example, Nancy Fraser critiqued the Patnaiks' description of 'capitalism's spontaneous behaviour', given that in her view the only truly spontaneous element in capitalism is the endless drive for accumulation, and therefore that imperialism itself cannot be understood by only focusing on this economic aspect, but that other forms of control must also be taken into account.[4] Notably, she argues that expropriation may be necessary for profitable exploitation in capitalism. In doing so, she expands the traditional notions of imperialism to encompass distinct forms of oppression, including racialized accumulation, by showing how exploitation and expropriation are distinguishable, yet intertwined (Fraser 2016). Furthermore, Fraser's (2019) recognition of the intertwinement of exploitation and expropriation allows for an integration of multiple forms of oppressions, along economic, political, ecological and gendered lines, including imperial dominance. This opens a wide research agenda for ways of studying various axes of uneven development that are intertwined with imperialism.[5]

Despite the partial retreat of the state in obedience to the need of international finance and limited state autonomy under capitalism (Patnaik 2018), the territorial state remains relevant and essential for capital, even in its global form (Wood 2003). Indeed, capital's economic power has not existed without support of extra-economic force, which today is 'primarily supplied by the state' (ibid.: 5). Centring imperialism, however, forces us to go beyond 'methodological nationalism', where the national territory is taken as the primary unit of analysis, and rather focus on the international system of exploitation itself (van der Linden 2008; Pradella 2014).

Wood (2003: 3) draws parallels between the difficulty of pinning down the precise actors in the exploitative imperialist relationship, and the relationship between capital and worker. While, as a Marxist, she acknowledges that the capitalist appropriates what the labour produces, she points out that this relationship is not at all transparent and that the means by which the capitalist appropriates this labour is by its very nature 'obscure'. She points out that it is even harder today than it was in earlier colonial empires to 'detect the transfer of wealth from weaker to stronger nations', even though it is 'painfully obvious that such a transfer is taking place' (ibid.: 3–4).[6] As coercion under capitalism is exercised not only personally and directly by means of superior force, but also indirectly and impersonally by the compulsion of the market, it becomes difficult to point at particular actors, as it is the structures of the system itself that drive exploitation. Centring imperialism means identifying how these structures manifest themselves, and the constraints they impose on developing economies.

CENTRING IMPERIALISM TO UNDERSTAND THE UNEVENNESS OF FINANCE

While interest in the links between finance, imperialism and capitalism dates back to Hilferding (1910/1980), or Marx (1867) for that matter, the debate about financialization really took off in the 1980s with the deregulation of finance and the rise of outsourcing through global value chains. There is now a significant body of work concerned with how financialization reflects and shapes the patterns and pace of accumulation (van der Zwan 2014). Empirically, the relevance and spread of financialization in the developing world is closely associated with the globalization of international capital flows (Akyüz 2013), the integration of national financial systems (Chesnais 2016), as well as the rise of neoliberalism (Duménil and Lévy 2011).

In Alami et al. (2021) we argue that to understand the challenges posed by international finance for developing economies today, it is necessary to see international financial subordination as a persistent and structural phenomenon related to developing economies' unequal historical integration into a hierarchical world economy. The important implication is that international financial subordination 'is not only a phenomenal expression of the crisis-ridden dynamics of accumulation, it is also a function of relations of empire and imperialism' (Alami et al. 2021: 12). The research agenda presented in Alami et al. builds on insights from an emerging body of literature that considers the contemporary role of finance in uneven development, including work drawing on structuralist, post-Keynesian, Marxist, dependency theory, institutionalist and critical international political economy traditions (e.g. Seabrooke 2007; de Paula et al. 2017; Purcell 2018; Dafe 2019; Bonizzi et al. 2019; Koddenbrock 2020; Tilley 2020; Gadha et al. 2021; Musthaq 2021; Raposo et al. 2021). Studying financial and monetary processes in the light of colonial legacies is also a way of responding to recent calls from postcolonial studies to better integrate the role of colonialism in social theory (e.g. Bhambra 2020).

An example of how imperialism can be placed at the centre of studies of global and uneven financialization is the innovative work of Musthaq (2021), who updates Samir Amin's conceptualization of 'imperialist rent' and the role of the peripheral state in perpetuating subordination. Amin's concept of 'imperialist rent' is derived from the idea of monopoly rent, associated with the dominance of a handful of corporations across all sectors (Amin 2019). Monopolies differ from other corporations in their ability to extract surplus value at a higher rate, which Amin dubbed imperialist rent, when the difference in wages between labour across nations is greater than the difference between their productivities, resulting in the superexploitation of labour in the periphery (see Higginbottom 2014 and Cogliano et al. 2021 for contemporary applications). Amin (2019) also described this phenomenon as global labour arbitrage. While this may have made sense at the time when Amin was originally formulating his ideas, Musthaq (2021) argues that the concept, which was originally tied to labour, requires a re-examination in the context of contemporary financialization. Drawing further on Amin's (2008) observation that an elite 'finance-oligopoly' benefited from price differences across national economies, Musthaq (2021) connects the theory of imperialist rent to financialization. As higher interest rates are offered in the global periphery, compared to the centre, there is also the potential for imperialist 'financial arbitrage' (see also Billingsley 2006; Jones 2016). The role of world money is central for the imperial power's dominance in a system of imperial financial arbitrage. Indeed, the currency at the top of the international hierarchy enjoys privileges such as 'seigniorage benefits, cheap savings and credit, and freedom from payment disciplines' (Musthaq 2021: 21). The growing responsiveness of capital movements to monetary policy in advanced countries worsens the situation for the countries in a subordinate monetary position in the global economy.[7]

While the work of Musthaq (2021) demonstrates aptly the utility of centring imperialism in the study of global monetary and financial relations, unpacking the historical evolution of such imperialist relations can deepen our understanding of financialization further. The empirical findings from my work studying the evolution of financial systems in Ghana and Senegal, co-authored with Kai Koddenbrock and Ndongo Samba Sylla (see e.g. Koddenbrock et al. 2020; Kvangraven et al. 2021a), suggest that much of the financialization literature today fails to account for the colonial histories of finance, and that centring imperialism is key for understanding how finance operates in Ghana and Senegal today. In an African context, the extractive nature of the colonial financial regime and its impact on contemporary economies were documented by Nkrumah (1965), Amin (1974), Pouemi (1980 [2000]), and others. Nkrumah and Amin both considered the neocolonial structures of the postcolonial banking sectors, which in turn limited the possibilities for autonomous industrialization and domestic investment. In line with this, we show that in both cases, the separation of the financial from domestic production is the result of political as well as economic domination, and that the extractive orientation of both production and finance endured throughout the colonial and postcolonial periods (Koddenbrock et al. 2020). While the postcolonial governments were able to partially reverse some of these structures right after independence (especially in Ghana), the crisis of the 1970s onwards undid those reversals through pressures to liberalize, privatize and deregulate.

We found that in Senegal, the Banque de l'Afrique Occidentale (BAO) was not at all oriented towards financing indigenous entrepreneurs or diversifying the colonial productive structure, and in 1949 it devoted 92 per cent of its resources to financing export and import activities (Koddenbrock et al. 2020; see also Dieng 1982). Furthermore, merchant firms lobbied aggressively against private property in land, to prevent local farmers from obtaining credit for agricultural production (Bernards 2019). Indeed, centring imperialism is important here to draw attention to the ways in which the colonial banking system worked in tandem with colonial business in the interest of colonial capital, and to the detriment of indigenous populations.

Similarly, it is impossible to understand the Ghanaian financial system without seeing it in light of the British Empire, as strong links were forged between the British colonial government, British industrialists and British finance in the City of London at that time (Koddenbrock et al. 2020; see also Cain and Hopkins 1987). Indeed, the early period of mining investments in Ghana took place in a period of financial expansion of the City as British domestic manufacturing was experiencing a decline. What is more, the establishment of the West African Currency Board in 1912 effectively amounted to an extension of the British Empire, with the colonial currency held at parity and readily convertible to sterling, and strict control on colonial currency issuance to eliminate the inflation risk (Koddenbrock et al. 2020; see also Narsey 2016). As in Senegal, then, the restrictive imperial setting meant that the main function of the colonial domestic banking system was to settle the accounts of the colonial economy, rather than to finance domestic investments. In short, colonialism made it possible for imperial capital to exploit colonized labour and raw materials more easily.

Since the end of formal colonialism, the nature of how imperialism has impacted upon Ghana's and Senegal's financial systems has, of course, changed. There was a period of resistance to colonial structures and anti-colonial 'world-making' in both countries in the first two decades after independence (Koddenbrock et al. 2020; Getachew 2009). However, since then, despite no direct formal control, the structural operation of finance in both countries has remained 'remarkably unaltered despite a diversification of financial instruments' (Koddenbrock et al. 2020: 10), along with the remaining colonial economic and monetary structures (Akolgo 2017; Boone 1990; Pigeaud and Sylla 2021). The crisis of the 1970s and the structural adjustment programmes (SAPs) led to a consolidation of the dominance of foreign capital in the banking systems, opening to foreign multinationals and easing regulation of them, and a tightening of banking and monetary policy that further limits public domestic investment (Kraus 2002; Koddenbrock et al. 2020). A central feature of the SAPs was precisely to impose economic imperatives and introduce compulsions of the market where they previously did not exist. While this led to a weakening of the state as a provider of active finance and public goods, it oriented the state's capacity towards facilitating the entry of global capital.

In line with the Wall Street Consensus (Gabor 2021), new financial markets are being developed in both Senegal and Ghana, such as local currency capital markets (Koddenbrock et al. 2020; see also Banse 2021). This means a stronger focus on maintaining financial stability and improving the reputation of the banking sectors among international investors. Again, this means orienting the financial sector to the interest of global capital rather than to the needs of the domestic population. What is more, we find that while the colonial period involved direct coercive financial and economic repression, inflation targeting, which is a policy actively pushed by international institutions, plays a similar role today. This repression of inflation in the postcolonial world is in line with Patnaik and Patnaik's (2017) view of the contemporary global imperialist system working to maintain the value of money in the centre. In short, again, we see that the logic of how the financial system is shaped is similar to what it was under formal colonial control, although today it is to the benefit of global capital rather than colonial capital.

Centring a historical analysis of imperialism of the financial systems of Ghana and Senegal allows us to see how the current orientation of the domestic financial sector towards foreign capital is an enduring feature that was established during the colonial period (with a short period of resistance to this structure in the 1960s and 1970s). This point is important, as even within theories of imperialism, colonial legacies may be displaced from the centre of analysis (Bhambra 2020). What is more, studying Ghana's and Senegal's financial systems in isolation from imperatives of the power of the colonizer, foreign capital and international institutions would leave us with a limited under-standing of what shapes these systems. Furthermore, these cases demonstrate that a serious engagement from a Global South perspective with the logics of imperialism can not only improve our understanding of financial systems but also 'tone down the claim of novelty found in the financialisation literature' (Koddenbrock et al. 2020: 3).

Moreover, as Wood (2003) observes, the predominance of the economic imperatives in contemporary imperialism means that the specific actors of exploitation are more difficult to identify, leaving us to study how the structures of international exploitation shape the economies of Ghana and Senegal instead, in addition to the enforcers of these structures, such as states and international organizations. Indeed, the reorientation of the state towards global capital, under pressure from international financial institutions, is absolutely essential to understand the operation of financial systems in Ghana and Senegal today (see also Mkandawire 1999). This is just one example of a 'new' phenomenon – financialization – that can benefit from historicizing and centring imperialism in order to not lose valuable information that helps us better to understand how it unfolds in the Global South.

CONCLUSION

The debates about how to conceptualize imperialism have been complex. Unfortunately, in mainstream development analysis, there has been a deep failure to acknowledge how capitalist development was dependent on colonial exploitation and appropriation, and how such exploitation and appropria-tion, though mutated, continues to operate in an imperialist global political economy. As Patnaik and Patnaik (2017: 184) put it, this seems to be the result of an 'almost deliberately cultivated ignorance'. However, with ine-qualities increasing across the world in the wake of the COVID-19 pandemic, it becomes increasingly relevant to think about how imperialism is driving such inequalities. For example, Jayati Ghosh sees the system for intellectual property rights relating to vaccines as embedded in imperialism (Polychroniou 2021).

There may not be one single theory of imperialism applicable at all times, but rather several, that correspond to multiple historical manifestations of imperialism (Roy 2018). Scholars writing about imperialism today no doubt recognize that imperial arrangements of exploitation have evolved over time, and that the measures employed to achieve imperialist goals have changed. How exactly this power structure has changed is a source of intense debate. While the traditional Marxist theorists of imperialism had their heyday in the early 20th century, the debate has neither been resolved nor ended, as research agendas centred on imperialism are still being shaped across the Global North and Global South, as is evidenced in the special issue on imperialism's relevance in *Third World Quarterly* (Narayan and Sealey-Huggins 2017) and the rich edited volume on *The Changing Face of Imperialism* by Sunanda Sen and Maria Cristina Marcuzzo (2018). There have also been a series of recent books where scholars fruitfully centre imperialism (e.g. Desai 2013; also Narsey 2016; Norfield 2016; Getachew 2019; Suwandi 2019; Patnaik and Patnaik 2021; Gadha et al. 2021).

This chapter discusses the utility of centring imperialism in the study of uneven development specifically. It charts out the ways this can be done, and what such an approach reveals about different issues in development today. To show how centring imperialism has potential for understanding modern phenomena that have evolved since the heydays of imperialism scholarship, the chapter shows how centring imperialism is particularly helpful for understanding the role of finance and financialization in shaping and perpetuating uneven development. As new financial practices and instruments continue to spread through the world, centring imperialism will help us to understand how these developments will have variegated and uneven impacts.

ACKNOWLEDGEMENTS

I am grateful to Kai Koddenbrock and Ndongo Samba Sylla for our multiple and extensive discussions on how to understand and apply theories of imperialism over the past couple of years. Those discussions have certainly shaped the exposition of this chapter. The usual disclaimers apply.

NOTES

1. Notably, Marx also contributed to colonial drain theory, as he wrote about 'an annual drain of wealth' from the English colonies to England, through a transfer mechanism built into the colonies' public finance and trade system. These writings can be found in a series of articles which Marx wrote on British rule in India in the *New York Daily Tribune* in 1853–1858 (see Guha 1968).
2. Indeed, while Lenin's work inspired many dependency theorists to incorporate imperialism into their analysis, this prompted Arrighi (1978) to complain that Marxists were increasingly creating confusion around the concept of imperialism in the 1960s, by presenting different theoretical approaches to imperialism, and all paying tribute to Lenin, regardless of whether their theoretical concepts were compatible with Lenin's theory of imperialism.
3. See, for example, Wolfe (1997), Brenner (2006), Narayan and Sealey-Huggins (2017) and Sen and Marcuzzo (2018) for reviews.
4. The debate between Nancy Fraser, Prabhat Patnaik and other Marxists, which took place at the New School, is summarized in Kvangraven (2017).
5. See, for example, Valiani (2012) and Gündüz (2013) on the imperialism of migration and caring labour; Sealey-Huggins (2017) and Ajl (2021) on the existential threat posed by climate change and how it is structured by contemporary

social relations that are imperialist in character; and Miapyen (2020) on the racial relations undergirding imperialist oil extraction and dispossession in Nigeria.

6.   Kari Polanyi-Levitt made a similar observation in an interview with Fischer (2018: 558), where she noted that unequal exchange between nations is 'so obvious that it is not even interesting'.
7.   For similar findings on the financial and monetary constraints imposed on the periphery, yet slightly different interpretations, see Vasudevan (2008), Alves (2017), de Paula et al. (2017), Alami (2020) and Lampa (2021).

REFERENCES

Ajl, Max. 2021. *A People's Green New Deal*. London: Pluto Press.
Akolgo, Isaac Abotebuno. 2017. 'Afro-euphoria: is Ghana's economy an exception to the growth paradox?' *Review of African Political Economy* 45(155): 146–157.
Akyüz, Yılmaz. 2013. *The Financial Crisis and the Global South: A Development Perspective*. London: Pluto Press.
Alami, Ilias. 2020. *Money Power and Financial Capital in Emerging Markets Facing the Liquidity Tsunami*. Abingdon: Routledge.
Alami, Ilias, Carolina Alves, Bruno Bonizzi, Annina Kaltenbrunner, Kai Kodddenbrock, et al. 2021. 'International financial subordination: a critical research agenda.' Greenwich Papers in Political Economy No. 33233.
Alves, Carolina Cristina. 2017. Stabilisation or financialisation: examining the dynamics of the Brazilian public debt. PhD thesis. SOAS University of London.
Amin, Samir. 1974. *Accumulation on a World Scale*. Hassocks: Harvester Press.
Amin, Samir. 2008. '"Market economy" or oligopoly-finance capitalism?' *Monthly Review* (April): 51–61.
Amin, Samir. 2019. 'The New Imperialist Structure.' *Monthly Review* (August): 32–45.
Arrighi, Giovanni. 1978. *The Geometry of Imperialism: The Limits of Hobson's Paradigm*. London: New Left Books.
Arrighi, Giovanni. 1994. *The Long Twentieth Century: Money, Power and the Origins of our Times*. London and New York: Verso.
Banse, Frauke. 2021. 'The German push for local currency bond markets in African Countries: a pathway to economic sovereignty or increased economic dependency?', in Maha Ben Gadha, Fadhel Kaboub, Kai Koddenbrock, Ines Mahmoud and Ndongo Samba Sylla (eds), *Economic and Monetary Sovereignty in 21st Century Africa*. London: Pluto Press.
Bernards, Nick. 2019. '"Latent" surplus populations and colonial histories of drought, groundnuts, and finance in Senegal.' *Geoforum* 126: 441–450.
Bhambra, Gurminder. 2020. 'Colonial global economy: towards a theoretical reorientation of political economy.' *Review of Political Economy* 28(2): 307–322.
Billingsley, Randall. 2006. *Understanding Arbitrage: An Intuitive Approach to Financial Analysis*. Upper Saddle River, NJ: Wharton School Publishing.
Bonizzi, Bruno, Annina Kaltenbrunner and Jeff Powell. 2019. 'Subordinate financialization in emerging capitalist economies', in Phil Mader, Daniel Mertens and Natasha van der Zwan (Eds), *The International Handbook of Financialization*. Abingdon: Routledge.
Boone, Catherine. 1990. 'State Power and Economic Crisis in Senegal.' *Comparative Politics* 22(3): 341–357.

Brenner, Robert. 2006. 'What Is, and What Is Not, Imperialism?' *Historical Materialism* 14(4): 79–105.

Cain, Peter J. and Antony Gerald Hopkins. 1987. 'Gentlemanly Capitalism and British Expansion Overseas II: The New Imperialism, 1850–1945.' *Economic History Review* 40(1): 1–26.

Chesnais, François. 2016. *Finance Capital Today: Corporations and Banks in the Lasting Global Slump*. Boston, MA: Brill Academic Publishing.

Chilcote, Ronald H. 1974. 'Dependency: a critical synthesis of the literature.' *Latin American Perspectives* 1(1): 4–29.

Chowdhury, Subhanil. 2018. 'Is imperialism a relevant concept in today's world?', in Sunanda Sen and Maria Cristina Marcuzzo (eds), *The Changing Face of Imperialism*. New York and Abingdon: Routledge.

Cogliano, Jonathan F., Roberto Veneziani and Naoki Yoshihara. 2021. 'The Dynamics of International Exploitation.' Department of Economics, UMass Boston Working Paper 2021-02.

De Paula, Luiz Fernando, Barbara Fritz and Daniela Magalhães. 2017. 'Keynes at the periphery: currency hierarchy and challenges for economic policy in emerging economies.' *Journal of Post Keynesian Economics* 40(2), 183–202.

Dafe, Florence. 2019. 'Fuelled power: oil, financiers and central bank policy in Nigeria.' *New Political Economy* 24(5): 641–658.

Desai, Radhika. 2013. *Geopolitical Economy: After US Hegemony, Globalization and Empire*. London: Pluto Press.

Dieng, Amady Aly. 1982. *Le Rôle du système bancaire dans la mise en valeur de l'Afrique de l'Ouest*. Dakar: Les Nouvelles Éditions Africaines.

Duménil, Gérard and Dominique Lévy. 2011. *The Crisis of Neoliberalism*. Cambridge, MA: Harvard University Press.

Fischer, Andrew. 2018. Debt and development in historical perspective: the external constraints of late industrialisation revisited through South Korea and Brazil. *World Economy* 41(12): 3359–3378.

Foster, John Bellamy. 2010. 'The age of monopoly-finance capital.' *Monthly Review* 61(9): 1–13.

Fraser, Nancy. 2016. 'Expropriation and exploitation in racialized capitalism: a reply to Michael Dawson.' *Critical Historical Studies* 3(1): 163–178.

Fraser, Nancy. 2019. 'Is capitalism necessarily racist?' *Political Letters*, Presidential address delivered in one hundred fourteenth Eastern Division meeting of the American Philosophical Association in Savannah, GA, on 5 January 2018.

Gabor, Daniela. 2021. 'The Wall Street Consensus.' *Development and Change* 52(3): 429–459.

Gadha, Maha Ben, Fadhel Kaboub, Kai Koddenbrock, Ines Mahmoud and Ndongo Samba Sylla (eds). 2021. *Economic and Monetary Sovereignty in 21st Century Africa*. London: Pluto Press.

Getachew, Adom. 2019. *Worldmaking after Empire: The Rise and Fall of Self-Determination*. Princeton, NJ: Princeton University Press.

Guha, Amalendu. 1968. 'Karl Marx and the drain theory.' *Journal of the Gokhale Institute of Politics and Economics* 10(3-4): 477–495.

Gündüz, Zuhal Yeşilyurt. 2013. 'The feminization of migration: care and the new emotional imperialism.' *Monthly Review*, 1 December.

Hardt, Michael and Antonio Negri. 2000. *Empire*. London: Harvard University Press.

Higginbottom, Andy. 2014. '"Imperialist rent" in practice and theory.' *Globalizations* 11(1): 23–33.

Hilferding, Rudolph. 1910/1980. *Finance Capital: The Study of the latest Phase of Capitalist Development.* London: Routledge & Kegan Paul.

Hobson, John Atkinson. 1902. *Imperialism: A Study.* New York: Cosimo Classics.

Jones, Campbell. 2016. 'The world of finance.' *Diacritics* 44(3): 30–54.

Koddenbrock, Kai. 2020. 'Hierarchical multiplicity in the international monetary system: from the slave trade to the CFA Franc in West Africa.' *Globalizations* 17(3): 516–531.

Koddenbrock, Kai, Ingrid Harvold Kvangraven and Ndongo Samba Sylla. 2020. 'Beyond financialisation: the need for a longue durée understanding of finance in imperialism.' *OSF PrePrints.* DOI: 10.31219/osf.io/pjt7x.

Kraus, Jon. 2002. 'Capital, power and business associations in the African political economy: a tale of two countries, Ghana and Nigeria.' *Journal of Modern African Studies* 40(3): 395–436.

Kvangraven, Ingrid Harvold. 2017. 'Is "imperialism" a relevant concept today? A debate among Marxists.' *Developing Economics* 21 May.

Kvangraven, Ingrid Harvold. 2021. 'Beyond the stereotype: restating the relevance of the dependency research programme.' *Development and Change* 52(1): 76–112.

Kvangraven, Ingrid Harvold. Kai Koddenbrock and Ndongo Samba Sylla. 2021a. 'Financial subordination and uneven financialisation in 21st century Africa.' *Community Development* 56(1): 119–140.

Kvangraven, Ingrid Harvold, Maria Dyveke Styve and Ushehwedu Kufakurinani. 2021b. 'Samir Amin and beyond: the enduring relevance of Amin's approach to political economy.' *Review of African Political Economy* 48(167): 1–7.

Lampa, Roberto. 2021. 'Capital flows to Latin America (2003–17): a critical survey from Prebisch's business cycle theory.' *Review of Political Economy* 33(1): 103–125.

Lenin, Vladimir. 2000. *Imperialism the Highest Stage of Capitalism.* New Delhi: LeftWordbooks.

Luxemburg, Rosa. 1913/1951. *The Accumulation of Capital.* London: Routledge and Kegan Paul.

Marx, Karl. 1867. *Das Kapital – Kritik der politischen Oekonomie.* Hamburg: Verlag von Otto Meisner.

Marx, Karl. 1993. 'The method of political economy', in *Grundrisse, Foundations of the Critique of Political Economy.* London: Penguin.

Miapyen, Buhari Shehu. 2020. 'The capital, state and the production of differentiated social value in Nigeria.' *Identities.* DOI: https://doi.org/10.1080/1070289X.2020.1785182.

Mkandawire, Thandika. 1999. 'The political economy of financial reform in Africa.' *Journal of International Development* 11: 321–342.

Musthaq, Fathimath. 2021. 'Dependency in a financialised global economy.' *Review of African Political Economy* 48(167): 15–31.

Narayan, John and Leon Sealey-Huggins. 2017. 'Whatever happened to the idea of imperialism?' *Third World Quarterly* 38(11): 2387–2395.

Narsey, Wadan. 2016. *British Imperialism and the Making of Colonial Currency Systems.* Basingstoke: Palgrave Macmillan.

Nkrumah, Kwame. 1965. *Neocolonialism: The Last Stage of Imperialism.* London: Thomas Nelson & Sons.

Norfield, Tony. 2016. *The City – London and the Global Power of Finance.* London and New York: Verso.

Pachter, Henry. 1970. 'The problem of imperialism.' *Dissent* 17(September–October): 461–488.

Patnaik, Prabhat. 2018. 'Reflections on contemporary capitalism', in Sunanda Sen and Maria Cristina Marcuzzo (eds), *The Changing Face of Imperialism*. New York and Oxford: Routledge.

Patnaik, Utsa and Prabhat Patnaik. 2016. *A Theory of Imperialism*. New York: Columbia University Press.

Patnaik, Utsa and Prabhat Patnaik. 2021. *Capital and Imperialism: Theory, History, and the Present*. New York: Monthly Review Press.

Pigeaud, Fanny and Ndongo Samba Sylla. 2021. *Africa's Last Colonial Currency: The CFA Franc Story*. London: Pluto Press.

Polychroniou, C.J. 2021. 'The World Trade Organization Is Threatening Vaccine Equity and Climate Goals – An Interview with Jayati Ghosh.' *Global Policy Journal*, 1 June.

Pouemi, Joseph Tchuindjang 1980. [2000]. *Monnaie, servitude et liberté: La répression monétaire de l'Afrique*. Paris: Menaibuc.

Pradella, Lucia. 2014. 'New developmentalism and the origins of methodological nationalism.' *Competition and Change* 18(2): 180–193.

Pradella, Lucia. 2015. 'Imperialism and capitalist development in Marx's Capital.' *Historical Materialism* 21(2): 117–147.

Purcell, Thomas F. 2018. 'Hot chocolate: financialized global value chains and cocoa production in Ecuador.' *Journal of Peasant Studies* 45(5–6): 904–926.

Raposo, Bruna Ferraz, Niemeyer Almeida Filho and Marisa Silva Amaral. 2021. 'The pattern of capital reproduction in dependent and financialized capitalism.' *Latin American Perspectives*. https://doi.org/10.1177/0094582X211061878.

Reinert, Erik. 2007. *How Rich Countries Got Rich ... and Why Poor Countries Stay Poor*. London: Constable.

Robinson, William. 2005. 'The new transnationalism and the folly of conventional thinking.' *Science and Society* 69(3): 316–328.

Rodney, Walter. 1972. *How Europe Underdeveloped Africa*. London: Bogle-L'Ouverture Publications.

Roy, Satyaki. 2018. 'Imperialism, the "old" and the "new": departures and continuities', in Sunanda Sen and Maria Cristina Marcuzzo (eds), *The Changing Face of Imperialism*. New York and Oxford: Routledge.

Seabrooke, Leonard. 2007. 'Everyday legitimacy and international financial orders: the social sources of imperialism and hegemony in global finance.' *New Political Economy* 12(1): 1–18.

Sealey-Huggins, Leon. 2017. '"1.5°C to stay alive": climate change, imperialism and justice for the Caribbean.' *Third World Quarterly* 38(11): 2444–2463.

Sen, Sunanda and Maria Cristina Marcuzzo. 2018. 'Introduction', in Sunanda Sen and Maria Cristina Marcuzzo (eds), *The Changing Face of Imperialism*. New York and Oxford: Routledge.

Smith, John. 2018. 'Marx's Capital and the global crisis', in Sunanda Sen and Maria Cristina Marcuzzo (eds), *The Changing Face of Imperialism*. New York and Oxford: Routledge.

Suwandi, Intan. 2019. *Value Chains: The New Economic Imperialism*. New York: Monthly Review Press.

Tilley, Lisa. 2020. 'Extractive investability in historical colonial perspective: the emerging market and its antecedents in Indonesia.' *Review of International Political Economy* 28(5): 1099–1118.

Valiani, Salimah. 2012. 'South–North nurse migration and accumulation by dispossession in the late 20th and early 21st centuries.' *World Review of Political Economy* 3(3): 354–375.

van der Linden, Marcel. 2008. *Workers of the World: Essays toward a Global Labor History*. Leiden, Netherlands and Boston, MA, USA: Brill.

van der Zwan, Natascha. 2014. 'Making sense of financialization.' *Socio-Economic Review* 12(1): 99–129.

Vasudevan, Ramaa. 2008. 'Finance, imperialism, and the hegemony of the dollar.' *Monthly Review* 59(11): 35–50.

Wolfe, Patrick. 1997. 'History and imperialism: a century of theory, from Marx to postcolonialism.' *American Historical Review* 102(2): 388–420.

Wood, Ellen Meiksins. 2003. *Empire of Capital*. London and New York: Verso.

8.   Imperialism: a note on the unequal treaties of modern China and Japan

Xuan Zhao

Western industrial policy towards the rest of the world—starting with England's—was very succinctly described by English economist Joshua Gee, in a bestselling 1729 work:

> That all Negroes shall be prohibited from weaving or spinning or combing of Wool, or manufacturing hats … Indeed, if they set up manufactures, and the Government afterwards shall be under a Necessity of stopping their progress, we must not expect that it will be done with the same ease that now it may. (Gee 1729: 121)

The word referring to race is not important here. It was clear at the time that England—by prohibiting export of woolen cloth from Ireland in 1699—had the same policy there (Hely-Hutchinson 1779). This English policy created a reaction in the form of pro-industrial policies in the rest of the world, and the main defender of such industrial policy against English theory and policy became German economist Friedrich List (1789–1846). In a recent book, *The Neomercantilists*, Eric Helleiner traces the industrial latecomers, dedicating a large section to Japan and China (Helleiner 2021: 201–280).

As a contemporary observer, Johann Heinrich Gottlob von Justi (1717–1771), the most important German economist in the 18th century and the epitome of the German mercantilism-cameralism, summarized that—via English theory and policy—nations such as Britain were in very advantageous positions, because they could lock their colonies into being the producers of the cheap raw materials demanded by their industries. And this was "the essential aim of those colonies" (Justi 1758: 145). Justi saw that, for several centuries, this economic imperialism was practiced only by the Europeans, and that their deeds "cannot be recalled without making human nature tremble" (Justi 1762: 321). Justi tried to evoke self-questioning in those European imperialists by alerting them to imagine how they would react if "the Chinese fleet appeared at the coast of Europe" and if the Chinese committed all the crimes the European did (ibid.: 324–325). But clearly the Europeans never listened to Justi's lectures carefully. Because China and Japan had long been established as strong states, Western economic dominance took a very different form here than in traditional colonialism. The economic imperialism in East Asia was embodied in what the Chinese and Japanese called 'the unfair treaties' or 'the unequal treaties' (不平等条约/不平等条約). These were the early commercial treaties between the West and China and Japan, and they came to be called 'unfair' or 'unequal' because they were not negotiated between equal partners, but rather imposed by the West on China and Japan.

Before the first unfair treaty signed in 1842, China, contemporarily under the rule of the Qing dynasty, conducted its maritime trade with European countries through a dozen licensed companies in Canton, or Guangzhou, the largest coastal city in the south (Wakeman 1978: 163–164). Before the Opium Wars of 1839–1842 and 1856–1860, China had been admired for its self-sufficiency. European mercantilists in the 17th and 18th centuries envied this self-sufficiency and raised China as the living example of the aim they chased for: an autarkical and populous economy with prosperous domestic commerce and sophisticated manufacturing industries such as silk textile and porcelain making (see Botero 1589 [1956]: 143; Hörnigk 1684 [2018]: 153; Justi 1762: 310–330). Meanwhile, Europeans had also been fascinated by the chance of penetrating the vast but nearly closed-up home market of China to seek a market for their rising manufacturing. Among them, Britain was the most enthusiastic. At first, in the 16th and 17th century, the British tried to capture the Chinese market with the products of their national industry: woolen textiles (Tan 1974: 411). However, they found that China was well satisfied with its home-spun cotton and silk, and not interested in their national products; but instead, tea—the Chinese local specialty—became the national drink of Britain starting in the eighteenth century.

In the 1770s Britain bought 33 percent of the tea exported from Canton, in the 1790s that share rose to 74 percent, in the 1800s it increased to 80 percent, and tea made up more than 90 percent of the expenditure the British East India Company (EIC) spent on Chinese goods (ibid.: 412). Britain and the EIC exhausted their means to balance this trade with British manufacturing, but they still failed. And the final solution they devised was to utilize the India-produced opium, nearly the only foreign good which the Chinese people were enthusiastic about and which could be monopolized by the EIC. Based on tea and opium, from the end of the 18th century the EIC carried out the triangle trade between Britain, China and India (ibid.: 416; Wakeman 1978: 171–172). Through this triangle trade in Asia, British merchants received the revenue which accumulated in the British domestic financial sector and became a source of capital to fund the industrializing British manufacturers (Tan 1974: 424). In this way, the opium trade with China became of national interest in Britain.

On the other side, however, the Chinese imperial government became worried and developed a growing aversion to the opium trade (but not to the

British merchants or government) (ibid.). The Emperor and his officials found that the trade brought enormous outflows of silver. In 1810s, China accumulated $26 million in foreign trade surplus, but during the years between 1828 and 1836 it lost $38 million in importation, of which the majority was opium (Wakeman 1978: 171–173). Apart from the economic devastation, imperial officials also noticed that the physical health of Chinese people was weakened by the drug, and their social morality was corrupted (ibid.: 178–181). As a result, in 1839, the Chinese Emperor approved severe actions against the opium trade and its consumption in Canton (ibid.: 185). The British national interest was therefore violated, and thereupon the First Opium War started. However, it is interesting to note that Friedrich List, the main contemporary objector to the hypocritical British free trade doctrine, actually praised contemporary China's strict repression of opium. He wrote that according to the "theory of values" advocated by the free trade economics, the opium trade was lucrative to both British exporters and Chinese importers, so it should be promoted; but luckily the Chinese officials saw its damage to the national productive forces (List 1839: 6–7). And List believed that this case served as "the differentiation of the theory of productive forces from the theory of values" (ibid.: 7). Following List's perspective, the history of China's unfair treaties started with the struggle between two nations over the extension and protection of their own national productive forces.

As a land-focused empire whose only enemy for the past 200 years had come from Inner Asia, the Chinese navy was unable to match the British. As a result, China was forced to negotiate and sign the Nanking Treaty (南京条约) with Britain on August 29, 1842. This was the first unfair treaty in Chinese history. It mainly stipulated that China was to: (1) open up Canton, Foochow, Amoy, Ningpo, and Shanghai as five free trade ports for British merchants, where British consuls were established; (2) abolish the monopoly of the licensed Canton companies on foreign trade; (3) cede Hong Kong Island to Britain; and (4) compensate the British with an indemnity of $21 million (Wakeman 1978: 212; Wang 2011: 18). More than a year later, on October 8, 1843, China and Britain signed the Treaty of the Bogue (虎门条约), which was the supplementary to the Nanking Treaty and confirmed the General Regulations of Trade (五口通商章程) released unilaterally by Britain on July 22, 1843 regarding the arrangements of China–Britain trade. The Treaty of the Bogue, or the General Regulations, mainly stipulated: (1) that the tariff rate of China's imports and exports with Britain should be no more than 5 percent of the value of the goods; (2) the extraterritoriality of Britain in China: namely, that all British subjects in China were not under the jurisdiction of Chinese laws, but under the British consuls; (3) the unilateral most-favored nation treatment of Britain; (4) permission for Britain to station gunships in all five trade ports to guarantee the implementation of the Regulations (Fairbank 1978: 221–222;

Wang 2011: 20–21). From then on, free trade was imposed on China by force: China had lost its tariff and custom sovereignty, and its defense against foreign industry was dismantled. China's import tariff rate was 5 percent of goods value at most; but in comparison, the import tariff rate of contemporary European countries was 15–60 percent of the goods value (ibid.: 20). China quickly accepted this unfair tariff system, partly because of the threat posed by British ship cannons, and partly because as a passive trader which waited for foreign traders to come to Canton, China was unaware of how high the tariff rates were in Europe (Zheng 1994 [1894]: 214). Had China had such knowledge, it would probably have not given in so easily. The overwhelming triumph of Britain over what had been seen as the all-powerful celestial empire stimulated other nations of the West. Following the pattern of Britain, in order to acquire the same privileges, the United States (US) and France successively signed unfair treaties with China in July and October of 1844.

The Nanking Treaty and the treaties that followed had already violated China's sovereignty, but merchants and industrialists of the West were still unsatisfied. They wanted to further open the Chinese market, not to be confined to only five trade ports (Wang 2011: 23). Therefore, after the first batch of the unfair treaties, Britain, France and the US were all seeking the chance to get more from China. In 1856, a French missionary was executed by the Chinese government for shielding the criminal activities of his Chinese believers, and a British merchant ship and its sailors were detained under suspicion of smuggling (ibid.). Using the excuse of these events, Britain and France again forged an alliance after the Crimean War and launched an expedition to China. Anglo-French naval forces occupied Canton in December 1857, and in May 1858 they occupied Tientsin (Tianjin), the largest coastal city in North China, less than 100 miles from Peking (Beijing), the capital city of China (Fairbank 1978: 243–249). The empire was shocked and sent envoys to Tientsin to negotiate. Meanwhile, the US and Russia also sent their ambassadors to Tientsin to require the same privileges that Britain and France were about to receive (Wang 2011: 24). In June 1858, China successively signed treaties with the US, Russia, Britain and France, in exchange for the withdrawal of foreign troops. This batch of treaties, known as the Treaties of Tientsin (天津条约), mainly stipulated that: (1) China should pay indemnity to its invaders; (2) embassies of Western states should be set up in Peking; (3) missionary actions should be free in China; (4) foreigners should be free to travel inside China; and (5) nine more trade ports were opened up: five along the coast, and four along the Yangtse River (ibid.: 24–25).

To the Chinese imperial court, the Treaties of Tientsin were merely an action to pacify the Anglo-French alliance and stop their expedition, so that it could concentrate on dealing with the Taiping Rebellion (1851–1864), the largest peasant war in Chinese history, sweeping the southern half of Chinese territory (ibid.: 24; Fairbank 1978: 252–253). In order to guarantee the validity of the treaties, Britain and France insisted that the treaty ratifications should be exchanged in Peking, but China insisted otherwise. After a series of frictions, the Anglo-French alliance restarted their expedition in 1860. In August, they occupied Tientsin again; in September, the Chinese Emperor fled the capital; and in October, Peking was occupied by the Anglo-French army (ibid.: 256–258). In October and November of 1860, China had to sign the Treaties of Peking (北京条约) with Britain, France, Russia and the US (Wang 2011: 27). Besides reconfirming the Treaties of Tientsin, the Treaties of Peking stipulated: the cession of Kowloon to Britain; opening Tientsin, the front gate of Peking, as a trade port; increased indemnity; and permission for Chinese laborers to work abroad, which essentially facilitated the existing import of slaves ("coolies") from China to the New World (Jung 2005: 690).

After the Treaties of Peking, a semi-colonial situation of China took shape: "consular jurisdiction over treaty power nationals (extraterritoriality), foreign administrative control of concession areas in treaty ports, foreign warships in Chinese waters and troops on Chinese soil, foreign shipping in China's coastal trade and inland navigation, and tariffs limited by treaty" (Fairbank 1978: 259).

The semi-colonial situation, the threat of European armies, the superiority of Western technology, the destitute economy, the suffering people, and the devastation caused by the Taiping Rebellion and other civil wars in the middle of the 19th century, all stimulated the proud Chinese Confucian literati, and after pacifying the country from peasant wars, from the late 1860s China started self-strengthening programs in order to save the Chinese political and social order through catching up with Western advanced military and industrial technologies (Kuo 1978). Through these government-initiated endeavors, new armies with modernized weapons were organized, and a modern naval fleet of ironclads was built. Investments were made in dozens of mechanized factories to supply the products of the ongoing technological revolution: textiles, iron and steel, steam engines and ships, machinery, and rifles and guns following the Western models. A merchant marine was built. New schools were established to teach modern engineering, Western military arts, and foreign languages. Government-sponsored students were sent abroad to study in foreign universities. Foreign classical texts were translated. Construction of a national telegraph and railway network was started. And the Westernized way of diplomacy was adopted. When those unfair treaties were signed, China had no knowledge about the conventional form of Western diplomacy. After Chinese ambassadors were sent to Europe, the mandarins found that those treaties were truly unfair, and they felt deeply ashamed and regretful. Apart from foreign troops on their homeland soil and the ceded territories, two issues specifically drew their attention: tariff sovereignty and extraterritoriality. Guo Songtao (郭嵩涛) (1818–1891), who was the Chinese ambassador to Britain and France during 1876–1878, noticed that the Chinese tariff rate was fixed at 5 percent, but the tariff rates of Britain, France and the US were very much higher: they could even reach 100 percent (Wang 2011: 36). Ambassador Guo's successor, Zeng Jize (1839–1890) (曾纪泽), found that in the West there was only diplomatic immunity, and Western countries did not relinquish their jurisdiction over non-diplomatic foreign subjects to foreign embassies; therefore, China had been fooled to provide indiscriminate extraterritoriality to all foreigners (ibid.: 36–37). As China started to industrialize itself, it discovered the tricks of the West, especially the trick of so-called "free trade."

On the ideological level, Chinese mercantilism started to grow because of the stimulus of the superiority of the Western economies and the disaster China had fallen into. The earliest epitome of the Imperial Chinese mercantilism was Zheng Guanying [郑观应] (1842–1921), a successful transnational merchant from Shanghai and a participant of the self-strengthening programs (Helleiner 2021: 238–245). Zheng's most famous argument was his advocacy of "commercial warfare" (商战) against the West, to protect and extend China's industries. Zheng picked the strong word "warfare" to describe China's commercial situation because he believed China's that industry and commerce were as endangered by the Western invasions as China's territory, so a warfare-like economic policy should be urgently adopted (Zheng 1994 [1894]: 238). Zheng's design of commercial warfare was typically mercantilist: trade protection, industrial education, technology transfer, reverse engineering, subsidizing entrepreneurs and inventors, promoting modern sciences and mechanization, and building laws and institutions feasible for modern industry (ibid.: 238–266). The immediate target of Zheng's commercial warfare was the unfair tariff system. As he observed, high tariffs were imposed on China's rice exported to the US, but the US's flour exported to China was tariff-free; China's silk exported to the US was charged a tariff of 50 percent of the value, but the US's silk exported to China was charged only 5 percent (ibid.: 132). Zheng said that in this situation, "even if both countries' industries were equally capitalized, their prices would not be equal", so "how can the Chinese industries not suffer?" (ibid.: 248) Zheng wanted to copy the Western tariff principle: light or zero tariffs on necessities, mainly raw materials; high tariffs (about 60–100 percent of goods values) on "the goods which usurped the profit of national industries"; and prohibition of harmful goods, such as opium (ibid.: 212). Zheng never had the chance to see his proposals implemented, but his thoughts enlightened a generation of mercantilist and nationalist Chinese economic thinkers, including Dr Sun Yat-sen (1866–1925), the father of republican China (Helleiner 2021: 246–247). During the 1860s to 1890s, the West had been quite satisfied with the existing treaty system and did not make any major new treaties.

However, in the East, Japan started on the path of imperialism just as the West, and therefore gradually became the major enemy of China. Japan and China had very similar experiences in opening themselves up to the modern world. Since the regime of Tokugawa Shogunate was set up in the early 17th century, Japan closed itself to foreign trade except for keeping Nagasaki as the only commercial port to trade, and only with China and Holland, under strict government supervision. In the 17th and 18th centuries, Japan left the Europeans with the impression that "the Japanese people lived peacefully and richly although the country had only very limited foreign trade" (Kanamori 2009: 112). Johann von Justi was very much interested in the isolated Japan. He believed that Japan was the living example of the nation with "happiness through isolation." From the cases of Japan and China, Justi concluded that when a nation's manufacturing industries were dynamic enough and its inland trade was prosperous enough to provide full employment to its people, "foreign trade is lucrative to a nation, but it is not necessary at all" (Justi 1758: 13). The cases of Japan and China were the sources of inspiration which helped German economists to form their conventional principle that manufacturing was more important to a nation's economic welfare than foreign trade.

What happened to China in the 1840s alerted the contemporary Japanese, because Japan was the second-largest country in East Asia, which meant that it would probably be the next target of the West (Jansen 1980: 340). Fukizawa Yukichi (福沢谕吉) (1835–1901)—a pioneer in the process of enlightening the opened-up and modernizing Japan—went as far as saying that Japan should "go out of Asia into Europe," lest it follow in the steps of China and Korea as another victim of Western imperialism (Sugiyama and Mizuta 1988: 14).

Compared with the experience of China, the opening-up of Japan was initiated by the US instead of Britain, with the purpose of searching for locations of supplies for US ships on the Far East sea route, instead of conquering the market for domestic industries (Beasley 1989, 261, 267–268). After several attempts at negotiation were rejected by the Japanese government, in July 1853 the US sent Commodore Matthew Perry (1784–1858) to lead a squadron of gunships to Edo Bay, the front gate of Edo (later known as Tokyo), which was the capital city of the Tokugawa regime, in order to deliver the contemporary US President's letter to the Japanese Emperor to request "friendly commercial intercourse" (ibid.: 269). Then Perry left Tokugawa Bakufu, Japanese shogun's government, some time to consider the proposal in the letter, and withdrew to the China coast for maintenance. In February 1854, Perry's squadron showed up in Edo Bay again for negotiations (ibid.: 270). The result was the Kanagawa Treaty (神奈川条約), or Perry Treaty, signed on March 31, 1854. This was the first unfair treaty in Japanese history. It stipulated that Japan would: (1) open up Shimoda and Hakodate as ports for US ships to acquire coal and other supplies; (2) help shipwrecked sailors; (3) permit a US consul at Shimoda; and (4) offer the US the most-favored nation treatment (ibid.).

Just as France and the US followed Britain to settle treaties with China after the Nanking Treaty, so Britain and Russia also followed the US to sign treaties with Japan. In October 1854, Britain and Japan signed a treaty following the template of the Kanagawa Treaty (ibid.: 270–271). In Feburary 1855, Russia also achieved its treaty which, apart from including what was already there in the Kanagawa Treaty, also divided the Kuril Islands between Russia and Japan, and opened Nagasaki for Russia (ibid.: 271).

The Kanagawa Treaty and the following treaties only gave the West a base for ship supplies and maintenance in Japan, but did not open Japan for trade, and Japanese foreign trade was still conducted through Nagasaki under government supervision (ibid.: 275). Therefore, as the tension between China and the West intensified in 1856, and the Anglo-French alliance launched the expedition to the Far East, the West decided to take the chance to further open up Japan while extending the opening-up of China. The first US consul arrived in Japan in 1856, and he was ordered to settle a commercial treaty in a similar form as the one the US received from China in 1844 (ibid.: 277). Intimidated by what was happening in China, and fearing that declining the US request would bring gunships to Edo Bay again, Bakufu agreed to negotiate in 1857 (ibid.: 278). As a result, on July 29, 1858, the Treaty of Amity and Commerce between the United States and the Empire of Japan (日米修好通商条約) was signed. The Treaty mainly stipulated: (1) that Americans were permitted to freely buy and sell without Japanese government intervention; (2) that Kanagawa, Nagasaki, Niigata, and Hyogo were opened as trade ports; (3) that trade in Edo and Osaka, respectively the largest and wealthiest metropolises in East and West Japan, was permitted; (4) that a US embassy was permitted in Edo and consuls in all opened trade ports; (5) the extraterritoriality of the US subjects; and (6) that the tariff rate on Japanese exports was fixed at 5 percent, and the tariff rate on most imports was set at 20 percent; but the tariff on raw silk, which was the most important Japanese export commodity, and other goods, were 5 percent (ibid.: 280).

Clearly, this was a treaty following the Chinese template. "Any Western diplomat who had been involved in negotiations with China would have recognized most of this" (ibid.). Just like China, Japan was forced to open trade ports, lost its trade protection and tariff sovereignty, and had to provide extraterritoriality to foreign subjects. However, it seemed that Japan was more benevolently treated by the West than China, because the treaty prohibited exporting opium to Japan, which did not exist in China's treaties, and it did not demand permission to station troops and gunships in Japanese territory. Following the US pattern, in August 1858, Japan signed similarly modeled treaties with Holland, Russia, and Britain, and in October with France (ibid.:

283). This batch of treaties was known as the Ansei Five-Power Treaties (安政五カ国条約]), and "Ansei" was the Japanese era name for the years from 1854 to 1860. This was Japan's unfair treaty system.

These diplomatic catastrophes, along with the social and economic crisis at the twilight of the Tokugawa regime, and the extended political conflict between the Bakufu and feudal lords (*daimyos*, 大名), turned to the antagonism of *daimyos* and their samurais, with the ambition of reforming Japan against the Tokugawa Shogunate. These crystalized as the movement of Sonnō Jōi (尊皇攘夷): restoring the power of the Japanese Emperor, overthrowing Bakufu, and expelling the barbarians (Jansen 1989). The movement finally led to a civil war (1868–1869). In the end, with the support of anti-Bakufu *daimyos* and reformist samurais, the Meiji Emperor restored the sovereign power of the Japanese Emperor which had been usurped by shoguns for more than 600 years.

After the Meiji Restoration, Japan started its self-strengthening movement. Stimulated by China's experience and shocked by the power of the West, Japan embraced Westernization. "The most important result of the Japanese perception of Chinese disasters was the resolve not to repeat the Chinese experience" (Jansen 1980: 342). Japan's self-strengthening movement deployed similar military and economic programs as its Chinese counterpart (Beasley 1962: 472–475). However, Japan reformed itself much more thoroughly. It created a new state administration system, introduced the compulsory education of citizens, reformed social institutions and structure, refreshed national culture, organized the national parliament, and promulgated a constitution (ibid.: 465–472, 475–482). Contemporary China never did any of this. Japanese reformers had become the actual decision-makers of the state through the Sonnō Jōi movement and the civil war, whereas Chinese reformers were only a group of provincial governors who had some weight with the central government, but still had to struggle within the framework set by traditions and conservative-minded leaders of the state.

Just like their Chinese colleagues, Japanese reformers also understood the problem of unfair treaties, and they started to solve them after the Meiji Restoration. "Attempts to secure the abolition of extra-territoriality and tariff control, both embodied in the so-called 'unequal treaties' of the late Tokugawa period, became a major theme of Japanese foreign policy after 1878" (ibid.: 482). After a series of tough negotiations, in 1894, Japan and the Western powers agreed to abolish extraterritoriality; and in 1911, after the old treaties expired, Japan retrieved its tariff sovereignty (ibid.). Japan ended its unfair treaty system much earlier than China.

Japan developed the ambition of imperialism at least from the 16th century. It dreamed of becoming a world empire by conquering Ryukyu, Korea, China, and even India. After the Meiji Restoration and overall reforms, a refreshed

Japan embarked on its long-dreamed-of path of expansion. After a series of conflicts with China over Ryukyu, Taiwan, and Korea, in 1894, the First Sino-Japanese War broke out. Surprising the world, Japan prevailed. China's intimidating fleet of ironclads was nearly annihilated and its new armies could not block the Japanese army (Hsu 1980: 106–107). As a result, China was forced to negotiate and accept a new major unfair treaty with Japan, the Shimonoseki Treaty (马关条约) signed on April 17, 1895. The treaty stipulated that China was to: (1) cease Korea's status as one of her vassal states and recognize its full independence; (2) pay a huge indemnity (more than the sum of all previous indemnities to the West) to Japan; (3) cede Taiwan and the Pescadores Islands to Japan; (4) open Chungking, Soochow, Hangchow, and Shashi as trade ports; and (5) permit Japan to open factories and engage industries in China (ibid.: 108). According to the unilateral most-favored nation treatment China had ceded to the Western powers, the West now automatically acquired the chance to directly invest in China, just as Japan. With the Shimonoseki Treaty, China was forced to open to the foreign direct investment. Chinese industrialists had to directly face the foreign factories equipped with advanced technologies in their home market.

Moreover, the catastrophe of China in the First Sino-Japanese War revealed to the Western Powers that even after self-strengthening, China was weak, just as it was in 1840, so the Western powers, who were in the last round of division of the world before the First World War, started a struggle for the partition of China (ibid.: 109–115). Their interference in China triggered Chinese people's anti-foreign movement under the patronage of government, known as the Boxer Rebellion. In order to protect their interests, major Western powers formed an alliance and invaded China in June 1900; on July 14, the Western army took Tientsin; and a month later Peking fell (ibid.: 123–125). China was forced to negotiate again, and on September 17, 1901, signed the Boxer Protocol, which provided for: (1) the punishment of the Chinese officials who were responsible for motivating the Boxer Rebellion; (2) indemnity to the Western powers; (3) apology missions to Germany and Japan; (4) the establishment of a permanent legation guard; (5) the destruction of all forts between Peking and the coast of Tientsin; and (6) permission to station Western troops in key locations around Peking (ibid.: 126–127; MacMurray 1921: vol. 1, 278–320).

These were the major unfair treaties in Chinese history, which were the pillars of China's treaty system with the West before 1949, and provided the legal framework for the other hundreds of treaties and agreements between Chinese central and local governments and foreign countries regarding more specific and detailed issues.

Unfair treaties and the two major problems caused by them—extraterritoriality and tariff sovereignty—were the central diplomatic concerns of all Chinese regimes between 1911 when the last Emperor abdicated and the Republic of China was set up, and 1949 when the People's Republic of China was established. Constant attempts had been made to resolve them. The extraterritoriality was officially abolished in January 1943, when the US and the United Kingdom (UK) tried to strengthen their alliance with China against Japan in the Pacific War (Wang 2011: 108–112). As for the tariff sovereignty, in July 1928, the US gave up the fixed tariff rate and recognized the tariff sovereignty of the Nanking KMT government, which was established in 1927 under the support of the US; but in exchange for the tariff sovereignty, China had to recognize the most-favored nation treatment of the US (ibid.: 102). Following the example of the US, Germany, the UK, France, and Japan, all made the same deal with China during 1928 to 1930 (ibid.). Therefore, although China could now decide its tariff rate, its home market was still forced to open to the West. The full retrieval of China's sovereignty in foreign trade did not happen until 1949, when the newborn People's Republic of China rejected all previous treaties and started to create a whole new diplomatic relationship with foreign countries.

The history of unfair treaties ended in China. But this episode has become a crucial component of modern Chinese political ideology. Unfair treaties branded modern Chinese minds with two universally known idioms: 丧权辱国 (lose sovereignty and humiliate motherland) and 割地赔款 (cede territories and pay indemnity), both of which summarized the unfair treaties and symbolized the worst political failure which every Chinese regime after Qing has tried its best to avoid. Unfair treaties made the Qing dynasty, which was one of the most successful conquerors and state administrators in both Chinese and global history and the creator of modern China in many aspects, a shameful age in modern Chinese minds. However, it cannot be denied that the English theory and policy summarized by Joshua Gee as the ideology behind the unfair treaties has prevailed even up to now. The British Empire died out, but its successor in many ways, the United States, still insisted on strategy to stop the progress of latecomers' industry. The world has already witnessed the ongoing exertion of this strategy. Threatened by the Chinese national industrial strategy, Made in China 2025, which aimed at building China's competitiveness in nearly all advanced manufacturing sectors, the United States openly discarded the doctrine of free trade and globalization which it had insisted on for decades, and launched a trade war against China (Dodwell 2018). And when the Chinese government was negotiating with the United States to settle a truce, the shameful history of unfair treaties of China and Japan was recalled again by the Chinese public, alerting them to stay vigilant against any possible "Joshua Gee strategy" by the advanced industrial powers (Forsyth 2019).

REFERENCES

Beasley, W.G., "Japan," in *The New Cambridge Modern History*, Vol. XI, ed. F.H. Hinsley, pp. 464–486, London: Cambridge University Press, 1962.

Beasley, W.G., "The foreign threat and the opening of the ports," in *The Cambridge History of Japan*, Vol. 5, ed. Marius B. Jansen, pp. 259–307, London: Cambridge University Press, 1989.

Botero, Giovanni, transl. P.J. Waley. *The Reason of State* (1589), London: Routledge & Kegan Paul, 1956.

Dodwell, David, "The real target of Trump's trade war is 'Made in China 2025'," June 17, 2018, *South China Morning Post*, https://www.scmp.com/business/ globaleconomy/article/2151177/real target trumps trade war made china 2025.

Fairbank, John K., "The creation of the treaty system," in *The Cambridge History of China*, Vol. 10, ed. John K. Fairbank, pp. 213–263, London: Cambridge University Press, 1978.

Forsyth, Randall W., "What China wants to avoid in trade talks: becoming the next Japan," 17 May 2019, *Barrons*, https://www.barrons.com/articles/what-china-wants -to-avoid-in-trade-talks-becoming-the-next-japan-51558139518.

Gee, Joshua, *The Trade and Navigation of Great-Britain Considered*, London: Printed by Sam. Buckley, in Amen-Corner, 1729.

Helleiner, Eric, *The Neomercantilists: A Global Intellectual History*, Ithaca, NY: Cornell University Press, 2021.

Hely-Hutchinson, John, *Commercial Restraints of Ireland Considered in a Series of Letters Addressed to a Noble Lord*, Dublin: William Hallhead, 1779.

Hörnigk, Philipp Wilhelm, transl. Keith Tribe, intro. Philipp Robinson Rössner, *Austria Supreme (if It So Wishes) (1684); A Strategy for European Economic Supremacy*, London: Anthem Press, 2018.

Hsu, Immanuel C., "Late Ch'ing foreign relations, 1866–1905," in *The Cambridge History of China*, Vol. 11, eds John K. Fairbank and Kwang-ching Liu, pp. 70–141, London: Cambridge University Press, 1980.

Jansen, Marius, "Japan and the Chinese Revolution of 1911," in *The Cambridge History of China*, Vol. 11, eds John K. Fairbank and Kwang-ching Liu, pp. 339–374, London: Cambridge University Press, 1980.

Jansen, Marius, "The Meiji Restoration," in *The Cambridge History of Japan*, Vol. 5, ed. Marius B. Jansen, pp. 308–366, London: Cambridge University Press, 1989.

Jung, Moon-Ho, "Outlawing 'Coolies': Race, Nation, and Empire in the Age of Emancipation," *American Quarterly*, 57(3), 2005, pp. 677–701.

Justi, Johann Heinrich Gottlob, *Vollständige Abhandlung von denen Manufacturen und Fabriken*, Vol. 1, Copenhagen: Rothenschen Buchhandlung, 1758.

Justi, Johann Heinrich Gottlob, *Vergleichung der Europäischen mit den Asiatischen und andern vermeintlich Barbarischen Regierungen,* Berlin, Stettin, and Leipzig: Johann Heinrich Rüdiger, 1762.

Kanamori, Shigenari, "Justi and Japan," in *The Beginning of Political Economy*, ed. Jürgen Backhaus, pp. 111–116, Erfurt: Springer, 2009.

Kuo, Ting-yee, "Self-strengthening: the pursuit of Western technology," in *The Cambridge History of China*, Vol. 10, ed. John K. Fairbank, pp. 491–542, London: Cambridge University Press, 1978.

List, Friedrich, *Das Wesen und der Wert einer nationalen Gewerbsproduktivkraft*, Berlin: Weltgeist-Bücher Verlagsgesellschaft m.b.H., 1839.

MacMurray, John V.A., *Treaties and Agreements With and Concerning China, 1894–1919*, 2 vols, New York: Oxford University Press, 1921.

Sugiyama, Chuhei and Hiroshi Mizuta, *Enlightenment and Beyond: Political Economy Comes to Japan*, Tokyo: University of Tokyo Press, 1988.

Tan, Chung, "The Britain–China–India Trade Triangle (1771–1840)," *Indian Economic and Social History Review*, 11(4), 1974, pp. 411–431.

Wakeman, Frederic, "The Canton trade and the Opium War," in *The Cambridge History of China*, Vol. 10, ed. John K. Fairbank, pp. 163–212, London: Cambridge University Press, 1978.

Wang, Dong, transl. Zhiwei Gong. *China's Unequal Treaties: Narrating National History* [中国的不平等条约：国耻与民族历史叙述], Shanghai: Fudan University Press, 2011.

Zheng, Guanying [郑观应]. *Sheng Shi Wei Yan* [Words of warning in a flourishing age, 盛世危言] (1894), Shenyang: Liaoning People's Publishing House, 1994.

PART III

Understanding mechanisms that create and
prevent inequality

9. Physiocracy, guillotines and antisemitism? Did economics emulate the wrong Enlightenment?

Andrea Saltelli and Erik S. Reinert

INTRODUCTION

In this book we have attempted to understand uneven development, paying particular attention to the history of economic thought and its legacies. Thus, our work would be incomplete if we neglected the main economic theory of the French Enlightenment: physiocracy. Stephen Pinker's (2018b) book *Enlightenment Now* has brought this period into focus again.

In our view this Enlightenment theory started the tradition that made it possible to base economic theory on far-fetched assumptions and still appear reasonable to the majority of people for a time. This was an approach that would make it possible to create theories tailor-made to fit the vested interests of specific economic groups: the interests of the feudal landlords during the Enlightenment, and of financial capital today.

Briefly we would also like to point to other problems with the French Enlightenment, which appears to be Pinker's main reference point. In 1789, Joseph-Ignace Guillotin had the idea that would lead to a very efficient way of killing people during revolutionary France. In 1793–1794 about 17 000 people – aged from 14 to 92 – were guillotined in France. Some 25 years earlier, the Italian Enlightenment scientist Cesare Beccaria in his 1764 book *On Crime and Punishment* (Beccaria 1788 [1764]), had come up with a much better idea: prohibit torture and the death penalty altogether. The different Italian version of the Enlightenment: that of Milan (see S. Reinert 2018) and that of Naples (with economists such as Antonio Genovesi and jurist Geatano Filangeri) had approaches, values and contexts very different from the French version.[1]

Antisemitism was an ugly part of the French Enlightenment. In his 1764 *Philosophical Dictionary*, Voltaire addresses the Jews: 'you are calculating animals; try to be thinking animals' (Voltaire 1824 [1764]). In the 1770s the majority of contributors to the famous *Encyclopédie* 'who were busy defending the civil rights of the black inhabitants of the Antilles, the Hurons of North America, or other tribes, forgot got to plead for the emancipation of their immediate neighbours, the Jews of France, and instead covered them with accusations and mockery' (Birnbaum 2017). On the other hand, Italy was one of the few countries at the time where Jews had no restrictions.

There is a direct connection between physiocratic economic theory and the guillotine. What we could call 'the crowning achievement' of physiocracy – the main economic theory of the French Enlightenment – was the shortage of bread in Paris that became the direct cause of the outbreak of the French Revolution. Adam Smith (1776) tells us that it is not by the goodness of the baker that we get our daily bread, but because of the baker's own self-interest. But in France in the 1770s, more money could be made by moving grain (wheat) out of the city, and making money as prices went up, than by baking bread. In other words, in opposition to Adam Smith's teachings, the logic of the market showed that there was more money to be made by not baking bread. High prices and shortage of bread created increasing discontent in Paris, and the French Revolution broke out on 14 July 1789, the day that news reached Paris that the last antiphysiocrat in power, Jacques Necker, had lost his job as Minister of Finance (Kaplan 2015). Feudalism and financial speculation not only were the two basic causes of the French Revolution, but are still, in general, the two main institutions that prevent the growth of the real economy and a fair distribution of income.

RENAISSANCE: THE MISSING PIECE IN THE PUZZLE

Some years ago, a young man known to both authors started studying economic history at the London School of Economics (LSE). He wrote home scandalized that LSE seemed to think that the history of civilization started with the Enlightenment, totally skipping the Renaissance.

We think he had a point. In Europe, the human mind was first liberated with the Renaissance. To mediaeval minds all knowledge worth having was found in the Bible and in Aristoteles. An early philosopher and natural scientist, Franciscan monk Roger Bacon (c. 1214–1292), went outside these borders. Bacon extolled experimentation so ardently that he has sometimes been viewed as a harbinger of modern science, but he was condemned to prison by his fellow Franciscans because of certain 'suspected novelties' in his teaching (Taylor 1914: II, 514–538). Bacon was an early forerunner of Renaissance values, representing practical inventions, but also what Thorsten Veblen centuries later would call 'idle curiosity'.

Modern society started with the Renaissance, when neo-Platonist ideas from the Byzantine Empire reached Florence in the early 15th century. Mankind having been created in the image of God, their duty was to also be creative

(Reinert and Daastøl 1997). As has been mentioned in the introduction to this book, the new respect for knowledge expressed itself in that the prestige that cities had previously won from stealing bodies of saints – such as Venice stealing the body of St Mark from Alexandria in AD 828 – now came from stealing the bodies of important philosophers. The body of Georgios Gemistos Plethon (who died in Greece in 1452) can now be visited in Rimini.

One important point which distinguished the Renaissance was the interest in inventions, technical knowledge and machinery. Two recent books raise this issue: *The Italian Renaissance of Machines* (Galluzzi 2020) and *Renaissance Invention* (Markey 2020). Leonardo da Vinci (1452–1518) not only produced fine paintings, but also designed irrigation canals, a prototype tank and a prototype flying machine (ornithopter). Techniques of visualization and quantification also received a momentous impulse in the Italian Renaissance (Crosby 1996).

The brief entry on 'technology' in the *Encyclopaedia of the Enlightenment* (Delon 2002: 1317–1323) informs us that few articles on technology in the paradigm-carrying *Encylopédie* of the French Enlightenment cover technology. This was the forum where the physiocrats presented their theories. Supporting the intuition of our young man at LSE, regarding technology the *Encyclopaedia of the Enlightenment* states: 'Indeed, most of the objects, systems and procedures represented in that work date back to earlier centuries, and some of them even figure in the notebooks and treatises of Renaissance engineers' (Delon 2002: 1317).

Technology, the key preoccupation of the Italian Renaissance, was marginal to the Enlightenment: 'an age of humanity, an age of rapid material progress and social upheaval of which the Enlightenment had only offered a glimpse'. Physiocracy, a French economic theory that appeared shortly before 1760, argued for the primacy of agriculture as the only source of value. Adding value to raw materials using technology and machinery was seen as 'sterile': the theory was in practice 'anti-technology'. In a large German book on the Enlightenment (*Aufklärung*), eminent German economic historian Bertram Schefold jumps all the way to Charles Babbage (1832) to find a good understanding of mechanization (Schefold 2012).

We think the young man at LSE had a point. The Renaissance was an important foundation for later human development. In the introduction to this book, we see how German historian Leopold von Ranke (1795–1886) explains how progress and economic development came to a halt in Italy with the end of the Renaissance, and progress moved northwards in Europe. Stephen Toulmin (1992) had perhaps a point when he devoted a full chapter of his *Cosmopolis* to the '17th Century Counter-Renaissance'.

ALTERNATIVE ENLIGHTENMENTS

The core idea of this book is to understand uneven development. From that point of view, it is important that, up to this point, economics had everywhere – from Ancient China to Ancient Greece and the Arab world – been part of the larger subject of philosophy. With the French Enlightenment the school of physiocracy was born. As the first economic science with a narrow horizon and a completely arbitrary assumption at its core – the idea that only agriculture created value – economics changed into a science easily manipulated by vested interests. Similarly today, economics has arbitrarily stopped distinguishing between productive capital and potentially unproductive financial capital – between what you can buy for money, and money itself – a distinction that was important from the Bible until Joseph Schumpeter. The result is the process of financialization: a relatively sharp increase in size and importance of a country's financial sector relative to its overall economy.

Economic theory during the French Enlightenment clearly favoured the vested interests of the feudal landlords, against what we could call the industrializing bourgeoisie. With a theory based on the completely arbitrary assumption that labour was void of any skills – negating the role that knowledge plays – David Ricardo (1817) managed to 'prove' that the world would become richer if England specialized in being the only industrialized country in the world, with the rest of the world supplying raw materials and buying their industrial products. All countries that are presently wealthy have, for long periods, disregarded David Ricardo's trade theory. The sad thing is that even now the recommendations of the World Bank and the International Monetary Fund are essentially based on Ricardo's trade theory, leaving still today a large part of the world population with a comparative advantage in being poor and ignorant. While new knowledge was the core of the Renaissance, Ricardo's trade theory represents its antithesis: the participants in his theory of trade possess no qualifications whatever. Not only that, Ricardo's theory of international trade – which is the main theory underlying today's capitalism – is curiously also void of capital.

Physiocracy is given disproportionally high coverage in the history of economic thought, but it was carried out in practice only in two limited geographical areas outside France: in the Duchy of Baden-Baden in Germany, and in Tuscany. Still, in Paul Samuelson's *Economics* – the textbook that formed economics for generations from 1948 onwards – key physiocrat Quesnay is one of the two lines directly inspiring Adam Smith, from whom Samuelson lets all later economics descend, including Marx (Samuelson 1976, inside back cover).

If Samuelson was the only information we had on the subject, we would have thought that Adam Smith was a follower of physiocracy. That is not the case. A contemporary report on physiocracy lists European economists into two categories, physiocrats and antiphysiocrats (Will 1782: 71–72). In England, Adam Smith ends up on the side of the antiphysiocrats.

Porter and Teich (1981) provide a useful overview of the Enlightenment in several national contexts, including Austria, the Netherlands, Russia, Scotland, Sweden and Switzerland. Jacob (2019) makes a similar *tour de force* from the point of view of religion. In such works the Scottish Enlightenment stands out as a strong and independent movement. In Scotland – in contrast to France – the Enlightenment was characterized by a thoroughgoing empiricism and pragmatism, aiming for improvement and virtue in society as a whole. No arbitrary assumptions such as those of physiocracy. Comparing Adam Smith to the other economists of the Scottish Enlightenment, we find that he was much closer to liberalism than his Scottish contemporaries. Indeed, economists in the English-speaking periphery – Ireland, Scotland and North America – tended to be protectionists rather than free traders (Reinert 2015). Two important economists of the Scottish Enlightenment – quasi-contemporaries of Adam Smith – who went against the teachings of Adam Smith, are briefly discussed below.

The writings of the Edinburgh-born James Steuart (1713–1780) can probably be seen as the highest point of mercantilism, the theory which – empirically correctly even today – claimed that a country needed manufacturing in order to be wealthy. Steuart's two-volume work published in 1767, *An Inquiry into the Principles of Political Economy*, was the first to use the term 'political economy' in a book title in English. Steuart's voluminous work was published in at least ten editions, in English, German and French, before 1850.

Another important economist of the Scottish Enlightenment was the Earl of Lauderdale (James Maitland, the 8th Earl of Lauderdale, 1759–1839). Lauderdale's *Inquiry into the Nature and Origin of Public Wealth* was published in Edinburgh in 1804,[2] Adam Smith's most important quasi-contemporary in the United Kingdom. Noteworthy points where Lauderdale takes exception to Adam Smith are: (1) economic growth owes much more to the use of machinery than to the division of labour per se; (2) demand is much more important for economic growth than savings, that is, Adam Smith's 'parsimony'; and (3) a clear distinction between public and private wealth, where parsimony may make the latter grow, but not the former.[3]

Scottish economist James Anderson (1739–1808) is credited by Schumpeter (1954: 263) as being the first to see how economic growth is a result of what Schumpeter calls 'historical increasing returns': a combination of increasing returns and innovations. These are two distinctly different factors that are perfectly separable in theory, but not in practice. Since Henry Ford's mass production technology was not available at the scale that cars were previously built, the two factors in practice become inseparable.

German economic theory during the Enlightenment[4] shows the exact opposite of the physiocratic theory. In German cameralism of the period we find a cult of manufacturing industry, not of agriculture. An important book by Johann Friedrich von Pfeiffer (1718–1787) carried the title *The Antiphysiocrat* (Pfeiffer 1780) (Figure 9.1); thus attacking the ideological enemy head on. The rest of Europe tended to do as the Germans did: supporting manufacturing rather than agriculture.

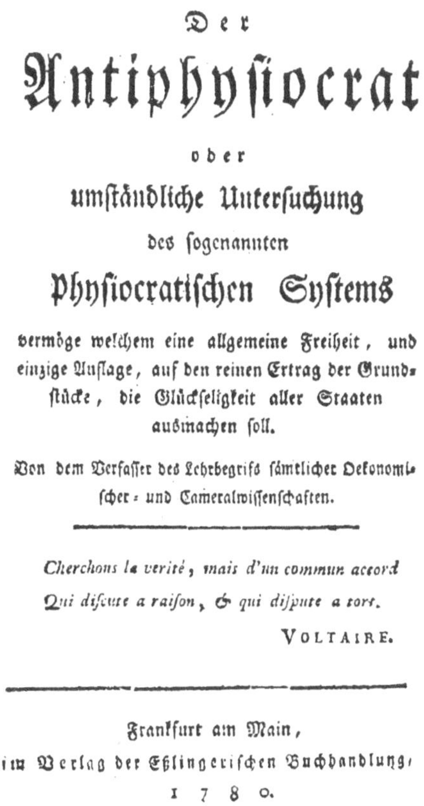

Der

Antiphysiocrat

o b e r

umständliche Untersuchung

des sogenannten

Physiocratischen Systems

vermöge welchem eine allgemeine Freiheit, und
einzige Auflage, auf den reinen Ertrag der Grundstücke, die Glückseligkeit aller Staaten
ausmachen soll.

Von dem Verfasser des Lehrbegrifs sämtlicher Oekonomi-
scher- und Cameralwissenschaften.

*Cherchons la verité, mais d'un commun accord
Qui discute a raison, & qui dispute a tort.*

VOLTAIRE.

Frankfurt am Main,
im Verlag der Eßlingerischen Buchhandlung,
1 7 8 0.

Source: Pfeiffer (1780).

Figure 9.1   *Antiphysiocracy was the idea that won the day in terms of practical policy during the Enlightenment*

We should also briefly mention the Spanish Enlightenment, which shows us an example of experience-based economics winning over vested interests. At the time, the Spanish economy was relatively backward, with the power vested in the same feudal interest as in France. The inflow of gold and silver from the New World had led to de-industrialization and inflation. The economic decadence of Spain did not occur due to a lack of competent economic advice from its native economists, says the main authority on the subject, Earl Hamilton: rather, the authorities were not keen on listening to their advice (Hamilton 1932, 1935).

The writings of Spanish economist Gerónimo de Uztáriz (1670–1732) were inspired by his military career of almost 20 years in Holland, which was under Spain until 1714. Uztáriz attended the Royal Academy at Brussels and served in the Low Countries both during his military service and later as a captain in the infantry, before becoming Prime Minister to the Spanish Viceroy of Sicily in 1705 (Hamilton 1935; Reyes 1999). His main work was the influential *Teórica y practica de comercio y de marina* (Uztáriz 1751 [1724]). The work contains many references to the wealth of the Dutch Republic, and advice on how to create a similar economic structure – with manufacturing – in Spain. Lacking official approval, the first edition had a very limited print run.

Also with Uztáriz we can observe how ideas travelled in Europe at the time. His book was translated into English, French and Italian. Uztáriz' first publication was the foreword to the 1717 Spanish translation of Huet's *Commerce de Hollande*. Uztáriz' conclusion is in line with the contemporary mainstream, completely the opposite of the later physiocracy outside France: '[Manufactures] is a mine more fruitful of gain, riches, and plenty, than those of Potosí',[5] and he presents a long list of policy measures aimed at making the Spanish economy more like that of the Dutch Republic. On our point about the Renaissance versus the Enlightenment: while Uztáriz clearly wrote during the period which we normally call the Enlightenment, one of his biographers (Wilson 1978) refers to him creating 'an intellectual foundation for the Spanish Renaissance'. 'Renaissance' being any period when technology and manufacturing comes into focus.

WHO WON THE SCIENTIFIC REVOLUTION?

In the French Enlightenment, different visions of science, knowledge and progress came to life. Among those, the vision of Rousseau appealed to a knowledge that would be at the service of a moral and social regeneration, bringing fairness where privilege and class had reigned before. An alternative vision, held by Voltaire, had a more limited programme for science, in which science was not to be mixed with ethical, political or social concerns. This tension in turns reflects a much older tension: that between the science of the crafts and that of the academies.

In his *A People's History of Science: Miners, Midwives and 'Low Mechanicks'*, Clifford D. Conner (2005) sets out to show how the history of science – often presented as the achievement of 'great minds', owes more than we normally acknowledge to the work of artisans, midwives, brewers, blacksmiths, sailors and other ordinary non-titled people. For Conner, in many circumstances the 'knowing how' of empirical crafts alimented the knowledge of 'knowing why' nurtured by academic elites.

In this long and erudite work, Conner shows how the fight between the science of craftspersons and academic science was part and parcel of a power struggle, which in the Enlightenment and the ensuing French Revolution had a moment of climax. His analysis of the prodigies of Francis Bacon first, and of Tycho Brahe and Robert Boyle later, shows how these great thinkers were at the same time creature of their time and social class, accepting as natural an order where 'low mechanicks' have no place in the progress of science.

Conner also discusses how artisans, whose names are in many cases lost, in fact performed the celebrated experiments of the titled virtuosi of natural philosophy. He tells us about the diaspora of the artisans who, following the death of Tycho Brahe in 1601, abandoned the observatory on the island of Hven in the strait between contemporary Sweden and Denmark, de facto infusing European science with a new current. For the first time, a new class of middle-class scholars became visible (Conner 2005: 352).

According to Conner, in the course of this struggle, the official science of academies became the owner of the knowledge generated by artisans from the lower classes; including with the use of patent regimes that appropriated the ownership of artisans' ingenuity. The French Revolution initially gave a voice to Rousseau's ideal of a science integrating moral and social values, and paved the way for a flourishing of artisans' associations. These openly battled against the power and the programmes of elite science, for example in contrasting Condorcet's educational plans for a 'super-academy' with absolute power of control of scientific and technological life in France. While artisans in the end obtained the patent law they demanded, the elitist tendencies of Enlightenment science – moulded on the Baconian and Newtonian ideals upheld by Voltaire – in the end prevailed. The Thermidorean period consolidated a conservative vision of science that would not disrupt existing social arrangements. This was associated to ideas of the neutrality of science and to the specialization of science into separate disciplines that persist to this day.

Thus, the Enlightenment harboured different possible scientific futures, one of which, that of a democratized science with a mission of social better-ment, did not come into being. In the end, the Enlightenment and the French Revolution set science on a different path. This led from the 'small science' of

the disinterested gentlemen philosophers who – like Boyle – preferred 'lucif-
erous' to 'lucriferous' experiments, to the academies of the 19th century. This
eventually led to the present 'big science' configuration (de Solla Price 1963),
with its power asymmetries (Ravetz 1990), convulsions and crises (Saltelli and
Funtowicz 2017).

Nobody incarnates better the optimistic vision of the Enlightenment than
Nicolas de Condorcet (1743–1794), who in the last chapter of his *Sketch for
a Historical Picture of the Advances of the Human Mind* illustrates thus his
vison of the future to come: 'All the errors in politics and in morals are founded
upon philosophical mistakes, which, themselves, are connected with physical
errors' (Condorcet 1955 [1795]: Ninth Epoch).

Thus, for Condorcet, once the Enlightenment programme has solved the
physical-philosophical problems of humanity, true progress will have been
achieved. As an example, overpopulation and war due to scarcity of resources
will not happen, because technical progress and ethical progress will go hand
in hand:

> The only foundation of faith in the natural sciences is the principle, that the general
> laws, known or unknown, which regulate the phenomena of the universe, are regular
> and constant; and why should this principle, applicable to the other operations of
> nature, be less true when applied to the development of the intellectual and moral
> faculties of man? (ibid.: Tenth Epoch)

Man will understand that his duty 'will consist not in the question of giving
existence to a greater number of beings, but happiness' (ibid.: Tenth Epoch).
This extraordinary vision of intellectual and moral vision going hand in hand,
of knowledge of the law of nature leading to moral progress, represents the
great promise of the Enlightenment to achieve 'the destruction of inequality
between different nations; the progress of equality in one and the same nation;
and lastly, the real improvement of man' (ibid.: Tenth Epoch).

THE CARTESIAN DREAM AGAIN

In describing how the vision of the Enlightenment has shaped modernity,
many authors talk about a 'Cartesian dream' (Pereira and Funtowicz 2015),
referring to Descartes' famous sentence about man as master and possessor of
nature, capable of controlling and putting to good use the forces of nature for
the betterment of man. In Chapter 4 of this book the authors, including the two
authors of the present chapter, have attempted to link the Cartesian dream to

a Ricardian dream, this latter based on the use of abstract theorems to describe economic activity. Also for Davis and Hersh, our age can be said Cartesian:

> Now the ingredients of the method as reported in Descartes' Discours de la Methode are vague except in geometry. There they have been so fruitful, extending to all of mathematics and to science in general, that it would not be a mistake to call our age and all its scientific aspirations Cartesian. (Davis and Hersh 1986: 260)

Thus mathematics – loved by Descartes for algebra and geometry, and by Condorcet for his work on decision theory algorithms – was an important element of the dream. For Alfred W. Crosby (1996), it was a particular aspect of mathematics, its capacity to permit quantification and visualization (via prospective), that was responsible for the extraordinary success of the West after the Renaissance; a thesis that Crosby illustrates with extraordinary effectiveness.

In a sense, it is difficult to blame Descartes for his inebriation with geometry and mathematics. As discussed by cognitive psychologists Lakoff and Núñez (2001), the popping up of the Greek π from circles and squares, or of Neper's e from compound interest computations, can inspire awe. How can one fail to believe that these numbers are divine, or that they attend to something fundamental and unchangeable in the writing of the book of Nature, as noted by Galileo? They point to a paradox here, in that: 'it follows from the empirical study of numbers as a product of mind that it is natural for people to believe that numbers are not a product of mind!' (Lakoff and Núñez 2001).

For the already quoted Davis and Hersh (1986: 235), only the introduction of non-Euclidean geometries challenged this dream of Divine mathematics. This discussion of mathematics and quantification may appear to be a digression from the theme treated in this chapter, were it not for the fact that understanding the project of the Enlightenment, for the good and for the bad, needs its quantification agenda. As per the bad, when when the state started measuring its subject, it did not forget the antisemitic programme of enlightenment (Hacking 1990). Much of present-day algorithmic revolution, and the present impending dystopia of surveillance capitalism (Zuboff 2019) or governance by numbers (Supiot 2017), is the most evident sign of the presence of the dream in our times (Saltelli et al. 2021a).

DIFFERENT VISIONS OF THE ENLIGHTENMENT

The classic text of critique of the Enlightenment remains to this day the work of Theodor W. Adorno and Marx Horkheimer entitled *Dialectic of Enlightenment* (Adorno and Horkheimer 1997 [1947]). Here the two authors from the School of Frankfurt set out to investigate the broken promise of enlightenment in crude terms: 'Why mankind, instead of entering into a truly human condition, is sinking into a new kind of barbarism.'

Written just after World War II and published in 1947, the book dissects the dialectic link between enlightenment and domination, and ultimately cruelty and suffering, illustrated with the lucid folly of Sade and the conflicted awareness of Nietzsche (ibid.: 81–119). As per the promises of enlightenment, 'Its herald Bacon dreamed of many things "which kings with their treasure cannot buy, nor with their force command, [of which] their spials and intelligencers can give no news." As he wished, they fell to the burghers, the enlightened heirs to those kings' (ibid.: 42).

By opening the way to market-based domination of man on man, enlightenment, empowered by a subservient science, paved the way for a return to myth, illustrated by Nazi Germany and by antisemitism: 'Anti-Semitism is a deeply imprinted schema, a ritual of civilization; the pogroms are the true ritual murders. They demonstrate the impotence of sense, significance, and ultimately of truth'.

Reflecting what happened during the French Enlightenment, the barbarism of antisemitism thus becomes the valve through which the masses, cheated by the unfulfilled promises of happiness and equality of enlightenment, can release their destructive lust. With enlightenment, science lends itself to a self-oblivious instrumentalization; it reflects hierarchy and coercion, and in its neo-positivistic version, metamorphoses the criticism of the encyclopaedists into affirmation and apology (ibid.: xii).

Coming to more recent authors, and to the issue of the legacy of enlightenment in our global governance, political philosopher John Gray (1998) notes how a 'worldwide free market embodies the western Enlightenment ideal of a universal civilization'. Both Marxian socialism and a global free market share thus the nature of delusive Enlightenment-inspired experiments in social engineering. For Gray (1995): 'The legacy of the Enlightenment project – which is also the legacy of Westernization – is a world ruled by calculation and wilfulness which is humanly unintelligible and destructively purposeless.'

Steven Shapin (2019) describes the crisis of modern science in terms of its extraordinary 'historical success in enfolding scientific inquiry and scientific findings into modern civic life, especially the practices of government and commerce', as a result of the 'asymmetric alliance between science, the state, and industry'. This integration of science into all aspects of life comes at a price. This has been described in terms of a 'new endarkenment' in the sense of an undoing of the Enlightenment (Millgram 2015), dystopias (Saltelli and Boulanger 2019), and the loss of the Renaissance element of modernity (Toulmin 1992). These and other authors variously lament the loss of understanding for oneself: making sense of things in a world increasingly complexified by technology (Millgram 2015). Other elements of the picture are the loss of knowledge as a source of emancipation and personal maturation (Lyotard 1979), rationality winning over reasonableness (Toulmin 1992), and in more recent times a new acceleration of a crisis entangling science, technology and policy (Saltelli and Boulanger 2019).

For Jerome Ravetz the rapid transformations taking place in the collective image of science correspond to the maturing of structural contradictions, among which that between science's image and science's role is the most important (Ravetz 2011). Most of the authors just quoted allude in some form or another to an undoing of the ideals of the Enlightenment.

WEAPONIZING THE ENLIGHTENMENT

Steven Pinker (2018b) also calls for a return to the Enlightenment; or, we should say, his vision of the Enlightenment's salient features. Pinker's (2018b) *Enlightenment Now: The Case for Reason, Science, Humanism and Progress* has had a mixed reception, ranging from unreserved enthusiasm to stern condemnation. This polarized reception, coupled with Pinker's candour in sharing with the reader his radical vision of salvation via a return to his enlightenment, allows us to analyse in detail precisely those problematic elements of enlightenment that are the focus of this chapter.

Bill Gates calls Pinker's book 'My new favourite book of all time.' The book is particularly appreciated by those who dislike the so-called fear-mongers (*The Economist* 2018), that is, persons who disproportionately fear technology instead of appreciating it for its gifts.

To the opponents, the purpose of Pinker's book is to reassure liberals that they are on 'the right side of history' (Gray 2018), and to endorse a Manichean vision of reason against darkness which robs the Enlightenment of its principal attributes, that of a vigilant scepticism (Riskin 2019). According to a comment in the *New York Times* (Szalai 2018):

> [Pinker] admits that the presidency of Donald J. Trump might be a 'setback' to the forward march of progress. But as long as he can consign Trump and authoritarian populism to 'a pushback of elements of human nature,' he can stay in thrall to the wonders of 'Enlightenment institutions' – and ignore the possibility that such institutions, with their blithe consolidation of power in the name of progress, might have helped to stoke such populist rage.

The academic limits of the work of Pinker are evident, as are the contradictions: 'Left-wing and right-wing political ideologies have themselves become secular religions', he notes, while pushing his own candid version of scientism, a confusing mixture where enlightenment – as Pinker defines it – can be 'called humanism, the open society, the cosmopolitan or liberal or classical liberalism' (Pinker 2018b: 4). He is at best superficial in how he interprets the thought of both friends such as David Hume, Adam Smith and Denis Diderot, and foes from Friedrich Nietzsche to the 'cultural pessimists' who treat science with scepticism. Few philosophers are spared his elemental fury, from the school of Frankfurt to the deprecated postmoderns and the scholars of science studies (ibid.: 396).

In spite of these limits, Pinker's unfettered apology for free market capitalism may be considered as mainstream, practised by what has been called 'the Davos set' (Hickel 2019). Pinker is undoubtedly on the side of techno-optimists, such as the current of the so-called ecomodernists (Shellenberger and Nordhaus 2015; Pinker 2018a), for whom technology is the best solution to the problem created by technology. To exemplify, Pinker welcomes nuclear power, genetically modified crops and geoengineering to adapt to climate change.

While Pinker considers himself 'something of a watchdog for politically correct dogma in academia' (ibid.: 138), he attacks unceremoniously the part of the same academia that he dislikes: the 'second culture', the leftist intellectuals, the ecologists, and those who burden medical and psychological research with ethical protocols (ibid.: 402).

All industrial actors, from pharma to agrochemical, from nuclear to information technologies, can find in Pinker a champion incarnating a vision of progress where these technologies must be allowed to roam free. For Pinker, decarbonization, dematerialization and densification are just around the corner, provided fearmongers and cultural pessimists can be silenced. Perhaps the main contradiction of Pinker's work is in discounting how many of today's conquests are due to the fathers of the ecological movement, and to the upholders of women's and workers' rights. When published in 1962, Rachel Carson's *Silent Spring* received the same kind of broadsides from 'defenders of DDT' that Pinker reserves for present-day ecologists. Needless to say, today Carson is considered the champion of the birth of the ecological sensibilities espoused by Pinker.

While much discussion (Hickel 2019; Lent 2018) surrounding *Enlightenment Now* is about whether we really 'never had it so good', as argued by Pinker – with the end of war, hunger, enslavement, and the world having already passed 'peak populism' (ibid.: 451) – we are concerned here with a less-discussed part of his work. The last chapters of his book are devoted to science and humanism, and it is here that we find with unexpected clarity the most sinister elements of Pinker's programme.

In an opening move, Pinker turns the tables by presenting science as cornered and under attack: 'today the beauty and power of science are not just unappreciated but bitterly resented' (ibid.: 387). He resents the positions of the 'demonizers of scientism', and 'cultural institutions [that] cultivate a philistine indifference to science that shades into contempt' (ibid.: 395), and engages in an all-out defence of science's role in eugenics, the Tuskegee experiment on syphilis, and denies the existence of social Darwinism. His target is the perceived 'anti-science humanities program', without forgetting social sciences in general. An attack on the famous 'feminist glaciology' paper (ibid.: 397) seals his theorem.

The author's true enemies are the sceptical intellectuals, the humanists and social scientists just across the corridor of his faculty building. Not the economists, though, whose effort at quantifying the real he praises (ibid.: 403–404). His 'science under siege' vision is unrealistic; but so were Ayn Rand's novels about a West collapsing under the weight of a socialist ideology. Yet these novels fortified the resolve of generations of laissez-faire economists. Pinker's candid version of scientism, his weaponization of enlightenment and his praise of the victories of neoliberalism, similarly aim to fortify the present techno-economic orthodoxy.

CONCLUSIONS

The Enlightenment strove to eliminate superstitions about nature; in the process, it enthroned superstitions about science. This superstition thrives in the present dominating neoliberal vision of world affairs. We mentioned in our analysis the important role that Enlightenment-inspired technologies of measurement and quantification played in constructing modernity. On the same ground as we should revisit our ideas about a Platonic mathematics as holding the key to the fabric of the real, without abandoning mathematics as the extraordinary creation of the human mind that it is, our affection to the ideals of the Enlightenment would need to be carefully reappraised. What is in that project that deserves preserving, and what has become a problematic legacy?

At the time of writing this chapter, the fight for the control of the public imaginary sees the values of the Enlightenment at the forefront of the battle. A short example may help here: when it comes to protecting our common environment, a new generation of self-appointed 'guardians of reason' defend science against its purported enemies by calling them anti-science, fearmongers, and the like (Foucart et al. 2020). The guardians are in fact stealth actors in a fight between corporate interests, for example in the agrochemical sectors, against activists concerned with the use of pesticides, or genetically modified substances or nuclear energy. As discussed by Foucart et al. (2020), the guardians also manage to enrol in this battle well-meaning individuals and associations, who sincerely share the vision of Pinker discussed above. These actors may fail to realize that whatever the merits or demerits of the specific technology being discussed or defended, they may happen to be manipulated in a high-level exercise of regulatory capture (Saltelli et al. 2021b). They are the ideal recipients of the theses discussed in this chapter.

Pinker's idea of the economy as a relentless forward-moving machinery ultimately relies on the simplifying assumptions by Anglo-Saxon economists as described in the Introduction and Chapter 1 in this book: the basic one being that all economic activities are qualitatively alike. Renaissance economics (Italian economist Antonio Serra 2011 [1613]) describes the simple dichotomy that produced wealth and poverty: that of increasing and diminishing returns to scale (see Reinert 1980). Pinker (2018b: 95) provides an example of the wonders of modern technology: South Indian small fishermen 'increased their income and lowered the price of fish' by using their mobile phones at sea to find the market that offered the best price that day. Chapter 10 in this book, by Sylvi Endresen, explains how diminishing returns and resulting technological retrogression had impoverished the same South Indian fishermen. The increase in income through cell phones is completely dwarfed by the decrease in catch and income caused by diminishing returns and technological retrogression.

The philosopher who Pinker seems to hate the most, Friedrich Nietzsche, explains why Pinker fails: 'There is only a perspective of seeing, only a perspective of "knowing"; and the more affects we allow to speak about one thing, the more eyes, different eyes, we can use to observe one thing, the more complete will our "concept" of this thing, our "objectivity", be' (Nietzsche 1999 [1877]). By accepting the assumptions of neoclassical economics as his only angle, Pinker fails to see qualitative differences between economic activities, between fishing in South India and producing software in the United States. By using only the angle produced by neoclassical economics – assuming all economic activities to be qualitatively alike – Pinker's analysis clearly fails Nietzsche's 'objectivity test'.

NOTES

1.   To his credit, Pinker approvingly cites Beccaria.
2.   A second revised edition appeared in 1819. Lauderdale possessed an impressive collection of books and pamphlets on economics subjects, now housed at Tokyo Keizai University Library.
3.   For a comparison of Lauderdale and Adam Smith, see Suguiyama (1996). Suguiyama had access to Lauderdale's own copy of Adam Smith's *Wealth of Nations*.
4.   Cassirer (2007) and Stackelberg (1996) provide excellent treatises on Enlightenment philosophy.
5.   Potosí, at about 4000 metres in present-day Bolivia, was the richest of all mines in the world. At the time it was the second-largest city in the world after London.

REFERENCES

Adorno, Theodor W. and Max Horkheimer (1997 [1947]), *Dialectic of Enlightenment*, New York: Verso.

Babbage, Charles (1832), *On the Economy and Machinery and Manufactures*, London: Charles Knight.

Beccaria, Cesare (1788 [1764]), *On Crime and Punishment*, Edinburgh: printed by James Donaldson.

Birnbaum, Pierre (2017), *Est-il des moyens de rendre les Juifs plus utiles et plus heureux? le concours de l'Académie de Metz* (1787), Paris: Seuil.

Carson, Rachel (1962), *Silent Spring*, Cambridge MA: Riverside Press.

Cassirer, Ernst (2007), *Die Philosophie der Aufklärung*, Hamburg: Felix Meiner.

Condorcet, Nicolas de (1955 [1795]), *Sketch for a Historical Picture of the Advances of the Human Mind*, New York: Noonday Press.

Conner, Clifford D. (2005), *A People's History of Science: Miners, Midwives and 'Low Mechanicks'*, New York: Nation Books.

Crosby, Alfred W. (1996), *The Measure of Reality: Quantifications in Western Europe, 1250–1600*, Cambridge: Cambridge University Press.

Davis, Philip J. and Reuben Hersh (1986), *Descartes' Dream: The World According to Mathematics*, Dover Science Books, London: Penguin Books.

Delon, Michel (ed.) (2002), *Encyclopaedia of the Enlightenment*, 2 vols, Chicago, IL: Fitzroy Dearborn Publishers.

The Economist (2018), 'A Future Perfect. Steven Pinker's "Case for Optimism: Enlightenment Now" Explains Why the Doom-Mongers are Wrong', 24 February.

Foucart, Stéphane, Stéphane Horel and Sylvain Laurens (2020), *Les Gardiens de la Raison. Enquête sur la Désinformation Scientifique*, Paris: Éditions La Découverte.

Galluzzi, Paulo (2020), *The Italian Renaissance of Machines*, Cambridge, MA: Harvard University Press.

Gray, John (1995), *Enlightenment's Wake: Politics and Culture at the Close of the Modern Age*, London: Routledge.

Gray, John (1998), *False Dawn: The Delusions of Global Capitalism*, London: New Press.

Gray, John (2018), 'Unenlightened Thinking: Steven Pinker's Embarrassing New Book is a Feeble Sermon for Rattled Liberals', *New Statesman*, 22 February.

Hacking, Ian (1990), *The Taming of Chance*, Cambridge: Cambridge University Press.

Hamilton, Earl (1932) 'Spanish Mercantilism before 1700', in Arthur H. Cole, A.L. Dunham and N.S.B. Gras (eds), *Facts and Factors in Economic History, Articles by Former Students of Edwin Francis Gay*, Cambridge MA: Harvard University Press.

Hamilton, Earl (1935), 'The Mercantilism of Gerónimo de Uztáriz: A Reexamination', in Norman Humes (ed.), *Economics, Sociology and the Modern World. Essays in Honor of T.N. Carver*, Cambridge MA: Harvard University Press.

Hickel, Jason (2019), 'Bill Gates says Poverty is Decreasing. He Couldn't Be More Wrong', *The Guardian*, 29 January.

Jacob, Margaret C. (2019), *The Secular Enlightenment*, Princeton, NJ, USA and Oxford, UK: Princeton University Press.

Kaplan, Steven (2015), *Bread, Politics and Political Economy in the Reign of Louis XV*, London: Anthem.

Lakoff, George and Rafael Núñez (2001), *Where Mathematics Come From: How the Embodied Mind Brings Mathematics into Being*, New York: Basic Books.

Lauderdale, James Maitland, Earl of (1804), *Inquiry into the Nature and Origin of Public Wealth*, Edinburgh: Constable.

Lent, Jeremy (2018), 'Steven Pinker's Ideas are Fatally Flawed. These Eight Graphs Show Why', *Open Democracy*, 21 May.

Lyotard, Jean-François (1979), *La Condition Postmoderne: Rapport sur le Savoir*, Paris: Éditions Minuit.

Markey, Lia, ed. (2020), *Renaissance Invention. Stradanus's Nova Reperta*, Evanston IL: Northwestern University Press.

Millgram, Elijah (2015), *The Great Endarkenment: Philosophy for an Age of Hyperspecialization*, New York: Oxford University Press.

Nietzsche, Friedrich (1999 [1887]), *Genealogy of Morals, Third Essay*, New York: Oxford University Press.

Pereira, Ângela Guimarães and Silvio Funtowicz (2015), *Science, Philosophy and Sustainability: The End of the Cartesian Dream*, London: Routledge.

Pfeiffer, Johann Friedrich von (1780), *Der Antiphysiokrat, oder umständliche Untersuchungen des sogenannten physiokratischen Systems für eine allgemeine Freyheit und eine einzige Auflage auf den reinen Ertrag der Grundstücke*, Frankfurt a. M: Schäfer.

Pinker, Steven (2018a), *Enlightenment Environmentalism: The Case for Ecomodernism*, Oakland, CA: Breakthrough Institute.

Pinker, Steven (2018b), *Enlightenment Now: The Case for Reason, Science, Humanism, and Progress*, New York: Viking.

Porter, Roy and Mikulás Teich (eds) (1981), *The Enlightenment in National Context*, Cambridge: Cambridge University Press.

Ravetz, Jerome R. (1990), *The Merger of Knowledge with Power: Essays in Critical Science*, London: Mansell.

Ravetz, Jerome R. (2011), 'Postnormal Science and the Maturing of the Structural Contradictions of Modern European Science', *Futures* 43(2): 142–148.

Reinert, Erik S. (1980), 'International Trade and the Economic Mechanisms of Underdevelopment', PhD thesis, Cornell University (University Microfilm).

Reinert, Erik S. (2015), 'Daniel Raymond (1820): A US Economist Who Inspired Friedrich List, with Notes on Other Forerunners of List from the English-Speaking Periphery', in Helge Peukert (ed.) *Festschrift to Jürgen Backhaus*, Marburg: Metropolis.

Reinert, Erik S. and Arno Daastøl (1997), 'Exploring the Genesis of Economic Innovations: The Religious Gestalt-Switch and the *Duty to Invent* as Preconditions for Economic Growth', *European Journal of Law and Economics*, 4(2–3), pp. 233–283; and in Christian Wolff, 1998, *Gesammelte Werke*, 3rd series, Vol. 45, Hildesheim: Georg Olms Verlag.

Reinert, Sophus (2018), *The Academy of Fisticuffs: Political Economy and Commercial in Enlightenment Italy*, Cambridge MA: Harvard University Press.

Reyes, Fernández Duran (1999), *Jerónimo de Uztáriz (1670–1732). Una Política Económica para Felipe V*, Madrid: Minerva.

Ricardo, David (1817), *On the Principles of Political Economy and Taxation*, London: John Murray.

Riskin, Jessica (2019), 'Pinker's Pollyannish Philosophy and Its Perfidious Politics', *Los Angeles Review of Books*, 15 December.

Saltelli, Andrea, A. Andreoni, W. Drechsler, J. Ghosh, R. Kattel, et al. (2021a), 'Why Ethics of Quantification is Needed Now', UCL Institute for Innovation and Public Purpose WP 2021/05. London: UCL Institute for Innovation and Public Purpose.

Saltelli, Andrea and Paul-Marie Boulanger (2019), 'Technoscience, Policy and the New Media. Nexus or Vortex?', *Futures* 115: 102491. doi: 10.1016/FUTURES.2019.102491.

Saltelli, Andrea, D.J. Dankel, M. Di Fiore, N. Holland and M. Pigeon (2021b), 'Science, the Endless Frontier of Regulatory Capture', *Futures*. doi: 10.1016/j. futures.2021.102860.

Saltelli, Andrea and Silvio Funtowicz (2017), 'What is Science's Crisis Really About?', *Futures* 91: 5–11.

Samuelson, Paul (1976), *Economics*, New York: McGraw-Hill.

Schefold, Bertram (2012), 'Bedürfnisse und Gebrauchswerte in der deutschen Aufklärung: Zum wechslenden Status der Waren bei Kameralisten, ökonomischen Klassikern und frühen Anhängern der historischen Schule', in Berndt Frauke and Daniel Fulda (eds), *Die Sachen der Aufklärung*, Hamburg: Felix Meiner Verlag.

Schumpeter, Joseph (1954), *History of Economic Analysis*, New York: Oxford University Press.

Serra, Antonio (2011 [1613]), *A 'Short Treatise' on the Wealth and Poverty of Nations (1613)*, edited by Sophus Reinert, London: Anthem.

Shapin, Steven (2019), 'Is there a Crisis of Truth?', *Los Angeles Review of Books*, 2 December.

Shellenberger, Michael and Ted Nordhaus (2015), *An Ecomodernist Manifesto*, Oakland, CA: Breakthrough Institute.

Smith, Adam (1776), *Wealth of Nations*, London: Strahan & Cadell.

de Solla Price, D.J. (1963), *Little Science, Big Science*, New York: Columbia University Press.

Stackelberg, Jürgen von (1996), *Humanismus und Aufklärung. Aus der Werkstatt eines Romanisten*, Bonn: Romantischer Verlag.

Steuart, James (1767), *An Inquiry into the Principles of Political Economy*, 2 vols, London: Millar & Cadell.

Suguiyama, Chuhei (1996), *Lauderdale's Notes on Adam Smith's Wealth of Nations*, London: Routledge.

Supiot, Alain (2017), *Governance by Numbers: The Making of a Legal Model of Allegiance*, Oxford: Bloomsbury Press.

Szalai, Jennifer (2018), 'Steven Pinker Wants You to Know Humanity is Doing Fine. Just Don't Ask About Individual Humans', *New York Times*, 28 February.

Taylor, Henry Osborn (1914), *The Medieval Mind. A History of the Development of Thought and Emotions in the Middle Ages*, 2 vols. London: Macmillan.

Toulmin, Stephen E. (1992), *Cosmopolis: The Hidden Agenda of Modernity*, Chicago, IL: University of Chicago Press.

Uztáriz, Gerónimo de (1751 [1724]), *Theorica y Practica de Comercio*, Madrid.

Voltaire (François-Marie Arouet) (1824 [1764]), *A Philosophical Dictionary*, 2nd edn, London: Printed for J. & H.L. Hunt.

Will, Georg Andreas (1782), *Versuch über die Physiocratie, deren Geschichte, Litteratur, Inhalt und Werth*, Nürnberg: Raspe.

Wilson, Charles (1978), 'Gerónimo de Uztáriz, un Fundamento Intelectual para el Renacimiento Económico Español del Siglo XVIII', in *Dinero y Crédito, (Siglos XVI al XIX): Actas del Primer Coloquio Internacional de Historia Económica*, Madrid: Moneda y Crédito.

Zuboff, Shoshana (2019), *The Age of Surveillance Capitalism: The Fight for a Human Future at the New Frontier of Power*, New York: PublicAffairs.

10. Technological retrogression and persistent poverty

Sylvi B. Endresen

INTRODUCTION

Early in the morning Adil prepares for work. When the tide is at its lowest, it is safe to tread the muddy shore. Equipped with a heavy box which he pushes in front of him, he gathers clams on the beach. The work is heavy and the working hours are long, but Adil is still young and strong. He has been doing this for just a few years. He started his career 17 years old as a crewman on purse seiners, but advanced quickly to trawlers. What made him, who had experience with advanced technology only, turn to the lowest form of technology available in the village, at only 33 years old? His justification for the technology choice was as follows: he paradoxically finds that he can earn more by producing less. He created his own job when he was dissatisfied with the masters aboard the modern boats. He claimed that the owners' share of the catch was unreasonably large. On some trips, the crewmen were left with nothing. But the work he does now is hard and risky, in terms of both health and income. In future, he wishes to invest in a small boat with an outboard engine.

Adil is but one of the many of fishermen who experienced technological retrogression in the cases I have studied. My theory, published in the book *Technological Retrogression: A Schumpeterian Interpretation of Modernization in Reverse* (Endresen 2021), seeks to explain this phenomenon. The theory is based on two empirical analyses of technological retrogression in Asian fisheries (Sri Lanka and Malaysia), undertaken during the historical periods of modernization of the fishing fleet. A substantial reversal of modernization was caused by increased prices of input in one case, and overexploitation of resources in the other. These were cases of technological retrogression by necessity. Technological retrogression, while enabling the immediate survival of producers, held no promise for improving living conditions of poor fishermen. Rather, labour productivity fell, and poverty was cemented as modernization reversed. Technological retrogression is thus an engine of increased inequality and the persistence of poverty.

Technological retrogression is neglected in economic theory. No wonder: it is invisible in production statistics, and difficult to observe. But more surprising is that the classical economists' analysis of increasing versus diminishing returns to scale has sunk into oblivion. This central argument of Malthus and other 19th century economists was, however, rescued by Alfred Marshall (1890) for a few decades, only to fall even more out of fashion among economists during the liberal and neoliberal eras. However, in contemporary economics, the importance of these processes is highlighted by Erik S. Reinert (1980, 2004, 2007). Formulating the theory of technological retrogression, I rely heavily upon his analyses of the necessity of industrialization to escape diminishing returns and, thereby, underdevelopment and poverty. After reading this chapter I hope readers will understand why Alfred Marshall – in his founding work of neoclassical economics – suggests:

> One simple plan would be the levying of a tax by the community on their own incomes, or on the production of those goods which obey the Law of Diminishing Returns, and devoting the tax to a bounty on the production of those goods with regard to which the Law of Increasing Returns acts sharply. (Marshall 1890: 452)

Another source of inspiration is Joseph Schumpeter (1934/2017). Since he is the major analyst of technological progress, you may wonder why. Through creative destruction new opportunities of applying high-productive technology emerge, turning economic downturns into upturns, setting cumulative spirals of economic growth into motion. But when economic downturns necessitate the choice of less advanced technologies which reduce labour productivity, spirals of economic decline result. My theory of technological retrogression is thus 'Schumpeter in reverse'. Producers who (re)turned to traditional technologies saw their modernization vanish, and with it, the prospects of an improved standard of living.

The aim of this chapter is to introduce the concept and theory of technological retrogression as formulated in Endresen (2021). It provides a short introduction to the major findings and main arguments of the book. Theoretical discussions as well as empirical findings are (painfully) condensed, leaving just enough to establish the relationship between technological retrogression and marginalization, and thus persistent poverty. After clarifying the concept of technological retrogression, I describe the work history method. Then follows a section on the reconstruction of transitions. This section provides substance to the next two, on technological and socio-economic polarization, and on diminishing returns and lock-in. Empirical findings and their explanations are the building blocks of the theory of technological retrogression, discussed in the concluding section, on Schumpeterian dynamics in reverse.

THE CONCEPT OF TECHNOLOGICAL RETROGRESSION

The concept of technology has a tool component, 'techno', and a knowledge component, 'logy'. There are two levels of knowledge involved: knowledge linked to the immediate operation of a tool (as found in instruction manuals, for instance), and knowledge on how production should be organized for tools to function. In Figure 10.1 the concepts of technological change are presented. 'Retrogression of tools' refers to 'from tractor to horse'; or rather, in this context, 'from sails to oars'. 'Retrogressive mobility of labour' may refer to retrogression at the sector level as well as counter-historical flows of labour from secondary and tertiary industries to agriculture. Choice of technology is analysed at the level of the production unit and economic sector, and may also involve geographical mobility of labour. In theory, technological retrogression may cause entire subsectors to retrograde, causing market withdrawal and production for subsistence.

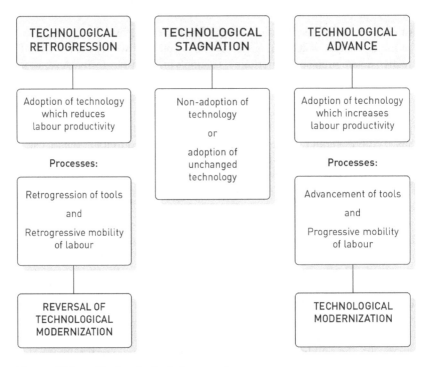

Figure 10.1   Technological change: the concepts

At the societal level, aggregate outcomes of individuals' actions (their concrete choices and adoption of technologies) can be studied in terms of technological advance, retardation, stagnation and retrogression. This characterizes the direction of change: societies may modernize technologically – progress; if modernization slows down, they move very slowly forward – retardation; they may also stagnate; or, as is the present object of analysis, they may move 'backwards' – retrogression. Technological advance and retrogression may be considered converse processes. In cases where the technological gap (difference in technology levels in terms of labour productivity) is closing, the process is termed technological convergence. But productivity levels may also move further apart, in the process of technological divergence.

Historically, ancient technologies are gradually replaced by more advanced technologies. In fishing societies, new and profitable technologies attracted young and strong fishermen, and they were also the obvious choice of the new boatowners. Allowing their young sons to join modern crews also spread the risk of losing family breadwinners, challenging ancient recruitment practices. The crew on traditional crafts became older and older, and artisan production died with its old users. Technologies may thus diffuse smoothly in a population, but the process may be impeded for some reason. When I claim that the fishing communities studied have stagnated in their technological advance, I mean that the process of diffusion of modern technology has slowed down or even stopped. This description of the process of technological change reveals that I expect diffusion of modern technology to follow some sort of normal course; in fact, it indicates a belief in predestination: one expects artisanal fisheries to disappear, and highly productive modern boats to take over. The basis of such a modernization hypothesis is an empirical generalization of the process of technological change within industrial countries. The underlying model of diffusion of technology is made explicit in Figure 10.2. The figure is based on the logistic curve depicting the pattern of diffusion of innovations over time (Lloyd and Dicken 1977: 63).

Modernization theory was the major source of inspiration for development strategists of Sri Lanka and Malaysia during the decades following World War II. A major tenet of this system of belief is the inevitability of progress. For centuries, this idea dominated Western thought. Modern technology and infrastructure as well as Western values, due to an assumed superiority, would soon dominate. Artisanal, low-productive technologies would be reduced to a traditional sector in decay. The idea of 'dual societies' was born. When approaching the modernization of fisheries in the societies in question, these grand narratives of progress were part of my theoretical heritage. But equally important was the critique of dualism of the dependency school of thought. These theorists, many inspired by Marxism, relentlessly pointed at prolonged transition periods in underdeveloped countries, even 'blocked' development.

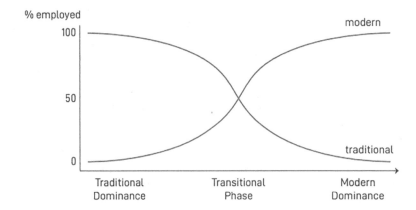

Figure 10.2   Ideal spread of modern technology

The origin of development constraints was colonialism, placing developing countries in subordinate positions in the world economic system. A prominent spokesman among them was Samir Amin (1976), whose analysis of peripheral capitalism became a major inspiration in my analysis of technological retrogression when first I encountered the phenomenon.

THE WORK HISTORY METHOD

I came across the phenomenon of technological retrogression when reading a newspaper article on the return to traditional fishing technology in Negombo, west Sri Lanka, in the early 1980s. I uncovered the process on the southern coast of the country by applying the work history method, which I designed for this purpose. In Endresen (2021), you will find a thorough description and discussion of the limitations of this method.

Even if reliable boat statistics had existed, analysing work histories would have been the only way to reconstruct technological change and document the mobility of labour between different technology levels. When interviewing the producers about their choices of technology, every change they made during their careers was minutely recorded in a matrix (see Table 10.1). The matrix shows the year, their age, and the reason why they made every decision. Any remarkable or unexpected course of events, such as movement of labour *from advanced to traditional* can be detected. Figure 10.3, however, sketches an interview with a boatowner who followed a common modernisation path of upward career mobility.

Table 10.1   *The work history matrix*

Year	Age	Time	Craft	Ownership	Method	Reasons for changes
1950	15	10 years	Oru with sails	Father's	Handlining	Better catch of modern boats
1960	25	5 years	Mechanized boat	Own	Longlining	Nylon nets more productive
1965	30	15 years	Same	Same	Driftnet	
1980 (present)	45		Same	Same		

The individual experiences recorded are the basis for the reconstruction of technological change at village levels. They are also used to analyse the relationship between level of living and technology level (see below).

The fisherman whose career path is presented in Figure 10.3 has steadily moved upwards, from a low form of technology, via intermediate, ending up in the high form of technology category. His career path reflects social mobility

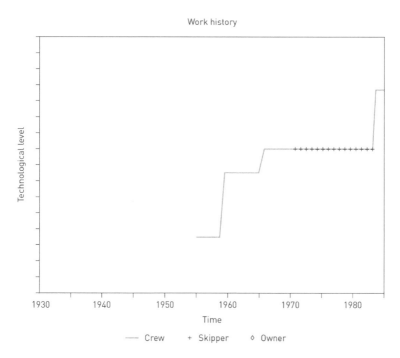

Figure 10.3   *Career path depicting technological modernization*

as well, since he started as an ordinary crewman, then became skipper, and in the end, he owns a boat.

He started to go fishing with his father aboard a *perahu* with sails, becoming a full-time crewman in 1954, when he was 15 years old. At 20 years old, he left his father's craft to become one of four crewmen aboard an inboard boat. For seven years he had this job, until he got the chance to work aboard a purse seiner, where he advanced to skipper in 1972. All through the 1970s, he worked aboard the purse seiner, and was during that time able to save enough to buy his own small trawler in 1985. He was 47 years old at the time of the study. Every change of technology he made to increase his income, he claimed, and had saved enough to buy his family a better house to live in.

The fisherman whose career path is presented in Figure 10.4 you already know; it is Adil, who I introduced you to in the first paragraph of this chapter. After years of work as a modern crewman, he now uses the technique of ancient gatherers, as old as humanity itself. Is this fisherman one of the 'failures' who could not cope with modernization? Perhaps, but I do not think so; he hoped to earn enough to invest in a small modern boat. Furthermore, he has shown considerable initiative by creating his own job when he was dissatisfied

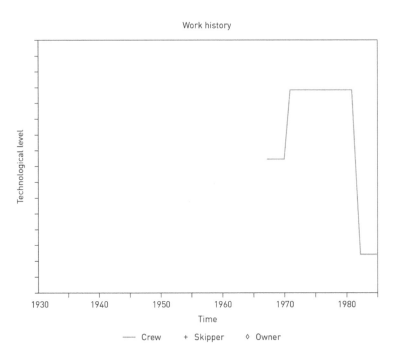

Figure 10.4   Career path depicting technological retrogression

with his masters. When he was a trawler crewman, he changed boat five times; he was dissatisfied with what he earned. He claimed that the owners' share of the value of the catch was unreasonably large. In terms of standard of living, they were as poor as when they got married, living in a shack attached to his wife's parents' house. In this Malaysian village, as in most fishing villages of the world, the owners of boats and gear are far better off than crewmen. Due to increased capital intensity, the more modern the fishing methods, the less equal the sharing of the catch. Modern owners as well as crew may be hit hard by diminishing returns, but owners may for some time – through the catch share system – transfer the burden of the hard times to their crews.

RECONSTRUCTING TRANSITIONS

Using work histories, several analyses can be undertaken. Individual career paths can be computed, searching for patterns. And when work histories are collected from a representative sample of fishermen, the data can be analysed at village level as well. One way is to establish groups of fishermen according to technology as well as age and owner/skipper/crewman dimensions, to establish how modernization affected the standard of living. This was undertaken in both studies, showing the expected improvement of living standards with technological modernization.

But these data can be used for another purpose as well. Since all changes of technology that the fishermen had made were timed during the interviews and recorded in the matrix, the course of technological change at the village level could be reconstructed. For every year, I figured out the relative share of the different forms of technology. I could follow the adoption of the first modern vessels, the growth period, the decline, and finally the stagnation of the transition became visible when diminishing returns hit the industry. Still, data at the individual level had to be used to document the movement of labour between technology levels, which is hidden in aggregate data.

Yet another technological change, unexpected (but logical) was detected using the work history method: when modern technologies were introduced, artisanal fisheries were negatively affected. Figure 10.5 shows the distribution of labour using artisanal technologies over time. When mechanized boats were introduced, the flow of labour from artisanal to industrial fisheries started. This affected the internal distribution of labour within artisanal fisheries: that is, the relative weight on the techniques *oru* with sails, *oru* without sails and *ma del*. The sailing catamarans were the most advanced, requiring sailing and navigation skills. These craft could harvest pelagic species far out at sea, and these fishermen easily got jobs on the modern boats. As time went by, artisanal fisheries came to consist of rowing craft and a few beach seine (*ma del*) fishermen. Mechanization thus had the unexpected result that artisanal fisheries

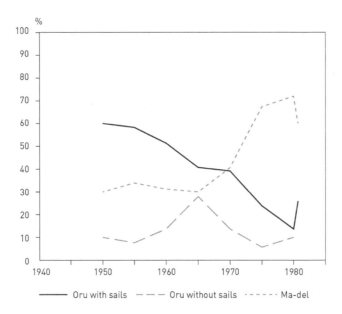

Figure 10.5   Artisanal technologies become less advanced (Sri Lanka)

became less advanced due to selective recruitment to modern fisheries. The importance of this became evident when the retrogression process started: the traditional fisheries they turned or returned to were technologically less advanced, and confined to species found inshore. Over time, sailing craft and therefore sailing skills were lost. However, the curves of Figure 10.5 show that a few daring fishermen returned to traditional *orus* with sails.

In the Malaysian case the same pattern, from sails to oars, was found, and during the last part of my stay there some fishermen, like Adil, stopped using craft altogether, some of them even reintroduced primitive crab traps. Again, there was a selective recruitment to modern fisheries, involving a drain of sailing and navigation skills from artisanal fisheries. Thus, when modern fishermen return to artisanal fisheries, they do not return to the fisheries they left; there was a radical change because of retrogression of tools.

Now let us leave internal variations of artisanal technology, and turn to the overall picture. According to the ideal model (Figure 10.2), we should expect three distinct phases: traditional dominance, a transitional phase, and modern dominance.

In Figure 10.6, which depicts technological change in a Sri Lankan village, the contours of a transition are visible, but just a few years after its introduction, technological modernization seems to stagnate. Artisanal technology

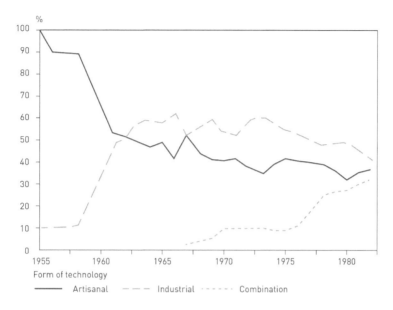

Figure 10.6   Prolonged transitional phase (Sri Lanka)

is not yet a dying remnant: artisanal, modern and the combination form of technology are equally important. The transitional phase is prolonged or has stopped. A new development, the combination of modern and artisanal technology, increased in importance in the 1970s.

However, these aggregate figures disguise variation at individual level. When examining the career paths of the fishermen, it appears that about half of the artisanal fishermen earlier worked onboard modern boats. The most frequent reason given for leaving modern boats was insufficient and irregular incomes, and increased expenses due to the increased price of oil. It is noteworthy that the fishermen who returned were relatively young, and that fewer owners than crewmen returned to artisanal fisheries. When the catch is shared, the owner and the boat get their share, and the rest is divided among the crew. This means that the owner can cover his costs while the crew, in the worst case, get close to zero when expenses for food during the trip are deducted. Through the share system the boat owners are 'insured', and some of the risk is transferred to the crew. The share system now promotes inequality, and fighting against it is difficult, especially in the case of absentee ownership of the boats. Absentee ownership loosens the bonds between owner and crew, and reduces local control over production. When crewmen on modern boats give up and leave the boat for good, the owners can pick and choose among a large reserve army of labour to replace them.

Turning to the Malaysian case, a similar and quite dramatic course of events appears. Figure 10.7 presents the transitional phase, again based on reconstructed employment figures obtained through the work history method. The two advanced forms of technology (purse seining and trawling) are combined, and contrasted to artisanal, low-technology forms. Technological modernization was first rapid, then stagnated. The contours of an ideal spread of modern technology are visible until about 1970. The most interesting period to explain is thus from then onwards. Although an upturn of artisanal technology is visible, I am reluctant to claim that this should be interpreted as more than a slowdown of modernization. However, during this latter period, modern fishermen turned to artisanal fisheries to survive. So instead of dying out, the strength of artisanal as compared to industrial fisheries increases. And the (re) turning fishermen are, as in Sri Lanka, relatively young.

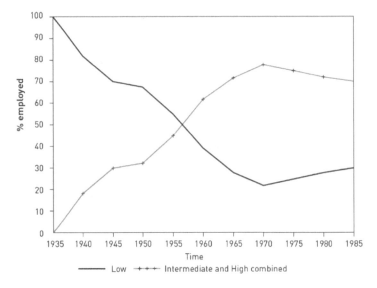

Figure 10.7   *The transition comes to a halt (Malaysia)*

Summing up major findings: in total, 86 fishermen in the Malaysian case moved from a higher to a lower level of technology in terms of labour productivity, which is 40 per cent of the sample. In Sri Lanka, the percentage was 50. The fishermen retrograded to inshore fisheries. Most fishermen who experienced technological retrogression were crewmen, not owners. Few were 'target workers' who worked aboard modern crafts in order to save money to buy a traditional craft. It is interesting to note that in the Malaysian case, slightly more fishermen who experience technological retrogression have no experience with the technology they move to. They are not old and tired (only three gave that reason), and they are generally positive towards modern fishing methods. Furthermore, they are poor: in both cases, 90 per cent of the fishermen who had experienced technological retrogression score below the middle standard of living variable. It is thus highly probable that retrogressive mobility is a strategy of the poor to improve their living standard; but it is equally probable that they try to prevent their standard of living from deteriorating. Their situation is rather dramatic; they become crewmen aboard artisanal craft, and such crewmen are the poorest group in the villages. In contrast to these fishermen's adaptations, fishermen of industrial countries who face similar situations move upwards in terms of technology, or leave the industry.

The main explanatory factor for technological retrogression in the Sri Lankan case was the increased price of inputs. In the Malaysian case, resources decreased dramatically during the period studied: overfishing caused severe resource depletion, aggravated by violations of zone regulations. As an artisanal fisherman smilingly put it, when asked about the resource situation in inshore fisheries: 'Everybody goes inshore these days. Even the trawlers.' A probable hypothesis is that the decrease in inshore resources caused the slowing down of the retrogression trend in the 1980s.

TECHNOLOGICAL AND SOCIO-ECONOMIC POLARIZATION

We can observe at the beginning of technological modernization a flow of labour to highly productive modern technology, creating economic growth and prosperity in the villages. Technological modernization thus led to the betterment of many households' standard of living. Boat owners increased their incomes tremendously, whereas such prosperity never quite reached the crew; although the greater the share of advanced technology in the fisherman's technological past, the better off his household. Economic growth and social inequality go hand in hand: the gap between rich and poor has increased immensely. So far in the analysis we do not need any new theory to explain this course of events; any modernization theory building on experience from industrial capitalist countries will do.

But then something went wrong: with diminishing returns, the return to labour on modern boats dropped like a stone. The modern fishermen had embraced modernization of the fleet, experiencing increasing returns for years, but with diminishing fish stocks and reduced catches, they had to deal with reduced incomes to the extent that they turned or returned to less advanced technologies; and were thereby hit by further diminishing returns.

Technological progress may counteract a tendency of diminishing returns, but this 'will depend on the outcome of the race between the diminishing returns pulling worker productivity down and technological development which works to bring productivity up' (Reinert 1980: 190). In the cases studied, there were no investments in ultra-modern fishing technologies which could exploit deep-sea resources and thereby escape diminishing returns. The owners' capital was eroded to the extent that equipment was run down, and savings for technology improvements depleted. When the wage reductions became unbearable, there was a flow of labour, mainly crewmen, back to artisanal technology. Boat owners were the last to turn to retrogression for survival.

One might expect that the flow of labour from industrial to artisanal fisheries would lead to a shortage of labour on the modern boats. But there is an ample supply of labour in the villages, of young fishermen willing to try their luck; there is an unlimited demand for workplaces, to paraphrase Lewis (1954). There were attempts at establishing the number of 'surplus fishermen' in Malaysia during modernization; thousands of fishermen were considered 'too many'. Then, what did such 'surplus fishermen' do? My best bet is that they do what fishermen normally do: they go fishing, even without a craft, with home-made gear. Technological retrogression is overlooked, hidden in aggregate figures.

Some of the technologies which modern fishermen (re)turned to were extremely low-productive and ancient, resulting in economic decline and persistent poverty. Diminishing returns necessitated a change of technology, but the choice of technology which further reduced labour productivity did not lead to an escape from poverty. To the contrary, when many chose to (re)turn to artisanal technology – 'inshore crowding' – pressure upon inshore resources led them deeper into further diminishing returns. To paint the picture even more grimly, artisanal technology had become less advanced during the modernization period. We may safely say that fishermen are locked into inshore fisheries as well. If proponents of 'small is beautiful' are still among us, they should note that beauty depends on scale of production. It is of no significance to the fish which type of technology led to its extinction. Producers are driven into diminishing returns unless measures are taken not to exhaust nature's carrying capacity.

The relative strength of artisanal versus industrial technology in terms of technology has been stable for a long time, and a backwards movement is identified. The latter is not necessarily set against the modernization hypothesis: it can be interpreted as a temporary setback of modernisation. But this period is so long-lasting that a fisherman can live his entire working life during 'setback'; a continuous, permanent 'crisis' is a contradiction in terms. If not blocked, the transition seems frozen, requiring more than just time to thaw, and this depends mainly on external factors.

DIMINISHING RETURNS AND LOCK-IN

When searching for explanations of the phenomenon of technological retrogression, the starting point is, firstly, whatever motivation the producers who experienced the retrogression have. Secondly, the circumstances under which the changes occur should be investigated; in the cases analysed, diminishing returns were decisive. But why did the fishermen (re)turn to artisanal technology instead of leaving the industry or the village in search of a new livelihood? A hypothesis may be that the skill which fishermen possess does not easily convert to other occupations. However, fisheries have steadily modernized in many countries, and fishermen who were made 'superfluous' have been absorbed into other industries, in their villages or in other places where jobs could be found. In both societies studied, the fishermen found few options for other work elsewhere. The fishermen considered themselves confined to their village and trade.

Situations where the producers face diminishing returns and lack alternative employment opportunities, are analysed by Reinert (1980: 177) in terms of a lock-in effect. Where there is a large oversupply of cheap labour, real wages are reversible 'until the level of physical subsistence is reached, since there is no employment in alternative activities giving a better pay'. Marginal resources are therefore utilized much longer in developing countries; such immiserizing development may continue for decades.

But there is a level beyond that of physical subsistence: starvation. Ricardo's 'iron law of wages' is of significance: where there is an oversupply of labour, wage levels may drop to what the most desperate of workers are willing to accept (Ricardo 1817), even if it means working just for a meal for your family. Ricardo's conclusion was, however, Malthusian, since he anticipated that the resulting misery would reduce the number of workers and thus lead to an increase in the wage rate. Technological retrogression can be studied in terms of reproduction of labour below the subsistence level. Diminishing returns and technological retrogression may spur flows of migrants desperately seeking to escape this poverty trap. Indeed, international migration tends to be from countries specializing in diminishing-returns activities (agriculture, fisheries and mining) to countries where increasing-returns activities (industry) dominate. This brings us back to the wise suggestion from Alfred Marshall quoted above.

PERIPHERAL CAPITALISM AND MECHANISMS OF MARGINALISATION

In developing countries, real wages are reversible. They are not in industrial countries 'where strong labor unions [can refuse] to take the cut in real wages' (Reinert 1980: 219). In industrial countries, economic activities subject to diminishing returns 'die a natural death in the competition for labor with other economic activities' (Reinert 1980: 178). Working-class struggles resulted in the increased price of labour, spurring technological progress. In capitalist industrial countries, from the mid-19th century onwards, political struggles led to greater security for the lower classes of society. Old-age pensions, sick leave, unemployment compensation, and other welfare measures, were gradually introduced.

I identified technological retrogression in two Third World capitalist countries that, in a historical perspective, built capitalism in a 'colonial' context. For centuries, these economies had been outward-oriented, and production was directed towards the needs of the 'mother country'. Differentiation of the economy is lacking and industrialization is insufficient to absorb labour made superfluous in primary production during modernization. Modernization held a promise that was kept for some years, but then the poorest became worse off, with resources depleted and technology more labour-intensive; they are victims of a marginalization process.

Mechanisms of marginalization are, according to Amin (1976), the manifestation of the peripheral capitalist nature of Third World economies. Positive effects of technological modernization are way out of reach of many producers; their living conditions may even deteriorate because of modernization. Technological retrogression has the characteristics of a marginalization process. My contribution to development theory is thus that technological heterogeneity enables technological retrogression when labour exploitation deepens, resources are exhausted, and when weak economies are hit by increased world market prices of essential raw materials.

When modern technologies are chosen, the capacity to absorb labour is less than it would have been if increased production were achieved through a gradual expansion of artisanal fisheries. The introduction of highly productive boats generated a labour surplus which would not have existed if a lower rate of resource exploitation had been chosen. In both cases studied, the choice of more productive technologies made parts of the labour force superfluous. Retrogressive mobility of labour did not lead to a situation of undersupply: new recruits immediately replaced those who exited industrial boats. The reproduction of artisanal fisheries secures a labour reserve which may seize any chance for even a slight betterment of the prospects of income. According to Amin (1976), a large reserve army is functional for further capital accumulation, since it lowers the wage rate. Therefore, the unlimited supply of labour (Lewis 1954) partly explains why wages in industrial fisheries remain low. The fishermen who accept these wages have no other choice, they are willing to work for almost any wage: an iron law of wages is at work. But, as I have shown, there is a threshold which is reached when labour starts to flow from industrial to artisanal fisheries. The (re)turners believe that, at least in the short run, they will gain by doing so. Given the low standard of living of artisanal fishermen, I doubt that they consider their long-term prospects to be very promising.

There is, however, an additional explanation of the pressure on the wage rate: industrial fishermen can accept a low wage because traditional security nets are being reproduced; and they are being reproduced because the wages are low. Artisanal as well as modern fishermen depend upon the preservation of ancient redistribution mechanisms, anchored in value systems. These security nets maintain a more egalitarian society and protect the poor against starvation. The growth of an industrial production system, capitalist in nature, put traditional security nets under pressure. The availability of traditional technologies can be considered part of the security system of modern producers: 'preservation of the relations with the village and the familial community is an absolute requirement for the wage-earners, and so is the maintenance of the traditional mode of production as the only one capable of ensuring survival' (Meillassoux 1980: 198). But the continuation of redistribution mechanisms typical of an artisanal production system was insufficient to maintain the egalitarian society. Under peripheral capitalism, the gap between the privileged and the needy became immense. Unlike in the core economies, there is a non-correspondence between productivity improvements and the wage rate (Amin 1976). The low wages benefit consumers in the First World as well as capital owners. I have found, however, that not only consumers and the elites benefited from technological modernization: there is ample evidence that, for some time, technological modernization improved the material living conditions of the producers. For a long time, therefore, technological retrogression appeared as a paradox to me. On the other hand, socio-economic inequality, even polarization, is well documented, which supports Amin's theory; the owners of the means of production got the lion's share of the surplus resulting from technological modernization. Furthermore, that so many fishermen stay on the craft, while their incomes reduce, demonstrates that real wages are reversible in lock-in situations, affecting the shares of owners as well as those of crewmen.

The technological changes that I have described cannot be explained without theories which explicitly address Third World development. The processes of technological stagnation and retrogression are inexplicable without them.

Moreover, the phenomenon of technological retrogression cannot even be discovered without theories of Third World development. It would have been easy not to observe the process: when you see a fisherman using an ancient cast net on the shore, day after day, do you consider it a matter of course that he earlier worked aboard a trawler? And if you try to reconstruct the process of technological change by means of boat statistics, you will not observe retrogression at all: it is an intra-industry mobility of labour, which only will become visible when many modern boats lie permanently idle.

I set out with conventional conceptions of how technological innovations diffuse in a population; my understanding is considerably shaken. I now find the causes of non-adoption of modern technology far more interesting than the causes of its adoption. At the heart of theories of diffusion of technology are modernization theories, based on empirical generalizations of historical experiences of industrial countries. These theories lack explanations of technological retrogression, which in simple words means that they offer no concepts which may characterize the process. Maybe those who reject modern technology have always been ignored? When explained in terms of modernization theory, knowers but non-adopters are considered either as Luddites or simply as stubborn traditionalists. It is often explicitly assumed that they are future adopters: it is only a matter of time, and we all will be modern. The ideology of progress is ingrained in our minds, especially the minds of students of technological change.

CONCLUSION: SCHUMPETERIAN DYNAMICS IN REVERSE

To formulate a general economic theory based on my empirical findings, observations should be stripped of context. Cast in Schumpeterian terms, we find at the beginning of technological modernization the creative destruction of low-productive technologies, and high-productive modern technology that created positive spirals of economic growth and prosperity in the village. This can be termed Schumpeterian progressive economic dynamics. Then diminishing returns sets in, setting in motion retrogressive economic dynamics: technological retrogression, the resurrection of artisanal technology, some of which is extremely low-productive and ancient, resulted in poverty and broken dreams of improved living conditions. We may term the process 'Schumpeterian dynamics in reverse'. When I observed this, progressive and retrogressive economic dynamics existed simultaneously, producing unprecedented social inequality.

Diminishing returns, low capital formation and lock-in trap the economies in poverty, aggravated by immiserizing spirals of economic decline set in motion by technological retrogression. Myrdal's (1957) analysis of 'cumulative causation' is of relevance to capture such retrogressive economic dynamics, as is Reinert's metaphor of 'cascading fragilities'. Cascading fragilities are economic mechanisms, often induced by external shocks, that may precipitate chains of events producing retrogression, measured as falling real wages, increased mortality, use of less capital-intensive technologies, environmental degradation and energy shortages. Economies may move from financial fragility (Hyman Minsky's term) to wage fragility, livelihood fragility and, lastly, into a state of technological fragility. Understanding the last state of fragility is the core of my theory.

According to Schumpeter, the economy turns from decline to development during the downswing of a cycle, when entrepreneurs start adopting new technology. As demonstrated, Schumpeterian dynamics have an evil twin: retrogressive dynamics that are set in motion where (un)favourable contextual preconditions such as lock-in prevail. Whereas Schumpeter discusses technological changes that result in increasing returns and economic progress, my theory discusses changes that result in diminishing returns and economic decline. The resurrection of technologies and production systems previously swept away by gales of creative destruction may, for some of you, have positive connotations. But in my book, there is no nostalgia: the phenomenon of technological retrogression is considered detrimental to economic growth, and social and regional development.

Throughout the history of economic prosperity, we find technological modernization at the core. Capital-strong production units innovate their way out of recessions through technological progress, adopting more advanced production equipment that improves productivity, forming virtuous spirals of growth. When producers resort to technologies which secure survival, but which result in low labour productivity, the possibility of capital accumulation diminishes and thus modernization that could form an escape from poverty: vicious spirals of decline are formed. Therefore, the reversal of technological modernization is closely related to marginalization, increased inequality and persistent poverty.

REFERENCES

Amin, Samir. 1976. *Unequal Development*. Hassocks: Harvester Press.

Endresen, Sylvi Birgit. 2021. *Technological Retrogression: A Schumpeterian Interpretation of Modernization in Reverse*. London: Anthem.

Lewis, W. Arthur. 1954. *Economic Development with Unlimited Supplies of Labour*. Manchester: Manchester School of Economic and Social Studies.

Lloyd, Peter E., and Peter Dicken. 1977. *Location in Space: A Theoretical Approach to Economic Geography*, 2nd edn. New York: Harper & Row.

Marshall, Alfred. 1890. *Principles of Economics*. London: Macmillan.

Meillassoux, Claude. 1980. 'From Reproduction to Production: A Marxist Approach to Economic Anthropology'. In Harold Wolpe (ed.), *The Articulation of Modes of Production*. London: Routledge & Kegan Paul, 189–201.

Myrdal, Gunnar. 1957. *Economic Theory and Under-developed Regions*. London: Gerald Ducksworth.

Reinert, Erik S. 1980. *International Trade and the Economic Mechanisms of Underdevelopment*. Ann Arbor, MI: University Microfilms.

Reinert, Erik S. 2004. 'Globalization in the Periphery as a Morgenthau Plan: The Underdevelopment of Mongolia in the 1990s'. In Erik S. Reinert (ed.), *Globalization, Economic Development, and Inequality: An Alternative Perspective*. Cheltenham, UK and Northampton, MA, USA: Edward Elgar Publishing, 157–214.

Reinert, Erik S. 2007. *How Rich Countries Get Rich ... and Why Poor Countries Stay Poor*. London: Constable.

Ricardo, David. 1817. *Principles of Political Economy and Taxation*. London: Everyman's Library.

Schumpeter, Joseph. 1934/2017. *The Theory of Economic Development. An Inquiry into Profits, Capital, Credit Interest, and the Business Cycle*. London: Routledge.

PART IV

When nations and systems decline and collapse

11. When nations collapse: a note on Jacob Bielfeld's 'On the Decline of States' (1760)[1]

Erik S. Reinert

In a period when we observe major shifts among the world powers, it is interesting to read a work theorising around the fall of nations during a period where the experience base was so much broader than today. After the Thirty Years War, the Treaty of Westphalia (1648) included formal recognition for 365 German principalities as autonomous states. In 1789, about 30 years after Bielfeld wrote, the number was around 40. Not that Bielfeld wrote about German states in particular; these numbers are included to illustrate the large number of cases from which he could generalise.

The subject of economic decline – the notion that societies are born to follow the cyclical patterns of nature in birth, life and decline – has of course been with us for a very long time. We find it in the Greek philosophy of Plato and in the Arab philosophy of Ibn-Khaldun in the 1300s. During the Renaissance the West freed itself from the random vicissitudes of the blindfolded goddess Fortuna and opened for rational economic policy to prevent boom and bust.

The author of the chapter discussed here belonged to a rational school which held that if one understood the reasons for decline, it could be prevented. Jacob Friedrich von Bielfeld (1717–1770) was born in Hamburg. His main work, the two-volume *Institutions Politiques* which contains the chapter 'On the Decline of States', was published in the Hague in Holland, in 1760. As was normal in the Prussian setting at the time, the work was written in French. Despite its voluminous text – 358 plus 344 pages in a large quarto format – the work became an international bestseller with a total of 12 editions, including translations into German (1761), Italian (1764), Spanish (1767) and Russian (1768/1775). An abbreviated translation in Portuguese even made it to Brazil and was published there in 1823 (Pires 1823). It is worth noticing that Bielfeld's chapter on the subject was published 16 years before the first volume of Edward Gibbon's extremely influential six-volume *The History of the Decline and Fall of the Roman Empire* (Gibbon 1776–1789).

Compared to the other important 18th century economists,[2] Bielfeld's background in high society was atypical for the time. As an important advisor to Frederick the Great of Prussia, Bielfeld is frequently mentioned in the literature, but there is not much on Bielfeld himself. The literature is limited to two relatively slim theses (*Inauguraldissertationen*) on him, from 1928 (Voss 1928) and 1937 (Stössl 1937). We also have an *Eloge* published after he passed away (Fournay 1772).

Born into a family of merchants in Hamburg, Jakob Friedrich von Bielfeld's life was international from an early age. In 1732, age 17, he started his university studies in Leyden, Holland, and travelled in Holland, France and England. In 1738 he met and befriended then Crown Prince Frederick of Prussia. Like Frederick, Bielfeld was a freemason. With Fredrick's ascent to the Crown in 1740, Bielfeld started his diplomatic and later administrative career in the service of Prussia. He became tutor to Prince August Ferdinand, curator of Prussia's universities and director of Berlin's famous Charité hospital, and was ennobled as Baron. After 15 years of service to Prussia, at the age of 38, he withdrew from public service to his properties in Altenburg in the eastern part of Germany in 1755.

Bielfeld's letters and inside anecdotes from the Prussian Court were popular at the time (Bielfeld 1768). In addition to the *Institutions Politiques* (Bielfeld 1760), the letters and the journal, Bielfeld had already written an interesting work on the recent progress of Germany (Bielfeld 1752), and later produced an encyclopedic work in the Enlightenment tradition (Bielfeld 1768). The English translation of this is entitled *The Elements of Universal Erudition: Containing an Analytical Abridgment of the Sciences, Polite Arts, and Belles Lettres* (Bielfeld 1770/1771). In this work Bielfeld is acknowledged as having used the term 'statistics' for the first time, defined as 'the science that teaches us what is the political arrangement' of all modern states of the known world'.[3]

Bielfeld's volumes of *Institutions Politiques* are written in the venerable *Fürstenspiegel* – or 'Kings' Mirror' – tradition. Going back to Greek (Aristotle) and Roman (Pliny the Younger) writers, this type of work lists the virtues and duties of rulers and princes, establishing the necessary wisdom and principles for good governance. An important German predecessor – 100 years before Bielfeld – was Veit Ludwig von Seckendorff (1626–1692) with his *Teutscher Fürsten-Staat*, published in 1656 (Seckendorff 1656), staying continuously in print for about 100 years. Seckendorff and Bielfeld were both employed by rulers who represented the best intellectualism of Enlightened Despotism: Ernest the Pious of Gotha and Frederick the Great of Prussia, respectively. Frederick the Great's (1740) *Anti-Machiavel* – his criticism of Nicolò Machiavelli – represented a curious incident inside the *Fürstenspiegel* tradition in that the *Fürst* (the Ruler) himself participated in the debate.

Bielfeld's approach is taxonomic and typical of his time. Like Linnaeus (1707–1778) did in the world of plants and animals, Bielfeld attempts to create order in the economic and political world by creating the necessary categories of forces at work. In an important early economic treaty, Antonio Serra (1613) also used a taxonomic approach, and the same approach was found in English economics before Adam Smith (S. Reinert 2011). In contrast with his predecessors, Smith eliminated important taxonomies as found, for example, in King (1721) – that of 'good' and 'bad' trade among them – and introduced the counterintuitive proposal that all economic activities are qualitatively alike as agents of economic wealth.[4] As one important example of the different results of Bielfeld's taxonomic and qualitative approach compared to that of the English classical economists: Portugal having neglected its manufacturing sector, Bielfeld (1760) sees that nation's position vis-à-vis Britain as one of unfortunate dependency. This is of course completely the opposite to David Ricardo (1817), who uses Portugal as an example of the blessings created by free trade.

The experience-based knowledge and wisdom contained in Bielfeld's work reminds one of the teachings and wisdom of Benjamin Franklin's *Way to Wealth*, which was first published in 1757. Franklin aimed his wisdom at the common man; Bielfeld's *Institutions* aimed at the rulers and administrators of Europe, while his (1770) *Universal Erudition* had been aimed at the common man. Contrary to what could be expected, Benjamin Franklin's *Way to Wealth* – not Adam Smith's *Wealth of Nations* – is the most published economics book in history, judged by the number of different editions (S. Reinert 2015). It is certainly dramatic that this kind of economics – at both the macro and micro levels – has now virtually disappeared from economic science.

In the following there is an attempt at a résumé of Bielfeld's chapter, paraphrasing and citing Bielfeld. Numbers in brackets refer to the relevant paragraph in the translation in the 2014 chapter referred to initially.

In sharp contrast to today's equilibrium economics, Bielfeld starts out his chapter 'On the Decline of States' with the basic assumption that everything in the world is characterised by instability: 'The most formidable empires are subject to the law of change and inconstancy'. When change occurs in 'great bodies' (such as empires), these are called revolutions, Bielfeld states, and that is when the 'face of the universe is changed'.

A 'universal history of the world' investigates both the causes and effects of revolutions, Bielfeld says. He distinguishes between two kinds of revolutions: the natural and the political. The former are 'grievous effects of nature, such as earthquakes, floods, plagues and like scourges'. The latter revolutions are 'caused by men, and alter only the system of states, by changing the form of their government, or by subjecting their peoples to alien laws', which is the subject of Bielfeld's inquiry.

Bielfeld's taxonomy starts by distinguishing between internal and external causes of decline. The power of the state may be real or relative, as is shown by external threats to the state. The internal power of state may also be founded upon 'the local situation, or on opinion, or accessory'. The local situation may be affected by natural disasters, and responses to it may be strengthened or weakened given the circumstances of the country. On opinion (or ideology), Bielfeld states that:

> The power of opinion becomes weaker, and falls into decline, in proportion as the opinion upon which this power is based dissipates in the mind of men; and as a consequence one must not find it at all strange that those who are at the head of such a state seek to perpetuate this opinion, whether it be true or false.

There are also direct and indirect causes of decline: 'Among the great number of direct or indirect causes that can abbreviate the life of a government, change the system of states, and overturn empires, we will only indicate the principal causes, and those that produce the most sudden effects.'

I have organised Bielfeld's points into a taxonomy that distinguishes between eight external (alien) and 18 internal (intrinsic) causes of decline. In this résumé I have numbered the external factors from E-1 to E-8, and the internal ones from I-1 to I-18. One can imagine using these categories today for a summary diagnosis of national problems, and since I first read Bielfeld's chapter about 20 years ago, I feel that things have changed. In some areas, Bielfeld strangely feels gradually more relevant.

Twenty years ago, the prospect of migration, Bielfeld's factor E-1 in our taxonomy, seemed much less remote than it is now. The dramatic migration events in the Mediterranean, in Greece, and at the southern United States border, have brought this factor higher on everybody's list of problems, and – at the time of writing – a migration incident on the border between Belarus and Poland looks increasingly ugly. With the coronavirus pandemic, factor I-12 (epidemics and occupational health), has of course taken on new importance, and in some countries this factor seems to combine strongly with I-16 (constant internal wrangling).

In the United States there has recently been a focus on systemic failures. *How Democracies Die* is a 2018 book on the subject written by two political scientists from Harvard (Levitsky and Ziblatt 2018). These authors add to the worries expressed over a period of time by Thomas Frank, from his 2004 *What's the Matter with Kansas?* onwards (Frank 2004). The United States may presently be seen as suffering from E-4 (imperial overextension), I-8 (neglect of production and science,[5] de-industrialisation), I-15 (debt), increasingly I-16 (constant internal wrangling), probably also I-7 (too much freedom destroying social cohesion). With Trump and subsequent events, one is tempted to add category I-2 (defective public administration/insane sovereign).

From Bielfeld's perspective, the events in Afghanistan brought internal differences between different variants of Muslim religions, I-5 (excessive religion) and I-6 (oppression), to the surface. Bielfeld's phrase, 'External devotion too easily leads to enthusiasm, to superstition, to fanaticism, to idleness, to indolence, to a disregard for worldly matters which is so harmful to the progress of the arts, talents and commerce', is clearly valid for the Muslim Council in Kabul, but not for the Muslim Council of Singapore. With this excessive religion (I-5), came E-2 (war), E-5 (dependency), I-1 (unwise constitutions), I-2 (defective public administration/insane sovereign), and definitely I-8 (decline of production and science).

We have divided Bielfeld's arguments into the following categories.

EXTERNAL (ALIEN) CAUSES OF DECLINE

E-1.   Migration

It is remarkable that, writing during the 18th century, Bielfeld would put migration as the top external danger to a nation. At the time, the Indian Nations of North America were being ruined by migration from Europe, but as expected this was not what Bielfeld had in mind:

> Among the alien causes one can count first of all the great migrations of peoples, such as the spectacle that the fourth and fifth centuries offered Europe. Now hordes of Goths, Vandals and other Barbarians stream from the depths of the north to flood Europe, extending their conquests to Spain, to Italy and even Africa; now the peoples who inhabit the most northerly countries attack their neighbours towards the south, forcing them to leave their home. These last are then constrained in turn to fall upon other peoples who were their southern neighbours; and so, little by little, move around each other in turns, constantly pushing towards the most equable climates. (5)
> Indeed, each nation changed place, kingdoms, empires and republics were destroyed, or founded, or transported to other lands ... Is it unthinkable that one day there will arise from the Australian lands, from the almost unknown African interior, from Ethiopia, from the depths of Asia, from the upper Americas, an innumerable swarm of men, stronger, more robust, more indefatigable than the Europeans, and put to rout all the skill, all the facility of the latter in the art of war, and all their policy? (5) I concede that such a revolution seems far removed, but it is not impossible; and without wishing to anticipate remote evils, there are dangers in this respect that are much closer to us. (6)

E-2.   War

War, unjust or equitable, can cause the decline of states. Wars may result in states declining by degrees rather than through one-off battles. All the writers on the rights of peoples maintain that the right of conquest is a legitimate right; but even if it were not, the greatest part of the changes occurring in empires, and in the world since its origin right up to the present day, have they not been occasioned by force of arms? Fortunate wars elevate states, just as the unfortunate ruin them. It is however a rarity that one war alone destroys at once an empire.

... Princes, ministers, generals need to be persuaded of a Divine Providence ruling all, but act as if they do not believe this, and as if good or bad outcomes depend upon their own prudence; for indeed experience proves that all incidents of war, as in all other affairs of the world, derive always from natural causes. It is only visionaries, or spirits too slothful or stupid, who attribute each accident to the immediate and miraculous guidance of the Supreme Being; if they open their eyes, if they examine properly, then they will find this cause to be a side effect. (7)

E-3.   Excessive Demands from Neighbouring States

'When a neighbouring power makes excessive advances in all objects of policy, its expansion can become the third cause, whether proximate or more remote, of the decline of another state.' Excessive demands between states, in a context of a zero sum game, may lead to the decline of a state. Setting strategic long term objectives is crucial, and prudent negotiations can forestall war:

Europe's political system is today in general such that one state is not able to raise itself except at the expense of another, whether it be by conquest, or by commerce etc. Each degree of real power which it acquires gives it at least one more degree of relative power, and the degree that it gains is a loss for its rivals. Ultimately, going from strength to strength, it comes imperceptibly to engender terror among the other sovereigns, finally setting their measure. Nearly all statesmen have felt this truth. The lengthy disputes between the Austrian and Bourbon Houses, between the northern powers etc. have been ruled by no other principle; but cabinets only too rarely adopt the most fitting measures to prevent this excessive elevation of powers which is capable of inspiring in them a proper jealousy. Such cabinets can be seen to favour minor interests over major, ceding the most essential, constant advantage to a passing one, and sometimes concluding alliances with rivals which not only serve in turn to fortify the latter against themselves, but also against their natural allies, with whom they should make common cause by opposing in concert the expansion of these same rival powers. The Latin tag which is so true, and so politic, *obstare principiis*, that it is necessary to act quickly if not to be acted upon, is too much neglected by those who conduct affairs of state, and sometimes a century of war is needed to gain what one could have been able to forestall by a few strokes of the pen.

E-4.   Imperial Overextension

'The over-extension of an empire nearly always becomes a cause of its decline.' Bielfeld here makes the same point about imperial overstretch which Paul Kennedy was to make about the United States more than 200 years later (Kennedy 1987). To Bielfeld, uniting all lands under one empire is a 'chimerical undertaking' because a central power cannot know what is happening in the distant parts of the empire. The governance structures of the empire in far-off places are susceptible to breaking down at any moment. Rebellions and internal wars are viewed as more dangerous than external ones. The local senates that have to be established in the provinces form numerous, almost independent, states; and the loose relationship they enjoy with the principal government can break down at any moment. Rebellions and internal wars are more dangerous than external wars, hence the dismembering of provinces, and the decline, fall and destruction of the state (9).

E-5.   Dependency

Bielfeld here raises the issue which, starting in the 1960s, created such a huge debate in Latin America: that of dependency. The contemporary example he uses, that of Portugal vis-à-vis Britain, seems very well taken. 'The absolute dependence of a state on another power is yet another cause of its gradual weakening', says Bielfeld. The dependency of one nation upon another may be for reasons of idleness, or because of the need for protection ('vice of police'), or regarding its basic needs (foodstuffs, manufactures and other primary needs).

The origin of dependence may be the result of bad policy. The dependent state may become way too entangled with its powerful ally. It may sell all or most of its produce to it, and rely too much on the 'subsidies' it receives. Bielfeld warns that 'These are involvements which go further than one thinks':

> This dependence can come from national idleness, or from a vice of police [policy] such that for most foodstuffs, manufactures and other prime needs the country is compelled to provide for itself through another strong people, not being able to do otherwise in this regard. Portugal is almost in this situation vis-à-vis Britain. However, this dependence finds its origin in an inferior system of policy embraced by the government, in which it espouses all the disputes of a powerful ally, taking its part too deeply, attaching its fortune to that of that same ally through almost indissoluble links, and above all when it sells to this ally more or less all its forces and in return becoming too reliant on subsidies. These are involvements which go further than one thinks. Sailing in a stormy sea, one's barque is attached to a first-rate vessel with chains which one would not know how to break when this vessel is imperilled, and the barque is dragged with it into the abyss. (10)

E-6.   Grandiosity of Independence

'The decline of the state may also be occasioned by the affectation of a great independence and an authority capable of casting into shade other sovereigns.' A state that becomes overconfident in its ability to be independent may provoke the ire of other states, which may result in other states uniting against it. It may also lead to undertakings that are beyond the means of the state. Power ought to be exercised judiciously and excess avoided.

A state that wishes to concern itself entirely with itself, breaking off all liaisons, whether of commerce or of friendship, with the rest of Europe: such a state revolts all other powers. There is an art in hiding all the power that is possessed, and policy demands that one never makes use of it on small occasions, but reserves it for major occasions (11).

The state can enfeeble itself through the excessive indolence of those who govern it and those who do not know how to make use of all its advantages, render its laws valued, and render it respected by its neighbours. It can also be plunged into irreparable misfortune by a sovereign who embarks upon vain, chimerical, perilous undertakings that are absolutely beyond his powers, such as if he ventures into commerce that he would not be able to protect, if he seeks justice by armed force against a power that can crush him, if he demands prerogatives and extraordinary honours, if he conceives projects of conquest that are too extensive. This point is obviously also relevant for modern democracies.

E-7.   Division of Empire (or 'Balkanisation')

This is another issue which has re-emerged in Europe, reinforced by the global financial crisis. 'The state also suffers loss by the monarch dividing his empire.' Splitting up of territories weakens the state, in terms of pursuit of the 'good life' in the nation, and more especially as regards external threats. Splitting up the empire is against natural law and leaders should not be allowed to whimsically divide up territory.

There is a difference between what constitutes the empire's possessions and those of its sovereign. The latter may be divided up, but division of the former needs to be thought of in different terms. Saxony, the richest and most extensive province of Germany, lost its unity through the territorial divisions and subdivisions which were successively made between the different lines of the House of Saxony and the diverse branches of each line. This division of states is both unjust and futile. The least reflection on the origins of peoples and of civil government reveals that men are united in the body of society so that they might be stronger, and only consent to be ruled over by a sovereign so that they might be happier by their union, and to be able to oppose the attentions of their enemies with greater vigour under a common chief. But this chief has no right to partition a country and a people that the ancients have once brought together, and for which providence has conferred upon it a government with the tacit and express condition that it maintain the country and people as entire as it is able. All the deference that people show to their sovereign is given only on the condition that they do not break the knot that binds them, and which keeps them in a *corps d'état*.

Ultimately natural law, the rights of peoples, and the founding constitutions of the greater part of countries, are opposed to such partitions. One most essential part of the happiness of peoples must not depend on the caprice of a sovereign, and once a province is incorporated into the state, it can only be detached by *force majeure*, which silences all consideration of equity, and all policy. But policy, whose principal object is that which is useful, does not lose sight of that which is equitable.

There is also a great difference between the succession of sovereigns and that of private persons. One cannot divide up men and people as one divides up other goods of fortune; and considering the matter closely, sovereignty is not a good over which its possessor has disposal, but rather a responsibility, an office with which he is endowed (14). Here, Bielfeld's discussion of luxury and on the roles of princes is also most interesting.

E-8.   Single Sovereign (or Sovereignty is Indivisible)

There cannot be two sovereigns for the same state. Such attempts can become a direct cause for decline of a state. The political axiom stating that sovereignty is indivisible, since power divided is power enfeebled, also shows us why two princes cannot simultaneously occupy the same throne. Such an arrangement thus becomes a very direct cause for the decline of a state.

INTERNAL (INTRINSIC) CAUSES OF DECLINE

I-1.   Unwise Constitutions Leading to Inequity

Again it is interesting that Bielfeld chooses as his first cause, in this case of internal decline, constitutions which lead to inequity:

> Similar states, seemingly defective edifices where burdens and support are poorly distributed and the proportions irregular, crumble of themselves and succumb under their own weight. The ancient Greeks, who groped unceasingly for the best form of government for their republics, fell into bad hands, and their legislators, lacking theory and experience, made monsters of republics which destroyed themselves whereas their citizens performed prodigies of valour against their external enemies.

I-2. Defective Public Administration/Insane Sovereign

An insane sovereign can lead to the decline of the state, and should be removed or replaced by a guardian acting in his stead: 'The constant mistakes committed by an extravagant prince occasion the decline of his state before the wisest ministers are able to remedy them.'

I-3. Requirements of State (Public Administration)

In Bielfeld's discussion here we see the outlines of a description of a Weberian bureaucracy. The state needs to be supported by loyal ministers. It is not sufficient for the state to be regular, certain and predictable, and the leader wise: loyal ministers are also needed. It is not enough that the form of a government be regular, and the prince wise: for the preservation of the state one also needs loyal ministers.

As only God can do everything, even the greatest king has need of support in governing, and in carrying out his wishes. Imagine a state that falls into the hands of incompetent, or ill-intentioned, ministers. Every occasion to do good for the country is missed, all the misfortunes that can befall a country are not forestalled. Success will never follow the wisdom or generosity of a prince's resolve, for it will sour in execution; such failures unsettle the prince, and make him uncertain of the measures that he should take in future (22).

I-4. Relaxation of Morals (Importance of Morals and Rule of Law)

'The relaxation of moeurs, in the maintenance of good order and of society, in the observance of laws – these are all once again a direct and intrinsic cause of the decline of a state.' Mediocre laws that are observed are preferable to wiser laws that are neglected. It is the people who make up the state; if the people abandon themselves to all sorts of vices, only one or two generations are needed for them to become debilitated; this is a fact based upon centuries of experience.

Laws are not promulgated as a vain speculation, to occupy doctors and schoolmen, but to be put into practice. Well-observed, but somewhat mediocre, laws make the state stronger than do wiser laws that go neglected. The impunity with which crimes are committed becomes the source of 1000 evils in the state, and as a consequence of its decay.

I-5. Excessive Religion

'Those who argue that religion is of no use in the government of a state, and that cunning and the gallows is sufficient to deter malefactors and maintain good order, are talking claptrap.' Religion is important to a state. However, religion has to subordinate itself to the king, and to do so wisely. Religion should not be too dominant. 'Let us beware!' As soon as positive religion spreads in a country, taking the place of natural religion – too speculative and too uncertain for the multitude, since each man is different in sentiment and insight – then the country is on the way to decline:

> This nation [England], the most political of all, recognises that its happiness, its tranquillity, the maintenance of its power, depend to a great extent upon the main-tenance of its religion. Here religion has subordinated itself to the king, and does so wisely. (24) But as much as it is necessary for the good of the state for religion and a solid piety to prevail in the nation, it is fatal if the state allows it to become too ascendant. A people of devotees, of whatever religion, would be a people both ridiculous and feeble. The reasons for this are so palpable that they require no elaboration. External devotion too easily leads to enthusiasm, to superstition, to fanaticism, to idleness, to indolence, to a disregard for worldly matters which is so harmful to the progress of the arts, talents and commerce. (25)

I-6.   Oppression / Limits on Liberty (or Despotism)

Where despots limit the liberty of the people, the state cannot be powerful, as at all times the ruler is at risk of losing the rulership. The means used to main-tain domination and obedience of the people weakens the state. In other words, oppression is not a sustainable form of government.

In countries where the natural liberty of men is oppressed under a purely despotic yoke, the state cannot be very powerful. There is not one moment when the despot is not in danger of perishing on his throne, and it costs a thousand-fold more to achieve obedience to absolute power than to the power of the law. The measures that such a despot is obliged to continually take to maintain the people in a state of obedience, and to prevention sedition, absorb half of the natural forces of the state; each popular riot, which occurs despite all precautions, weakens it all the more, and each revolution that overthrows the monarch shakes the state to its foundations. Hence the previously unimag-inable weakness of the Ottoman Empire, and other Asiatic monarchies which would, in the absence of this vice, shake all Europe. It appears that slavery renders men worthless.

I-7.   Excess of Liberty

Too much liberty and freedom can limit the need for restraint that is essential for the creation of social cohesion and the 'general good' (*ben commune*). In modern terms this could be translated as a focus on individual rights at the expense of the correlative obligations that flow from such rights, to both individuals and collectives/communities. Likewise it could be expressed as an exclusive focus on 'freedoms to' (for example, to carry a gun), at the expense of 'freedoms from' (for example, from being shot): 'A people which seeks to become too free gives to its neighbours the means to forge its chains. To make men combine for the general good there is need of a restraint that will render them obedient, and a power that will make them all subjects' (27).

I-8. Decline of Production; Neglect of Agriculture, Commerce, Sciences, Useful Arts; and Passion for Liberal Arts and Frivolity

'When a nation neglects to perfect agriculture, commerce, the sciences and the useful arts (i.e. handicraft and manufactures), giving itself with too great a passion to the liberal arts and frivolous objects, it can only become weak, and the state languishes' (28). This point is obviously extremely relevant for Europe and the United States at the moment, and how the financial crisis of 2007/2008 was handled.

I-9. Arrogance, Pride and Idleness

This is an argument much in line with economist Thorstein Veblen's (1899) *Theory of the Leisure Class*:

> Another very direct cause of the weakness and decline of a state is the pride and idleness of the nation. It was a great political idiot who was the first to seek to persuade the nobility into believing that they demean themselves through honest employment of their own hands. The author of the Persian Letters[6] admirably depicts the arrogance, the indolence, and the dislike of labour in the Spanish nation, especially among the nobility. He writes that nobility is acquired through sitting around.
>
> The nobility sets a dangerous example for the people. Their inactivity introduces idleness to that class of citizens whose work buttresses the state ... Nobody has ever told me that the nobility are sufficiently occupied by warfare. Wars are short and the peace is long. (29)

I-10. Senseless Laws

Laws need to be wise in and of themselves but also take into account the context in which they are applied or made: 'We remarked above all that laws must not only be full of wisdom in themselves, but also quite appropriate to the countries for which they are made.' In other words, context is very important. What use is it if, while the state is well-founded, the prince wise, ministers excellent, moeurs good, the laws are ridiculous? (31)

Here follows criticism of other religions, Catholicism and Jewry (32, 33). Bielfeld's ugly anti-Semitism is unfortunately rather typical of the period, and is similar to that of Voltaire (with whom Bielfeld corresponded).

I-11.   Excessively Large Colonies

Compared to the mechanistic understanding of trade in David Ricardo, Bielfeld in this paragraph (indirectly) explains why colonial trade differs from symmetrical trade among equal nations: 'Excessively large colonies which the state establishes in distant provinces, and above all in other parts of the world, enfeeble the state, and moreover become an intrinsic cause of its decline.' Large colonies need to be managed to gain the advantages from them, without becoming a cause of decline:

> I say excessively large, since one should not imagine that my remarks bear upon the colonies that Holland, England and France, for example, maintain, and almost constantly refresh in their Asian and American possessions. For apart from these nations being extremely numerous in themselves, and that they enrol as many foreign subjects as they can for their transport, it has to be considered that these colonies procure to the metropole five significant advantages which abundantly repay the losses incurred by the citizens removed, and who remain dependent on the state, constantly contributing to the good of the state. These advantages are 1. a much greater consumption of the products of the land which the metropole sends there; 2. the addition of a greater number of manufacturers, artisans etc. who serve the needs of the colonies; 3. the augmentation of navigation and of all workers contributing to it; 4. the export of a greater quantity of foodstuffs that are necessary in these colonies; 5. a much greater superfluity of foodstuffs and merchandise which these colonies provide, and which the metropole provides to other peoples, which leads to the continual growth of its commerce.

I-12.   Epidemics and Occupational Health

'Epidemics greatly ravage the people and weaken the state, depriving it for a considerable period of the resources necessary to defend itself against an unjust aggressor.' Failing to maintain the people, and the armies, in good health enfeebles the nation:

> If one persists in establishing some good citizens in a country where the air is bad, sending them into mines which exhale sulphureous vapors, employing them in the cultivation of rice which grows only in mires constantly inundated with stagnant water and so on; such action constantly enfeebles the state's people, and as a result slowly leads, almost unfailingly, to the decline of the state. (35)

I-13.   Abuse of Spirits and Strong Liquors

'The abuse the people make of spirits and other strong liquors; we add here that liquors can weaken a nation if they are made use of without due moderation.' As an example, Bielfeld uses the excess of alcohol consumption in England in 1734 and 1735, before wise legislation made the English again turn to 'healthy beer'.

I-14.   Relaxation of Military Discipline

'The relaxation of military discipline also leads a state into unfailing loss':

> Women who have such influence over the hearts of men, priests, merchants, manufacturers, artisans, cultivators – they all desire peace, and look upon it with the greatest happiness. They are right in one sense, but they do not at all see that a lengthy peace corrupts the soldiery, relaxes discipline, allow the officer and the soldier to become unpracticed in their art, and softens them. One would wish that in time of war the entire army would be composed only of lions, and in time of peace of sheep; but this is to ask for a contradiction, to want a chimera. Many people find military discipline too harsh in a peacetime garrison; it seems much too gentle when they march on the enemy. Men are never in agreement with themselves. They learn that peace is made to accustom officer and soldier to war, that discipline must be constantly upheld in an army, that the most skillful princes set up exercise encampments, carry out maneuvers, marches, reviews, all to keep their troops up to the mark, making them practiced, and not allowing them to forget the fatigue of serious campaigns, nor the art of winning. (37)

I-15.   Debt

Bielfeld distinguishes between two kinds of debt: sovereign debt and debt accrued in commercial transaction:

> a state can have two kinds of debt: one whose real value is employed in manufactures, commerce, and all sorts of useful establishments for the relief of the people; the other in which the fund is consumed by the sovereign in frivolous expenditure. The excess of this latter kind of debt can only enervate the state, and lead it into a certain ruin.

Today we can observe that democratic governments may also engage in frivolous expenditure and assume large debts:

> If the country in question has no kind of equivalent for the debt contracted upon its credit, if it has insufficient means to regain through the balance of its commerce the interests which the state pays annually on the borrowed capitals, not long is needed before it falls into decline. (38)

I-16.   Constant Internal Wrangling

'The continual wrangling between ministers, generals and others in monarchies, and in republics the divisions between Senate and People, between magistrates and the heads of government – both can easily lead the state into decline, and from decline to fall.' Constant wrangling between ministers, generals and others in monarchies, and senate and people in republics, can lead to state decline because 'that every kingdom divided against itself will be reduced to a desert, and every city or house divided against itself cannot persist'. However, it is recognised that 'real boats rock', and that divisions are 'a necessary consequence of the republican state'.

While one can of course imagine the most perfect form of government, and set out the wisest maxims of policy, it is always necessary to place conduct of the diverse branches of government into different departments, which is to say, in the hands of men who are full of passion. If these passions blind them, if their views of matters are too diverse, if they are divided among themselves, their actions will unfailingly be at cross-purposes, and the state will fall into anarchy. Such divisions are more frequent and more dangerous in republics, for there is no authority as great or as active as in monarchies, capable of reuniting all employees under the banner of the public good, and making everyone address their own tasks in spite of themselves. Divisions are a necessary consequence of the republican state; they always have been, and always will be. Sovereign power cannot make itself felt too quickly to suppress disunion and bring its progress to a sudden halt, even with the greatest rigour (39).

I-17.   Interfering with Fundamental Laws of Government

When a republic interferes with the fundamental laws that regulate the constitution of its government the state runs a very great risk of running to ruin.

I know that different times call for different ways, and that laws have to follow those changes that occur in the world's state of affairs; but the constitution of the state must never alter, and the laws bearing upon this must remain as far as possible immutable. Every political arrangement has its disadvantages, and it is better to deal with those that arise from an established system than to change a system that has long supported a state. Experience is here in agreement with theory and principles. (40)

I-18.   Regicide or Assassination of the Sovereign

The killing of the sovereign is an indirect cause that can bring about the decline or overthrow of a state, weakening its resilience. One thinks that these evil deeds, whose seed was sown in the works of Machiavelli and his disciples, have been stifled by the philosophical spirit which has, over the last few centuries, improved Europe's police and, it has been said, made Europe more virtuous:

> all the citizens of a country, in submitting themselves to monarchical government, feel that their individual wills are united in the single person of the sovereign, to whom they accord an authority necessary to this end, and related powers to set it to work; that the person of the monarch has been rendered sacred and inviolable by the universal consent of all civilised nations, and the king is endowed with the title of 'majesty' to impress upon the hearts of all men a greater veneration for their dignity. One also sees that it is not permissible for any member of society, of whatever estate, and whatever degree he might be, to believe his own interest, or that of the state in general, to be hurt in any particular, or betrayed by the decrees of his sovereign, such that he acquires the slightest trace of a right to make an attempt on the monarch; for on the contrary, each citizen is individually wounded by this same attentat. (41)

NOTES

1. The full English text of Bielfeld's chapter can be found in Reinert (2014).
2. For a discussion of German economic theory in this period, see Reinert (2019).
3. Bielfeld is mentioned for this in modern textbooks, eg. in Gupta (2004: Section 15.1). See also Ycart (2016).
4. For a discussion of Adam Smith's role in this, see Reinert (1999).
5. An early warning here was Magaziner and Reich (1982)
6. This refers to Montesquieu's (1721) *Lettres persanes*.

REFERENCES

Bielfeld, Jacob Friedrich von, *Progrès des allemands dans les sciences: les belles-lettres & les arts, particulièrement dans la poésie & l'eloquence*, Amsterdam: F. Changuion, 1752.

Bielfeld, Jacob Friedrich von, *Institutions Politiques*, 2 vols, The Hague: Chez Pierre Gosse Junior, 1760.

Bielfeld, Jacob Friedrich von, *Letters of Baron Bielfeld: Secretary of Legation to the King of Prussia; Preceptor to Prince Ferdinand; Chancellor of the Universitys in the dominions of his Prussian Majesty, F.R.A.B. &c. Author of the Political Institutes: Containing Original Anecdotes of the Prussian Court for the Last Twenty Years*, London: J. Robson, 1768.

Bielfeld, Jacob Friedrich von, *The Elements of Universal Erudition: Containing an Analytical Abridgment of the Sciences, Polite Arts, and Belles Lettres*, 3 vols, London: G. Scott, for J. Robson, 1770; Dublin edition: Printed for H. Saunders, J. Potts, etc, 1771.

Fournay, Johann Heinrich Samuel, 'Eloge de M. de Bielfeld', in *Nouveaux Mémoires del'Académie Royale des Sciences de Berlin*, Berlin: Voss, 1772.

Frank, Thomas, *What's the Matter with Kansas?*, New York: Metropolitan Books, 2004.

Franklin, Benjamin, *The Way to Wealth*. Philadelphia, PA: Printed and sold by B. Franklin and D. Hall, 1757.

Frederick the Great, *Anti-Machiavel, ou Essai de critique sur le Prince de Machiavel*, Publié par M. de Voltaire A Bruxelles, Chez François Foppens, 1740.

Gibbon, Edward, *The History of the Decline and Fall of the Roman Empire*, London: Strahan & Cadell, 1776–1789.

Gupta, B.D., *Mathematical Physics*, New Delhi: Vikas, 2004.

Kennedy, Paul, *The Rise and Fall of the Great Powers*, New York: Random House, 1987.

King, Charles, *The British Merchant; or, Commerce Preserv'd*, 3 vols, London: John Darby, 1721.

Levitsky, Steven and Daniel Ziblatt, *How Democracies Die*, New York: Crown, 2018.

Magaziner, Ira C., and Robert Reich, *Minding America's Business: The Decline and Rise of the American Economy*, New York: Harcourt Brace Jovanovich, 1982.

Montesquieu, Charles de Secondat, baron de, *Lettres persanes*, 1721.

Pires, Ferreira Gervásio, *Resumo das Instituições Políticas do Barão de Bielfeld, parafraseadas e acomodadas à forma actual do governo do Império do Brasil, oferecido à mocidade brasiliense por um seu compatriota pernambucano*, Rio de Janeiro: Tipografia Nacional, 1823.

Reinert, Erik S., 'The Role of the State in Economic Growth', *Journal of Economic Studies*, 26 (4/5), 1999, pp. 268–326.

Reinert, Erik S., 'Jacob Bielfeld's On the Decline of States (1760) and its Relevance for Today', in Backhaus, Jürgen (ed.), *Great Nations at Peril*, New York: Springer, 2014, pp. 133–172.

Reinert, Erik S., *The Visionary Realism of German Economics. From the Thirty Years' War to World War II*, London: Anthem, 2019.

Reinert, Sophus A. (ed.), *Antonio Serra, A 'Short Treatise' on the Wealth and Poverty of Nations (1613)*, London: Anthem, 2011.

Reinert, Sophus A. 'The Way to Wealth Around the World: Benjamin Franklin and the Globalization of American Capitalism', *American Historical Review*, 120 (1), 2015, pp. 61–97.

Ricardo, David, *The Principles of Political Economy and Taxation*, London: John Murray, 1817.

Seckendorff, Veit Ludwig von, *Teutscher Fürsten-Staat*, Frankfurt: Götz, 1656.

Serra, Antonio, *Breve trattato che possono far abbondare li regni d'oro & ergeno, dove non sono miniere*, Naples: Lazzaro Scorriggio, 1613.

Stössl, Friedel, *Jakob Friedrich von Bielfeld: sein Leben und Werk im Lichte der Aufklärung*, Forchheim: O. Mauser, 1937.

Veblen, Thorstein, *Theory of the Leisure Class*, New York: Macmillan, 1899.

Voss, Gerda, *Jakob Friedrich Freiherr von Bielfeld; Ein Jugendfreund Friedrich des Großen*, introduction by Stephan Kekulé von Stradonitz ['Unter Förderung der Grossen National-Mutterloge "Zu den drei Weltkugeln" und "des Vereins deutscher Freimaurer"'], Berlin: Curtius, 1928.

Ycart, Bernard, 'Jacob Bielfeld (1717–1770) and the Diffusion of Statistical Concepts in Eighteenth Century Europe', *Historia Mathematica*, 43 (1), 2016, pp. 26–48.

12. Free trade with the former COMECON countries as unequal exchange

Marta Kuc-Czarnecka, Andrea Saltelli, Magdalena Olczyk and Erik S. Reinert

Two authors of this chapter were born to the east of what was once the Iron Curtain and two to the west. From both angles, the two systems – capitalism and communism – seemed to be as contrary to each other as possible. Few people are aware that in terms of industrial and trade policy, both classical capitalism and communism had a common root in the theories of German economist Friedrich List (1789–1846) (List 1841). In fact, for the 200th anniversary of his birth in 1989, both East Germany (DDR) and West Germany's Deutsche Bundespost celebrated Friedrich List's anniversary with postage stamps. The two enemies who had split Germany between them even chose the same portrait of their common hero.

However, after the collapse of the Berlin Wall, the policy that was forced upon the former Council for Mutual Economic Assistance (COMECON) countries was not the old capitalism honoured by West Germany in 1989. Capitalist theory (but not practice) had given way to neoliberalism, a system that does not see any difference between economic activities. The theory that came out as a winner at the end of the Cold War was essentially David Ricardo's (1817) theory of international trade (Ricardo 1974 [1817]), restated by United States (US) economist Paul Samuelson. Samuelson 'proved' that free trade, regardless of what was traded, would create a movement towards factor price equalization (that the price of the factors of production, capital and labour) would tend to equalize across the globe. This neoliberal theory was immediately forced upon the former communist countries, leading to different degrees of deindustrialization.

List's theories became the theoretical foundation for the countries that followed England's path to capitalist industrialization. There are also two crucial links between the bourgeois economist Friedrich List and communism. The first was his influence on Karl Marx (1818–1883). It seems that Marx only started writing about economics after having read List's main work from

1841. 'Paradoxically enough, Marx was introduced to political economy, not by reading the Western classics, but by their chief German critic' (Szporluk 1988: 21). Thoroughly understanding List's theory, Marx at one point states: 'the Free Trade system works destructively ... and carries antagonism of proletariat and bourgeoisie to the uttermost point. In a word, the Free Trade System hastens the Social Revolution. In this revolutionary sense alone, gentlemen, I am in favor of Free Trade.'[1]

The second important link to communism was through Sergei Witte (1849–1915), the Russian Minister of Finance under the last two tsars. In 1889, when Witte had just entered government, he wrote a lengthy pamphlet on the work of Friedrich List. Inspired by List, Witte saw the future of his country in terms of industrialization and railway building. After the 1917 Russian Revolution people found to their surprise that the industrial policy of the Bolsheviks was essentially the policy prescribed by Sergei Witte starting 30 years earlier (Von Laue 1963).

Interestingly the first warning against the harmful effects of the policy that followed after the fall of the Berlin Wall, presenting 'a dramatically different view of how to help post-Soviet economies', was published in 1992, with Jan Kregel (who wrote Chapter 16 in this book) as one of the authors (Kregel et al. 1992).

INTRODUCTION

In this chapter, we examine the consequences of the largest opening and enlargement of the European Union (EU) in terms of uneven economic development and resulting migration: (1) for the countries of Central and Eastern Europe (CEE); (2) for the European Union as a whole; and (3) also for the former CEE countries that remained outside the European Union (such as Belarus, Moldova and Ukraine).

The study is divided into two periods. The first period begins with the end of the Eastern European free trade zone (COMECON) in 1991 and ends in 2004. The second period starts with the so-called 'Big Bang' EU enlargement, that is, integrating a large number of former COMECON countries into the European Union, on 1 May 2004 (Bulgaria and Romania followed in 2007). Both periods led to varying degrees of deindustrialization and emigration from the CEE countries.

In 1991, and even more so in 2004, European ideology underwent a remarkable transformation. The value placed on industry and manufacturing gradually disappeared, giving way to a neoliberal vision (Reinert 2020a). According to this school of thought, accession to world markets and the European Union promised alignment with Western European living standards for the CEE countries (Kijek and Matras-Bolibok 2020). The view of international trade as it developed during the Cold War is consistent with US economist Paul Samuelson's interpretation of David Ricardo's 1817 theory of trade (Samuelson 1948, 1949), according to which international trade would tend to lead to factor price equalization: that is, that prices for labour and capital would tend to equalize among nations. In this theory, all economic activities are considered qualitatively equal. Thus, if we were to send all the shoe shiners to one country and all the high-tech engineers to another, both countries and the workers would tend to become equally rich. As previously in Latin America (Reinert and Kattel 2004), this theory has caused considerable economic damage in CEE countries.

Despite sceptical voices warning as to the excessive diversity and inadequate preparation of the CEE countries, attitudes toward accessions were generally positive. The elimination of existing geographic, socio-economic and, in a sense, cultural boundaries toward a common destiny had now become one of the principles of the EU, as expressed by President Juncker when he stated that 'the notion of convergence is at the heart of our economic union' (Juncker 2015). An early lone voice firmly opposed to the optimistic folly of factor price equalization was Harvard economic historian David Landes, who wrote to one of the authors in 1999 (Reinert 2007: 294): 'If we ever achieve factor price equalization, who says it will go up?' Landes had an inkling of what would happen: integration with an Eastern European low-wage area led to downward pressure on wages in the old EU countries (Reinert and Kattel 2007, 2004). Incidentally, it is increasingly argued these days that similar dynamics are at play in China–US relations (Hirsh 2020).

It seems that both CEE countries and the EU were not fully prepared for this enlargement (Borg and Diez 2015; Reinert 2006). Moreover, various phenomena that could not be foreseen in the prevailing neoclassical economic framework, such as the economic crisis, the refugee crisis, and the rise of anti-European political forces, exposed shortcomings and inefficiencies in the foundations of integration, leading to a high risk of dissatisfaction among the intended recipients of EU policies (Czech and Krakowiak-Drzewiecka 2019; Skare and Porada-Rochoń 2019). Undoubtedly, the European model of integration of two completely different economies was unprecedented in the world. Nevertheless, it showed uneven and unequal territorial effects of industrial change and globalization, associated with differing opportunities and living standards. Therefore, investigating these questions is very important in order to create guidelines for future policies.

PREVIOUS WORKS

It has been argued that with the Eastern enlargement, the European Union has abandoned its earlier implicit strategy of symmetric integration and emphasized the role of solid manufacturing industries in all member states (Reinert and Kattel 2004). It has also been noted that the relationship between 'donors' and 'recipients' of democracy promotion is asymmetric (Grimm and Grimm 2019), meaning that in the context of administrative changes, 'donor countries' have greater influence than 'recipient countries', which ultimately behave as passive actors in the international arena.

As indicated earlier, neoclassical economic theory assumes that economic integration, together with free trade and market competitiveness, leads to equal remuneration of the factors of production – labour and capital – around the world. In practice, growth rates and wage levels depend heavily on local factors and the specific structure and context of individual economies; in other words, economic growth is 'activity-specific'. An old tradition that began with the work of Antonio Serra (Serra [1613] 2011), is still very much alive in Alfred Marshall's founding work on neoclassical economics (Marshall 1890), and was briefly revived by Paul Krugman in 1981 (Krugman 1981), explains how inequalities can be exacerbated – rather than mitigated – by economic integration (Cieślik and Hien Tran 2019). These theories simply distinguish between economic activities that are subject to diminishing returns to scale (where a factor of production is inherently limited) and where production costs increase beyond a certain point, and those that are subject to increasing returns to scale, where higher production leads to higher productivity and decreasing costs. Reinert (1980) showed how the major export commodities of three Latin American countries – Bolivia, Ecuador and Peru – produced well into the range of diminishing returns: whenever production volume was reduced, production costs fell. A recent Organisation for Economic Co-operation and Development report (OECD 2018) on Chile proves that the same exact mechanisms in Chilean copper mining are at work.

It is important to note that within a country or region, rising revenues lead to higher barriers to entry into an industry, resulting in imperfect competition, and rents that are passed on to the country or region in the form of higher profits, higher wages and higher taxable income. Goods produced with diminishing returns are usually commodities subject to perfect competition (commodity competition). When productivity increases, the benefits – by definition – tend to be passed on to consumers in the form of lower prices (Reinert 1994). Activities with increasing returns have a triple blessing: decreasing costs under imperfect competition and high profits. In contrast, activities with diminishing returns face a triple curse: rising costs (beyond a certain point) with perfect competition and low profits. When these mechanisms come into play – for example, between the colonial power and its colonies – increased economic integration can lead to the rapid development of the wealthier and more prosperous regions at the expense of the peripheral areas.

Most of the literature on EU enlargement has focused on explaining the successful aspects of this integration (Crescenzi and Giua 2016, 2018; Heider 2018; Rapacki and Prochniak 2019). The relatively small number of critical approaches focus mainly on political inequality and the uncertainty associated with further integration (Hodson and Puetter 2019; Hooghe and Marks 2019), the polarization of policies (Kuhn 2019; Rauh et al. 2019), shortcomings of the European Monetary Union (Koyama 2016), and social dumping (Bernaciak 2014; Ricci 2019). Relatively few studies have addressed industrialization in this setting (Duman and Kurekova 2012; Medve-Balint and Scepanovic 2019; Pavlinek 2018), nor have they followed James Kenneth Galbraith's intuition of the looming dangers that 'if the East Europeans fall asleep on the train to Stockholm, they may wake up as the boat docks in Buenos Aires' (Galbraith 1991).

The questions of which regions have benefited most from the combination of cohesion and industrial policy, and what factors influence the success of integration, remain largely unanswered. In this chapter, we adapt some of the theses of the evolutionary (Schumpeterian) and historical schools of economic development (Reinert 2007) to examine the different stages of the development of the EU project. We revisit some of the theses of the 1988 Cecchini report (Cecchini et al. 1988) regarding the expected benefits of the EU project in terms of increasing returns to scale in manufacturing. We examine the scope and limits of EU industrial policy by focusing on CEE countries, which are classic examples of dependent market economies. We examine whether the rapid opening of their economies and subsequent accession deprived the CEE countries as a whole of economic activities in which productivity gains spread 'collusively' – in the form of higher profits and higher wages – and left them with low-tech activities in which the benefits from productivity gains spread as they are assumed to do under perfect competition: namely, as lower prices for consumers (who may be located abroad). Note that without entry, the CEE countries would have been able to retain at least some of the collusive opportunities. The term 'collusive' here refers to the development and retention of activities where increased productivity leads to higher wages rather than lower prices, and to policies that bring government and industry together as accomplices in developing an advanced manufacturing sector with increasing returns (Reinert 1994). We recognize that the differences among the countries are enormous, and we try to take them into account as we look for common trends.

RESEARCH HYPOTHESES

Our research questions cover a long period, from the fall of the Berlin Wall in 1989 to the present, focusing on the impact of the opening of the markets of the CEE countries and their subsequent accession to the European Union in 2004–2007.

We skip the earlier stages of the EU economic development and start with the period 1957–1993, which is a continuation of the economic ideology of the highly successful Marshall Plan of 1947. According to this philosophy, the presence of manufacturing in all countries is necessary for them to achieve a satisfactory standard of living. Thus, Paolo Cecchini, in his co-authored 1988 report entitled 'Europe 1992, The Overall Challenge' (Cecchini et al. 1988), was correct in noting that the main benefits from the single market (estimated at ECU 200 billion or more at the time of the report) would come as a result of increasing returns to scale in the manufacturing industry. The opportunities for 'economies of scale' and for 'fixed investment costs with increased sales volume' were highlighted in the report.

This was the ideology on which the Marshall Plan and the European Economic Community (EEC) had been built. The Maastricht Treaty instead was signed in the spirit of the triumphalism of the market that followed the fall of the Berlin Wall in 1989, the spirit that began with Paul Samuelson's 1948/1949 articles built on David Ricardo's 1817 theory of international trade. Cecchini's very explicit assumptions about the key role of manufacturing in creating benefits for participating nations were seemingly forgotten. However, the free trade shock of 1990 wiped out large parts of the manufacturing sector in the former COMECON countries. The introduction of the euro in 1999, the freezing of exchange rates and the elimination of the main adjustment mechanism among European nations, had the undesirable consequence of causing many peripheral countries to lose their (manufacturing) industries with increasing returns, which formed the core of Cecchini's argument (Reinert 2017, 2018; Reinert and Kattel 2007, 2019). Cecchini had no way to antici-pate that some countries would largely lose their manufacturing as a result of changing economic paradigms.

On this basis, we test the theory that countries prevented from developing export goods in increasing returns industries end up exporting people instead (Reinert 2007). In other words, we postulate the same relationship between economic structure and population density as Hoover did in his 1947 postwar analysis of the effects of the deindustrializing Morgenthau Plan on the pop-ulation density of a deindustrialized Germany: 'There is an illusion that the New Germany remaining after the annexations can be reduced to a "pastoral state." This is not possible unless we annihilate or expatriate 25 000 000 people' (Hoover, in a letter to President Truman, 18 March 1947). This letter to Washington was undoubtedly an essential factor in the establishment of the Marshall Plan – the opposite of the Morgenthau Plan – a few months later (in June 1947). That diminishing returns cause migration had already been stated by the founder of neoclassical economics, Alfred Marshall (1890). Krugman

(1981) also takes up a model of the US economist Frank Graham (1923) and places increasing returns and the lack thereof in the context of what he calls a 'Hobson–Lenin view' based on the works on imperialism by Hobson (1902) and Lenin (1939).

On this basis, we will look at the phenomenon of migration within the EU – which is usually presented as an opportunity for both sides, that is, both exporting and importing countries – as a process that can potentially produce winners and losers. To this end, we will look at the number, gender and skills of economic migrants, and the entrepreneurial activities of migrants in the host countries. Other hypotheses put to the test in this chapter concern the economic structure of the CEE countries and the industrial composition of their economies. Finally, we address the question of what happened in the periphery of the periphery, that is, what shocks were transmitted from CEE countries to countries beyond their borders, including Belarus, Moldova and Ukraine.

EMPIRICAL ANALYSIS

Our analysis was performed based on publicly available data on the relationship between gross domestic product (GDP) and the stock and flow of labour. The analysis covers two periods: the period of CEE countries' integration with world markets after the collapse of COMECON, 1991–2019; and the period of transformation and international migration flow after the largest EU enlargement in 2004–2007.

Integration of Disintegration? A Long Way to the Global Economy

It is vital to realize that there are various types of deindustrialization. There are three key differentiating factors: (1) per capita income from which the deindustrialization process begins; (2) the nature of the manufacturing activities in relative decline and the non-manufacturing activities that are relatively growing; and (3) the dynamics of the process (Tregenna 2009, 2011, 2014). In short, the adverse effects of deindustrialization are expected to be greater, the lower the level of economic development at which it initiates. Moreover, there is enormous variability within sectors regarding cumulative productivity and contribution to the balance of payments. Thus, deindustrialization does not occur when the employment share in manufacturing decreases due to more rapid productivity growth here than in other sectors, as long as this takes place with a simultaneous increase in the employment level in manufacturing and an increase in the manufacturing share in GDP.

Table 12.1 includes economic indicators used for detecting deindustrialization (understood as a decrease in the share of manufacturing value-added in GDP) in CEE countries since 1990. Comparing those countries with Germany,

Table 12.1   Percentage change in manufacturing value-added as a percentage of GDP

Period		ISO code										
	BU	CZ	DE	EE	HR	HU	LT	LV	MD	PL	SK	UA
1995–2000	-3.33	9.68	0.04	-9.14	-9.47	5.05	0.21	-22.78	-37.53	-17.10	4.95	-47.30
1995–2019	-23.79	4.15	-5.33	-24.31	-35.18	0.24	-3.33	-42.40	-51.25	-13.13	-2.88	-64.99

Notes: BU – Belarus, CZ – Czechia, DE – Germany, EE – Estonia, HR – Croatia, HU – Hungary, LT – Lithuania, LV – Latvia, MD – Moldova, PL – Poland, SK – Slovakia, UA – Ukraine. (Bulgaria: lack of data).
Sources: Based on data from World Bank and OECD.

a significant decline in the industrial potential in all countries can be observed, both in the short term (1995–2000) and in the long term (1995–2019). Severe deindustrialization occurred in Latvia, Moldova, Romania and Ukraine, where the decrease in manufacturing value-added share in GDP in 1995–2019 ranged from 30 to 60 per cent (Table 12.1). A slower pace of deindustrialization can be observed in Czechia, Hungary, Lithuania and Slovakia, which had a rate of change close to Germany's economy, which is probably the result of the substantial inflow of foreign direct investment (FDI) to these countries between 1990 and 2015 (Cieślik 2019). The most worrying phenomenon is the permanent decline in the share of manufacturing value-added of all countries in the period 2005–2019; therefore, it is not limited to the initial period of the analysis.

Deindustrialization can also be analysed through the prism of employment. Table 12.2 reveals that in all CEE countries in 1995–2009, the average wage in manufacturing has dwindled compared to wages in the entire economy. This tendency is opposite to that observed in the German economy, in the face of the common opinion of manufacturing as the 'wage leader' in national econo-mies. The compensation of work in manufacturing was significantly reduced in the post-accession period, which could be explained by low productivity growth in manufacturing compared to other industries. Another explanation is a slow change in manufacturing structure, with the persistence of a substantial fraction of low-wage sectors, such as textiles or wood industries. This hypoth-esis is also supported by the data included in Table 12.3, that is, showing the technological intensity in the manufacturing sector as research and develop-ment (R&D) expenditure measured as a fraction in the added value.

Table 12.3 underlines a significant difference in the technology intensity between Germany and CEE countries. Estonia, Poland and Slovakia achieved no more than 20 per cent of the technological power of Germany. Only Czechia and Hungary recorded an increase in R&D expenditure in manufac-turing (as a fraction of value-added). Radosevic (2017) notes that the EU is moving towards manufacturing modernization based on large-scale invest-ments in smart specialization and highly innovative R&D activities. From that perspective, the CEE countries can be perceived as peripheral.

Since the beginning of the transformation in the 1990s, small CEE coun-tries have been strongly export-oriented. In almost every CEE country in 1993–2008, the share of manufacturing products in total exports exceeded 80 per cent. In Czechia, Estonia, Hungary, Latvia and Slovakia, the ratio of exported goods and services to GDP is the highest in the EU, and manufactur-ing is the dominant export sector (Table 12.4). Czechia, Hungary and Slovakia focus their export activities mostly on automotive, telecommunications and electrical products, due to substantial investments of Volkswagen and Skoda. The significant share of telecommunications products in Estonian exports

Table 12.2   Labour compensation per employee in manufacturing relative to the total economy, 1995–2009

ISO	Year														
	1995	1996	1997	1998	1999	2000	2001	2002	2003	2004	2005	2006	2007	2008	2009
CZ	100.8	101.4	100.2	102.4	103.3	103.4	103.0	102.5	100.7	102.4	102.0	101.5	102.6	101.2	96.9
EE	89.6	90.7	98.0	96.8	92.9	93.9	92.3	99.8	95.5	91.1	91.8	97.4	94.2	88.3	87.4
DE	128.7	130.0	131.4	133.1	134.1	136.9	137.4	138.0	139.0	141.5	142.5	146.3	146.6	146.0	142.3
HU	110.1	110.0	109.3	104.7	106.3	109.2	101.6	94.5	92.1	92.9	93.2	92.4	93.2	91.4	91.8
PL	112.9	114.7	115.7	116.8	115.8	119.8	113.4	114.6	112.0	110.7	108.3	106.3	106.9	105.3	104.3
SK	100.6	99.0	96.9	96.7	97.8	101.9	102.8	102.0	103.9	103.2	101.2	105.1	105.0	107.2	103.8

Source: Based on data from OECD STAN.

Table 12.3   *R&D intensity using value-added for the manufacturing sector*

Year	ISO code					
	CZ	EE	DE	HU	PL	SK
1995	2.14	1.13	6.75	1.32	0.97	1.08
2009	2.85	1.06	8.23	2.48	0.62	0.75

Source: Based on data from OECD STAN.

Table 12.4   *Manufacturing export in a total of goods export (%)*

Year	ISO code				
	CZ	DE	HU	PL	SK
1993	88.21	94.58	91.33	86.24	97.20
2008	95.68	91.14	94.24	94.48	95.24

Source: Based on data from OECD STAN.

is due to the strong Swedish branch of Ericsson. Latvia and Lithuania are exporters of raw materials and wooden products, and Poland exports furniture and ships.

The literature (Deardorff 1980; Greenhalgh et al. 1994) treats trade balance as a good approximation of international competitiveness, expressing a country's ability to succeed in the global market. Inability to meet the domestic demand, leading to an increase in imports, is reflected in a negative trade balance and indicates the lack of competitiveness of domestic industries. Such a trade balance can become permanent if the export structure cannot adjust to the global market's needs.

Figure 12.1 reveals that in 1992–2008, a negative trade balance was observed in the analysed CEE countries. The worst situation occurred in Poland, where imports exceeded exports for almost the whole period after the transformation. Since 2003–2004, only Czechia, Hungary and Slovakia strengthened their GDP growth through a positive trade balance.

Figures 12.2 and 12.3 present GDP growth in the former Soviet Union and CEE countries belonging to the European Union. The scale on both visualizations is fixed to allow direct comparisons. It can be noticed that GDP growth curves in the former Soviet Union countries were steeper than those in CEE countries.

Uzbekistan is a remarkable country that successfully implemented the old-fashioned strategy of substituting imports from Latin America.[2] Such a policy favours the domestic industry by imposing high tariffs on imported goods. With the help of Japanese companies, Uzbekistan even managed to start local production of buses and trucks. Thus, Uzbek policy is similar to the

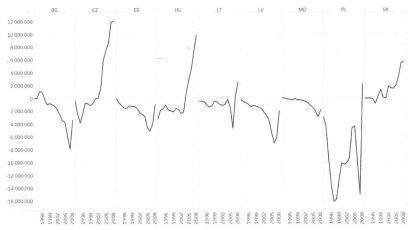

Source: Based on data from OECD STAN.

Figure 12.1   The trade balance in manufacturing, 1992–2009

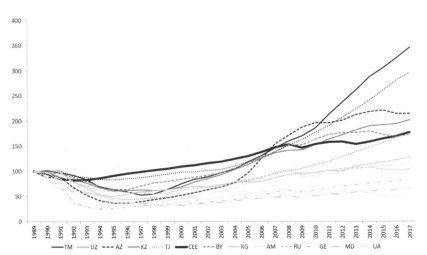

Note: TM – Turkmenistan, UZ – Uzbekistan, AZ – Azerbaijan, KZ – Kazakhstan, TJ – Tajikistan, KG – Kyrgyzstan, AM – Armenia, RU – Russia, GE – Georgia.
Source: Based on data from Popov (2019).

Figure 12.2   GDP growth in the Former Soviet Union, 1987–2017

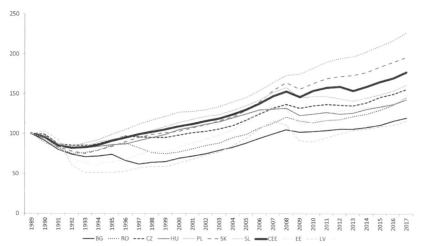

Source: Based on data from Popov (2019).

Figure 12.3   GDP growth in the Central and Eastern European countries belonging to the EU, 1987–2017

19th century US policy, which allowed for free import of raw materials, but the tariffs were set based on the standard that 'the higher the added value, the higher the import duty'.

Migration

The labour markets and the demographic situation in the newly associated countries were formed by the economic performance in the CEE countries and the EU's free movement of people policy. In 2004, migrations were a relatively marginal phenomenon: CEE residents usually migrated to 1–2 selected countries (mainly Germany and the United Kingdom), while their presence in the remaining EU15 countries was negligible. However, the migration processes intensified over the analysed 15-year period from 2004 to 2019. The fraction of Bulgarians living in the 'old EU' countries in 2004 was 0.71 per cent, and it was the highest migration rate among the CEE countries. In 2004, 0.33 per cent of all Poles lived in Germany, which was nearly 70 per cent of Polish emigrants. In 2004, Czechia had the lowest ratio of emigrants, with only 0.05 per cent of inhabitants living in EU15 countries, mainly Germany.

By 2019, the situation had changed radically; the number of emigrants residing in the EU15 had skyrocketed. The negligible Czech emigration from 2004 increased to almost 6 per cent in 2019, with nearly 80 per cent of Czech emigrants living in Germany. Currently, the largest outflow is observed in Romania, where around 15 per cent of the population lives abroad (mainly in Italy, Spain and Germany). Germany and the United Kingdom are still the most desirable migration destinations for CEE inhabitants. A interesting linguistic pattern can be observed as people move to countries within the same linguistic families: Italy being the primary destination for Romanians, and Finland for Estonians.

A comet chart in Figure 12.4 reveals that the migrant stock from CEE countries in 2004 did not exceed 1 per cent of the inhabitants of the origin country (comet tail, in light grey). The highest shares were observed in Romania (0.9 per cent of inhabitants), Bulgaria (0.7 per cent) and Latvia (0.6 per cent). Fifteen years later, the increase and diffusion of migration can be observed (comet head, in dark grey). Today, 15 per cent of Romanians, 11.27 per cent of Latvians, 10.63 per cent of Croats, 9.91 per cent of Bulgarians, and 9.45 per cent Poles live abroad.

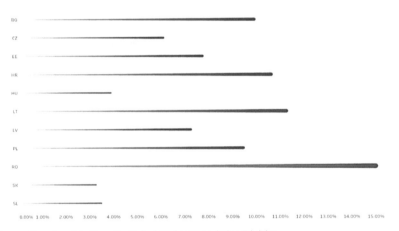

Source: Based on data from the United Nations Population Division.

Figure 12.4   *Percentage of CEE's population living in the 'old' European Union countries, 2004 and 2019*

In 2004, a positive net migration was documented in 11 countries, and none of them were CEE countries (Figure 12.5). In 2004, the highest net migration ratio reaching 1.32 per cent was observed in Cyprus and the second-highest (1.14 per cent) in Luxemburg. In 2019, all CEE countries still had a negative net migration. However, changes took place in the volume of migrants to the EU15 countries, which resulted from the expanded outflow of people from CEE countries. In 2019, looking at immigrants by country of destination,

Luxemburg had the highest percentages of immigrants (27 per cent), followed by Austria and Germany (4.5 per cent), Belgium (4 per cent), United Kingdom and Sweden (over 3 per cent). At the same time, Romania recorded a negative net migration of over -15 per cent; Lithuania of -13 per cent, Bulgaria of -9.5 per cent, and Poland of almost -9 per cent.

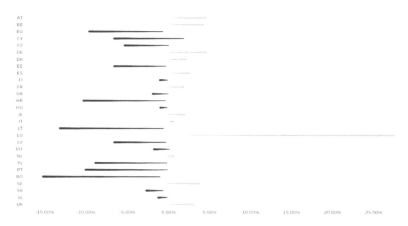

Note: Migration to and from non-EU countries was not taken into consideration.
Source: Based on data from the United Nations Population Division.

Figure 12.5   *Net migration rate among EU countries as a percentage of the population*

Considering differences in the gender of emigrants between countries, it turns out that women constituted a more significant proportion (up to 6 per cent difference in 2019). This number did not rise meaningfully over the analysed period (see Table 12.5). In Italy, 67 per cent of migrants are Moldovan women.

Table 12.6 displays the distribution of migrants from Belarus, Ukraine and Moldova in mid-2005 and mid-2019. For these three countries, Russia is the main target (approximately 7.5 per cent of the residents of each country are

Table 12.5   *Women as a percentage of total migrants, 2004 and 2019*

Year	ISO code											
	BG	CZ	EE	HR	HU	LT	LV	MD	PL	RO	SK	SL
2004	53.00	55.52	54.81	52.41	50.98	56.41	55.03	52.16	54.64	53.12	52.72	55.76
2019	56.77	55.40	54.96	51.67	50.04	55.14	55.16	53.24	51.52	53.14	53.55	53.89

Source: Based on data from the United Nations Population Division.

Table 12.6   The percentage of Belarusians, Ukrainians and Moldavians living abroad, 2005 and 2019

Destination*	Country of origin (2005)			Country of origin (2019)		
	BY	MD	UA	BY	MD	UA
CA	---	0.20	0.12	---	0.53	0.14
CZ	---	0.15	0.16	---	0.23	0.18
DE	0.21	0.49	0.40	0.21	0.60	0.44
EE	0.14	---	---	0.15	---	---
ES	---	0.24	0.13	---	0.54	0.15
FR	---	0.11	---	---	0.2	---
GR	---	0.23	---	---	0.28	---
IE	---	---	---	---	0.12	---
IL	0.27	0.47	0.31	0.28	0.3	0.35
IT	0.17	2.41	0.25	0.18	5.32	0.28
KG	0.15	0.11	---	0.16	---	0.1
KZ	0.59	0.28	0.60	0.61	0.35	0.67
LT	0.53	---	---	0.55	---	---
LV	0.68	---	0.10	0.71	---	0.11
PL	0.94	---	0.56	0.97	---	0.63
PT	---	0.31	---	---	0.57	---
RO	---	1.13	---	---	5.00	---
RU	8.67	7.93	6.99	8.96	8.29	7.85
US	0.48	0.71	0.63	0.50	1.34	0.71
UZ	0.29	---	0.28	0.30	---	0.32

Notes: * CA – Canada, US – the Unitied States of America. Only values higher than 0.1 per cent are displayed.
Source: Based on data from the United Nations Population Division.

living there). A comparison of data included in Table 12.6 does not indicate significant fluctuations in migration patterns between 2005 and 2019. A dramatic change can be seen in the increased fraction of Moldavians living in Romania (from 1.13 per cent to 5 per cent). No other significant changes have been seen over the past 15 years. In the case of Belarus, the number of emigrants increased by 0.1 percentage points, whereas in Moldova the growth was lower than 1 percentage point. In Ukraine, the number of emigrants rose by 0.2 percentage points. To conclude, the outflow of CEE inhabitants to EU15 countries has not been compensated by a parallel inflow from the former COMECON countries.

DISCUSSION AND CONCLUSIONS

According to Hirsh (2020) economists are now 'on the run' after their analysis seriously misfired, with Krugman reciting the most explicit *mea culpa* after realizing the damage done to US wages by competition with China. Unlike the United States, part of Europe, mainly the 'old' part, managed to profit from the asymmetric trade balance by using EU12 inhabitants as a source of cheap labour. Reinert (2020b) has defined this process as 'assumption-based rent': rents that accrue to richer countries due to the basic assumption of neoclassical economics. Migration movements within the European Union are not a hot political topic, compared to refugees and economic migrants from Africa and the Middle East. Undoubtedly, the import of cheap labour has hurt wages in the wealthier EU15 countries. Wage levels in the United Kingdom construction sector have been considerably reduced. There also seem to be somewhat negative migration hierarchies, or 'trickledown' effects. Paradoxically, in Western Ukraine, the good news is that the construction workforce migrates to Poland to replace employees who have migrated elsewhere. At the same time, in Moldova, we are told that the good news is that there are many construction jobs in Ukraine. Despite the official EU narrative of the enlargement as a path to wealth for all (Cecchini et al. 1988), it obviously produced many losers.

One problematic aspect of migration that is not explicitly treated in this work is the resulting loss of essential professions and skills. For example, the outflow of physicians and nurses may render the country of origin more vulnerable, as we are witnessing due to the COVID-19 pandemic (Szpakowski et al. 2019; Żuk et al. 2019). Moreover, deindustrialization always leads to increased migration, sometimes as an unstoppable sequence of deindustrialization, de-agriculturization and depopulation (Reinert 2017, 2013). In Mexico, an extreme case is Chiapas; another case is Moldova in Europe, where children tend to grow up with their grandparents because both parents are working abroad. It can be argued that lower wages also produce winners and losers in 'old' Europe. Some of the emigrant CEE citizens would prefer to remain in their homeland if they did not lack chances in the present quasi-colonial organization.

While we do not possess a valid counterfactual, the contrast of Figures 12.4 and 12.5 suggests that it is legitimate to wonder whether the CEE countries would have fared better economically by not joining the EU. The introduction of the common currency has made things worse for the periphery, where inflation continued in Italy and Greece, but stopped immediately in Germany. Whereas devaluations of the local currencies previously solved such imbalances within the European Union (be they liras, drachmas or escudos), the only adjustment mechanism now left is moving people, often against the will of both the migrant-exporting and the migrant-importing countries. The euro has worsened the migration problem, and one can assume that the relative success of Poland is partly due to avoiding pressure to replace zlotys with euros.

At the time of eastern expansion, experienced economists argued passionately against the 'shock therapy' generally unanimously recommended by Western economists. Kregel et al. (1992) encouraged a more gradual approach to avoid the shock therapy that in effect happened in 2004. Opening up for free trade inside the old COMECON countries at the time of the 1989 collapse would have eased the transition considerably by letting countries at similar levels of technological level 'learn' to compete inside a market economy. Apparently, there are only a few regrets. When will Europe's CEE countries finally awake from the lethargy of the 'Samuelsonian/Ricardian dream' (Reinert 2020a; Reinert et al. 2021) of factor price equalization?

ACKNOWLEDGEMENTS

We want to express our great gratitude to Professor Vladimir Popov for his courtesy and help, and for providing us with the raw data from Popov (2019).

The authors are grateful to the journal *Structural Change and Economic Dynamics* for permitting redrafting and shortening the text published as Kuc-Czarnecka et al. (2021).

NOTES

1. In Marx's 'Speech on the Question of Free Trade', quoted in Szporluk (1988: 20).
2. See also Vladimir Popov's Chapter 14 in this book.

REFERENCES

Bernaciak, M., 2014. 'Social dumping and the EU integration process', ETUI Working Paper, 2014.06.
Borg, S., Diez, T., 2015. 'Postmodern EU? Integration between alternative horizons and territorial angst', *JCMS: Journal of Common Market Studies*, 54, 136–151. https://doi.org/10.1111/jcms.12327.
Cecchini, P., Catinat, M., Jacquemin, A., 1988. *The European Challenge, 1992: The Benefits of a Single Market*. Aldershot: Wildwood House.
Cieślik, A., 2019. 'Bezpośrednie inwestycje zagraniczne w Polsce: stan obecny i perspektywy rozwoju', *Rocznik Instytutu Europy Środkowo-Wschodniej*, 17, 245–263. https://doi.org/10.36874/riesw.2019.1.11.
Cieślik, A., Hien Tran, G., 2019. 'Determinants of outward FDI from emerging economies'. *Equilibrium. Quarterly Journal of Economics and Economic Policy*, 14, 209–231. https://doi.org/10.24136/eq.2019.010.

Crescenzi, R., Giua, M., 2016. 'The EU cohesion policy in context: does a bottom-up approach work in all regions?', *Environment and Planning A: Economy and Space*, 48, 2340–2357. https://doi.org/10.1177/0308518X16658291.

Crescenzi, R., Giua, M., 2018. 'One or many cohesion policies of the European Union ? On the diverging impacts of cohesion policy across member states', SERC Discussion Papers.

Czech, S., Krakowiak-Drzewiecka, M., 2019. 'The rationale of Brexit and the theories of European integration'. *Oeconomia Copernicana*, 10, 589–602. https://doi.org/10 .24136/oc.2019.028.

Deardorff, A.V., 1980. 'The general validity of the law of comparative advantage', *Journal of Political Economy*, 88, 941–957. https://doi.org/10.1086/260915.

Duman, A., Kurekova, L., 2012. 'The role of state in development of socio-economic models in Hungary and Slovakia: the case of industrial policy', *Journal of European Public Policy*, 19, 1207–1228. https://doi.org/10.1080/13501763.2012.709018.

Galbraith, J.K., 1991. 'The false metaphor of transformation', in Joseph Lee and Walter Korter (eds), *Europe In Transition: Political, Economic and Security Prospects for the 1990s*. Austin, TX: Lyndon B. Johnson School of Public Affairs, pp. 29–42.

Graham, F.D., 1923. 'Some aspects of protection further considered', *Quarterly Journal of Economics*, 37, 199. https://doi.org/10.2307/1883929.

Greenhalgh, C.A., Taylor, P., Wilson, R., Greenhalgh, C., Taylor, P., Wilson, R., 1994. 'Innovation and export volumes and prices – a disaggregated study', *Oxford Economic Papers*, 46, 102–35. https://doi.org/10.1093/oxfordjournals.oep.a042115.

Grimm, S., Grimm, S., 2019. 'Democracy promotion in EU enlargement negotiations: more interaction, less hierarchy', *Democratization*, 26, 851–868. https://doi.org/10 .1080/13510347.2019.1590701.

Heider, B., 2018. 'The impact of EU Eastern enlargement on urban growth and decline: new insights from Germany' s Eastern border', *Papers in Regional Sciences*, 98, 1443–1468. https://doi.org/10.1111/pirs.12407.

Hirsh, M., 2020. 'Economists on the run', *Foreign Policy*, 22 October.

Hobson, J.A., 1902. *Imperialism: A Study*. New York: Pott & Co..

Hodson, D., Puetter, U., 2019. 'The European Union in disequilibrium: new inter-governmentalism, postfunctionalism and integration theory in the post-Maastricht period', *Journal of European Public Policy*, 26, 1153–1171. https://doi.org/10.1080/ 13501763.2019.1569712.

Hooghe, L., Marks, G., 2019. 'Grand theories of European integration in the twenty-first century', *Journal of European Public Policy*, 26, 1113–1133. https://doi .org/10.1080/13501763.2019.1569711.

Juncker, J.-C., 2015. *The Five Presidents' Report: Completing Europe's Economic and Monetary Union*. Background documents on economic and monetary union. https:// ec.europa.eu/info/publications/five-presidents-report-completing-europes-economic -and-monetary-union_en.

Kijek, A., Matras-Bolibok, A., 2020. 'Technological convergence across European regions', *Equilibrium. Quarterly Journal of Economics and Economic Policy*, 15, 295–313. https://doi.org/10.24136/eq.2020.014.

Koyama, Y., 2016. 'Systemic defects in the EMU and small countries in Central and Eastern Europe', *Finanse Rynki Finansowe i Ubezpieczenia*, 1, 687–704. https://doi .org/10.18276/frfu.2016.79-55.

Kregel, J., Grabher, G., Matzner, E., 1992. *The Market Shock: An Agenda for the Economic and Social Reconstruction of Central and Eastern Europe*. Vienna: Austrian Academy of Sciences.

Krugman, P., 1981. 'Trade, accumulation, and uneven development', *Journal of Development Economics*, 8, 149–161. https://doi.org/10.1016/0304-3878(81)90026-2.

Kuhn, T., 2019. 'Grand theories of European integration revisited: does identity politics shape the course of European integration?', *Journal of European Public Policy*, 26, 1213–1230. https://doi.org/10.1080/13501763.2019.1622588.

Kuc-Czarnecka, M., Saltelli, A., Olczyk, M., Reinert, E.S., 2021. 'The opening of Central and Eastern European countries to free trade: a critical assessment', *Structural Change and Economic Dynamics*, 58, 23–34. https://doi.org/10.1016/j.strueco.2021.04.005.

Lenin, V.I., 1939. *Imperialism: The Highest Stage of Capitalism*. New York: International Publishers.

List, F., 1841. *Das Nationale System der Politischen Ökonomie*. Stuttgart: Cotta.

Marshall, A., 1890. *Principles of Economics*. London: Macmillan. https://doi.org/10.1057/9781137375261_1.

Medve-Balint, G., Scepanovic, V., 2019. 'EU funds, state capacity and the development of transnational industrial policies in Europe's Eastern periphery', *Review of International Political Economy*. https://doi.org/https://doi.org/10.1080/09692290.2019.1646669.

OECD, 2018. *OECD Economic Surveys: Chile*. Paris.

Pavlinek, P., 2018. 'Global production networks, foreign direct investment, and supplier linkages in the integrated peripheries of the automotive industry', *Economic Geography*, 94, 141–165. https://doi.org/10.1080/00130095.2017.1393313.

Popov, V., 2019. 'Successes and failures of industrial policy: lessons from transition (post-communist) economies of Europe and Asia', MPRA Paper 95332, University Library of Munich, Germany.

Radosevic, S., 2017. 'Upgrading technology in Central and Eastern European economies', *IZA World Labor*, 338. https://doi.org/10.15185/izawol.338.

Rapacki, R., Prochniak, M., 2019. 'EU membership and economic growth : empirical evidence for the CEE countries', *European Journal of Comparative Economics*, 16, 3–40.

Rauh, C., Bes, B.J., Schoonvelde, M., 2019. 'Undermining , defusing , or defending European integration? Assessing public communication of European executives in times of EU politicization', *European Journal of Political Research*, 26(3), 344–365. https://doi.org/https://doi.org/10.1111/1475-6765.12350.

Reinert, E.S., 1980. 'International trade and the economic mechanism of underdevelopment', PhD thesis, Cornell.

Reinert, Erik S., 1994. 'Competitiveness and its predecessors – a 500 year cross-national perspective', Oslo. STEP Report No. 3/1994. (Also published in *Structural Change and Economic Dynamics*, Vol. 6, 1995, pp. 23–42, special issue on 'Changes in long-term competitiveness: an historical perspective'. Working paper version, https://mpra.ub.uni-muenchen.de/48155/1/MPRA_paper_48155.pdf. Republished 2020, https://www.networkideas.org/featured-articles/2020/11/competitiveness-and-its-predecessors-a-500-year-cross-national-perspective/.)

Reinert, E.S., 2006. 'European integration, innovations and uneven economic growth: challenges and problems of EU 2005', The Other Canon Foundation and Tallinn University of Technology Working Papers in Technology Governance and Economic Dynamics, No. 5.

Reinert, E.S., 2007. *How Rich Countries Got Rich and Why Poor Countries Stay Poor*. London: Constable.

Reinert, E.S., 2013. 'Primitivization of the EU periphery: how the European Union hollowed out Heinrich von Thünen's model and put both Friedrich List and Joseph Schumpeter into reverse gear', *IzR. Informationen Zur Raumentwicklung / Informations on Spatial Development*, 1/2, pp. 1–11.

Reinert, E.S., 2017. 'EU's three slippery concepts: an attempt to explain the lack of European cohesion', in: Allemand, F., Rassafi-Guibal, H. (eds), *État, Marché, Société: Un Ordre de Compétitivité*. Esch-sur-Alzette: Université du Luxembourg. https://resume.uni.lu/story/eus-three-slippery-concepts-an-attempt-to-explain-the -lack-of-europe.

Reinert, E.S., 2018. 'Smart Specialization: theory and brief case studies', A Report to the European Commission, JRC Seville, The Other Canon Foundation and Tallinn University of Technology Working Papers in Technology Governance and Economic Dynamics. No. 81.

Reinert, E.S., 2020a. 'The inequalities that could not happen: what the Cold War did to economics', in: Fullbrook, E., Morgan, J. (eds), *The Inequality Crisis*. Bristol: World Economics Association, pp. 387-430.

Reinert, Erik S., 2020b. 'The inequalities that could not happen: what the Cold War did to economics', *Real-World Economics Review*, 92: 186–206.

Reinert, E.S., Di Fiore, M., Saltelli, A., Ravetz, J.R., 2021. 'Altered states: Cartesian and Ricardian dreams', UCL, Institute for Innovation and Public Policy WP2021/07.

Reinert, E.S., Kattel, R., 2004. 'The qualitative shift in European integration: towards permanent wage pressures and a "Latin-Americanization" of Europe?', Praxis Working Papers, Tallinn. Reproduced as Chapter 16 in Reinert, E.S., 2019. *The Visionary Realism of German Economics: From the Thirty Years' War to the Cold War*. London: Anthem, pp. 477–512.

Reinert, E.S., Kattel, R., 2007. 'European eastern enlargement as Europe's attempted economic suicide?' The Other Canon Foundation and Tallinn University of Technology Working Papers in Technology Governance and Economic Dynamics, No. 14.

Reinert, E.S., Kattel, R., 2019. *The Visionary Realism of German Economics, From the Thirty Years' War to the Cold War*. London: Anthem.

Ricardo, D., 1974 [1817]. *The Principles of Political Economy and Taxation*. London and New York: Dent.

Ricci, A., 2019. 'Is there social or monetary dumping in the European Union? Manufacturing competitiveness in Central and Eastern Europe', *Entrepreneurial Business and Economics Review*, 7, 159–180. https://doi.org/10.15678/EBER.2019 .070109.

Samuelson, 1948. 'International trade and the equalisation of factor prices', *Economic Journal*, 58, 163–184.

Samuelson, Paul A., 1949, 'International factor-price equalisation once again', *Economic Journal*, 59, 181–197.

Serra, A., 2011. *A Short Treatise on the Wealth and Poverty of Nations (1613)*, edited by Sophus Reinert. London: Anthem Press.

Skare, M., Porada-Rochoń, M., 2019. 'Tracking financial cycles in ten transitional economies 2005–2018 using singular spectrum analysis (SSA) techniques', *Equilibrium. Quarterly Journal of Economics and Economic Policy*, 14, 7–29. https://doi.org/10.24136/eq.2019.001.

Szpakowski, R., Dykowska, G., Fronczak, A., Zając, P., Czerw, A., 2019. 'Migrations of nurses and doctors from Poland: data for the years 2014-2020 based on the sample of capital city of Warsaw', *Archives of Medical Scienes*, 15, 811–820. https://doi.org/10.5114/aoms.2017.70331.

Szporluk, R., 1988. *Communism and Nationalism. Karl Marx vs. Friedrich List*. New York: Oxford University Press.

Tregenna, F., 2009, 'Characterising deindustrialisation: an analysis of changes in manufacturing employment and output internationally', *Cambridge Journal of Economics*, 33(3). https://doi.org/10.1093/cje/ben032.

Tregenna, F., 2011, 'Manufacturing productivity, deindustrialization, and reindustrialization', WIDER Working Paper 2011/057. Helsinki: UNU-WIDER.

Tregenna, F., 2014, 'A new theoretical analysis of deindustrialisation', *Cambridge Journal of Economics*, 38(6). https://doi.org/10.1093/cje/bet029.

Von Laue, T., 1963. *Sergei Witte and the Industrialization of Russia*. New York: Columbia University Press.

Żuk, P., Żuk, P., Lisiewicz-Jakubaszko, J., 2019. 'Labour migration of doctors and nurses and the impact on the quality of health care in Eastern European countries: the case of Poland', *Economic and Labour Relations Review*, 30, 307–320. https://doi.org/10.1177/1035304619847335.

13. Escaping the poverty trap in China: the co-evolution of diversity in property and economic development

Ting Xu

INTRODUCTION

Seeking solutions for China to escape the poverty trap is a development policy of China (e.g., State Council Information Office of the PRC 2001, 2011, 2021). The idea that 'external aid can only temporarily alleviate poverty (*fupin*); development is the only way to escape poverty (*tuopin*)', was proposed by the Chinese government in 1986 and has become China's national policy since 1994 (e.g., General Office of the State Council 1986; State Council of the PRC 1994).[1] Development is regarded as the key to escaping poverty. For example, Professor Erik Reinert's 2007 book *How Rich Countries Got Rich ... and Why Poor Countries Stay Poor* explained modern economic development in relation to poverty and poverty traps.[2] His 2009 article on 'The Terrible Simplifiers' (Reinert 2009a) discussed how Korea escaped the poverty trap. Professor Peer Vries's 2013 book *Escaping Poverty: The Origins of Modern Economic Growth* examined how the West escaped poverty through a systematic comparison of Great Britain and China and emphasised the role of 'an active developmental state' in this process. Professor Yuen Yuen Ang's 2016 book *How China Escaped the Poverty Trap* discussed why and how development happened in China. Ang (2016: 3) argued that development is 'a co-evolutionary process': 'States and markets interact and adapt to each other, changing mutually over time.'[3]

When a country industrialises, the rural areas always stay behind. But the implementation of the 'development-oriented' poverty alleviation policy in China (State Council Information Office of the PRC 2011) provides a different experience. Major initiatives for promoting poverty reduction started from the rural areas. The white paper published by the State Council Information Office of the PRC in 2001 stated:

> The reform that China started in 1978 was, first and foremost, a reform of the land management system, i.e., replacing the collective management system of the people's commune with the household contract responsibility system. This change of the land system kindled the peasants' real enthusiasm for labor, thus greatly liberating the productive forces and improving the land output.

China's experience clearly demonstrates that one of the most important factors contributing to China's escape from the poverty trap is its reform of property in rural land. Here 'property' refers to both a resource and the way a resource is managed and regulated. The latter connotation of 'property' entails that property is an institution.[4] As a property lawyer who has worked on the co-evolution of property and economic development for many years, writing a chapter on China's escape from the poverty trap by focusing on property and economic development has become a natural choice. I need to answer three questions: (1) what kind of property as an institution can promote economic development? (2) What kind of economic development is crucial to the country's escape from the poverty trap? (3) What is the relationship between property and economic development?[5]

An analytical framework based on neoclassical economics cannot provide satisfactory answers to the three questions raised above, for neoclassical economics is 'a theory of accumulation of capital and allocation of resources, rather than of the creation and assimilation of new knowledge' (Reinert 2006: 5). According to neoclassical economics, free markets, individual liberty and private property rights protected by 'the rule of law' are the *sine qua non* for sustained economic growth. But one of the surprising cases that challenge this assumption is how China started growing very fast at the end of the Cold War, at a time when the Soviet Union entered a period of shock therapy.[6] An analytical framework based on neo-institutional economics cannot explain this puzzle either. While neo-institutional economics is interested in 'studying the institutional structures necessary for economic development', it 'tends to discuss institutions independent of the type of productive structure they support' (Reinert 2006: 1). By contrast, the 'old' institutional schools 'saw institutions as an integral part of a particular production system' (Reinert 2006: 1). According to the 'old' institutional schools, different production systems need different institutions; an institution by itself cannot alter the production system and promote economic development (Reinert 2006: 1). This approach to studying institutions originates from the work of Thorstein Veblen (1857–1929) (Reinert 2006: 1). Given the limitations of both the neoclassical and neo-institutional approaches, it is necessary to find an alternative analytical framework to answer the three questions above.

To answer the three questions above, this chapter proposes three hypotheses:

Hypothesis 1: Diversity in property, rather than clarity of property rights, has helped China to escape the poverty trap.

Hypothesis 2: The kind of economic development needed for countries including China to escape the poverty trap requires structural change, which is not a smooth process.

Hypothesis 3: Diversity in property and economic development co-evolves; new property regimes play a crucial role in introducing new production systems and in furthering economic development.

Here 'diversity in property' refers to different property arrangements in the same space at the same time, which will be further elaborated in the following sections.

To examine the three hypotheses, this chapter provides a new synthesis of the three areas of research I have done since embarking on my academic career: examining diversity in institutions, including diversity in property and an extended conception of 'the market'; bringing Darwinian ideas into the arena of studying property regime transformation in China; and studying the co-evolution of property in land and economic development. It draws insights from several research fields including law, governance and development; evolutionary and institutional economics; and political economy. In so doing, it advances the research field of examining poverty traps in relation to China through applying and developing approaches from evolutionary economics and legal studies.

This chapter first highlights the importance of diversity as a development strategy for a country to escape the poverty trap. Drawing on Darwinian ideas and insights from institutional and evolutionary economics, especially Veblenian and Schumpeterian institutions, it then offers a nuanced approach to studying the co-evolution of property and economic development, which contains key mechanisms including variation (diversity), inheritance, and selection (selective adaptation). For economic development, selection needs to be prompted by innovation and emulation. Employing this approach does not intend to theorise the co-evolution of property and economic development. Rather, it specifies the processes and mechanisms driving the co-evolution of property and economic development. The three mechanisms plus the 'innovation' and 'emulation' elements discussed in this chapter were proposed by Jean-Baptiste Lamarc (1744–1829), Charles Darwin (1809–1882), Thorstein

Veblen (1857–1929) and Joseph Schumpeter (1883–1950), and have been discussed by evolutionary economists (for example, Reinert and Hodgson) for a long time. The works of those scholars, including Lamarc, Darwin, Veblen, Schumpeter, Reinert and Hodgson, have influenced me to develop the analytical framework of applying the three mechanisms in the context of property and economic activities in China. Schumpeter's work is particularly relevant to the analysis of the importance of innovation in institutional change. The chapter then elaborates these key mechanisms in the context of the co-evolution of diversity in property and economic development in China.

At this introductory stage, it is also necessary to define the scope of this study. Due to limited space, the study focuses on the period between the late 1970s and the late 1990s, although property practices in late imperial China are briefly discussed as an example of institutional continuity ('inheritance'). It should also be noted that 'emulation' discussed in the existing literature focuses on practices in the industrial sector. But this chapter focuses on China's agricultural sector, although the intersection of the agricultural and industrial sectors is also analysed to highlight the fact that innovation in the agricultural sector has paved the way for industrialisation. The reason is that China always faces a pressing need to feed the country's large population, and fixing issues in relation to land policy and property rights in rural land is crucial to alleviating poverty.

DIVERSITY AS A DEVELOPMENT STRATEGY TO ESCAPE THE POVERTY TRAP

Since China's economic reform commenced in 1978, diversity has existed in China's 'socialist market economy' with a mix of state-owned, collectively owned rural township enterprises and village enterprises, as well as private and foreign joint venture sectors. Moreover, within the collective ownership of rural land, individual property rights[7] co-exist with communal property rights. Here communal property refers to 'a resource over which a community and its members together have overall control and the way a resource is managed and regulated by a community for its collective purposes' (Xu 2017: 514). There is a mix of individual property rights and communal property rights in such a resource.[8]

As diversity in property is one of the key issues to be examined in this chapter, it is important to define the meaning of 'diversity' and to highlight its role in economic development. 'Diversity is the fact of many different types of things or people being included in something; a range of different things or people' (*Cambridge Dictionary* n.d.). Diversity concerns a variety of things or people existing in the same space at the same time. Diversity is part of nature's strategy for the suvival of species from natural shocks of all kinds, but diversity as a strategy is also consciously employed in human societies for the same reason (Reinert and Xu 2013: 4). Diversity constitutes a key element in economic development; this is not unique to China. Starting in the 1400s, Europe – and later the West in general – experienced an explosion of intellectual creativity and economic development, due to increasing diversity in polities, policies, cultures and ideas (Reinert and Xu 2013: 2). Simultaneously with China's process of de-diversification in that period and falling behind, Europe forged ahead.[9]

Despite the crucial role of diversity in the rise of Europe and the West in general, today's mainstream economics is ill-positioned to handle diversity and its implications (Reinert 2009a: 2–3). At its very core stands a de facto negation of diversity, largely due to the legacies of Adam Smith (1723–1790) and David Ricardo (1772–1823) (Reinert 2009a: 2). In developing economic theories, both managed to create order by converting the enormous diversity in production and trade into one single common denominator: labour hours (Reinert 2009b). The labour hour-based economics founded by Smith and Ricardo neglected labour hours of different quality. For example, labour hours spent doing surgery in a hospital are qualitatively different from those spent cleaning the floors of the same hospital, and a country inhabited by surgeons would have a higher income than one inhabited by cleaning personnel (Reinert and Xu 2013: 3). Further, if we follow Ricardian logic of comparative advantage, the cleaning personnel would specialise in 'a comparative advantage in being poor' (Reinert and Xu 2013: 3).

The labour hour-based economics combined with Richardian logic of comparative advantage has led some developing countries to believe that it is in their interest to let developed countries specialise in manufacturing industry; these developing countries subsequently fall into a poverty trap (Reinert 2007). Here, I agree with Ang's point made in her working paper (Ang 2017: 3) that 'China's escape from the poverty trap' does not mean that all of China has been out of poverty, as many areas in central and western China remain poor. That said, China's escape from the poverty trap as discussed in this chapter is specifically concerned with the fact that China has escaped the trap of specialising in 'a comparative advantage in being poor' (Reinert and Xu 2013: 3). I argue that diversity in property in rural land has given rise to 'innovative property transformation'[10] in China, which has contributed to China's escape from this kind of poverty traps.

The failure of modern economics to incorporate the role of diversity has serious implications. These implications are now becoming visible in a relative decline of the West and the re-emergence of China and Asia (Reinert and Xu 2013). Although diversity was reintroduced to economics by evolutionary economists (Nelson and Winter 1982), this approach has been limited to relatively narrow studies of innovation and studies of innovation systems on the national level. It is important to bring the work of Veblen to life to examine the importance of diversity in economic development. Veblen was one of the key figures in developing the 'old insitutionalism', which emphasises the importance of diversity in institutional change (Reinert 2006). Veblen is also regarded as the father of evolutionary and institutional economics (Hodgson 2012). As Hodgson (2012: 287) argued, Veblen's contribution to evolutionary and institutional economics is to 'bring Darwinian ideas into the economic arena'. The combination of Darwinian ideas with studies of the economic sphere by Veblen is important to analyse the co-evolution of institutions and economic activities. Recognising the importance of diversity in institutions and institutional change also helps to develop the extended conception of the market as an intellectual ground to test different ideas and experiments (Reinert and Xu 2013). Institutions that build this kind of market are not necessarily 'good institutions'[11] from the neoclassical perspective.

DIVERSITY IN PROPERTY AND ECONOMIC DEVELOPMENT: KEY CONCEPTS AND MECHANISMS

The proposition that only 'strong and clear' property rights can promote economic growth remains influential in theoretical analysis and has profound appeal in the context of many research publications commissioned and supported by the World Bank.[12] The importance of diversity in property has been neglected in this proposition. To overcome the 'tragedy of the commons' (Hardin 1968), privatisation is often offered as the solution. However, we can contest this solution by looking at property regimes in Europe and elsewhere. For example, legal historian Paolo Grossi (1981: xi) argued that 'collective landholding arrangements had existed side by side with properties individually owned from the Middle Ages through the nineteenth century and that these collective arrangements were often economically efficient'. China's property regime since the late 19th century has undergone sea changes, with the meaning of ownership being framed in some 'big moments'[13] that include revolutions and reforms: the legal reforms of the late 19th and early 20th centuries, the collectivisation movement (1953–1978), and the economic reform that commenced in 1978 (Xu 2017: 498). That said, diversity existed in most parts of China's long-term property regime transformation, except the collectivisation period.

The following discussion of diversity in property and its relationship with economic development draws upon insights from institutional and evolutionary economists such as Veblen and Schumpeter, who have developed nuanced approaches to studying institutions and institutional change:

> Institutions are, in substance, prevalent habits of thought with respect to particular relations and particular functions of the individual and of the community ... The situation of today shapes the institutions of tomorrow through a selective, coercive process, by acting upon men's habitual view of things, and so altering or fortifying a point of view or a mental attitude handed down from the past ... The evolution of society is substantially a process of mental adaptation on the part of individuals under the stress of circumstances which will no longer tolerate habits of thought formed under and conforming to a different set of circumstances in the past. (Veblen 1899/2007: 126–127)

For Veblen, 'shared habits with respect to particular relations' constitute 'the formative material of institutions' (Hodgson 2012: 286). Based on this assumption, Veblen proposes an alternative framework for conceiving of the evolution of institutions in which 'activity and habit formation precede rational deliberation' (Hodgson 2012: 285). This framework challenges much traditional thought on institutions manifest in 'the static model of old-style classic economics' (Banta 2007: x), and in the same way, it prompts us to rethink diversity in property. If we follow Veblen's argument on the evolution of institutions, property cannot be only understood as a fixed set of rules that are assumed to directly govern human behaviour; rather, property consists of diverse (could be competing and even conflicting) ideas and practices, which constantly co-evolve with socio-economic circumstances in dynamic processes (Xu 2017: 502).

This evolutionary process, according to Veblen, is that 'instinct is prior to habit, habit is prior to belief and belief is prior to reason' (Hodgson 2012: 286). This evolutionary account enables us to examine the origin, development, persistence and change of institutions at 'both the instinctive and the cultural levels' (Hodgson 2012: 288), as well as at both the individualist and collective levels. As Hodgson (2012: 287) argued, Veblen's contribution to evolutionary and institutional economics is to 'bring Darwinian ideas into the economic arena'. I would like to argue that Veblen also contributes to studying diversity in property, bringing Darwinian ideas to the analysis of the co-evolution of diversity in property and economic activities.

The (Darwinian) evolution of property can be elucidated not only by drawing analogies to Darwinian concepts of variation, inheritance, and selection, but also by broadening the scope of the Darwinian framework, from the biological world to human interactions in society.[14] By 'variation', I mean that there exists diversity in ideas, practices and institutions in accordance with dynamic socio-economic conditions.

By 'inheritance', I mean the persistence and continuity of the old institutions despite changes. It is worth mentioning that the mechanism of 'inheritance' in my analytical framwork comes closer to 'Lamarckism' (Jean-Baptiste Lamarck, a French zoologist, 1744–1829) rather than 'Darwinism'. Lamarck assumed that acquired characteristics could be inherited in future generations.[15] Darwin also 'belived in the inheritance of acquired characters' (Hodgson 2012: 287–288). 'Whether this happens in reality is an empirical question. Even if it were true, the Darwinian principles of variation, inheritance and selection would be required to complete the explanation' (Hodgson 2012: 288).

By 'selection', I mean that changing socio-economic contexts may shift and reframe 'perceptions and dispositions within individuals' and give rise to new 'habits of thought and behaviour' (Hodgson 2012: 287) and thus new forms of institution. Veblen (1899/2007) termed this phenomenon 'selective adaptation'. That said, Veblen 'did not make the context, criteria or mechanisms of selection entirely clear', although he 'generally saw institutions as units of selection in a process of economic evolution' (Hodgson 2012: 291). Ang (2016: 12) also raised questions about the key mechanisms of co-evolution in her analytical framework; she did not comment on Veblen's work:

> Each of these mechanisms raises concrete questions that guide our mapping of co-evolutionary paths, as follows. *Variation*: Were new options and strategies being produced, and by whom? *Selection*: What shaped the motivation for selection at a given juncture? Was an adaptive choice retained or abandoned for a new selection, and why? *Niche creation*: Was a unit in question trying to differentiate from other members of the system or blindly replicating the strategies of others?

Veblen's emphasis on changing socio-economic contexts may help us to answer some of the questions, but it also raises a new question: What are the driving forces behind the changes in socio-economic contexts? These forces may be internal or external, including changes in natural conditions, wars, regime change (for example, the demise of the former Soviet Union), financial crises, and external threats (for example, the Meiji revolution in Japan).[16] Institutions are created or modified in order to selectively adapt to the changes in socio-economic contexts. But institutions which enable economic development are often brought about by emulation and innovation beyond adaptation.

'Emulation' is defined in the *Oxford English Dictionary* (2011) as 'effort to match or surpass a person or achievement, typically by imitation'. 'Emulation', an alternative to 'envy', signifies 'the desire to imitate and improve on superiors without harming them in the process' (Reinert 2011: 2). Emulation constitutes one of the key elements that contributed to the rise of Europe (Reinert 2009b). For example, the Renaissance in Europe is an 'Age of Emulation' when diverse actors including architects, artists, humanists, and sovereigns emulated the 'past glory of Rome' (Reinert 2011: 29). This period also saw the rise of northern states in the European periphery through emulating the Italian core (Reinert 2011: 29). The rise of Europe and the United States is not through free trade but through emulation and innovation, which brought about qualitative changes, or economic development (Reinert 2009b, 2011). 'Emulation' should come before 'comparative advantage' (Reinert 2009b: 16). Further, emulation is closely linked to a broader conception of the 'market', which is much more than a mechanism setting prices. This kind of 'market' extends to being an arena where different ideas, in the form of laws, types of governance, and economic and industrial policies, are tested against each other (Reinert and Xu 2013: 4). Emulation can help to build this kind of market, which is crucial to the promotion of innovation and economic development.

Veblen (1899/2007: 22) discussed the role of emulation in the development of the institution of ownership:

> The motive that lies at the root of ownership is emulation; and the same motive of emulation continues active in the further development of the institution to which it has given rise and in the development of all those features of the social structure which this institution of ownership touches.

Veblen's writing also indicates that institutions can 'affect the dynamics of changing modes of production' (Reinert 2006: 18; see also Veblen 1904/2013: 37–48). In order to further illustrate this point of view and the importance of innovation for economic development, we need to bring in Schumpeterian institutions (for example, patents, tariffs, scientific academies), which are concerned with the importance of innovation in generating new knowledge and modes of production, which helps to move the economic activities to the next 'stage' or 'paradigm' (Reinert 2000: 11). Schumpeterian institutions focus on production, and this stands in sharp contrast to the view of institutions adopted by mainstream economics, which focuses on the free market and trade and favours export-led and foreign direct investment (FDI)-driven economic growth (Reinert 2006: 2–3). For example, patents are creating the opposite of a 'free market'.[17]

For Schumpeter, there exists a fundamental difference between economic development and economic growth. Economic development is driven by endogenous technological advance (Schumpeter 1943/2010: 96),[18] and 'comes from within the economic system and is not merely an adaptation to changes in external data; it occurs discontinuously, rather than smoothly; it brings qualitative changes or "revolutions," which fundamentally displace old equilibria and create radically new conditions' (Elliott 2012: xix). Mere quantitative growth does not amount to economic development: as Schumpeter argued, 'add successively as many mail coaches as you please, you will never get a railway thereby' (Schumpeter 1934/2012: 64). Further, to examine the process of institutional change, it is important to look at the process of 'creative destruction' developed by Schumpeter: '[a] process of industrial mutation ... that incessantly revolutionizes the economic structure *from within*, incessantly destroying the old one, incessantly creating a new one' (Schumpeter 1943/2010: 73).

Schumpeterian institutions have significant implications for aiding one in thinking of the relationship between institutional change and economic activities: 'an institution that suits one production system may not suit another' (Reinert 2006: 1).[19] Schumpeter's argument has been developed by many others, for example by Nelson and Winter (1982) and by Perez (1983, 2004). In developing Schumpeter's work, Perez has invoked the concept of a 'techno-economic paradigm':[20] 'different eras are dominated by different fundamental technologies ... The [institutions] suitable for an earlier set of fundamental technologies may be quite inappropriate for the new' (Nelson 1995b: 80). However, these points have been ignored by neoclassical economists. For them, rather than institutions and economic activities co-evolving, institutions determine economic activities.

The work of institutional and evolutionary economics, especially that of Veblen and Schumpeter and that on the importance of emulation, helps me to develop a framework for analysing the co-evolution of diversity in property and economic development with key mechanisms:

1. Variation: the existence of diversity in property and the market in accordance with dynamic socio-economic conditions.
2. Inheritance: the persistence and continuity of the old property regime despite socio-economic changes.
3. Selection: the formation of new forms of property due to changes in socio-economic contexts (but for economic development, selection will need to be prompted by emulation and innovation beyond adaptation).

To further illustrate the co-evolution of diversity in property and economic development, a contextualised analysis of the approach developed above is required, using China's experience as a case study.

DIVERSITY IN CONTEXT: THE CO-EVOLUTION OF PROPERTY AND ECONOMIC DEVELOPMENT IN CHINA

Following discussion of diversity in the previous sections, diversity in property in the Chinese context (in three key periods of property regime transformation) discussed in this section focuses on two levels: (1) the co-existence of private property and communal property; and (2) within one type of property (private

*Table 13.1   Diversity in property (rural land) in China's long-term
property regime transformation*

Property regime transformation (the vertical dimension)	Diversity in property (the horizontal dimension)
Late imperial China (Ming 1368–1644 and Qing 1644–1840) 'variation, inheritance, selection'	(1) The co-existence of private property (owned by the household) and communal (lineage) property (2) The co-existence of individual and communal (household) interests within private property ('two/three lords to one field')
1978–1980s 'variation, inheritance, selection, innovation and emulation'	(1) The revival of private property (through the introduction of the 'household responsibility system' as an innovative property institution) and the co-existence of private property and communal property (2) The co-existence of individual and communal interests within communal property
The 1990s 'variation, inheritance, selection, innovation and emulation'	(1) The emergence of new types of communal property (through rural shareholding co-operatives) as innovative property institutions and the co-existence of private and (old and new types of) communal property (2) The co-existence of individual and communal interests within new types of communal property

or communal), the co-existence of individual and communal property interests (Table 13.1).

Diversity in Property and Socio-economic Activities in Late Imperial China

Variation existed in property in rural land throughout the history of late imperial China.[21] The general practice was that land owned by the household was alienable, subject to sale, purchase and inheritance (Pomeranz 2008: 113),[22] with exceptions such as lineage property. The plot of land which a household owned and cultivated is often regarded as private property. Diversity existed in ecosystems: while in the north root vegetable cultivation helped farmers to survive harsh winters, in the south farmers relied on rice-growing, as there were floods and more water. However, rice-growing required intensive cultivation, and the costs to landlords of the supervision of intensive farming were increasing (Heijdra 1998: 526). Diversity in the property regime was intensified subsequently, a process galvanised by the emergence of permanent tenancy (*yongdian*) in the 18th century ('selective adaptation').[23] Permanent tenancy helped landlords to reduce these costs, and at the same time provided an incentive for tenants (organised in the unit of the household) to improve the land and increase its value (Heijdra 1998: 526). Moreover, tenants were able to work on a larger piece of land that might be owned by different landlords (Zhao and Chen 2006: 297). As a result, landlords tended to charge a household a fixed rent, and the household was given a permanent tenancy to farm a parcel of land in return (Palmer 1987: 27; Heijdra 1998: 526). A change of landlord could not deprive the tenants of their right to the land, but tenants were nevertheless restricted from transferring their rights to others.

Yet in practice more and more rich tenants functioned as secondary landlords and transferred their rights to others without the landlord's permission. The practice was called *siquan xiangshou*, which was later transformed into the 'habit' of 'two lords to one field': the topsoil rights or interests referred to the permanent entitlements to farm the land and could be inherited (Yang 1988: 100; Liang 2014: 400). This practice recognised various property interests in the same piece of land, based on long-term social practice which adapted socio-economic conditions (Elvin 1973: 253; Perdue 2004: 51). The establishment of property interests in topsoil often led to the transfer of these property interests by topsoil holders (Pomeranz 2008: 117). As topsoil holders did not need to pay taxes and were not controlled by government registers, they could circumvent the involvement of the government when selling property interests in topsoil.

A more complex land system which consisted of multi-layer holders – for example, 'three lords to one field' (*yitian sanzhu*) – of the same piece of land evolved from the social practices of permanent tenancy and the 'two lords to one field', a typical example that contains the three mechanisms of 'variation, inheritance and selection'; this system continued later on (through 'inheritance') in Republican China (1911–1949). In the period between 1650 and 1850, China experienced an exponential growth of population, from 100 million to almost 425 million (Chen and Myers 1976: 1). It was not accidental that the practice of multi-holders claiming property interests in the same piece of land was prevalent in Fujian province, where the land per person ratio was one of the most excessive in the empire and multiple claims were attached to the same piece of land (Heijdra 1998: 533). The practice of 'three lords to one field' was composed of at least three tiers: small rent landlords (*xiao zuzhu*), large rent landlords (*da zuzhu*), and the actual cultivators of the land (*diannong*). These three levels of land holders were closely interlinked to issues concerning agricultural production, tax payment and rent (Heijdra 1998: 533). Small rent landlords were the original landowners, who sold both their rights of collecting rents from the cultivators and their tax obligations to large rent landlords, who then had the rights to collect rents from cultivators and became the taxpayers. Cultivators paid the rents and got the permanent rights to use and farm the land. Even Ellickson (2012: 284, 293), who questioned the institutions of subjecting land rights to the former seller's right of redemption in late imperial China, acknowledged that 'in many instances, arrangements of [the division of ownership across time] are advantageous to all involved', and that topsoil rights 'stimulated improvements to agricultural land'.

Such kind of diversity in property was eliminated by collectivisation (1956–1978), which abolished private ownership and established collective proprietorship of rural land. This was modelled on post-1917 Soviet collectivisation, but ignored diversity in natural conditions, socio-economic activities, and the governance structure between the countryside in China and in the USSR. Russian farmers traditionally worked in communes (the *mir* or *obshchina*) (Heinzen 2004: 11–46); whereas China had limited urbanisation and a huge rural area, and farmers were governed by lineages, especially in South China. The elimination of private ownership and gentry governance in rural China left an empty space to be filled by the central government. However, geographical, social and economic variations made it impossible to develop and execute a comprehensive rural development plan (Xu 2017: 512). Although collective ownership provided machinery and irrigation services and did promote consolidated farming in some areas, socio-economic conditions in Chinese society, for the most part, were not ready to accommodate large-scale collective ownership. Farmers were forced to pool resources, not due to shared common values and belief, but due to political pressure. Further, the introduction of collective ownership removed the breadth of diversity inherent in the property regime, and the single form of collective ownership in rural China reduced the resilience of the property regime in times of natural disasters and economic and political crises, such as in the time of the famine that occurred in 1959–1961 (Xu 2017: 512).

Diversity in Property and Economic Development from 1978 to the 1980s

The communes began to be dismantled at the start of the economic reform process commenced in 1978, and collectivised agriculture was gradually abandoned through the introduction of the 'household responsibility system'.[24] This system was first set up in 1978 by a small group of farmers, 18 rural households in total, in Fengyang County in Anhui Province, who were driven by the need to grow more food and to prevent their families from starving. This initiative was supported by Wan Li (1916–2015), who then served as the provincial Party leader in Anhui province, among other reformists in charge of implementing rural reforms (Chen and Xia 1998: preface). This initiative then became popular and was widely emulated, especially in poor and hilly areas (Lin 1987: 410). It was considered to be a success, and so was increasingly recognised by Party policies. It was expanded on a nationwide scale between

1980 and 1983.[25] The emergence of the household responsibility system was not simply due to 'selective adaptation'. Rather, it was an innovative property institution which emerged in a small locality in 1978 and was expanded nation-wide through emulation by other regions of China.

The question here is what constituted the socio-economic and political conditions that made the re-emergence of diversity in the property regime described above possible. Although the pre-1978 Chinese economy is gener-ally labelled as one of 'central planning', decentralisation in China has roots dating back to the 1950s, especially in the first Five-Year Plan (1953–1958) (Lardy 1978: 3–4).[26] At that time, central control was constrained by diversity and variation in China's geography, transportation conditions, and commu-nications capacity (Lardy 1978: 20). Unlike the former Soviet Union, where strong central control sidestepped local discretion and allocated plans directly to enterprises, 'the Maoist system decentralized economic and administrative power to the localities', and most of the reform initiatives were from the 'bottom up' (Oi 1995: 1134). Although decentralisation in the 1950s did not change the entire central-planned scheme in the pre-1978 era, this kind of decentralisation increased a certain degree of economic power at the local levels that survived into the 1960s and 1970s.

In the process of market reforms from the late 1970s to the late 1990s, central control declined further, and political and economic power gradually devolved to local government. While the centre still had political control over the local through the system of Party-sanctioned appointments of officials, its fiscal capacity went into decline. The term 'federalism' has been widely used to characterise the changes that have taken place in the Chinese polity (Goldstein 1995: 1127). Scholars have described (albeit in different ways) the nature of decentralisation from the central government to local governments in contemporary China as quasi-federal or simply federal,[27] although China's political and legal systems lack the institutional infrastructure of 'constitutional federalism' and local governments in China do not have 'formal political [and legal] autonomy *vis-à-vis* the centre' (Tsai 2004: 4). Some scholars argue that this kind of de facto federalism is market-preserving and underpins economic growth in China.[28] I argue that de facto federalism that took shape in 1980s China made selective adaptation, emulation and the emergence of the extended 'market' possible. China in this period bore a resemblance to Renaissance Europe, where each state in Europe at that time had a different economic and cultural context, and a different intellectual agenda; Europe became a huge laboratory where a plethora of ideas flourished (Reinert and Xu 2013: 2). That said, it must be noted that de facto federalism or the kind of decentralisation in China is not the same as the existence of literally hundreds of small states in Renaissance Europe where emulation took place. Emulation in China is distinctive in that it occurs within a state, rather than from state to state.

In the process of decentralising power from central to local government, the previously assumed 'zero-sum model' of the relationship between the centre and the local is no longer sufficient.[29] Local governments developed various kinds of strategy to cope with the central government in decentralisation. Some scholars reminded us of the possible check function of local governments. For example, various reform initiatives took place across different regions in China. It was difficult for the centre to bring local reforms to a halt and restore central planning completely, due partly to the resistance of local leaders (Huang 1996: 1–2). Regional inequality and variations should also be taken into account when examining the transformation of the governance system (Yang 1997: 137–139). This kind of 'involuntary' decentralisation has promoted a certain degree of diversity in China, especially in the area of economic policy. For example, since the 1980s, Special Economic Zones[30] have been set up in coastal regions including Shenzhen, Zhuhai and Shantou in Guangdong Province, Xiamen in Fujian Province, and the entire Hainan Province. Special Economic Zones were developed in China as 'a strategy for reform and opening up, as well as promoting industrialization and fostering its technological capacities' (Oqubay and Lin 2020: 4). They enjoy special economic policies and more power in making governmental decisions. For example, the first auction of land use rights took place in Shenzhen on 1 December 1987, although this practice obviously contravened the Constitution; four months later, on 12 April 1988, the Constitution was amended to allow the transfer of land use rights (Clause 4 of Article 10).

Turning to the introduction of the household responsibility system, contractual management rights have been granted to farmers, in the form of contracts, for the possession and use of rural land for farming purposes. Therefore, farmers have individual property rights/interests in rural land for farming purposes. The collective issues contracts to the household, which has responsibility for the management of farming an area of land called 'responsibility land'. The 'responsibility land' is therefore subject to the farmer's individual property interests, and various layers of communal property interests including the household's interest and the collective's interest. For farmers, once they had discharged their duty to meet the grain quota imposed by the state, they could retain their additional production: the grain produced over and above the required quota.

The introduction of the household responsibility system was driven by farmers' belief in 'land to the tillers', and the household-based production system matched the economic conditions in most areas. As discussed above, this system also represents an innovative initiative whereby individual land rights came to be selectively readmitted and integrated into collective land rights.[31] Individuals in the household have come to see the responsibility land as de facto private property, and therefore have the incentive to engage effectively in agricultural production. In the meantime, the household functions as a close-knit community that organises agricultural production, enabling the existence of private land rights in a collective land system. Diversity in property has been reintroduced to the rural land system where individual property rights and communal property rights co-exist. This system shares some common features with the land system in late imperial China (the mechanism of 'inheritance' operates), but it includes new mechanisms such as restrictions on transfers of farmers' individual property rights to sustain communal property. If the farmer ceases to be a member, or no longer relies on farming to make a living, the farmer's individual property rights automatically cease and revert to the household the farmer belongs to. If the household ceases to exist, property rights held by its previous members revert to the collective. These restrictions are in line with China's land policy on conservation of farmland, and the pressing need to feed 1.4 billion people.

One phenomenon, however, is often overlooked in endorsing the function of the household responsibility system: that is, 'if a production team heavily relied on machinery for its production, it would be difficult to break down the production into household-based operations' (Lin 1987: 413). This phenomenon indicates that when techno-economic development in agricultural production requires an innovative property regime for promoting cooperation and consolidated/industrialised farming, an old (inherited) property system such as the household responsibility system, which was once an innovative initiative that promoted economic development, may have come to function as a roadblock to further development (Xu 2017: 513). The gap between the development of techno-economic conditions and the development of an innovative property regime may well explain a puzzle that occurred in the late 1980s: although the household responsibility system was widespread, economic growth stagnated (Lin 1992: 39).

Diversity in Property and Economic Development in the 1990s

In the early 1990s, farmers began to pool resources and circulate land use rights in responding to the needs of agricultural production and the market, although some of the initiatives contradicted the formal, written law. Various initiatives were emerging. Some were promoted by farmers; others were led by local governments or even commercial companies. In many places 'recollectivisation' of individual and household property rights became the trend. For example, farmers at Xiaogang Village – the first village that distributed land use rights to farmers – recollectivised their dispersed land use rights for more efficient use and management of land (Xu 2010: 567). Farmers transferred their contractual use rights to one commercial company specialising in intensive and co-operative farming and management of rural land, to gain more income.

More initiatives emerged in coastal regions to address a further roadblock to farmers' engagement with marketisation and enjoyment of benefits from industrialisation occurring in the urban areas: the transfer of land use rights for construction purposes by farmers[32] (if not reclaimed by the state first) is banned. One initiative was called the Nanhai model (*nanhai moshi*). In 1992, a farmland shareholding co-operative system (*tudi gufen hezuo zhi*)[33] was experimented with in Nanhai, a county-level city of Guangdong Province.[34] The value of rural land for construction purposes owned by the collective was appraised and divided into shares owned by farmers. A shareholding co-operative was formed by the administrative village. Plots of rural land for construction purposes were then rented out by the co-operative to investors and enterprises. In this way, rural land could be used for industrial purposes, but not through land acquisition by the state. Farmers could thus enjoy the profits of industrialisation according to the shares they had, while the collective retains ownership of rural land. But one of the shortcomings of this model is that this kind of shareholding co-operative is controlled by the administrative village. Farmers could not monitor the operation of the co-operatives. The administrative villages, rather than farmers, enjoyed most of the profits.

Another initiative, called the Kunshan model (*kunshan moshi*), also emerged in the early 1990s.[35] Kunshan is a county-level city of Jiangsu Province. In this model, the collective obtained quotas of rural land for construction purposes through land reclamation, and then rural households within the collective could bid for these quotas. These rural households later formed co-operatives. Land use rights for construction purposes were thus held by co-operatives of farmers rather than administrative villages. These co-operatives then built factories and shops rented by outside investors. There was less government involvement in this property arrangement than that in the Nanhai model.

The Sunan and Nanhai models represent innovative property regimes for promoting cooperation and consolidated farming in the 1990s, albeit with limits. Further local reforms – through the emulation of the two models – allowed farmers to contribute rural land contractual management rights as shares to enterprises or joint ventures.[36] Inland regions started to emulate those experiments initiated in coastal areas. For example, despite the contradictory laws and regulations, on 1 July 2007, farmers in Chongqing were allowed to contribute land use rights to joint enterprises or joint ventures as shares, provided that the use purpose of arable land is not changed.

CONCLUSION

This chapter examines one of the most important factors contributing to China's escape from the poverty trap by looking at the ways in which diversity in property in land and economic development co-evolved from the late 1970s to the 1990s. It brings Darwinian ideas into the arena of studying the co-evolution of institutions and economic development, and develops insights from institutional and evolutionary economics, especially those of Veblen and Schumpeter, in the context of property regime transformation in China. In so doing, it offers a nuanced approach to studying the co-evolution of diversity in property and economic development, which contains key mechanisms including variation (diversity), inheritance, and selection (selective adaptation as well as innovation and emulation). This approach also extends the conception of the market as an intellectual ground to test different ideas and experiments. Institutions that build this kind of market are not necessarily 'good institutions' in the neoclassical sense. An analysis of China's long-term property regime transformation from the 17th century to the late 1990s has demonstrated that economic activities and diverse property institutions co-evolved with occasional institutional innovations underpinning upswings in (Schumpeterian) economic development. The conclusions confirm the three hypotheses raised in the introduction of this chapter.

The analytical framework employed in this chapter highlights the importance of diversity and qualitative changes in economic development. It is necessary to first look at 'stages' of economic development from the standpoint of production (for example, agricultural and industrial stages);[37] and then to examine changing contexts, in particular techno-economic change over time rather than a linear, normative series of changes such as from communal property to private property, as the inevitable result of property regime transformation. Of course, focusing on the context does not mean that property regime transformation is spontaneous, at the mercy of geographical and climatic conditions. New property regimes (innovative property regimes) play a crucial role in introducing new products, processes, and production systems and in furthering economic development. These are Schumpeterian institutions, which have been largely overlooked by the mainstream study of the relationship between property and economic activities.

The case study of China challenges much traditional thought on the relationship between property and economic activities, and in the same way, it prompts us to rethink the ways in which institutions and economic development co-evolve. It is possible to impose changes on institutions from above or externally, such as through revolutions and wars; the changing circumstances may reframe new ideas, perceptions, habits and practices, giving rise to new institutions. However, fundamental aspects of the old institutions may persist and continue, despite modifications, if the economic conditions have not been fundamentally changed. Economic development, or qualitative changes, need institutions enabled by innovation and emulation beyond selective adaptation. Matching policies to context, which enables innovation and emulation, is the key to escaping the poverty trap.

ACKNOWLEDGEMENTS

The author would like to thank Dr Wei Gong, Dr Dimitrios Kyritisis, Professor James Penner, Professor Erik Reinert, Mrs Fernanda Reinert and all participants in the seminar jointly organised by the Private Law Research Group and the Centre for Asian Legal Studies of the National University of Singapore on 25 October 2021, for their comments on an earlier draft of this chapter. All remaining errors are my responsibility.

NOTES

1. A lot of research on China in relation to poverty traps has been done. A quick search through the library catalogue using keywords such as 'the poverty trap in China' and 'escape the poverty trap' gives rise to hundreds of relevant studies from 1993 to 2015; at least 100 studies have these keywords in their titles. Examples include Hung and Makdissi (2004), Cao et al. (2009), Knight et al. (2009, 2010), Le Van et al. (2010), Wang and Zhu (2013).
2. See also Reinert (1996).
3. 'Co-evolution' is the 'signature term' of Richard Nelson of Columbia University. His 1982 book with Sidney Winter, *An Evolutionary Theory of Economic Change*, represented the start of the neo-Schumpeterian wave. Most evolutionary economists use the term 'co-evolution'. For Nelson's works on co-evolution see, for example, Nelson (1994, 1995a). For other relevant works, see, for example, Norgaard (1984: 528) who argued that 'agricultural development can be viewed as a coevolutionary process'; and Peters and Verghis (1993: 3) who argued that 'the interaction between the state and markets plays an essential role in the economic development of [developing countries]'.
4. See, for example, Dagan (2011).
5. For a discussion of the co-evolution of property and economic development, see Xu (2017).
6. See, for example, Weber (2021).
7. Here I use 'individual property rights' as opposed to 'private property rights'. Individual property rights are property rights held by a human being, whereas private property rights can be held by a human being or an artificial legal entity. See more detailed discussion of this distinction in Xu and Gong (2020: 138).
8. See the next section for detailed discussion.
9. 'Falling behind' and 'forging ahead' are terms introduced by Abramowitz (1986).

10. It may be helpful to distinguish between three interrelated terms: property regime transformation, innovative property transformation and property evolution: 'Property regime transformation in the broad sense does not indicate either a clear trend or a foreseeable outcome; it need not be progressive. By contrast, innovative property transformation ... conveys a positive connotation of enabling economic development and structural change, which may not be a smooth process. Property evolution in the broad sense conveys a positive connotation (it may even contain a teleological element), but not necessarily the identical form of connotation found in innovative property transformation' (Xu 2017: 499).

11. See, for example, World Bank (2002: 99), discussing 'the greater capacity of rich countries to provide good institutions' and arguing that '[g]ood governance matters for growth and poverty reduction'.

12. See, for example, World Bank (2004, 2015). For criticism of the World Bank's approach to development, see, for example, Kennedy (2011), offering a critique of 'accepting conventional neo-liberal wisdom about the importance of "clear" or "strong property rights" for economic development'; and Kindama (2014), arguing that '[the World Bank forces] developing countries to follow a pre-prescribed model of development, based on the neoliberal principles of privatization, deregulation, low corporate taxation and "free market" fundamentalism'.

13. See, for example, Ackerman (1993), examining American constitutional development by focusing on 'critical junctures' or 'critical moments'; Capoccia and Keleman (2007), using 'critical junctures' or 'critical moments' to describe fundamental institutional change; and Davidson and Dyal-Chand (2011), describing the transformations in property as 'property moments'.

14. My analytical framework draws upon Hodgson (2012) where he clearly discussed 'the Darwinian principles of variation, inheritance and selection' (p. 288). I finished the first draft paper discussing the three mechanisms including variation, inheritance and selection in the context of the property regime transformation in China in late 2015 and presented my work in early 2016 in three workshops in the United Kingdom: 'Towards an Evolutionary Theory of Property?', the Annual Seminar on the History and Theory of Property Law, School of Law, Queen Mary University of London, 21 April 2016; 'Property as an Evolutionary Process: The Case of Property Regime Transformation in China', Workshop on Legalism: Property and Ownership, St John's College, University of Oxford, 29–30 January 2016; and 'Legalising Property in China: An Evolutionary Account', workshop on Communal Property in China and the UK, School of Law, University of Sheffield, 21 January 2016. Ang (2016: 12) also discussed 'three signature mechanisms of coevolution', drawing on these concepts:
    1   *Variation*: generation of alternative
    2   *Selection*: selection among and assembly of alternatives to form new combinations
    3   *Niche creation*: crafting of distinct and valuable roles among heterogenenous units within a system.
    For other discussions of the relevant concepts, see also Parker (1980), discussing variation, selection and creation; and Luksha (2008), discussing coevolution, variation, selection, adaption, creation, niche and niche construction.

15. Thanks to Professor Erik Reinert for raising this point.

16. See, for example, Williamson (2000: 598–599).

17. Thanks to Professor Erik Reinert for raising this point.

18. See also Nelson (1995b: 68).

19. See also Reinert (2007).
20. Here technological change should not be seen as 'an engineering phenomenon but as a complex social process involving technical, economic, social and institutional factors in a web of interactions'. See Perez (2004: 219).
21. Historical materials on property in late imperial China has been discussed in detail in Xu (2017).
22. See also Zhang (2014: 174).
23. Some scholars argue that permanent tenancy emerged as early as the Southern Song Dynasty (1127–1279). See, for example, Wu (1987), Palmer (1987), Xie (1999).
24. For a discussion of the communes, see, for example, Shue (1984).
25. For Chinese rural policy in the late 1980s, see, for example, Christiansen (1992).
26. For a discussion of the central–local relationship in China, see, for example, Xu (2014: 106–111).
27. See, for example, Cao et al. (1999), Huang (1996), Tsai (2004).
28. See, for example, Qian and Weingast (1996, 1997), Weingast (1995). Critiques of this arguement pointed out that it is rather 'market-thwarting federalism'; see Tsai (2004).
29. See, generally, Li (1998).
30. For a discussion of the role of industrial hubs including special economic zones in facilitating economic growth and in 'the climbing of the development ladder', see Oqubay and Lin (2020).
31. See, for example, Clarke (2013). See also Penner (2020: 206), arguing that '[any] sensible characterization of what is *owned* by "common owners" involves the summation of what each has actually possessed'. For a discussion of 'community-based individual property rights', see Xu and Gong (2020).
32. Parts of rural land are set for construction purposes such as for building farmers' residential plots and rural factories.
33. For shareholding co-operatives (*gufen hezuozhi*), see, for example, Vermeer (1999).
34. For a discussion of the Nanhai model, see also Xu and Murphy (2008), Xu (2010).
35. For a discussion of the Kunshan model, see Xu (2010).
36. The Land Contracting Law (2002) and the Land Administration Law (2004) conflict at this point. Article 42 of the Land Contracting Law allows farmers to contribute rural land contractual management rights as shares. According to Article 60 of the Land Administration Law, farmers cannot contribute land use rights to joint enterprises or joint ventures as investments, or assign land use rights to township enterprises without approval from the government at or above county levels.
37. See, for example, Reinert (2000), pointing out that German economist Karl Bücher argues that each 'stage' of development tends to develop its own institutions, including land use and land tenure. See also Reinert (2006: 22).

REFERENCES

Abramovitz, Moses (1986) 'Catching Up, Forging Ahead, and Falling Behind', *Journal of Economic History* 46 (2): 385–406.

Ackerman, Bruce (1993) *We the People: Foundations (Volume 1)*, new edn. Cambridge, MA: Harvard University Press.

Ang, Yuen Yuen (2016) *How China Escaped the Poverty Trap*. Ithaca, NY, USA and London, UK: Cornell University Press.

Ang, Yuen Yuen (2017) 'Industrial Transfer and the Remaking of the People's Republic of China's Competitive Advantage', ADBI Working Paper 762. Tokyo: Asian Development Bank Institute. Available at: https://www.adb.org/publications/industrial-transfer-and-remaking-prc-competitive-advantage.

Banta, Martha (2007) 'Introduction' to Thorstein Veblen, *The Theory of the Leisure Class: An Economic Study in the Evolution of Institutions* (1899/2007). Oxford: Oxford University Press, vii–xxvi.

Cambridge Dictionary Online (2009) Available at: https://dictionary.cambridge.org/dictionary/english/diversity?q=diversity+.

Cao, Shixiong; Wang, Xueqing and Wang, Guosheng (2009) 'Lessons Learned from China's Fall into the Poverty Trap', *Journal of Policy Modelling* 31: 298–307.

Cao, Yuanzheng; Qian, Yingyi and Weingast, Barry R. (1999) 'From Federalism, Chinese Style to Privatization, Chinese Style', *Economics of Transition* 7 (1): 103–131.

Capoccia, Giovanni and Keleman, R. Daniel (2007) 'The Study of Critical Junctures: Theory, Narrative, and Counterfactuals in Historical Institutionalism', *World Politics* 59 (3): 341–369.

Chen, Fu-Mei Chang and Myers, Ramon (1976) 'Customary Law and the Economic Growth of China during the Chíng Period', *Ch'ing shih wen-t'i* 3 (5): 1–33.

Chen, Huairen and Xia, Yurun (1998) *The Origin: Documenting the Emergence of the Household Responsibility System in Fengyang (Qiyuan: fengyang dabaogan shilu)*. Hefei: Huangshan shushe.

Christiansen, Flemming (1992) 'Stability First! Chinese Rural Policy Issues 1987–1990', in Eduard B. Vermeer (ed.), *From Peasant to Entrepreneur: Growth and Change in Rural China*. Wageningen: PUDOC, 21–40.

Clarke, Alison C. (2013) 'Integrating Private and Collective Land Rights: Lessons from China', *Journal of Comparative Law* 7(2): 177–193.

Dagan, Hanoch (2011) *Property: Values and Institutions*. Oxford: Oxford University Press.

Davidson, Nestor M. and Dyal-Chand, Rashmi (2011) 'Crisis and the Public–Private Divide in Property' in Robin Paul Malloy and Michael Diamond (eds), *The Public Nature of Private Property*. Farnham, UK and Burlington, VT, USA: Ashgate, 65–87.

Ellickson, Robert C. (2012) 'The Costs of Complex Land Titles: Two Examples from China', *Brigham-Kanner Property Rights Conference Journal* 1: 281–302.

Elliott, John E. (2012) 'Introduction' to Joseph Schumpeter, *The Theory of Economic Development: An Inquiry into Profits, Capital, Credit, Interest, and the Business Cycle*, 16th edn. New Brunswick, NJ: Transaction Publishers, vii–lix.

Elvin, Mark (1973) *The Pattern of the Chinese Past: A Social and Economic Interpretation*. Stanford, CA: Stanford University Press.

General Office of the State Council of the PRC (1986) 'Minutes of the First Plenary Meeting of the State Council's Leader's Group for Economic Development in Poor Areas', *Gazette of the State Council of the People's Republic of China* (1986, No. 16), 10 June. Available at: http://www.gov.cn/gongbao/shuju/1986/gwyb198616.pdf.

Goldstein, Steven M. (1995) 'China in Transition: The Political Foundations of Incremental Reform', *China Quarterly* 144: 1105–1131.

Grossi, Paolo (1981) *An Alternative to Private Property; Collective Property in the Juridical Consciousness of the Nineteenth Century*. Chicago, IL: University of Chicago Press.

Hardin, Garrett (1968) 'The Tragedy of the Commons', *Science* 162 (3859): 1243–1248.

Hayford, Charles (1998) 'The Storm over the Peasant: Orientalism and Rhetoric in Construing China', Lund East Asia Working Paper Series on Language and Politics in Modern China, Lund University.

Heijdra, Martin (1998) 'The Socio-Economic Development of Rural China during the Ming', in Dennis Twitchett and Frederich W. Mote (eds), *The Cambridge History of China. Vol. 8, The Ming Dynasty, 1368–1644, Part II*. Cambridge: Cambridge University Press, 417–575.

Heinzen, James W. (2004) *Inventing a Soviet Countryside: State Power and the Transformation of Rural Russia, 1917–1929*. Pittsburgh, PA: University of Pittsburgh Press.

Hodgson, Geoffrey M. (2012) 'Thorstein Veblen: The Father of Evolutionary and Institutional Economics', in Erik S. Reinert and Francesca Lidia Viano (eds), *Thorstein Veblen: Economics for an Age of Crises*. London: Anthem Press, 283–295.

Huang, Yasheng (1996) *Inflation and Investment Controls in China: The Political Economy of Central-Local Relations During the Reform Era*. New York: Cambridge University Press.

Hung, Nguyen Manh and Makdissi, Paul (2004) 'Escaping the Poverty Trap in a Developing Rural Economy', *Canadian Journal of Economics / Revue canadienned'économique* 37 (1): 123–139.

Kennedy, David (2011) 'Some Caution about Property Rights as a Recipe for Economic Development', *Accounting, Economics, and Law* 1 (1): 1–62.

Kindama, Ishmael (2014) 'Land Campaigners Criticise World Bank Doing Business and Benchmarking of the Business of Agriculture in Africa'. Available at: http://www.ethiopianreview.com/index/51384.

Knight, John; Li, Shi and Deng, Quheng (2009) 'Education and the Poverty Trap in Rural China: Setting the Trap', *Oxford Development Studies* 37 (4): 311–332.

Knight, John; Li, Shi and Deng, Quheng (2010) 'Education and the Poverty Trap in Rural China: Closing the Trap', *Oxford Development Studies* 38 (1): 1–24.

Lardy, Nicholas R. (1978) *Economic Growth and Distribution in China*. Cambridge, UK and New York, USA: Cambridge University Press.

Le Van, Cuong; Schubert, Katheline and Nguyen, Tu-Anh (2010) 'With Exhaustible Resources, Can a Developing Country Escape from the Poverty Trap?', *Journal of Economic Theory* 145 (6): 2435–2447.

Li, Linda Chelan (1998) *Centre and Provinces – China 1978–1993: Power as Non-Zero-Sum*. New York: Oxford University Press.

Liang, Gengyao (2014) *The Social History of China (Zhongguo shehui shi)*. Taipei: National Taiwan University Press.

Lin, Justin Yifu (1987) 'The Household Responsibility System Reform in China: A Peasant's Institutional Choice', *American Journal of Agricultural Economics* 69 (2): 410–415.

Lin, Justin Yifu (1992) 'Rural Reforms and Agricultural Growth in China', *American Economic Review* 82 (1): 34–51.

Luksha, Pavel (2008) 'Niche Construction: The Process of Opportunity Creation in the Environment', *Strategic Entrepreneurship Journal* 2 (4): 269–283.

Nelson, Richard R. (1994) 'The Co-evolution of Technology, Industrial Structure, and Supporting Institutions', *Industrial and Corporate Change* 3 (1): 47–63.

Nelson, Richard R. (1995a) 'Co-evolution of Industry Structure, Technology and Supporting Institutions, and the Making of Comparative Advantage', *International Journal of the Economics of Business* 2 (2): 171–184.

Nelson, Richard R. (1995b) 'Recent Evolutionary Theorizing about Economic Change', *Journal of Economic Literature* 33 (1): 48–90.

Nelson, Richard R. and Winter, Sidney G. (1982) *An Evolutionary Theory of Economic Change.* Cambridge, MA: Harvard University Press.

Norgaard, Richard B. (1984) 'Coevolutionary Agricultural Development', *Economic Development and Cultural Change* 32 (3): 525–546.

Oi, Jean C. (1995) 'The Role of the Local State in China's Transitional Economy', *China Quarterly* 144: 1132–1149.

Oqubay, Arkebe and Lin, Justin Yifu (eds) (2020) *The Oxford Handbook of Industrial Hubs and Economic Development.* Oxford: Oxford University Press.

Oxford English Dictionary (2011) New York: Oxford University Press.

Palmer, Michael (1987) 'The Surface-Subsoil Form of Divided Ownership in Late Imperial China: Some Examples from the New Territories of Hong Kong', *Modern Asian Studies* 21 (1): 1–119.

Parker, Gary (1980) 'Creation, Selection, and Variation', *Acts and Facts* 9 (10). Available at: https://www.icr.org/article/creation-selection-variation.

Penner, James (2020) *Property Rights: A Re-Examination.* Oxford: Oxford University Press.

Perdue, Peter (2004) 'Constructing Chinese Property Rights: East and West', in Islamoglu Huri (ed.), *Constituting Modernity: Private Property in the East and West.* London: I.B. Tauris & Co., 35–68.

Perez, Carlota (1983) 'Structural Change and the Assimilation of New Technology in the Economic and Social System', *Futures* 15 (5): 357–375.

Perez, Carlota (2004) 'Technological Revolutions, Paradigm Shifts and Socio-Institutional Change', in Erik S. Reinert (ed.), *Globalization, Economic Development and Inequality: An Alternative Perspective.* Cheltenham, UK and Northampton, MA, USA: Edward Elgar Publishing, 217–242.

Peters, Enrique Dussel and Verghis, Mathew A. (1993) 'The State, Markets, and Development', A Rapporteurs' Report, Working Paper #196 – June 1993. Available at: https://dusselpeters.com/218.pdf.

Pomeranz, Kenneth (2008) 'Land Markets in Late Imperial and Republican China', *Continuity and Change* 23 (1): 101–150.

Qian, Yingyi and Weingast, Barry R. (1996) 'China's Transition to Markets: Market-Preserving Federalism, Chinese Style', *Journal of Policy Reform* 1: 149–185.

Qian, Yingyi and Weingast, Barry R. (1997) 'Federalism as a Commitment to Preserving Market Incentives', *Journal of Economic Perspectives* 11 (4): 83–92.

Reinert, Erik S. (1996) 'Diminishing Returns and Economic Sustainability: The Dilemma of Resource-Based Economies under a Free Trade Regime', in Stein Hansen, Jan Hesselberg and Helge Hveem (eds), *International Trade Regulation, National Development Strategies and the Environment: Towards Sustainable Development?* Oslo: Centre for Development and the Environment, University of Oslo, 119–150.

Reinert, Erik S. (2000) 'Karl Bücher and the Geographical Dimensions of Techno-Economic Change: Production-Based Economic Theory and the Stages of

Economic Development', in Jürgen Backhaus (ed.), *Karl Bücher: Theory–History–Anthropology–Non Market Economies*. Marburg: Metropolis-Verlag, 177–222.

Reinert, Erik S. (2006) 'Institutionalism Ancient, Old and New: A Historical Perspective on Institutions and Uneven Development', UNU-WIDER (World Institute for Development Economics Research), Research Paper No. 2006/77.

Reinert, Erik S. (2007) *How Rich Countries Got Rich ... and Why Poor Countries Stay Poor*. New York: Carroll & Graf Publishers.

Reinert, Erik S. (2009a) 'The Terrible Simplifiers: Common Origins of Financial Crises and Persistent Poverty in Economic Theory and the New "1848 Movement"', DESA Working Paper No. 88.

Reinert, Erik S. (2009b) 'Emulation versus Comparative Advantage: Competing and Complementary Principles in the History of Economic Policy', Working Papers in Technology Governance and Economic Dynamics no. 25, The Other Canon Foundation, Norway; Tallinn University of Technology, Tallinn.

Reinert, Erik S. and Xu, Ting (2013). 'Declining Diversity and Declining Societies: China, the West, and the Future of the Global Economy', Uno Newsletter Working Paper Series 2 (13): 1–21. Available at: http://www.unotheory.org/files/2-13-3.pdf.

Reinert, Sophus (2011) *Translating Empire: Emulation and the Origins of Political Economy*. Cambridge, MA: Harvard University Press.

Schumpeter, Joseph (1934/2012) *The Theory of Economic Development: An Inquiry into Profits, Capital, Credit, Interest, and the Business Cycle* (16th edn). New Brunswick, NJ, USA: Transaction Publishers.

Schumpeter, Joseph (1943/2010) *Capitalism, Socialism and Democracy*. London, UK and New York, USA: Routledge.

Shue, Vivienne (1984) 'The Fate of the Commune', *Modern China* 10 (3): 259–283.

State Council Information Office of the PRC (2001) 'Rural China's Poverty Reduction', White Paper. Available at: http://en.people.cn/features/PRpaper/pr.html.

State Council Information Office of the PRC (2011) 'Progress in Development-Oriented Poverty Reduction in Rural China', White Paper. Available at: http://en.people.cn/features/PRpaper/pr.html.

State Council Information Office of the PRC (2021) 'Poverty Alleviation: China's Experience and Contribution', White Paper. Available at: http://www.xinhuanet.com/english/download/2021-4-6/FullText.pdf.

State Council of the PRC (1994) 'Seven-Year State Plan for Aiding the 80 Million People Who Still Live below the Poverty Line and Poverty Elimination in China by the End of this Century (1994–2000)', *The Gazette of the State Council of the People's Republic of China* (1994, No. 12), 28 June 1994. Available at: http://www.gov.cn/gongbao/shuju/1994/gwyb199412.pdf.

Tsai, Kellee S. (2004) 'Off Balance: The Unintended Consequences of Fiscal Federalism in China', *Journal of Chinese Political Science* 9 (2): 1–26.

Upham, Frank (2018) *The Great Property Fallacy: Theory, Reality, and Growth in Developing Countries*. Cambridge: Cambridge University Press.

Veblen, Thorstein (1898) 'The Beginnings of Ownership', *American Journal of Sociology* 4 (3): 352–365.

Veblen, Thorstein (1899/2007) *The Theory of the Leisure Class: An Economic Study in the Evolution of Institutions*. Oxford: Oxford University Press.

Veblen, Thorstein (1904/2013) *The Theory of Business Enterprise*. Mansfield Centre, CT: Martino Publishing.

Vermeer, Eduard B. (1999) 'Shareholding Cooperatives: A Property Rights Analysis', in Jean C. Oi and Andrew G. Walder (eds), *Property Rights and Economic Reform in China*. Stanford, CA: Stanford University Press, 123–144.

Vries, Peer (2013) *Escaping Poverty: The Origins of Modern Economic Growth*. Goettingen: V& R unipress GmbH.

Wang, Luolin and Zhu, Ling (eds) (2013) *Breaking Out of the Poverty Trap: Case Studies from the Tibetan Plateau in Yunnan, Qinghai and Gansu*. Hackensack, NJ: World Century Publishing.

Weber, Isabella M. (2021) *How China Escaped Shock Therapy: The Market Reform Debate*. Abingdon: Routledge.

Weingast, Barry R. (1995) 'The Economic Role of Political Institutions: Market-Preserving Federalism and Economic Development', *Journal of Law, Economics and Organization* 11 (1): 1–31.

Williamson, Oliver E. (2000) 'The New Institutional Economics: Taking Stock, Looking Ahead', *Journal of Economic Literature* 38 (3): 595–613.

World Bank (2002) *World Development Report 2002: Building Institutions for Markets*. New York: Oxford University Press. Available at: https://openknowledge .worldbank.org/handle/10986/5984.

World Bank (2004) *Initiatives in Legal and Judicial Reform*. Available at: http:// documents.worldbank.org/curated/en/139831468778813637/Initiatives-in-legal -and-judicial-reform.

World Bank (2015) 'Doing Business 2016: Measuring Regulatory Quality and Efficiency', 27 October. Available at: http://www.doingbusiness.org/reports/global -reports/doing-business-2016.

Wu, Tingyu (1987) *Zhongguo Lidai Tudi Zhidu Shigang (The History of Land Institutions in China)*. Jilin: Jilin Daxue Chubanshe.

Xie, Zaiquan (1999) *Mingfa wuquan lun (Rights in Rem in Civil Law)*. Beijing: Zhongguo Zhengfa daxue Chubanshe.

Xu, Ting (2010) 'The End of the Urban–Rural Divide? Emerging Quasi-Commons in Rural China"', *Archiv für Rechts und Sozialphilosophie (Archives for Philosophy of Law and Social Philosophy)* 96 (4): 557–573.

Xu, Ting (2014) *The Revival of Private Property and its Limits in Post-Mao China*. London: Wildy, Simmonds & Hill Publishing.

Xu, Ting (2017) 'Towards an Evolutionary Theory of Property? A Longitudinal Analysis of Property Regime Transformation in China', *Journal of Comparative Law* 12 (2): 496–517.

Xu, Ting and Gong, Wei (2020) 'Community-based Individual Property Rights: Developing the "Bundle of Rights" Perspective in the Chinese Context' *Asia Pacific Law Review* 28(1): 138–158.

Xu, Ting and Murphy, Tim (2008) 'The City as Laboratory and the Urban–Rural Divide: The Revival of Private Property and its Limits in Urban China', *China Perspectives* 4: 26–34. (Published in both English and French.)

Yang, Dali (1997) *Beyond Beijing: Liberalization and the Regions in China*. London: Routledge.

Yang, Guozhen (1988) *Mingqing Tudi Qiyue Wenshu Yanjiu (The Research into Land Titles and Contracts in the Ming and Qing)*. Beijing: Renmin Chubanshe.

Zhang, Taisu (2014) 'Social Hierarchies and the Formation of Customary Property Law in Pre-Industrial China and England', *American Journal of Comparative Law* 62 (1): 171–220.

Zhao, Gang and Chen, Zhongyi (2006) *Zhongguo tudi zhidu shi (The History of Land Institutions in China)*. Beijing: Xinxing Chubanshe.

14. Recent experiences of successful economic policies: the case of Uzbekistan

Vladimir Popov

UZBEKISTAN'S ECONOMIC PERFORMANCE DURING TRANSITION

After the collapse of the Union of Soviet Socialist Republics (USSR) and the market-oriented reforms in successor states, the comparative performance in the post-Soviet space varied greatly (Figures 14.1 and 14.2). In retrospect, it is clear that rapid economic liberalization did not pay off: many gradual reformers (labelled procrastinators at the time) from the former Soviet Union (FSU) performed better than the champions of big bang liberalization (the Baltic States and Central Europe). In Belarus, Turkmenistan, and Uzbekistan, for instance, privatization was slow; over 50 percent of gross domestic product (GDP) is created in state enterprises (Figure 14.3), yet their performance is superior to that of more liberalized economies. Recently, when resource prices were high, resource abundance helped exporters such as Azerbaijan, Kazakhstan, Russia, and Turkmenistan to maintain higher income. Uzbekistan also exported commodities—cotton, gold, and gas—which have experienced an increase in average prices in several past decades. However, this was not a *sine qua non* for growth: resource-poor Belarus, and Uzbekistan, self-sufficient in fuel and energy, did much better than resource-rich Russia.

As recent research shows, the crucial factor in economic performance is the ability to preserve the institutional capacity of the state (see Popov 2007, 2011 for surveys). The story of transition was very much a government capability, rather than a market failure. In all former Soviet republics and in the Eastern European countries, government spending fell during transition, and the provision of traditional public goods, from law and order to health care and infrastructure, worsened. This led to an increase in income inequalities, shadow economy, corruption, crime, and mortality.[1] But in countries with the smallest decline in government spending (countries which are diverse in other

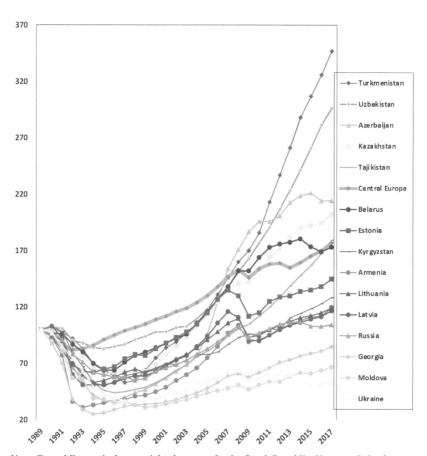

Note: Central Europe is the unweighted average for the Czech Republic, Hungary, Poland, Slovakia, and Slovenia.
Source: Based on data from European Bank for Reconstruction and Development (EBRD) Transition Reports for various years.

Figure 14.1   GDP change in economies of the former Soviet Union, 1989 = 100%

respects: Central Europe, Estonia, Belarus, Uzbekistan), these effects were less pronounced and the dynamics of output was better (Popov 2014c).

The other important reasons for superior performance are good macroeconomic and industrial policies. Here Uzbekistan is unique: it is the only country in the post-Soviet space that succeeded in increasing the share of industry in GDP, and the share of machinery and equipment in the total industrial output,

Sources: Based on data from World Development Indicators (WDI). For Baltic States (Estonia, Latvia, Lithuania), Moldova and four former Yugoslav republics (Bosnia and Herzegovina, Montenegro, Croatia, Serbia) comparable WDI data for 1990–94/97 are missing, so the data are taken from EBRD Transition Reports, 1995–2002. GDP growth rate for Serbia and Montenegro are assumed to be that of Yugoslavia and FR Yugoslavia before 1997. For Bosnia and Herzegovina, it is assumed that GDP fell by 90 percent in 1990–1995 (Wikipedia).

Figure 14.2   Average GDP growth rate in 1990–2019, %

and exports. It created a competitive export-oriented auto industry from the ground up.

Overall, Uzbekistan is an economic success story in the post-Soviet space. Its transformation-stage recession was very mild compared to other countries

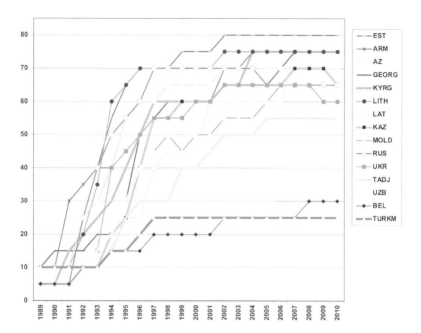

Note: Data for years after 2010 are unavailable.
Source: Based on data from Transition Report, EBRD.

*Figure 14.3   The share of private sector in GDP in former Soviet
republics, 1989–2010, %*

of the former Soviet Union: its GDP more than tripled in 1989–2019, a better
result than even in Central European countries (Figure 14.1); its population's
life expectancy, currently at 72 years, may have not increased much, but it
did not fall as it did in other former Soviet republics in the 1990s; its population increased from 20 million in 1989 to nearly 35 million in 2021; and its
murder rate—the reliable objective indicator of institutional capacity of the
state (Popov 2011)—is low: it fell from 5.2 cases per 100 000 inhabitants in
1993, to 1.1 cases in 2017, against 5 in the United States (US). In 2009, during
the "great recession", only resource-rich Kazakhstan and Azerbaijan showed
higher economic growth rates than Uzbekistan, whereas most post-communist
countries experienced a reduction of output.

True, Uzbekistan's performance is not as spectacular as that of China; nevertheless, it is exceptional for the post-Soviet space (Figure 14.2). In 2011, it
became the first country in post-Soviet space and the 15th country in the world
to launch a high-speed train line (between Tashkent and Samarkand). This

was extended from Samarkand to Bukhara in 2016. The train is made by the Spanish Talgo and runs a distance of 600 km in 3 hours 20 minutes.

The inclusiveness of growth appears to be higher in Uzbekistan as well. In 2012, Uzbekistan's official estimate for the Gini coefficient was just above 30 percent (World Bank estimates suggest that the Gini coefficient fell from 45 percent in 1998, to 35 percent in 2003). This is lower than in most transition economies. Meanwhile, in the more liberalized economies of Russia, Lithuania, and Georgia, income distribution was noticeably more uneven, ranging between 0.38 and 0.45 (Figure 14.4).

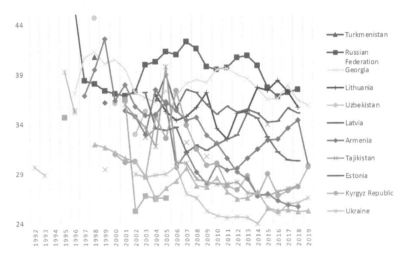

Source: Based on data from WDI.

Figure 14.4   *Gini coefficient of income distribution in post-Soviet states since 1992, %*

Another indicator of income distribution is the number of billionaires.[2] The 2013 Forbes count placed Russia and Georgia ahead in billionaire-intensity—number of billionaires per $1 trillion purchasing power parity (PPP) GDP—followed by Ukraine, the Czech Republic, and Kazakhstan (Table 14.1). Other former USSR countries do not have billionaires yet, although their PPP GDP is higher than that of Georgia. For example, Azerbaijan and Uzbekistan are supposed to have about three billionaires had they the same level of billionaire-intensity as Russia. But in fact, they do not.

Its relatively successful economic performance is even more impressive given that Uzbekistan is not a major oil and gas exporter, and that it is one of

Table 14.1   *Billionaires in the former USSR, Eastern Europe, China, and Vietnam, 2012*

	Number of billionaires	Total wealth	PPP GDP, 2012	Number per trillion PPP GDP	Wealth of billionaires to PPP GDP, %
China	122	260.9	12471	9.8	2.1
Russia	110	403.8	3380	32.5	11.9
Ukraine	10	31.3	338.2	29.6	9.3
Kazakhstan	5	9.2	233	21.5	3.9
Czech Republic	4	14.0	277.9	14.4	5.0
Poland	4	9.8	844.2	4.7	1.2
Georgia	1	5.3	26.6	37.6	19.9
Vietnam	1	1.5	322.7	3.1	0.5
Romania	1	1.1	352.3	2.8	0.3
Uzbekistan	0	0	107	0.0	0.0

Sources: Based on data from Forbes billionaires list (http://www.forbes.com/billionaires/ #page:1_sort:0_direction:asc_search:_filter:All%20industries_filter:All%20countries_filter:All %20states); WDI.

two double-landlocked countries[3] in the world (the other being Liechtenstein). It is important, however, to distinguish between growth rates and the level of per capita income. Uzbekistan remains a poor country with PPP GDP per capita of below US$8000 in 2021, against close to $30 000 in Russia and Kazakhstan, about $20 000 in China, over $17 000 in Turkmenistan, and $15 000 in Azerbaijan. Many Uzbeks are migrating to find jobs in Russia.

It is necessary to separate the effects associated with the dynamics of output from the effects of the terms of trade and financial flows. At the end of the Soviet period, in the 1980s, real incomes in Uzbekistan were about half of those in Russia. After the collapse of the USSR, real incomes in non-resource republics fell dramatically due to the change in relative prices: oil, gas, and other resources became several times more expensive relative to ready-made goods. Uzbekistan was a large importer of oil, and its trade with all countries, including other Soviet republics, if recalculated in world prices, yielded a deficit of 9 percent of GDP (Soviet Economy 1991). To make matters worse, after the collapse of the Soviet Union the financial flows from Moscow dried up. In 1990, interbudgetary transfers from the Soviet Union budget amounted to 31 percent of the revenues of the republican budget (Soviet Economy 1991).

Hence, the sharp reduction of real incomes in Uzbekistan in the early 1990s was larger than the reduction of output, and was primarily due to the poor external environment and circumstances, rather than policy and choice. However, the dynamics of real output—that is, the physical volume of output

(Figure 14.1), which is dependent on both circumstances and policy, but not dependent directly on terms of trade (world prices)—was better than in all countries of Eastern Europe and the former USSR with the exception of Turkmenistan.

Uzbekistan so far appears to be quite successful in fighting the coronavirus pandemic: its COVID-19 deaths per million inhabitants in 2020 were only around 20, whereas in most developed and many developing countries the numbers were in the hundreds (Figure 14.5).

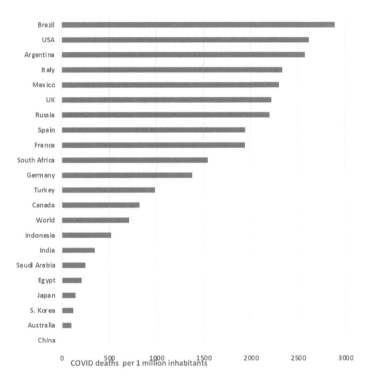

Source: Based on data from Worldometers (https://www.worldometers.info/coronavirus).

Figure 14.5   *Death rate from COVID-19 in G20 countries, per 1 million inhabitants (by January 2022)*

The more reliable indicator of excess deaths from all causes—that is, the increase in the mortality rate in 2020–2021 as compared to several previous years—was also low. By May 2021, Uzbekistan (together with Tajikistan and Belarus) had one of the lowest excess mortality rates as compared to the preceding years among all former Soviet republics: less than 1 per 1000 inhabitants, as compared to over 3 per 1000 in Russia and Lithuania.[4] By March 2022, excess deaths in Uzbekistan (1 per 1000) were lower than in other Central Asian countries, and lower by an order of magnitude than in some other post-communist countries such as Bulgaria and Russia (Figure 14.6).

EXCESS DEATHS PER 100 PEOPLE

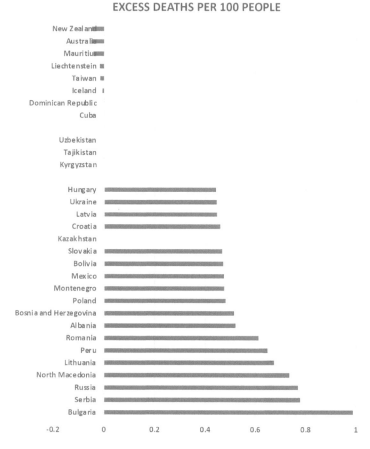

Source: Based on data from *The Economist*, March 11, 2022.

Figure 14.6   Excess deaths since country's first 50 COVID-19 deaths

Economic performance during the coronavirus pandemic was better in Uzbekistan than in most countries of the world. Its GDP increased by 1.7

Table 14.2   *GDP growth rates, % (2021, IMF economic forecast, April 2021)*

Country	2019	2020	2021 (Estimate)	2022 (Forecast)	2023 (Forecast)
Argentina	-2.1	−9.9	10.0	3.0	2.5
Australia	1.9	−2.2	4.2	4.1	2.5
Brazil	1.4	−3.9	4.7	0.3	1.6
Canada	1.9	−5.2	4.7	4.1	2.8
China	5.8	2.3	8.1	4.8	5.2
France	1.5	−8.0	6.7	3.5	1.8
Germany	0.6	−4.6	2.7	3.8	2.5
India	4.0	−7.3	9.0	9.0	7.1
Indonesia	5.0	−2.1	3.3	5.6	6.0
Italy	0.3	−8.9	6.2	3.8	2.2
Japan	0.3	−4.5	1.6	3.3	1.8
Korea	2.0	−0.9	4.0	3.0	2.9
Mexico	-0.1	−8.2	5.3	2.8	2.7
Russia	2.0	−2.7	4.5	2.8	2.1
Saudi Arabia	0.3	−4.1	2.9	4.8	2.8
South Africa	0.2	−6.4	4.6	1.9	1.4
Spain	2.0	−10.8	4.9	5.8	3.8
Turkey	0.9	1.8	11.0	3.3	3.3
United Kingdom	1.4	−9.4	7.2	4.7	2.3
United States	2.2	−3.4	5.6	4.0	2.6
Uzbekistan	5.7	1.7	6.1	5.4	5.5

Sources: Based on data from World Economic Outlook, January 2022 Update. IMF, 2022.

percent in 2020, while only two G20 countries, Turkey and China, were able to achieve positive growth rates in 2020; all the other G20 countries experienced a recession, sometimes as deep as 5 to 10 percent reduction of annual GDP (Table 14.2).

CHANGES IN UZBEKISTAN'S ECONOMIC STRUCTURE

Industrial structure matters for economic development. The Chenery (1960) hypothesis states that countries at similar levels of economic development should have similar patterns of resource allocation between sectors. But in theoretical models it is often assumed that there are externalities from industrialization and industrial export (Murphy et al. 1989; Polterovich and Popov 2004, 2005). There is growing evidence that countries which are more industrialized, and countries with more technologically sophisticated industrial export, are growing faster than others (Hausmann et al. 2006; Rodrik 2006). There are still no cases of "economic miracles" based on agriculture or services.

Not all countries are able to climb the technological ladder, diversify, and upgrade the structure of their economy and exports. In most transition economies a "primitivization" of the industrial structure occurred (Popov 2020). Secondary manufacturing and high-tech industries proved to be uncompetitive, and their output was curtailed after the deregulation of prices and the opening of the economy. As a matter of fact, an increase in the share of the service sector, especially trade and finance, at the expense of industry (deindustrialization) occurred in all post-communist economies.

Previously in the centrally planned economies, the service sector, in particular trade and finance, were underdeveloped. It seems, however, that in many of these economies deindustrialization went too far. In Tajikistan, for example, the share of services in GDP nearly doubled, increasing from about 30 percent in the early 1990s to 57 percent in 2010, whereas the share of manufacturing in GDP fell from 25 percent in 1990 to 10 percent in 2010. In Russia the share of industry in GDP fell from about half in 1990 to about one-third in the mid-1990s, whereas within industry itself the share of the primary sector (fuel, energy, steel, and non-ferrous metals) in the total industrial output increased from 25 percent to over 50 percent.

The share of industry as a whole (which includes not only manufacturing, but also mining and utilities—electric energy, water, and gas distribution—Figure 14.7[5]), as a rule of thumb, despite sharp fluctuations, did not decline much in resource-rich countries (Azerbaijan, Kazakhstan, Russia, Turkmenistan), but declined in non-resource rich countries. The only exception is Uzbekistan, which has a medium resource abundance (self-sufficient in energy), but managed to increase the share of industry to over 30 percent after it fell from 35 to below 20 percent in 1987–2002 (Figure 14.7).

The structure of exports in most post-Soviet states also became more primitive within two decades; the share of manufactured goods in total exports either declined or did not show any clear tendency towards increase. This was partly caused by the increase in resource prices and the resource boom: the expansion of fuel production and exports in Azerbaijan, Kazakhstan, Russia, and Turkmenistan. In Russia the share of fuel, minerals, metals, and diamonds in total exports grew from 52 percent in 1990 (USSR) to 67 percent in 1995, and 81 percent in 2012. In contrast, the share of machinery and equipment in total exports fell from 18 percent in 1990 (USSR) to 10 percent in 1995, and 4.5 percent in 2012.

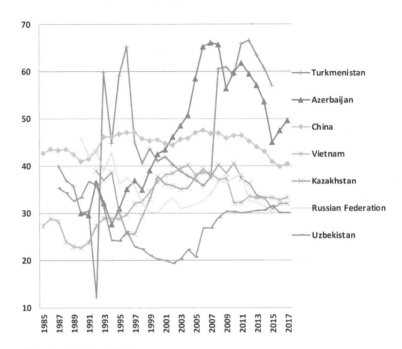

Source: Based on data from WDI.

Figure 14.7   *The share of industry value added in GDP in China, Vietnam, and the resource-rich FSU in 1985–2017, %*

Such changes in the industrial structure were not solely the result of an "invisible hand of the market." As Greenwald and Stiglitz (1986, 2013) point out, market failures are pervasive, and private rewards and social rewards virtually always differ. Governments, then, are inevitably involved in shaping the industrial structure of the economy, by what they both do and do not do. As many authors point out, the secret of "good" industrial policy in East Asia, as opposed to "bad" industrial policy in the former Soviet Union, Latin America, and Africa, may be associated with the ability to reap the benefits of export externalities (Khan 2007a; Gibbs 2007). Exporting to world markets, especially to developed countries, enables the upgrade of quality and technology standards, and yields social returns in excess of the returns to particular exporters. The greatest increases in productivity are registered at companies that export to advanced (Western) markets and which export hi-tech goods (Harris and Li 2007; Shevtsova 2012). In addition, it has been shown that the gap between the actual level of development and the hypothetical level, which corresponds to the degree of sophistication of a country's exports, is strongly correlated with productivity growth rates (Hausmann et al. 2006). In other words, it pays off to promote exports of sophisticated and high-tech goods. Not all countries which attempt to promote such exports succeed, but those that do not try, virtually never engineer growth miracles.[6]

It is worth noting that there is an opposite view (Gill et al. 2014). Gill et al. conclude that it is not clear whether diversifying exports and production is necessary for development, and that governments need concern themselves less with the composition of exports and profile of production, and more with their "national asset portfolios": the natural resources, built capital, and economic institutions. But the example of Uzbekistan is yet another proof to the contrary.

Since independence in 1991, Uzbekistan encouraged and carried out three important structural shifts in its economy: (1) a decrease in cotton production and exports, and an increase in food production, achieving food self-sufficiency; (2) an attainment of energy self-sufficiency and an achievement of net fuel exporter status; and (3) an increase in the share of industry in GDP, and the share of machinery and equipment in industrial output and exports (Popov 2014a).

After independence, an automobile industry was created in Uzbekistan from the ground up. Car production was supported by the government and by the Korean auto company Daewoo. After Daewoo declared bankruptcy, US General Motors became the government's partner. The government also bought a stake in Turkey's Koc in SamKochAvto, a producer of small buses and lorries. Afterwards, it signed an agreement with Isuzu Motors of Japan to produce Isuzu buses and lorries. In 2014, Uzbekistan produced 250 000 cars, and nearly a quarter were exported.[7] In 2011, a joint venture of State Auto Company and General Motors, the engine plant in Tashkent, became operational with a capacity of 360 000 engines a year. In 2021, after the decline associated with the COVID-19 pandemic, the auto industry produced nearly 300 000 vehicles; about 10 percent of them were exported, mostly to Kazakhstan.

Uzbekistan's exports increased dramatically: from $2 billion in 1992 to $15 billion in 2011, or from $100 to $500 per capita. The share of former USSR countries in exports fell from over 60 percent in 1992 to less than 40 percent in 2012. The share of cotton in exports fell from 65 percent in 1992 to only 9 percent in 2012, while the share of fuel (mostly gas) and oil products increased from 4 to 38 percent. The share of machinery and equipment increased from 2 to 7 percent, and the share of chemical products from 6 to 9 percent. In imports, the share of food fell from 43 to 10 percent, whereas the share of machinery and equipment increased from 10 to 46 percent (Popov 2014a).

In the 2010s the second round of industrial policy focused on heavy chemicals: Shurtan Gas Chemical Complex and the planned production of synthetic liquid fuels based on purified methane together with South African Sasol and Malaysian Petronas; liquefied natural gas production at Mubarek gas processing plant; Dehkonobod Potash Fertilizer Plant; and Ustyurt gas chemical complex at Surgil deposit (Popov 2014b).

MACROECONOMIC POLICY

In 2000–2021 Uzbekistan was growing at a rate of 4–9 percent, with the exception of the 2020 pandemic year (when growth fell to 2 percent) and a barely visible decline in growth rates during the 2008–2009 recession (Figure 14.8). Inflation was brought under control in the beginning of the 2000s; it it has remained quite high since then, mostly running at double digits, but only once (in 2010) exceeded 30 percent a year (Figure 14.8). The government finances were in good order, the current account balance was positive until the 2008–2009 recession (Figure 14.9), and the debt to GDP ratio in 2002–2015 was falling (Figure 14.10).

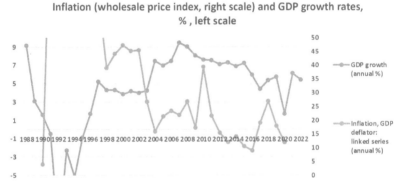

Inflation (wholesale price index, right scale) and GDP growth rates, % , left scale

Source: Based on data from WDI database.

Figure 14.8   Economic growth and inflation in Uzbekistan, 1988–2022

Foreign exchange reserves at the end of 2012 were estimated at about $40 billion (15 months of imports, against five months in 2004), not including about $5 billion (2010) in the Reconstruction and Development Fund of Uzbekistan.[8] By 2020, the foreign exchange reserves were also 15 months of imports, like in China, and higher than in other Central Asian countries (Figure 14.11).

Some problems emerged after the global 2008–2009 recession: the exchange rate of the *som* was allowed to appreciate, the current account balance turned

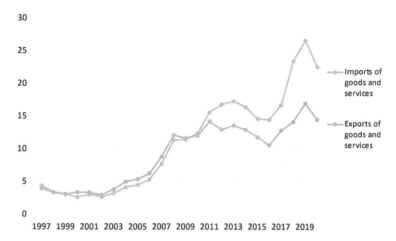

Source: Based on data from WDI database.

Figure 14.9   Exports and imports of Uzbekistan in 1997–2020, billion dollars

negative (Figure 14.9), and external debt to GDP ratio increased (Figure 14.10), whereas economic growth slowed down (Figure 14.8). However, in 2017 the new leadership started economic reforms, including deregulation of the exchange rate, which led to a considerable devaluation. The share of

Source: Based on data from WDI database.

Figure 14.10   External debt of Central Asian countries and China in 1992–2020

Source: Based on data from WDI database.

Figure 14.11   Foreign exchange reserves of Central Asian countries and China in 1982–2020

investment in GDP increased from around 30 percent in 20052016 to about 40 percent in 2019–2020 which helped to sustain economic growth (Figure 14.12).

In the area of macroeconomic policy, Uzbekistan is not exceptional. Many countries of the former USSR have managed to put their government finances in order in recent years, and they enjoy budget surpluses, moderate inflation,

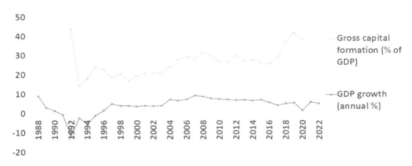

Source: Based on data from WDI database.

Figure 14.12   Share of investment in GDP and economic growth rates in Uzbekistan in 1988–2022

and growing foreign reserves. What makes Uzbekistan different, even unique, is a policy of low exchange rate. This promotes export-oriented development similarly to that seen in Japan in the 1950s–1970s, South Korea in the 1960–1980s, and China and Association of Southeast Asian Nations (ASEAN) countries since the 1990s (Dollar 1992; Easterly 1999; Polterovich and Popov 2004; Rodrik 2008; Bhalla 2012). Undervaluation of the exchange rate via accumulation of foreign exchange reserves, in fact, becomes a powerful tool of industrial policy, creating stimuli for tradable goods at the expense of non-tradables (Greenwald and Stiglitz 2013). Former communist countries of Eastern Europe and the USSR did not carry out such a policy; on the contrary, their exchange rates often were and are overvalued, especially in countries that export resources (they suffer from the Dutch disease).

UNDERVALUATION OF THE EXCHANGE RATE: THE MAIN TOOL OF INDUSTRIAL POLICY

Since 2000, Uzbekistan is probably the only country in the post-Soviet space which carries out predictable and gradual nominal devaluation of the currency that is somewhat greater than needed to counter the differences in inflation rates between Uzbekistan and its major trading partners, so that the real effective exchange rate depreciates slowly. The real exchange rate of the *som* versus the US dollar has somewhat appreciated, though not as much as the currencies of other countries (Figure 14.13).

Ratio of national prices to the US prices (PPP conversion factor (GDP) to market exchange rate ratio)

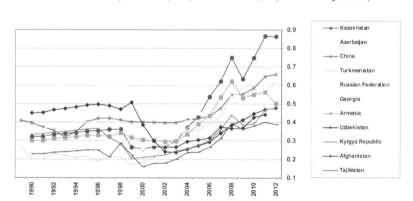

Source: Based on data from WDI.

Figure 14.13   Real exchange rate with the US dollar for selected countries

However, the real effective exchange rate of the som (that is, with respect to currencies of all major trading partners) decreased by over 50 percent in 2000–2007 (Popov 2014a); and after the increase in 2008–15, declined again in 2015–20 (Figure 14.14). This is in sharp contrast to other transition countries of the region (North and Central Asia and Caucasus) for which data are available (Figure 14.15). Other, more traditional tools of industrial policy exist: for example, the tax stimuli to manufacturing exporters mentioned earlier, government orders, and government investment. However, undervaluation of the exchange rate is probably the most important instrument.

Note: Ratio of PPP exchange rate to the official exchange rate.
Source: Based on data from WDI database.

Figure 14.14   Real exchange rate of Uzbek som in 1995–2020, World Bank estimate

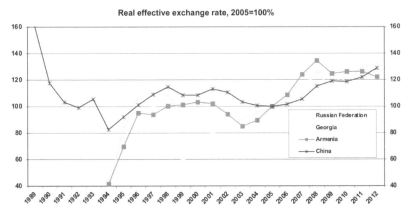

Sources: Based on data from WDI, IMF.

Figure 14.15   Real effective exchange rate of selected countries

WHICH INDUSTRIES SHOULD DEVELOP AT A FASTER PACE?

The reduction in the share of industry in GDP and the increase in the share of services is an objective process; but in the fast-growing countries (for example, China) this decline was slower than in others. At the same time, it appears that the increase in the share of machinery and equipment in manufacturing output, as in China, usually accompanies rapid growth or even becomes the engine of growth. Cases of rapid growth ("economic miracles") that are based on an accelerated growth of the service sector are yet to occur.

The question of "What are the particular manufacturing industries which could become the engine of growth?" is a difficult one. Unfortunately, economic theory does not suggest any definite clues, with the exception of the idea that these industries should have the highest externalities, that is, their social returns should be higher than private returns. Yet, it is not easy to measure these externalities. Upon examination of the literature and the experience of countries with industrial policy, it is possible to isolate methods which can help in our identification of industries that should be supported (Chowdhury and Popov 2016).

For example, one can support several industries which seem promising with the condition that assistance ends if the increase in exports is not achieved within, for example, five years. This is called "EPconEP": effective protection conditional on export promotion (Jomo 2013). Economic policy-makers in this case are similar to the military commander who begins an offensive on several fronts, but deploys reserves where there has been a breakthrough.

Alternatively, one can attempt to predict the specific industries where limited investment can give the greatest effect, leading to the creation of globally competitive production. Most likely, these would be industries that lag behind in total factor productivity in the most advanced countries, but by less than other industries.

It is also possible to choose at random. In this case, it is important to be consistent by embarking on the path of support for a particular industry without withdrawal, even if there is no immediate success or breakthrough in world markets. After all, the modern theory of international trade explains country specialization not by comparative advantage, but rather by "learning by doing."

If a country does not have any comparative advantages, similarly to post-war Japan for example, it is necessary to create them ("dynamic comparative advantages") by mastering the production of goods that have not been produced before. Supporting such production and consistently encouraging exports, without withdrawal for some time, is likely to have the learning by doing effect, allowing the country to gradually become competitive. As the saying goes, if Japan, which does not possess any minerals or extensive agricultural land, were to rely on comparative advantages, its exports today would not even be sushi (which includes rice), but only sashimi.

There are two opposing views on how advanced in technology the industries supported in the framework of industrial policy ought to be. Justin Lin, former Chief Economist of the World Bank, developed the idea of comparative advantages following (CAF) and comparative advantages defying (CAD) industrial strategy. The best result, according to his argument, could be achieved if countries develop industries that are consistent with their comparative advantages, as determined by their endowment structure, and do not try to overleap necessary stages aiming at exporting the goods which are exported by very advanced countries (Lin 2011).

This view is consistent with the "flying geese" paradigm: as more competitive countries move to more advanced types of exports, the vacated niches are occupied by less-developed countries. It is known that relatively poor countries began to export textiles and shoes, then moved on to the export of steel products and heavy chemicals, then to the export of cars and electrical consumer products such as washing machines and refrigerators, then to consumer electronics and computers. In this case, the newcomers could benefit from the experience of other countries by trying to replicate their success.

The transition from one exported good to another could be dictated by the cycle of innovations. As Lee (2013) suggests, the cycle is short for electronics, and long for pharmaceuticals and chemicals. This may explain why East Asian countries which focused mostly on industries with short cycles managed to avoid growth slowdowns while moving from one export niche to another.

Justin Lin appears to believe that Uzbekistan should not leap over the consecutive stages by going from processing agricultural goods directly to auto and heavy chemistry industries. He suggests that Uzbekistan could gain greater benefits by developing less sophisticated industries such as food, textiles and leather goods.[9] The share of research and development (R&D) expenditure in GDP in Uzbekistan was indeed falling in the recent two decades: from 0.36 percent in 2000 to 0.13 percent in 2018 (Table 14.3). The arguments against, however, are supported by the examples of Israel and Finland which, at the end of the 20th century, mastered the production of high-tech goods (electronics) and are now leading the world in the share of R&D expenditure to GDP ratio (Figure 14.16).

In contrast, Ricardo Haussmann, Jason Hwang and Dani Rodrik (Hausmann and Rodrik 2006; Hausmann et al. 2006; Rodrik 2006) hypothesize that the more technologically sophisticated the export structure, the greater the stimuli for economic growth. China in 1992 and 2003, for example, had the greatest gap between the hypothetical per capita income (computed based on the tech-

Table 14.3   *R&D expenditure as a % of GDP in Uzbekistan in 2000–2018*

Year	R&D spending as % of GDP	Year	R&D spending as % of GD
2000	0.36	2009	0.20
2001	0.35	2010	0.20
2002	0.29	2011	0.19
2003	0.27	2012	0.20
2004	0.27	2013	0.20
2005	0.24	2014	0.16
2006	0.22	2015	0.17
2007	0.22	2016	0.18
2008	0.19	2017	0.16
2009	0.20	2018	0.13

Source: Based on data from WDI.

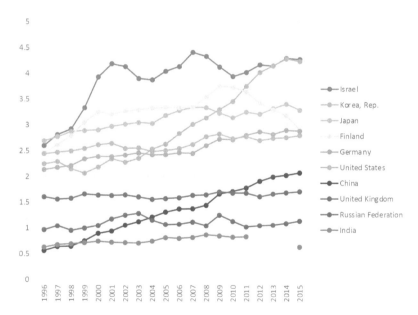

Source: Based on data from WDI.

Figure 14.16   *R&D expenditure in selected countries, % of GDP*

nological sophistication of export structure) and the actual per capita income. That is to say, the structure of the Chinese exports was similar to that of countries with several-fold higher levels of economic development.

In another article (Hausmann and Rodrik 2006) the process of transition from the production and export of one group of goods to the other is compared to the movement of monkeys in a forest from closer to more distant trees. The trees rich with fruit are far away, whereas closer trees do not have as much. Thus, the monkeys must compare the movement costs with the benefits of reaching the more fruit-abundant trees. Similarly to the monkeys, firms and society as a whole must compare the cost of mastering the new output and exports (low for "nearby" industries which are close to existing technologies and high for "far away" industries with totally new technological processes) with the benefits (externalities) associated with developing particular industries (theoretically the higher the costs, the more sophisticated these industries are).

A similar debate took place between Justin Lin and Ha-Joon Chang (Lin and Chang 2009). The latter was defending the idea of CAD industrial policy which favours industries that defy the country's comparative advantages. Such industries take time to develop, yet they could be worthwhile. For example:

> Japan had to protect its car industry with high tariffs for nearly four decades, provide a lot of direct and indirect subsidies, and virtually ban foreign direct investment in the industry before it could become competitive in the world market. It is for the same reason that the electronics subsidiary of the Nokia group had to be cross subsidized by its sister companies for 17 years before it made any profit. History is full of examples of this kind, from eighteenth-century Britain to late twentieth-century Korea. (Lin and Chang 2009)

Chang's and Rodrik's positions are similar, but there is a subtle distinction between the CAD strategy and the policy to promote high-tech industries and R&D in relatively poor countries. The CAD strategy does not necessarily imply a transition to more technologically sophisticated industries, but rather, to industries that are not linked to comparative advantages of a particular country. Theoretically, it could be a transition from chemicals to machine building with the same, or even lower, level of R&D intensity and technological sophistication. Rodrik's idea is that externality returns from the production and export of new products are proportional to the degree of their technological sophistication, which is measured by the comparison of export structures of rich versus poor countries. High-income countries export more high-tech products on average. Developing high-tech production in poor countries may be costly, yet the returns from such a policy could be greater. It may well pay off for a relatively poor country to make "a big leap forward" by investing heavily in the education of the labour force and high-tech industries, bypassing the intermediate stages of producing goods with medium research intensity. The implication for Uzbekistan is that investment in the auto and heavy chemistry industries could be well justified.

Uzbekistan's creation of a car industry from the ground up was an undisputable success of industrial policy: a breakthrough to world markets with the products of a medium-level research intensity, previously achievable only by countries of a higher-level development. It remains to be seen, however, whether the second round of industrial policy, with a focus on heavy chemistry, will succeed.

CONCLUDING REMARKS

The general reason for the better performance of slow liberalizers with rather authoritarian regimes in the post-communist world (Azerbaijan, Belarus, China, Kazakhstan, Turkmenistan, Uzbekistan, Vietnam) is the ability to preserve the strong institutional capacity of the state. The economic model in these countries is close to what is usually described as "developmental authoritarianism": a market economy with a strong state that is successfully providing public goods (law and order, protection of property rights and contracts, education, health care, infrastructure, social welfare) and is growth-oriented.

Economic liberalization alone cannot be credited for the economic successes of developmental states. In other regions of the world, economic liberalization did not produce such impressive results. On the contrary, in Latin America, where it was tried after the debt crisis of the early 1980s (the Washington Consensus), it led to the economic stagnation and "lost decade" of the 1980s. Then came the turn of sub-Saharan Africa with the same results in the 1990s, and of the former Soviet Union and Eastern Europe (also in the 1990s) with a dramatic reduction of output on a scale larger than the Great Depression of the 1930s. Why economic liberalization work in Uzbekistan (as it did in China and Vietnam), but not in other regions?

The answer is that reforms which are needed to achieve success are different for countries with different backgrounds. Manufacturing growth is like cooking a good dish: all the ingredients should be in the right proportion; if only one is under- or overrepresented, the "chemistry of growth" will not happen. Fast economic growth can materialize in practice only if several necessary conditions are met at the same time. Rapid growth is a complicated process that requires a number of crucial inputs: infrastructure, human capital, even land distribution in agrarian countries, strong state institutions, economic stimuli, among other things. Once one of these crucial necessary ingredients is missing, the growth just does not take off. Economists talk today about "binding constraints" that hold back economic growth; finding these constraints is the task of "growth diagnostics" (Rodrik et al. 2005). In some cases, these constraints are associated with the lack of market liberalization; in others, with the lack of state capacity or human capital or infrastructure.

In Uzbekistan, like in the other former Soviet republics and other former socialist countries (Eastern Europe, China, Vietnam, Mongolia), the preconditions for the post-reform success were created mostly in the preceding pre-reform period. But in many of these countries strong state institutions—the precious heritage of the socialist era—were destroyed during the transition period, when the state failed in the provision of such public goods as law and order (contract and property rights in particular), welfare, education, health care, and infrastructure. On the contrary, in Uzbekistan and other developmental states there was no government failure, so the other crucial ingredient of the economic miracle—an efficient state apparatus—was not lacking.

On top of that, Uzbekistan is remarkable in another respect: it is the only country in the post-Soviet space that had a largely export-oriented industrial policy. Eastern European countries did not use any particular industrial policy, relying predominantly on market forces, and resource-rich FSU countries (Azerbaijan, Kazakhstan, Russia, Turkmenistan) had a variant of Dutch disease (subsidization of all domestic producers and consumers through low domestic prices for fuel and energy and overvalued exchange rate). In contrast, Uzbekistan, more like China and Vietnam, promoted export-oriented development via an undervalued exchange rate, even though it became virtually self-sufficient in fuel and energy (Popov 2020). This is the most remarkable difference between Uzbekistan and Belarus, which also adopted the model of developmental authoritarianism, but without the export-oriented industrial policy.

NOTES

1. State capacity is understood as the ability of the state to enforce rules and regulations, and is measured by objective indicators such as crime rate, murder rate, the share of shadow economy, i. e. the degree of compliance with tax rules and criminal code (the murder rate is better than the crime rate due to statistical registration problems: grave crimes, such as murders, are registered more accurately than other crimes, especially in developing countries; see Popov 2008).
    There are well-known problems with subjective measures of institutional capacity, such as the corruption perception indices of Transparency International and the World Bank indices of government effectiveness, rule of law, and so on (Khan 2007b; Popov 2011). The institutional capacity declined dramatically in the 1990s in many transition economies; all three traditional monopolies of the state (on violence, tax collection and issuance of currency) were undermined (Popov 2004).
2. The statistics on the number of billionaires published annually by Forbes allegedly characterize income distribution at the very top of the wealth pyramid. The

number of billionaires depends mostly on the total size of the country's GDP. Much less important is the per capita GDP. The relationship is non-linear:
Number of billionaires in 2007 = $-0.9 + 0.367y - 0.0049y^2 + 2.6Y^2$,
where:
y is PPP GDP per capita in thousand $ in 2005,
Y is PPP GDP in 2005 in trillions.
N = 181, R^2 = 0.95, all coefficients significant at 1% level.
Countries which exceed the predicted number of billionaires considerably (by two times and more) are: Canada, Israel, Germany, Spain, the United Kingdom, India, Turkey, Saudi Arabia, Egypt, Hong Kong, Malaysia, the Philippines, Brazil, Russia, Ukraine, and Kazakhstan. In contrast, countries where the number of billionaires is considerably lower than predicted are Japan, China, most countries of Western Europe, Oman, Argentina, Romania, and the Czech Republic (Popov 2014c).

3. Double-landlocked countries are countries completely surrounded by other landlocked countries.

4. Excess Mortality across Countries in 2020. Centre for Evidence-Based Medicine, March 3, 2021 (https://www.cebm.net/covid-19/excess-mortality-across -countries-in-2020/); Statista (https://www.statista.com/statistics/).

5. Unfortunately, there are no comparable statistics on the share of mining industry and utilities separately.

6. One exception could be Botswana, which had one of the highest rates of per capita GDP growth in the last 50 years (5 percent during 1960–2010), which was primarily driven by exports of primary commodities (namely, diamonds) and not of high-tech goods. The other exception may be Oman: out of 20 economies with average growth rates of GDP per capita in 1950–2010 of 3 percent and more a year, Oman was the only oil-rich state (nearly 5 percent growth a year) (Popov and Jomo 2017). True, many other oil and gas exporters in the Persian Gulf and elsewhere quickly became rich in recent decades, but not due to higher growth rates of output (it was moderate), but due to the improvement of the terms of trade; their income from resource exports grew much faster than their output and exports.

7. In 2013, Uzbekistan sold over 60 000 cars to Russia and 33 000 to Kazakhstan. In 2014–2015 exports fell dramatically due to a recession in Russia. In 2014, car output was 246 000 including over 55 000 for export (38 000 to Russia, the rest to Kazakhstan, Azerbaijan, Ukraine, Belarus, and also to Indonesia, Brazil, Turkey, South Korea). The share of the joint venture company GM Uzbekistan in the Russian car market fell to 1.5 percent in 2014 from 2.2 percent in 2013 (UzDaily. uz, 2015, http://www.uzdaily.uz/).

8. In 2006, Uzbekistan's Fund for Reconstruction and Development (FRD) was established. It has been used primarily for sterilization and accumulation of foreign exchange revenues, but officially it was presented as a financial institution for providing government-guaranteed loans and equity investments to strategic sectors of the domestic economy. It was established by Uzbekistan's Cabinet of Ministers, Ministry of Finance, and the five largest state-owned banks. The equity capital of the fund reached US$5 billion in 2010. The FRD provides debt financing for modernization and technical upgrade projects in sectors that are strategically important for the Uzbek economy (energy, chemicals, non-ferrous metallurgy, and so on). All loans require government approval. The credit portfolio of the FRD reached US$871 million in 2010 (BEEBA 2011).

9.   Personal communication with Justin Lin. In its general form the theory is presented in Lin (2011).

REFERENCES

BEEBA (2011). 2011 Investment Climate Statement—Uzbekistan. 2011 Investment Climate Statement. Bureau of Economic, Energy and Business Affairs. March. http://www.state.gov/e/eb/rls/othr/ics/2011/157382.htm.

Bhalla, Surjit (2012). Devaluing to Prosperity: Misaligned Currencies and Their Growth Consequences. Peterson Institute for International Economics.

Chenery, Hollis (1960). Patterns of Industrial Growth. *American Economic Review*, 50 (3), 624–654.

Chowdhury, Anis and Vladimir Popov (2016). What Uzbekistan Tells Us about Industrial Policy that We Did Not Know? DESA working paper No. 147. February.

Dollar, David (1992). Outward-Oriented Developing Economies Really Do Grow More Rapidly: Evidence from 95 LDCs, 1976–1985. *Economic Development and Cultural Change*, 40 (3), 523–544.

Easterly, William (1999). *The Lost Decades: Explaining Developing Countries Stagnation 1980–1998*. World Bank.

Forbes (2013). The World Billionaires. Forbes, http://www.forbes.com/billionaires/list/

Gibbs, Murray (2007). *Trade Policy*. UN DESA.

Gill, Indermit S., Ivailo Izvorski, Willem van Eeghen and Donato De Rosa (2014). Diversified Development. Making the Most of Natural Resources of Eurasia. World Bank.

Greenwald, Bruce and Joseph Stiglitz (1986). Externalities in Economies with Imperfect Information and Incomplete Markets. *Quarterly Journal of Economics*, 101 (2), 229–264.

Greenwald, Bruce and Joseph Stiglitz (2013). Learning and Industrial Policy: Implications for Africa. In: Stiglitz, J., Lin, J., and Patel, E. (eds), *The Industrial Policy Revolution II. Africa in the XXI Century*. IEA series. London: Palgrave Macmillan.

Harris, Richard and Qian Cher Li (2007). Learning-by-Exporting? Firm-Level Evidence for UK Manufacturing and Services Sectors. http://www.gla.ac.uk/media/media_36279_en.pdf.

Hausmann, Ricardo and Dani Rodrik (2006). Doomed to Choose: Industrial Policy as Predicament. Harvard University. September 2.

Hausmann, Ricardo, Jason Hwang and Dani Rodrik (2006). "What You Export Matters," NBER Working Paper, January.

Jomo, Kwame Sundaram (2013). The Best Approach to Economic Development is Pragmatism. In: P. Dutkiewicz and R. Sakwa (eds), *22 Ideas to Fix the World Conversations with the World's Foremost Thinkers*, New York: New York University Press.

Khan, Mushtaq (2007a). Governance, Economic Growth and Development since the 1960s. DESA Working Paper No. 54, August. http://www.un.org/esa/desa/papers/2007/wp54_2007.pdf.

Khan, Mushtaq (2007b). *Investment and Technology Policies*. UN DESA.

Lee, Keun (2013). *Schumpeterian Analysis of Economic Catch-up Knowledge, Path-Creation, and the Middle-Income Trap*. Cambridge University

Press. https://www.cambridge.org/core/books/schumpeterian-analysis-of-economic-catchup/E4B005F1B831664F2B016B1D6BABF38F.

Lin, Justin Yifu (2011). From Flying Geese to Leading Dragons. New Opportunities and Strategies for Structural Transformation in Developing Countries. Policy Research Working Paper 5702. June.

Lin, Justin and Ha-Joon Chang (2009). Should Industrial Policy in Developing Countries Conform to Comparative Advantage or Defy it? A Debate Between Justin Lin and Ha-Joon Chang. *Development Policy Review*, 27 (5), 483–502

Murphy, Kevin M., Andrei Shleifer and Robert W. Vishny (1989). Industrialization and the Big Push. *Journal of Political Economy*, 97 (5), 1003–1026.

Polterovich, Victor, and Vladimir Popov (2004) Accumulation of Foreign Exchange Reserves and Long Term Economic Growth. In: Tabata, S. and A. Iwashita (eds), *Slavic Eurasia's Integration into the World Economy*. Sapporo: Slavic Research Center, Hokkaido University. http://www.nes.ru/%7Evpopov/documents/EXCHANGE%20RATE-GrowthDEC2002withcharts.pdf.

Polterovich, Victor and Popov, Vladimir (2005). *Appropriate Economic Policies at Different Stages of Development.* NES. http://www.nes.ru/english/research/pdf/2005/PopovPolterovich.pdf.

Popov, Vladimir (2004). The State in the New Russia (1992–2004): From Collapse to Gradual Revival? PONARS Policy Memo No. 342, November.

Popov, Vladimir (2007). Shock Therapy versus Gradualism Reconsidered: Lessons from Transition Economies after 15 Years of Reforms. *Comparative Economic Studies,* 49 (1), 1–31.

Popov, Vladimir (2008). Getting Better? Or Getting Worse? Murder Rate under Putin. *EURUS Newsletter*, 25 (2), 1–3. https://carleton.ca/vpopov/wp-content/uploads/Murder-rate-under-Putin.pdf.

Popov, Vladimir (2011). Developing New Measurements of State Institutional Capacity. PONARS Eurasia Policy Memo No. 158, May. MPRA Paper 32389, August.

Popov, Vladimir (2014a). An Economic Miracle in the Post-Soviet Space: How Uzbekistan Managed to Achieve What No Other Post-Soviet State Has. MPRA Paper No. 48723.

Popov, Vladimir (2014b). Can Uzbekistan Economy Retain Its High Growth Rate? Scenarios of Economic Development in 2015–30. PONARS Eurasia Working Paper, December.

Popov, Vladimir (2014c). *Mixed Fortunes: An Economic History of China, Russia and the West*. New York: Oxford University Press.

Popov, Vladimir (2020). Successes and Failures of Industrial Policy: Lessons from Transition (Post-Communist) Economies of Europe and Asia. In: Oqubai, A., Cramer, C., Chang, H.-J., and Kozu-Wright, R. (eds), O*xford Handbook on Industrial Policy*. Oxford: Oxford University Press.

Popov, V. and K.S. Jomo (2017). Are Developing Countries Catching Up? *Cambridge Journal of Economics*, 42 (1), 33–46.

Rodrik, Dani (2006). What's so Special about China's Exports? Harvard University, January. http://www.hks.harvard.edu/fs/drodrik/Chinaexports.pdf.

Rodrik, Dani (2008). The Real Exchange Rate and Economic Growth. October. http://www.hks.harvard.edu/fs/drodrik/Research%20papers/RER%20and%20growth.pdf.

Rodrik, D., R. Hausmann and A. Velasco (2005). Growth Diagnostics. https://tinyurl.com/y2nnyo3l.

Shevtsova, Yevgeniya (2012). International Trade and Productivity: Does Destination Matter? Discussion Papers in Economics 12/18. Heslington: University of York.

Soviet Economy (1991). *A Study of the Soviet Economy*, Vols 1, 2, 3. IMF, World Bank, OECD, EBRD.

PART V

Finance versus the real economy

15. Uneven development, financialised capitalism and subordination

Bruno Bonizzi, Annina Kaltenbrunner and Jeff Powell

INTRODUCTION

What role does finance play in our understanding of uneven development? Orthodox economics typically limits its analysis to the fallout from the financial volatility experienced in developing countries, generally pinning the blame on underdeveloped domestic financial systems, low-quality institutions, macroeconomic and regulatory mismanagement, and market failure. In contrast, heterodox analyses both within and outside economics have taken a greater interest in the role of financial actors from the core, and the power imbalances integral to and amplified through the global financial architecture. Alami et al. (2022) urges learning from three such traditions. In dependency theory, in the context of the colonial legacy, interactions between domestic class formations, multinational corporations (MNCs) and foreign governments are analysed, highlighting linkages of the interests of financial actors of the core to exploitation of workers in the periphery. Post-Keynesian economists have shone a light on the monetary subordination of emerging capitalist economies' (ECEs) currencies which occupy lower ranks in the hierarchical international monetary system; this is variously attributed to their lower liquidity premium (a kind of financial rent), that is, their inability to store value, and/ or unwillingness of private actors to issue and hold liabilities denominated in ECE currencies on their balance sheet. Marxist analysis, overlapping with some of dependency theory, emphasises class relations and the interrelationship of production and finance, relations of empire and imperialism, and how these relations are internalised within states in both the core and the periphery.

The flipside of this question is to ask what role uneven development plays in (necessarily heterodox) theories of financialisation. There is a growing literature on financialisation in ECEs, ranging from cross-country assessments of the (largely) macroeconomic effects of a growing engagement with finance, to studies looking at the diversity of financialisation experiences across different, especially non-financial, sectors (agriculture, mining and manufacturing), to detailed examinations of the 'financialisation of everyday life' as experienced, for example, through increased reliance on household indebtedness, or projects to expand so-called 'financial inclusion'. Much of this literature is not concerned with the question of the relationship of the experience under study with financialisation dynamics elsewhere in the world. Where this question is posed, there are different understandings of whether external actors or domestic institutions and dynamics should be seen as the prime drivers of financialisation in ECEs. Regardless of where this literature falls on this question, the implicit understanding is usually one of discrete nation-state units interacting (with disagreement over the degree and direction of influence), rather than parts of an uneven global system.

In what follows we will argue that much of what is studied under the heading of 'financialisation' should be located within a global system of financialised capitalism, in which ECEs adopt a specific subordinate role, in both production and finance. The lived experiences of financialised capitalism differ based on where one sits in an uneven hierarchy of classes and nation-states. From the perspective of actors in ECEs, agency is neither absent nor absolute, but circumscribed by their position in global capitalism. In the next section, we elaborate our theory of (subordinate) financialised capitalism. This is followed by a more detailed discussion of the key transformations in the circuits of productive and financial capital that distinguish capitalist dynamics in recent decades; then an exploration of the interlinkages between the two circuits; and a specific look at the subordination of ECEs in those circuits and their interaction. The last section concludes.

A THEORY OF (SUBORDINATE) FINANCIALISED CAPITALISM

It is important to first distinguish between cyclical processes of 'financialisation' and the secular stage of 'financialised capitalism'. Growth in the relative weight of finance in a particular period and/or place, may be sustained – even for a surprisingly long time – through the expansion of various forms of credit. However such 'bubbles' are by no means unique to contemporary capitalism, and inevitably have given way to 'de-financialisation'. In contrast, the contemporary period is marked by the intertwined combination of such processes of financialisation (upon which the global economy has become increasingly reliant to overcome problems of realisation), along with a qualitative change in the role of finance in the establishment, maintenance and expansion of the world market.

We distinguish this qualitative change through the use of the term 'financialised capitalism' (FC). FC has emerged under the specific historical conditions that have accompanied the substantive completion of the internationalisation of the circuits of capital. Previously limited to financing and commodity circulation, in the last three decades this process of internationalisation has come to encompass production itself, a process first theorised in the 1970s with the emergence of MNCs (Palloix 1975; Hymer 1979). The passage of capital through its various forms now takes place primarily at the global level, rather than within any single nation-state.

Critical to sustaining FC has been the nature of the subordinate integration of the periphery into the world economy, premised upon the emergent and uneven operation of the law of value at the global level. The internationalisation of production has allowed the extraction and transfer of value from workers in the periphery to agents disproportionately located in the core. Importantly, an increasing share of this value is captured by financial capital, thanks to its supporting role and opportunistic position with respect to the internationalisation of capital. The proliferation of circuits of capital across time and space has demanded a vastly increased role for market-based finance in the funding and governance of accumulation, while affording finance lucrative new opportunities for capturing a greater share of value created through a variety of methods, legal and otherwise.

On a lower level of abstraction, FC is characterised by the restructuring of production and finance at the global level. First, production has been restructured into disaggregated, hierarchically structured global value chains (Gereffi and Korzeniewicz 1994; Coe and Yeung 2015), perhaps more accurately referred to as global production networks (GPNs). Multinational firms headquartered in the core occupy monopsonistic lead positions in GPNs, from where they are able to exploit wage and profit differentials, and take control of strategic assets, especially intangible assets such as design patents, intellectual property and branding. Within these networks, financial actors play an essential role in controlling the mechanisms through which value is extracted, transferred and stored. Second, finance has been transformed into a globalised United States (US) dollar market-based system (Gabor 2020). This system allows a flexible and elastic supply of credit and hedging mechanisms, as well as mechanisms to govern production through its ability to move and store financial wealth offshore. It exerts pressures, through both ostensibly 'market' incentives and explicitly coercive governance, over the financial system reform in ECEs, resulting in increasing interconnection and dependency. The rise of global market-based finance thus represents the other side of the coin of FC to global production, offering the instruments and infrastructures to support the restructuring of production and the transfer of value.

In both finance and production, peripheral countries assume a subordinate position which is both inherent to the working of FC and shapes the experience of actors therein; whereas subordination in production creates the value, subordination in finance ensures its safe transfer to, realisation and storage as financial wealth, primarily (but not only) in the core and its offshore centres. This is why we place the word 'subordinate' in parentheses in '(subordinate) financialised capitalism'; FC is inherently a system of super- and subordination. This systemic view provides us with a very different perspective on the debate highlighted in the introduction over whether financialisation is primarily an externally or internally driven dynamic. Peripheral countries are a part of FC, and experience the pressures exerted by it, whether or not they are experiencing the typical 'symptoms' associated with financialisation (especially in the core). Capturing the precise nature of the insertion of agents from a particular country into global circuits of production and finance requires careful study of historical and institutional specificities and examination of inter- and intra-class dynamics both within and across borders. To be clear, however, this is not to make a teleological argument: there is agency, even though it is circumscribed, and there will emerge different strategies for attempting to move within the dynamic hierarchies of FC.

TRANSFORMATIONS IN THE CIRCUITS OF PRODUCTIVE AND FINANCIAL CAPITAL

The last half century has witnessed initial attempts by MNCs to source low-cost inputs abroad or find additional end markets, evolving into diverse, often complex, multi-layered GPNs, which slice production processes into constituent steps and relocate them geographically in an effort to exploit differences in labour costs and productivity. As a result, MNCs, whose headquarters and shareholders are overwhelmingly located in the core, have become much more international, with an increasing share of assets, sales and employment emanating from foreign operations.

This transformation has profound implications for the size and nature of the transfer of value from the working classes of the periphery to the capitalists of the core. Following Ricci's (2019, 2021) pathbreaking work empirically documenting unequal exchange, we can distinguish inter- and intra-industry transfer of surplus value from its site of creation to a distinct site of realisation. Inter-industry transfers, a differential rent, emerge out of differences between industries which dominate in the core versus those prominent in the periphery; these differences can be in wages, profit rates and capital intensity. Intra-industry transfers, an absolute rent, reflect differences between firms in the core and those in the periphery in the same industry, either in wages adjusted for labour productivity or in profit rates owing to the growth of monopoly.

In ECEs, Lewis (1954) first argued that a 'traditional' sector puts downward pressure on wages in the 'modern' sector. Productivity growth in the latter, given pressures towards the equalisation of profit rates, results in lower export prices, declining terms of trade for ECEs, and a value transfer to advanced capitalist economies (ACEs). Evidence of persistent gaps in unit labour costs between core and periphery suggest that while labour productivity in the periphery has risen, nominal wages have been restrained (Suwandi 2019). Prebisch (1950) and Singer (1950) famously linked declining terms of trade to specialisation in low-value primary exports, while core firms export manufactured goods. Industrial manufacturers, thanks to the higher income and price elasticity of demand for their exports, and often assisted by monopolistic market positions, are able to capture greater benefits from trade. While firms in the periphery have made progress in manufacturing, some two-thirds of the profits of the top 2000 TNCs accrue to firms headquartered in the core (UNCTAD 2018), dominating the most profitable industries such as pharmaceuticals, media, and information and communication technology (ICT). Firms in these industries enjoy barriers to entry from economies of scale, network effects, technological advantage, and institutional or regulatory factors. Finally, surplus value transfer may arise out of inter-industry differences in capital intensity. Grossman (1992 [1929]) showed how a higher organic composition in the advanced countries means that a higher rate of surplus value may co-exist with a lower profit rate. The tendency for the equalisation of profit rates ensures that core goods sell above their price of production, while those of the periphery sell below it. Additional surplus value is captured by the advanced-country capitalist through the exchange of non-equivalents, as long as core producers are not compelled by competition to lower their selling price to the price of production. Enormous global expenditures in marketing, and various tariff and non-tariff trade barriers, serve to achieve these ends.

But as an increasing share of global trade is transacted within GPNs, consideration of intra-industry transfers becomes ever more critical. Emmanuel (1972) first highlighted the importance of wage differentials to intra-industry transfer of surplus value, putting emphasis on the role of differences in trade union density. Smith (2016) deploys the concept of 'super-exploitation' to describe the circumstances where workers are remunerated below their social reproduction costs. This draws attention to the gendered basis of value transfers (Dunaway 2013), through both women's direct exploitation (in, for example, the garment industry), and the indirect exploitation of women's roles in social reproduction activities which determine socially necessary labour time. Complementing the arguments which emphasise wage differentials are those which put stress on profit differentials. Building on the initial work on monopoly capitalism of Baran and Sweezy (1968), a growing body of labour process theory literature (for example, Parker et al. 2018) documents the ways that GPN lead firms are able to capture 'strategic assets', including technology, intellectual property, marketing and design, in order to extract a form of rent. Milberg and Winkler (2013) provide evidence of lead firms' monopsony power vis-à-vis their suppliers, which allows them to push down on costs, maintaining high mark-ups and distributing gains in the form of higher dividends and share buybacks. Suwandi (2019) describes this process as 'systemic rationalization', involving measures such as directly controlling suppliers' overheads, holding suppliers responsible for meeting delivery times and flexibility in product changes, or forcing the costs of compliance with international certification onto suppliers. These arguments support Starosta's (2010) assertion that lead firms in GPNs capture surplus value from 'small capitals' which do not take part in the equalisation of the rate of profit at the general level.

While the geographical transfer of value (GTV) is not new, it has taken on new forms and risen in quantitative terms to unprecedented levels in the postwar period. Ricci's (2019) empirical work suggests a doubling of the GTV between 1995 and 2007; a period during which intra-industry transfers increased from less than half to two-thirds of the total transfer. Limiting his estimate to only that part of the transfer of value related to differences in labour productivity, Ricci (2021) finds that for the period from 1990 to 2019 for which data is available, core regions have enjoyed a consistent and growing value inflow, reaching a peak of 8.5 per cent of their GDP in 2008 (plateauing at approximately that level since). Outflow value transfers from the poor periphery, especially South and Southeast Asia, have grown both in absolute terms and as a share of GDP throughout the period, exceeding 20 per cent of GDP throughout. This highlights the growing importance of GPNs in channelling surplus value from its site of creation in the global periphery to its realisation predominantly in the core.

We turn now to the changing appearances of finance which accompanied this internationalisation of the circuits of capitalist accumulation. The story of finance in FC is a restructuring around market-based finance and the domination of the US dollar. This process has been heterogeneous, and significant cross-country differences remain in national financial systems. But the global tendency has been one towards a greater 'Americanisation' of finance (Gowan 2009; Fichtner 2017; Gabor 2020), with market-based institutional structures becoming ever more central to the functioning of the system, and US dollar funding markets becoming central (Murau et al. 2020). These transformations have been discussed within the financialisation literature focused on the transformation of banking (Erturk and Solari 2007; Lapavitsas 2013), but even more so in the so-called 'critical macro-finance' literature (Gabor 2020): this literature draws on the work of Hyman Minsky and focuses on the way liquidity is systemically organised and produced, with particular attention to developments in money and derivative markets, where collateralisation of financial relations has significantly enhanced the power of borrowers over lenders, and

Table 15.1   Characteristics of finance within financialised capitalism

Characteristics	Main location	Empirical manifestations
Institutionalisation of wealth	Long-term securities markets	Expansion of long-term securities markets Growth of institutional investors
Transformation of banking	Money and credit markets	Collateralised lending and borrowing Credit to households Originate to distribute
Production of new securities	Derivative and 'alternative asset' markets	Securitisation Growth of interest rate and exchange rate derivative markets
Internationalisation of finance	Foreign exchange markets	Growth of cross-border transactions and positions Currency trading volumes
Governing through financial markets	Public finance and monetary policy	Central banks' dealer of last resort function and quantitative easing Rise of public debt through bond markets

the linked liquidity dynamics to asset prices (Sissoko 2019). While by necessity a simplification, Table 15.1 summarises the key characteristics of finance within FC.

Firstly, FC is characterised by the institutionalisation of wealth as managed financial assets. As value is created and transferred, its accumulation takes the form of financial wealth that is to be managed and stored in financial markets. This has created large pools of wealth, managed by a highly concentrated sector. Secondly, banks have reoriented their business from corporate to household lending and fee-generating activities, such as trading, and have a larger proportion of their balance sheet devoted to market-based activities. These trends have weakened but not reversed since the global financial crisis in 2008–2009. Thirdly, complementing the previous two trends has been significant innovation in the creation of new securities and traded financial instruments. This includes new asset classes to store the ever larger amounts of managed wealth, and instruments such as derivatives for risk management (and speculative) purposes.

Fourthly, all these transformations have taken place at an increasingly global level. There has been a dramatic increase in cross-border asset positions and financial flows, both in size among ACEs, and in scope involving a larger number of countries. Finally, there is a tighter interconnection between financial markets and public governance. This is particularly clear in the case of monetary policy, which entirely works through the circuits of market-based finance, but also more widely in the pursuit of public and international policy objectives by states.

It is important to reassert here that these transformations, much like those in production, are hierarchical. The US dollar remains dominant across the five characteristics outlined above. Most debt contracts, financial securities, funds offered by asset managers and collateral requirements are denominated in US dollars. The financial sector intermediating these relations, especially the booming passive fund management sector (Braun 2020), is also heavily concentrated in the US and a few other ACEs. The mode of governing through financial markets is not only pioneered by the US with significant global spill-overs, but is very often promoted on a global scale by US institutions (Gabor 2021).

So, all in all, FC has been marked by the uneven restructuring of production and finance. But what are the specific ways in which these transformations are linked? And how do they generate and perpetuate subordination for ECEs? We take up these questions in the following sections.

THE INTERLINKAGES OF PRODUCTIVE AND FINANCIAL CAPITAL

The concurrent development of GPNs and globalised (but US dollar-based) market-based finance is more than coincidental. The two processes are in fact intertwined: on the one hand the global transfer of value allows the appropriation of value that sustains the profits of global finance and its greater weight in the global economy; on the other hand, global market-based finance has been key to supporting the process of global production and value creation/extraction, its realisation as profits, and its transfer and storage as financial wealth.

Firstly, with regard to value creation/extraction, globalised US dollar market-based finance provides key support to GPNs. GPNs require significant financing, both in the form of foreign direct investment to be established, and in the form of working capital to be maintained, as a 'payment chain' develops alongside the long production chain until the point of sale. This financing is ultimately originating in US dollar funding markets, either by larger banks reliant on wholesale funding (Bruno and Shin 2021), or directly through issuance of corporate bonds. Access to US dollar financing is also enhanced by the development of derivative markets, which allow hedging of financial risks, but can also – through foreign exchange swaps – provide access to short-term dollar loans secured against foreign currency collateral (Borio et al. 2017).

Global market-based finance also imposes a disciplining role on global production. Market-based financial mechanisms standardise return and profit expectations (and their distribution to asset owners), and significantly enhance the power of creditors over borrowers thanks to collateralised financial relationships. This is because borrowers need to provide collateral, which is repriced daily and thus forces them to provide liquidity at short notice.

Secondly, global market-based finance supports the transfer of value through and out of GPNs and its storage as accumulated wealth. Parallel to GPNs, global wealth chains have been established, which govern the transfer of value downstream (Coe et al. 2014; Quentin and Campling 2018). These do not simply follow the structure of the productive networks, but extract value from them at various points through, for example, the creation of investment vehicles which exist solely for the purposes of exploiting jurisdictional differences in tax rules. In this way, profits are channelled to where they can be 'stored' as financial wealth, minimising taxation. Offshore financial centres play an important role in this, especially as the nominal location of intangible assets against which profits are booked in order to avoid taxes (Bryan et al. 2017). The production of new securities allows for storage of wealth by the owners of capital, who need stores of value as their profits accumulate (Lysandrou 2018).

Finally, global market-based finance is crucial to the realisation of profits in FC at the global level. The GTV implies a greater extraction of surplus value from workers in the ECEs, which cannot, however, be realised through sale in the location of its creation in its entirety. Indeed, much of this value is transferred upstream unrealised, with the point of sale and thus realisation often being several steps away from production. Among the consequences of GPNs therefore is the geographical and temporal separation between the location of production and value creation, and the location of final sale and profit realisation.

In FC the elasticity of the financial system is significantly enhanced to sustain aggregate demand globally and thus postpone the realisation problem. The significant accumulation of debt, backed by rising asset prices, boosts global demand. The key transformations of finance described in the previous section allow this to take place more easily; debt is secured against collateral and/or securities, offloading much of the risk from lenders to borrowers, supported by an ever-greater provision of liquidity by central banks.

At a national level, viable growth regimes have to confront this global structure. As a result, debt-driven and export-oriented growth appear as the only viable regimes for sustained capital accumulation (Stockhammer 2012, 2016): either countries engage directly with debt accumulation to finance demand, or they do so by relying on exports, and thus exploit other countries' willingness to accumulate debt. This is consistent with a world increasingly dominated by GPNs, where countries have to either rely on exports downstream, or be the ultimate location of sale where profits are realised.

The arguments presented so far indicate how FC unfolds unevenly, due to the existing uneven structures and the new ones created by GPNs and global market-based finance. As indicated above, in both finance and production, peripheral countries assume a subordinate position which is both inherent to the working of FC and shapes the experience of actors therein. It is this subordination that we turn to in more detail next.

FINANCIALISED CAPITALISM AND SUBORDINATION

The literature on GPNs, among others, has shown the constitutive role of ECEs' subordination in production which creates the value underpinning the global accumulation of financial wealth. ECEs' subordination in finance, in turn, ensures the safe transformation of this wealth, its storage, and transfer (primarily) to the core and its offshore centres.

At the point of value extraction, as ECEs become embedded into GPNs, they simultaneously become exposed to the dollar-based financing system behind them. Dollar financing eliminates the exchange rate risk for operators from the core, and reinforces the dollar's dominance and monetary subordination in ECEs. Indeed, in FC, dollar financing – increasingly through market-based forms, and frequently offshore – becomes a necessity to participate in the global economy. For example, data from the Bank for International Settlements shows that foreign currency (offshore) debt by ECE non-financial corporations has surged over recent years, creating potential currency mismatches and embedding those firms more closely into the global financial cycle (Aldasoro et al. 2021). At the same time, controlling access to US dollar finance becomes a position of power within GPNs, which can be used by downstream firms to discipline suppliers (Baud and Durand 2012).

With regard to the transformation of that value into financial wealth, and its safe storage and transfer to the core, ECEs' subordination in international money and financial markets manifests through several processes. For one, ECEs' assets are characterised by structurally higher financial returns (for example, as in the notorious carry trade phenomenon) to compensate for potential risks to core agents and ensure the value-stable storage of financial wealth. Often these risks arise from institutional and governance conditions which differ from those in core economies, creating transaction costs and uncertainty for core agents (for example, the lack of liquid exchanges, different regulation, and so on). For that reason, ECEs are subject to significant pressures, ranging from explicit policy conditionality to 'market-based' investor demands, to undertake institutional transformations towards market-based systems and implement macroeconomic constraints to ensure the safe transfer of financially realised value to the core.

Whereas, in bank-based systems, direct relationships between lenders and borrowers supported the realisation of financial returns, in market-based systems the provision of liquidity – that is, the ability to sell an asset at any time and at little cost – becomes essential to investor security. As a result, the ECE assets sought by foreign investors have become more varied and dominated by tradable instruments, such as different types of bond market securities, equities, exchange traded funds and derivatives. The domestic corollary has been the push to develop domestic bond and equity markets for government and firm financing and derivatives markets to hedge interest and exchange rate risk. In addition to the shift of domestic institutional structures to market-based financing, risk to global financial capital has been reduced by the institution of similar macroeconomic regimes and governance standards. These include: inflation targeting plus (managed) floating exchange rate regimes; a general move towards capital account liberalisation (complemented by macroprudential regulations); massive reserve accumulation; and Anglo-Saxon governance and property rules.

These features of ECEs' position in FC are subordinate on two counts. Firstly, higher returns contribute to the GTV in financial form, for both public and private ECE agents. Secondly, the institutional transformations and macroeconomic features of FC constrain agency in ECEs and undermine developmental structural transformations. For example, capital account liberalisation and floating exchange rate regimes can lead to increased volatility in the exchange rate and domestic asset prices, dependent on the global financial cycle. This volatility increases uncertainty, undermines competitiveness and/ or destabilises domestic balance sheets (in particular in the case of currency mismatches mentioned above), which weigh on investment decisions.

Finally, ECEs assume a subordinate role in the global system of profit realisation, with significant implications for their domestic growth regimes. While the export-led versus debt-led growth regime dichotomy within FC remains a useful simplification, it assumes subordinate characteristics in ECEs. Our argument here is consistent with recent literature, suggesting how the insertion into the global economy through GPNs is key to understanding the development of their growth model (Akcay et al. 2022; Schedelik et al. 2021; Smichowski et al. 2021). Their downstream position within GPNs limits their ability to retain value produced domestically, making any profit realisation dependent on demand conditions elsewhere. Their ability to circumscribe this through finance is constrained by their peripheral position in the circuits of market-based finance, and the limited capacity to sustain (private) debt accumulation given by lower incomes and collateral offered by ECE residents.

Autonomy within such subordinate growth regimes is therefore constrained. The dynamics of exports depend on global demand distributed through GPNs, and financed through global US dollar markets. The latter makes traditional macroeconomic policy levers harder to use, as a strong US dollar tends to have depressing impacts on activity, thus neutralising any positive impact from exchange rate depreciation (Bruno and Shin 2019). Domestic consumption and investment, too, can be constrained by the need to acquire US dollars, which is contingent on the state of global liquidity. In sum, the key sources of aggregate demand in ECEs have become exposed to GPNs and market-based finance, over which ECEs have little control.

Nevertheless, this subordination of ECEs in FC does not imply a convergence to a single uniform 'subordinate financialised' growth model. One possibility is the explicit pursuit of export-led growth models, which can be found in the 'exportist' regimes of East Asia (Jessop and Sum 2006) or 'dependent growth regimes' of Eastern Europe (Bohle 2018). These models reproduce some of the features of mercantilist ACEs such as Germany, but their dynamics are largely dependent on the demand and finance fed through GPNs.

Other countries can be similarly outward-oriented but as part of less explicit and stable export-led strategies. This has been the case of many Latin American economies, which benefited from GPNs but have not achieved sustained export surpluses, or have largely based their exports on primary commodities (Levy-Orlik 2014; Guevara et al. 2018). Where exports are insufficient to drive domestic demand, forms of debt-led accumulation take place, although these are by necessity more limited than in ACEs, given the lower wealth and income of workers, and higher reliance on foreign credit (Karwowski 2018).

Finally, growth models that are less exposed to GPNs and/or private borrowing necessarily see a much larger role of the state. The state can have the capacity, through industrial policy, to upgrade the position of domestic production within and beyond GPNs. Further, in many ECEs the only actor that has a significant borrowing capability is the state, which can therefore act as a stabiliser for domestic aggregate demand. Active role of the state has become more prevalent since the global financial crisis, as many ACEs have moved towards mercantilism, thus limiting the potential for mercantilism in ECEs (Akcay et al. 2022).

CONCLUSION

This chapter has set out a theory of subordinate financialisation, which puts the uneven development of the global economy at the core of its analysis. In contrast to large parts of the literature on financialisation in ECEs, which focuses on concrete national manifestations (externally induced or otherwise), we have highlighted the need to adopt a systemic understanding of financialisation processes. Financialisation, in our view, needs to be located within a global system of financialised capitalism, in which ECEs adopt a specific subordinate role, in both production and finance. This subordinate position is inherent to FC and circumscribes the agency of ECE actors.

Financialised capitalism, we argued, is characterised by the substantive completion of the internationalisation of the three circuits of capital. On a lower level of abstraction, it manifests in the global disaggregation of production in the form of GPNs, and the rise of US dollar-dominated market-based finance. These two processes have emerged in an interdependent way, where the value generated in global GPNs has provided the basis for the extreme accumulation of financial wealth, whilst the rise and institutional transformations of global finance enabled the near complete internationalisation of production. In both processes, ECEs assume a subordinate role: whereas the greater exploitation of labour in ECEs creates the value, subordination in finance ensures the appropriation of that value and its safe transformation, storage and transfer (frequently abroad) as financial wealth. With regard to the realisation of this value as profit, we argued that the temporal and spatial separation between production and realisation at the global level constrains the growth models of ECEs, which remain subordinate in such global processes.

These processes of (subordinate) FC amplify existing inequalities; both directly through extraction from the working class and enrichment of (financial) capitalists, and indirectly by shaping the class struggle which determines state action. Moreover, they fundamentally constrain ECEs' autonomous and transformational development trajectory. Low wages and exploitative labour conditions not only mean abhorrent living conditions for many, but also undermine the domestic demand stimulus necessary for autonomous development. High domestic financial returns (interest rates), and the volatility and uncertainty of key macroeconomic prices such as the exchange rate, weigh on productive investment. So do the institutional transformations to market-based financial and Anglo-Saxon governance systems, alien to many of these economies, and not fit for funding long-term industrial transformations. Only with a significant and active role of the state can ECEs hope to carve out some space to determine their own growth strategies, still mindful of their own global insertion into FC.

Though many herald the end of globalisation, these subordinate processes are likely to deepen with the impending climate breakdown. Whereas the innovations necessary to replace carbon-intensive sectors are largely produced in the core, ECEs will be the first and hardest hit by the physical and transitional risks attached to climate chaos. FC as a system, in turn, predisposes us to maintain (if reshape, in response to new threats) GPNs and a market-based finance approach to responding to climate breakdown (for example, in the form of carbon markets, state de-risking of private sector green investment, and so on) and hence ECEs' subordinate position in that system. Therefore, national policy measures – for example, industrial policy, capital account re-regulations, or the use of development banks – whilst of course important, will only go so far to mitigate ECEs' international subordination. Only truly transformational system change on the global level, which addresses both the structure of global production and that of international finance, will be able to create a fairer and more just global society.

REFERENCES

Akcay, Ü., Hein, E. and Jungmann, B. (2022) Financialisation and Macroeconomic Regimes in Emerging Capitalist Economies Before and After the Great Recession, *International Journal of Political Economy*. https://doi.org/10.1080/08911916.2022.2078009

Alami, I., Alves, C., Bonizzi, B., Kaltenbrunner, A., Koddenbrock, K., Kvangraven, I.H. and Powell, J. (2022) International Financial Subordination: A Critical Research Agenda, *Review of International Political Economy*. https://doi.org/10.1080/09692290.2022.2098359

Aldasoro, I., Hardy, B. and Tarashev, N. (2021) Corporate Debt: Post-GFC through the Pandemic, *BIS Quarterly Review,* June, pp. 1–14.

Baran, P.A. and Sweezy, P.M. (1968) *Monopoly Capital: An Essay on the American Economic and Social Order*, Harmondsworth: Penguin.

Baud, C. and Durand, C. (2012) Financialization, Globalization and the Making of Profits by Leading Retailers, *Socio-Economic Review*, 10 (2), pp. 241–266.

Bohle, D. (2018) European Integration, Capitalist Diversity and Crises Trajectories on Europe's Eastern Periphery, *New Political Economy*, 23 (2), pp. 239–253.

Borio, C., McCauley, R.N. and McGuire, P. (2017) FX Swaps and Forwards: Missing Global Debt?, *BIS Quarterly Review*, September, pp. 37–54.

Braun, B. (2020) American Asset Manager Capitalism, *SocArxiv Papers*. https://osf.io/preprints/socarxiv/v6gue.

Bruno, V. and Shin, H.S. (2019) Dollar and Exports, BIS Working Paper, 819.

Bruno, V. and Shin, H.S. (2021) The Effects of Currency Strength on International Trade, VoxEu Online Source, https://voxeu.org/article/effects-currency-strength-international-trade.

Bryan, D., Rafferty, M. and Wigan, D. (2017) Capital Unchained: Finance, Intangible Assets and the Double Life of Capital in the Offshore World, *Review of International Political Economy*, 24 (1), pp. 56–86.

Coe, N.M., Lai, K.P.Y. and Wójcik, D. (2014) Integrating Finance into Global Production Networks, *Regional Studies*, 48 (5), pp. 761–777.

Coe, N.M. and Yeung, H.W.-C. (2015) *Global Production Networks: Theorizing Economic Development in an Interconnected World*, Oxford: Oxford University Press.

Dunaway, W.A. (ed.) (2013) *Gendered Commodity Chains: Seeing Women's Work and Households in Global Production*, Stanford, CA: Stanford University Press.

Emmanuel, A. (1972) *Unequal Exchange: A Study of the Imperialism of Trade*, New York: Monthly Review Press.

Erturk, I. and Solari, S. (2007) Banks as Continuous Reinvention, *New Political Economy*, 12 (3), pp. 369–388.

Fichtner, J. (2017) Perpetual Decline or Persistent Dominance? Uncovering Anglo-America's True Structural Power in Global Finance, *Review of International Studies*, 43 (1), pp. 3–28.

Gabor, D. (2020) Critical Macro-Finance: A Theoretical Lens, *Finance and Society*, 6 (1), pp. 45–55.

Gabor, D. (2021) The Wall Street Consensus, *Development and Change*, 52 (3), pp. 429–459.

Gereffi, G. and Korzeniewicz, M. (eds) (1994) *Commodity Chains and Global Capitalism*, Westport, CT: Praeger.

Gowan, P. (2009) Crisis in the Heartland: Consequences of the New Wall Street System, *New Left Review*, 55, pp. 5–29

Grossman, H. (1992 [1929]) *The Law of Accumulation and the Breakdown of the Capitalist System: Being also a Theory of Crises*, London, Pluto Press.

Guevara, D., Guevara, C. and Cómbita, G. (2018) Structural Change in Colombia: From Import Substitution to Export-Led Growth Illusion, in Levy, N. and Bustamante, J. (eds), *Financialisation in Latin America: Challenges of the Export-Led Growth Model*, London: Routledge.

Hymer, S. (1979) *The Multinational Corporation: A Radical Approach*, Cambridge: Cambridge University Press.

Jessop, B. and Sum, N.-L. (2006) A Regulationist Re-Reading of East Asian Newly Industrializing Economies: From Peripheral Fordism to Exportism, in Jessop, B. and Sum, N.-L. (eds), *Beyond the Regulation Approach: Putting Capitalist Economies in Their Place*, Cheltenham, UK and Northampton, MA, USA: Edward Elgar Publishing.

Karwowski, E. (2018) Corporate Financialization in South Africa: From Investment Strike to Housing Bubble, *Competition and Change*, 22 (4), pp. 413–436.

Lapavitsas, C. (2013) *Profiting Without Producing: How Finance Exploits Us All*, London: Verso.

Levy-Orlik, N. (2014) Financialisation in Unsuccessful Neo-Mercantilist Economies: External Capital Inflows, Financial Gains and Income Inequality, *LIMES+*, 11, pp. 147–175.

Lewis, W.A. (1954) Economic Development with Unlimited Supplies of Labour, *Manchester School*, 22 (2), pp. 139–191.

Lysandrou, P. (2018) *Commodity: The Global Commodity System in the 21st Century*, New York: Routledge.

Milberg, W. and Winkler, D. (2013) *Outsourcing Economics: Global Value Chains in Capitalist Development*, New York, Cambridge University Press.

Murau, S., Rini, J. and Haas, A. (2020) The Evolution of the Offshore US-dollar System: Past, Present and Four Possible Futures, *Journal of Institutional Economics*, 16 (6), pp. 767–783.

Palloix, C. (1975) *L'economie mondiale capitaliste*, Paris: François Maspero.

Parker, R., Cox, S. and Thompson, P. (2018) Financialization and Value-based Control: Lessons from the Australian Mining Supply Chain, *Economic Geography*, 94 (1), pp. 49–67.

Prebisch, R. (1950) *The Economic Development of Latin America and its Principal Problems*, New York: United Nations.

Quentin, D. and Campling, L. (2018) Global Inequality Chains: Integrating Mechanisms of Value Distribution into Analyses of Global Production, *Global Networks*, 18 (1), pp. 33–56.

Ricci, A. (2019) Unequal Exchange in the Age of Globalization, *Review of Radical Political Economics*, 51 (2), pp. 225–245.

Ricci, A. (2021) *Value and Unequal Exchange in International Trade: The Geography of Global Capitalist Exploitation*, London: Routledge.

Schedelik, M., Nölke, A., Mertens, D. and May, C. (2021) Comparative Capitalism, Growth Models and Emerging Markets: The Development of the Field, *New Political Economy*, 26 (4), pp. 514–526.

Singer, H.W. (1950) The Distribution of Gains between Investing and Borrowing Countries, *American Economic Review*, 40 (2), pp. 473–485.

Sissoko, C. (2019) Repurchase Agreements and the (de)Construction of Financial Markets, *Economy and Society*, 48 (3), pp. 315–341.

Smichowski B.C., Durand, C. and Knauss, S. (2021) Participation in Global Value Chains and Varieties of Development Patterns, *Cambridge Journal of Economics*, 45 (2), pp. 271–294.

Smith, J. (2016) *Imperialism in the Twenty-First Century: Globalization, Super-Exploitation, and Capitalism's Final Crisis*, New York: Monthly Review Press.

Starosta, G. (2010) The Outsourcing of Manufacturing and the Rise of Giant Global Contractors: A Marxian Approach to Some Recent Transformations of Global Value Chains, *New Political Economy*, 15 (4), pp. 543–563.

Stockhammer, E. (2012) Financialization, Income Distribution and the Crisis, *Investigación Económica*, 71 (279), pp. 39–70.

Stockhammer, E. (2016) Neoliberal Growth Models, Monetary Union and the Euro Crisis. A Post-Keynesian Perspective, *New Political Economy*, 21 (4), pp. 365–379.

Suwandi, I. (2019) *Value chains: The New Economic Imperialism*, New York: Monthly Review Press.

UNCTAD (2018) *Trade and Development Report 2018: Power, Platforms and the Free Trade Delusion*, New York and Geneva: UNCTAD.

16. Unequal growth and the single currency: the fiscal policy paradox

Jan Kregel

The promise of free trade based on comparative advantage is that the mutual benefits should accrue to all trading partners. Whether or not convergence occurs the implication is that there should be convergence in the rewards to labour and capital across trading partners, even if the functional distribution remains unequal within countries. The thrust of the modern amendments to Ricardo's theory was to show that trade could be a viable substitute for freedom of circulation of labour and capital. Thus the post-war European project initially sought to open trade in the 1957 Treaty of Rome creating the European Economic Community (EEC). The rapid increase in cross-border trade accompanying recovery from the war was in decline by the 1980s and attention turned to the creation of an integrated single market in goods, capital and labour via the Single European Act. A central pillar of this approach was the creation of a single currency and a European Central Bank.

THE SINGLE CURRENCY AND EXCHANGE RATE STABILITY

A single European currency had already been considered in the 1970 Werner Report, drafted in the context of the Bretton Woods global fixed exchange rate system. Although this system collapsed shortly after the report was published, the EEC continued to pursue the equivalent of an irreversible fixed rate system via a single currency, issued by a supra-national monetary authority, despite most of its trading partners having implemented floating exchange rates. Whether or not the introduction of the single currency would have provided the support necessary to achieve the expected benefits of the Single European Act, its introduction in a world of floating rates produced novel and unexpected results that paradoxically led to increasing divergence in the performance of the member states.

The introduction of the single currency in these conditions produced two unintended results. First, the adoption of an irreversible internal fixed exchange rate system in the presence of an international system of floating rates eliminated exchange rate adjustment amongst member states, but also made it impossible for individual members to use exchange rate adjustment to influence their trading relations with the rest of the world.[1] Second, it created a currency issued by an institution without any direct linkage to a national government or influenced by government expenditure decisions on the bank's balance sheet,[2] eliminating direct coordination between the creation of domestic liquidity and individual governments' fiscal policy. Indeed, this problem was resolved by making fiscal policy subservient to the single currency via the Protocol to Section 104 of the Maastricht Treaty.

While the single currency eliminated bilateral exchange rates for national currencies of member states, it did not eliminate the impact of the exchange rate of the single currency on the performance of individual countries via variations in the rate of the single currency vis-à-vis the other, floating, currencies of international trading partners. Instead it made the impact of variation in the exchange of the single currency relative to the rest of the world uniform across member states with wide differences in their domestic production structure and the structure of their external trade with the rest of the world. In the same way as uniform monetary policy that accompanied the single currency had a differential impact on member states depending on their particular economic conditions, uniform exchange rate changes had differential impacts across countries due to differences in domestic economic conditions. Thus changes in investor preferences for United States (US) dollar-denominated holdings, or changes in global capital flows, could produce positive or negative impacts on domestic conditions that were counter to desired domestic policy requirements.

INTERNAL ADJUSTMENT TO EXTERNAL IMBALANCES

While the single currency eliminated national exchange rate adjustments as a policy to influence economic performance, fiscal policy was also eliminated, because it was thought that divergences in national debt and deficits would be inimical to the success of the single currency. As a result, the remaining domestic policy instrument was domestic wage and price adjustments relative to eurozone and non-eurozone trading partners. Since such adjustments would have a differential impact on relative competitiveness within and outside the eurozone, their direct impact on domestic conditions was difficult to determine. Since many of the European Union (EU) member countries had used devaluation as a means of supporting domestic activity through exports, this could only be achieved via reductions in the rate of increase in domestic wages and prices relative to trading partners. Since many of the strongest EU countries gave policy priority to wage and price stability, this created the potential for a deflationary bias similar to that prevalent in the pre-war gold standard. Countries with above-average inflation and external deficits were under greater pressure and incentive to adjust via measures to reduce relative prices and activity relative to the surplus countries and to their trading partners in the rest of the world. While variation in the external value of the single currency could provide aggregate adjustment of the eurozone external balance, the impact of these changes would not have an equal impact across all members of the eurozone, while the enabling Protocol provided no formal fiscal policy mechanism to redistribute or offset this impact on productive and social conditions in individual countries.

At the same time, the re-denomination of the sovereign debt of national governments in a currency issued independently of national member governments' budgets, or national central bank policy, sharply constrained the ability to finance domestic adjustment policies to offset the differential impact of the exchange rate of the single currency. In essence, government financing of domestic fiscal policy expenditures became formally identical to that of any private institution. Financing of expenditures had to be covered by fiscal revenues, or by borrowing from the domestic or foreign private sector, or by sale of assets to the domestic private or external sector. If government used borrowing to finance a shortfall of fiscal revenues, then to meet debt service on the sovereign debt thus created would require governments to generate tax receipts greater than expenditures, engage in additional borrowing (debt rollover), or sell public assets.

Just as different private borrowers have different credit risks and face different risk-adjusted borrowing rates, 'sovereign' borrowers should have different credit risks determined by the ability of governments to raise revenue as determined by conditions of the domestic economy and institutions. However, after the introduction of the single currency, the fact that government borrowing was denominated in the liability of an external central bank appears to have led private lenders to overlook national risk differentials in the first ten years of the euro's existence. Thus, countries with higher borrowing and debt stocks were little penalized by the market imposing higher borrowing rates, leading to an allocation of private sector liquidity within the eurozone which reinforced economic imbalances and contributed to the European financial crisis after the collapse of US financial markets.

This market anomaly allowed many individual governments to access private market financial support at attractive interest rates, to implement domestic income support measures to avoid the implementation of wage/price adjustment mechanisms compatible with the new single currency system, in a process that resembled the financing of Latin American governments' deficit by private capital flows in the 1970s.

However, when this private sector market interest rate uniformity anomaly disappeared after the 2008 financial crisis, and economic conditions made it difficult for governments to generate higher fiscal revenues to replace the with-drawal of private financing, maintaining the financial stability of government and private financial institutions required financial support at the EU level in the form of the creation of the European System of Financial Supervision (ESFS), subsequently replaced by the European Stability Mechanism (ESM), the extension of International Monetary Fund (IMF) programme support, and eventually the direct intervention in government securities markets by the President of the European Central Bank (ECB) to 'do what it takes' to prevent a destructive financial collapse of government bond markets and private finan-cial institutions. The necessity of an EU-level response to the crisis should have made it obvious that the existing framework of fiscal policy management at the national level was incompatible with the new system.

EARLY RECOGNITION OF IMPACT OF MONETARY POLICY AND FISCAL CONSTRAINTS

Many commentators had already noted the difficulty created by a monetary policy managed by a central institution, that was independent of fiscal policies managed at the national level and subject to aggregate constraints. Wynne Godley (1993: 9) had noted that while the Maastricht Treaty explicitly outlined monetary arrangements, it offered no insight on the question:

> how is the rest of economic policy to be run? As the Treaty proposes no new insti-tutions other than a European bank, its sponsors must suppose that nothing more is needed. But this could only be correct if modern economies were self-adjusting systems that didn't need any management at all.

He also pointed out that:

> the Maastricht criteria for the establishment of 'convergence' were far too narrowly conceived. To fulfil the conditions necessary for a successful currency union it is not nearly enough that member countries agree to follow simple rules on budgetary policy ... They need to reach a degree of structural homogeneity such that shocks to the system as a whole do not normally affect component regions in drastically different ways. (ibid.: 9).

He noted that:

> if Europe is not to have a full-scale budget of its own ... you will still have, by default, a physical stance of its own made up of the individual budgets of compo-nent states. The danger, then, is that the budgetary restraint to which governments are individually committed will impart a dis- inflationary bias that locks Europe as a whole into a depression it is powerless to lift. The useful comparison can be made with the US ... The analogy is useful because United States does so obviously need

a federal budget as well as a federal bank, and the activities of the two authorities have to be coordinated. If there is a recession remedial (expansionary) fiscal policy at the federal level is the only proper response; it is inconceivable that corrective action should be left to component states, which have neither the perspective nor the coordinating machinery to do the job. If there is a federal budget there must obviously be a legislative and executive apparatus that executes it, and is democratically accountable for it. (Godley 1997: 24)

Prominent members of the Bundesbank had also noted this mismatch between monetary policy imposed on the level of the EU, and fiscal policy left to decisions of member states within the constraints in support of the single currency. Otmar Issing, a member of the German Bundesbank and eventual Chief Economist of the ECB, noted in a review of the Maastricht process that:

historical experience shows that national territories and monetary territories normally coincide ... the relevant legislation, as a rule, defines monetary sovereignty in relation to a national territory ... In contrast to the normal rule, the Maastricht Treaty implies a clear discrepancy between the intentionally rather modest political integration and monetary integration. (Issing 1966)

THE 2009 FINANCIAL CRISIS AND EXTRAORDINARY FISCAL POLICY

The experience of the 2009 financial crisis highlighted this difference between an EU-level monetary policy and fiscal policy decisions left to the decisions of the member states, but independently of the differential conditions that the single currency and exchange rate produce in economic performance: differences that would normally be met by fiscal policy measures appropriate to individual conditions, but which were constrained by the conditions to support the single currency. Even if the earlier critiques were ignored, the most recent experience should have suggested the need for an alternative mechanism of financial support for government policies to respond to macroeconomic imbalances that were compatible with the concern to avoid government default and maintain the integrity of the euro. Instead the response was to strengthen the constraints on individual governments' domestic expenditure policies to support the stability of their fiscal balance and thus the stability of the euro, rather than the stability of the macroeconomy. However, this simply reinforced the recessionary bias that was already implicit in the relation of the new single currency and its issuance by a central bank without a political/institutional base, and made it more difficult to offset the impact on domestic economic conditions of international changes in exchange rates.

REINFORCING FISCAL CONSTRAINTS REDUCE FLEXIBILITY IN CRISIS RESPONSE

While the formal specification of these constraints on government expenditure contained in the Protocol to section 104c(2) of the Maastricht Treaty, and subsequent reinforcements in the Stability and Growth Pact in response to the crisis – for example, the Six Pack (2011), the Two Pack (2013), plus Title III of the Fiscal Stability Treaty (the Fiscal Compact) that are considered necessary conditions for the stability and success of the euro – were introduced in order to improve coordination of national fiscal policies, they also reduced the flexibility of national governments in responding to financial crisis, and to intra-EU imbalances created by the single currency in a global floating exchange rate system. This mismatch in monetary and fiscal policy decisions – the former at the EU level, and the latter at the national level – and the mismatch in the flexibility of monetary policy management relative to the increasingly rigid fiscal policy objectives, created potential financial instability in the euro area and undermined the operation of monetary policy.

FISCAL STABILITY AND FINANCIAL FRAGILITY

Minsky's analysis of financial fragility may provide a guide to the paradox of measures to support euro stability leading to national financial instability. The extensions of the prior fiscal constraints in the recently introduced Fiscal Compact imply that most governments should always have financing profiles that generate fiscal balance or surplus. The Fiscal Compact is the equivalent of a policy of imposing what Minsky defined as hedge financing as a common EU policy. That is, always having more than sufficient resources to meet financial commitments without recourse to external financing. In Minsky's approach this financial profile should provide extreme financial stability, as governments will always have the resources to finance their expenditure commitments on current expenditures and on debt service.

However, this condition contains a paradox, and a virtual impossibility theorem for countries that currently have debt and deficit ratios above the Stability and Growth Pact (SGP) limits, as this requires not only budget balance, but a rising fiscal surplus that can only be achieved through a combination of higher growth and taxation. Since governments cannot produce this growth through appropriate demand management policies, it must come from either domestic consumption and investment, or from net foreign demand. But increased domestic expenditures cannot be generated by reducing government expenditures or raising taxes to generate the required fiscal surplus, since this only reduces domestic demand. Improving the external account can no longer be achieved by exchange rate adjustment, but must involve domestic wage and price adjustment, which also exerts a negative impact on domestic incomes and investment incentives. Further, these adjustments must be relative to major trading partners who may also be engaged in domestic price adjustments, making the required adjustments even greater.

FISCAL STABILITY, FINANCIAL FRAGILITY: THE PARADOX OF (GOVERNMENT) SAVINGS

As noted, for Minsky, financial stability is similar to the requirements of the Stability and Growth Pact and the Fiscal Compact: hedge financing for the government. This requires that tax yields are greater than expenditure by a margin (T>>G) to provide for debt reduction. But, as noted, higher tax yields in the absence of fiscal measures to produce higher growth require the private sector to increase tax payments, which can only be done by reducing private expenditure. Thus, the ability of the private sector to increase tax payments and repay debt requires the private sector to spend less than its income. Thus, if households net save (Y − C >> 0) and firms earn net profits, which is equivalent to net saving, this means that for the combined private sector, saving should exceed investment (S>I). But this contradicts the condition for macroeconomic equilibrium for a closed system to maintain output levels: 0 = (S − I) + (T − G).

So, for the compact conditions to hold, S<I and the private sector must finance its deficit expenditure by increasing its indebtedness, increasing private sector financial fragility. In a closed system, the public and private sectors cannot both be engaged in hedge financing at the same time. Figure 16.1 shows the Minskyan financial profiles for the private sector compared to the government sector.

Private Sector	**Sovereign**
• 1 Hedge: S>I	• 1 Hedge: T>G
But macroeconomic balance requires 0 = (S-I) + (T-G):	
so if T>G then S<I and:	so if S>I then T<G and:
• 2 Speculative: some more debt or:	• 2 Speculative: some more debt or:
• 3 Ponzi: S<I more debt, sell assets	• 3 Ponzi: G>T more debt, asset sales

Figure 16.1   Minsky financial instability profiles

For a closed system Figure 16.1 shows that it is not possible for both sectors to employ hedge finance, as would be required for Minsky's definition of financial stability. One sector has to be in deficit if the other is in surplus. The only way that both can be in surplus is if the measures indicated in lines 2 or 3 are implemented, increasing indebtedness or divesting assets, neither of which are sustainable processes for the private sector, and which are constrained by the Fiscal Compact conditions. These same relations can be shown in a graphic representation of the national accounts for a closed economic system.

From the aggregate income identity, we know that national income is determined by the aggregate of private and government expenditure. We also know that aggregate expenditure is determined by household decisions to consume, business decisions to invest, and government net expenditures. It is usually assumed that the private sector net saves (households spending less than their income more than offsets business spending in excess of profits). But, irrespective of the balance between the position of households and firms, in a closed economy the combined private sector cannot save on net more than the net deficit of the government sector, and vice versa. While no individual economic unit can spend more than it earns without borrowing from some other unit, this is not true for the aggregate economy as a whole without some adjustment in another sector or in the level of income. This is the basis for the argument given above, and is based on the national accounting definition of income and expenditure:

$$Y = C + I + (G - T)$$

where Y is national income, C is consumption expenditure, I investment expenditure, G government expenditure and T taxation of income:

since $C = Y - S$ so $Y = (Y - S) + I + (G - T)$

This means that the net position of any given sector will be conditioned on the behaviour of the other if income is not to adjust to restore the balance, for example, $(S - I) = (G - T)$.

In Figure 16.2, the private sector financial balance $(S - I)$ is represented on the horizontal axis, positions on the right of the origin indicate that on balance household saving exceeds firms' decisions to invest, and households are acquiring financing assets with those savings. On the left of the origin, firms are investing more than households are willing to save. The vertical axis represents the government balance: above the origin the government receives taxes in excess of its expenditure, while below it is in deficit and must issue liabilities to cover the gap between expenditures and tax yields.

The dotted line shows all the possible combinations of government and private sector balances for a given level of income. For any combination not represented on this line, income will adjust. For example, in the first quadrant, which shows combinations of fiscal surplus and private sector surplus,

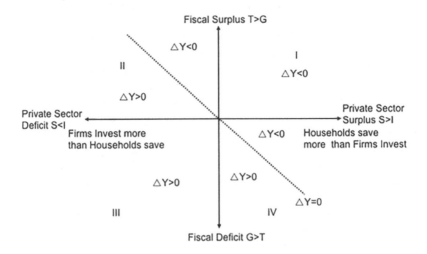

Figure 16.2   Government and private sector financial balances

expenditures are less than income and thus income will decline. On the other hand, in the third quadrant the opposite occurs, and income will be increasing. For the second and fourth quadrants the behaviour of income depends on the relative balance of surpluses and deficit positions. When surplus positions exceed deficits, income will decline, and vice versa as indicated on the graph. Thus the above-mentioned paradox. It is impossible for the government to run a hedge financing scheme without sacrificing growth, unless the private sector increases its indebtedness. But it will only be willing to do this if it expects income and profits in the future to justify the higher expenditure. But, as was shown in the Great Depression of the 1930s and in the 2000s, this is unlikely to occur without an exogenous boost to activity, which normally can only come from higher government expenditures via fiscal policy. If the government must run a surplus that is sufficient to eliminate its excess debt over time, then the result will simply be to substitute private debt for government debt, or for national incomes to fall, producing a permanent condition of stagnation. Both these conditions create fragility for households, who are forced to borrow to meet debt service, and for firms, as lower growth means reduced revenues available to meet their financial commitments, with a clear impact on non-performing loans of the financial system.

Is there a way out of this paradox and perpetual economic underperformance as the price for stability of government debts and the success of the euro? Yes:

the answer is to be found in the external sector. For an open economy, macroeconomic equilibrium in the level of income requires:

$$0 = (S - I) + (T - G) - (X - M).$$

It is possible for the private and public sectors to be in surplus (S>I and T>G) if
and only if there is a current account surplus (X>M) sufficiently large to compensate. This means that the Fiscal Compact conditions can only be met with
an external surplus sufficiently large to offset the savings of the government
and the private sector. At the EU level this means that since some countries will
only require fiscal balance, while excess-debt countries will require surpluses,
the euro can only survive if the EU as a whole produces an external surplus.
But this means that the financial fragility, deficit spending and increasing
indebtedness are shifted to the rest of the world; in current conditions, to the
United States. Figure 16.3 summarizes these arguments.

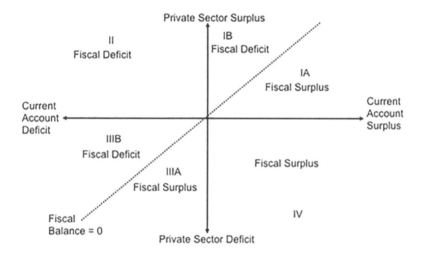

Figure 16.3   Financial instability at the global level

These relations can be presented graphically by transforming Figure 16.2,
following a suggestion of Robert Parenteau (2010), to include the external
account balance. Figure 16.4 represents three balances but only two dimensions, so the graph is normalized on the basis of balance in one of the three
sectors to show the compatible positions of the other two. To present the role
of the Fiscal Compact this graph is normalized around the 45 degree line

through the origin, which shows the combination of private sector and external sector positions compatible with government fiscal balance (T – G = 0).

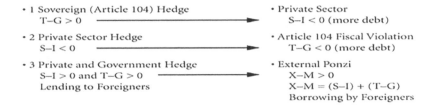

- 1 Sovereign (Article 104) Hedge
  T–G > 0
- 2 Private Sector Hedge
  S–I < 0
- 3 Private and Government Hedge
  S–I > 0 and T–G > 0
  Lending to Foreigners

- Private Sector
  S–I < 0 (more debt)
- Article 104 Fiscal Violation
  T–G < 0 (more debt)
- External Ponzi
  X–M > 0
  X–M = (S–I) + (T–G)
  Borrowing by Foreigners

Figure 16.4   Fiscal balance

The vertical axis shows the financial position of the combined private sector, with a saving surplus represented by a positive sign (above the horizontal line) and a deficit position of increasing debt a negative sign (below the horizontal line). The horizontal axis shows a current account surplus as a positive sign (to the right of the vertical line) and a deficit as a negative sign (to the left of the vertical line). The graph is thus a handy way of identifying the private and external sector positions that are compatible with the Fiscal Compact pledge of a balanced government budget.

Starting from the origin, both the private sector and the foreign sector are in balance, $S - I = 0$ and $X - M = 0$, so the government is also in balance: $T - G = 0$. As noted, on any point along the 45-degree line, the government budget expenditure is balanced by tax receipts. However, the private sector can only net save and have a hedge profile along with the government in quadrant IA, in which the external surplus exceeds the private sector surplus. In quadrant IB, the current account is not sufficiently large to offset private saving, and the government is in deficit.

To represent the Fiscal Compact's requirement for a fiscal surplus, or for a country with an excess debt position, the 45-degree line would be shifted downward to the right, as in Figure 16.5.

The figure also shows that the area in quadrant IV compatible with a fiscal surplus requires an increase in private sector indebtedness matched by a higher current account surplus. For positions in quadrant IA the external surplus must be sufficiently large to offset a private sector surplus. The shaded area in the graph provides a representation of the conditions that could be required for countries such as Italy and Greece, which have very large debt ratios, under say a 3 per cent fiscal surplus target. For these countries, given the condition of household balance sheets it is unlikely that they can borrow to meet expenditure in excess of income, so that quadrant IV is not a viable solution.

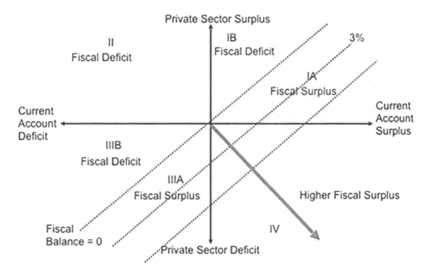

Figure 16.5   Higher fiscal balance

The graph can also be normalized on private sector equilibrium as in Figure 16.6, with the 45-degree line showing the conditions in the other two sectors, given S = I balance. Unless the private sector is able to finance expenditure via deficit spending, the Fiscal Compact viable positions lie in quadrant IA, with a current account surplus sufficient to offset the combined net saving of the government and the private sector. If uncertainty or monetary restriction leads the private sector to increase saving, as shown along the bold arrow in quadrant IV, the current account balance must be even higher in order to allow a fiscal surplus. Of course, the crucial question is whether the external sector can be expanded by the amounts required to support equilibrium.

These diagrams suggest that the ability to obtain an external surplus is crucial to the ability of the private and government sectors to meet the fiscal targets. Since the external account is the mirror image of the net balance of the private and government sectors of its foreign trading partners, domestic adjustment to allow debtors to fully repay creditors can only occur with the cooperation of the debtors' trading partners. However, the differential combination of the three sectoral balances will have an impact on country growth performance.

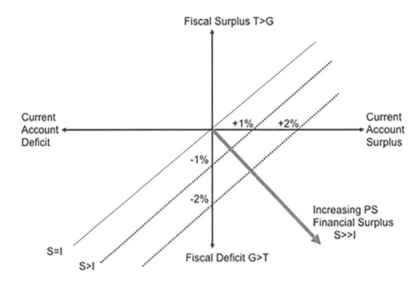

Figure 16.6   PS surplus S>1

THE BALANCE POSITIONS OF MAJOR EUROZONE COUNTRIES

As noted, the major eurozone economies show major differences in their debt, deficit and external balance positions. Italy and France have been constrained by their ability to improve their growth performance: first, because they cannot use their traditional reliance on exchange rate adjustment; second, because internal wage and price adjustment would just reduce their domestic demand performance; and third, because the other major northern eurozone economies are enjoying much higher current account surpluses, which produces euro appreciation. This conundrum is exacerbated by the fact that to gain competitive advantage not only do wages and prices have to be reduced, but they must be below the already low rates in the export surplus northern countries.

Finally, internal demand stimulus is limited by the Fiscal Compact restraint on government expenditures. Thus, low growth creates increased financial instability, as incomes are not sufficient to service financial liabilities and produce the growth of non-performing loans in the financial system.

The paradox is even stronger in eurozone economies that do not show current account surpluses. This includes France and Belgium as well as most of the smaller member states. For these countries the -3 per cent fiscal constraint

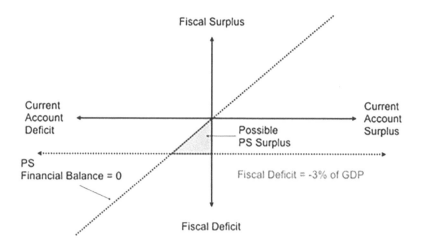

Figure 16.7   The policy conundrum: no devaluation to impact CAB

and an external deficit means that they can only achieve a position of private sector hedge financing by operating in the shaded triangle in Figure 16.7.

The paradoxal position facing smaller indebted EU periphery countries that seek to expand by means of domestic demand and investment above domestic savings would produce conditions such as shaded area in Figure 16.8. Here, increasing private sector deficits will be compatible with higher external deficits and an improved fiscal position. This again highlights the fact that government stability only comes with an increase in private sector indebtedness in the absence of the ability to access external demand by selling into external markets.

CAN THE EURO SURVIVE WITHOUT EXTERNAL SURPLUSES?

This leaves external demand as the only solution to survival of the euro, given the insistence on fiscal balance. But without the ability to improve external competitiveness through exchange rate adjustment, internal depreciation through wage reductions or productivity increases in advance of wage increases will be required. However, this is also a policy that reduces domestic demand, offsetting the benefits of higher foreign demand. And here is the paradox: all the policies proposed to increase growth of incomes and generate fiscal surpluses ultimately have a negative impact on income growth. Keynes called it the paradox of saving; here, it is the paradox of euro survival.

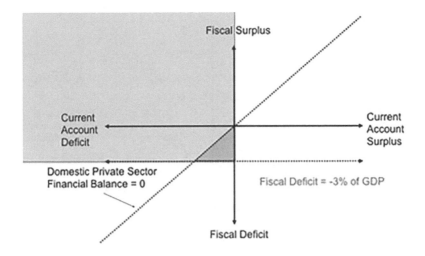

Figure 16.8   *The Economic and Monetary Union and the Stability and Growth Pact can increase the odds of private sector financial fragility*

Historically, deflations have produced financial crises just as easily as inflation. While Germany pleads for more political control and integration, the EU may disintegrate through political reaction to prolonged stagnation.

IS THE EUROZONE A PONZI SCHEME?

But is this solution financially stable? In the 1940s, the United States considered a policy of supporting domestic demand through a permanent current account surplus. Evsey Domar (1950) showed that a stable share of export surplus to GDP was feasible and stable, on one condition: the rate of increase of the outstanding foreign lending was greater or equal to the interest rate charged on the loans. But, on reflection, note that this is the definition of a Ponzi scheme. And the reduction in efficiency wages and/or currency depreciation required to keep the surplus would dampen domestic demand, producing stagnation. The survival of the euro based on a permanent export surplus seems to require the permanent maintenance of a Ponzi scheme or stagflation to keep imports from growing more rapidly than exports.

Thus, given the inability to improve external competitiveness in the short term, it is impossible to have both the private and fiscal balances in surplus. If the public sector is to remain within the 3 per cent deficit limit, the private sector will have to be in deficit. As shown clearly in Figure 16.8, this can only occur if a country has a current account surplus. It is thus clear that if a country has a debt to GDP position higher than 60 per cent it can only comply with the convergence conditions if it manages to situate itself in quadrant IA. But this is precisely the adjustment conundrum raised by the fiscal and debt constraints, for this means that there must be other member states that are in quadrants II and III within the deficit limit of 3 per cent.

Just as it is inappropriate to extend the analysis of the household budget constraint to the economy as a whole, it is also inappropriate to extend it to the analysis of national solvency in the international context. Indeed, it may be the case that the policies of foreign governments are a major determinant of domestic performance. This was the conclusion that Keynes came to in his work on German postwar reparations. Germany could repay the Allies only if the Allies were willing to boost their consumption of German goods. The solution that was eventually adopted – increasing short-term private lending to Germany rather than increasing imports of German goods – laid the basis for both the 1929 US stock market crash and the rise of fascism in Germany.

THE IMPACT OF RELATIVE WAGE AND PRICE ADJUSTMENT IN PLACE OF EXCHANGE RATE ADJUSTMENTS

It is also important to note the limitations on wage and prices adjustments: they must be relative to those of a country's major trading partners. Consider the policies introduced by the German government after reunification in 1990. Wage growth was slowed below the growth in productivity and unit labour costs fell, and inflation dropped below that in the rest of the eurozone. The impact was the same as if German had depreciated its currency, and is equivalent to an implicit subsidy for exporters, and a tax on imported consumption goods. Interest rates set by the ECB on the basis of average EU inflation rates in the presence of lower German inflation produced a higher relative real interest rate in Germany, and thus an incentive to private saving. As a result of these policies, Germany's government deficit fell and its external surplus rose, boosting the German savings rate. leading to a private sector surplus and an external surplus: a position in quadrant IA. With a lowered government deficit, the external position had to more than offset it, or the growth rate would have fallen; which is in fact what occurred. The result is growth in German GDP in excess of the growth of consumption, and a rising German savings rate. It should be obvious that this result is independent of whether or not the Germans were more parsimonious than the Italians or Greeks, either ethnically or culturally. The German private sector was simply responding to policy incentives introduced in order to pay for reunification.

But within a monetary union such as the euro, this domestic policy means that Germany has to be a net lender to the rest of the world, and in particular to the rest of the European Union, to the extent that it has a positive external balance within the EU; which is in fact the case. And this is precisely what happened in the 2000s. German banks lent to private and government borrowers in the periphery in order to allow them to run deficits and buy imports, many of them from Germany. The result: Italian, Greek and Portuguese fiscal and external deficits, which produced a rate of growth of income below the rate of growth of consumption, a low savings ratio, and a rising debt ratio. It is thus not surprising that some of the largest exposures to peripheral borrowers such as Greece were German (and French) banks. But, if the borrowers are insolvent, then the loans on German and French bank balance sheets were impaired and could not be redeemed without the creation of the European Financial Stability Facility/European Financial Stability Mechanism to purchase the loans.

But this does not mean that those countries with weaker fiscal balances and external debt are more profligate than Germany is parsimonious. It is the policy mix that makes them so, not any inherent cultural characteristic. The real cost of a potential default will be borne by the lending banks. As already noted, unless there is cooperation to increase flexibility in terms of domestic policy, there is nothing that the highly indebted eurozone countries can do to change their behaviour. Italy cannot adjust its exchange rate if it wants to remain in the eurozone. It could attempt to reduce real wage growth to below the rate of productivity growth, but this would have to be at a rate higher than that practiced in Germany, and would cause a reduction not only in demand and employment but also in saving. It would also reduce saving in Germany, since its growth rate would also fall due to a declining net external surplus. Germany can only continue its behaviour by finding export markets external to the eurozone, which is what occurred as Germany increased exports to China. But, given the new US policy, this is going to be more and more difficult. The bottom line is that highly indebted countries will not be able to repay outstanding debts through fiscal austerity, nor by expanding their external surplus; the solution lies in fiscal policy coordination in the EU and in the global economy, not in the Fiscal Compact. Highly indebted countries can grow their way out of debt; they cannot export their way out of debt by domestic depreciation and raising exports. But to do this requires a reform of the conditions on fiscal policy in the EU to support and share domestic growth and employment.

NOTES

1.   Diverse exchange rate systems remain part of the European Union (EU), with some countries holding exemptions from the presumption to introduce the euro, and others retaining their national currencies with fixed/flexible rates relative

to the euro, and flexible rates vis-à-vis the rest of the world. This simultaneous maintenance of fixed and flexible rates for non-eurozone and for eurozone countries was not envisaged in the initial discussions of the single currency. It has produced the concept of 'variable velocity' or 'concentric convergence' in which member states can choose the speed at which they introduce the various requirements for membership.

2. While most central banks have restrictions on their ability to finance government expenditures directly, they are all subject to some degree of representative democratic political control, despite the claims of central bank independence. It is also commonly accepted that coordination between monetary and fiscal policy is an essential element of the efficiency of economic policy. The ECB was created in the Maastricht Treaty and is only subject to the conditions in EU Treaties and the power granted to it by the European Commission, not the European Parliament.

REFERENCES

Domar, E. 1950. 'The Effect of Foreign Investments on the Balance of Payments', *American Economic Review* 40, 805–826

Godley, Wynne, 'Derailed', *London Review of Books*, Vol. 15 No. 16, 19 August 1993, p. 9.

Godley, Wynne, *London Observer*, 31 August 1997, p. 24.

Issing, Otmar 'Europe: Political Union through Common Money?', Occasional Paper 98, London: Institute of Economic Affairs, 1966.

Parenteau, R. 'Minsky and the Eurozone Predicament: Transcending the Dismal Science', Presented at the 19th Annual Hyman P. Minsky Conference, After the Crisis – Planning a New Financial Structure, New York, 15 April 2010.

PART VI

Ecology

17. Identifying ecologically unequal exchange in the world-system: implications for development

Alf Hornborg

INTRODUCTION

The renewed liberalization of the world market that has characterized the past four decades has resulted in widening global inequalities and accelerated environmental degradation (Milanovic 2011; Alvaredo et al. 2013, 2017; Chancel and Piketty 2015; Woodward 2015; Teixidó-Figueras et al. 2016). Much as Karl Polanyi ([1944] 1957) could have predicted, economic globalization has had severely detrimental consequences for what he called the "fictitious" commodities of labor and land. As labor time and natural space have been increasingly commodified, low wages and lax environmental legislation serve as competitive advantages that attract capital investment to the Global South. The gaps between developed and developing (or less-developed) nations have widened in terms of both economic and ecological conditions. These trends are difficult to account for using established theories of development or underdevelopment. However, the theory of ecologically unequal exchange (EUE) offers a framework that simultaneously explains economic and ecological polarization and impoverishment by focusing on asymmetric transfers of non-monetary, biophysical resources and environmental harms (Bunker 1985, 2007; Odum and Arding 1991; Odum 1996; Hornborg 1998, 2001, 2009, 2013, 2019; Jorgenson 2006, 2016; Rice 2007a, 2007b, 2009; Jorgenson and Clark 2009; Jorgenson et al. 2009; Hornborg and Martinez-Alier 2016; Oulu 2016a; Gellert et al. 2017; Frey et al. 2019a, 2019b; Givens et al. 2019; Dorninger et al. 2021). In this chapter I discuss the theoretical foundations of EUE and provide a cursory review of the literature on methods for empirically identifying EUE and testing hypotheses derived from the theory.

While development theory since World War II has discussed the causes of uneven development from several perspectives, the roles played by the material substance of traded commodities have generally been neglected. Although most theorists have shared the observation that reliance on resource extraction and exports of primary goods tends to be associated with lower levels of development and affluence, while industrial processing is associated with higher levels, this division of labor has been accounted for in terms of social institutions, historical conditions, market mechanisms, and a range of other factors that disregard the material features of the global flows of goods. To put it briefly, development theorists have mostly discussed what are the best ways to guide countries to transition from extraction to industry, without pursuing the question of why industry is an economically more successful strategy than extraction. Even structural theories emphasizing that the terms of trade for primary products will deteriorate compared to those for manufactured goods (the Prebisch–Singer hypothesis) refer to divergent income elasticities of demand rather than the material consequences of exchanging the two kinds of commodities. This neglect of the material dimension of world trade undoubtedly reflects the focus of neoclassical economic theory on monetary metrics and market mechanisms, and its concomitant failure to address the irreversible physical degradation of resources as they are processed in human economies (Georgescu-Roegen 1971). In contrast, EUE theory does take this physical aspect of economic processes into consideration, which means acknowledging that industrial cores are economically rewarded for dissipating resources, with more resources to dissipate, while extractive peripheries lose their most accessible and highest-quality resources and suffer increasing environmental degradation.

Common to the many studies and discussions of EUE is thus a concern with other metrics than money in assessing the consequences of international trade and related global production networks. Efforts are made to quantify the resources that have been extracted—or the amount of pollution generated—in the production of a commodity. The resource demands and/or pollution history represented by a commodity are said to be "embodied" in it. Non-monetary metrics thus embodied in a commodity include greenhouse gas emissions, requisite land area, volumes of water, volumes of materials, expended energy, invested labor time, and so on. What all these measures have in common is that they refer to objective biophysical phenomena rather than to human assessments of exchange values. In contrast to superficial understandings of EUE that denote the transfers of matter and energy represented by the traded commodities, measures of embodied resources refer to all the resources that have been used throughout the production process. Such measures can thus not be determined by examining the commodities themselves, but must be reconstructed using methods such as life cycle assessments (e.g., Oulu 2016b) or multi-regional input–output modelling (e.g., Dorninger et al. 2021).

A common response to the conundrum of EUE is to attempt to estimate the monetary value of the biophysical deficits generated by unequal exchange (cf.

Emmanuel 1972; Amin 1976). However, such attempts do not acknowledge the relational character of money prices. The hypothetical, alternative prices of "underpaid" labor and other resources are fantasies based on prices generated by current market arrangements, which presuppose EUE. It is logically flawed to represent alternatives to the currently asymmetric biophysical flows in measures that are contingent on the existence of those flows. It would obviously be misleading, for instance, to estimate the value of net transfers of embodied resources from the Global South to the Global North in terms of the average prices of embodied resources exported from the North, as this would completely neglect the value added of industrial manufacturing processes in the North. The asymmetric transfers of embodied resources must thus be represented and understood in other than monetary terms, which implicates biophysical realities beyond the horizons of economics. The relevance of biophysical asymmetries in international trade thus lies not in underpayment, but in their contributions to the uneven growth of material infrastructures for profit-generating production, their indications of skewed patterns of consumption, and their implications for the unequal distribution of resource exhaustion and environmental degradation.

EUE theory has raised some major theoretical issues and generated several methodological approaches. This chapter addresses theoretical aspects of the EUE concept, then briefly reviews some of the methodologies that have been applied to empirically test for the occurrence and consequences of EUE.

THEORETICAL AND CONCEPTUAL ISSUES

EUE in Relation to Neoclassical Economic Theory

According to standard textbooks in mainstream economics (e.g., Krugman and Wells 2018), there is no such thing as "ecologically unequal exchange." In fact, there does not even seem to be such a thing as "unequal exchange." In Paul Krugman and Robin Wells's monumental book *Economics*,[1] which continues to shape the minds of countless economists implementing its logic in every imaginable context, there is no mention of unequal exchange. This is noteworthy, but not surprising. For most mainstream economists, the concept of unequal exchange is an oxymoron. The conceptual framework of neoclassical economics, focusing on the processes which determine market prices, logically precludes considerations of unequal exchange.[2] Assuming that exchange is conducted by means of (all-purpose[3]) money in freely price-setting markets, transactions are equal and reciprocal by definition. If measured in money prices, exchange is necessarily balanced. This follows from the exclusive concern with monetary metrics. To be sure, this focus on money suffices to generate the complex field of analysis introduced by Krugman and Wells, yet the conceptual framework of neoclassical economics never analytically penetrates the material world beyond the societal flows of exchange values. Much as Karl Marx observed, mainstream economics has constructed an elaborate framework for tracing the logic of money, but remains alienated from the non-monetary aspects of reality which it veils.

How should we account for the fact that ecologically unequal exchange is excluded from the field of vision of mainstream economics? The social sciences have produced several approaches to such cognitive or linguistic blind spots, whether explained in terms of ideology—that is, support for power structures (as theorized, for instance, by Marx, Foucault, and Derrida)—or more generally as the social production of ignorance (Proctor and Schiebinger 2008). Rather than imply that the field of economics is part of an insidious conspiracy intentionally concealing the reality of unequal exchange, it will suffice to observe that its preoccupation with societal configurations of supply and demand is consistent with the modern conceptual separation of society and nature. In the 19th century, the discipline of economics aspired to understand the transformations of human societies in terms that did not reduce market phenomena to mere reflections of natural features such as physical geography. The original ambition to produce an autonomous and non-reductionist science of society is understandable, but the extent to which the influential—indeed, hegemonic—field of modern economics has proven incapable of accommodating interdisciplinary insights on sustainability (for instance, climate change) is becoming alarmingly evident. The creation of an autonomous social science of economics has unfortunately entailed a conceptual insulation from natural science. As the urgency of transdisciplinary approaches to global environmental issues and inequalities intensifies, the conceptual framework of conventional economics remains strikingly myopic. Its preoccupation with money frequently entails a complete disregard for how material factors such as biology, thermodynamics, and global ecology impinge on economic processes, and vice versa. However, a long line of theorists in Marxist and ecological economics—here classified as "heterodox" in relation to the orthodoxy of mainstream economics—have offered alternative frameworks that assign causal relevance also to non-monetary factors such as embodied labor-power and embodied energy.

EUE in Relation to Heterodox Economic Theories

EUE and Marxist economics

The concept of unequal exchange as used by Marxist economists (Emmanuel 1972; Amin 1976) and world-system analysts (Wallerstein 1974) has generally been based on the labor theory of value. Emmanuel's (1972) classic study demonstrated that the exchange of commodities between a low-wage and a high-wage country will be unequal in the sense that the former will export more embodied labor in exchange for less. However, given the labor theory of value, Marxists generally refer to such asymmetric transfers in terms not of embodied labor, but of surplus value. This means that the net flows between the two countries—and the gains of one country at the expense of the other—are conceptualized as quantifiable in money. In this approach, unequal exchange is understood as the appropriation of surplus labor value through trade. In contrast with EUE theory, that which is asymmetrically transferred is thought of as measurable in money, rather than some material metric (here: labor time) applicable to biophysical resources. Moreover, as Marxist theory posits that labor-power is the only source of surplus value and capitalist profits, it cannot adequately conceptualize ecologically unequal exchange in the sense of asymmetric transfers of other surplus-yielding resources than embodied labor. It thus cannot identify exploitation and accumulation in terms of net flows of natural resources unless such flows represent net flows of embodied labor (conceived as "labor value") invested in their extraction.

EUE and ecological economics
Almost simultaneously with Emmanuel's (1972) study on "the imperialism of trade," the systems ecologist Howard T. Odum (1971) published an early introduction to his concept of "emergy," originally meant as a shorthand for "embodied energy." He has proposed that unequal exchange between two countries can be identified in terms of net transfers of value measured as past investments of energy in the commodities exchanged (Odum and Arding 1991; Odum 1996). In a similar vein, Stephen Bunker (1985) argued that Marxist and world-systems analyses of exploitation were too confined to considerations of labor value, and thus blind to asymmetric flows of what he called "energy values" between different economic sectors within and between countries. To Bunker, such net transfers of energy from extractive sectors are fundamental to the polarization of developed core areas and their underdeveloped peripheries. Odum's and Bunker's concerns with asymmetric transfers of energy recognized how biophysical transfers are essential to the expansion of economic cores, but they both adhered to the mainstream convention of conceptualizing such transfers in terms of underpaid values, rather than simply as material transfers organized by price differences.

As Stephen Lonergan (1988) has shown, labor and energy theories of value are formally identical in that they both explain exploitation in terms of differences between prices and values. Some Marxists have found Odum's approach to "unequal ecological exchange" congenial to their own concerns, recognizing his focus on embodied energy as related to Marx's emphasis on embodied labor-power (Foster and Holleman 2014). Both approaches conceptualize exploitation and accumulation as the net appropriation of some form of objective value that is underpaid on the market. While Odum's and Bunker's efforts to theorize the unequal exchange of energy were seminal, they raised questions about whether the asymmetrically traded commodities should be conceptualized as underpaid values, or as neutral records of the material history of their production, or in terms of the implications of their inherent physical properties (Hornborg 1998). Given that the productive potential of energy diminishes throughout the production process (Georgescu-Roegen 1971), the concept of "embodied energy" must refer to an item's history rather than to its current physical properties. It illuminates the material context of a commodity's production and exchange, which in labor and energy theories of value is tantamount to assessing its value. However, to choose a particular biophysical input as the criterion of some putatively objective measure of value is unwarranted and contestable. The theory of ecologically unequal exchange does not refer to asymmetric flows of values, but to net transfers of material resources and the uneven biophysical repercussions of their extraction, transformation, and consumption. Although such asymmetries are obviously generated by regularities in how commodities are evaluated and priced, it is misleading to conceptualize them in terms of an underpayment of objectively "real" values or a disregard for "externalities," because this suggests, like mainstream environmental economics, that ecological degradation can be understood through a monetary metric. The inclination to think of uneven resource appropriation in terms of "underpaid" or "unpaid" values is an analytical fallacy to which several Marxist and ecological economists have succumbed (Bunker 1985; Odum 1996; Foster and Holleman 2014; Moore 2015). Such expressions imply that higher prices would more adequately correspond to the putatively "real" value of resources, as if such objective values could be established, and as if money could compensate for increases in entropy. Although generally aware that monetary valuation cannot adequately represent EUE, or what has been conceptualized as the North's "ecological debt" to the South, theorists of global environmental justice tend to be constrained by the monetary idiom in which exchange and indebtedness are conventionally framed (Martinez-Alier 2002; Warlenius 2017). Arguably, the very notion of "value," which remains a central topic of deliberation among heterodox economists, ultimately derives from habits of thought generated by the phenomenon of money (Hornborg 2019).

AN EUE PERSPECTIVE ON THE ONTOLOGY OF TECHNOLOGY

The disregard within mainstream economics for the material substance of trade is paradoxical, given the discipline's great emphasis on technology, which clearly has a material dimension. Krugman and Wells (2018: 672–673) explain that "increased productivity is the key to long-run economic growth" and that the three main reasons for growth in productivity are (1) increases in physical capital, that is, "manufactured resources such as buildings and machines"; (2) increases in human capital, generally referred to as education and knowledge;[4] and (3) technological progress, defined as "an advance in the technical means of the production of goods and services." Both the volume of physical capital and the state of technology must have a bearing on the quantities of material inputs such as metals and energy, yet the relative quantities of such inputs are addressed only in specialized fields such as industrial ecology. They are evidently not a concern for mainstream models of economic growth and development. It is noteworthy that Krugman and Wells (ibid.) quantify physical capital in dollars rather than physical metrics: "The average U.S. private-sector worker today is backed up by more than $350,000 worth of physical capital— far more than a U.S. worker had 100 years ago and far more than the average worker in most other countries has today." This use of monetary measures to represent the quantity of material infrastructure illustrates the incapacity of mainstream economics to properly conceptualize the materiality of the world organized by money.

Global satellite images of night-time lighting confirm that the accumulation of physical capital is strongly correlated with the density of monetary income. The geographical distribution of technological infrastructure closely coincides with gross domestic product density per km^2 (Hornborg 2019: 60, fig. 3). The economists' conviction that growth in physical capital is requisite to economic growth is clearly valid, but the question remains why the net flows of materials that are required to accumulate physical capital are not a key concern for neo-classical economics. As the ratios by which physical inputs to production are maintained must hinge on relative market prices, the market can be understood as a social institution that organizes net flows of materials to core sectors of the economy. Yet this material aspect of the market remains out of sight for mainstream economists, for whom free market transactions are axiomatically symmetric, reciprocal, and fair. Money prices project an illusion of reciprocity that obscures the asymmetric transfers of physical, productive potential from extractive sectors, largely located in the Global South, to productive cores in the Global North. This illusion hinges on the conviction that economic exchange values are somehow more "real" than the tangible, physical metabolism of industrial metropoles.

The conceptual sequestration of money and exchange values from material resource flows enables neoclassical economics to approach "physical capital" and "technological progress" as non-material phenomena contingent on dollar investments and profitable innovations. This permits them to acknowledge the significance of technological infrastructure without considering the asymmetric physical resource flows through which it is reproduced. Although it can be empirically demonstrated that core regions of the world economy are net importers of embodied labor, land, energy, and materials (Dorninger and Hornborg 2015; Dorninger et al. 2021), such asymmetric material transfers are not regarded as essential to the reproduction of infrastructure in the cores. If economists had recognized them as crucial to the growth and maintenance of physical capital, EUE would be a central consideration in economics and development theory. From a metabolic perspective, the growth of "techno-mass" (Hornborg 1992) is as dependent on net inputs of energy and other biophysical resources as is the growth and metabolism of biomass.

The peculiarly non-material understanding of growth in infrastructure—or, rather, the absence of a conceptual connection between the growth of physical capital and trade, understood in non-material terms—was a product of discursive boundaries (between economics and engineering) constructed in early industrial Britain. Paradoxically, it also characterized the outlook on technology in the historical materialism of Karl Marx. In several respects, Marx's perspective was entrenched in the debate on political economy in 19th-century Britain. Marxist theory thus celebrates what is perceived as the development of the "productive forces," without concerning itself with the extent to which local technological progress is contingent on asymmetric resource transfers in the world-system. This is particularly problematic as Marxist theory is perceived as both materialist and centrally concerned with asymmetric exchange. The conundrum highlights how fundamentally our understanding of the phenomenon of EUE must transform our hopes for a "green" technology that will make modern society sustainable (Bonds and Downey 2012; Hornborg 2013, 2016).

METRICS AND METHODOLOGIES FOR TESTING EUE

In developing a range of methods for testing for the occurrence and consequences of EUE, scholars have investigated global trade in terms of both embodied resources (goods) and embodied impacts (harms). A number of studies have identified a recurrent tendency of countries in the Global South to export resources to countries in the North while experiencing negative impacts such as resource exhaustion, land degradation, pollution, and biodiversity loss. Such impacts are theoretically predictable illustrations of how EUE enables the Global North, in outsourcing its extraction of resources as well as its elimination of waste products, to achieve environmental load displacement to the South. The global movements of goods and harms are two sides of the same coin, providing the Global North with both sources of new resources and sinks for its metabolic waste. The following subsections provide a list of some of the parameters that exemplify the biophysical asymmetries between the North and the South, and the methods that have been used to study them. Due to limitations of space, the list is very cursory and serves mainly as a guide to further reading. Taken together, however, the studies listed here offer a formidable verification of the occurrence of EUE.

While this literature generally validates the expectations of EUE theory, we should keep in mind that categories such as core/periphery and North/ South cannot be perfectly delineated as coinciding with the territories of nations or continents. These concepts refer to statistical tendencies and polarizations indicating asymmetric relations that recur at several levels of the world-system. Such asymmetries can also be identified within nations, but as most data on trade refer to the international level, the studies tend to deal with EUE relations between nations.

Embodied Land

The most well-known measure of embodied land is the ecological footprint. Ecological footprint accounting estimates the extent to which the production of commodities requires eco-productive space, and to which different consumption patterns thus imply unequal claims on abstract land (Rees and Wackernagel 1994; Wackernagel and Rees 1996; Wackernagel et al. 1997, 1999; York et al. 2003; Jorgenson 2003; Jorgenson and Rice 2005, 2007; Rice 2007a, 2007b; Weinzettel et al. 2013; Asici and Acar 2016). The genealogy of the ecological footprint concept can be traced through the work of William Catton (1980) to the concept of "ghost acreages" conceived by Georg Borgström (1965). Ecological footprints are measured in average global hectares. Asymmetric claims on embodied land have also been calculated using multi-regional input–output (MRIO) analysis (Lugschitz et al. 2011; Yu et al. 2013), estimates of time-space appropriation (Hornborg 2013; Warlenius 2017), and studies of international land acquisitions (Seaquist et al. 2014; Frame 2019). The idea of ecological footprint has served as a template for concerns with other resource demands that are invisible to the consumer, giving rise to concepts such as "material footprint," "labor footprint," "biodiversity footprint," "water footprint," and "carbon footprint."

Embodied Materials

The volumes of materials required in production processes and thus embodied in trade goods have been measured through material flow analysis (MFA). The usual metric is tons. MFA measures not only the material content of the commodities in themselves, but also all materials claimed through their production (Fischer-Kowalski and Amann 2001; Muradian and Martinez-Alier 2001). It has been applied to calculating the "physical trade balances" of nations over time, as well as to assessing resource efficiency at national to global scales

(Pérez Rincón 2006; Eisenmenger and Giljum 2007; Wiedmann et al. 2015; Haas et al. 2015; Mayer and Haas 2016; Dorninger and Eisenmenger 2016; Martinez-Alier et al. 2016; Schandl et al. 2016a; Krausmann et al. 2017; Plank et al. 2018; Magalhães et al. 2019; Infante-Amate and Krausmann 2019). Transfers of materials in international trade have also been approached through studies of global commodity chains (Bunker and Ciccantell 2005; Ciccantell and Smith 2009; Ciccantell 2019).

Embodied Energy

The flows of energy in extraction, production, transport, and consumption have been conceptualized in terms of an unequal exchange between cores and peripheries, to the disadvantage of the latter (Bunker 1985; Odum and Arding 1991). In analogy with the development of organisms, Howard T. Odum (1996) coined the term "emergy" as a measure of the amount of energy that has contributed to the formation of a commodity. As Stephen Lonergan (1988) anticipated, Marxists such as John Bellamy Foster have found affinities between Odum's energy theory of value and the Marxist labor theory of value (Foster and Holleman 2014). Foster (2008) conceptualizes the core's appropriation of energy as "energy imperialism."

Embodied Labor Time

Human labor is a specific form of purposeful energy invested in production. Building on the Marxist labor theory of value, Emmanuel (1972) defined "unequal exchange" as the net transfer of embodied labor from low-wage to high-wage countries that results from international differences in the price of labor. The Marxist discourse on unequal exchange focuses on transfers of "labor value," measurable in money, rather than on transfers of labor time (cf. Gibson 1980). Studies focusing on international flows of embodied labor measured (as biophysical exertion) in person-year equivalents have illuminated global inequalities (Alsamawi et al. 2014; Simas et al. 2014; Pérez-Sánchez et al. 2021). Asymmetric transfers of labor time have also been highlighted through estimates of time-space appropriation (Hornborg 2013; Warlenius 2017).

Embodied Human Appropriation of Net Primary Production (HANPP)

HANPP is a measure of the proportion of net primary production from a given area that is appropriated by humans. It is thus an indicator of the extent to which humans dominate ecosystems. Global trade in biomass has been analyzed in terms of embodied HANPP (Erb et al. 2009; Haberl et al. 2012; Haberl et al. 2014; Temper 2016). Net exports of embodied HANPP tend to be linked to decreases in land productivity and losses of biodiversity.

Embodied Biodiversity Loss

Trade in biomass tends to increase biodiversity loss in net exporting areas. The concept of "biodiversity footprint" has been presented as measurable through MRIO models (Lenzen et al. 2012b). Many of the studies of biodiversity loss have focused empirically on land cover change and deforestation (Burns et al. 2003, 2006; Jorgenson 2006, 2010; Shandra et al. 2009a; Shandra et al. 2011; Kill 2016; Henderson and Shorette 2017; Austin 2010, 2017; Noble 2017; Sommer et al. 2019). Some studies also consider threats to animal species (Shandra et al. 2009b).

Marine Resources

Global fisheries and trade in marine resources have resulted in loss of marine biodiversity no less alarming than biodiversity loss and overall land cover change. These developments have been approached as consequences of EUE (Clark et al. 2019).

Embodied Water

Many exports, particularly agricultural products, embody significant quantities of water that have been used in their production. The concept of "water foot-print" has been applied to indicate the amount of water indirectly transferred as such goods are traded between nations (Fitzgerald and Auerbach 2016).

Embodied Pollution

Environmental load displacement from cores to peripheries has been studied in terms of the trade in toxic waste (Clapp 1994), and more recently in terms of pollution of air, water, or soil embodied in trade goods (Muradian et al. 2002; Muradian and Giljum 2007; Jorgenson 2009; Shandra et al. 2009c; Zhang et al. 2018).

Greenhouse Gas Emissions

Emissions of carbon dioxide are a category of air pollution that has received particular attention in the context of global climate change. While different nations hope to present accounts suggesting successful emission reductions, several studies emphasize the difference between production-based versus consumption-based emissions. The latter emissions are embodied in imports consumed within a country but frequently attributed to the country where the goods are produced. Carbon-intensive industries are often located in the Global South. Studies of "carbon footprints" focus on the global distribution of emissions resulting from the division of labor between cores and peripheries, and the trade in embodied emissions (Roberts et al. 2003; Roberts and Parks 2008, 2009; Lawrence 2009; Jorgenson 2011, 2012; Jorgenson and Clark 2012; Peters et al. 2011; Kanemoto et al. 2014; Givens and Jorgenson 2014; Prell and Sun 2015; Warlenius 2016; Isenhour and Feng 2016; Peng et al. 2016; Sommer and Kratena 2017; Bradford and Stoner 2017; Ciplet and Roberts 2019; Givens 2018; Huang 2018).

Aggregated Metrics

Some studies combine several different metrics to illuminate the multi-faceted character of EUE. A frequently applied methodology is environmentally extended multi-region input–output (MRIO) modelling (Lenzen et al. 2012a; Yu et al. 2014; Dorninger and Hornborg 2015; Schandl et al. 2016b; Wiedmann and Lenzen 2018; Dorninger et al. 2021).

Entropy

While difficult to quantify, the transformations of resources through extraction, manufacture, and transport inevitably result in increases in physical disorder, or entropy (Georgescu-Roegen 1971). Given that industrial cores must export their products at higher prices than they pay for the materials and energy used in the production of these exports, there will be an inexorable net transfer of physical order to cores and, as we have seen, a displacement of entropy to peripheries (Hornborg 1992, 1998, 2001; Frank 2007; Biel 2012; McKinney 2019). This is a more abstract way of conceptualizing unequal exchange, but it agrees with the general structure of EUE empirically identified by the other metrics reviewed here.

CONCLUSIONS

To posit that free market trade is in some sense "unequal" inevitably forces us outside the paradigm of neoclassical economics. But to articulate the very widespread understanding of world trade as exploitative in analytically rigorous terms presents conceptual difficulties for ecological economists and Marxists alike. Their intuitive understanding of global trade inequalities is that exports from less-developed countries are "underpaid." This is to imply that those exports have "real" values that are greater than their market price. But how could such values be ascertained? Long-standing efforts at constructing labor or energy theories of value notwithstanding, there is no analytically robust way of deriving some monetary measure of value from biophysical inputs such as labor or energy. We must finally concede that value is determined by the logic of the market.

Regardless of theories of value, proposals for a more just and equitable world often hinge on the imperative that exports from less-developed countries should be paid more than is currently the case. But how could higher prices compensate for the withdrawal and destruction of natural resources? Money cannot compensate for entropy. Higher prices might reduce the volume of trade, but to significantly rectify the imbalances of the modern world economy the prices would have to be raised so high that the continued existence of high-tech society in the developed countries would be unfeasible. This is to say that modern industrial civilization as inaugurated in early 19th-century Britain continues to be made possible by asymmetric global resource flows, which are in turn reproduced by the logic of market prices, through which products representing dissipated natural resources must be priced higher than the resources that are spent in their production. To envisage a civilization not based on such asymmetric flows should mean conceding that the artefact of all-purpose money itself will need to be redesigned; but this is a conclusion that neither mainstream nor heterodox economists are likely to take seriously.[5]

The global asymmetries addressed in this chapter appear to be inherent in the structural logic of the idea, inscribed in all-purpose money, that everything can be exchanged for everything else. To curb the increasingly globalized logic of EUE, a solution might be for each nation to establish a complementary, special-purpose currency used only for products and services that originate within a given radius from the point of purchase (Hornborg 2019). To limit the geographical reach of much of the world's money—rather than let globalization continue to reward long-distance transportation, low wages, and lax environmental legislation in the Global South—may ultimately be the only way to prevent market exchange from encouraging an intensifying exploitation of international differences in the price of labor and other resources. In alleviating the many detrimental consequences of EUE it would be a way of restraining the logic of the market from generating alarming global inequalities, ecological degradation, and climate change.

ACKNOWLEDGMENT

I am grateful to Andrew Jorgenson for suggesting some useful additions to a draft version of this chapter.

NOTES

1. The fifth edition of the book is over 1000 pages and has a 28-page, four-column index.
2. Some mainstream economists occasionally use the concept of "unequal exchange" to denote market power such as monopoly, that is, conditions where a market's price-setting mechanisms are not given free rein. This is a very different definition of unequal exchange than the one offered in this chapter.
3. The category of all- or general-purpose money was introduced by Karl Polanyi ([1957] 1968) to distinguish money that mediates exchanges of all kinds of goods and services from so-called special-purpose currencies, which are used within more narrow spheres of exchange.
4. Krugman and Wells (2018: 673) emphasize the kind of knowledge necessary to utilize physical capital: "It's not enough for a worker to have good equipment— he or she must also know what to do with it."
5. Given that Karl Marx's deliberations in *Capital* to a great extent did problematize the social and even ecological repercussions of money, it is frustrating to find his followers exclusively concerned with an abstract agent referred to as the "capitalist system." Capitalism is not an agent but an aggregate result of human transactions complying with conventions defined by the idea of all-purpose money.

REFERENCES

Alsamawi, Ali, Joy Murray, and Manfred Lenzen. 2014. The employment footprint of nations: Uncovering master–servant relationships. *Journal of Industrial Ecology* 18(1): 59–70.

Alvaredo, Facundo, Anthony B. Atkinson, Thomas Piketty, and Emmanuel Saez. 2013. The top 1 percent in international and historical perspective. *Journal of Economic Perspectives* 27(3): 3–20.

Alvaredo, Facundo, Lucas Chancel, Thomas Piketty, Emmanuel Saez, and Gabriel Zucman. 2017. *World Inequality Report 2018*. Paris: World Inequality Lab.

Amin, Samir. 1976. *Unequal development: An essay on the social formations of peripheral capitalism*. New York: Monthly Review Press.

Asici, Ahmet Atil, and Sevil Acar. 2016. Does income growth relocate ecological footprint? *Ecological Indicators* 61: 707–714.

Austin, Kelly F. 2010. The "hamburger connection" as ecologically unequal exchange: A cross-national investigation of beef exports and deforestation in less-developed countries. *Rural Sociology* 75(2): 270–299.

Austin, Kelly F. 2017. Brewing unequal exchange in coffee: A qualitative investigation into the consequences of the Java trade in rural Uganda. *Journal of World-Systems Research* 23(2): 326–352.

Biel, Robert. 2012. *The entropy of capitalism*. Chicago, IL: Haymarket Books.

Bonds, Eric, and Liam Downey. 2012. "Green" technology and ecologically unequal exchange: The environmental and social consequences of ecological modernization in the world-system. *Journal of World-Systems Research* 18(2): 167–186.

Borgström, Georg. 1965. *The hungry planet: The modern world at the edge of famine*. New York: Macmillan.

Bradford, John Hamilton, and Alexander M. Stoner. 2017. The treadmill of destruction in comparative perspective: A panel study of military spending and carbon emissions, 1960–2014. *Journal of World-Systems Research* 23(2): 298–325.

Bunker, Stephen G. 1985. *Underdeveloping the Amazon: Extraction, unequal exchange, and the failure of the modern state.* Chicago, IL: University of Chicago Press.

Bunker, Stephen G. 2007. Natural values and the physical inevitability of uneven development under capitalism. In *Rethinking environmental history: World-system history and global environmental change*, edited by Alf Hornborg, J.R. McNeill, and Joan Martinez-Alier, pp. 239–258. Lanham, MD: AltaMira Press.

Bunker, Stephen G., and Paul S. Ciccantell. 2005. *Globalization and the race for resources.* Baltimore, MD: Johns Hopkins University Press.

Burns, Thomas J., Edward L. Kick, and Byron L. Davis. 2003. Theorizing and rethinking linkages between the natural environment and the modern world-system: Deforestation in the late 20th century. *Journal of World-Systems Research* 9(2): 357–390.

Burns, Thomas J., Edward L. Kick, and Byron L. Davis. 2006. A quantitative cross-national study of deforestation in the late 20th century: A case of recursive exploitation. In *Globalization and the environment*, edited by Andrew K. Jorgenson and Edward L. Kick, pp. 37–60. Leiden: Brill.

Catton, William R., Jr. 1980. *Overshoot: The ecological basis of revolutionary change.* Urbana, IL: University of Illinois Press.

Chancel, Lucas, and Thomas Piketty. 2015. *Carbon and inequality: From Kyoto to Paris. Trends in the global inequality of carbon emissions (1998–2013) and prospects for an equitable adaptation fund.* Paris: Paris School of Economics.

Ciccantell, Paul S. 2019. Ecologically unequal exchange and raw materialism: The material foundations of the capitalist world-economy. In *Ecologically unequal exchange: Environmental injustice in comparative and historical perspective*, edited by R. Scott Frey, Paul K. Gellert, and Harry F. Dahms, pp. 49–73. Houndmills: Palgrave Macmillan.

Ciccantell, Paul, and David A. Smith. 2009. Rethinking global commodity chains: Integrating extraction, transport, and manufacturing. *International Journal of Comparative Sociology* 50(3–4): 361–384.

Ciplet, David, and J. Timmons Roberts. 2019. Splintering South: Ecologically unequal exchange theory in a fragmented global climate. In *Ecologically unequal exchange: Environmental injustice in comparative and historical perspective*, edited by R. Scott Frey, Paul K. Gellert, and Harry F. Dahms, pp. 273–305. Houndmills: Palgrave Macmillan.

Clapp, Jennifer. 1994. The toxic waste trade with less-industrialised countries: Economic linkages and political alliances. *Third World Quarterly* 15(3): 505–518.

Clark, Brett, Stefano B. Longo, Rebecca Clausen, and Daniel Auerbach. 2019. From sea slaves to slime lines: Commodification and unequal ecological exchange in global marine fisheries. In *Ecologically unequal exchange: Environmental injustice in comparative and historical perspective*, edited by R. Scott Frey, Paul K. Gellert, and Harry F. Dahms, pp. 195–219. Houndmills: Palgrave Macmillan.

Dorninger, Christian, and Alf Hornborg. 2015. Can EEMRIO analyses establish the occurrence of ecologically unequal exchange? *Ecological Economics* 119: 414–18.

Dorninger, Christian, and Nina Eisenmenger. 2016. South America's biophysical involvement in international trade: The physical trade balances of Argentina, Bolivia, and Brazil in the light of ecologically unequal exchange. *Journal of Political Ecology* 23: 394–409.

Dorninger, Christian, Alf Hornborg, David J. Abson, Henrik von Wehrden, Anke Schaffartzik, et al. 2021. Global patterns of ecologically unequal exchange: Implications for sustainability in the 21st century. *Ecological Economics*. Online publication before print. https://www.sciencedirect.com/science/article/pii/ S0921800920300938.

Eisenmenger, Nina, and Stefan Giljum. 2007. Evidence from social metabolism studies for ecological unequal trade. In *The world system and the Earth system: Global socioenvironmental change and sustainability since the Neolithic*, edited by Alf Hornborg and Carole L. Crumley, pp. 288–302. Walnut Creek, CA: Left Coast Press.

Emmanuel, Arghiri. 1972. *Unequal exchange: A study of the imperialism of trade*. New York: Monthly Review Press.

Erb, Karl-Heinz, Fridolin Krausmann, Wolfgang Lucht, and Helmut Haberl. 2009. Embodied HANPP: Mapping the spatial disconnect between global biomass production and consumption. *Ecological Economics* 69: 328–334.

Fischer-Kowalski, Marina, and Christof Amann. 2001. Beyond IPAT and Kuznets Curves: Globalization as a vital factor in analysing the environmental impact of socio-economic metabolism. *Population and Environment* 23(1): 7–47.

Fitzgerald, Jared B., and Daniel Auerbach. 2016. The political economy of the water footprint: A cross-national analysis of ecologically unequal exchange. *Sustainability* 8(12): 1–16.

Foster, John B. 2008. Peak oil and energy imperialism. *Monthly Review* 60(3): 12–33.

Foster, John B., and Hanna Holleman. 2014. The theory of unequal ecological exchange: A Marx–Odum dialectic. *Journal of Peasant Studies* 41(2): 199–233.

Frame, Mariko. 2019. The role of the semi-periphery in ecologically unequal exchange: A case study of land investments in Cambodia. In *Ecologically unequal exchange: Environmental injustice in comparative and historical perspective*, edited by R. Scott Frey, Paul K. Gellert, and Harry F. Dahms, pp. 75–106. Houndmills: Palgrave Macmillan.

Frank, Andre G. 2007. Entropy generation and displacement: The nineteenth-century multilateral network of world trade. In *The world system and the Earth system: Global socioenvironmental change and sustainability since the Neolithic*, edited by Alf Hornborg and Carole L. Crumley, pp. 303–316. Walnut Creek, CA: Left Coast Press.

Frey, R. Scott, Paul K. Gellert, and Harry F. Dahms, eds. 2019a. *Ecologically unequal exchange: Environmental injustice in comparative and historical perspective*. Houndmills: Palgrave Macmillan.

Frey, R. Scott, Paul K. Gellert, and Harry F. Dahms. 2019b. Introduction: Ecologically unequal exchange in comparative and historical perspective. In *Ecologically unequal exchange: Environmental injustice in comparative and historical perspective*, edited by R. Scott Frey, Paul K. Gellert, and Harry F. Dahms, pp. 1–10. Houndmills: Palgrave Macmillan.

Gellert, Paul K., R. Scott Frey, and Harry F. Dahms. 2017. Introduction to ecologically unequal exchange in comparative perspective. *Journal of World-Systems Research* 23(2): 226–235.

Georgescu-Roegen, Nicholas. 1971. *The entropy law and the economic process*. Cambridge, MA: Harvard University Press.

Gibson, Bill. 1980. Unequal exchange: Theoretical issues and empirical findings. *Review of Radical Political Economics* 12(3): 15–35.

Givens, Jennifer E. 2018. Ecologically unequal exchange and the carbon intensity of well-being, 1990–2011. *Environmental Sociology* 4(3): 311–324.

Givens, Jennifer E., Xiaorui Huang, and Andrew K. Jorgenson. 2019. Ecologically unequal exchange: A theory of global environmental *in*justice. *Sociology Compass* 2019(13): e12693.

Givens, Jennifer E., and Andrew K. Jorgenson. 2014. Global integration and carbon emissions , 1965–2005. In *Overcoming global inequalities*, edited by Immanuel Wallerstein, Christopher Chase-Dunn, and C. Suter, pp. 168–183. New York: Routledge.

Haas, Willi, Fridolin Krausmann, Dominik Wiedenhofer, and Markus Heinz. 2015. How circular is the global economy? An assessment of material flows, waste production, and recycling in the European Union and the world in 2005. *Journal of Industrial Ecology* 19(5): 765–777.

Haberl, Helmut, Karl-Heinz Erb, and Fridolin Krausmann. 2014. Human appropriation of net primary production: Patterns, trends, and planetary boundaries. *Annual Review of Environment and Resources* 39: 363–391.

Haberl, Helmut, Julia K. Steinberger, Christoph Plutzar, Karl-Heinz Erb, Veronika Gaube, et al. 2012. Natural and socioeconomic determinants of the embodied human appropriation of net primary production and its relation to other resource use indicators. *Ecological Indicators* 23: 222–231.

Henderson, Kent, and Kristen Shorette. 2017. Environmentalism in the periphery: Institutional embeddedness and deforestation among fifteen palm oil producers, 1990–2012. *Journal of World-Systems Research* 23(2): 269–297.

Hornborg, Alf. 1992. Machine fetishism, value, and the image of unlimited good: Toward a thermodynamics of imperialism. *Man* (New Series) 27: 1–18.

Hornborg, Alf. 1998. Towards an ecological theory of unequal exchange: Articulating world system theory and ecological economics. *Ecological Economics* 25(1): 127–136.

Hornborg, Alf. 2001. *The power of the machine: Global inequalities of economy, technology, and environment*. Walnut Creek, CA: AltaMira Press.

Hornborg, Alf. 2009. Zero-sum world: Challenges in conceptualizing environmental load displacement and ecologically unequal exchange in the world-system. *International Journal of Comparative Sociology* 50(3–4): 237–262.

Hornborg, Alf. 2013. *Global ecology and unequal exchange: Fetishism in a zero-sum world*. Revised paperback version. London: Routledge.

Hornborg, Alf. 2016. *Global magic: Technologies of appropriation from ancient Rome to Wall Street*. Houndmills: Palgrave Macmillan.

Hornborg, Alf. 2019. *Nature, society, and justice in the Anthropocene: Unraveling the money–energy–technology complex*. Cambridge: Cambridge University Press.

Hornborg, Alf, and Joan Martinez-Alier, eds. 2016. Ecologically unequal exchange and ecological debt. *Journal of Political Ecology* Special Issue 23: 328–491.

Huang, Xiaorui. 2018. Ecologically unequal exchange, recessions, and climate change: A longitudinal study. *Social Science Research* 73: 1–12.

Infante-Amate, Juan, and Fridolin Krausmann. 2019. Trade, ecologically unequal exchange and colonial legacy: The case of France and its former colonies (1962–2015). *Ecological Economics* 156: 98–109.

Isenhour, Cindy, and Kuishuang Feng. 2016. Decoupling and displaced emissions: On Swedish consumers, Chinese producers and policy to address the climate impact of consumption. *Journal of Cleaner Production* 134: 320–329.

Jorgenson, Andrew K. 2003. Consumption and environmental degradation: A cross-national analysis of the ecological footprint. *Social Problems* 50(3): 374–394.

Jorgenson, Andrew K. 2006. Unequal ecological exchange and environmental degradation: A theoretical proposition and cross-national study of deforestation, 1990–2000. *Rural Sociology* 71(4): 685–712.

Jorgenson, Andrew K. 2009. Political economic integration, industrial pollution and human health: A panel study of less-developed countries, 1980–2000. *International Sociology* 24(1): 115–143.

Jorgenson, Andrew K. 2010. World-economic integration, supply depots, and environmental degradation: A study of ecologically unequal exchange, foreign investment dependence, and deforestation in less-developed countries. *Critical Sociology* 36(3): 453–477.

Jorgenson, Andrew K. 2011. Carbon dioxide emissions in Central and Eastern European nations, 1992–2005: A test of ecologically unequal exchange theory. *Human Ecology Review* 18(2): 105–114.

Jorgenson, Andrew K. 2012. The sociology of ecologically unequal exchange and carbon dioxide emissions, 1960–2005. *Social Science Research* 41(2): 242–252.

Jorgenson, Andrew K. 2016. The sociology of ecologically unequal exchange, foreign investment dependence and environmental load displacement: Summary of the literature and implications for sustainability. *Journal of Political Ecology* 23: 334–349.

Jorgenson, Andrew K., Kelly Austin, and Christopher Dick. 2009. Ecologically unequal exchange and the resource consumption/environmental degradation paradox: A panel study of less-developed countries, 1970–2000. *International Journal of Comparative Sociology* 50(3–4): 263–284.

Jorgenson, Andrew K., and Brett Clark, eds. 2009. Ecologically unequal exchange in comparative perspective. *International Journal of Comparative Sociology* 50(3–4): 211–409.

Jorgenson, Andrew K., and Brett Clark. 2012. Are the economy and the environment decoupling? A comparative international study, 1960–2005. *American Journal of Sociology* 118(1): 1–44.

Jorgenson, Andrew K., and James Rice. 2005. Structural dynamics of international trade and material consumption: A cross-national study of the ecological footprints of less-developed countries. *Journal of World-Systems Research* 11(1): 57–77.

Jorgenson, Andrew K., and James Rice. 2007. Uneven ecological exchange and consumption-based environmental impacts: A cross-national investigation. In *Rethinking environmental history: World-system history and global environmental change*, edited by Alf Hornborg, J.R. McNeill, and Joan Martinez-Alier, pp. 273–288. Lanham, MD: AltaMira Press.

Kanemoto, Keiichiro, Daniel Moran, Manfred Lenzen, and Arne Geschke. 2014. International trade undermines national emission reduction targets: New evidence from air pollution. *Global Environmental Change* 24: 52–59.

Kill, Jutta. 2016. The role of voluntary certification in maintaining the ecologically unequal exchange of wood pulp: The case of the Forest Stewardship Council's certification of industrial tree plantations in Brazil. *Journal of Political Ecology* 23: 434–445.

Krausmann, Fridolin, Dominik Wiedenhofer, Christian Lauk, Willi Haas, Hiroki Tanikawa, et al. 2017. Global socioeconomic material stocks rise 23-fold over the 20th century and require half of annual resource use. *PNAS* 114(8): 1880–1885.

Krugman, Paul, and Robin Wells. 2018. *Economics.* Fifth edition. New York: Macmillan Education.

Lawrence, Kirk S. 2009. The thermodynamics of unequal exchange: Energy use, CO_2 emissions, and GDP in the world-system, 1975–2005. *International Journal of Comparative Sociology* 50(3–4): 335–359.

Lenzen, Manfred, Keiichiro Kanemoto, Daniel Moran, and Arne Geschke. 2012a. Mapping the structure of the world economy. *Environmental Science and Technology* 46: 8374–8381.

Lenzen, Manfred, Daniel Moran, Keiichiro Kanemoto, Brendan Foran, L. Lobefaro, and Arne Geschke. 2012b. International trade drives biodiversity threats in developing nations. *Nature* 486: 109–112.

Lonergan, Stephen C. 1988. Theory and measurement of unequal exchange: A comparison between a Marxist approach and an energy theory of value. *Ecological Modelling* 41: 127–145.

Lugschitz, Barbara, Martin Bruckner, and Stefan Giljum. 2011. *Europe's global land demand: A study on the actual land embodied in European imports and exports of agricultural and forestry products.* Vienna: Sustainable Europe Research Institute.

Magalhães, Nelo, Jean-Baptiste Fressoz, Francois Jarrige, Thomas Le Roux, Gaëtan Levillain, et al. 2019. The physical economy of France (1830–2015): The history of a parasite? *Ecological Economics* 157: 291–300.

Martinez-Alier, Joan. 2002. *The environmentalism of the poor: A study of ecological conflicts and valuation.* Cheltenham, UK and Northampton, MA, USA: Edward Elgar Publishing.

Martinez-Alier, Joan, Federico Demaria, Leah Temper, and Mariana Walter. 2016. Trends of social metabolism and environmental conflicts: A comparison between India and Latin America. *Journal of Political Ecology* 23: 467–491.

Mayer, Andreas, and Willi Haas. 2016. Cumulative material flows provide indicators to quantify the ecological debt. *Journal of Political Ecology* 23: 350–363.

McKinney, Laura A. 2019. The entropy curse. In *Ecologically unequal exchange: Environmental injustice in comparative and historical perspective*, edited by R. Scott Frey, Paul K. Gellert, and Harry F. Dahms, pp. 143–165. Houndmills: Palgrave Macmillan.

Milanovic, Branko. 2011. A short history of global inequality: The past two centuries. *Explorations in Economic History* 48: 494–506.

Moore, Jason W. 2015. *Capitalism in the web of life: Ecology and the accumulation of capital.* London: Verso.

Muradian, Roldan, and Stefan Giljum. 2007. Physical trade flows of pollution-intensive products: Historical trends in Europe and the world. In *Rethinking environmental history: World-system history and global environmental change*, edited by Alf Hornborg, J.R. McNeill, and Joan Martinez-Alier, pp. 307–325. Lanham, MD: AltaMira Press.

Muradian, Roldan, and Joan Martinez-Alier. 2001. South–North materials flow: History and environmental repercussions. *Innovation: The European Journal of Social Science Research* 14(2): 171–187.

Muradian, Roldan, Martin O'Connor, and Joan Martinez-Alier. 2002. Embodied pollution in trade: Estimating the environmental load displacement of industrialised countries. *Ecological Economics* 41(1): 51–67.

Noble, Mark D. 2017. Chocolate and the consumption of forests: A cross-national examination of ecologically unequal exchange in cocoa exports. *Journal of World-Systems Research* 23(2): 236–268.

Odum, Howard T. 1971. *Environment, power, and society.* New York: Wiley-Interscience.

Odum, Howard T. 1996. *Environmental accounting: EMERGY and environmental decision making.* New York: John Wiley & Sons.

Odum, Howard T. and Jan E. Arding. 1991. Emergy analysis of shrimp mariculture in Ecuador. Working Paper, Coastal Resources Center, University of Rhode Island, Narragansett.

Oulu, Martin. 2016a. Core tenets of the theory of ecologically unequal exchange. *Journal of Political Ecology* 23: 446–466.

Oulu, Martin. 2016b. *Fair enough? Ecologically unequal exchange, international trade, and environmental justice.* Lund Dissertations in Human Ecology 3.

Peng, Shuijun, Wencheng Zhang, and Chuanwang Sun. 2016. "Environmental load displacement" from the North to the South: A consumption-based perspective with a focus on China. *Ecological Economics* 128: 147–158.

Pérez Rincón, Mario. 2006. Colombian international trade from a physical perspective: Towards an ecological "Prebisch Thesis." *Ecological Economics* 59: 519–529.

Pérez-Sánchez, Laura, Raúl Velasco-Renández, and Mario Giampietro. 2021. The international division of labor and embodied working time in trade for the US, the EU and China. *Ecological Economics.* https://doi.org/10.1016/j.ecolecon.2020.106909.

Peters, Glen P., Jan C. Mix, Christopher L. Weber, and Ottmar Edenhofer. 2011. Growth in emission transfers via international trade from 1990 to 2008. *PNAS* 108(21): 8903–8908.

Plank, Barbara, Nina Eisenmenger, Anke Schaffartzik, and Dominik Wiedenhofer. 2018. International trade drives global resource use: A structural decomposition analysis of raw material consumption from 1990–2010. *Environmental Science and Technology* 52: 4190–4198.

Polanyi, Karl. [1944] 1957. *The great transformation: The political and economic origins of our time.* Boston, MA: Beacon.

Polanyi, Karl. [1957] 1968. The semantics of money-uses. In *Primitive, archaic and modern economies: Essays of Karl Polanyi,* edited by George Dalton, pp. 175–203. Boston, MA: Beacon Press.

Prell, Christina, and Laixiang Sun. 2015. Unequal carbon exchanges: Understanding pollution embodied in global trade. *Environmental Sociology* 1(4): 256–267.

Proctor, Robert N., and Londa Schiebinger, eds. 2008. *Agnotology: The making and unmaking of ignorance.* Stanford, CA: Stanford University Press.

Rees, William E., and Mathis Wackernagel. 1994. Ecological footprints and appropriated carrying capacity: Measuring the natural capital requirements of the human economy. In *Investing in natural capital: The ecological economics approach to sustainability,* edited by A.M. Jansson, M. Hammer, C. Folke, and R. Costanza, pp. 362–290. Washington, DC: Island Press.

Rice, James. 2007a. Ecological unequal exchange: international trade and uneven utilization of environmental space in the world system. *Social Forces* 85(3): 1369–1392.

Rice, James. 2007b. Ecological unequal exchange: Consumption, equity, and unsustainable structural relationships within the global economy. *International Journal of Comparative Sociology* 48(1): 43–72.

Rice, James. 2009. The transnational organization of production and uneven environmental degradation and change in the world economy. *International Journal of Comparative Sociology* 50(3–4): 215–236.

Roberts, J. Timmons, Peter E. Grimes, and Jodie L. Manale. 2003. Social roots of global environmental change: A world-systems analysis of carbon dioxide emissions. *Journal of World-Systems Research* 9(2): 277–315.

Roberts, J. Timmons, and Bradley C. Parks. 2008. Fueling injustice: Globalization, ecologically unequal exchange and climate change. *Globalizations* 4(2): 193–210.

Roberts, J. Timmons, and Bradley C. Parks. 2009. Ecologically unequal exchange, ecological debt, and climate justice: The history and implications of three related ideas for a new social movement. *International Journal of Comparative Sociology* 50(3–4): 385–409.

Schandl, Heinz, Marina Fischer-Kowalski, James West, Stefan Giljum, M. Dittrich, et al. 2016a. *Global material flows and resource productivity: Assessment Report for the UNEP International Resource Panel*. Paris: United Nations Environment Programme.

Schandl, Heinz, Steve Hatfield-Dodds, Thomas Wiedmann, Arne Geschke, Yiyong Cai, et al. 2016b. Decoupling global environmental pressure and economic growth: Scenarios for energy use, materials use and carbon emissions. *Journal of Cleaner Production* 132: 45–56.

Seaquist, Jonathan W., Emma Li Johansson, and Kimberly A. Nicholas. 2014. Architecture of the global land acquisition system: Applying the tools of network science to identify key vulnerabilities. *Environmental Research Letters* 9: 1–12.

Shandra, John M., Christopher Leckband, and Bruce London. 2009a. Ecologically unequal exchange and deforestation: A cross-national analysis of forestry export flows. *Organization and Environment* 22(3): 293–310.

Shandra, John M., Christopher Leckband, Laura A. McKinney, and Bruce London. 2009b. Ecologically unequal exchange, world polity, and biodiversity loss: A cross-national analysis of threatened mammals. *International Journal of Comparative Sociology* 50(3–4): 285–310.

Shandra, John M., Eric Shircliff, and Bruce London. 2011. The International Monetary Fund, World Bank, and structural adjustment: A cross-national analysis of forest loss. *Social Science Research* 40(1): 210–225.

Shandra, John M., Eran Shor, and Bruce London. 2009c. World polity, unequal ecological exchange, and organic water pollution: A cross-national analysis of developing nations. *Human Ecology Review* 16: 53–63.

Simas, Moana, Richard Wood, and Edgar Hertwich. 2014. Labor embodied in trade: The role of labor and energy productivity and implications for greenhouse gas emissions. *Journal of Industrial Ecology* 19(3): 343–356.

Sommer, Mark, and Kurt Kratena. 2017. The carbon footprint of European households and income distribution. *Ecological Economics* 136: 62–72.

Sommer, Jamie M., John M. Shandra, and Carolyn Coburn. 2019. Mining exports flows, repression, and forest loss: A cross-national test of ecologically unequal exchange. In *Ecologically unequal exchange: Environmental injustice in comparative and historical perspective*, edited by R. Scott Frey, Paul K. Gellert, and Harry F. Dahms, pp. 167–193. Houndmills: Palgrave Macmillan.

Teixidó-Figueras, Jordi, Julia K. Steinberger, Fridolin Krausmann, Helmut Haberl, Thomas Wiedmann, et al. 2016. International inequality of environmental pressures: Decomposition and comparative analysis. *Ecological Indicators* 62: 163–173.

Temper, Leah. 2016. Who gets the HANPP (Human Appropriation of Net Primary Production)? Biomass distribution and the "sugar economy" in the Tana Delta, Kenya. *Journal of Political Ecology* 23: 410–433.

Wackernagel, Mathis, Larry Onisto, Patricia Bello, Alejandro C. Linares, Ina S.L. Falfán, et al. 1999. National natural capital accounting with the ecological footprint concept. *Ecological Economics* 29(3): 375–390.

Wackernagel, Mathis, Larry Onisto, Alejandro C. Linares, Ina S.L. Falfán, Jesus M. García, et al. 1997. *Ecological footprints of nations: How much do they use? How much nature do they have?* Xalapa, Mexico: Centre for Sustainability Studies, Universidad Anáhuac de Xalapa.

Wackernagel, Mathis, and William E. Rees. 1996. *Our ecological footprint: Reducing human impact on the Earth.* Gabriola Island, BC: New Society Publishers.

Wallerstein, Immanuel. 1974. *The modern world-system 1.* San Diego, CA: Academic Press.

Warlenius, Rikard. 2016. Linking ecological debt and ecologically unequal exchange: Stocks, flows, and unequal sink appropriation. *Journal of Political Ecology* 23: 364–380.

Warlenius, Rikard. 2017. *Asymmetries: Conceptualizing environmental inequalities as ecological debt and ecologically unequal exchange.* Lund Dissertations in Human Ecology 4.

Weinzettel, Jan, Edgar G. Hertwich, Glen P. Peters, Kjartan Steen-Olsen, and Alessandro Galli. 2013. Affluence drives the global displacement of land use. *Global Environmental Change* 23: 433–438.

Wiedmann, Thomas, and Manfred Lenzen. 2018. Environmental and social footprints of international trade. *Nature Geoscience* 11: 314–321.

Wiedmann, Thomas O., Heinz Schandl, Manfred Lenzen, Daniel Moran, Sangwon Suh, et al. 2015. The material footprint of nations. *PNAS* 112: 6271–6276.

Woodward, David. 2015. *Incrementum ad absurdum*: Global growth, inequality and poverty eradication in a carbon-constrained world. *World Economic Review* 4: 43–62.

York, Richard, Eugene A. Rosa, and Thomas Dietz. 2003. Footprints on the Earth: The environmental consequences of modernity. *American Sociological Review* 68: 279–300.

Yu, Yang, Kuishuang Feng, and Klaus Hubacek. 2013. Tele-connecting local consumption to global land use. *Global Environmental Change* 23: 1178–1186.

Yu, Yang, Kuishuang Feng, and Klaus Hubacek. 2014. China's unequal ecological exchange. *Ecological Indicators* 47: 156–163.

Zhang, Wei, Feng Wang, Klaus Hubacek, Yu Liu, Jinnan Wang, et al. 2018. Unequal exchange of air pollution and economic benefits embodied in China's exports. *Environmental Science and Technology* 52(7): 3888–3898.

Conclusion: what are the important lessons from history?

Erik S. Reinert and Ingrid Harvold Kvangraven

The successful cases where countries have been able to reverse uneven development are few and far between. However, there are some that are well worth drawing attention to, along with some of the key challenges associated with uneven development covered in this book.

Let us start with the challenges. In the Introduction to this book, we draw the reader's attention to the contra-intuitive reasonings of Adam Smith around the 'invisible hand', continuing with the even more abstract reasonings of David Ricardo. Originating in David Ricardo's 1817 book *Principles of Economics* we have the idea that free trade brings efficiency and benefits to all participating countries. Although Friedrich List, the great promoter of industrialization in Europe, called England's calls for free trade a form of 'kicking away the ladder', the principles of free trade were a part of the Bretton Woods meeting in 1944, when independent countries across the world, led by the United States (US) and the United Kingdom (UK), were trying to come up with a global governance system that could prevent another Great Depression following the end of World War II.

The result was that the World Bank was set up; initially meant to provide financing for long-term project loans and technical expertise to promote large-scale capital-intensive mega-investment projects through its International Bank for Reconstruction and Development (IBRD). This became crucial for financing rebuilding after the war. Meanwhile, the International Monetary Fund (IMF) was meant to cover short-term balance-of-payment problems (for example, due to a sudden drop in price of major export commodities or exchange rate difficulties). Finally, although John Maynard Keynes had ambitions for an International Trade Organization (ITO), this was not agreed on at Bretton Woods, but the countries agreed on a General Agreement on Trade and Tariffs (GATT), which promoted fairness in trade (no trading partner should be worse off than 'the most-favoured nation') alongside reductions in tariffs. Keep in mind that the world was very different in 1944: many countries across Africa and Asia were still colonies. India did not gain independence from the UK until 1947, and many African countries did not gain independence until the

1950s and 1960s. Thus, the Bretton Woods institutions were born to serve and stabilize a colonial economic system. This had implications for how they were governed then and how they are governed today, which is not much different from in 1944 (Wade 2013). Today, the US still has veto power in both the World Bank and the IMF, and the organizations' presidents are chosen by the US and Europe, respectively. The World Trade Organization (WTO) also has its origins in the Bretton Woods conference, but it was not finalized until 1994. In 1994, its mandate was expanded beyond trade and tariffs to also establish rules for investment, services and intellectual property. All in all, this led to a shrinking of policy space for countries in the Global South, as trade and industrial policy tools that were pursued by the UK, the US and the East Asian 'Miracle' countries as a part of their industrialization efforts became largely unavailable to countries in the Global South.

Despite – or perhaps because of – this challenge of a rather unequal and unfair global governance system, countries in the Global South did resist. The Bandung Conference in 1955 was the first large-scale Asian–African Conference, which was aimed to promote Afro-Asian economic and cultural cooperation and to oppose colonialism and neocolonialism. The conference was also an important step towards the eventual creation of the Non-Aligned Movement, which was founded by Kwame Nkrumah (Ghana), Josip Broz Tito (Yugoslavia), Sukarno (Indonesia), Jawaharlal Nehru (India) and Gamal Abdel Nasser (Egypt). Countries in the Global South were fighting for their independence, but they were also fighting for a more equal structured world. This is what led Adom Getachew to recently point out that these struggles were not limited to nationalism, but that it was rather a project of worldmaking (Getachew 2019).

Drawing on the problems Prebisch and Singer observed regarding the volatile prices of raw materials (see Chapter 6 in this book), Hans Singer wanted to create a soft loan fund for development, the Special United Nations Fund for Economic Development (SUNFED), to carry out projects such as for example buying up raw materials for a fixed price in case raw material prices fell, to create stability for raw material exporters; and also loans for investments in infrastructure (Shaw 2002). However, the US and UK blocked this project in the United Nations (UN) and instead led the establishment of the International Development Association (IDA) of the World Bank in 1960, which would provide soft loans to countries of the Global South.

Subsequently, Prebisch became a leading figure in the establishment of the UN Conference on Trade and Development (UNCTAD) in 1964 and led it as the first General Secretary. Prebisch's analysis was centred on the inherently asymmetric relationship between core and periphery, which became important for UNCTAD. Several of Prebisch's ideas are still highly influential today, although we do not always recognize them as stemming from Prebisch.

Examples are the political ideas of non-reciprocity in trade and policy space for development (Hannah and Scott 2017). Another example of an important South-led initiative includes the New International Economic Order (NIEO) – formally declared in the UN in 1974 – which was a set of proposals advocated by developing countries to end economic colonialism and dependency. UNCTAD and the Non-Aligned Movement were the main fora where the NIEO was discussed.

This history of global governance demonstrates that although the global economy has been rigged to serve countries that are already strong, resistance to this unequal system has been strong and important throughout global history, and it has created windows of opportunity for countries in the Global South. From the beginning of the end of formal colonialism, countries in the Global South knew that to gain autonomy they would need to challenge the global system. We see similar forms of resistance today, both within and outside hegemonic institutions, for example with Brazil and South Africa fighting for the waiver for COVID-19 vaccines within the WTO, or the BRICS countries (Brazil, Russia, India, China and South Africa) forming their own development bank to challenge the Bretton Woods institutions (the New Development Bank).

A challenge closely related to that of a constraining system of global governance is that of development theory. After all, it is a very particular kind of theory that legitimizes the current structures of global governance (see Chapter 1 in this book). Today, n-grams make it possible to study the history of thought from a new angle. It shows that David Ricardo – who Paul Samuelson places as the father of economics both right and left throughout the 19th century – in terms of references and citation was really a minor figure dwarfed by James Stuart Mill (1773–1836) and his son John Stuart Mill (1806–1873). John Stuart Mill, a liberalist, understood the importance of 'infant industry protection' for poor countries.

Historically, Manchester liberalism – the 18th century version of today's neoliberalism – was not really a brainchild of David Ricardo, but rather of Richard Cobden (1804–1865). An n-gram comparing the two authors shows Cobden already passing Ricardo in mentions in the early 1840s, and by the 1880s, Cobden has about six times as many mentions as Ricardo. The hatred towards the state that we later saw during the Cold War was already there in Manchester liberalism. John Bright (1811–1889) – Richard Cobden's partner in the free trade movement – was convinced that 'Most of our evils arise from legislative interference' (Vince 2005 [1898]). Here we find ourselves at the start of the school also represented by Ronald Reagan, when he in 1986 pronounced that 'The nine most terrifying words in the English language are: I'm from the government and I'm here to help.' In times of the coronavirus pandemic these statements again come across as particularly misplaced.

Ideologically, during the Cold War, much time was spent on conflicts between what Gustav Schmoller, Rector of the University of Berlin in 1897, called the irrational twin of the extreme left and the irrational twin of the extreme right (Schmoller 1897). Efforts in the Global South to create a non-aligned movement and carve out their own autonomous space in the world economy were often squashed with violence. There were solutions considered successful middle ways, such as the 1936 book *Sweden: The Middle Way*, first published in the United States (Childs 1936), but they did not produce the same ideological fervour that the 'irrational twins' did.

The Manchester School contrasts sharply with what was to be become, in Bright's lifetime, a very different approach in Germany. This volume is being published in the year after the 150th anniversary of the founding of the Verein für Socialpolitik (Association for Social Policy). Gustav Schmoller took the initiative to the first meeting in the autumn of 1872. This association, with its annual meetings, would bring forth the theories and practical policies for what became the European welfare state. By 1932, when the Verein ceased functioning, 188 volumes of proceedings – organized according to annual themes – had been published.

The reason for organizing the Verein für Socialpolitik was a problem which at the time was called *Die soziale Frage* (the social question). This was an inequality crisis similar to our present one; then, it was mainly seen as national, now it is global. In the founding meeting of the Verein, Gustav Schmoller expressed the worries of the time in the following way; also eerily relevant today:

> We believe the healthiest and most normal society can be expressed by a ladder containing rungs between different existences, depicting easy access from one step to another. Today's society threatens more and more to look like a ladder which grows fast at the top and at the bottom, but where the middle steps increasingly fall out, and where there is solid hold only at the very top and at the very bottom. (Verein für Socialpolitik 1873: 5)

Over the next 60 years the Verein was to build the institutional design of generalized European welfare, and the prescription was copied in many other countries. The starting points in the Verein's discussions were the practical problems at hand; and whether the private sector or the public sector would be the best agent to solve a specific problem was part of a pragmatic discussion. In the United Kingdom the 1942 Beveridge Report played a similar role of creating a holistic view of the social agenda. Today both Schmoller's ladder metaphor and William Beveridge's 'five giants' – want, squalor, ignorance, disease and idleness – ring a bell of recognition more than ever since World War II.

The two cosmopolitical ideologies that came to fight the Cold War – communism and neoliberalism – were already taking shape during the latter part of the 19th century. However, English economic theory at the time, represented by Cambridge economists Alfred Marshall, James Neville Keynes (John Maynard Keynes's father) and Herbert Somerton Foxwell,[1] was far more experience-based and pragmatic than English theories had been earlier in the century. They were all free from what Schumpeter called 'the Ricardian vice' – building extremely abstract theories that leave out key complexities of real life – and were closer to the German tradition.[2]

N-grams clearly show that David Ricardo's theory of 'comparative advantage' only reached popularity during the Cold War after Paul Samuelson's mathematized versions in 1948/49. There was a strong demand for ideas showing that capitalism was superior to communism, and Ricardo/Samuelson delivered 'proofs' that, regardless of whether your comparative advantage was in the Stone Age or in the Industrial Age, you should stick to that.

Strangely enough, history has disregarded that pre-neoliberal capitalism and communism had a key element in common: the belief in the need for industry to create national wealth. Celebrating the 150th anniversary of the birth of Friedrich List, the great promoter of industrialization in Europe, communist East Germany and capitalist West Germany each issued a postage stamp in his honour. They even used the same portrait. Here is where neoclassical economics and neoliberalism split with both the traditional capitalist and the communist tradition. And here they were both right. As former World Bank Chief Economist Justin Yifu Lin states: 'Except for a few oil-exporting countries, no countries have ever gotten rich without industrialization first' (Lin 2012: 350).

SOME PRINCIPLES THAT HAVE PROVEN TO BE USEFUL IN CREATING WEALTH AND FAIR SOCIETIES

With this in mind – the changing landscape of global governance, the need for theories that resonate with reality, and the importance of industry for generating welfare – we can gather some principles that may be useful for generating wealth and justice.

If we go back to look at what 'good' economic systems seem to have in common, history gives us some clues. For societies way back in history, we find Karl Polanyi's 'The Great Transformation' (1944) very useful. Polanyi describes societies of the kind Marx called *Urkommunismus*, which were organized before what Polanyi called the three fictitious commodities of the market economy were created: labour was not a commodity, there was no private ownership of land, and there was no money. Instead of trade there was reciprocity: when I marry, you help me build my house, while I provide the food. When you marry, the same thing is reciprocated. The problem is that this approach became impracticable when people no longer lived their whole lives together in small villages (or small systems). In other words, when it comes to fairness, scale is an issue. We can see how this principle works when a family shares what is in the refrigerator; we see that system working inside nomadic societies such as the economy of Sami reindeer herders in Northern Norway; but it is more difficult to envision when myriads of peoples share one planet where some economic activities are centralized due to enormous economies of scale (read: Bill Gates). A ruling economic theory where 'context does not matter' makes understanding these things more difficult.

Another element we can identify among long-lasting and relatively fair societies is the need for a balance of countervailing powers: an element of Montesquieu (1748) if you will, or what the Americans call checks and balances. We shall get back to this when discussing John Kenneth Galbraith below. In 1911, sociologist Robert Michels introduced his 'Iron Law of Oligarchy' as a natural development even of democracies; a phenomenon which any would-be fair society needs to be permanently aware of.

Decentralized systems can also help in several aspects that are important for sustaining decent societies. For example, decentralized community-centred social infrastructure has been important for effectively combating the COVID-19 virus, including in China (Li et al. 2021). The decentralized system in Kerala in India is often also held up as a beacon of democratic and well-organized social welfare, even under the restrictions of being fairly underfunded when compared to European welfare states (Véron 2001).

Similarly, the built-in radical uncertainty which surrounds technological change also calls for decentralized systems. The experience in the Soviet Union was that their system could produce excellency in some key areas only. The invention of the motor car is a case of such radical uncertainty. At the time, the logical choice would have been either the steam car (the power of the past) or the electric car (in 1881, electric trams were already in operation in Berlin). You need a system which is open enough to let the complete outsider Mr Benz experiment with his petroleum engine, who actually won the race. Centralized governments, and also democracies, would have financed research into kerosene which produced less soot; nobody would have asked Mr Edison to invent the electric light. The main dictionary in Scandinavia at the time said flatly that electric light did not have a future because it was harmful to the eyes.

In early capitalism we have some useful examples in the Italian city-states. There were so many of these states that there was room for emulation, for learning from other states. Werner Sombart claims that the two necessary institutions of capitalism were double-entry bookkeeping and bankruptcy. In both cases we are in Venice in the 1200s. In independent India, at one point they thought bankruptcy was a capitalist invention which they could live without, but found that without provision for bankruptcy there was chaos and increased corruption. Any slightly advanced system needs accounting systems; market societies or others all need a way to get rid of unhealthy economic organizations that become a burden.

The only European empire which has lasted more than 1000 years is, as far as we know, Venice. In early capitalism we have some useful rules from Venice and other Italian city-states. Siena, and then Florence, were also reasonably equal city-states. The Palazzo Pubblico in Siena (built 1297–1310) has some beautiful frescos on 'good government' and 'bad government', showing what is worth fighting for. Siena still has the world's oldest surviving bank, Monte dei Paschi di Siena (1472). Siena saw a relative decline, and Florence grew in importance. Florence was run by a council with frequently rotating members representing the different trades and professions. In Venice, these rulers were replaced every year. Looking at these governmental structures, one is struck by how they were obviously designed with some core ideas in mind:

1. Balancing different economic interests. We note that of the many members of the ruling council in Florence, there was only one representative from the banking sector, including sale of precious metals (Arte del Cambio) (Goldthwaite 2009).
2. Frequent circulation of people in order to prevent corruption. The council of the ten persons ruling in Florence were circulated every year. In Venice the election of a new Doge was such a complex ritual, involving so many steps, that the process looks laughable today (see Norwich 1982).
3. Avoiding heredity of power was a third principle in Venice. At times, especially in the early days, the son of a deceased Doge may have looked like the best candidate to be the successor. If so, the Senate might elect a very old person to be Doge, in order for the qualified son of the previous Doge to be able to take over relatively soon.

   On the other hand, it may be argued that the right of primogeniture is a useful institution. It helped to avoid land in Europe becoming so fragmented that one family could not make a living from it, and – to the extent that there are economies of scale in agriculture – it helped productivity. If we compare the unstable kingdoms in the Middle East, even today, with Western kingdoms, it seems clear that the right of primogeniture has been stabilizing in the West.
4. Adding value to raw materials locally. A core economic policy of Venice was free entry of raw materials without any duty, but severe protection of all activities adding value to raw materials. That included severe penalties for the importation of bread. The theoretic underpinning for this came from Giovanni Botero (1589).[3] This recalls the commercial policy of the young Republican Party of the United States, under Abraham Lincoln: no

duty on raw materials, but increasing duties as the degree of value added to the product increased. Silicon chips add more value to silicon sand than potato chips add to the potato, to use what was a popular US example. Looking at recent Chinese economic policy, one is able to see similarities. A colleague working a lot with China claims that Chinese economic policy is influenced by the unfair/unequal treaties – prohibiting industry – that were imposed upon them by the West (see Chapter 7 in this book).

5. Keeping feudalism out of power. Especially in the Republic of Florence, being surrounded by fertile agricultural land, keeping the feudal landlords away from power was a key issue. Cities were by definition 'havens' where the landlords had no power over their escaped serfs. In German, the saying 'city air makes free' still exists. Cities were ruled by their producers and traders; the feudal interests of the landlords were – almost by definition – in conflict with those of the city, and had to be kept away from power at any price. In Spain, on the other hand, the Mesta – the organization of the sheep-owners (Klein 1920) – had so much power that it would hinder the spread of agriculture, not to mention industry.

6. Avoiding speculation. One apparently curious law in Medieval Florence was the prohibition from bringing food out of the city. The importance of this became crystal clear under the French Revolution. Adam Smith tells us that 'It is not from the benevolence of … the baker that we expect our dinner, but from their regard to their own self-interest'. Just before the French Revolution it became clear that there was even more money to be made from carrying flour and wheat out of the city, waiting for prices to go up, than from baking bread. Not baking bread created huge profits, and this speculation caused the shortage of bread.[4]

The Bible (Matthew 25, 14–30) tells us that coins – the 'talents' – should not be buried, but invested. Early money theorist Nicolas Oresme complained in 1485 about too much money ending in treasure chests instead of being productively invested (Oresme 1995 [1485]). This is not why we created money, he writes. The Muslim prohibition against interest – *riba* – and the Christian prohibition from receiving interest up until the 1600s, must be seen in this perspective. Amassing fortunes without lifting a finger was seen as qualitatively very different from earning money by 'honest work', commerce and production.

Around 1600, Francis Bacon writes that money is like manure, only useful when spread. Through the whole history of civilization, we find the thread that the 'financial sector' is only useful when investing in the real economy. In 1834, Scottish-American economist John Rae created a useful distinction between money made by creating new goods or services, versus money made from already existing things increasing in price (Rae 1834). Today's financial sector ought to be revisited with these ideas in mind.

Getting back to the issue of countervailing power: John Kenneth Galbraith, in his 1952 book *American Capitalism: The Concept of Countervailing Power*, returns to this problem:

> The development of countervailing power requires a certain minimum opportunity and capacity for organization, corporate or otherwise. If the large retail buying organizations had not developed the countervailing power which they have used, by proxy, on behalf of the individual consumer, consumers would have been faced with the need to organize the equivalent of the retailer's power. This would have been a formidable task, but it has been accomplished in Scandinavia where the consumers' co-operative, instead of the chain store, is the dominant instrument of countervailing power in consumers' goods markets.

Galbraith sees the successful US capitalism at the time as a result of a balance between big labour, big business and big government. In the US, big government and big labour gradually disappeared, leaving the battlefield open to big business, which gradually shifted from being production capitalism to being financial capitalism.

In this context we should be open to the existence of enlightened despotism; which does not tend to be enlightened for very long. We saw some successful cases in the small German states, as with Ernest the Pious in Gotha (1601–1675). This was a period when German economists told princes that the success factors by which rulers were judged had changed: winning medieval tournaments was no longer the criterion for the success of a ruler. The health and well-being of their inhabitants were the criteria by which rulers would be judged from now on. Perhaps we now see a parallel to this in the US under Biden, where the economic well-being of its own citizens may take priority over foreign wars.

Furthermore, 'social democracy' is still a term which no one (to our knowledge) has used as a swearword. The 20th century Swedish model of capitalism represents John Kenneth Galbraith's balance of countervailing powers under capitalism: big business, big government and big labour. Although we recognize that there are many reasons why the Swedish model may not be replicable for countries in the Global South today, there are still relevant lessons to be learned, and for reasons that will be explained below, it is the easiest version of the history of social democracy to describe.

Swedish economists Gunnar Myrdal (1898–1987) – who had produced a theory where vicious and virtuous circles were dominating forces – and pragmatic economist Johan Åkerman (1896–1992) provided the theoretical background for the Swedish model. That country's industrial policy after World War II is didactically interesting because for a very long period it was dominated by just three individuals: industrialist Marcus Wallenberg (1899–1982), also the main shareholder of Stockholms Enskilda Bank;[5] Schumpeterian economist Erik Dahmén (1916–2005), who worked for the bank for several decades; and Labour Party politician Gunnar Sträng (1906–1992). Sträng held ministerial posts in the Swedish government from 1947 to 1976, the last 21 years as Minister of Finance.

Industrialist Wallenberg and his economic advisor Dahmén[6] – who had been working on 'development blocks'[7] – had lunch in the bank every Wednesday. Wallenberg and Sträng were also in close contact, seemingly also unofficially, to discuss economic policy. The result is what economists of the French regulation School refer to as 'the Fordist wage regime' (Boyer 2016). The fruits of innovations and productivity growth were divided between capital and labour: roughly, a 4 per cent productivity increase would give a 4 per cent wage increase. The ever-increasing real wages made labour increasingly more expensive in relationship to capital, while increasing demand was assured. This provided a very strong incentive for industrial mechanization, and in inflationary periods – such as in the 1970s – there is no doubt that the combination of ever-increasing wages, sometimes combined with negative costs of capital for the industrialists, helped mechanization. Wages developed in the industrial export sector, then spread to the whole economy, also for example to barbers – who had small possibilities for productivity improvement – and to the public sector as well.

Strangely enough, this wage policy also resulted in high real growth in Italy, although here the union-driven wage policy appeared to be irresponsible. During the 1970s and 1980s, one of us (Reinert) ran a small industrial company in Northern Italy. With a certain unwillingness he has come to think that the communist threat actually served the purpose of increasing the capital–labour ratio in industry and services, and thus creating labour-saving innovations, not only in manufacturing but also as exemplified by containers and self-service supermarkets. The high wage claims of the three Italian labour unions created inflation, which gave small entrepreneurs strongly negative interest rates and a strong incentive to invest in machinery. But the rising wages also increased general demand, creating virtuous circles in the productive sector. From the side of the financial markets, these events were an unmitigated disaster. Mario Draghi, who is two years older than Reinert, had inherited Italian Treasury Bonds (Boni del Tesoro) which at the time experienced negative interest rates of close to 10 per cent annually. As Head of the European Central Bank, Draghi later made sure that the financial sector got its revenge.[8]

A last important historical lesson we learned by what happened to Russia after the free trade shock imposed by the 'international community' after the fall of the Berlin Wall. With colleague Rainer Kattel, Reinert was asked by a Russian business magazine, *Expert*, to write a report on the Russian economy (Reinert and Kattel 2010). The most surprising part of the study was how much the Russian economy had been set back by the 'shock therapy' imposed by the

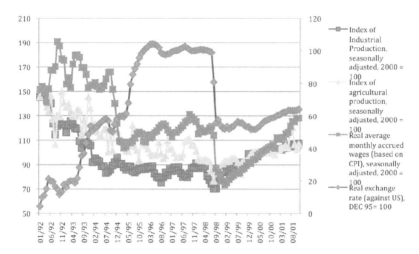

Figure C.1   *Exchange rate (right axis), real wages and production in Russia, 1992–2001*

Western world. Figure C.1 shows how, since statistics again became available from 1992 onwards.

Unsurprisingly for someone who studied Russia at the time, deindustrialization was massive. Between 1992 and 1997, industrial production was reduced by about 50 per cent. What was more surprising was that agricultural production was also reduced by around 50 per cent, and so were real wages. The really surprising thing was that, while the real economy was collapsing, the value of the ruble skyrocketed. Clearly, financial speculation was rampant until, in August 1997, there was a massive devaluation. In the meantime, Russian oligarchs had been able to get their rubles out of the country at extremely favourable exchange rates. As part of the same policy, domestic savings were severely penalized. A Russian colleague, Dean of the Higher School of Economics in Moscow, told Reinert that he had saved money to buy a car, but after the 1997 devaluation he could only afford a bicycle.

When these data were presented at the Gaidar Conference in Moscow in 2016, the chairman of the meeting suggested to send them to the prosecutor's office. In 2009 a study in the prestigious *Lancet* magazine correlated the shock therapy and the mass privatization to a decrease in life expectancy of Russian males by seven years (Stuckler et al. 2009). There is a debate around this, but it does seem that life expectancy in Russia reached its lowest point in 1994. In Figure C.1, this would correspond to the lowest point in real wages before the

1997 devaluation shock. After this shock real wages grew fast, after national production had received this enormous boost.

What is not well known is the scandal in the United States over the advice given to Russia by Harvard Institute of International Development (HIID), which was led by Professor Jeffery Sachs from 1995 to 1999. Our source here is *Harvard Crimson*, the internal magazine of Harvard University. A scandal erupted in 1996 when the US government declared that, as a contractor HIID, had 'abused the trust of the U.S. government by using personal relationships for private gain'. In 2000, the US department of Justice took Harvard to court, and five years later Harvard agreed to pay U$26.5 million to the US government. Andrei Schleifer, an economist who had advised Russia, had faced damages of up to U$104 million 'for conspiring to defraud the government while advising a U.S. funding program to privatize the Russian economy in the 1990s' (Harvard Crimson 2005). In the end he only had to pay $2 million, without admitting guilt. Somewhat curiously, the same Andrei Schleifer is now by far the world's most cited economist.[9]

Decades later, with the COVID-19 pandemic demonstrating the deepness of the unevenness of the global economy, we have not got much further in terms of challenging the polarizing and unequalizing nature of the global system. The IMF is still attaching conditions to its loans that restrict policy space and an active response to the pandemic on the behalf of countries in the Global South (Razavi et al. 2021). While there have been calls for a 'new' Bretton Woods, these calls have mostly come from within the West from people and policy-makers who see the rise of populist authoritarianism and the rise of China as a threat to global stability (Boughton 2022). However, the problem with the Bretton Woods system is not simply that it is outdated or that it is being undermined, but that it is also deeply undemocratic from the perspective of countries in the Global South. However, its counterpoint, the Bandung conference of 1955, was certainly not politically strong or broad enough to tilt the global economy in a more equal direction either. This has led Senegalese development economist Ndongo Samba Sylla to recently argue that what we need is not a 'new' Bretton Woods, but rather a 'Bandung Woods': a consideration of both multilateralism and the specific needs articulated by the countries of the Global South (Samba Sylla and Gabor 2022). Indeed, whatever the future holds, and regardless of whether we will see 'new' Bretton or Bandung Woods, we hope that this book does demonstrate that we need innovative and historically anchored thinking both to understand and, ultimately, to reverse the unevenness that continues to unfold across the world.

What is new since Bretton Woods is that not only the Third World, the Global South, but increasingly also the Second World (the former communist countries), and most recently also the First World (especially the United

States), see growing inequalities.[10] In Chapter 12 in this book the case of the Second World is discussed, showing how Ukraine is by far the worst case.

A HISTORY THAT RHYMES?

One of the several sayings that are attributed to Mark Twain is that 'History never repeats itself, but it does often rhyme'. In 1899, Thorstein Veblen published *The Theory of the Leasure Class*, a highly sarcastic and very efficient attack on the US upper classes who lived in splendour in the midst of often terrible poverty. Veblen, it was said at the time, held a mirror up to his fellow Americans – often migrants from Europe – showing them that they were now building a society similar to the feudal society they had left Europe to avoid.[11]

Ida Tarbell's (1904) attack specifically on the Rockefellers, and Veblen's attack on the capitalism of the age in general, were important inputs into the debate that shaped the growing antitrust laws. The New Deal policy that came following the crisis of 1929 can still be said to have been created in the spirit of Tarbell and Veblen.

Surprisingly, during the crisis in the 1930s in the United States, German economist Wilhelm Krelle (1962) in Figure C.2 shows that the percentage of

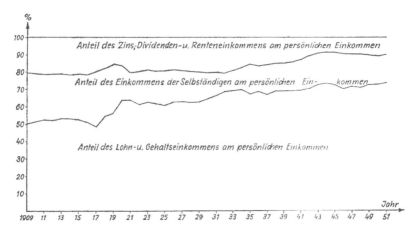

Note: Top: share of total US income from interest, dividends and rents. Middle: share of total US income from the self-employed (mostly farmers). Bottom: Share of total US income from salaries and wages. Total 100%. All incomes pre-tax. Social transfers have been added to salaries and wages. Profits retained in companies are not included.
Source: Krelle (1962: 12).

Figure C.2   United States: percentage of pre-tax income by sector, 1909–1951

gross domestic product (GDP) going to labour increased, meaning that capital income decreased more than labour income during the crisis. This would be the case if, in spite of high unemployment, the workers who kept their jobs tended to keep their wages. With the ratchet wheel of trade unionism intact, profits – rather than wage level – would be the factor suffering first during a recession. Today, due to the weakness of the labour unions and the high degree of financialization, this outcome will not occur again. Worst of all is that the key difference between raw materials and manufactured products – which was eliminated by Adam Smith and David Ricardo – has not been re-established. US economic historian Richard Goldthwaite shows that this dichotomy between raw materials and manufacturing lies at the root of European civilization. What is generally seen as Europe's 'commercial revolution', he argues, was in fact a process of import substitution: manufactured goods, that had previously been imported from the Levant, were now produced in Europe from the 12th century onwards (Goldthwaite 2009).

Like the mirror of feudalism that Thorstein Veblen held up to the American people, similar 'mirrors' are being produced today.[12] Hopefully we may avoid the rhyming effects. That requires getting rid of the colonial heritage in David Ricardo's trade theory.

NOTES

1. The most devastating criticism of Ricardo is found in Cambridge economist Herbert Foxwell's (1899) 110-page introduction to Anton Menger's *The Right to the Whole Produce of Labour*.
2. Unfortunately neoclassical economics came to be more based on Alfred Marshall's appendices and footnotes in his 1890 book than on his texts; that is, the necessary qualifications for these abstractions were left out.
3. Botero became the dominant economist in Europe for the next 70–80 years, with a large number of translations.
4. Kaplan (2015). The famous saying 'why don't they eat cake' appears in this context.
5. From 1972 *Skandinaviska Enskilda Banken*.
6. This story was told by Erik Dahmén at the 1996 Schumpeter conference in Stockholm.
7. Similar to what François Perroux called 'growth poles' and what Michael Porter later came to call 'clusters'.
8. This is discussed in detail in Reinert (2014).
9. https://ideas.repec.org/top/top.person.nbcites.html (accessed 6 February 2022).
10. This is treated in Reinert (2012).
11. For an overview of Veblen and his times, see Reinert and Viano (2012).
12. Examples are: Kotkin (2020); and a book by the *New York Times* Global Economics Correspondent Peter Goodman (2022) *Davos Man: How the Billionaires Devoured the World*.

REFERENCES

Botero, Giovanni (1589), *Dalla Ragion di Stato: Libri dieci, con tre Libri delle Cause della Grandezza e Magnificenza delle Città*, Venice: Giolitti.

Boughton, James (2022), 'How to Deal with a "Bretton Woods Moment"', Institute for New Economic Thinking, 10 February. https://www.ineteconomics.org/perspectives/blog/how-to-deal-with-a-bretton-woods-moment (accessed 2 October 2022).

Boyer, Robert (2016), 'Development and Régulation Theory', in Erik Reinert, Jayati Ghosh and Rainer Kattel (eds), *Handbook of Alternative Theories of Economic Development*, Cheltenham, UK and Northampton, MA, USA: Edward Elgar Publishing, pp. 352–385.

Childs, Marquis (1936), *Sweden: The Middle Way*, New Haven, CT: Yale University Press.

Foxwell, Herbert (1899), 'Introduction', in Anton Menger (ed.), *The Right to the Whole Produce of Labour*, London: Macmillan, pp. v–cx.

Galbraith, John Kenneth (1952), *American Capitalism: The Concept of Countervailing Power*, Boston, MA: Houghton Mifflin.

Getachew, Adom (2019), *Worldmaking After Empire: The Rise and Fall of Self-Determination*, Princeton, NJ: Princeton University Press.

Goldthwaite, Richard A. (2009), *The Economy of Renaissance Florence*, Baltimore, MD: Johns Hopkins University Press.

Goodman, Peter S. (2022), *Davos Man: How the Billionaires Devoured the World*, New York: Custom House.

Hannah, Erin and James Scott (2017), 'From Palais de Nations to Centre William Rappard: Prebisch and UNCTAD as Sources of Ideas in the GATT/WTO', in Matias Margulis (ed.), *The Global Political Economy of Raúl Prebisch*, London: Routledge, pp. 116–134.

Harvard Crimson (2005), 'Harvard to Pay $26.5 Million in HIID Settlement', 29 July. https://www.thecrimson.com/article/2005/7/29/harvard-to-pay-265-million-in/ (accessed 2 October 2022).

Kaplan, Steven (2015), *Bread, Politics and Political Economy in the Reign of Louis XV*, London: Anthem.

Klein, Julius (1920), *The Mesta: A Study in Spanish Economic History 1273–1836*, Cambridge, MA: Harvard University Press.

Kotkin, Joel (2020), *The Coming of Neo-Feudalism: A Warning to the Global Middle Class*, New York: Encounter Books.

Krelle, Wilhelm (1962), *Verteilungstheorie*, Tübingen: Mohr.

Li, Zhongjin, Ying Chen and Yang Zhan (2021), 'Building Community-Centered Social Infrastructure: A Feminist Inquiry into China's COVID-19 Experiences', Bologna, *Economia Politica*, See Building community-centered social infrastructure: a feminist inquiry into China's COVID-19 experiences – PubMed (nih.gov) (accessed 2 October 2022).

Lin, Justin Yifu (2012), *New Structural Economics: A Framework for Rethinking Development and Policy*, Washington, DC: World Bank Publications.

Marshall, Alfred (1890), *Principles of Economics*, London: Macmillan.

Michels, Robert (1911), 'Iron Law of Oligarchy', *Zur Soziologie des Parteiwesen. Untersuchungen über die Oligarchischen Tendenzen des Gruppenlebens*, Leipzig: Klinkhardt.

Montesquieu, Charles Louis de Secondat, Baron de (1748), *De l'Esprit des Loix*, Geneva: Barrillot & Fils.

Norwich, John J. (1982), *A History of Venice*, Harmondsworth: Penguin.

Oresme, Nicholas (1995 [1485]), *De Moneta*, Düsseldorf: Verlag Wirtschaft und Finanzen GmbH.

Polanyi, Karl (1944), *The Great Transformation*, New York: Rinehart & Company.

Rae, John (1834), *Statement of Some New Principles on the Subject of Political Economy, Exposing the Fallacies of the System of Free Trade, and of Some Other Doctrines Maintained in the 'Wealth of Nations'*, Boston, MA: Hilliard, Gray & Co.

Razavi, Shahra, Helmut Schwarzer, Fabio Durán-Valverde, Isabel Ortiz and Devika Dutt (2021), 'Social Policy Advice to Countries from the International Monetary Fund during the COVID-19 Crisis. Continuity and Change', ILO Working Paper 42, Geneva: ILO.

Reinert, Erik S. (2012), 'Neo-Classical Economics: A Trail of Economic Destruction since the 1970s', *Real-World Economics Review*, 60 (20 June), pp. 2–17.

Reinert, Erik S. (2014), 'Financial Crises and Countermovements. Comparing the Times and Attitudes of Marriner Eccles (1930s) and Mario Draghi (2010s)', in Dimitri Papadimitriou (ed.), *Contributions of Economic Theory, Policy, Development and Finance. Essays in Honor of Jan A. Kregel*. London: Routledge, pp. 319–344.

Reinert, Erik S. and Rainer Kattel (2010), 'Modernizing Russia: Round III. Russia and the Other BRIC Countries: Forging Ahead, Catching Up or Falling Behind?', The Other Canon Foundation and Tallinn University of Technology Working Papers in Technology Governance and Economic Dynamics, No. 32. http://hum.ttu.ee/wp/paper32.pdf (accessed 2 October 2022). Report for Global Policy Forum, Yaroslavl, Russia, September 2010. Published in Russian and English.

Reinert, Erik S. and Francesca Lidia Viano (eds) (2012), *Thorstein Veblen: Economist for an Age of Crises*, London: Anthem.

Ricardo, David (1817), *Principles of Economics*, London: John Murray.

Samba Sylla, Ndongo and Daniela Gabor (2022), 'Financial Empire'. https://thedigradio.com/podcast/financial-empire-w-daniela-gabor-ndongo-samba-sylla/ (accessed 2 October 2020).

Schmoller, Gustav A. (1897), 'Wechselnde Theorien und feststehende Wahrheiten im Gebiete der Staats- und Socialwissenschaften und die heutige deutsche Volkswirtschaftslehre', Rede bei Entritt des Rectorats gehalten in der Aula der Königlichen Friedrich-Wilhelms-Universität am 15 October, Berlin: W. Büxenstein. http://othercanon.org/wp- content/uploads/2020/02/Gustav_Schmoller_Wechselnde_Theorien_und_feststehende_Wahrheiten_im_Gebiete_der_Staats_und_Socialwissenschaften.pdf (accessed 2 October 2022).

Shaw, John (2002), *Sir Hans Singer: The Life and Work of a Development Economist*, London: Palgrave Macmillan.

Stuckler, David, Lawrence King and Martin McKee (2009), 'Mass Privatisation and the Post-Communist Mortality Crisis: A Cross-National Analysis', *Lancet*, 15 January.

Tarbell, Ida (1904*), The History of the Standard Oil Company*, New York: McClure.

Veblen, Thorstein (1899), *The Theory of the Leisure Class*, New York: Macmillan.

Verein für Socialpolitik (1873), *Verhandlungen der Eisenacher Versammlung zur Besprechung der Sozialen Frage am 6. Und 7. October 1872*. Leipzig, Ducker & Humblot.

Véron, René (2001), 'The "New" Kerala Model: Lessons for Sustainable Development', *World Development* 29 (4), pp. 601–617.

Vince, C.A. (2005 [1898]), *John Bright*, Whitefish, MT: Kessinger Publishing.

Wade, Robert (2013), 'The Art of Power Maintenance', *Challenge* 56 (1), pp. 5–39.

Index